Key to map symbols

C000199190

(22)	**Motorway with junction number**
	Primary route – dual/single carriageway
	A road – dual/single carriageway
	B road – dual/single carriageway
	Minor road – dual/single carriageway
	Other minor road – dual/single carriageway
	Road under construction
	Tunnel, covered road
(30) (30)	**Speed cameras** – single, multiple
	Rural track, private road or narrow road in urban area
	Gate or obstruction to traffic – restrictions may not apply at all times or to all vehicles
	Path, bridleway, byway open to all traffic, restricted byway
	Pedestrianised area
BS22	**Postcode boundaries**
	County and unitary authority boundaries
	Railway with station
	Tunnel
	Railway under construction
	Metro station
	Private railway station
	Miniature railway
	Tramway, tramway under construction
	Tram stop, tram stop under construction
	Bus, coach station

✚	**Accident and Emergency entrance to hospital**
H	**Hospital**
+	**Place of worship**
i	**Information centre** – open all year
	Shopping centre
P	**Parking**
P&R	**Park and Ride**
PO	**Post Office**
X	**Camping site**
	Caravan site
▶	**Golf course**
✕	**Picnic site**
Church	**Non-Roman antiquity**
ROMAN FORT	**Roman antiquity**
Univ	**Important buildings, schools, colleges, universities and hospitals**
	Built-up area
	Woods
River Medway	**Water name**
	River, weir
	Stream
	Canal, lock, tunnel
	Water
	Tidal water
87 / 58	**Adjoining page indicators**

The small numbers around the edges of the maps identify the 1-kilometre National Grid lines

The dark grey border on the inside edge of some pages indicates that the mapping does not continue onto the adjacent page

Abbreviations

Acad	**Academy**	Meml	**Memorial**
Allot Gdns	**Allotments**	Mon	**Monument**
Cemy	**Cemetery**	Mus	**Museum**
C Ctr	**Civic centre**	Obsy	**Observatory**
CH	**Club house**	Pal	**Royal palace**
Coll	**College**	PH	**Public house**
Crem	**Crematorium**	Recn Gd	**Recreation ground**
Ent	**Enterprise**	Resr	**Reservoir**
Ex H	**Exhibition hall**	Ret Pk	**Retail park**
Ind Est	**Industrial Estate**	Sch	**School**
IRB Sta	**Inshore rescue boat station**	Sh Ctr	**Shopping centre**
Inst	**Institute**	TH	**Town hall / house**
Ct	**Law court**	Trad Est	**Trading estate**
L Ctr	**Leisure centre**	Univ	**University**
LC	**Level crossing**	W Twr	**Water tower**
Liby	**Library**	Wks	**Works**
Mkt	**Market**	YH	**Youth hostel**

The map scale on the pages numbered in blue is 3½ inches to 1 mile
5.52 cm to 1 km • 1 : 18 103

0	¼ mile	½ mile	¾ mile	1 mile

| 0 | 250m | 500m | 750m | 1km |

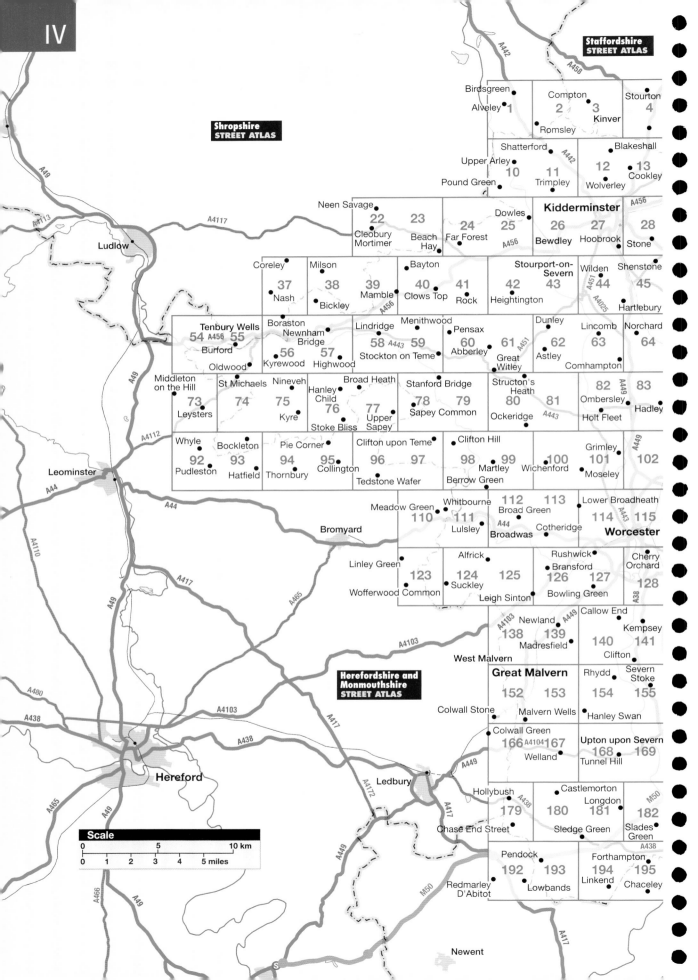

IV

Staffordshire
STREET ATLAS

Shropshire
STREET ATLAS

Birdsgreen
Alveley **1**
Compton
2 **3**
Kinver
Stourton
4

Romsley

Shatterford
Upper Arley
Pound Green
10
Trimpley
11

Blakeshall
12 **13**
Cookley
Wolverley

Neen Savage
22 **23**
Cleobury
Mortimer
Beach
Hay
24
Far Forest
Dowles
25

Kidderminster

26
Bewdley
27
Hoobrook
28
Stone

Coreley
37
Nash
Milson
38
Bickley
39
Mamble
Bayton
40
Clows Top
41
Rock
Stourport-on-
Severn
42
Heightington
43
Wilden
44
Shenstone
45
Hartlebury

Tenbury Wells
54 A456 **55**
Burford
Oldwood
Boraston
Newnham
Bridge
56
Kyrewood
57
Highwood
Lindridge
58 A443 **59**
Stockton on Teme
Menithwood
60
Abberley
Pensax
61
Great
Witley
Dunley
62
Astley
Lincomb
63
Comhampton
Norchard
64

Middleton
on the Hill
73
Leysters
St Michaels
74
Nineveh
75
Kyre
Hanley
Child
76
Stoke Bliss
Broad Heath
77
Upper
Sapey
Stanford Bridge
78
Sapey Common
79
Struncton's
Heath
80
Ockeridge
81
82 **83**
Ombersley
Holt Fleet
Hadley

Whyle
92
Pudleston
Bockleton
93
Hatfield
Pie Corner
94
Thornbury
95
Collington
Clifton upon Teme
96 **97**
Tedstone Wafer
Clifton Hill
98
Berrow Green
Martley
99
Wichenford
100
Moseley
Grimley
101
102

Meadow Green
110
Whitbourne
111
Lulsley
112 **113**
Broad Green
Cotheridge
Lower Broadheath
114 **115**

Bromyard
A44
Broadwas
Worcester

Linley Green
123
Wofferwood Common
Alfrick
124
Suckley
125
Leigh Sinton
Rushwick
Bransford
126
Bowling Green
127
Cherry
Orchard
128

Newland
138
Madresfield
139
Callow End
140
Clifton
Kempsey
141

West Malvern

Great Malvern
152 **153**
Colwall Stone
Malvern Wells
Rhydd
154
Hanley Swan
Severn
Stoke
155

Colwall Green
166 A4104 **167**
Welland
Upton upon Severn
168
Tunnel Hill
169

Hollybush
179
Chase End Street
Castlemorton
180
Sledge Green
Longdon
181
Slades
Green
182

Pendock
192
Redmarley
D'Abitot
193
Lowbands
Forthampton
194
Linkend
Chaceley
195

Ludlow

Leominster

Hereford

Herefordshire and
Monmouthshire
STREET ATLAS

Ledbury

Newent

Scale
0   5   10 km
0   1   2   3   4   5 miles

PHILIP'S

STREET ATLAS
Worcestershire

www.philips-maps.co.uk
First published in 2003 by
Philip's, a division of
Octopus Publishing Group Ltd
www.octopusbooks.co.uk
2-4 Heron Quays, London E14 4JP
An Hachette UK Company
www.hachettelivre.co.uk

Second edition 2009
First impression 2009
WORBA

978-0-540-09211-6 (spiral)

© Philip's 2009

Ordnance Survey®

This product includes mapping data licensed
from Ordnance Survey® with the permission
of the Controller of Her Majesty's Stationery
Office. © Crown copyright 2009. All rights
reserved. Licence number 100011710.

Contents

II	Mobile safety cameras
III	**Key to map symbols**
IV	**Key to map pages**
VI	**Route planning**
VIII	**Administrative and Postcode boundaries**
1	**Street maps** at 3½ inches to 1 mile
198	**Index** of towns, villages, streets, hospitals, industrial estates, railway stations, schools, shopping centres, universities and places of interest

Digital Data

The exceptionally high-quality mapping found in this atlas is available as digital data in TIFF format, which is easily convertible to other bitmapped (raster) image formats.

The index is also available in digital form as a standard database table. It contains all the details found in the printed index together with the National Grid reference for the map square in which each entry is named.

For further information and to discuss your requirements, please contact
victoria.dawbarn@philips-maps.co.uk

Mobile safety cameras

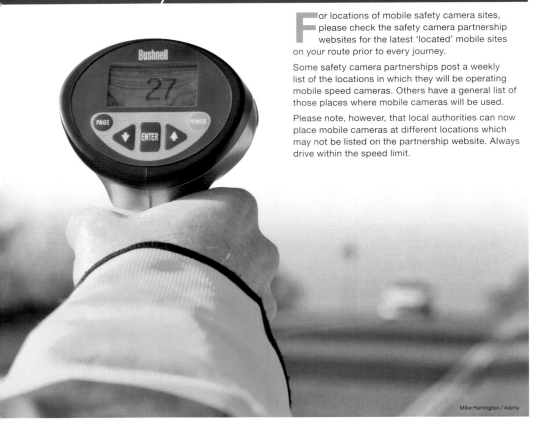

For locations of mobile safety camera sites, please check the safety camera partnership websites for the latest 'located' mobile sites on your route prior to every journey.

Some safety camera partnerships post a weekly list of the locations in which they will be operating mobile speed cameras. Others have a general list of those places where mobile cameras will be used.

Please note, however, that local authorities can now place mobile cameras at different locations which may not be listed on the partnership website. Always drive within the speed limit.

Mike Harrington / Alamy

Useful websites

Safer Roads Partnership in West Mercia
http://www.srpwestmercia.org.uk/

Staffordshire County Council
http://www.staffordshire.gov.uk/transport/cameras/

Warwickshire County Council
http://www.warwickshire.gov.uk/

Gloucestershire Safety Camera Partnership
http://www.glossafetycameras.org.uk/

West Midlands Casualty Reduction Scheme
http://www.wmsafetycameras.co.uk/

Further information
www.dvla.gov.uk
www.thinkroadsafety.gov.uk
www.dft.gov.uk
www.road-safe.org

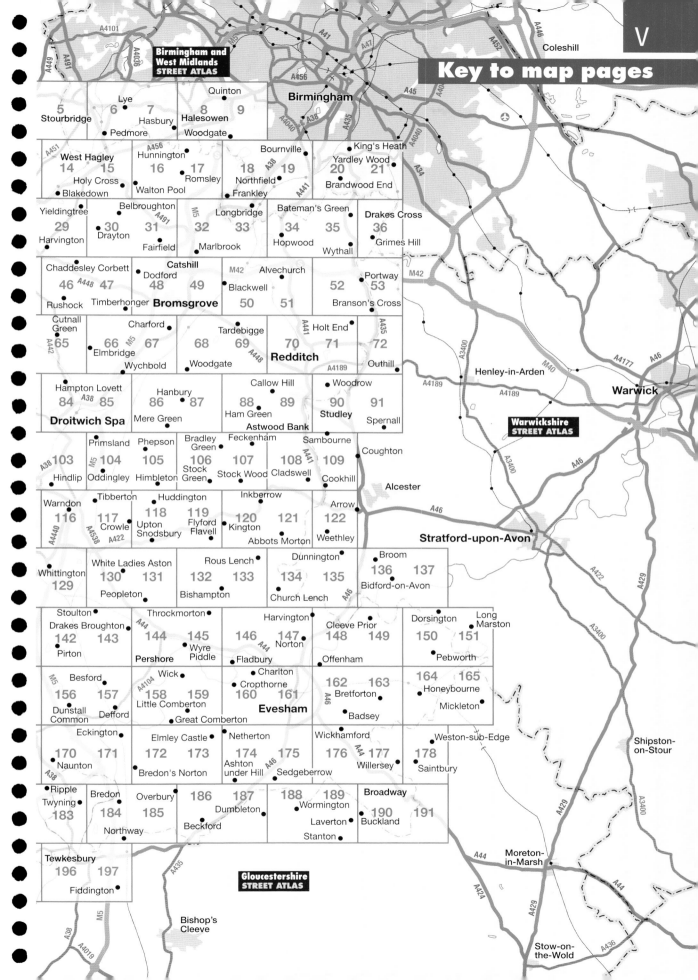

Birmingham and West Midlands STREET ATLAS

Coleshill

Quinton
Birmingham

5 Stourbridge
Lye
6 7 Hasbury 8 Halesowen 9
Pedmore Woodgate

Bournville
King's Heath
West Hagley
Hunnington
14 15 16 17 18 19 Yardley Wood 20 21
Holy Cross Romsley Northfield Brandwood End
Blakedown Walton Pool Frankley

Yieldingtree Belbroughton
29 30 31 32 Longbridge 33 Bateman's Green 34 35 Drakes Cross 36
Harvington Drayton Fairfield Marlbrook Hopwood Wythall Grimes Hill

Chaddesley Corbett Catshill
46 47 Dodford 48 49 Alvechurch 52 Portway 53
Rushock Timberhonger Bromsgrove Blackwell 50 51 Branson's Cross

Cutnall Green
65 66 67 68 Tardebigge 69 Holt End 70 71 72
Elmbridge Wychbold Woodgate Redditch Outhill

Hampton Lovett Henley-in-Arden
84 85 Hanbury 86 87 Callow Hill 88 89 Woodrow 90 91 Warwick
Droitwich Spa Mere Green Ham Green Astwood Bank Studley Spernall

Warwickshire STREET ATLAS

Primsland Phepson Bradley Green Feckenham Sambourne
103 104 105 106 107 108 109 Coughton
Hindlip Oddingley Himbleton Stock Green Stock Wood Cladswell Cookhill
Alcester

Warndon Tibberton Huddington Inkberrow
116 117 118 119 120 121 122 Arrow
Crowle Upton Snodsbury Flyford Flavell Kington Weethley
Abbots Morton
Stratford-upon-Avon

White Ladies Aston Rous Lench Dunnington Broom
Whittington 130 131 132 133 134 135 136 137
129 Peopleton Bishampton Church Lench Bidford-on-Avon

Stoulton Throckmorton Harvington Dorsington Long Marston
Drakes Broughton 144 145 146 147 Cleeve Prior 148 149 150 151
142 143 Wyre Norton Pebworth
Pirton Pershore Piddle Fladbury Offenham

Besford Wick Charlton
156 157 158 159 160 161 162 163 164 165 Honeybourne
Dunstall Little Comberton Cropthorne Bretforton Mickleton
Common Defford Evesham Badsey
Great Comberton

Eckington Elmley Castle Netherton Wickhamford Weston-sub-Edge
170 171 172 173 174 175 176 177 178
Naunton Bredon's Norton Ashton Sedgeberrow Willersey Saintbury
under Hill

Ripple Bredon Overbury Broadway
Twyning 184 185 186 187 188 189 190 191
183 Dumbleton Wormington
Northway Beckford Laverton Buckland
Stanton

Tewkesbury
196 197
Fiddington

Gloucestershire STREET ATLAS

Bishop's Cleeve

Shipston-on-Stour

Moreton-in-Marsh

Stow-on-the-Wold

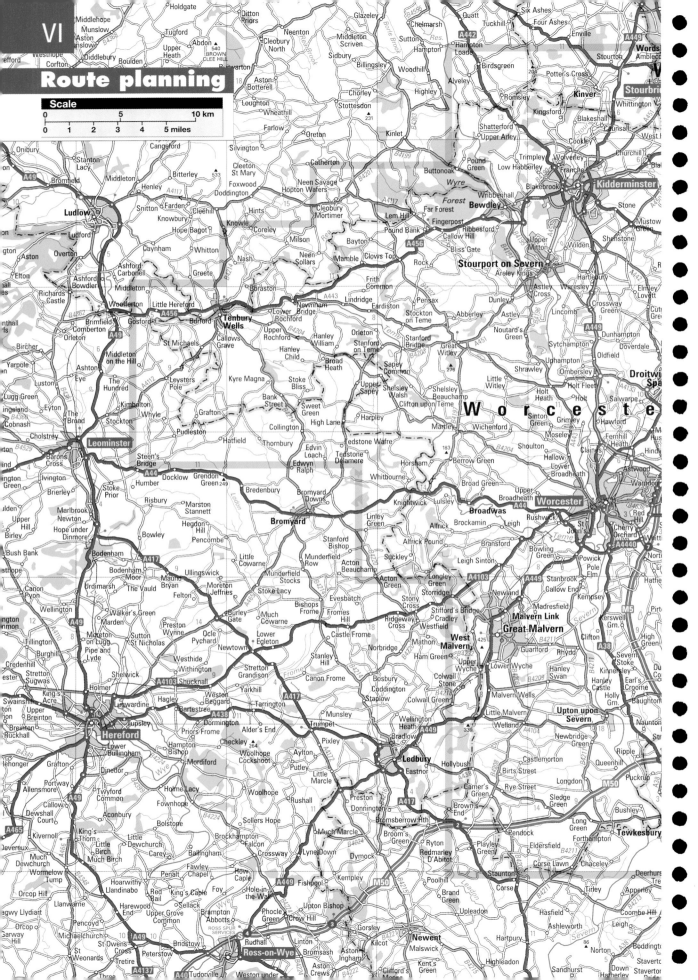

Scale

0   5   10 km
0   1   2   3   4   5 miles

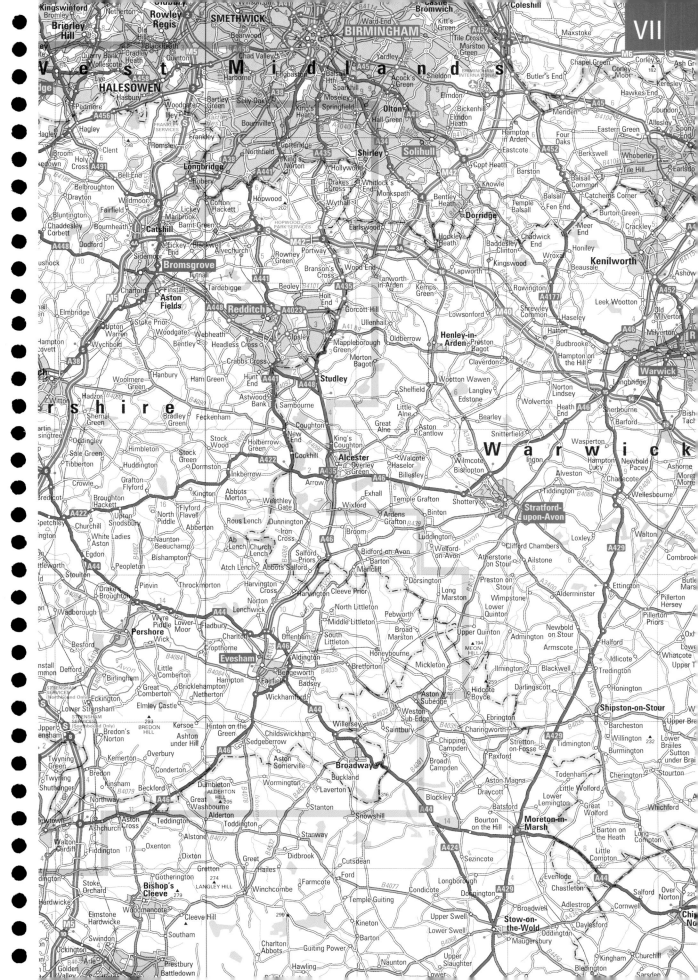

Administrative and
Postcode boundaries

County and unitary authority boundaries

District boundaries

Postcode boundaries

Area covered by this atlas

Scale

0   5   10   15   20   25 km
0   5   10   15 miles

SJ SK

SJ   SK
SO   SP

Birmingham and
West Midlands

Staffordshire

Shropshire

Birdsgreen
Alveley   WV15
WV16
Kingsford
DY12   DY11   Blakedown
Cleobury
Mortimer   DY14   Blakebrook
Bewdley   Kidderminster
DY7   Stourbridge
Kinver   DY8
Hagley
DY9   Romsley
Belbroughton
Catshill

DY5   DY64
Halesowen
B63   B32
B62   Frankley
B29   Bournville
B30   B14
B31   Longbridge
B45   B38
Barnt Green   B48   Alvechurch

B68 B67

B13

B28
B90
B47   B94
Wood End

Wyre Forest
SY8
Nash
SY8
HR6
Tenbury Wells   WR15
Callows Grave
Leysters
Whyle
Hatfield   Collington   HR7
Rock
Abberley
Great Witley
Bank Street
Clifton upon Teme
Collington
Stourport on Severn   Waresley
Holt Heath
Ombersley
WR6   Martley
Whitbourne

DY10

DY13
Elmley Lovett
Wychbold
Droitwich
WR9
Woolmere Green

Bromsgrove
B61   Bromsgrove
Aston Fields
B60
Feckenham   B96
Astwood Bank

Redditch
Beoley
Redditch   B98
B97   B80   Studley
Cladswell

B95

Worcestershire

Herefordshire

Broadwas
Alfrick
Suckley
WR2
WR1   Worcester
Rushwick
Cherry Orchard
Powick   Littleworth
Worcester
WR7

Fernhill Heath
Himbleton
WR3   Tibberton
Warndon   Crowle
WR4   Flyford Flavell
Bishampton

Inkberrow

B49   Warwickshire

Dunnington
Broom
Bidford-on-Avon
Church Lench   B50

Malvern Hills
Great Malvern
WR14
Colwall Stone
Malvern Wells
Upton upon Severn
Hanley Swan
Welland
WR13
Rye Street
HR8
Forthampton
GL19
Redmarley D'Abitot
Chaceley

WR5
Kempsey
WR8   Besford
Stoulton
Wadborough
Elmley Castle
Eckington
Longdon
Twyning Green
Bredon
Beckford
GL20   Tewkesbury
Fiddington

Pinvin
Pershore
WR10

Wychavon

Harvington
Evesham   Badsey
WR11
Cleeve Prior
Long Marston
CV37
Pebworth
Bretforton
Mickleton
Weston Subedge
Willersey
Broadway   GL55
WR12   Stanton   GL56
Ashton under Hill
GL54

Gloucestershire

SO SP

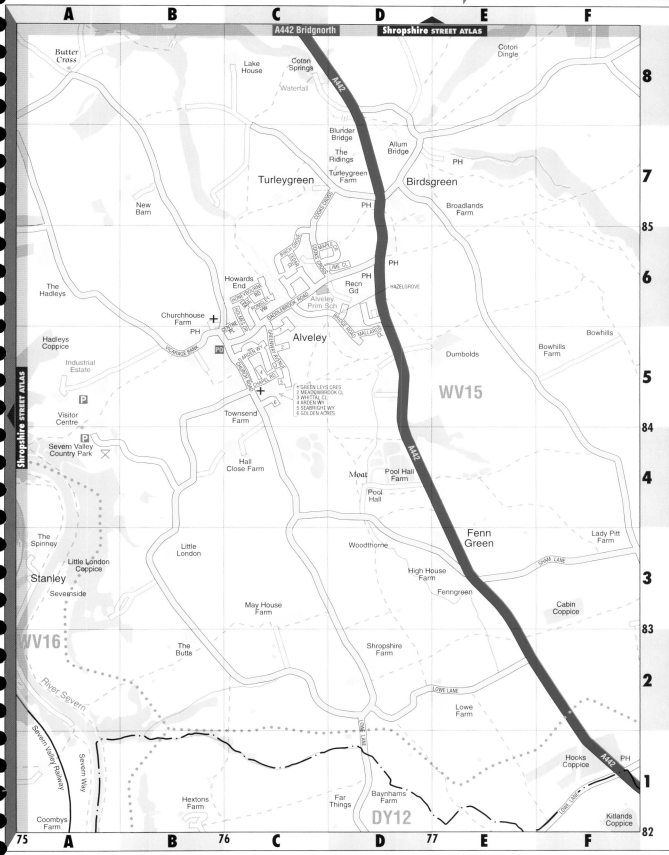

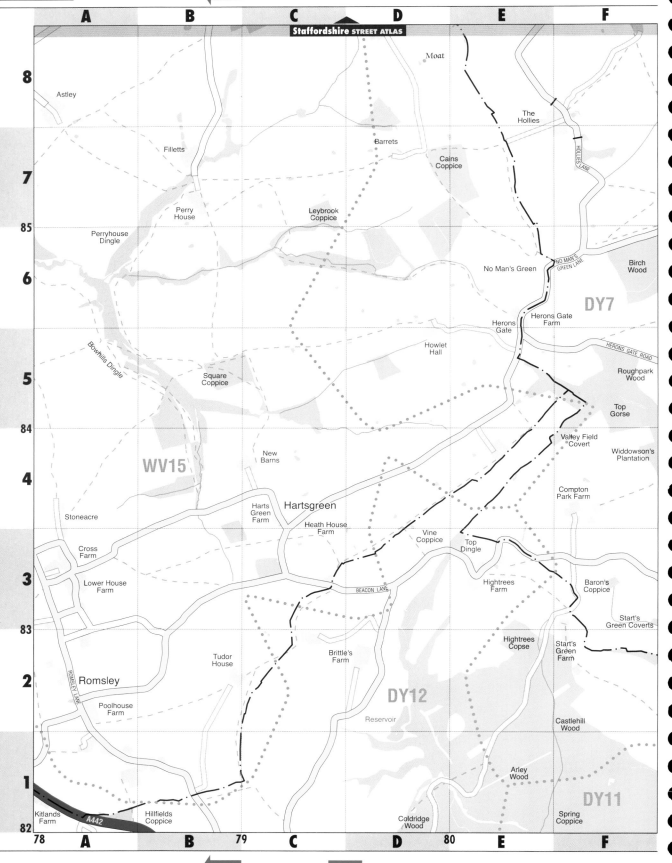

Staffordshire STREET ATLAS

DY7

WV15

DY12

DY11

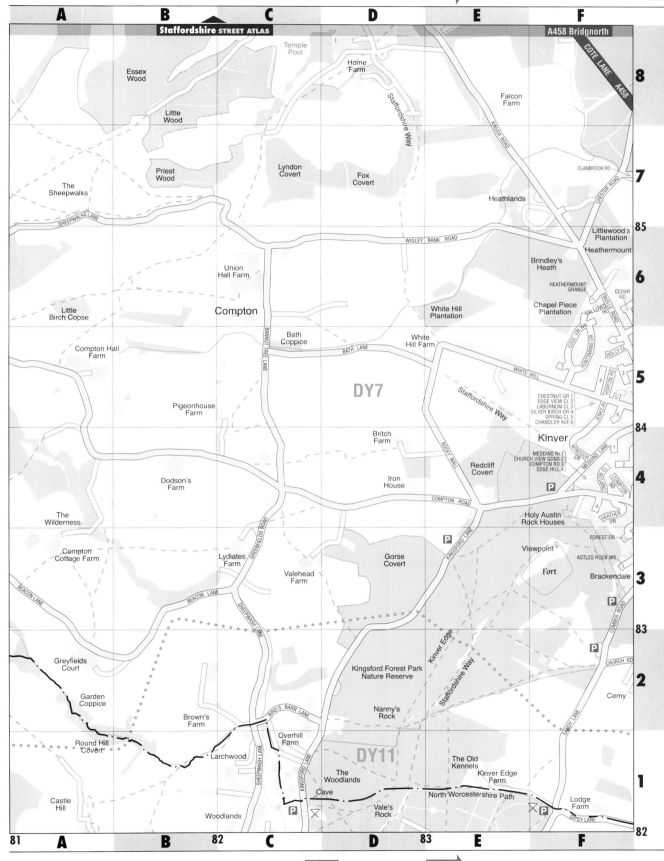

Staffordshire STREET ATLAS

A458 Bridgnorth

COTE LANE A458

A B C D E F

8
7
85
6
5
84
4
3
83
2
1
82

Essex Wood

Little Wood

Priest Wood

The Sheepwalks

SHEEPWALKS LANE

Temple Pool

Home Farm

Staffordshire Way

Lyndon Covert

Fox Covert

WIGLEY BANK ROAD

Union Hall Farm

Compton

Little Birch Copse

Compton Hall Farm

Pigeonhouse Farm

Dodson's Farm

The Wilderness

Compton Cottage Farm

Lydiates Farm

Valehead Farm

BEACON LANE

SHEEPWASH LANE

GREENFIELDS ROAD

BANNUT TREE LANE

Bath Coppice

BATH LANE

White Hill Farm

White Hill Plantation

Britch Farm

Iron House

ROCKY WALL

Gorse Covert

COMPTON ROAD

Kingsford Forest Park Nature Reserve

Nanny's Rock

KINGSFORD LANE

DY7

Falcon Farm

KINVER ROAD

CHESTER ROAD

Heathlands

CLANBROOK RD

Littlewood's Plantation

Heathermount

Brindley's Heath

HEATHERMOUNT GRANGE

ENVILLE ROAD

CEDAR GD

Chapel Piece Plantation

GALLOWS

EDGE VW WK

HUNTSMANS DR

HOLLY CL

WHITE HILL

Staffordshire Way

CHESTNUT GR 1
EDGE VIEW CL 2
LABURNUM CL 3
SILVER BIRCH DR 4
SPRING CL 5
CHANDLER AVE 6

JENKS AV

HORTON RD

Kinver

WINDSOR DR

MEDDINS LANE

MEDDINS RI 1
CHURCH VIEW GDNS 2
COMPTON RD 3
EDGE HILL 4

Redcliff Covert

COMPTON CL GD

COMPTON

Holy Austin Rock Houses

HEATHER DR

FOREST DR

Viewpoint

Fort

ASTLES ROCK WK

Brackendale

COMBER ROAD

CHURCH RD

Cemy

Kinver Edge

Staffordshire Way

SANDY LANE

GIPSY LANE

Greyfields Court

Garden Coppice

Round Hill Covert

Larchwood

Brown's Farm

BIRD'S BARN LANE

Overhill Farm

SHEEPWASH LANE

KINGSFORD LANE

DY11

The Woodlands

Cave

Woodlands

Vale's Rock

The Old Kennels

Kinver Edge Farm

North Worcestershire Path

Lodge Farm

Castle Hill

BEACON LANE

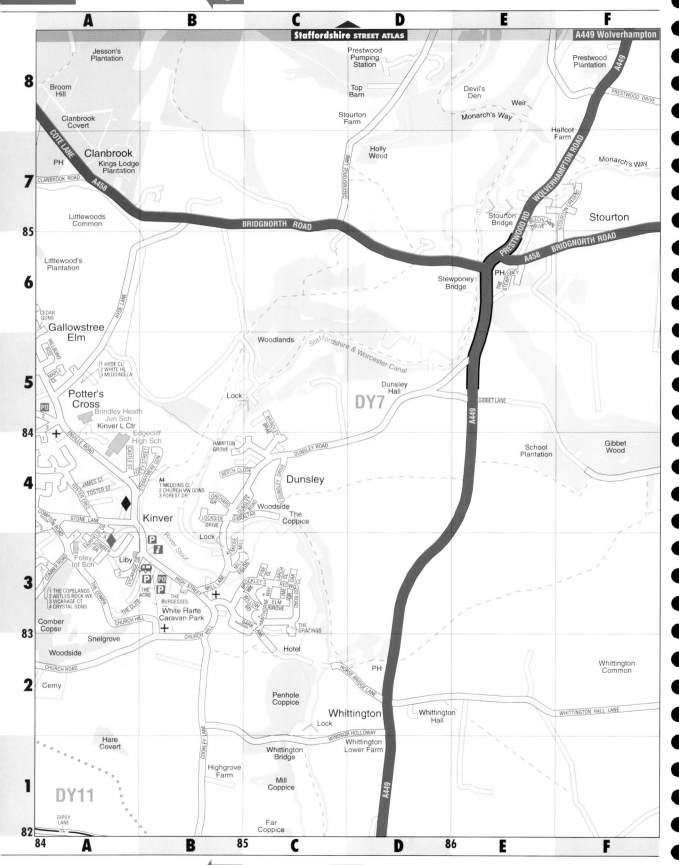

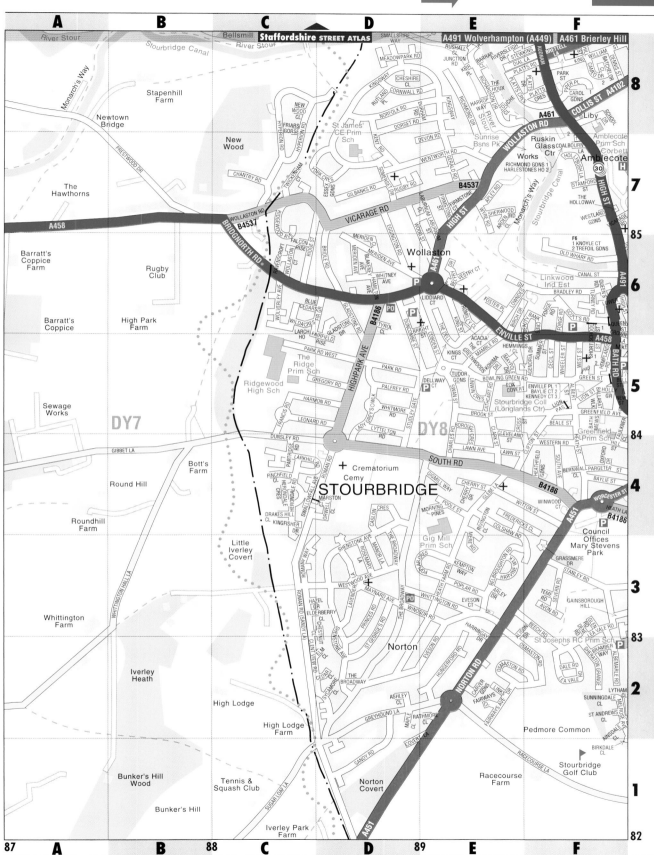

6
E8
1 STEWKINS CT
F8
1 CORBETT HO
2 DENNIS HALL

Staffordshire STREET ATLAS

A491 Wolverhampton (A449) A461 Brierley Hill

River Stour
Stourbridge Canal
Bellsmill
SMALLSHIRE WAY
River Stour

Monarch's Way

Stapenhill
Farm

Newtown
Bridge

New
Wood

New Wood

The Hawthorns

A458

WOLLASTON RD

BRIDGNORTH RD

B4537

Barratt's
Coppice
Farm

Rugby
Club

Barratt's
Coppice

High Park
Farm

Sewage
Works

DY7

GIBBET LA

Bott's
Farm

Round Hill

Roundhill
Farm

Little
Iverley Covert

Whittington
Farm

WHITTINGTON HALL LA

Iverley
Heath

High Lodge

High Lodge
Farm

Bunker's Hill
Wood

Tennis &
Squash Club

Bunker's Hill

Iverley Park
Farm

VICARAGE RD

St James'
CE Prim
Sch

Wollaston

The
Ridge
Prim Sch

Ridgewood
High Sch

HIGHPARK AVE

Crematorium
Cemy

STOURBRIDGE

DY8

SOUTH RD

B4186

Norton

THE BROADWAY

Gig Mill
Prim Sch

Norton
Covert

NORTON RD

A451

Ruskin
Glass
Works

Sunrise
Bsns Pk

Stourbridge Canal

Monarch's Way

Linkwood
Ind Est

ENVILLE ST

A458

Stourbridge Coll
(Longlands Ctr)

Mary Stevens
Park

Council
Offices

Pedmore Common

Birkdale
Cl

Stourbridge
Golf Club

Racecourse
Farm

RACECOURSE LA

Ambiecote
Prim Sch

Ambiecote

HIGH ST

COLLIS ST A4102

Liby

Corbett

F6
1 KNOYLE CT
2 TREFOIL GDNS

A491

BATH RD

B4186

WORCESTER ST

St Josephs RC Prim Sch

Gainsborough
Hill

6

A5
1 NEW ST
2 EDEN HO
3 The Crown Ctr
4 SMITHFIELDS
5 VICTORIA PASS

6 TALBOT PASS
7 Ryemarket Sh Ctr
8 FOSTER ST
9 COURT ST

5

A6
1 LOWER HIGH ST
2 ST GILES ROW
3 TREFOIL GDNS
4 JARDINE CL

B'ham & W. Midlands STREET ATLAS A4036 Dudley

A4102 Brierley Hill

Withymoor Village

BRIERLEY HILL

DY5

Peters Hill

Stambermill

Lye

Old Swinford

DY8

Wollescote

DY9

Old Swinford

Pedmore

Hodge Hill

5

5

15

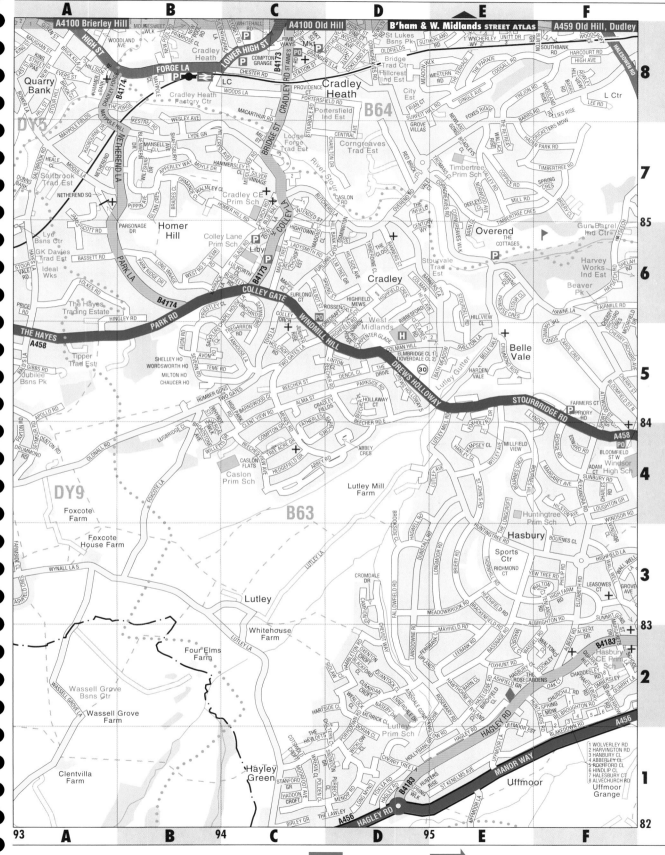

B'ham & W. Midlands STREET ATLAS

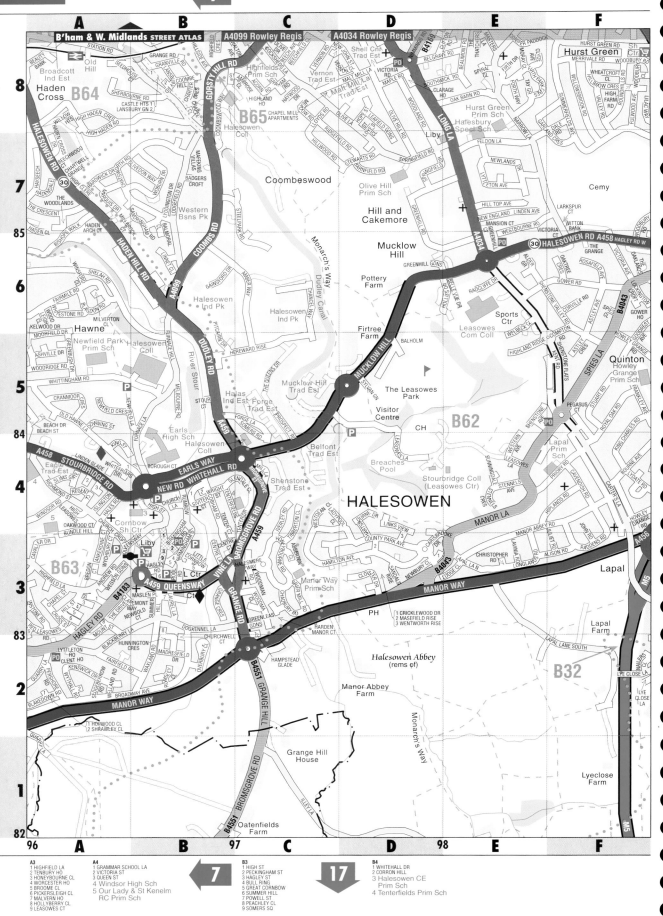

B'ham & W. Midlands STREET ATLAS

A3
1 HIGHFIELD LA
2 TENBURY HO
3 HONEYBOURNE CL
4 WORCESTER HO
5 BROOME CL
6 PICKERSLEIGH CT
7 MALVERN HO
8 HOLLYBERRY CL
9 LEASOWES CT

A4
1 GRAMMAR SCHOOL LA
2 VICTORIA ST
3 QUEEN ST
4 Windsor High Sch
5 Our Lady & St Kenelm
   RC Prim Sch

B3
1 HIGH ST
2 PECKINGHAM ST
3 HAGLEY ST
4 BULL RING
5 GREAT CORNBOW
6 SUMMER HILL
7 POWELL ST
8 PEACHLEY CL
9 SOMERS SQ

B4
1 WHITEHALL DR
2 CORRON HILL
3 Halesowen CE
   Prim Sch
4 Tenterfields Prim Sch

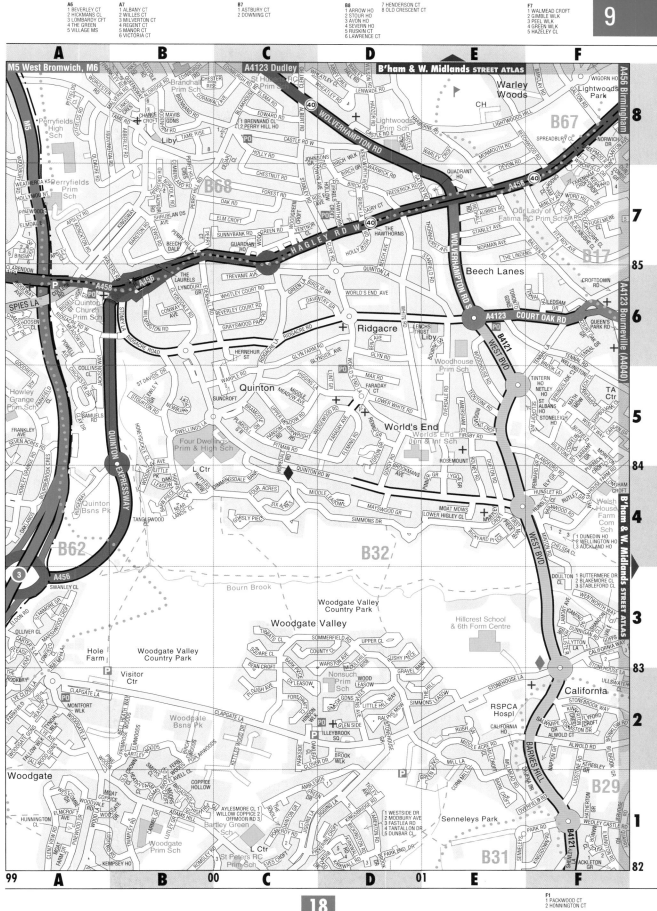

18

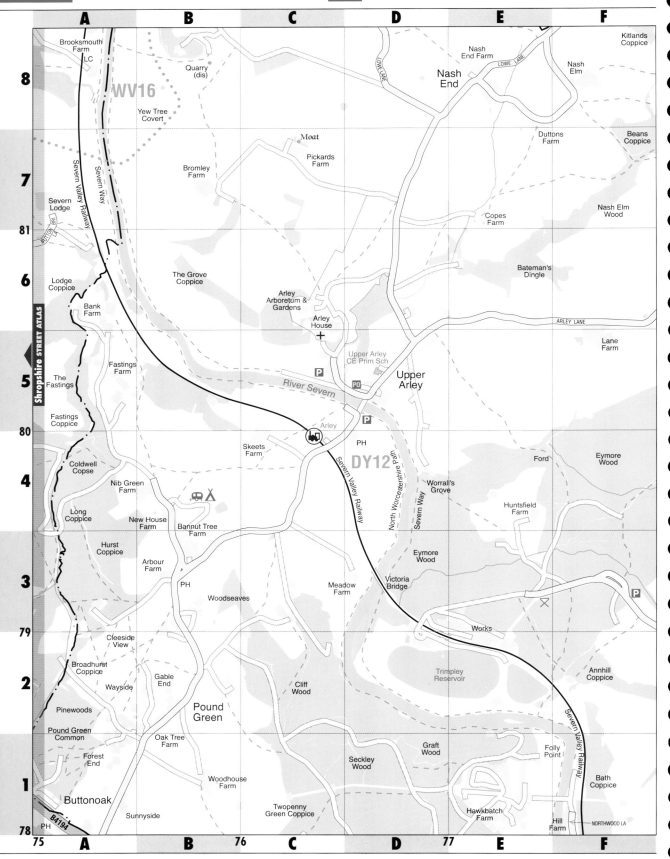

Shropshire STREET ATLAS

Row 8: Brooksmouth Farm, LC, WV16, Quarry (dis), Nash End Farm, Nash End, Kitlands Coppice, Nash Elm, Lowe Lane

Row 7: Yew Tree Covert, Bromley Farm, Moat, Pickards Farm, Copes Farm, Duttons Farm, Beans Coppice, Nash Elm Wood, Severn Valley Railway, Severn Way

Row 81: Severn Lodge, BUTTON BRI LA

Row 6: Lodge Coppice, Bank Farm, The Grove Coppice, Arley Arboretum & Gardens, Arley House, Bateman's Dingle, ARLEY LANE

Row 5: The Fastings, Fastings Farm, River Severn, Upper Arley CE Prim Sch, Upper Arley, PO, P, Lane Farm

Row 80: Fastings Coppice, Skeets Farm, Arley, PH, DY12, Ford, Eymore Wood

Row 4: Coldwell Copse, Nib Green Farm, New House Farm, Bannut Tree Farm, Severn Valley Railway, North Worcestershire Path, Worrall's Grove, Eymore Wood, Huntsfield Farm, Severn Way, Long Coppice

Row 3: Hurst Coppice, Arbour Farm, PH, Woodseaves, Meadow Farm, Victoria Bridge, P

Row 79: Cleeside View, Works

Row 2: Broadhurst Coppice, Wayside, Gable End, Cliff Wood, Trimpley Reservoir, Annhill Coppice, Pinewoods, Pound Green, Severn Valley Railway

Row 1: Pound Green Common, Forest End, Oak Tree Farm, Woodhouse Farm, Seckley Wood, Graft Wood, Folly Point, Bath Coppice, Hill Farm

Row 78: Buttonoak, B4194, PH, Sunnyside, Twopenny Green Coppice, Hawkbatch Farm, NORTHWOOD LA

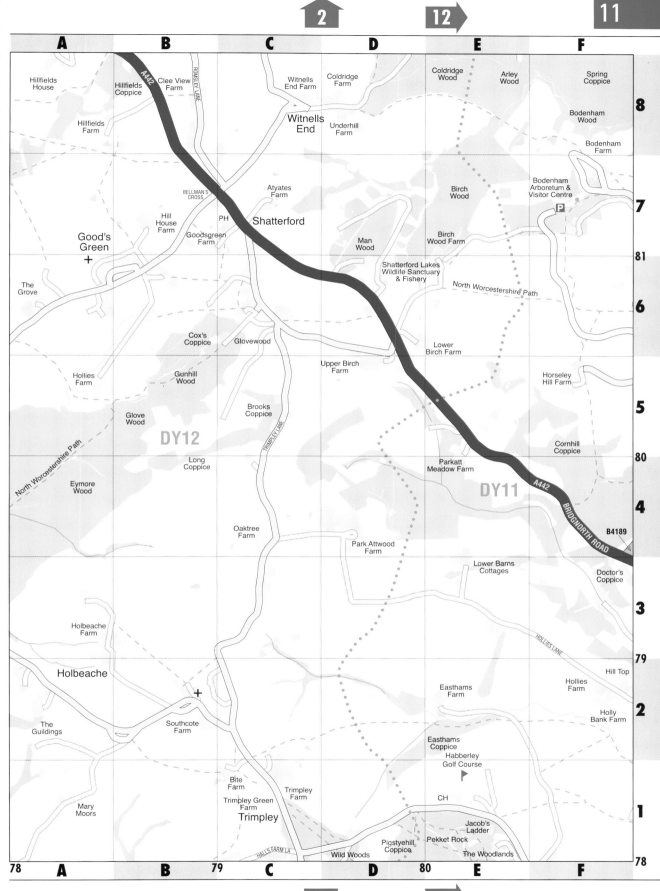

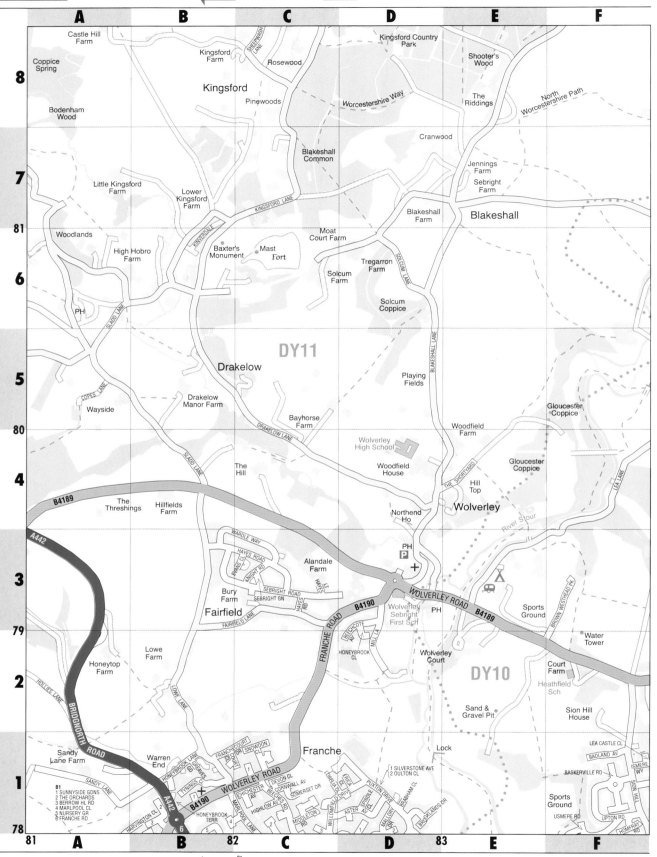

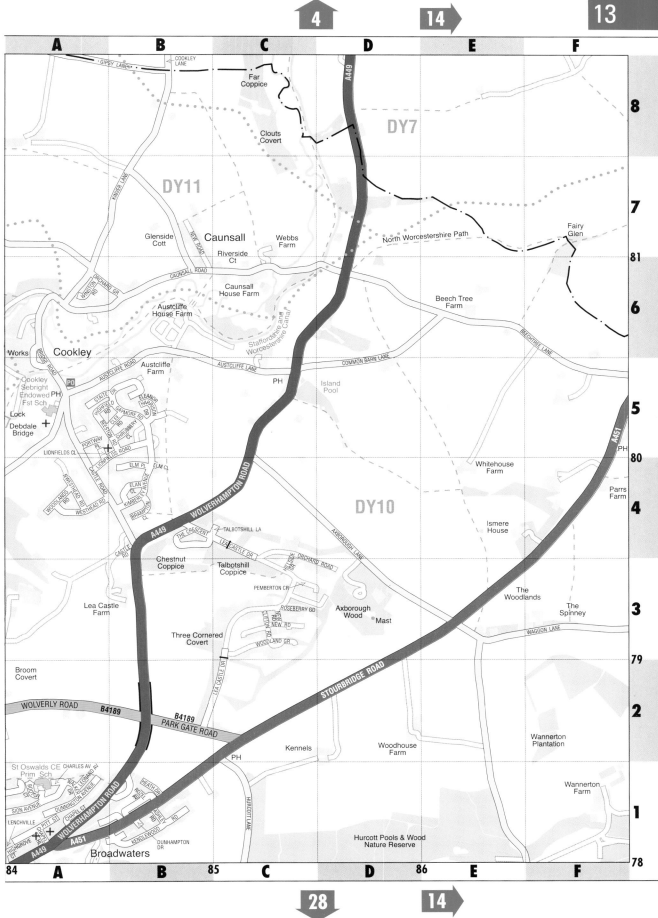

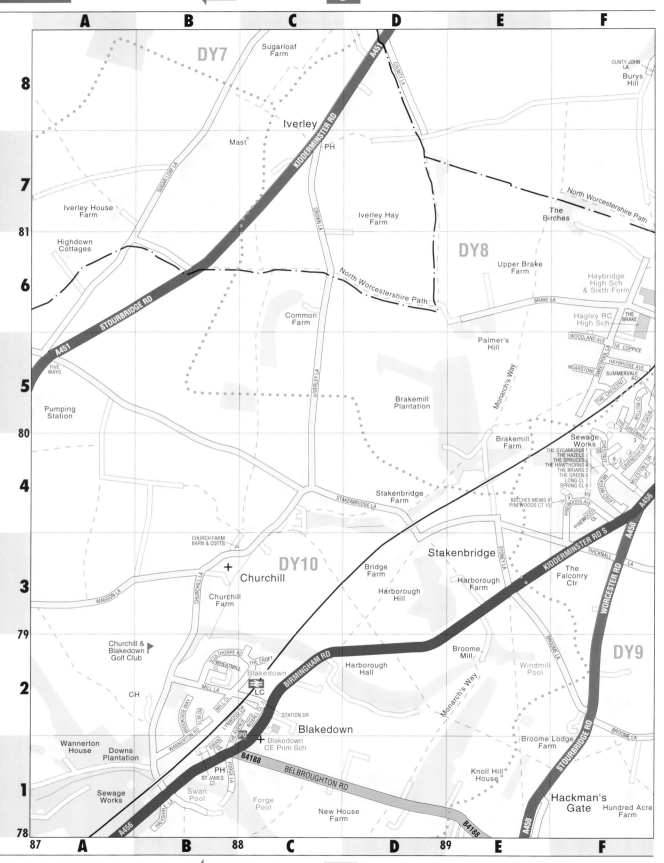

DY7

Sugarloaf Farm

COUNTY JOHN LA

Burys Hill

Iverley

North Worcestershire Path

Mast

PH

The Birches

Iverley House Farm

Iverley Hay Farm

DY8

Highdown Cottages

Upper Brake Farm

Haybridge High Sch & Sixth Form

North Worcestershire Path

STOURBRIDGE RD

Common Farm

Palmer's Hill

Hagley RC High Sch

THE BRAKE

A451

WOODLAND AVE

THE COPPICE

FIVE WAYS

HOARSTONE

SWEETPOOL LA

HAYBRIDGE AVE

SUMMERVALE RD

THE CRESCENT

Brakemill Plantation

Monarch's Way

WILLOW CL

THE OASIS

Pumping Station

THE GREENWAY

Brakemill Farm

Sewage Works

CHESTNUT

CAVENDISH DR

THE SYCAMORES 1
THE HAZELS 2
THE SPRUCES 3
THE HAWTHORNS 4
THE BRIARS 5
THE GREEN 6
LONG CL 7
SPRING CL 8

STAKENBRIDGE LA

Stakenbridge Farm

BEECHES MEWS 9
PINEWOODS CT 10)

PINEWOODS AVE

PINEWOODS CL

A456

CHURCH FARM BARN & COTTS

DY10

Stakenbridge

KIDDERMINSTER RD S

THICKNALL

WAGGON LA

CHURCHILL LA

Churchill

Bridge Farm

Harborough Farm

STONEY LA

The Falconry Ctr

A450

WORCESTER RD

Churchill Farm

Harborough Hill

Churchill & Blakedown Golf Club

Broome Mill

Windmill Pool

DY9

SOUTHORPE RD

THE CROFT

WHEATMILL CL

Harborough Hall

BIRMINGHAM RD

Monarch's Way

BROOME LA

Blakedown

CH

MILL LA

ELM CL

LC

Wannerton House

MILL CL

BROOKSIDE WAY

WANNERTON RD

THE AVENUE

LYNWOOD DR

ROYAL CL

STATION DR

Blakedown

Broome Lodge Farm

STOURBRIDGE RD

PO

Blakedown CE Prim Sch

Downs Plantation

SWAN

PH

ST JAMES CT

FORGE LA

B4188

BELBROUGHTON RD

Knoll Hill House

BROOME LA

Sewage Works

Swan Pool

Forge Pool

New House Farm

Hackman's Gate

A450

Hundred Acre Farm

HALESHIRE LA

A456

B4188

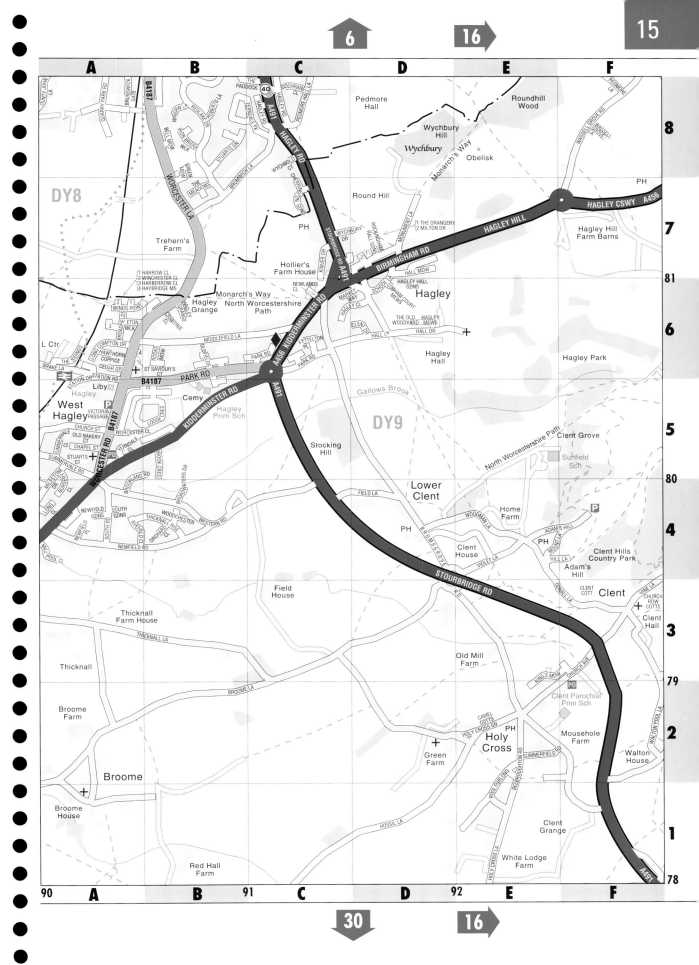

A B C D E F

CH

HAGLEY RD
A456
B63

8

B63

HAGLEY CAUSEWAY
A456

Hagley Wood

Bogs Wood

Uffmoor
Farm

7

LUTLEY LA
HAYLEY PARK RD
ABBEY RD
KELMELSTOWE
CRES
HODGETTS DR
WAUGH DR
CAUSEY FARM RD

81

HAGLEYWOOD LA

Spring
Farm

UFFMOOR LA

Uffmoor Wood

P

6

Nimmings
Plantation

Nimmings
Visitor Ctr
P

Penorchard
Farm

Chapel
Farm

CHAPEL LA

Short Wood

Clent Hills

St Kenelm's
Farm

Fox
Farm

Four
Oaks

5

The Four
Stones

High Harcourt
Farm
P

P

B62

ST KENELM'S RD

IVY LA

80

Clent Hills
Country Park

Monarch's Way

HOLT LA

Holt
Farm

THE ALDERS
THE HEDGEROWS
WAVERLEY CRES
DARK LA

4

Deep
Wood

Dark
Pool

Oatlands

SPRING LA

FIELDHOUSE LA

Fieldhouse
Farm

PH
VINE LA
CLATTERBACH LA

Walton Hill

Whitehall
Farm

RUMBOW LA

Nag Hill

Walton Hill
Farm

3

DY9

WALTON RISE

HIGHFIELD LA

Rumbow
Cottages

SHUT MILL LA

79

Walton Pool

Daleswood
Farm

2

Walton
Farm

Calcot
Hill

Dales Wood

DALESWOOD
PK

Squats
Wood

WINWOOD HEATH RD

North Worcestershire Path

FARLEY LA

MOOR HALL DR

Moorhall
Farm

Calcothill
Farm

1

Great Farley
Wood

ROMSLEY HILL
GRANGE

Farley
Farm

78

93 A B 94 C D 95 E F

8 ↑   **18** →

A   B   C   D   E   F

B63
Dovehousefields Farm
Hunnington
Blue Bird Pk
Goodrest Farm
B4551
M5
Illeybrook Farm
Illey LA
Innage Farm
PH
Illey
Potters Farm
Illey House Farm
Lower Illey

8

Breach Farm
THE CLOSE
RED HILL PL
Warstone Farm
Frankley Service Area

7

81

Hollies Farm
Hollyhurst Farm Caravan Site
Twiland Wood
Kettles Wood
Raven Hays Wood

6

Hunnington Farm
Horsepool Farm
Brookhouse Farm
FRANKLEY GN
FRANKLEY GREEN LA
Long Kettles Wood

5

Yewtree Farm
Porch House Farm
YEW TREE CL
ST KENELMS RD
EASTLEIGH DR
KENELM CT
BROMSGROVE RD
PO
PH
Romsley
St Kenelms CE Prim Sch
B62
WAVERLEY CRES
HILLCREST RD
WINSTON DR
POPLAR LA
DARK LA
PH
Ell Wood
Monarch's Way
Penny Fields
OXWOOD LA
OXWOOD LA
Newbrook Farm
B32
80

4

Yew Tree Farm
Dayhouse Wood
Long Saw Croft
Round Saw Croft
YEW TREE LA
Frankley Hill Farm
FRANKLEY HILL LA

3

Romsley Manor Farm
FARLEY LA
Mast
POUND LA
Lower Hill Barn
Frankley Hill

79

Romsley Hill
Mast
PUTNEY LA
Dayhouse Farm
OLD HOUSE LA
FORDRAUGHT LA
NEWTOWN LA
Newtown Farm
Sandhills Farm
Gannow Green Farm
BISHOP CL 1
PRINCE CHARLES CL 2
PRINCESS ANNE DR 3
PRINCE EDWARD DR 4
FISHER CL 5
QUEEN ELIZABETH RD
PRINCE ANDREW CRES
JUBILEE RD
FABIAN CL
NEW ST
B45
Holly Hill Methodist CE Inf Sch
Frankley Com High Sch
Liby

2

Dayhouse Bank
North Worcestershire Path
DAYHOUSE BANK
CHAPMAN'S HILL
B4551
M5
Gannow Green
GANNOW GREEN LA
Waseley Hills Visitor Ctr
P
Duck Pool Farm
Waseley Hills Country Park
DURANT CL
PEARMAN RD
CROMPTON CL
RYMAN CL
LYAL GDNS
HARLOE CRES
SKINNER CL
BARLEYFIELD ROW
GANNOW MANOR CRES
BLUTE CL
MITRE CL
CANVEY RD
ROMER RD
WOODHAM CL
RAMSEY CL
NEW INNS LA
ROBINIA CL
BOTTERY CL
DEVON CL
CORNWALL RD
BOLEYN RD
SHAFTINSAY DR
WESTBAY CL
KINTYRE CL
PHILIP RD
DORSET CL
NORFOLK
SUFFOLK
BROWNSLEA CL
ORMOND RD
CHALYBEATE CL
HIGH TIMBERS
MITTEN AVE
QUARRY CLOSE
WIDE ACRES
CROSS FARMS LA
RUBERY LA
GANNOW MANOR GDNS
HOLLY HILL
PO
P
Reaside Junior Sch
BRYHER WLK

1

78

32 ↓   **18** →

F1
1 BROOKDALE CL
2 CHADDERSLEY CL
3 RUBERY LA S
4 HOLLY HILL
5 CALDY WLK

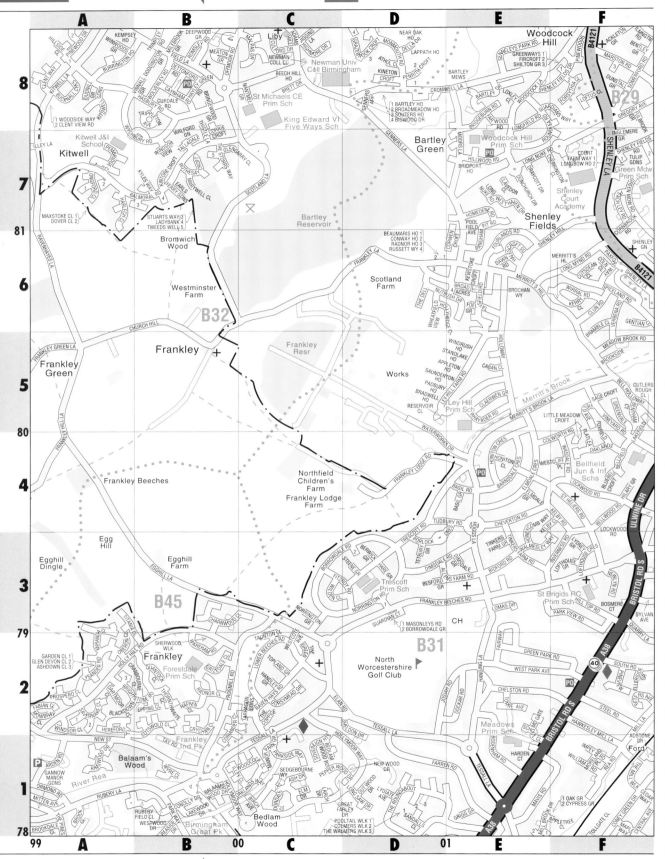

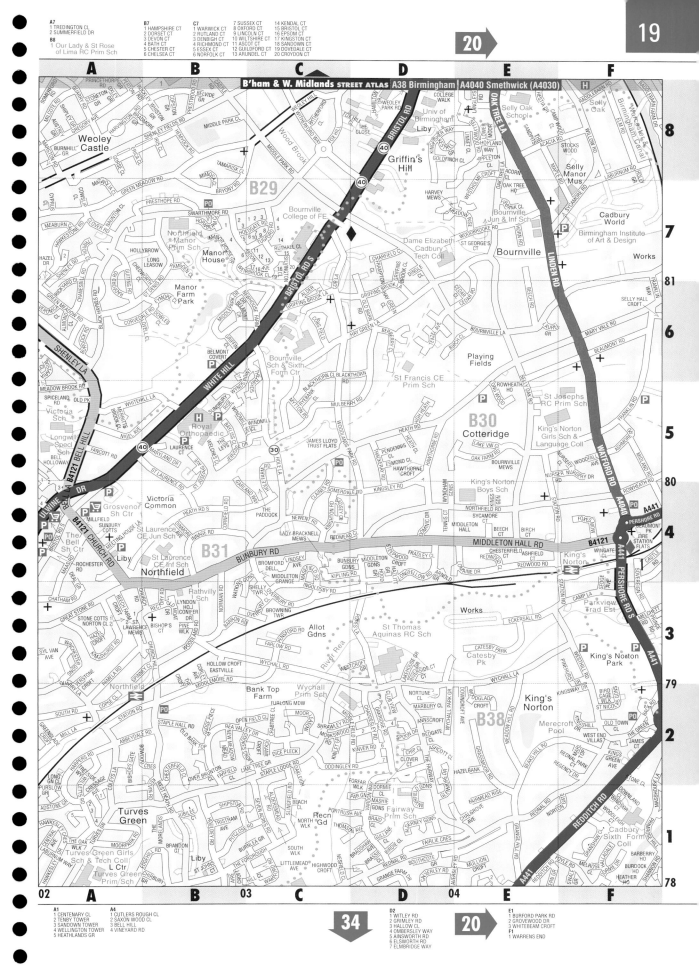

B'ham & W. Midlands STREET ATLAS A38 Birmingham A4040 Smethwick (A4030)

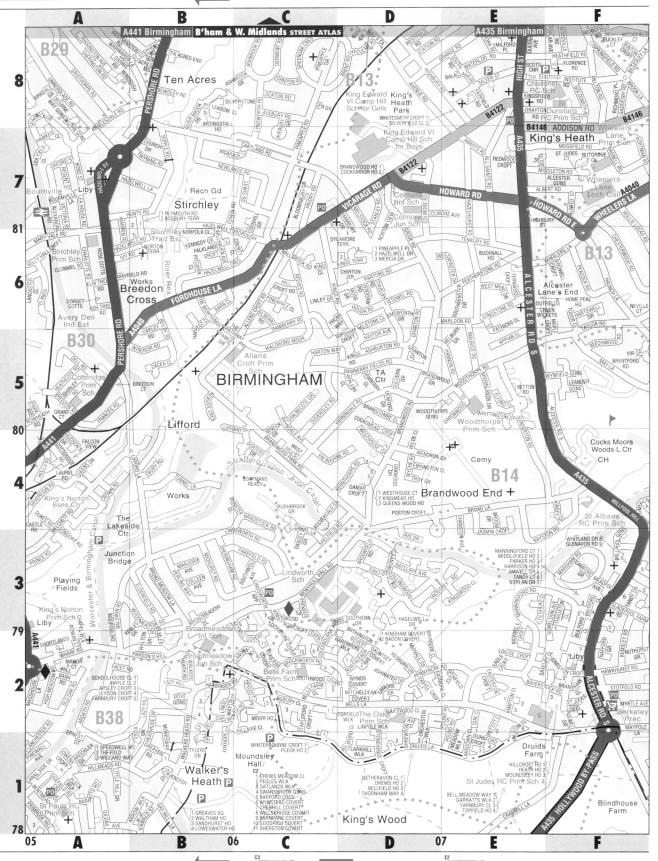

A441 Birmingham **B'ham & W. Midlands** STREET ATLAS A435 Birmingham

C3
1 BEECHWOOD CT
2 LINDSWORTH CT
3 ASHBURY COVERT
4 TAYNTON COVERT

E2
1 KINGSWOOD HO
2 SAXELBY HO
3 BARRATTS HO
4 BROOKPIECE HO
5 PITMEADOW HO
6 Baverstock Foundation Sch
& Specialist Sports Coll

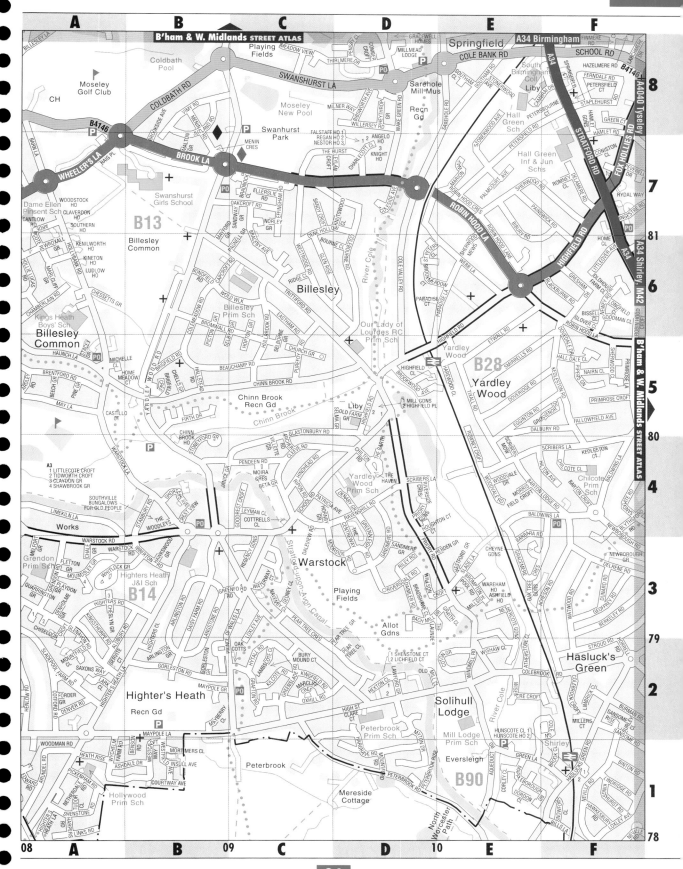

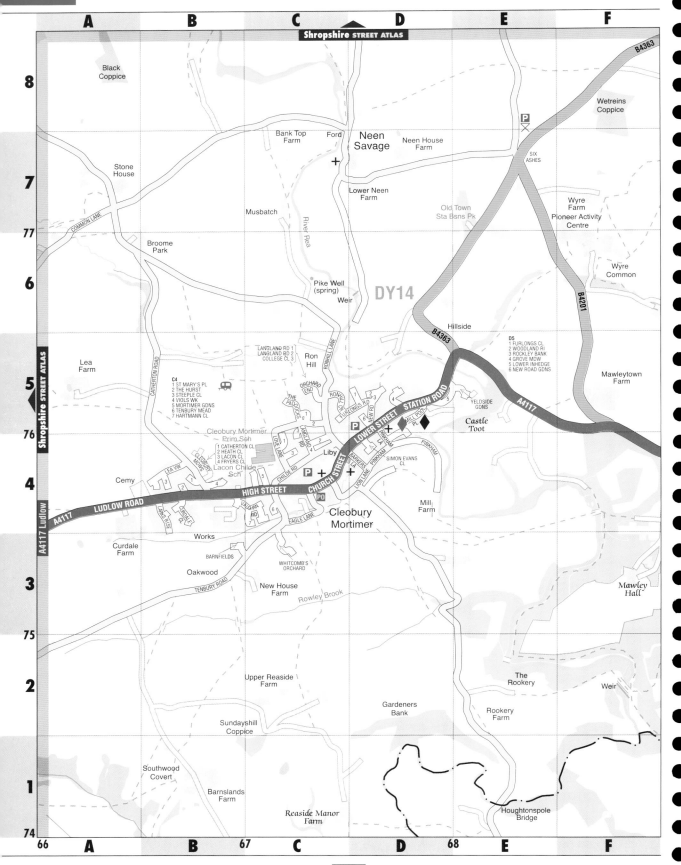

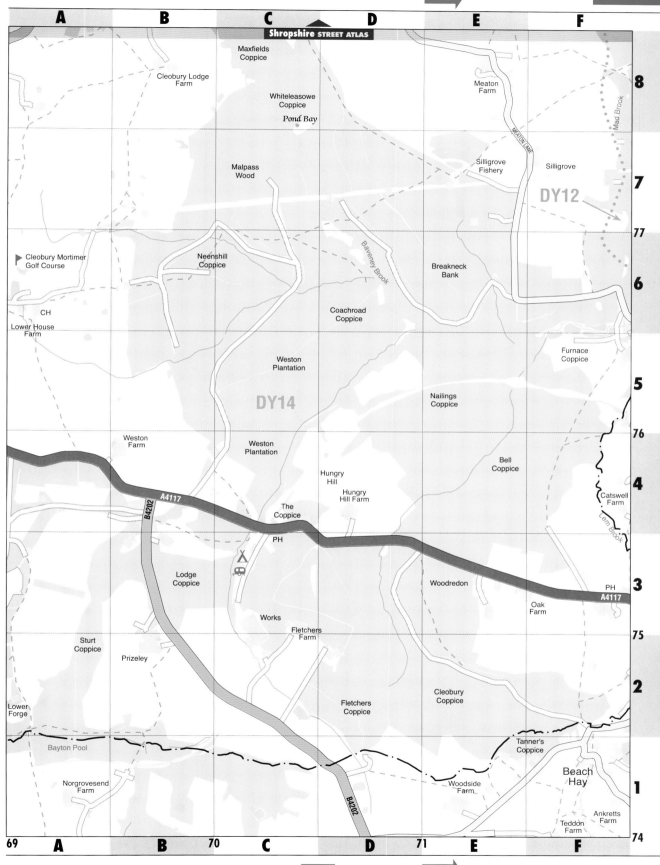

Shropshire STREET ATLAS

24

Maxfields Coppice

Cleobury Lodge Farm

Whiteleasowe Coppice

Pond Bay

Meaton Farm

Silligrove Fishery

Silligrove

Mad Brook

MEATON LANE

DY12

Malpass Wood

Neenshill Coppice

Baveney Brook

Breakneck Bank

Cleobury Mortimer Golf Course

CH

Lower House Farm

Coachroad Coppice

Furnace Coppice

Weston Plantation

DY14

Nailings Coppice

Weston Farm

Weston Plantation

Hungry Hill

Hungry Hill Farm

Bell Coppice

Catswell Farm

Lem Brook

The Coppice

A4117

B4202

PH

Lodge Coppice

Works

Fletchers Farm

Woodredon

Oak Farm

PH

A4117

Sturt Coppice

Prizeley

Fletchers Coppice

Cleobury Coppice

Lower Forge

Bayton Pool

B4202

Tanner's Coppice

Beach Hay

Norgrovesend Farm

Woodside Farm

Ankretts Farm

Teddon Farm

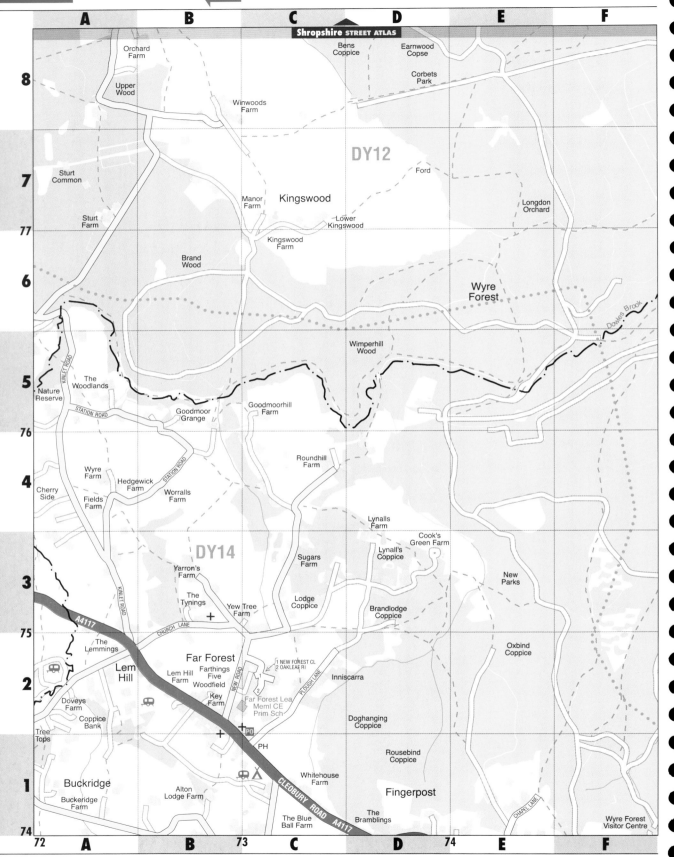

A **B** **C** **D** **E** **F**

8

DY12

7

77

6

Wyre Forest

5

76

DY14

4

3

75

Far Forest

2

Lem Hill

1

Buckridge Fingerpost

74

Orchard Farm
Bens Coppice
Earnwood Copse
Corbets Park
Upper Wood
Winwoods Farm
Ford
Sturt Common
Manor Farm
Kingswood
Longdon Orchard
Sturt Farm
Lower Kingswood
Kingswood Farm
Brand Wood
Wyre Forest
Wimperhill Wood
Dowles Brook
Nature Reserve
The Woodlands
KINLET ROAD
STATION ROAD
Goodmoor Grange
Goodmoorhill Farm
Wyre Farm
Hedgewick Farm
Fields Farm
Worralls Farm
STATION ROAD
Roundhill Farm
Cherry Side
Lynalls Farm
Cook's Green Farm
Sugars Farm
Lynall's Coppice
New Parks
Yarron's Farm
The Tynings
Yew Tree Farm
Lodge Coppice
Brandlodge Coppice
Oxbind Coppice
CHURCH LANE
The Lemmings
A4117
KINLET ROAD
1 NEW FOREST CL
2 OAKLEAF RI
Lem Hill Farm
Farthings Five Woodfield
NEW ROAD
PLOUGH LANE
Inniscarra
Doveys Farm
Key Farm
Far Forest Lea Meml CE Prim Sch
Doghanging Coppice
Coppice Bank
Tree Tops
PO
PH
Rousebind Coppice
Whitehouse Farm
Alton Lodge Farm
CLEOBURY ROAD A4117
The Blue Ball Farm
The Bramblings
CHAPEL LANE
Wyre Forest Visitor Centre
Buckeridge Farm

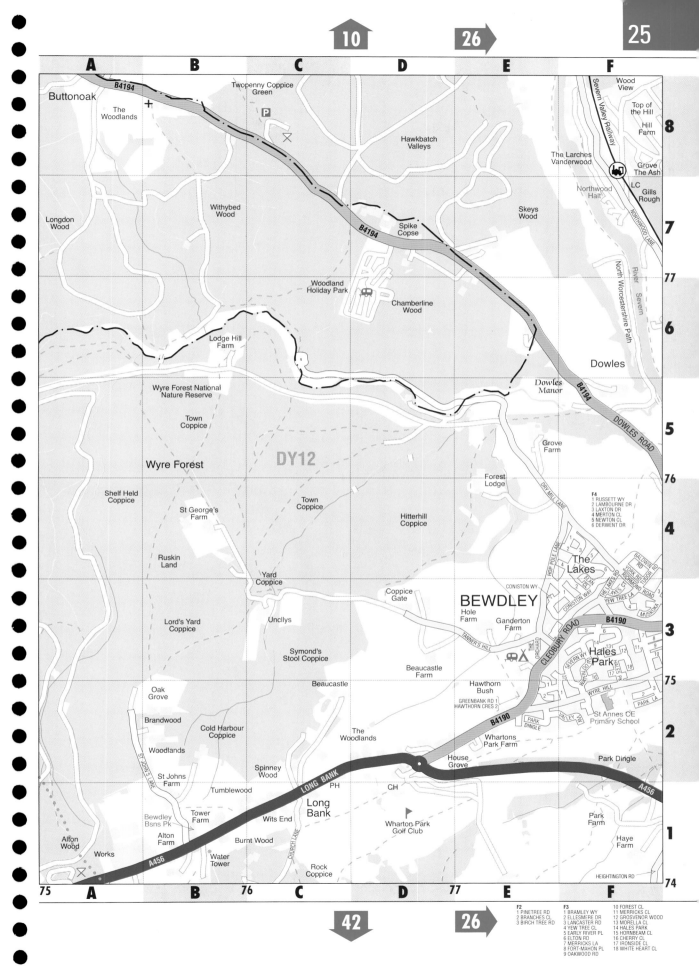

F2
1 PINETREE RD
2 BRANCHES CL
3 BIRCH TREE RD

F3
1 BRAMLEY WY
2 ELLESMERE DR
3 LANCASTER RD
4 YEW TREE CL
5 EARLY RIVER PL
6 ELTON RD
7 MERRICKS LA
8 FORT-MAHON PL
9 OAKWOOD RD

10 FOREST CL
11 MERRICKS CL
12 GROSVENOR WOOD
13 MORELLA CL
14 HALES PARK
15 HORNBEAM CL
16 CHERRY CL
17 IRONSIDE CL
18 WHITE HEART CL

F4
1 RUSSETT WY
2 LAMBOURNE DR
3 LAXTON DR
4 MERTON CL
5 NEWTON CL
6 DERWENT DR

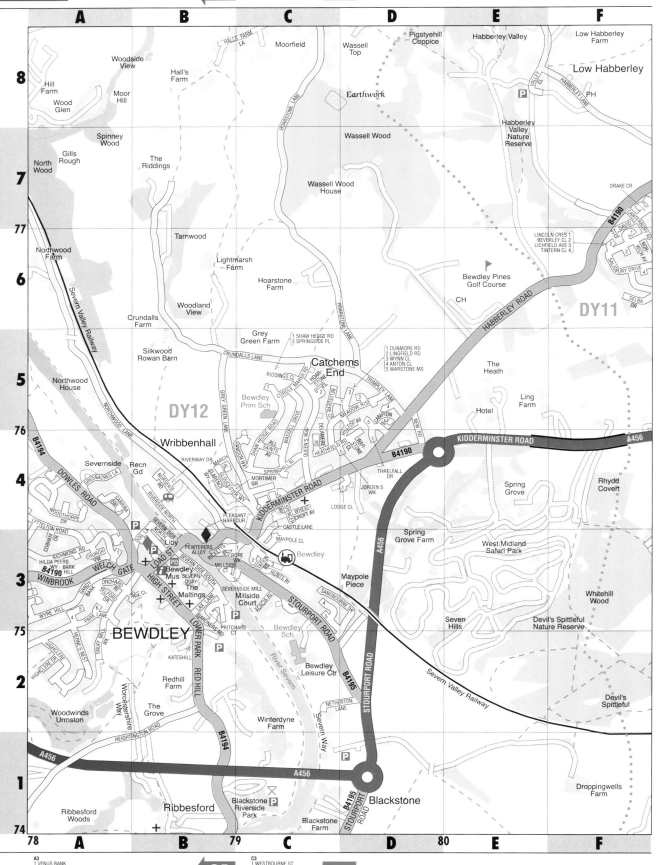

C6
1 HABBERLEY ST
2 BENNETT ST
3 ADAMS HO
4 WOODFIELD ST
5 ST JOHN'S ST
6 ST JOHN'S CL

D6
1 MILLERS CT
2 MILLFIELD GDNS
3 RUTH CHAMBERLAIN CT
4 PATERNOSTER ROW
5 PERRETT WLK
6 ROCK COTTS

E5
1 BRIDGE ST
2 MARLBOROUGH ST
3 WORCESTER CROSS
4 KIDDERMINSTER COLL

7 IDEAL BLDGS
8 LOWER MILL ST

E6
1 BLACK HORSE LA
2 CALLOWS LA
3 FREDA EDDY CT
4 KING CHARLES SQ
5 DERICK BURCHER'S MALL
6 SIR GEORGE'S MALL

7 SWAN SH CTR
8 SIR WALTER'S MALL
9 ROWLAND HILL SH CTR
10 ST GEORGES CT
11 GLADES ARENA L CTR

F5
1 AMBER TERR
2 FARFIELD STUDIOS
3 KIDDERMINSTER
  RAILWAY MUS

F6
1 TRINITY CT
2 VICTORIA CT
3 SOUTH ST

12   28

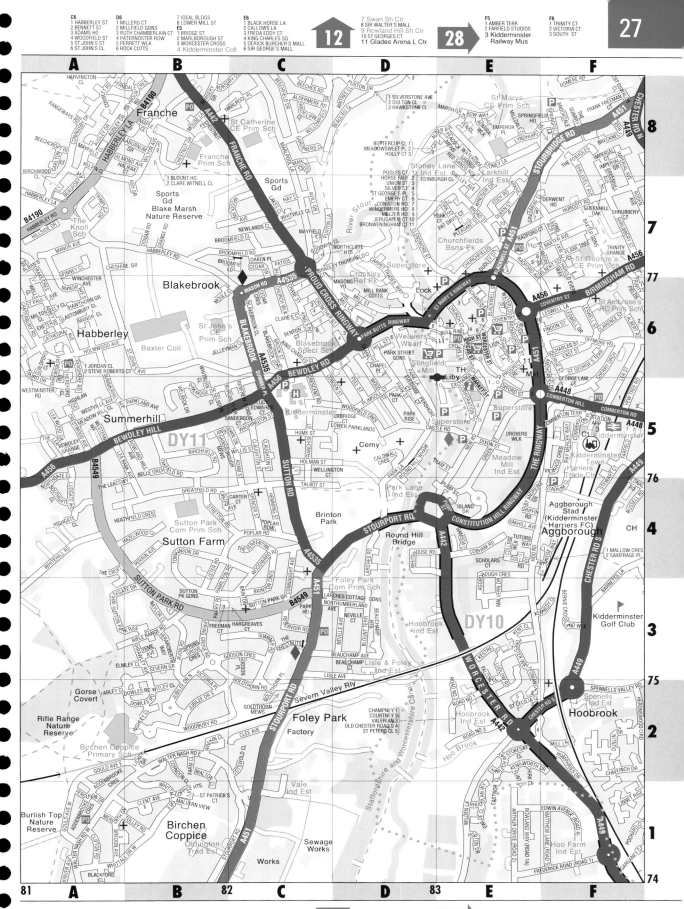

28

A5
1 THE HAWTHORNS
2 CHADDESLEY GDNS
3 SOMERLEYTON CT
4 COMBERTON MANS
5 COMBERTON CT

B6
1 MASEFIELD GDNS
2 GEORGE DANCE CL
3 KIPLING WLK
4 CHATTERTON WLK

◀ **27**   ▲ **13**

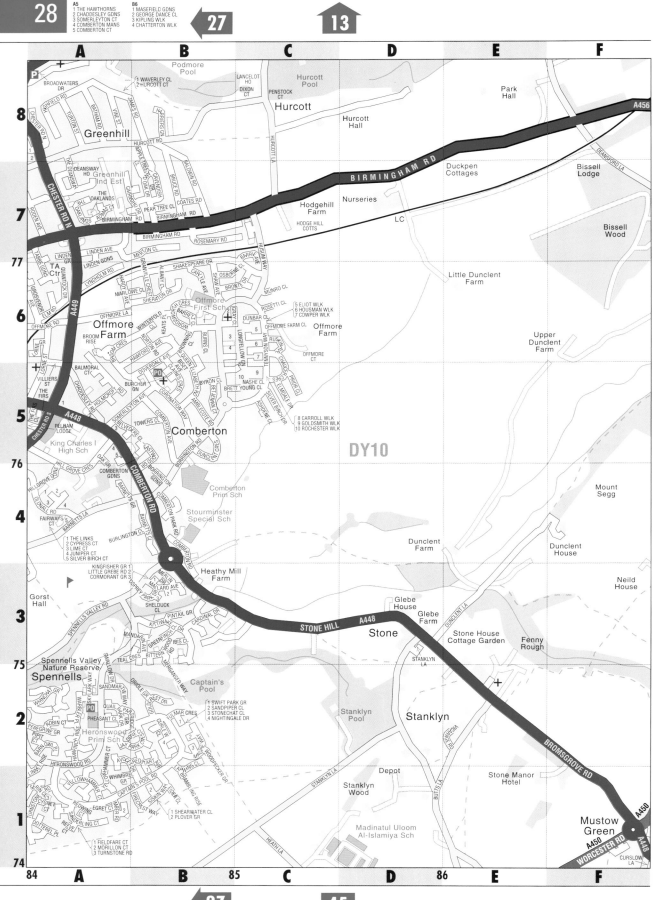

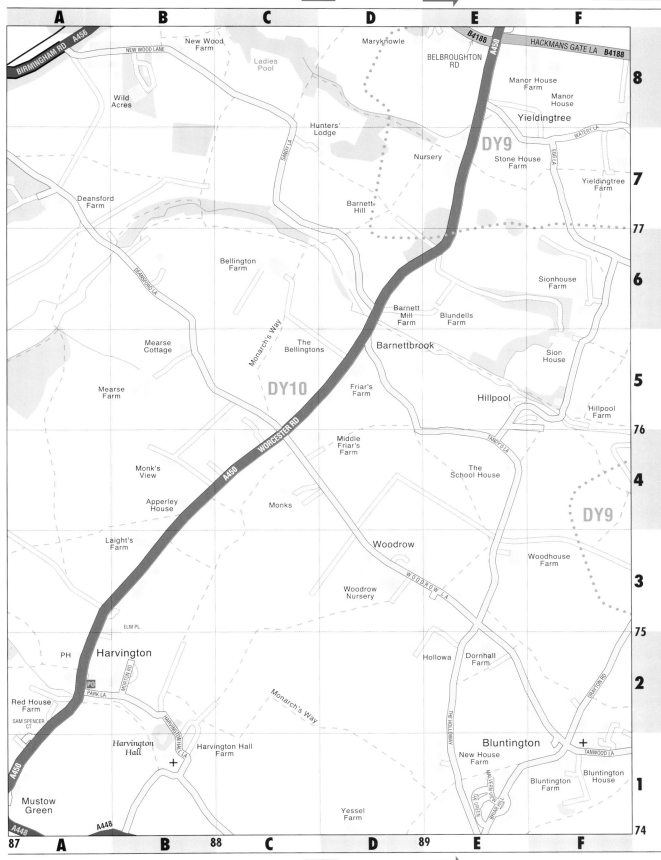

29
15

A B C D E F

8

7

77

6

5

76

4

3

75

2

1

74

B4188

Breach Farm

YEW TREE AVE

Giles Farm

A491 STOURBRIDGE RD

HACKMANS GATE LA

HORSILL LA

Brookfield Farm

Brookfield

HOLY CROSS LA

Yew Tree House

DARK LA

Branthill Farm

Field House Farm

WOODFIELD LA

Works

Belbroughton

B4188

FORGE LA

NASH LA

HIGH ST

PO

PINCHERS CL

WOODHOUSE ORCH

WOODGATE WAY

DRAYTON RD

QUEENS HILL

HARTLE LA

MEARSE LA

DY10

ESSO LA

Drayton Villa Farm

CHURCH HILL

CHURCH RD

THE GLEBE

GLEBE FIELDS

Hartle Farm

Hartle

Church Farm

Belbroughton CE Prim Sch

Sewage Works

Works

BRADFORD LA

Bradford House

New Barn

The Lydiate

DRAYTON RD

Drayton House

DY9

Drayton Pool

Drayton

Moorfields Farm

Hill Farm

Grove Farm

PH

WAYSTONE LA

Hurst Farm

Mount Farm

Waystone Farm

Shutt Hill

Villa Farm

Freemansfield Farm

HOCKLEY BROOK LA

Poolhouse Farm

Barrow Hill

Barrow Hill Farm

Broom Hill

Broomhill Farm

Woodlands Farm

75

The Fruit Farm

Drollis Farm

Tanwood House

TANWOOD BARNS

DORDALE RD

Whitehouse Farm

TANWOOD LA

DY10

Bournes Green

Tanwood

TANWOOD CROSS

Bournes Green Farm

Dordale Farm

Dordale

Swancote Farm

Hockley Brook

WOODDCOTE LA

Coalpit Coppice

Insetton House

Dordale Green Farm

WARBAGE LA

90 A B 91 C D 92 E F

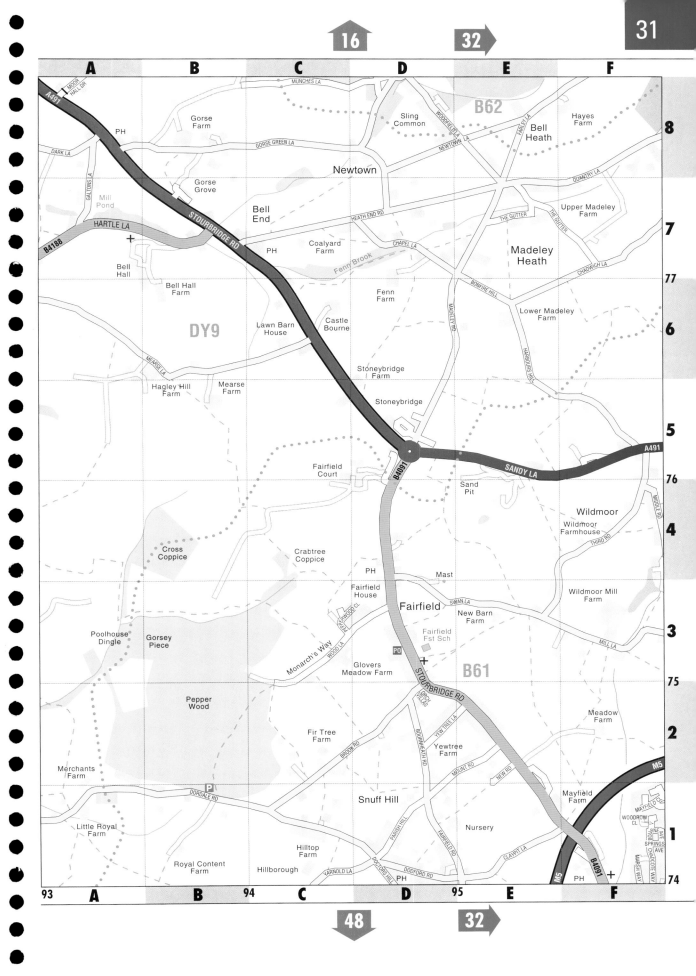

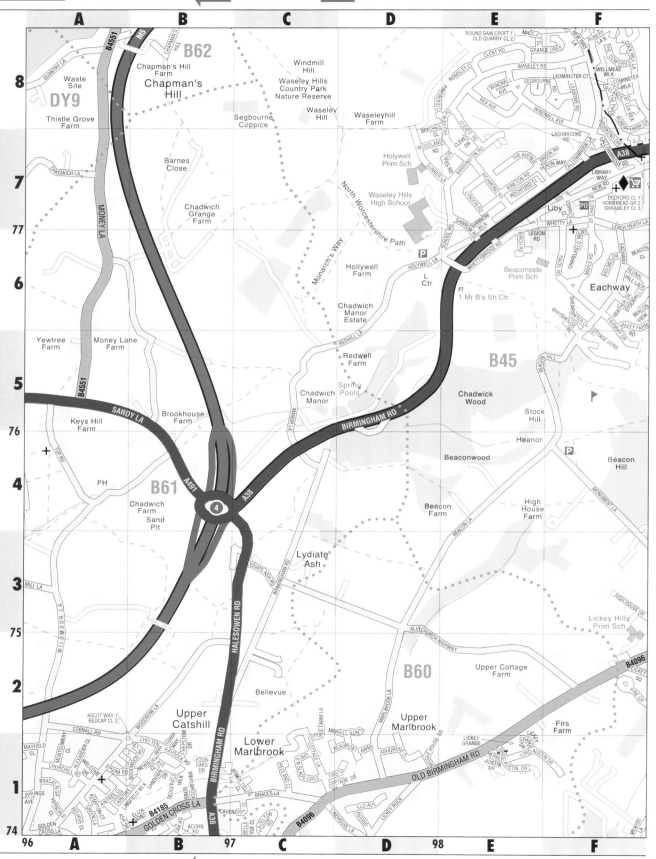

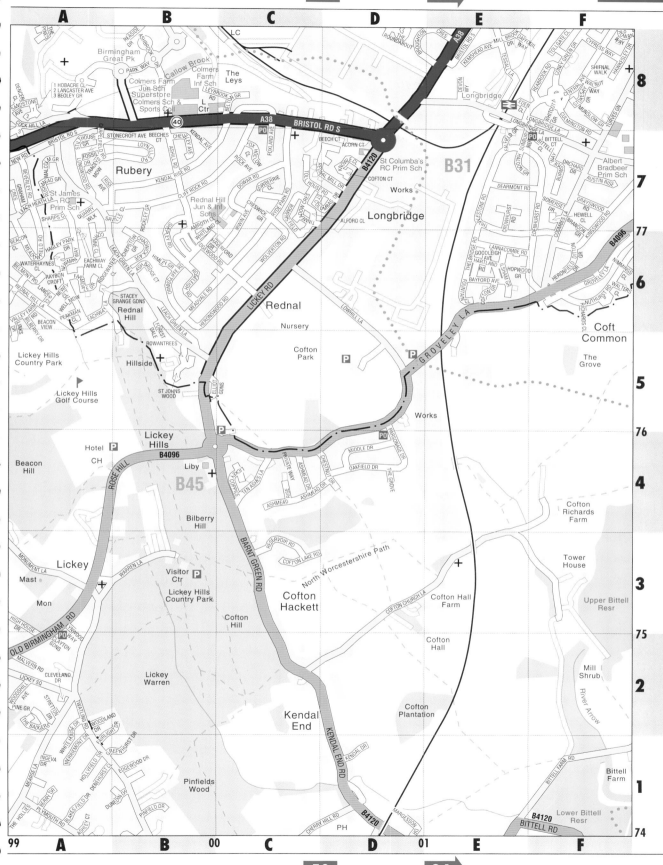

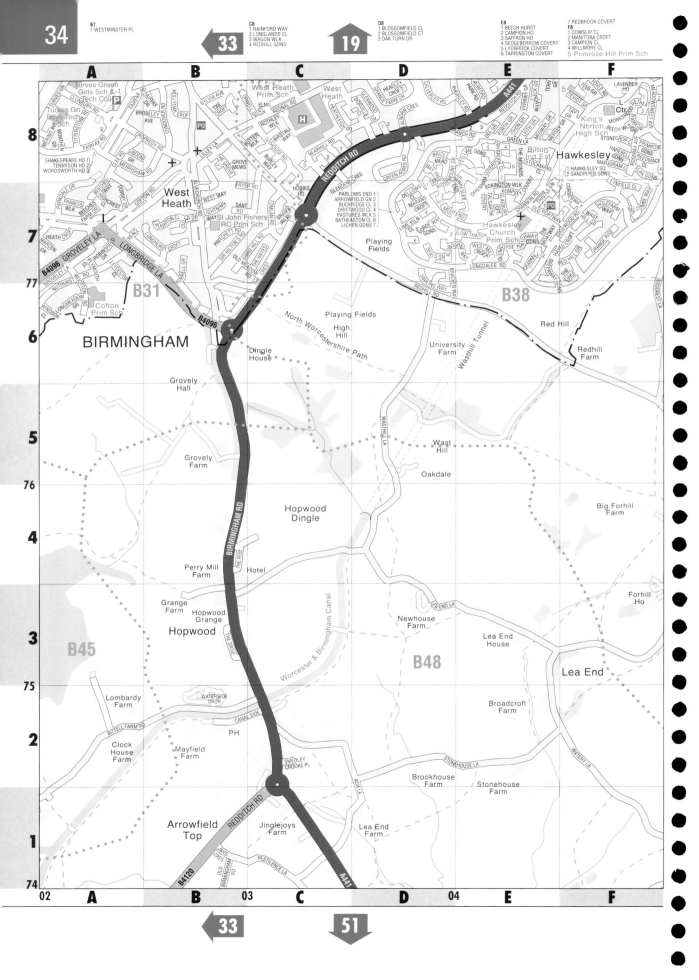

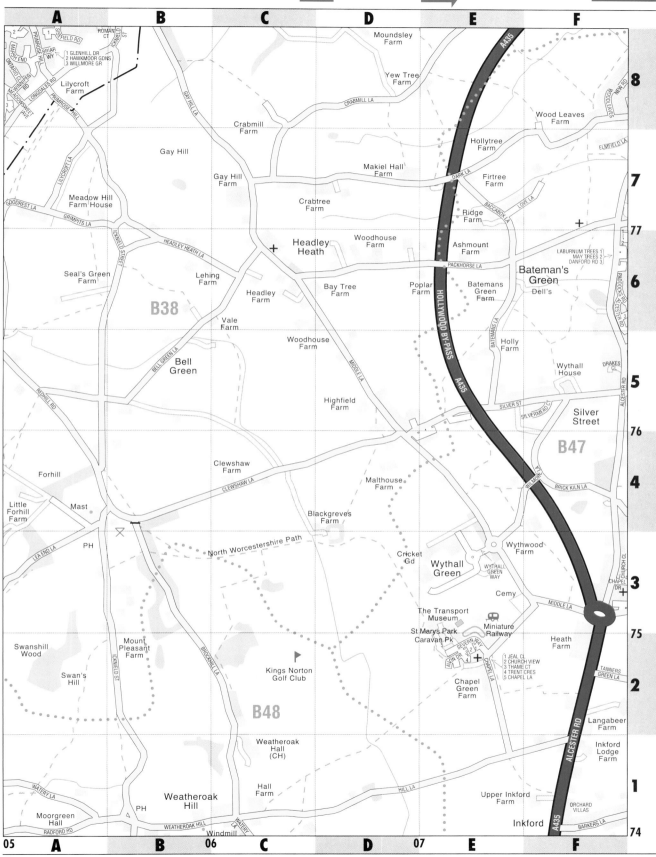

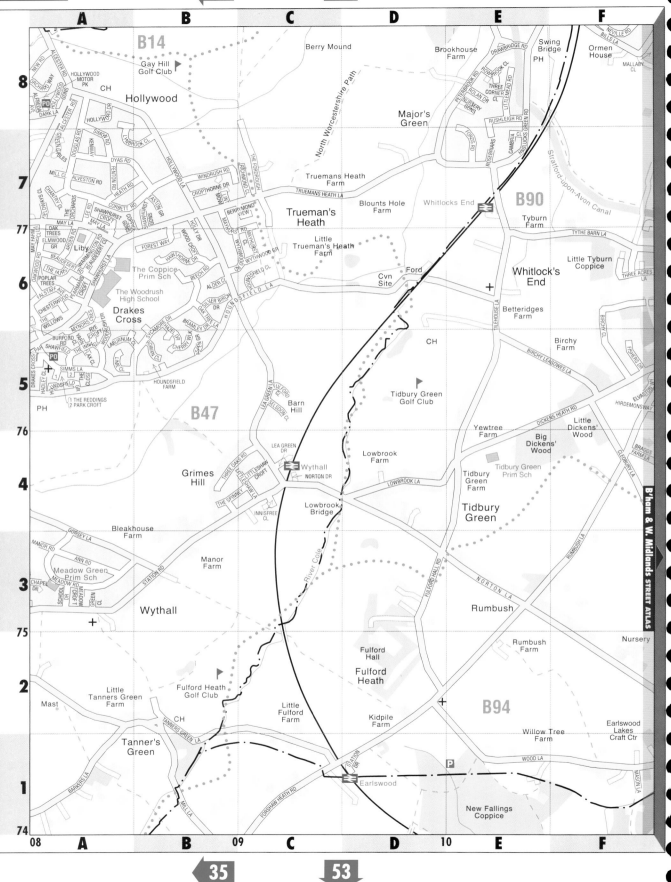

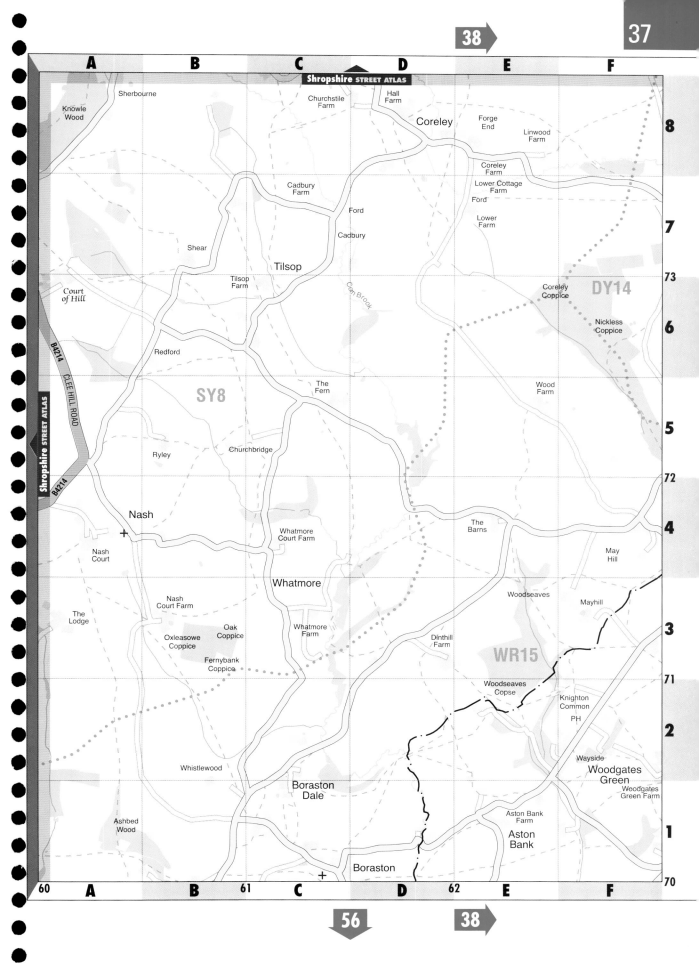

Knowle Wood
Sherbourne
Churchstile Farm
Hall Farm
Coreley
Forge End
Linwood Farm

8

Cadbury Farm
Ford
Coreley Farm
Lower Cottage Farm
Ford
Lower Farm

7

Shear
Tilsop
Cadbury
Coreley Coppice
DY14

73

Tilsop Farm
Court of Hill
Nickless Coppice

6

B4214
CLEE HILL ROAD
Redford
SY8
The Fern
Wood Farm

Shropshire STREET ATLAS

5

B4214
Ryley
Churchbridge

72

Nash
Whatmore Court Farm
The Barns

4

Nash Court
May Hill

The Lodge
Nash Court Farm
Whatmore
Woodseaves
Mayhill

3

Oxleasowe Coppice
Oak Coppice
Whatmore Farm
Dinthill Farm
WR15

Fernybank Coppice
Woodseaves Copse

71

Knighton Common
PH

2

Whistlewood
Wayside
Woodgates Green
Woodgates Green Farm

Boraston Dale

Ashbed Wood
Aston Bank Farm
Aston Bank

1

Con Brook

Boraston

70

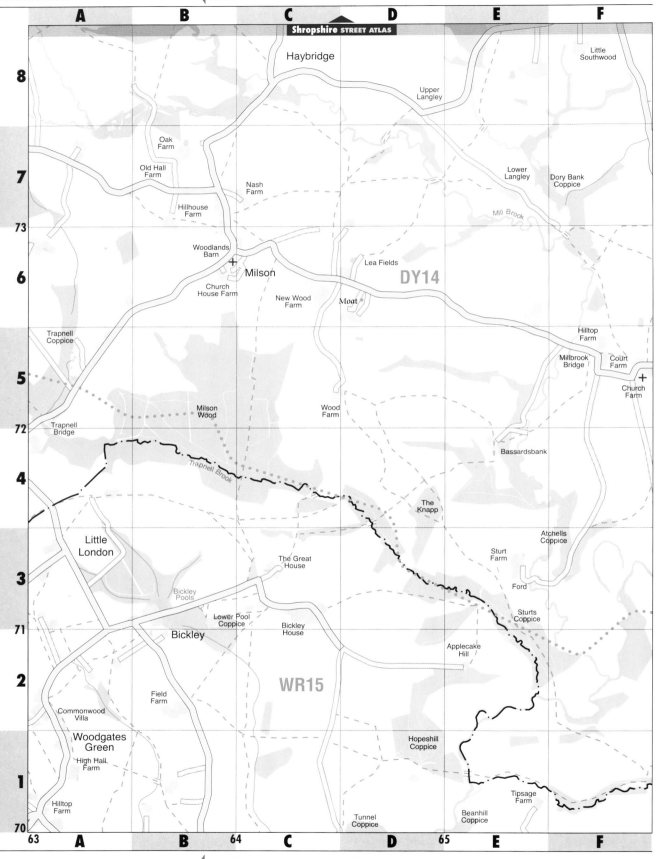

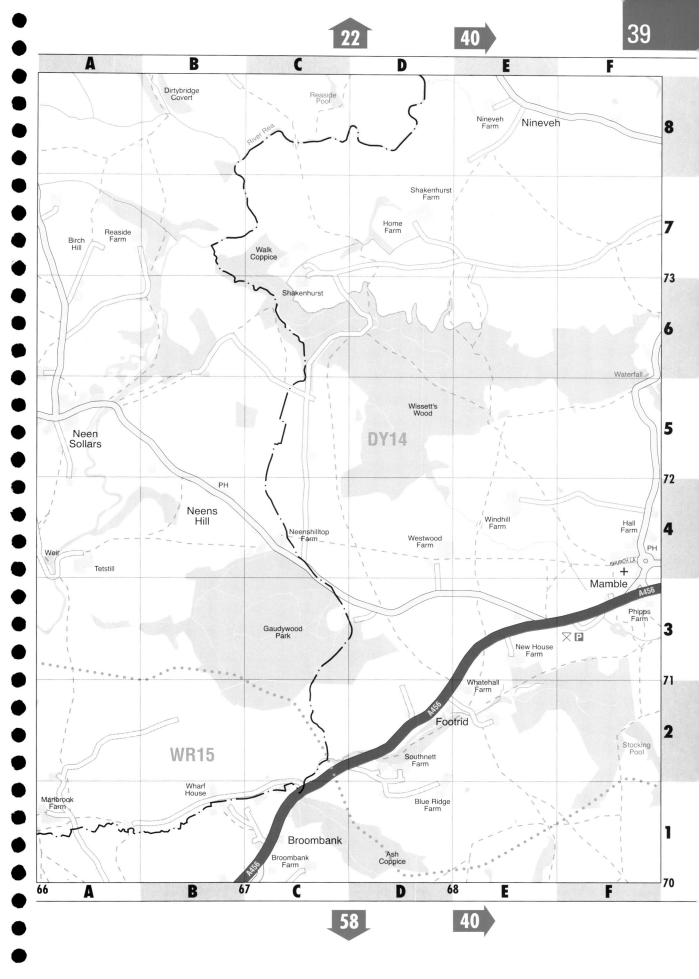

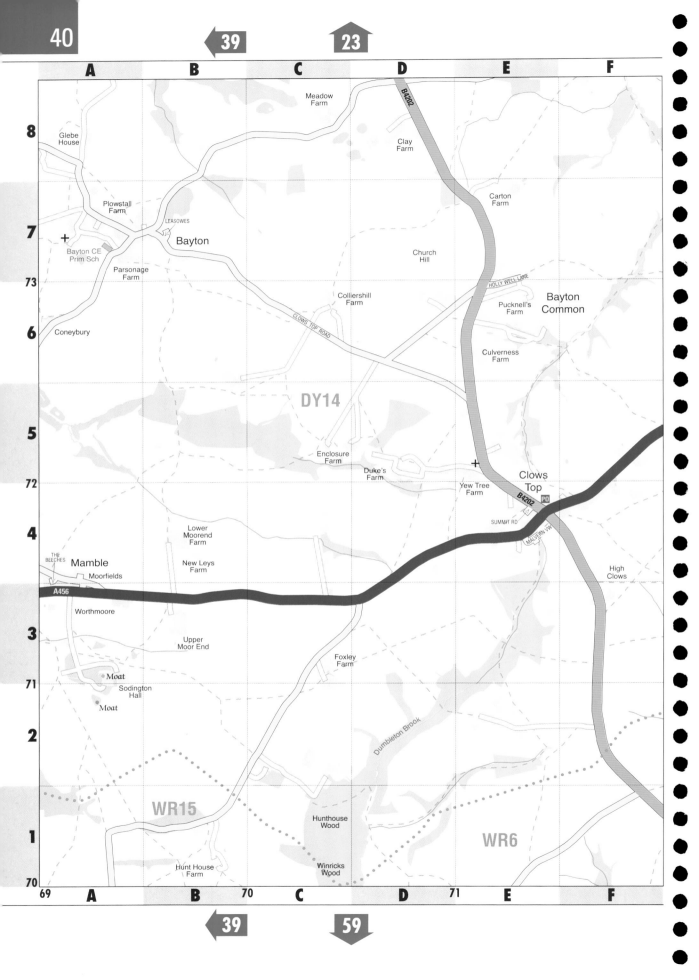

A B C D E F

8

Glebe House

Meadow Farm

Clay Farm

B4202

Carton Farm

7

Plowstall Farm

LEASOWES

Bayton

Church Hill

HOLLY WELL LANE

Bayton Common

73

Bayton CE Prim Sch

Parsonage Farm

Colliershill Farm

Pucknell's Farm

6

Coneybury

CLOWS TOP ROAD

Culverness Farm

DY14

5

Enclosure Farm

Clows Top

Duke's Farm

B4202

72

Yew Tree Farm

PO

SUMMIT RD

4

Lower Moorend Farm

MALVERN VW

THE BEECHES

Mamble

New Leys Farm

High Clows

Moorfields

A456

Worthmoore

3

Upper Moor End

Foxley Farm

Moat

71

Sodington Hall

Moat

2

Dumbleton Brook

WR15

Hunthouse Wood

1

WR6

Hunt House Farm

Winricks Wood

70

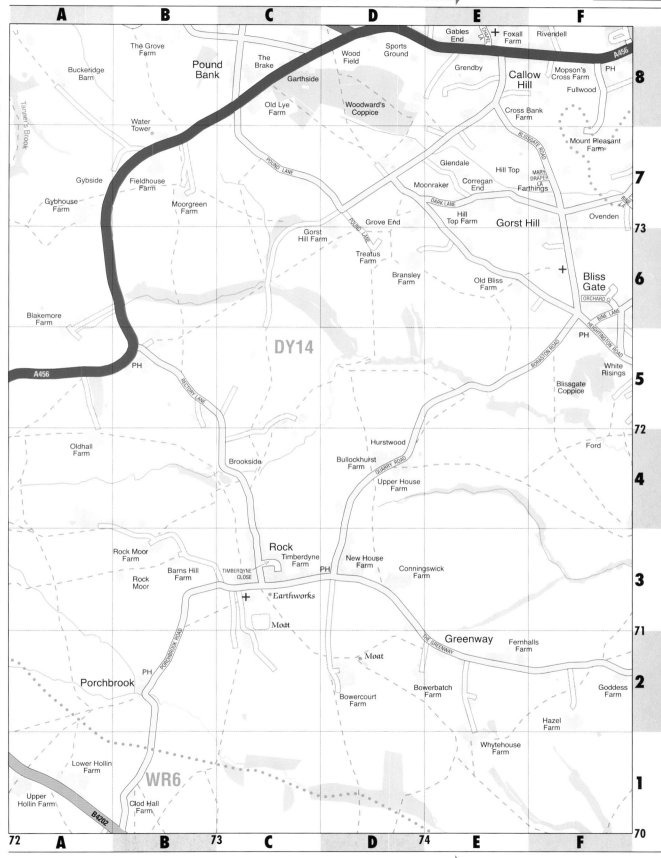

A   B   C   D   E   F

Tanner's Brook

Buckeridge Barn

The Grove Farm

Pound Bank

The Brake

Garthside

Wood Field

Sports Ground

Gables End

Foxall Farm

Rivendell

A456

PH

8

Grendby

Callow Hill

Mopson's Cross Farm

Fullwood

Old Lye Farm

Woodward's Coppice

Cross Bank Farm

BLISSGATE ROAD

Mount Pleasant Farm

Water Tower

POUND LANE

Glendale

Hill Top

MARY DRAPER LA

7

Gybside

Fieldhouse Farm

Moonraker

Corregan End

Farthings

BINE LA

Gybhouse Farm

Moorgreen Farm

DARK LANE

Ovenden

73

POUND LANE

Grove End

Hill Top Farm

Gorst Hill

Gorst Hill Farm

Treatus Farm

Bransley Farm

Old Bliss Farm

Bliss Gate

6

Blakemore Farm

ORCHARD CL

BINE LANE

DY14

HEIGHTINGTON ROAD

PH

A456

PH

RECTORY LANE

White Risings

5

BORASTON ROAD

Blissgate Coppice

72

Oldhall Farm

Brookside

Hurstwood

Ford

Bullockhurst Farm

QUARRY ROAD

Upper House Farm

4

Rock Moor Farm

Rock

Timberdyne Farm

New House Farm

Conningswick Farm

Barns Hill Farm

TIMBERDYNE CLOSE

PH

Rock Moor

Earthworks

3

Moat

71

PORCHBROOK ROAD

Greenway

Fernhalls Farm

THE GREENWAY

Moat

PH

Porchbrook

Bowerbatch Farm

Goddess Farm

2

Bowercourt Farm

Lower Hollin Farm

Hazel Farm

WR6

Whytehouse Farm

1

Upper Hollin Farm

Clod Hall Farm

B4202

70

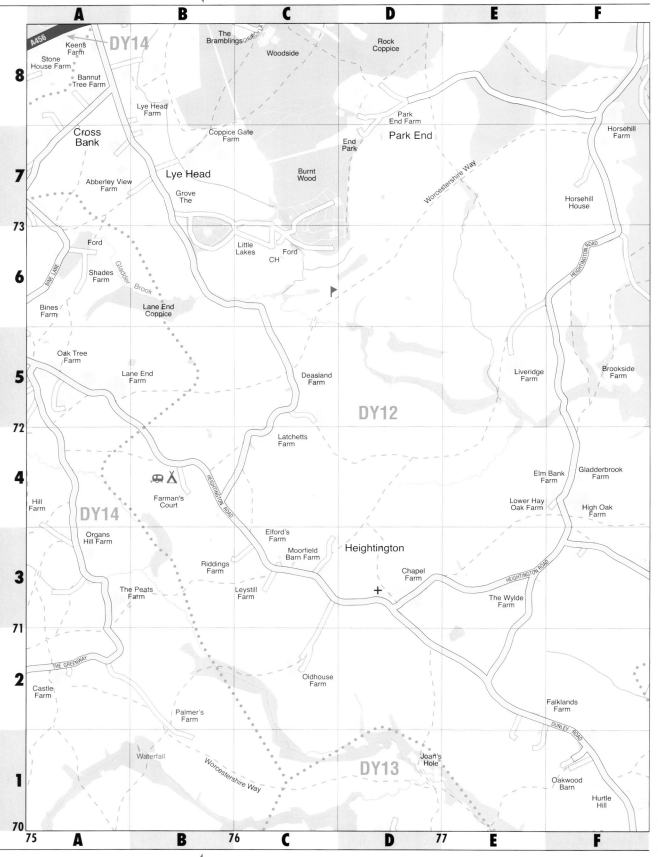

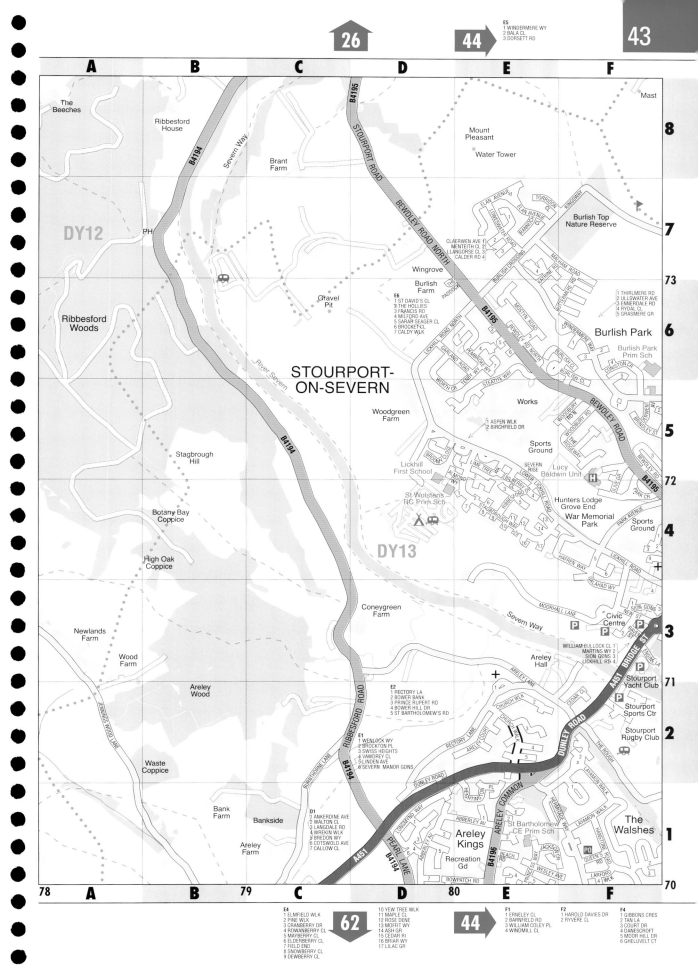

STOURPORT-ON-SEVERN

The Beeches

Ribbesford House

B4194

Severn Way

Brant Farm

B4195

STOURPORT ROAD

BEWDLEY ROAD NORTH

DY12

PH

Ribbesford Woods

River Severn

Gravel Pit

Mount Pleasant

Water Tower

Mast

ELAN AVENUE
TORRAON CL
LOWESWATER ROAD
ELAN AVENUE
RANNOCH CL
KINGSWAY

Burlish Top
Nature Reserve

CLAERWEN AVE 1
MENTEITH CL 2
LLANGORSE CL 3
CALDER RD 4

BURLISH CROSSING

MALHAM ROAD

KATRINE

Wingrove
Burlish Farm

THE PADDOCK

E6
1 ST DAVID'S CL
2 THE HOLLIES
3 FRANCIS RD
4 MILFORD AVE
5 SARAH SEAGER CL
6 BROCKET CL
7 CALDY WLK

LICKHILL ROAD NORTH

GARLAND ROAD

PEMBROKE CL

WORTH CR

TENBY WY

MOSTYN ROAD

BEWDLEY RD NORTH

BURLISH CL

STEATITE WAY

BURLISH CL

1 THIRLMERE RD
2 ULLSWATER AVE
3 ENNERDALE RD
4 RYDAL CL
5 GRASMERE GR

WINDERMERE WY

CONISTON CR

Burlish Park

Burlish Park
Prim Sch

B4195

BEWDLEY ROAD

Works

1 ASPEN WLK
2 BIRCHFIELD DR

WOODBURY RD
WOODBURY RD

THE RIDGEWAY

Sports Ground

BRINDLEY ST

BEWDLEY RD

BEWDLEY RD

PARK CR

Woodgreen Farm

Stagbrough Hill

B4194

BROOM CLOSE

ALMOND WY

LIME TREE WK

BILBERRY

STAGBOROUGH WAY

LOWER LICKHILL ROAD

RIBBESFORD DR

SEVERN RISE

Lucy
Baldwin Unit

H

OLIVE GR

PARK AVENUE

Botany Bay Coppice

Lickhill
First School

St Wulstans
RC Prim Sch

DY13

Hunters Lodge
Grove End

War Memorial
Park

Sports Ground

High Oak
Coppice

HAFREN WAY

GALAHAD WY

LICKHILL ROAD

Coneygreen
Farm

MOORHALL LANE

Severn Way

SION GDNS

NEW ST

RAVEN ST

Civic
Centre

P

P

WILLIAM BULLOCK CL 1
MARTINS WY 2
SION GDNS 3
LICKHILL RD 4

A451 BRIDGE ST

ENGINE LA

Newlands
Farm

Wood
Farm

JENNINGS WOOD LANE

Areley
Wood

Areley
Hall

ARELEY LANE

E2
1 RECTORY LA
2 BOWER BANK
3 PRINCE RUPERT RD
4 BOWER HILL DR
5 ST BARTHOLOMEW'S RD

RECTORY LANE

ARELEY COURT

CHURCH WLK

CHURCH WLK

CEDAR CL

DUNLEY ROAD

THE ROUGH

Stourport
Yacht Club

Stourport
Sports Ctr

Stourport
Rugby Club

P

Waste
Coppice

RIBBESFORD ROAD

BURNTHORNE LANE

B4194

E1
1 WENLOCK WY
2 BROCKTON PL
3 SWISS HEIGHTS
4 VAWDREY CL
5 LINDEN AVE
6 SEVERN MANOR GDNS

DUNLEY ROAD

LONGMYND WAY

HERGYTINO

ABBERLEY AV

ARELEY COMMON

LAVAMAN WALK

HERMITAGE WAY

LAVAMAN WALK

HANSTONE WAY

The
Walshes

Bank
Farm

Bankside

Areley
Farm

A451

PEARL LANE

B4194

D1
1 ANKERDINE AVE
2 WALTON CL
3 LANGDALE RD
4 WREKIN WLK
5 BREDON WY
6 COTSWOLD AVE
7 CALLOW CL

ABBERLEY AV

Areley
Kings

Recreation
Gd

B4196

St Bartholomew's
CE Prim Sch

BEACH

PRINCESS WAY

WESLEY AVE

JACKSON

QUEEN'S RD

PO

LARFORD

WLK

BOWPATCH RD

E4
1 ELMFIELD WLK
2 PINE WLK
3 CRANBERRY DR
4 ROWANBERRY CL
5 MAYBERRY CL
6 ELDERBERRY CL
7 FIELD END
8 SNOWBERRY CL
9 DEWBERRY CL

10 YEW TREE WLK
11 MAPLE CL
12 ROSE DENE
13 MOFFIT WY
14 ASH GR
15 CEDAR RI
16 BRIAR WY
17 LILAC GR

62

44

F1
1 ERNELEY CL
2 BARNFIELD RD
3 WILLIAM COLEY PL
4 WINDMILL CL

F2
1 HAROLD DAVIES DR
2 RYVERE CL

F4
1 GIBBONS CRES
2 TAN LA
3 COURT DR
4 DANESCROFT
5 MOOR HILL DR
6 GHELUVELT CT

8

7

73

6

5

72

4

3

71

2

1

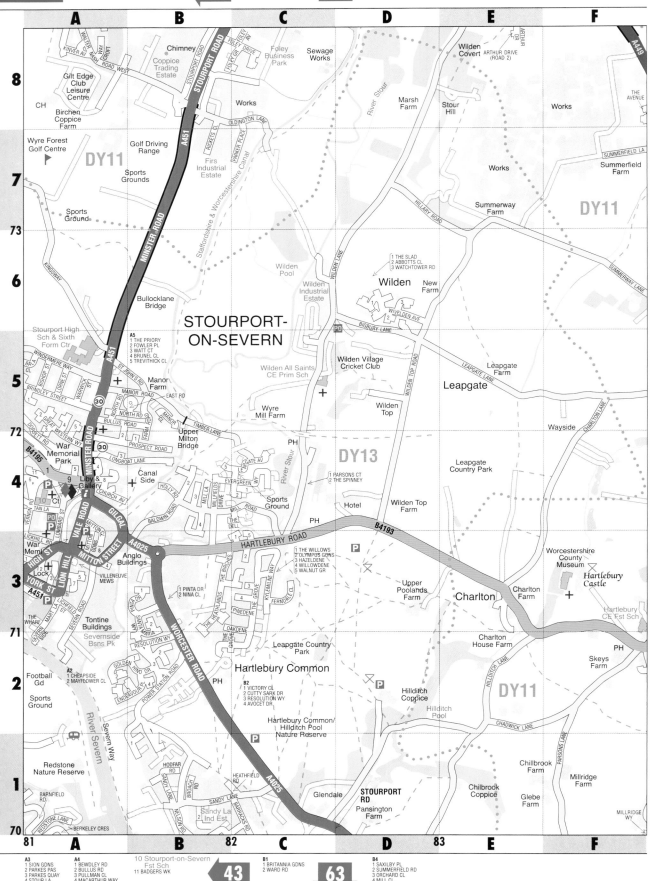

STOURPORT-
ON-SEVERN

DY11

DY13

DY11

Wilden

Leapgate

Charlton

Hartlebury Common

A5
1 THE PRIORY
2 FOWLER PL
3 WATT CT
4 BRUNEL CL
5 TREVITHICK CL

1 THE SLAD
2 ABBOTTS CL
3 WATCHTOWER RD

1 PARSONS CT
2 THE SPINNEY

1 THE WILLOWS
2 OLYMPUS GDNS
3 HAZELDENE
4 WILLOWDENE
5 WALNUT GR

1 PINTA DR
2 NINA CL

A2
1 CHEAPSIDE
2 MAYFLOWER CL

B2
1 VICTORY CL
2 CUTTY SARK DR
3 RESOLUTION WY
4 AVOCET DR

A3
1 SION GDNS
2 PARKES PAS
3 PARKES QUAY
4 STOUR LA
5 LODGE RD
6 BELL ROW
7 LODGECTS
8 MITTON WK

A4
1 BEWDLEY RD
2 BULLUS RD
3 PULLMAN CL
4 MACARTHUR WAY
5 ST MICHAEL'S CL
6 GIBBONS CRES
7 FOUNDRY ST
8 CHURCH DR
9 WORCESTER ST

10 Stourport-on-Severn
Fst Sch
11 BADGERS WK

B1
1 BRITANNIA GDNS
2 WARD RD

B4
1 SAXILBY PL
2 SUMMERFIELD RD
3 ORCHARD CL
4 MILL CL
5 MILLGATE CL

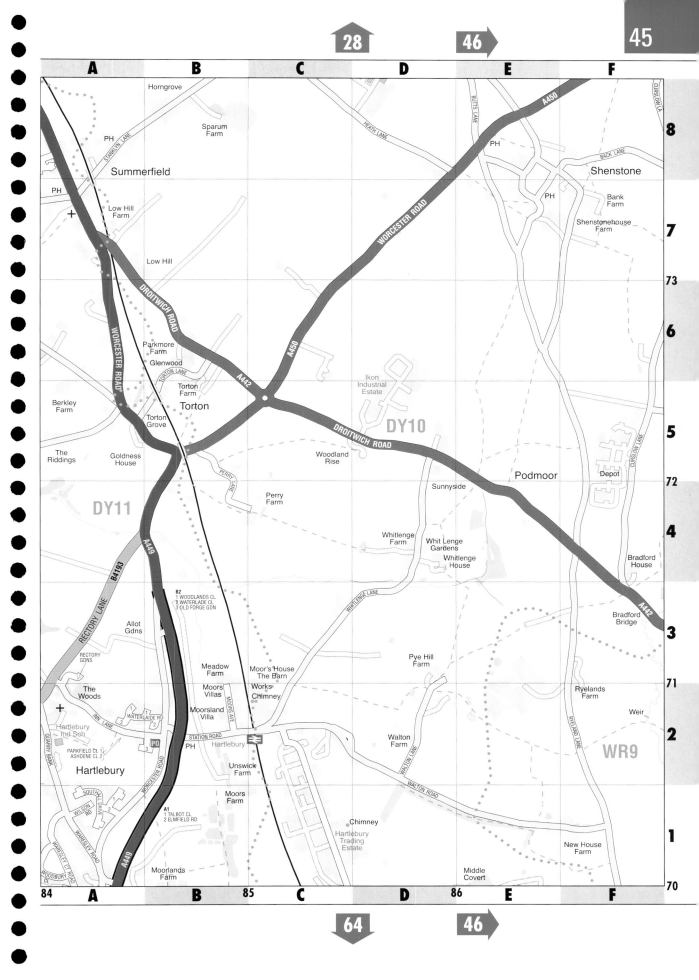

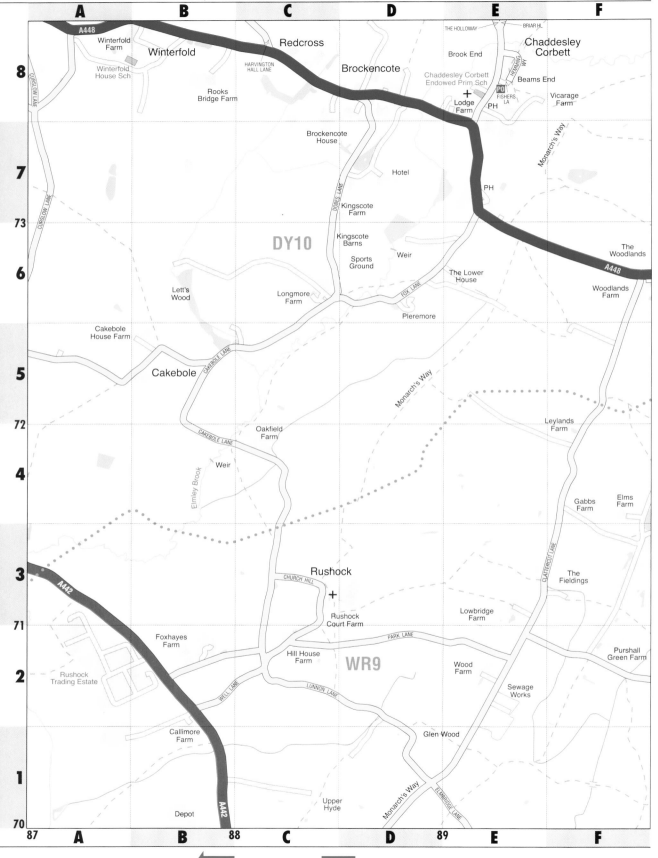

A448 Winterfold Farm
Winterfold
Redcross
Winterfold House Sch
HARVINGTON HALL LANE
Brockencote
Rooks Bridge Farm

THE HOLLOWAY
BRIAR HL
Brook End
Chaddesley Corbett
Chaddesley Corbett Endowed Prim Sch
PO
FISHERS LA
Beams End
Vicarage Farm
Lodge Farm
PH
Monarch's Way

CURSLOW LANE
CURSLOW LANE

Brockencote House

Hotel

DOBES LANE
Kingscote Farm

PH

DY10

Kingscote Barns

Sports Ground
Weir
The Woodlands
A448

Lett's Wood
Longmore Farm
FOX LANE
The Lower House
Woodlands Farm

Pleremore

Cakebole House Farm
CAKEBOLE LANE
Cakebole
Monarch's Way
Leylands Farm

CAKEBOLE LANE
Oakfield Farm

Elmley Brook
Weir
Gabbs Farm
Elms Farm

CLATTERCUT LANE

Rushock
CHURCH HILL
The Fieldings

Rushock Court Farm
Lowbridge Farm
Purshall Green Farm

A442
Foxhayes Farm
PARK LANE
71

Hill House Farm
WR9
Wood Farm

Rushock Trading Estate
WELL LANE
LUNNON LANE
Sewage Works

Callimore Farm
Glen Wood
ELMBRIDGE LANE

Monarch's Way

Depot
A42
Upper Hyde

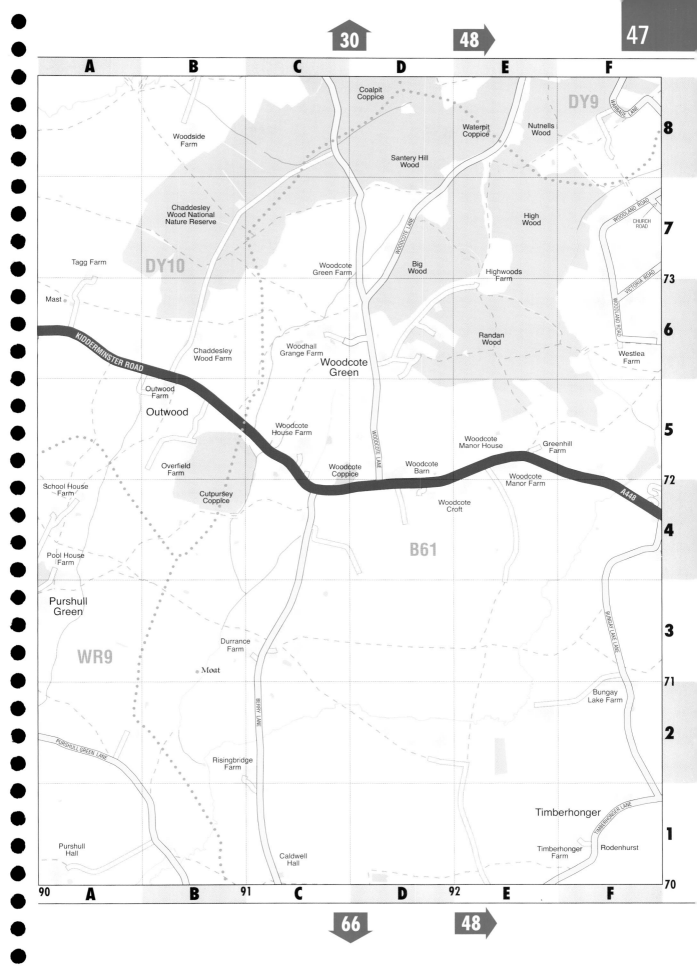

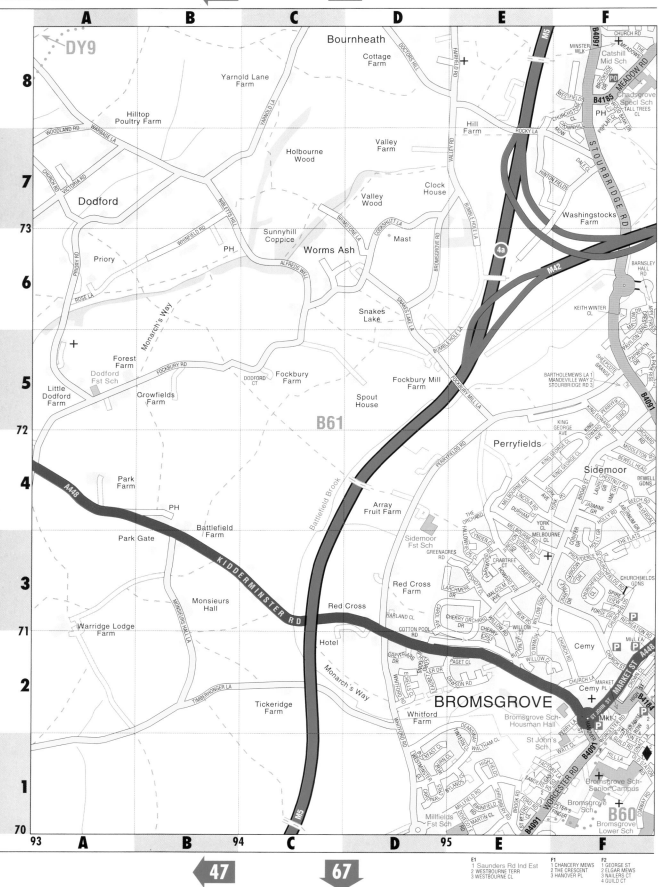

DY9

Bournheath

Cottage Farm

Yarnold Lane Farm

Hilltop Poultry Farm

WOODLAND RD   WARBAGE LA

VICTORIA RD   CHURCH RD

Holbourne Wood

DOCTORS HILL

FAIRFIELD RD

VALLEY RD

Hill Farm

ROCKY LA

M5

B4091

CHURCH RD
MINSTER WLK
THE MEADOWS

Catshill Mid Sch

WESTFIELDS
CHURCHSIDE CL
CROWNHILL
VICTO BANK DR

MEADOW RD
POPLAR CL

B4185   PH

Chadsgrove Specl Sch
TALL TREES CL

STOURBRIDGE RD

Dodford

CHURCH RD

Priory

ROSE LA

WHINFIELD RD

NIBLETTS HILL

Sunnyhill Coppice

PH

ALFREDS WELL

Worms Ash

BRIMSTONE LA

COCKSHUTT LA

Valley Farm

Valley Wood

Clock House

Mast

BROMSGROVE RD

BUMBLE HOLE LA

4a

M42

Washingstocks Farm

DALE CL

HINTON FIELDS

BARNSLEY HALL RD

KEITH WINTER CL

PAVILION DR
PIPWORTH DR
CRESSWELL DR
APPLETREE
LEA PARK RISE

Forest Farm

Dodford Fst Sch

FOCKBURY RD

DODFORD CT

Fockbury Farm

Snakes Lake

SNAKES LAKE LA

Spout House

Fockbury Mill Farm

FOCKBURY MILL LA

SHEEPCOTE GRANGE

B4091

Little Dodford Farm

Crowfields Farm

B61

BARTHOLOMEWS LA 1
MANDEVILLE WAY 2
STOURBRIDGE RD 3

KING EDWARD RD
PERRYFELDS CL
KING EDWARD AVE
KING EDWARD RD
ORCHARD RD

A448

Park Farm

PH

Battlefield Farm

Park Gate

Monsieurs Hall

KIDDERMINSTER RD

MONSIEURS HALL LA

Warridge Lodge Farm

TIMBERHONGER LA

Tickeridge Farm

PERRYFIELDS RD

Battlefield Brook

Array Fruit Farm

Sidemoor Fst Sch

GREENACRES RD

Red Cross Farm

LARCHMERE DR

HARLAND CL

Red Cross

COTTON POOL RD

Hotel

Monarch's Way

WHITFORD RD

Whitford Farm

Perryfields

KING GEORGE AVE

KING GEORGE CL

Sidemoor

CHESTNUT DR
BROAD RD
LAUREL GR
HOLLY RD
LIME GR
BEECH GR
JASMINE GR
ARDENNIM GR
SILVERDALE
THE FLATS
BEWELL HEAD
BEWELL GDNS
MIDDLETON RD

MELBOURNE AVE
LINCOLN RD
YORK AVE
MELBOURNE RD
MELBOURNE CL
YORK CL
DURHAM
CONIFER DR

THE ORCHARD
FALLOWFIELD
LYNDEN CL
CODWALL RD
CRABTREE LA
GRAFTON RD
MALCOLM AVE
HOWARD AVE
NEW RD
WILLOW GDNS

CRABTREE

BROMSGROVE

Monarch's Way

DEANSWAY
TINTERN RD
WALTHAM CL

Bromsgrove Sch-Housman Hall

CHERRY ORCHARD DR
CHERRY CRES
CHERRY RD
WILLOW RD
WILLOW CL
CHURCH LA
CHURCH RD

FORGE DR
SPIRE VIEW
RECREATION RD

CHURCHFIELDS GDNS

CHURCHFIELDS
MILL LA
A448

Cemy

St John's Sch

ST JOHN ST
HANOVER ST
WATT CL
B4091
HILL LA

WORCESTER RD

Cemy

MARKET ST
CROWN ST
MARKET PL

Mkt

High St
B4184

Whitford Farm

GREYFRIARS DR
PAGET CL
DAWSON RD

Millfields Fst Sch

ST PETERS RD
LORD RD
CARDINALS CRES
MILLFIELD RD
FACTORY RD
SANDERS RD
HIGH FIELDS
SHRUBBERY RD
BARNFIELD
LADY RD
BROOK RD
MARTIN CL
CONWAY RD

B4091

Bromsgrove Sch-Senior Campus

Bromsgrove Sch

Bromsgrove Lower Sch

B60

E1
1 Saunders Rd Ind Est
2 WESTBOURNE TERR
3 WESTBOURNE CL

F1
1 CHANCERY MEWS
2 THE CRESCENT
3 HANOVER PL

F2
1 GEORGE ST
2 ELGAR MEWS
3 NAILERS CT
4 GUILD CT

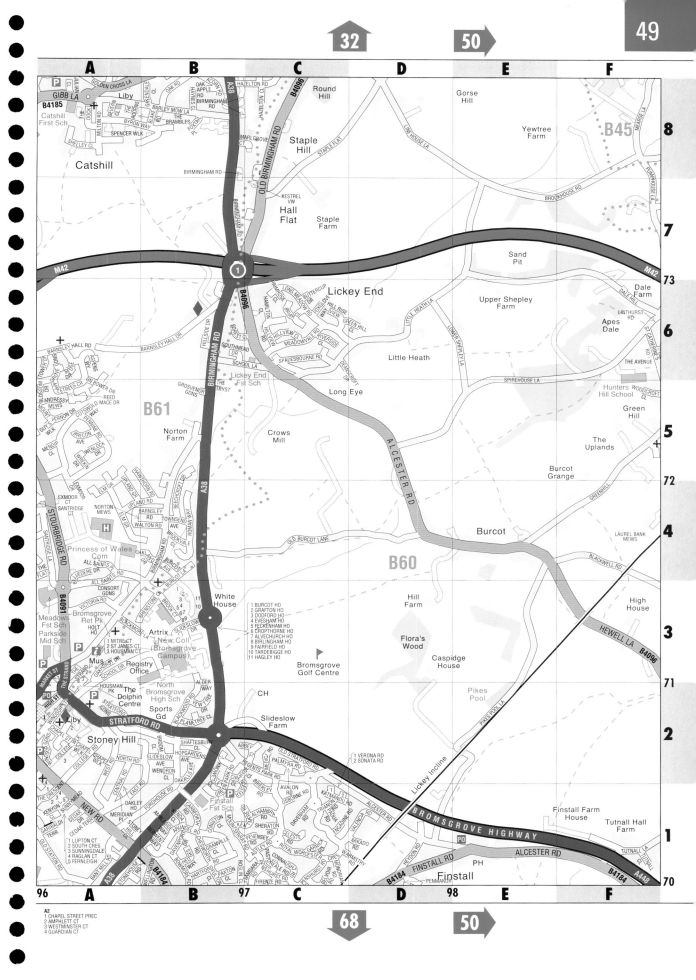

49
33

A **B** **C** **D** **E** **F**

8

PLYMOUTH DR 1
GORSE MEADOW DR 2

Brook
House

Barnt
Green

Fiery
Hill

Cherry
Gr

THE HAVEN
WOODSIDE DR
PLYMOUTH RD
WOOD END DR
TWATLING RD

BROOKHOUSE RD

SHEPLEY RD

SKINNER MDW

CHERRY HILL RD
BROOKWOOD DR
BEECH PARK DR
OAKGROVE DR

CHERRY HILL DR
FIERY HILL RD
ROSEWOOD DRIVE
FIERY HILL DR

CHERRY HILL RD
FIERY HILL RD

Barnt
Green

STATION APP

GREENBANK RD
PENZER DR
POPLAR DR

ORCHARD CROFT

HEWELL RD

HEWELL LA

THE LONGLANDS

SANDHILLS LA

B4120
BITTELL RD

LAUREL
GDNS

PO
Barnt Green
St Andrews
CE Fst Sch

BITTELL LA

SANDHILLS RD

D8
1 WILLOW TREE DR
2 ROSE TERR
3 COACH COTTS
4 VICTORIA MEWS

B4120
BITTELL RD

B4120

The
Paddocks

Billy LA

B45

SANDHILLS GN

7

Barnt
Green

SHEPLEY RD

BILLY LA

LINTHURST RD

Linthurst
Court

Sandhills
Farm

M42

73

M42

PIKE HILL

Masts

COOPERS HILL

Uplands

High
Croft

BIRCHES CL
Lock Keepers
Reach

6

PIKE
HILL

THE AVENUE

Linthurst

Blackwell
First School

ST CATHERINES RD

ST CATHERINES

TANGLEWOOD CL
THE GLEN
FOXES CL
 KINGSWAY

LINTHURST NEWTOWN

BLACKWELL RD

Withybed
Green

REAR
COTTS

FRONT
COTTS

FORWARD
COTTS

WITHYBED LA

P

B48

5

KIMBOLTON DR
CORNS GDNS
GLENEAGLES DR
BIRKDALE AVE
FAIRWAYS DR
WENTWORTH DR
STATION RD

Blackwell

CH

Wheeley
Farm

WHEELEY RD

FOXHILL
BARNS

FOXHILL LA

Gorsey Lane
Farm

Foxhill
House

SCARFIELD HILL

Scarfields
Farm

72

STATION
COTTS

AGMORE RD

Blackwell
Golf Course

COBLEY HILL

Scarfields
Dingle

4

Blackwell
Court

Mast

Cobley Hill
Farm

Cobley Hill

Andrew's
Coppice

GRANGE LA

3

Vigo

HOLLOWTREE LA

ASHMORE LA

B60

Cattespool

2

B4096

HEWELL LA

Hollow Tree
Farm

Robin Hill
Farm

STONEY LA

Stoney Lane
Farm

Sunny Bank
Farm

71

Stoney Lane
Cottage

Worcester & Birmingham Canal

Shortwood
Rough Grounds

1

TUTNALL LA

TUTNALL
GRANGE

Dolan Park
(Private)

WHARF LA

The Lower
House

Broad
Green

Works

BROCKHILL LA

B4096

B97

Shortwood Tunnel

Oxleasows
Farm

Little
Shortwood

B97

70

99 **A** **B** 00 **C** **D** 01 **E** **F**

49
69

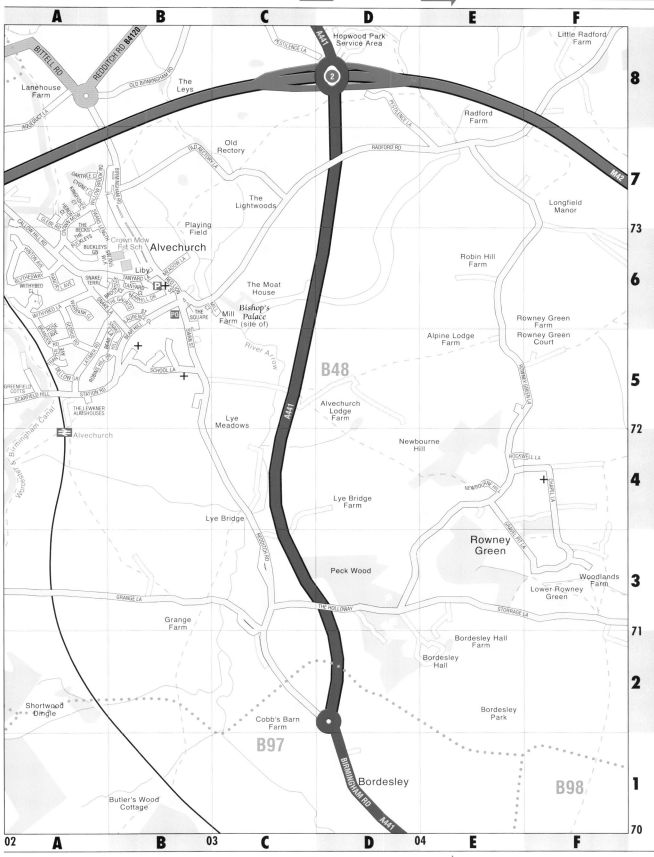

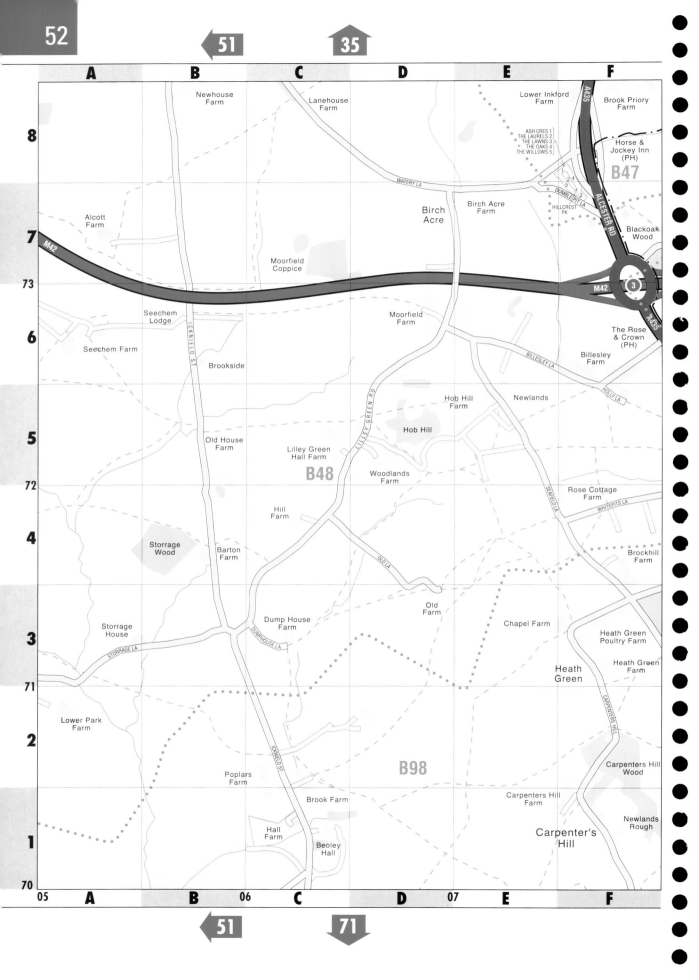

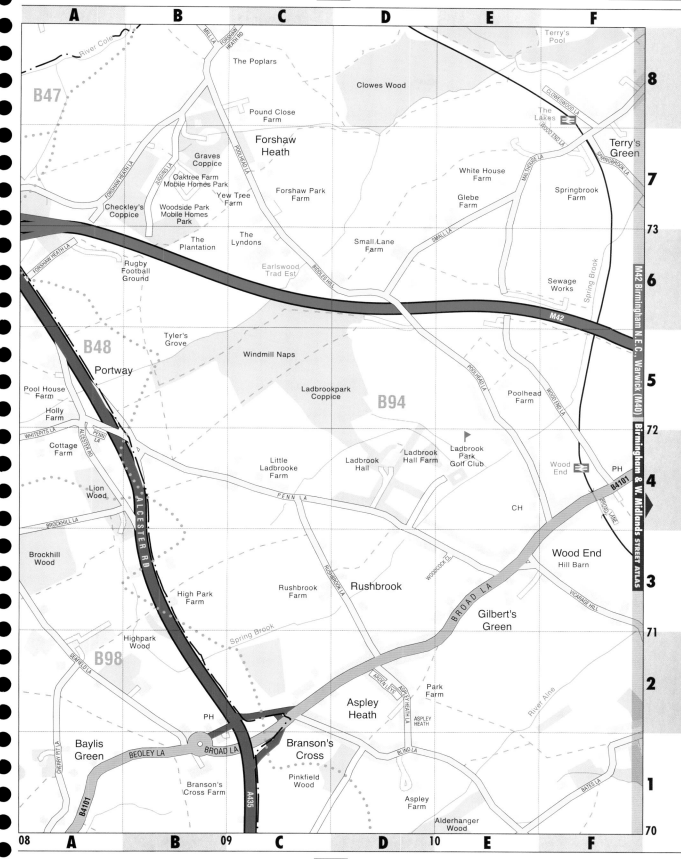

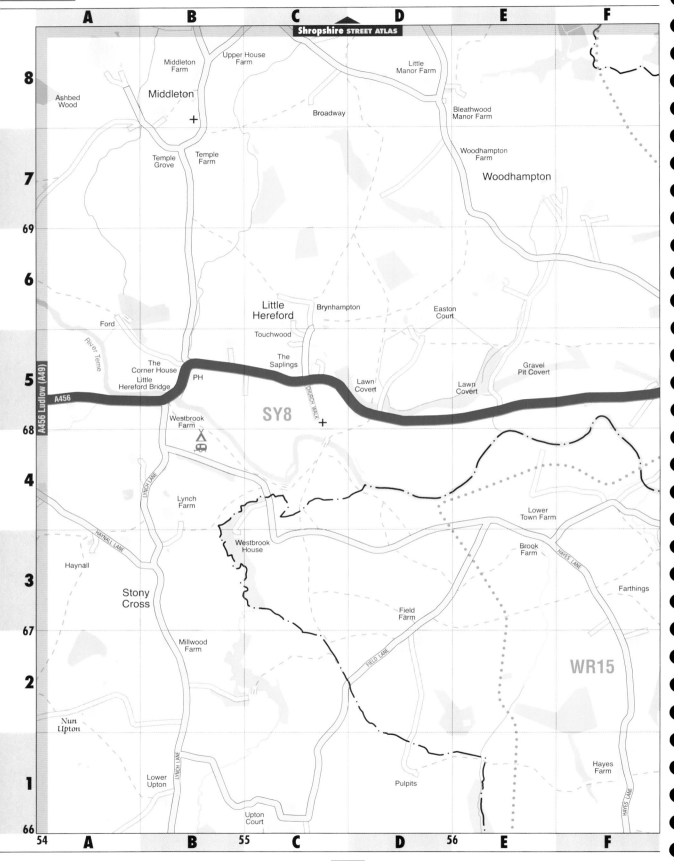

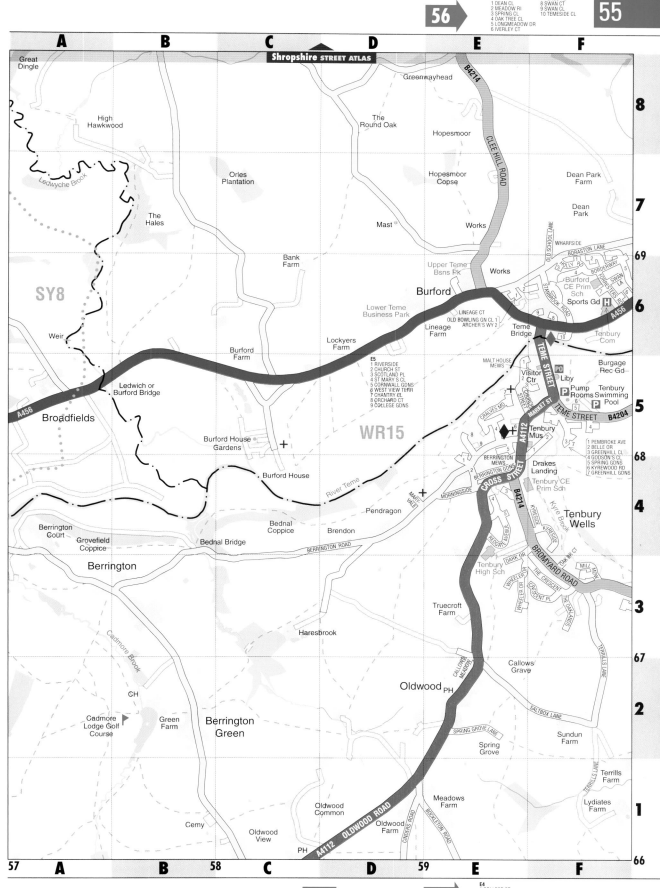

F6
1 DEAN CL
2 MEADOW RI
3 SPRING CL
4 OAK TREE CL
5 LONGMEADOW DR
6 IVERLEY CT
7 PENLU RD
8 SWAN CT
9 SWAN CL
10 TEMESIDE CL

Great Dingle

High Hawkwood

Ledwyche Brook

SY8

Orles Plantation

The Hales

Bank Farm

Greenwayhead

The Round Oak

Hopesmoor

Hopesmoor Copse

B4214

CLEE HILL ROAD

Dean Park Farm

Dean Park

Mast

Works

Works

Upper Teme Bsns Pk

Burford

Lower Teme Business Park

Lockyers Farm

Lineage Farm

Lineage CT

OLD BOWLING GN CL 1
ARCHER'S WY 2

WHARFSIDE

OLD SCHOOL LANE

BORASTON LANE

POLLY RD

BORDERWAY

FORESTERS

SWAN LA

DORCHESTER

STAMBROOK ROAD

Burford CE Prim Sch

Sports Gd H

A456

Teme Bridge

Tenbury Com

TEME STREET

PO

Liby

Pump Rooms

P

Burgage Rec Gd

Tenbury Swimming Pool

P

Weir

A456

Ledwich or Burford Bridge

Broadfields

Burford Farm

E5
1 RIVERSIDE
2 CHURCH ST
3 SCOTLAND PL
4 ST MARY S CL
5 CORNWALL GDNS
6 WEST VIEW TERR
7 CHANTRY CL
8 ORCHARD CT
9 COLLEGE GDNS

MALT HOUSE MEWS

Visitor Ctr

CHURCH STREET

GRAVES MD

MARKET ST

TEME STREET

B4204

5

WR15

Burford House Gardens

Burford House

River Teme

Tenbury Mus

A4112

Berrington Mews

BERRINGTON GDNS

Drakes Landing

Tenbury CE Prim Sch

68

1 PEMBROKE AVE
2 BELLE OR
3 GREENHILL CL
4 GODSON'S CL
5 SPRING GDNS
6 KYREWOOD RD
7 GREENHILL GDNS

Berrington Court

Grovefield Coppice

Bednal Bridge

Bednal Coppice

Brendon

Pendragon

MARE VALE

MORNINGSIDE

CROSS STREET

B4214

KYRESIDE

KYRESIDE

Kyre Brook

Tenbury Wells

4

Berrington

BERRINGTON ROAD

Tenbury High Sch

BELGRAVE AVENUE

DARK OR

WHEELER OR

CRESCENT PL

THE CRESCENT

OAK BR CT

THE OAKLANDS

BROMYARD ROAD

MILL

TERRILLS LANE

3

Cadmore Brook

Haresbrook

Truecroft Farm

CALLOWS MEADOW

67

CH

Oldwood PH

Callows Grave

SALTBOX LANE

Sundun Farm

2

Cadmore Lodge Golf Course

Green Farm

Berrington Green

A4112 OLDWOOD ROAD

SPRING GROVE LANE

Spring Grove

Terrills Farm

Lydiates Farm

1

Cemy

Oldwood View

Oldwood Common

PH

Oldwood Farm

CINDERS ROAD

ROCKLETON ROAD

Meadows Farm

66

E4
1 COLLEGE CT
2 BOG LA
3 MOUNT PLEASANT
4 MOUNT ORCH
5 BURLEIGH CL

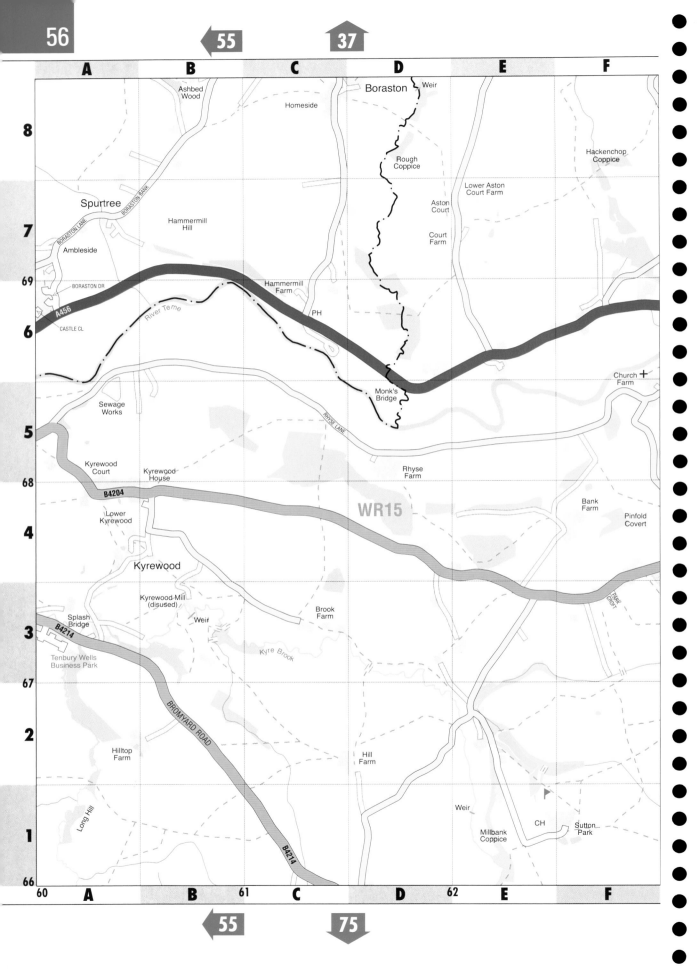

Boraston

Weir

Ashbed
Wood

Homeside

Rough
Coppice

Hackenchop
Coppice

Lower Aston
Court Farm

Spurtree

Aston
Court

Ambleside

Hammermill
Hill

Court
Farm

BORASTON BANK

BORASTON LANE

BORASTON DR

Hammermill
Farm

A456

River Teme

PH

CASTLE CL

Monk's
Bridge

Church
Farm

RHYSE LANE

Sewage
Works

Rhyse
Farm

Kyrewood
Court

Kyrewood
House

Bank
Farm

B4204

Pinfold
Covert

WR15

Lower
Kyrewood

Kyrewood

PARK CROFT

Kyrewood Mill
(disused)

Splash
Bridge

Weir

Brook
Farm

B4214

Kyre Brook

Tenbury Wells
Business Park

BROMYARD ROAD

Hill
Farm

Hilltop
Farm

Weir

CH

Sutton
Park

Millbank
Coppice

Long Hill

B4214

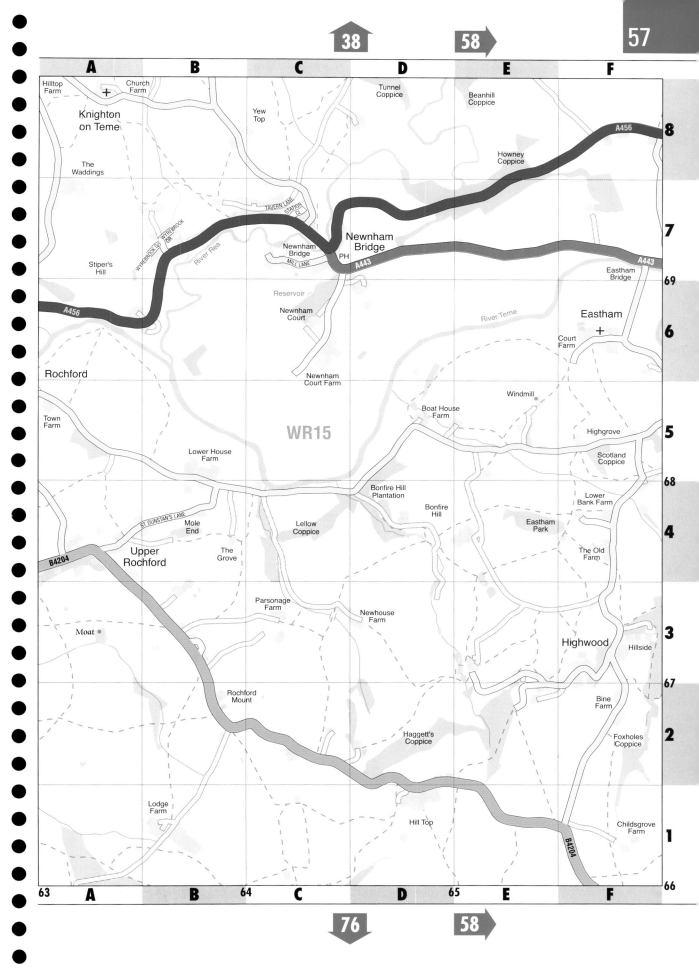

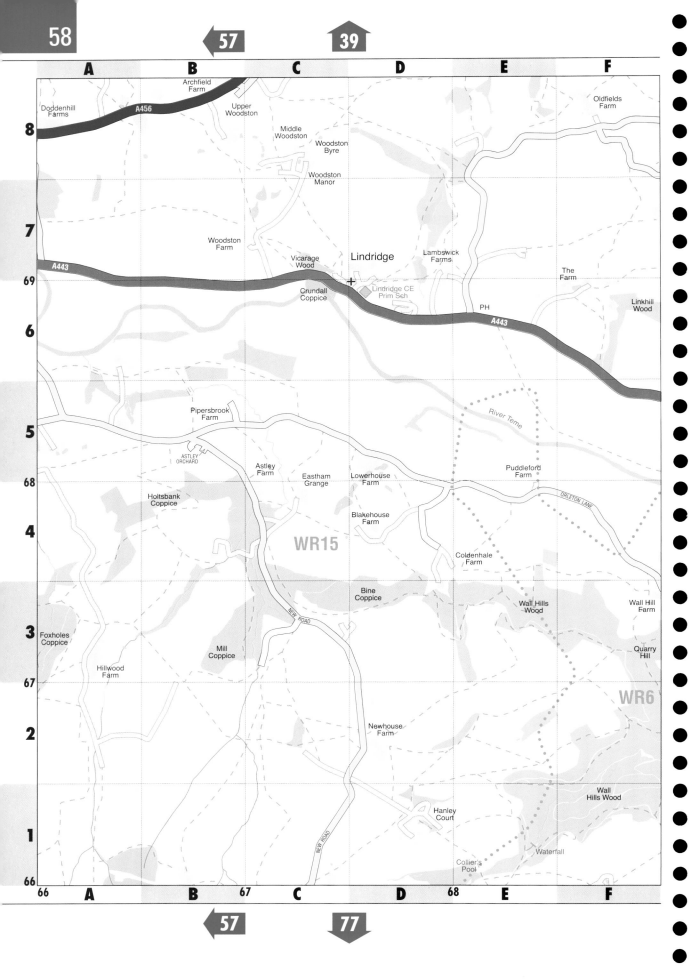

57
39

A B C D E F

8

7

69

6

5

68

4

3

67

2

1

66

Doddenhill Farms

A456

Archfield Farm

Upper Woodston

Middle Woodston

Woodston Byre

Woodston Manor

Oldfields Farm

Woodston Farm

A443

Vicarage Wood

Lindridge

Lambswick Farms

The Farm

Crundall Coppice

Lindridge CE Prim Sch

PH

A443

Linkhill Wood

Pipersbrook Farm

River Teme

ASTLEY ORCHARD

Astley Farm

Eastham Grange

Lowerhouse Farm

Puddleford Farm

ORLETON LANE

Holtsbank Coppice

Blakehouse Farm

WR15

Coldenhale Farm

Wall Hills Wood

Wall Hill Farm

Bine Coppice

Foxholes Coppice

NEW ROAD

Mill Coppice

Quarry Hill

Hillwood Farm

WR6

Newhouse Farm

NEW ROAD

Wall Hills Wood

Hanley Court

Waterfall

Collier's Pool

66 A 67 B C 68 D E F

57
77

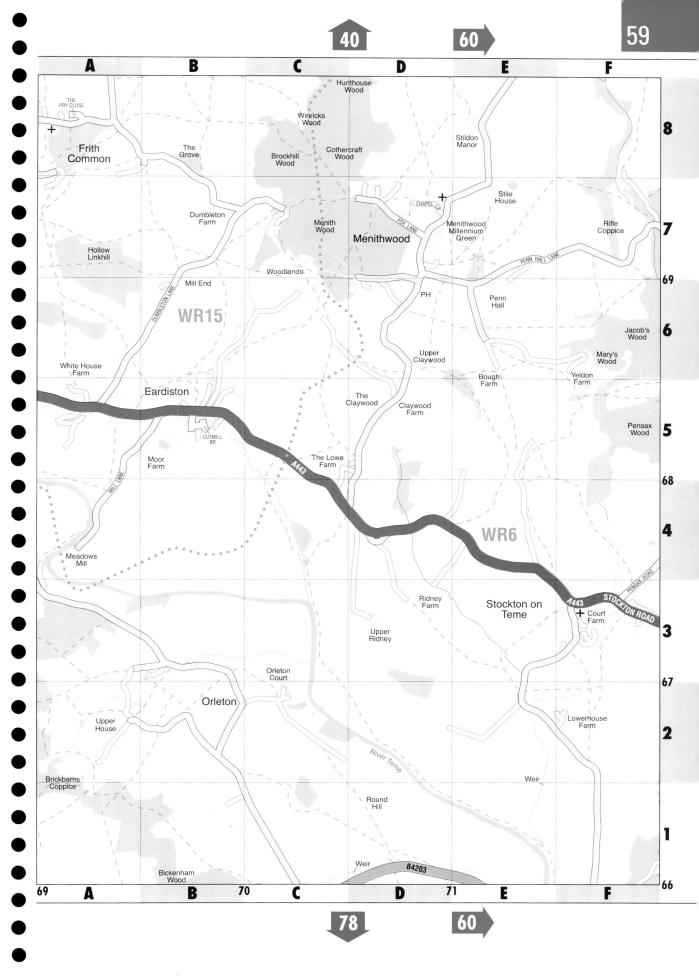

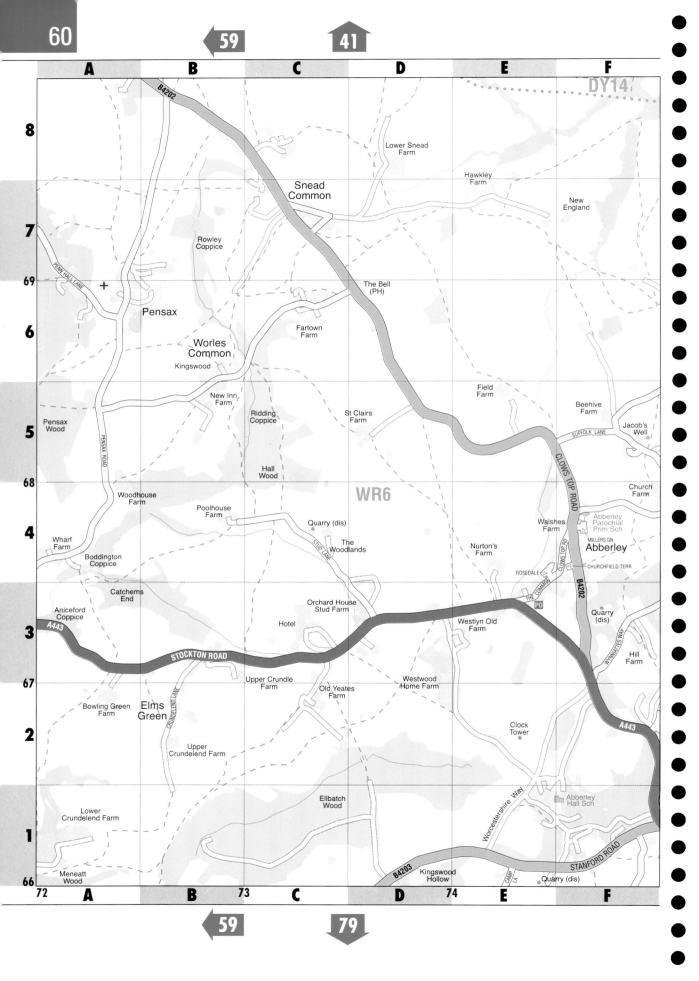

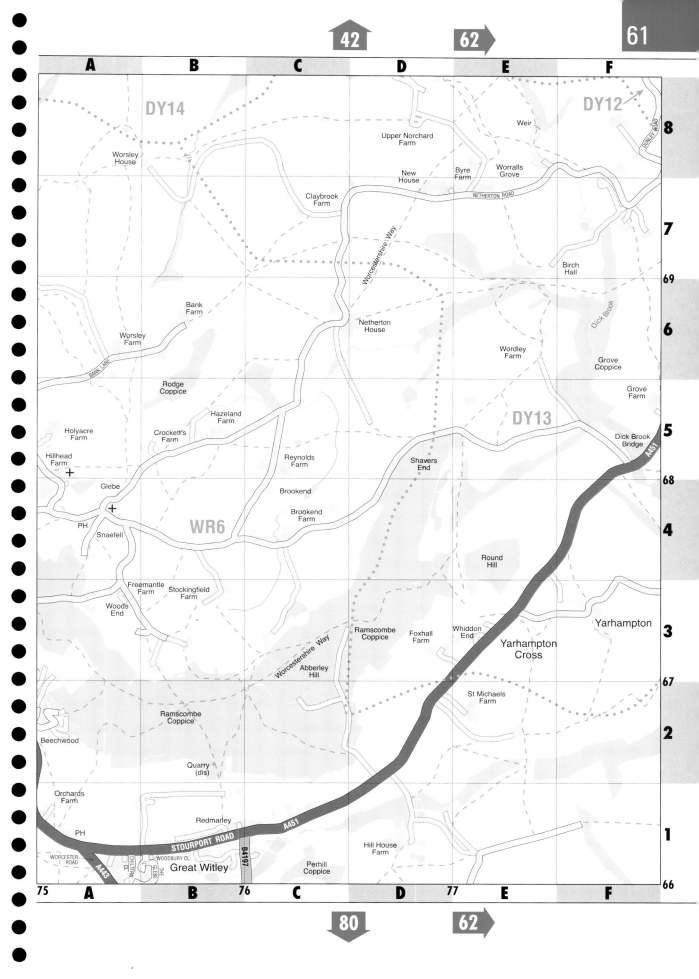

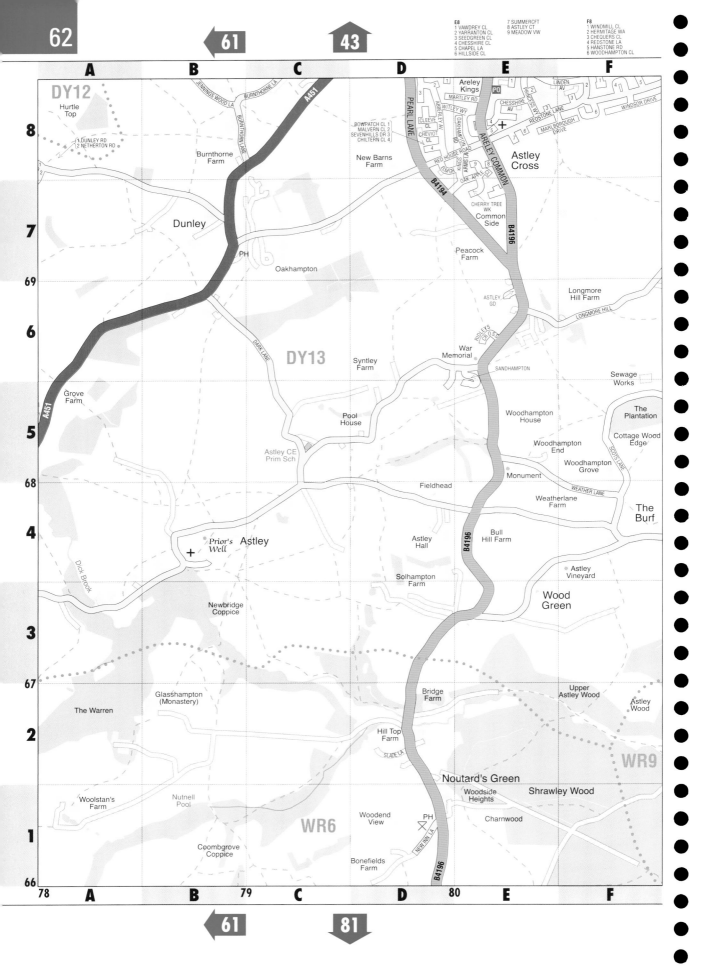

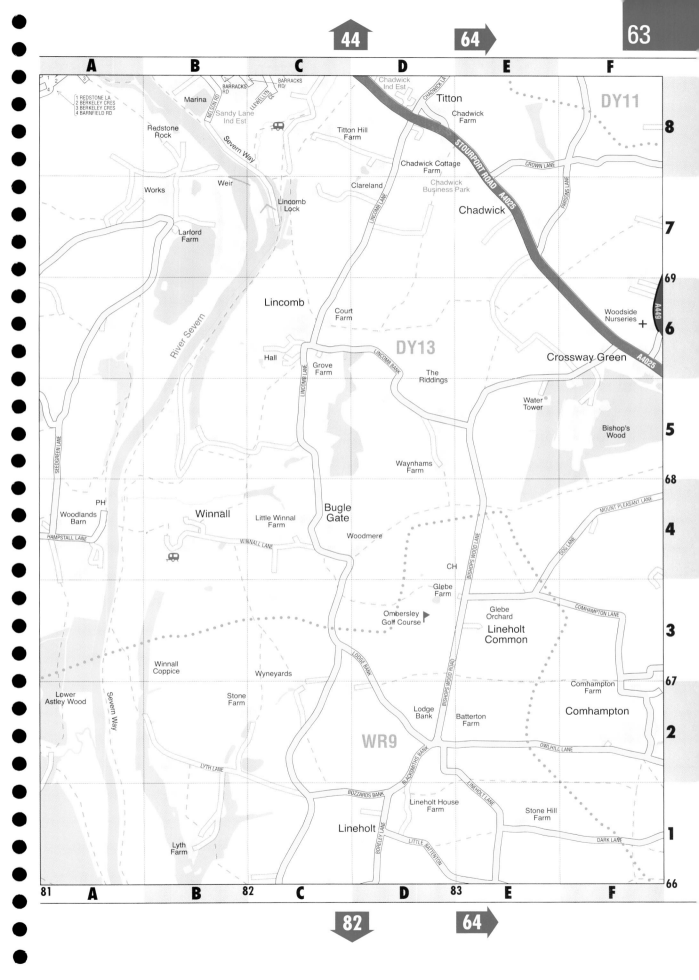

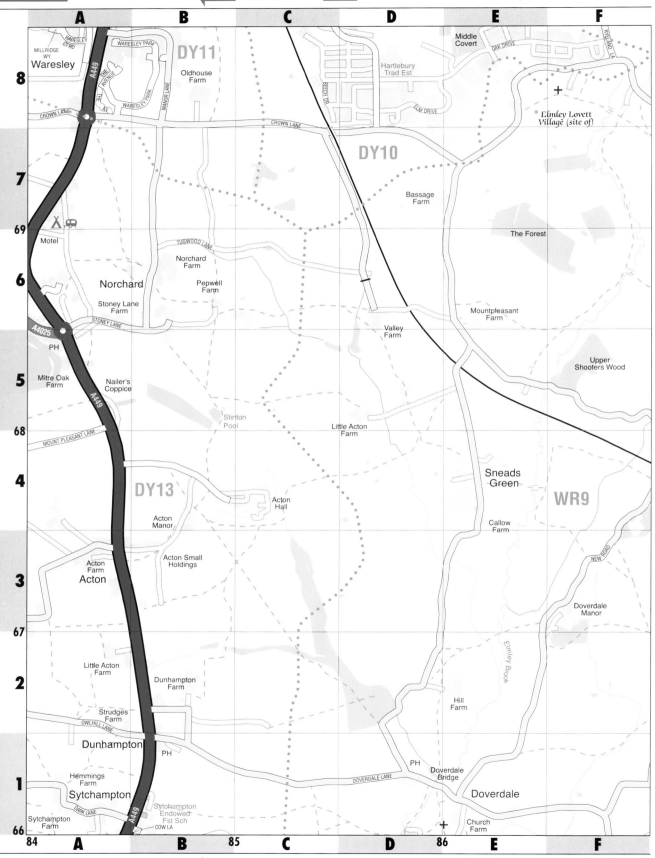

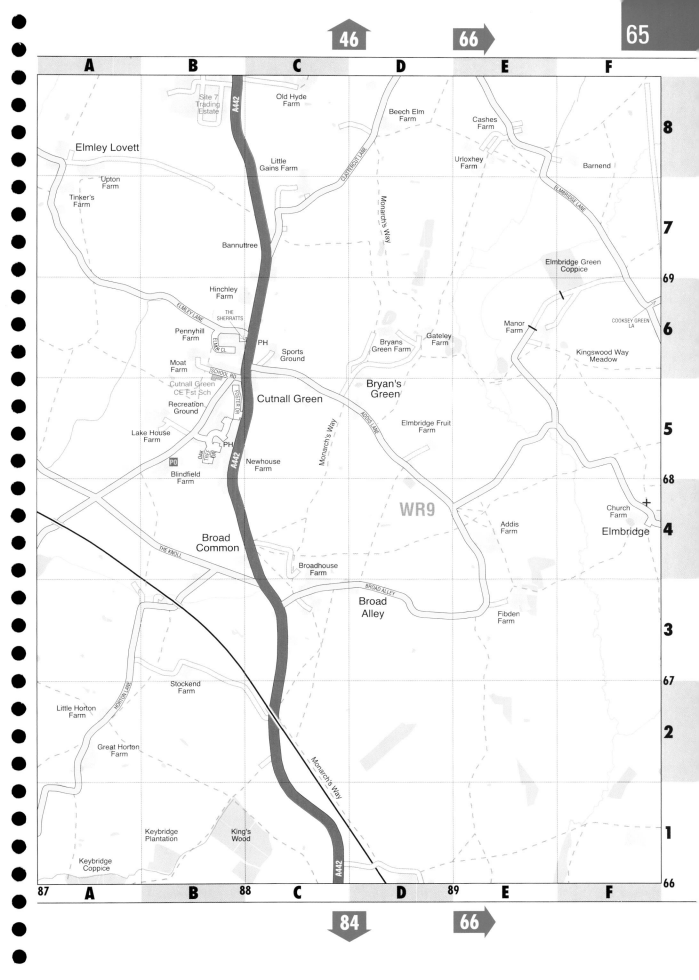

A B C D E F

8

Site 7 Trading Estate

Old Hyde Farm

Beech Elm Farm

Cashes Farm

Elmley Lovett

Little Gains Farm

Urloxhey Farm

Barnend

Upton Farm

Tinker's Farm

7

Bannuttree

Monarch's Way

Elmbridge Green Coppice

69

Hinchley Farm

THE SHERRATTS

Manor Farm

COOKSEY GREEN LA

6

Pennyhill Farm

PH

Sports Ground

Bryans Green Farm

Gateley Farm

Kingswood Way Meadow

Moat Farm

SCHOOL RD

Cutnall Green CE Fst Sch

Cutnall Green

Bryan's Green

Recreation Ground

Elmbridge Fruit Farm

5

Lake House Farm

PH

Monarch's Way

ADDIS LANE

68

PO

Newhouse Farm

WR9

Blindfield Farm

Church Farm

Elmbridge

4

Broad Common

THE KNOLL

Addis Farm

Broadhouse Farm

BROAD ALLEY

Broad Alley

Fibden Farm

3

67

Stockend Farm

HORTON LANE

Little Horton Farm

2

Great Horton Farm

Monarch's Way

Keybridge Plantation

King's Wood

1

Keybridge Coppice

A442

66

A B C 88 C D 89 E F 66

A B C D E F

8

Badge
Court

Badge Court
Farm

Cooksey Green Lane

PURSHULL GREEN LANE

Cooksey
Green

COOKSEY GREEN LANE

Longlands
Farm

Newhouse
Farm

NEWHOUSE LANE

TIMBERHONGER LANE

Forge House
Farm

Cooksey Green
Farm

BERRY LANE

7

COOKSEY GREEN LANE

Cooksey
Farm

Berry Lane
Farm

Cobbler's
Coppice

69

B61

6

Church Cottage
Farm

DOG LANE

West Lodge
Farm

Cooksey Lodge
Farm

SWAN LANE

5

The Hill
Farm

Cooksey
Corner

68

Radnall
Farm

Elmbridge

Coley Pits
Farm

4

ELMBRIDGE LANE

Newhouse
Farm

CRUTCH LANE

COLEY PITS LANE

Kingsland
Hill Farm

3

Grange
Farm

WR9

Withy Furlong
Farm

Little Gains
Farm

67

Radio
Masts

2

CROWN LANE

New Ridgeway
Farm

Radio
Transmitting
Station

PAPER MILL LANE

WORCESTER ROAD

New Ridge
Acre Farm

Old Ridgeway
Farm

M5

Radio
Masts

1

Crutch
Farm

Wyken
Farm

MILL LANE

Mill
Farm

A38

Wychbold

Crutch
Hill

BRINE PITS LANE

Ridgeway Court
Farm

Ridgeacre
Farm

Sewage
Works

Wychbold
Farm

CROWN LANE

CHURCH LANE

PH

66

90 A 91 B C 91 D 92 E F

E1
1 CHEQUERS LA
2 PEAR TREE WY

67

48 — E8
1 Millfields Fst Sch
2 St Peters RC Fst Sch

68

F6
1 Sugarbrook Ct
2 Aston Fields Trad Est
3 Silver Birches Bsns Pk
4 BGW Bsns Pk
5 The Courtyard Bsns Pk

A B C D E F

BROMSGROVE

M5

B61

Foxwalks Farm

East Lodge Farm

Breakback Hill

Mast

Grafton Manor House
Fish Pond

Grafton La

Bowling Green Farm

Rock Hill

B4091

Bromsgrove Lower Sch

South Bromsgrove High Sch Tech & Language Coll

Spadesbourne Brook

Monarch's Way

Charford

Charford Fst Sch

Stoke Rd A38

Sugarbrook

B4091 / Worcester Rd / Hanbury Rd

Redditch Rd

Superstore

Buntsford Gate Bsns Pk

West Ct

Buntsford Hill Bsns Pk

Sherwood Rd

A38

Stoke Heath

Oaklands Ct

Ploughmans Wlk

Avoncroft Mus of Historic Buildings

Avoncroft Com Arts Ctr

Windmill

Tanhouse Farm

Warren House

Sunningdale

Rectory Farm

THE BEECHES

Worcester Rd

PH

Fieldview House

Brickhouse La

E6
1 Waggoners Cl
2 Countinghouse Way
3 Kerry Hill
4 Martingale Cl
5 The Croft Bsns Pk

Fish House La

Brickhouse Farm

Little Brick House Farm

Stoke Prior Bridge

Stoke Prior

River Salwarpe

Hanbury Rd

Stoke Pound Farm

FARFIELD

Stoke Pound La

Little Intall Fields

Whitford Bridge Rd

Upton Warren

Swan La

RECTORY LA

Upton Warren Bridge

Moors Farm

The Christopher Cadbury Reserve

Foley Gardens

B60

Stoke Wharf

PH

A38

Sailing Lake

Hobden Hall Farm Ind Units

Hobden Hall Farm

Shaw La

PO

Ryefields Rd

Cloverdale

Orchard Cres

Stoke Prior Fst Sch

Ryefields Farm

Worcester and Birmingham Canal

Waste Pit

THE COURTYARD

Harris Bsns Pk

Saxon Bsns Pk

Sports Gd

Works

Hen Brook

Works

Shaw Lane Ind Est

Greenside

WR9

Sagebury Farm

Jubilee Cl

Jubilee Terr

Rosemary Dr
Verbena Dr
Sagebury Dr

PH

Wyche Cotts

Stoke Works

Westonhall Rd

Weston Hall Farm

Poolhouse Farm

B4091

Harbours Hill Farm

Little Harbours Farm

Morgate Rd

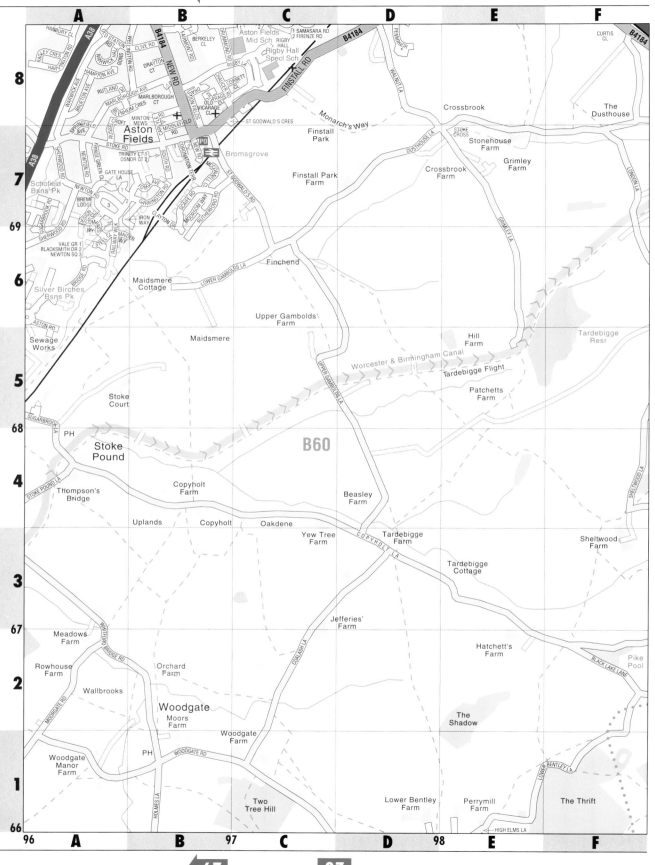

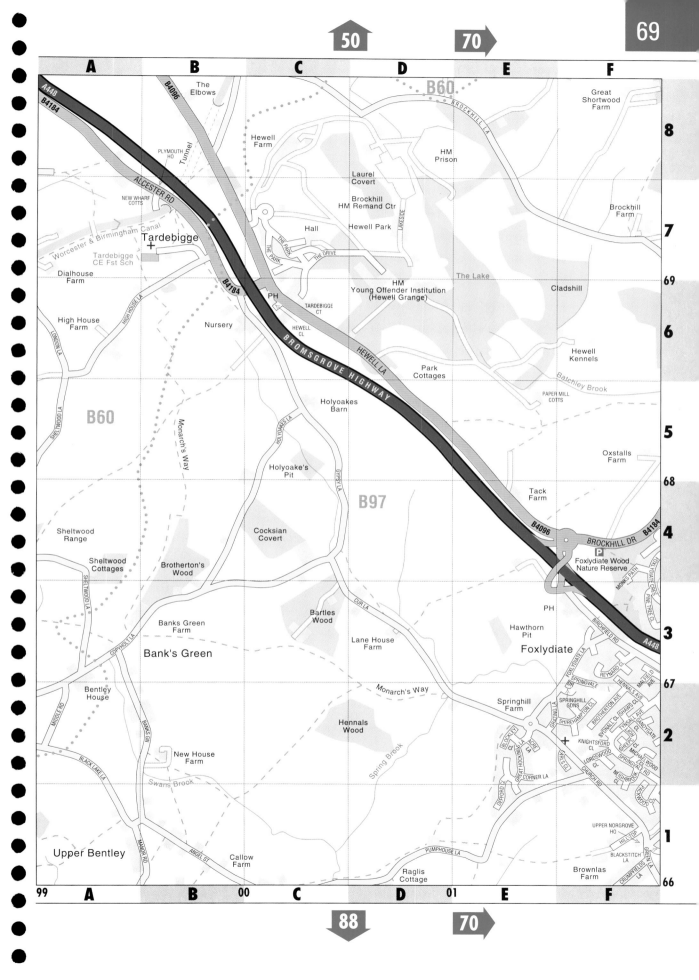

69 51

A B C D E F

8 7 69 6 68 5 4 67 3 2 1 66

Bordesley
Bordesley Park Farm

B4101 DAGNELL END RD B4101

BIRMINGHAM RD

PH
Abbey Park Golf Club

Butler's Hill Wood
Butler's Hill
Butler's Hill Farm
Weights Lane Bsns Pk
Weights LA
Weights Farm

Bordesley Bridge

River Arrow
HITHER GREEN LA
B98

Abbey Stad Sports Ctr

Greensleeves
B5
1 BLACKWELL LA
2 KERSWELL CL
3 DEVONPORT CL
4 ALDBOROUGH LA
5 GISBURN CL
6 ELLEN BROOK CL
7 CORNHAMPTON CL
8 AMBERGATE CL
9 DRAYCOTT CL
10 BIRCHENSALE FARM

Lowan's Hill Farm

Cemy
Crem
Bordesley Abbey (rems of)

Brockhill Wood

WHEELERS LA
OVERSLEY CL
PINK GN LA

Works
B4184
MIDDLEHOUSE

Bordesley LA

Needle Mill LA
Visitor Riverside Ctr
Forge Mill Needle Mus

Birchensale
BROCKHILL DR
Mast

LOWANS HILL COTTS
Red Ditch

WINDSOR RD
Enfield
Enfield Ind Est

Abbey Trading Centre
Superstore

St Stephen's CE First School
MASEY AVE
ST STEPHENS

HEWELL RD
ELIZABETH WAY

New Coll

Abbey Trad Ctr
CLIVE RD
CALBERT ST

ALVECHURCH HIGHWAY
B4160

Abbeydale
SANNINGDALE

Hewell Rd Swimming Pool
BRIDLEY MOOR RD
CEDAR PARK RD
BOWOOD CL

St Stephen's HO
ABBEY RD
GROSVENOR AVE

Registry Office
Empire Ct Bsns Pk
WELLINGTON ST

St George's Trinity High Sch & Sixth Form Ctr

A441

Birchensale Mid Sch
Holyoakes Field Fst Sch

New Coll

St Georges RD
PHILLIPS CT

Pitcheroak Specl Sch
B97
Valley Stad (Redditch FC)
1 KEMERTON HO
2 WILMCOTE HO
3 HANBURY HO
4 WOODGATE HO
5 LEDBURY HO
WIDNEY HO

J2OD ST
1 KINGFISHER WLK
2 KINGFISHER SQ
3 BATES HILL
4 ADELAIDE ST

New Redditch Coll

REDDITCH RINGWAY

Liby
TIC
Palace Theatre

BEDLEY RW

St Davids HO
ST DAVIDS HO
WILLOW WAY
PRIORS OAK

BROMSGROVE RD

Batchley Fst Sch
Batchley

PINVIN
MORTON RD

ALLWOOD HO

FERNEY HILL AVE
VICARAGE CRES
VICARAGE VIEW

CEMETERY LANE
STATION WAY

COVENTRY HIGHWAY
B4160

St Georges CE Fst Sch
The Trafford Pk

Foxlydiate Wood Nature Reserve

Pitcheroak Cotts
PITCHEROAK COTTS

HOLMWOOD CL
HOLWOOD HO

Cemy
BENTLEY CL

LUDLOW RD
OAKLY ST
SUMMER ST

HOLLOWAY

A448

Pitcheroak Wood Nature Reserve
REDDITCH

1 WOODSIDE AVE
2 SEACOLE HO
3 MUSKETTS CT
4 BIRCHFIELD CT
5 BIRCHES HO

PARTRIDGE HO 1
HAYNES HO 2
ROXBORO HO 3
CRESCENT HO 4

SMALLWOOD ALMSHOUSES
DINGLESIDE
TUNNEL

B98
NAILSWORTH RD
COLDFIELD DR

Webheath
Webheath Fst Sch

BROMSGROVE HIGHWAY
B4504

MAPLE HO
WESTBURY HO
MINWORTH CL

Smallwood

JUBILEE HO
LODGE POOL DR

Lodge Pool
Lodge Park

SHELTWOOD CL
COLEFORD CL
BIRCHFIELD CL
WOODEND CL
30

PLYMOUTH CL
WOOD CT

St Lukes CE Fst Sch

SOUTHCREST GDNS

Southcrest
Southcrest Wood Nature Reserve

CRABTREE CL
BARLICH WAY

WINDMILL DR
B4504

PLYMOUTH RD

A441
A4189

Marlpit Farm
MARLPIT LA

1 SPINNEY MEWS
2 SPINNEY WLK

St Luke's Cotts
ROOKERY CL
HEADLESS CROSS DR

A448

69 89

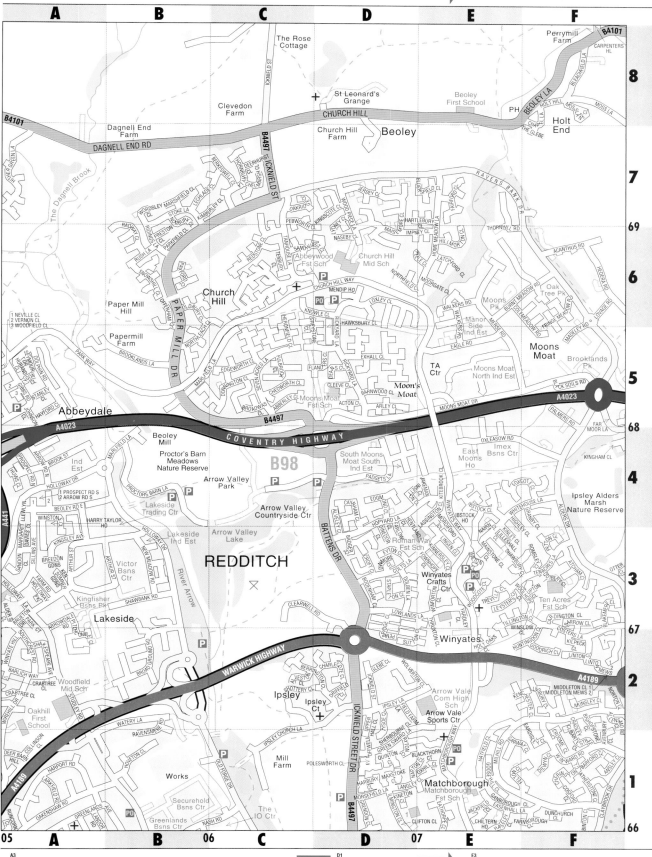

71
53

A **B** **C** **D** **E** **F**

BEOLEY LA
B4101

8

PINK GREEN LA

Pink
Green

ALCESTER
RD

A435

ALDERHANGER LA

FORDE HALL LA

Trap's
Green

ALDERHANGER LA

B94

TANWORTH LA

MOSS LA

Green Hills
Farm

7

WAPPING LA

69

HEDERA RD

B98

6

GORCOTT HILL

ULLENHALL LA

Gorcott
Hill

REDDITCH
Mast

Gorcott
Hall

PH

5

A4023 COVENTRY HIGHWAY

Oldberrow Hil
Farm

68

KINGHAM CL
ILLSHAW CL

HOLLYBERRY CL

B95

Skilts
Specl Sch

4

FURZE LA
FLAXLEY CL
LONGHOPE CL
CATELY CL
PRESTBURY CL
MERIDEN CL
KENDAL CL
FAR MOOR LA
HINDLIP CL
JAYS CL
DURSLEY LA
NEWENT CL
LINDRIDGE CL
OTTER CLOSE
CHESWICK

+

BIRMINGHAM RD

COMMON LA

Lower
Skilts
Farm

3

ABBOTS WOOD CL
ALDERS DR
BERKELEY CL

Mappleborough
Green

67

ARDENS CL

A4189
WARWICK HIGHWAY

A4189

HENLEY ROAD

B80

A4189 Warwick

A4189

2

CLAYBROOK DR

Mappleborough Green
CE J&I School
PH

Cracknut
Hill

Outhill

A435

Mappleborough
Green

HAYE LA

Gattax
Farm

1

66

08 **A** 09 **B** **C** 10 **D** **E** **F**

Warwickshire STREET ATLAS

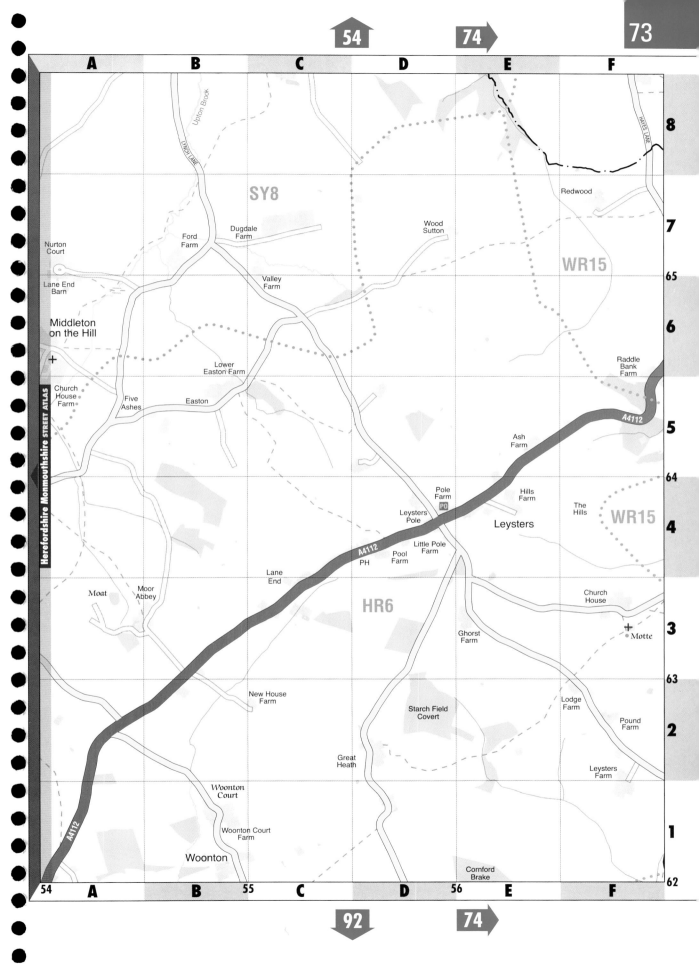

A B C D E F

8

Redwood

SY8

7

WR15

65

Nurton
Court

Dugdale
Farm

Wood
Sutton

Ford
Farm

Lane End
Barn

Valley
Farm

6

Middleton
on the Hill

+

Raddle
Bank
Farm

Lower
Easton Farm

Church
House
Farm

Five
Ashes

Easton

A4112

5

Ash
Farm

64

Pole
Farm
PO

Hills
Farm

The
Hills

WR15

Leysters
Pole

Leysters

4

A4112

Little Pole
Farm

PH

Pool
Farm

Lane
End

HR6

Church
House

+
Motte

3

Moat

Moor
Abbey

Ghorst
Farm

63

New House
Farm

Lodge
Farm

Pound
Farm

Starch Field
Covert

2

Great
Heath

Leysters
Farm

Woonton
Court

1

A4112

Woonton Court
Farm

Woonton

Cornford
Brake

62

Herefordshire Monmouthshire STREET ATLAS

Upton Brook

LYNCH LANE

HAYES LANE

A B C D E F

8

A4112

Oldwood Common

Currall Hall

St Michaels

Pool House

New House Farm

Cadmore Brook

St Michaels Farm

St Michael's Coll

College Walk

Little Redwood

7

Cadmore Bridge

Cinders Wood

Frith Farm

Oldwood Road

65

Gorsty Farm

Cinders Lane

6

A4112

Cinders

Birchley Farm

5

Lower Miles Hope Farm

Miles Hope

WR15

64

Wilden

4

Sunny Bank Dingle

Bockleton Road

Old Manor Farm

3

Hanging Grove

Hill Farm

Weston Farm

63

Prince's Grove

2

HR6

Ford

Newton Farm

Romers Common

Romers Farm

1

Cockspur Hall

Bockleton Country Study Centre

Middle Common

Home Farm

62

Cockspur Coppice

57 A B 58 C D 59 E F

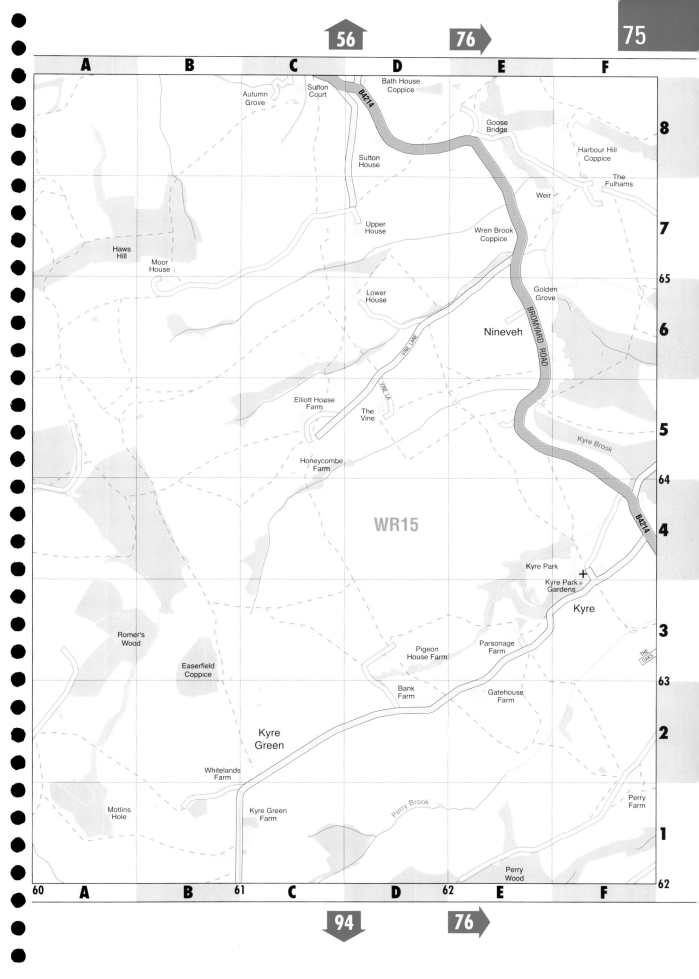

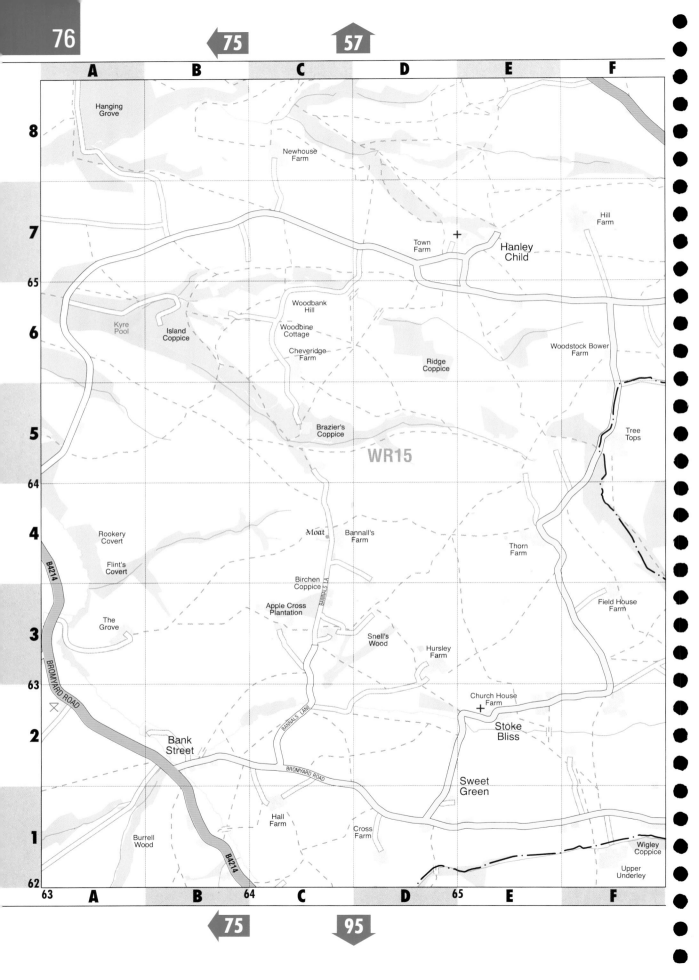

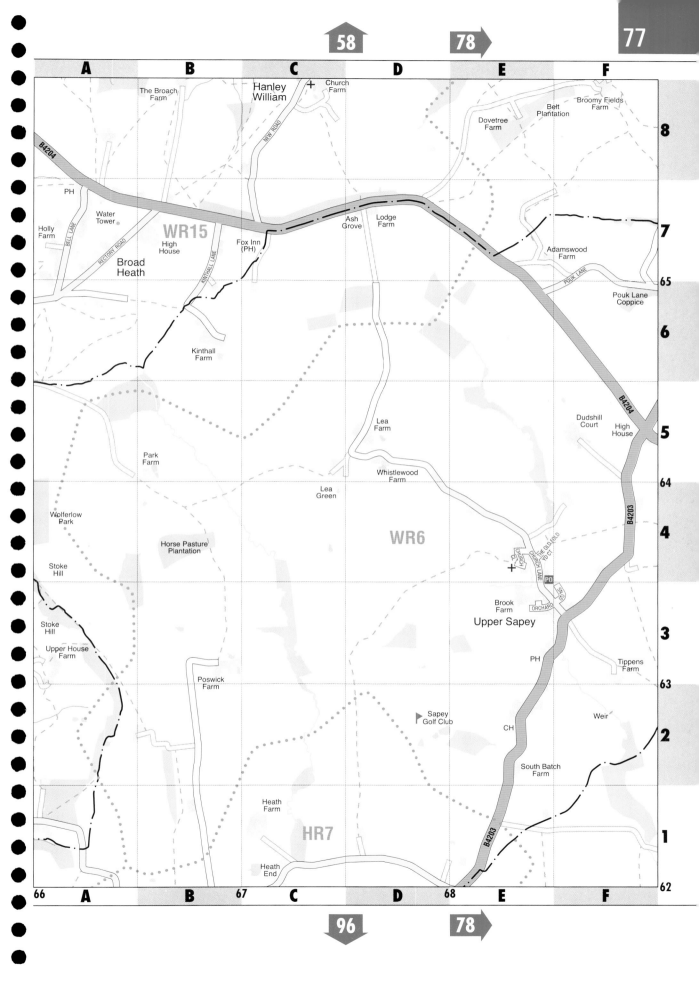

A | B | C | D | E | F

Stanford on Teme

Bickenham Wood

B4203

Home Farm

B4203

PH

8

Fall Farm

Stanford Court

Mill Farm

Stanford Bridge

7

Busk Coppice

River Teme

65

POUK LANE

Temple Dingle

Noverton Farm

Temeside

Nover Coppice

Pouk Lane Coppice

Park Farm

6

Park Plantation

Newbridge Coppice

Beehive Coppice

B4203

Wastehill Wood

5

Waters Farm

B4204

Sapey Common

PARK LANE

64

Yearston Court

ROCK LANE

Rock Coppice

Furnace Farm

4

Criftens Farm

WR6

Cliftonswood Farm

Devil's Den

James's Brake

3

Hell Hole

63

Ayton's Heath

Hill Climb

House Coppice

2

Safford Court Farm

Top Barn

1

Burton Court Farm

B4204

62

69 | A | B | 70 | C | D | 71 | E | F

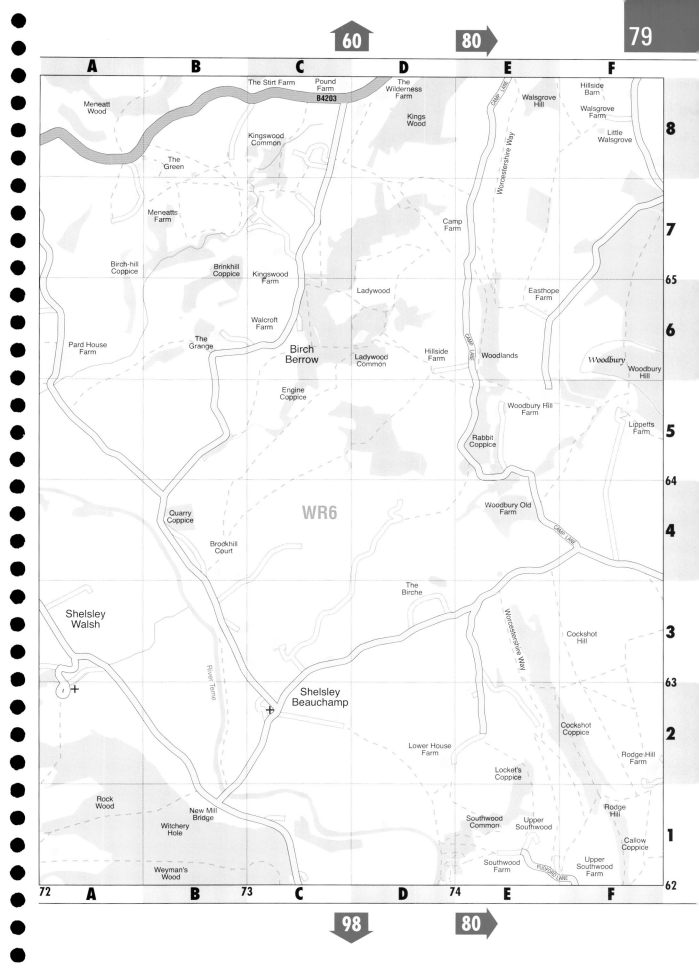

A B C D E F

8
7
65
6
5
64
4
3
63
2
1
62

Meneatt Wood

The Stirt Farm

Pound Farm

B4203

The Wilderness Farm

Kings Wood

Camp Lane

Walsgrove Hill

Hillside Barn

Walsgrove Farm

Little Walsgrove

The Green

Kingswood Common

Worcestershire Way

Meneatts Farm

Camp Farm

Birch-hill Coppice

Brinkhill Coppice

Kingswood Farm

Ladywood

Easthope Farm

Walcroft Farm

Pard House Farm

The Grange

Birch Berrow

Ladywood Common

Hillside Farm

Camp Lane

Woodlands

Woodbury

Woodbury Hill

Engine Coppice

Woodbury Hill Farm

Lippetts Farm

Rabbit Coppice

WR6

Woodbury Old Farm

Quarry Coppice

Camp Lane

Brookhill Court

Shelsley Walsh

The Birche

Worcestershire Way

Cockshot Hill

River Teme

Shelsley Beauchamp

Cockshot Coppice

Lower House Farm

Rodge Hill Farm

Locket's Coppice

Rock Wood

New Mill Bridge

Witchery Hole

Southwood Common

Upper Southwood

Rodge Hill

Callow Coppice

Weyman's Wood

Southwood Farm

Pudford Lane

Upper Southwood Farm

72 A B 73 C D 74 E F

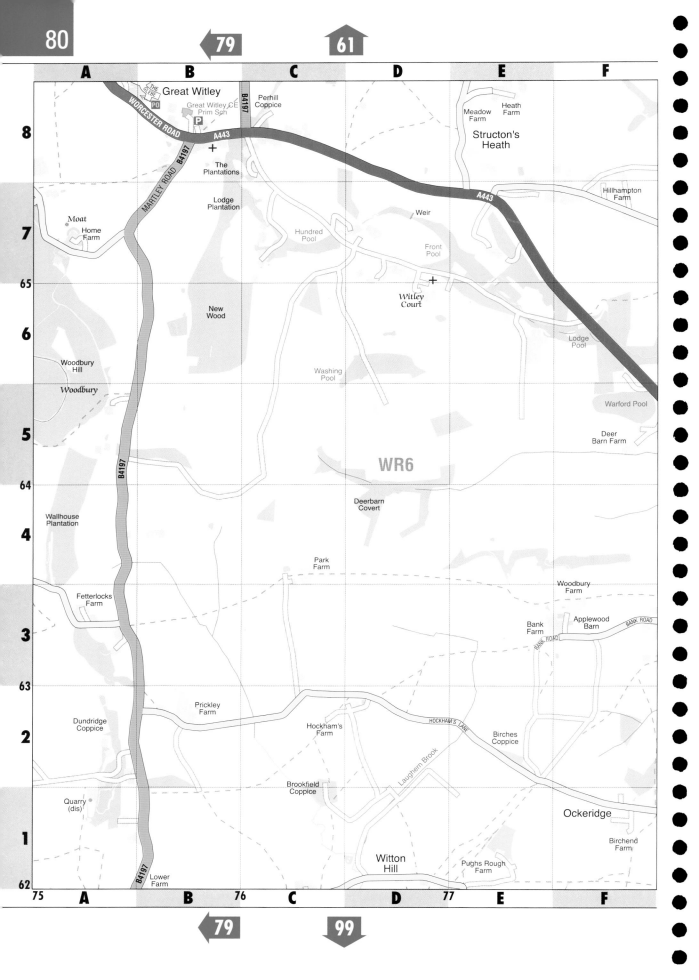

Great Witley

WORCESTER ROAD

THE GLEBE

PO

Great Witley CE
Prim Sch

P

Perhill
Coppice

Meadow
Farm

Heath
Farm

Structon's
Heath

A443

The
Plantations

Hillhampton
Farm

MARTLEY ROAD B4197

Lodge
Plantation

Weir

Moat

Home
Farm

Hundred
Pool

Front
Pool

Witley
Court

New
Wood

Lodge
Pool

Woodbury
Hill

Washing
Pool

Warford Pool

Woodbury

Deer
Barn Farm

B4197

WR6

Wallhouse
Plantation

Deerbarn
Covert

Park
Farm

Woodbury
Farm

Fetterlocks
Farm

Bank
Farm

Applewood
Barn

BANK ROAD

BANK ROAD

Prickley
Farm

HOCKHAM'S LANE

Dundridge
Coppice

Hockham's
Farm

Birches
Coppice

Laughern Brook

Brookfield
Coppice

Ockeridge

Quarry
(dis)

Birchend
Farm

Witton
Hill

Pughs Rough
Farm

B4197

Lower
Farm

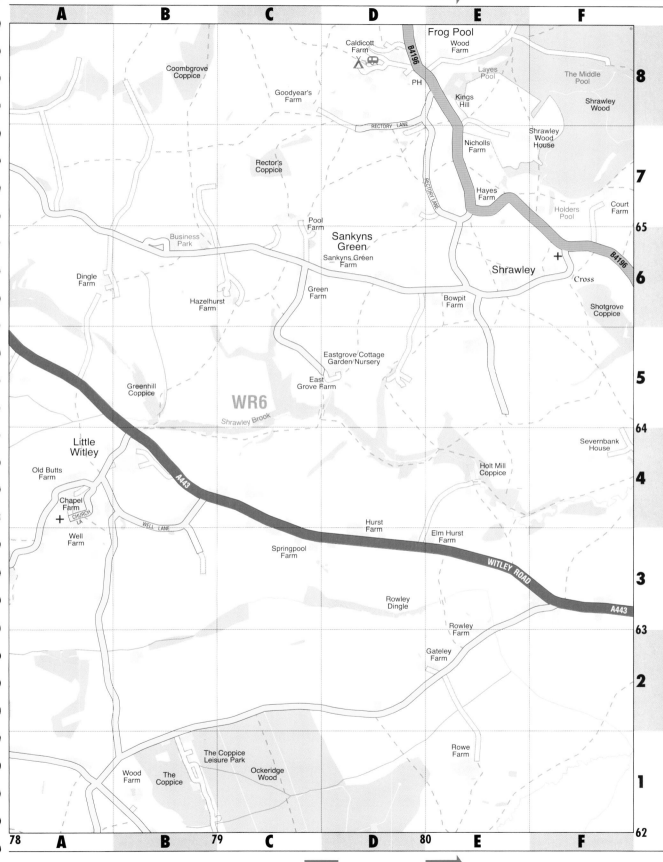

A B C D E F

8

7

65

6

5

64

4

3

63

2

1

62

Frog Pool

Caldicott Farm

Wood Farm

Layes Pool

The Middle Pool

Coombgrove Coppice

Goodyear's Farm

PH

B4196

Kings Hill

Shrawley Wood

RECTORY LANE

Nicholls Farm

Shrawley Wood House

Rector's Coppice

RECTORY LANE

Hayes Farm

Holders Pool

Court Farm

Pool Farm

Sankyns Green

Shrawley

Cross

B4196

Business Park

Sankyns Green Farm

Dingle Farm

Green Farm

Bowpit Farm

Shotgrove Coppice

Hazelhurst Farm

Eastgrove Cottage Garden Nursery

WR6

East Grove Farm

Greenhill Coppice

Shrawley Brook

Severnbank House

Little Witley

Holt Mill Coppice

Old Butts Farm

A443

Hurst Farm

Elm Hurst Farm

Chapel Farm

CHURCH LA

WELL LANE

Springpool Farm

WITLEY ROAD

A443

Well Farm

Rowley Dingle

Rowley Farm

Gateley Farm

The Coppice Leisure Park

Ockeridge Wood

Rowe Farm

Wood Farm

The Coppice

← 81
↑ 63

A **B** **C** **D** **E** **F**

8

BORELEY LANE

Shrawley
Wood

Clack's
Farm

Battenton
Green

Eden
Farm

Yewtree
House

New
Pool

Broomhall
Farm

Severn Way

Woodfield
House

7

River Severn

Boreley

Woodfield
Farm

Woodfield
Barn

NORTHAMPTON LANE

Mast

Northampton

65

Boreley
Farm

Carpenter's
Farm

WR9

6

B4196

Daneswood
Farm

BORELEY LANE

Sarah House
Farm

Uphampton

BORELEY LA

Baytree
Farm

PH

Shotgrove
Coppice

Boreley
House

Chapel
Farm

Birds
Farm

5

Brook
Farm

PH
Hotel

Parsonage

64

Bennett's
Farm

4

Holt
Fleet

Holt Fleet
Farm

PARSONAGE LANE

HOLT FLEET ROAD

Hollingshead
Farm

Weir

Holt
Lock

PH

Powers
Farm

3

CHERRY OR 1
THE HEATH 2
WOODBURY PK 3
LAMBOURNE OR 4
SEVERN HTS 5
APPLE TREE CL 6

Holt Fleet
Bridge

PH

P

B4196

5

2

6

Wychavon Way

Heath Farm

A443 WITLEY ROAD

CHERRY OR

1

A4133

A4133

PH

U4

3

63

PO

Holt
Heath

Fish
Pond

2

WR6

Severn Way

Bentley
Farm

Holt

+

Tower

1

A443

River Severn

62

Northington
Farm

Naunton
Farm

Top Barns
Quarry

← 81
↓ 101

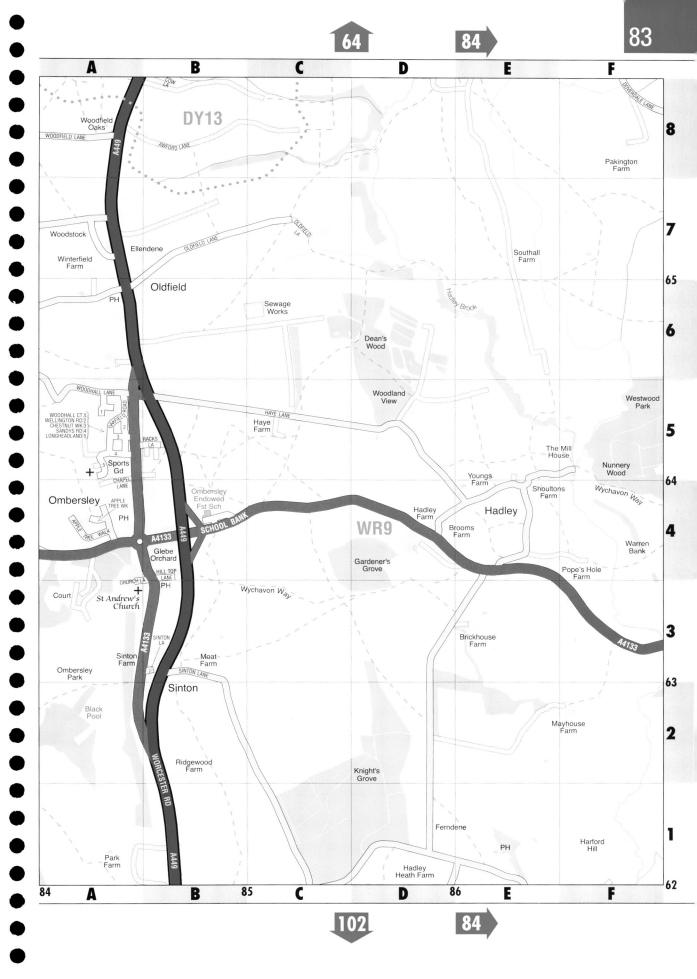

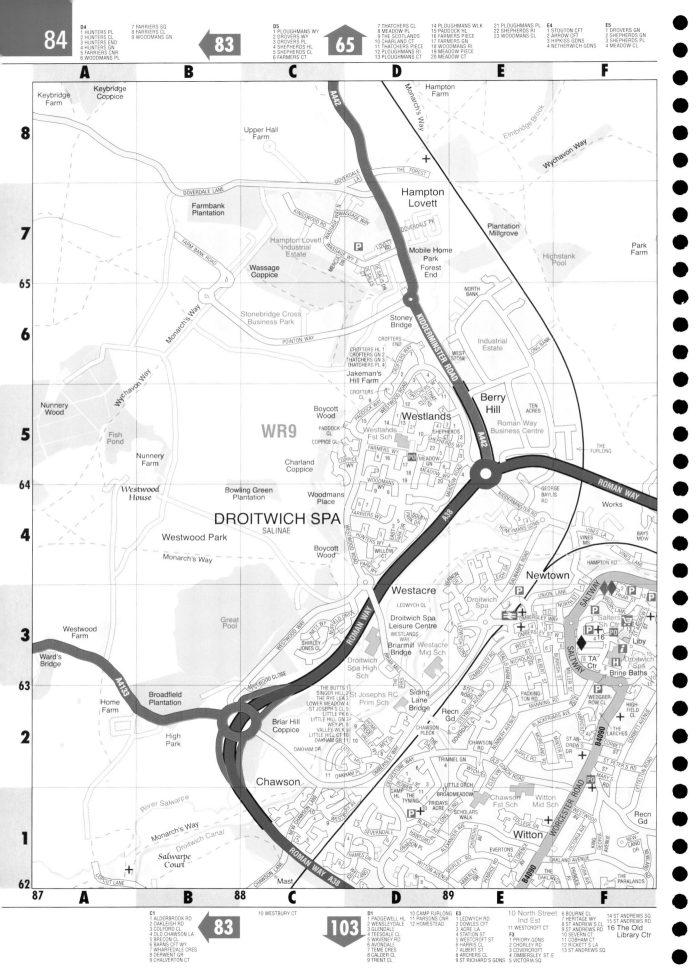

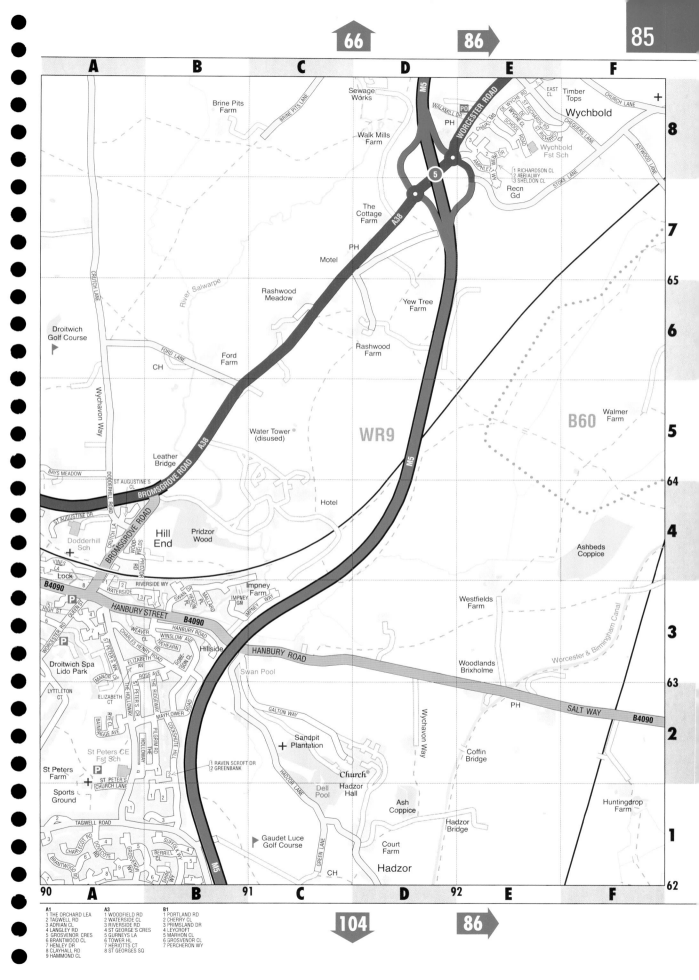

85
67

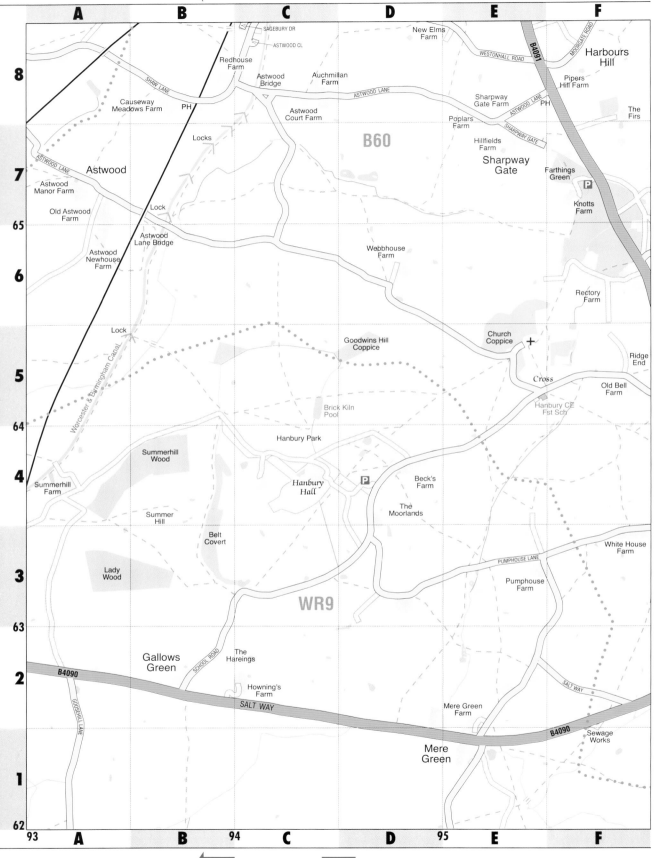

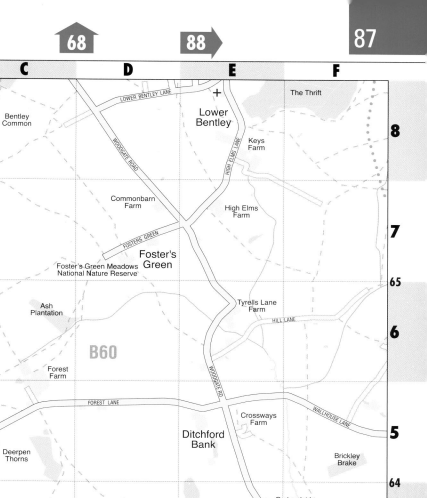
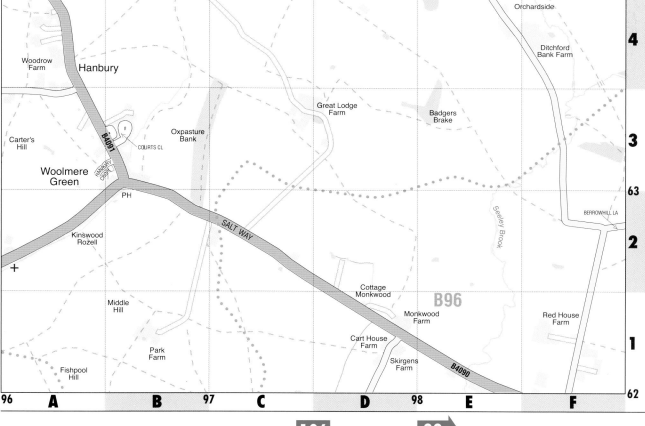

A B C D E F

8

7

65

6

65

Piper's
Hill

Pipers Hill
Farm

Vicarage
Farm

HOLMES LANE

Holmes
Farm

Bentley
Common

LOWER BENTLEY LANE

Lower
Bentley

The Thrift

Keys
Farm

HIGH ELMS LANE

Commonbarn
Farm

WOODGATE ROAD

FOSTERS GREEN

Foster's
Green

High Elms
Farm

Foster's Green Meadows
National Nature Reserve

Ash
Plantation

Forest
Hill

B60

Forest
Farm

Tyrells Lane
Farm

HILL LANE

Valley
Farm

HANBURY ROAD

The
Mount

FOREST LANE

WOODGATE RD

Crossways
Farm

Ditchford
Bank

WALLHOUSE LANE

Brickley
Brake

SCHOOL ROAD

Jinney Ring
Craft Centre

Resr

Deerpen
Thorns

Orchardside

64

Ditchford
Bank Farm

4

Woodrow
Farm

Hanbury

Great Lodge
Farm

Badgers
Brake

Carter's
Hill

B4091

Oxpasture
Bank

COURTS CL

HANBURY GROV

Woolmere
Green

PH

SALT WAY

Seeley Brook

BERROWHILL LA

3

63

2

Kinswood
Rozell

+

Middle
Hill

Park
Farm

Cottage
Monkwood

B96

Monkwood
Farm

Red House
Farm

Cart House
Farm

Fishpool
Hill

Skirgens
Farm

B4090

1

62

96 A B 97 C D 98 E F 62

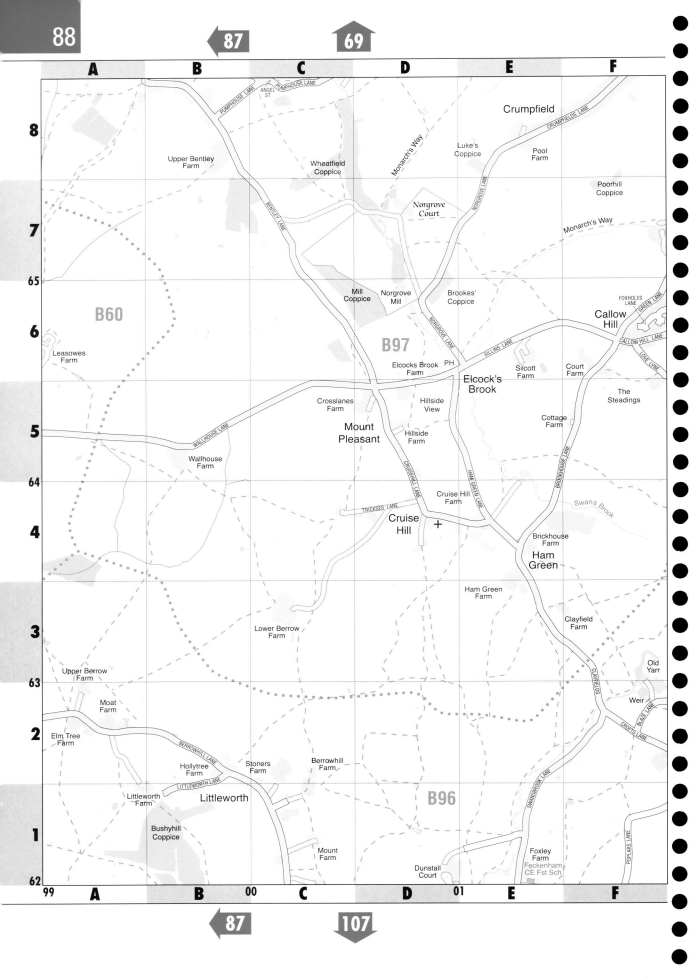

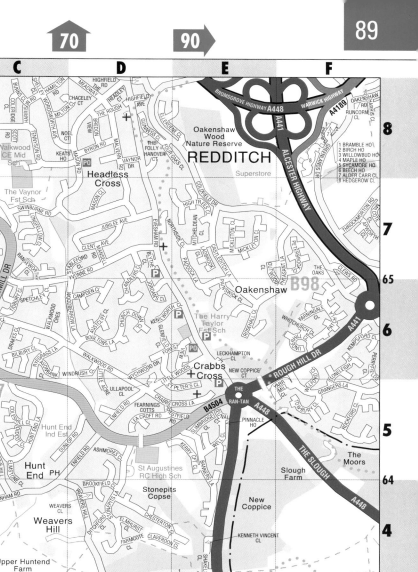

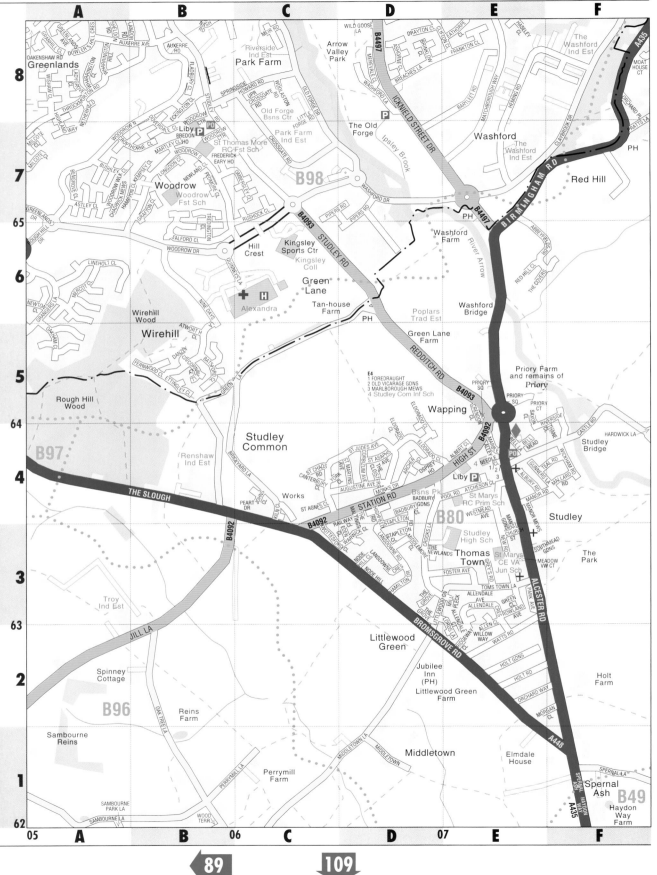

89 71

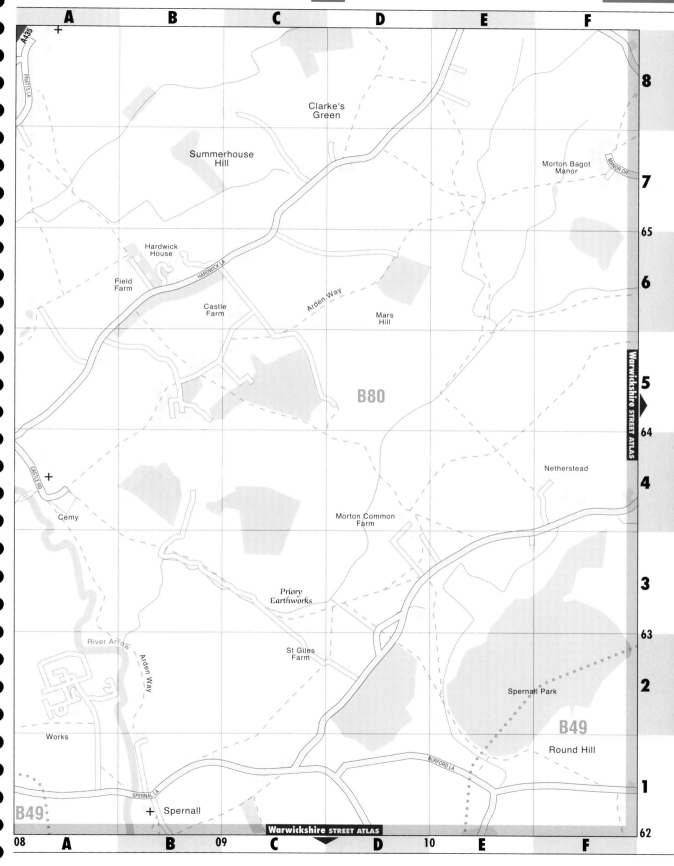

Warwickshire STREET ATLAS

A4112 Leominster (A49)

Herefordshire Monmouthshire STREET ATLAS

WR15

Perry Wood

North Field Covert

Cornford Brake

Rosedale

Rosedale Pool

Olden Farm

Lower Bach

Golderfield Farm

Whyle

Golder Field

Brook Farm

BELL LANE

Highfield Farm

Barnfield Farm

Bach Camp Fort

HR6

Home Farm

WHYLE LANE

Rectory Farm

Ghorst Farm

Court Farm

Pudleston

Upper Hamnish

Brockmanton

Pudleston Court

Pound Farm

Whyle Brook

Gorst Pool

Humber Brook

Stretford Brook

Moat

Ford Abbey

Fort

The Batches

Alderwood Farm

The Woodlands

Ford Abbey Farm

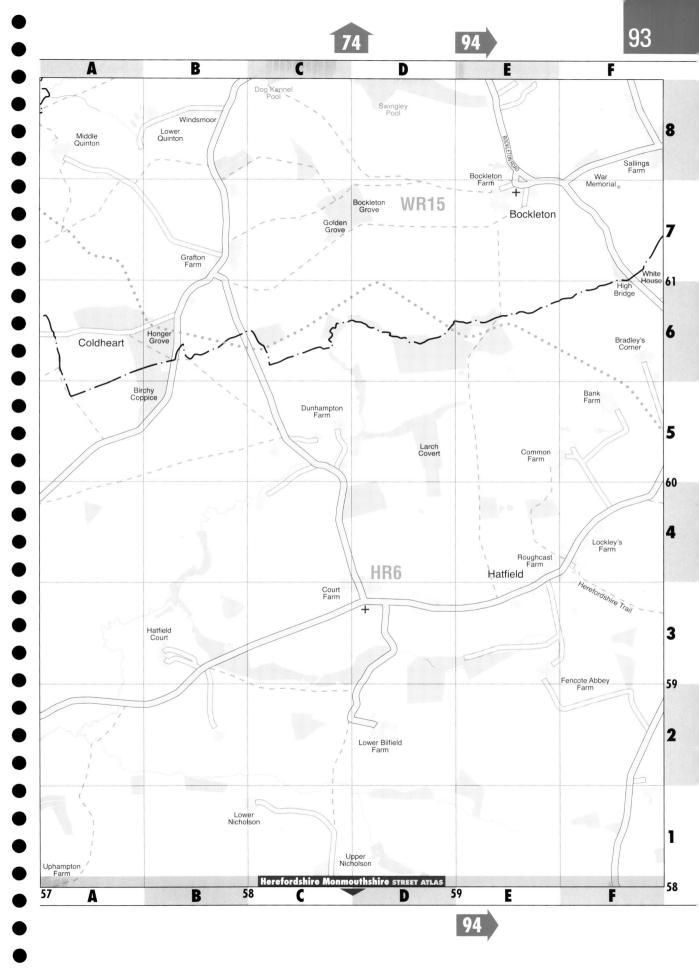

A B C D E F

8

Middle Quinton
Windsmoor
Lower Quinton
Dog Kennel Pool
Swingley Pool

BOCKLETON ROAD

Bockleton Farm

WR15

Sallings Farm
War Memorial

Bockleton Grove
Bockleton

Golden Grove

7

Grafton Farm

White House

61

High Bridge

Coldheart
Honger Grove

6

Bradley's Corner

Birchy Coppice

Dunhampton Farm

Bank Farm

5

Larch Covert

Common Farm

60

4

Roughcast Farm
Hatfield
Lockley's Farm

HR6

Herefordshire Trail

Court Farm

Hatfield Court

3

Fencote Abbey Farm

59

Lower Bilfield Farm

2

Lower Nicholson

1

Uphampton Farm

Upper Nicholson

57 A 58 B C 58 D 59 E F 58

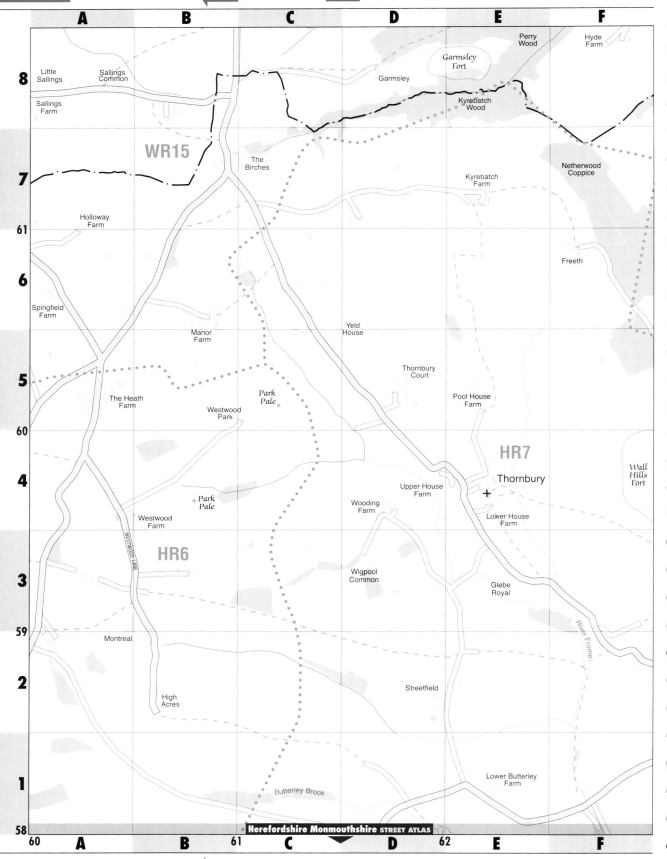

WR15

The Birches

Little Sallings
Sallings Common
Sallings Farm

Garmsley
Garmsley Fort
Perry Wood
Hyde Farm

Kyrebatch Wood

Netherwood Coppice

Kyrebatch Farm

Freeth

Holloway Farm

Spingfield Farm

Manor Farm

Yeld House

Thornbury Court

Pool House Farm

HR7

Thornbury

Wall Hills Fort

The Heath Farm

Park Pale

Westwood Park

Park Pale

Upper House Farm

Lower House Farm

Wooding Farm

HR6

Westwood Farm

WESTWOOD LANE

Wigpool Common

Glebe Royal

River Frome

Montreal

High Acres

Streetfield

Butterley Brook

Lower Butterley Farm

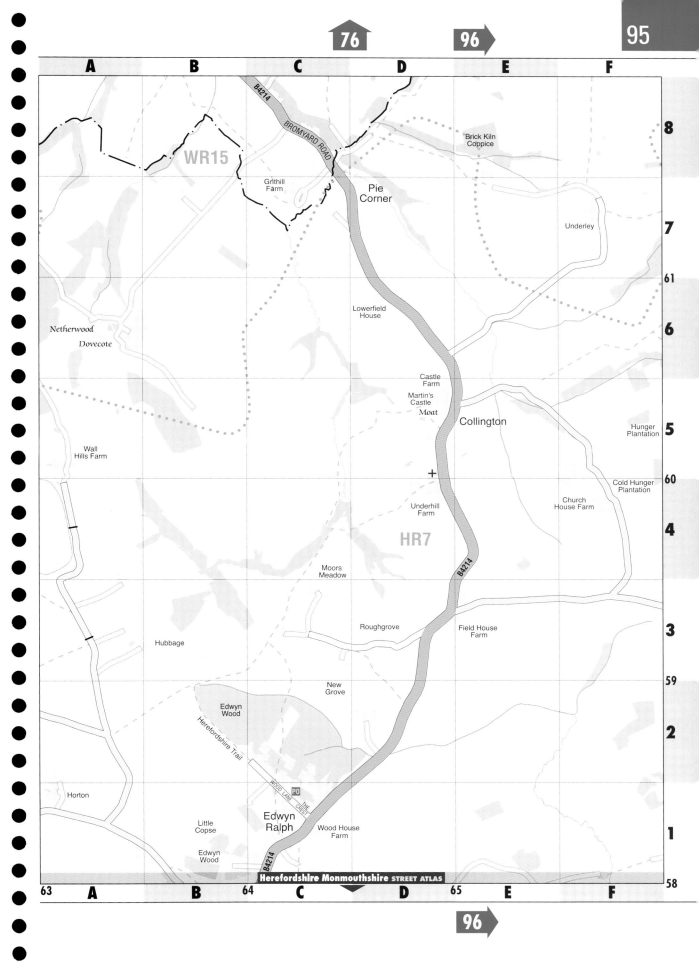

A   B   C   D   E   F

8

7

61

6

5

60

4

59

2

1

58

WR15

BROMYARD ROAD

B4214

Grithill
Farm

Pie
Corner

Brick Kiln
Coppice

Underley

Lowerfield
House

Netherwood
Dovecote

Castle
Farm

Martin's
Castle
Moat

Collington

Hunger
Plantation

Wall
Hills Farm

Cold Hunger
Plantation

Underhill
Farm

Church
House Farm

HR7

B4214

Moors
Meadow

Roughgrove

Field House
Farm

Hubbage

New
Grove

Edwyn
Wood

Herefordshire Trail

Horton

WOOD LANE

THE CREST

PO

Edwyn
Ralph

Wood House
Farm

Little
Copse

Edwyn
Wood

B4214

Herefordshire Monmouthshire STREET ATLAS

63   A   B   64   C   D   65   E   F

A   B   C   D   E   F

8   Upper House
     Farm

     Medieval Village
     of Wolferlow
     Wolferlow   B4203

                                                  Landymoor   Rose Furlong
                                                                           Farm

7   Harpley
                                    Forty   PITCHARD
                                    Acres Farm   CL
61   Cwmwood   Harpley
         Farm   PH   House

         Cwm   High   Home
6   Farm   Lane   Covert   WR6

                                    Cutnells

         Cwm
5   Wood   Vilt's
                                    ROMAN FORTLET   HIGH   Coppice
                                    (site of)   LANE

60   Acton
         Cold Hunger   Coppice
         Plantation
                                                             B4203
4   HR7

                                                                 Hedge House
                        Stoney   Farm
                        Bridge

                        Hetherings
3   Wildperry   Green   St James's Tedstone
         Farm   Farm   Church   Wafer

         Hope   DELAMERE ROAD
59   Farm   Court   Upper
                                    Farm   Grounds

2   Hill Cross

                        Ford
                                                                            Vinschurch
                                                                            Plantation
         Church
                                                                 Ram
1   Edvin   Sawpit   Plantation
         Loach   Covert

                   Barnfield   B4203   Upper   Bevan's
58   Wood   Norton   Wood

66   A   B   67   C   D   68   E   F

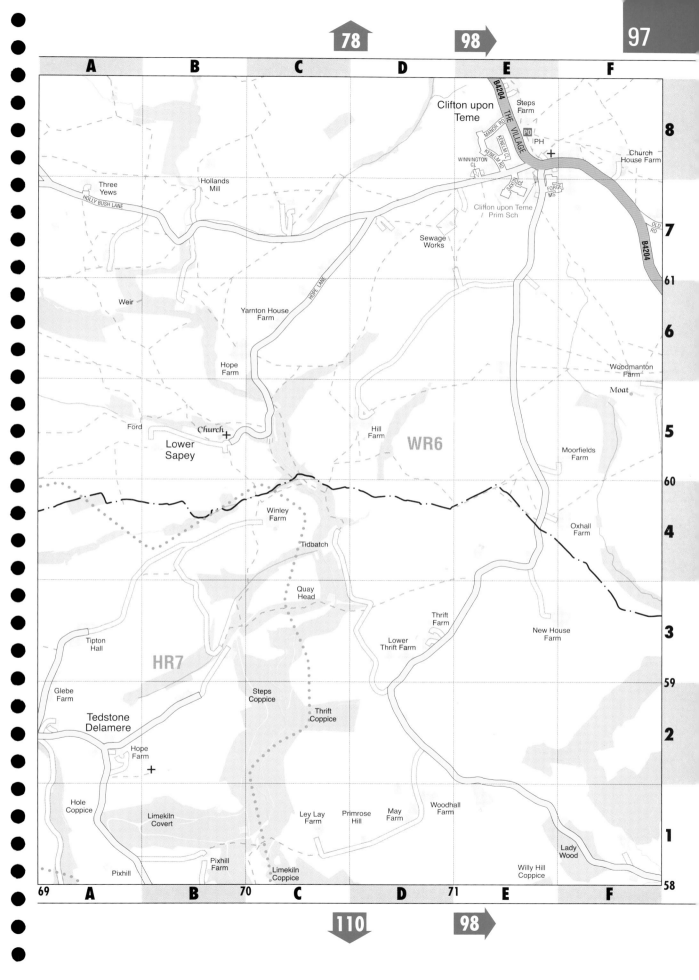

A   B   C   D   E   F

Clifton upon Teme

B4204

Steps Farm

MANOR RD

THE VILLAGE

PO

KENELM CL

KENELM RD

PH

WINNINGTON CL

Church House Farm

Clifton upon Teme Prim Sch

FORGE

MS

OLD RD

B4204

Three Yews

Hollands Mill

HOLLY BUSH LANE

Sewage Works

Weir

HOPE LANE

Yarnton House Farm

Hope Farm

Woodmanton Farm

Moat

Ford

Church

Hill Farm

WR6

Moorfields Farm

Lower Sapey

Winley Farm

Oxhall Farm

Tidbatch

Quay Head

Thrift Farm

New House Farm

Tipton Hall

HR7

Lower Thrift Farm

Glebe Farm

Steps Coppice

Thrift Coppice

Tedstone Delamere

Hope Farm

Hole Coppice

Limekiln Covert

Ley Lay Farm

Primrose Hill

May Farm

Woodhall Farm

Lady Wood

Pixhill Farm

Pixhill

Limekiln Coppice

Willy Hill Coppice

97 79

A   B   C   D   E   F

8

Weyman's Wood

Hamcastle Plantation

Motte

Homme Castle Farm

Pudford Coppice

Callow Farm

Pudford Hill

Pudford Farm

Callow Coppice

River Teme

Worcestershire Way

7

Slashes Coppice

OLD ROAD

Hambridge Coppice

Ham Bridge

PUDFORD LANE

61

PH

Clifton Hill

Pitlands Farm

B4204

Hambridge Farm

Hillend Farm

The Tee Farm

6

Marlpits Coppice

Indhouse Coppice

Tee Bank Coppice

B4204

Mason's Covert

5

Dale End Farm

Noak Farm

WR6

Kingswood Common

60

Kingswood

4

Ham Farm

Little Birch Hill Coppice

Ayngstree Farmhouse

Birch Hill Coppice

Worcestershire Way

3

Ham Wood

59

Berrow Farm

Tedney House

Ox Leasow Coppice

2

Tedney Bank

Berrow Hill (fort)

Scarr Coppice

Teme Side

River Teme

PH

Firs Farm

1

Glendale

Lower Hill Top

Berrow Green

Whitbourne Ford

Hill Top

Hill Top Farm

B4197

58

72   A   73   B   73   C   D   74   E   F

97 111

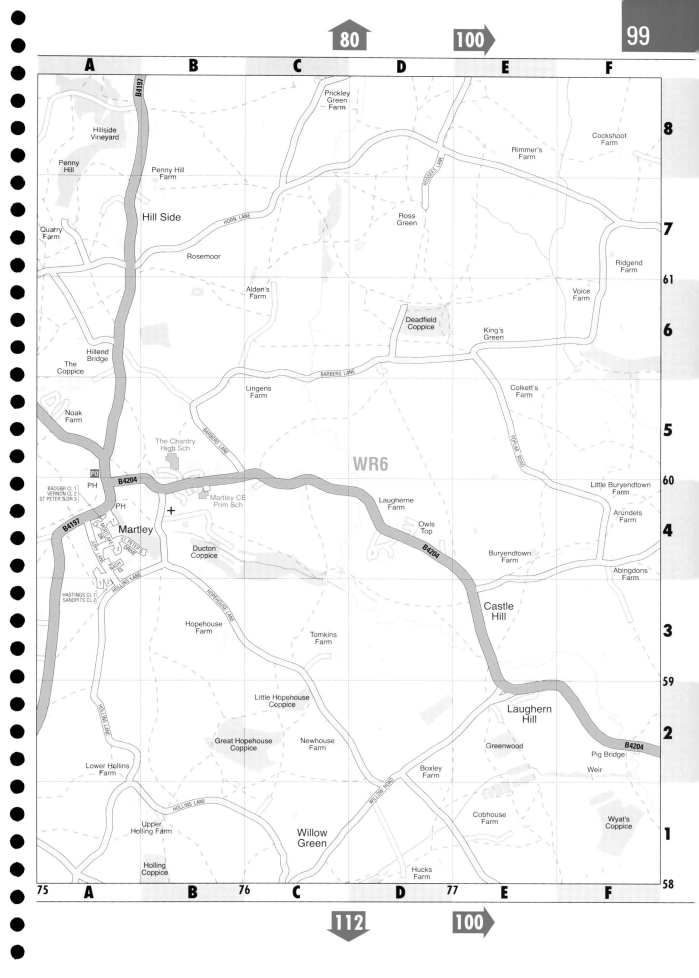

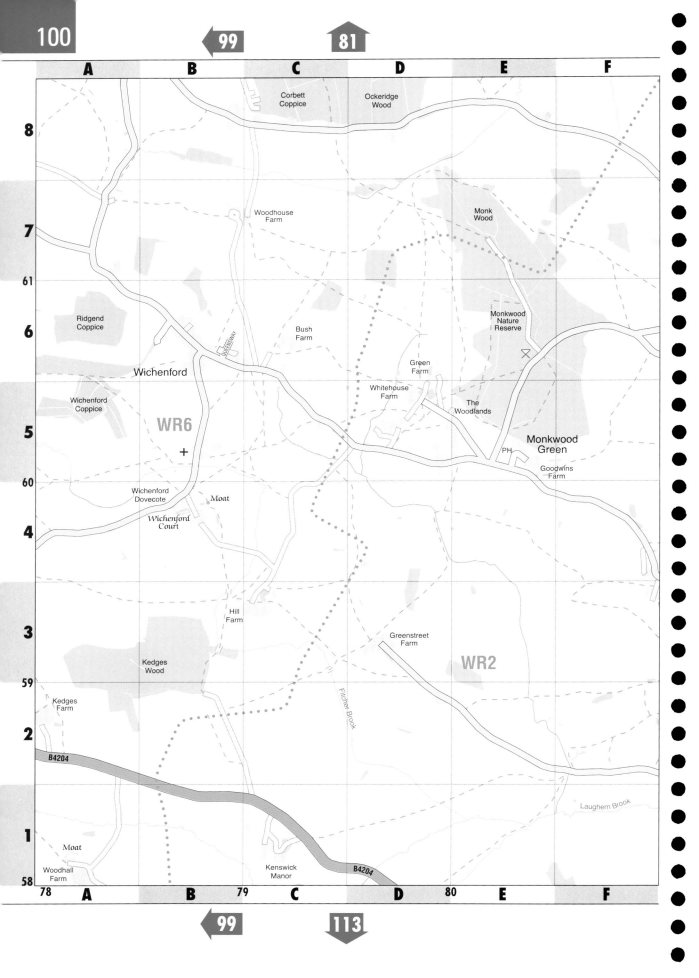

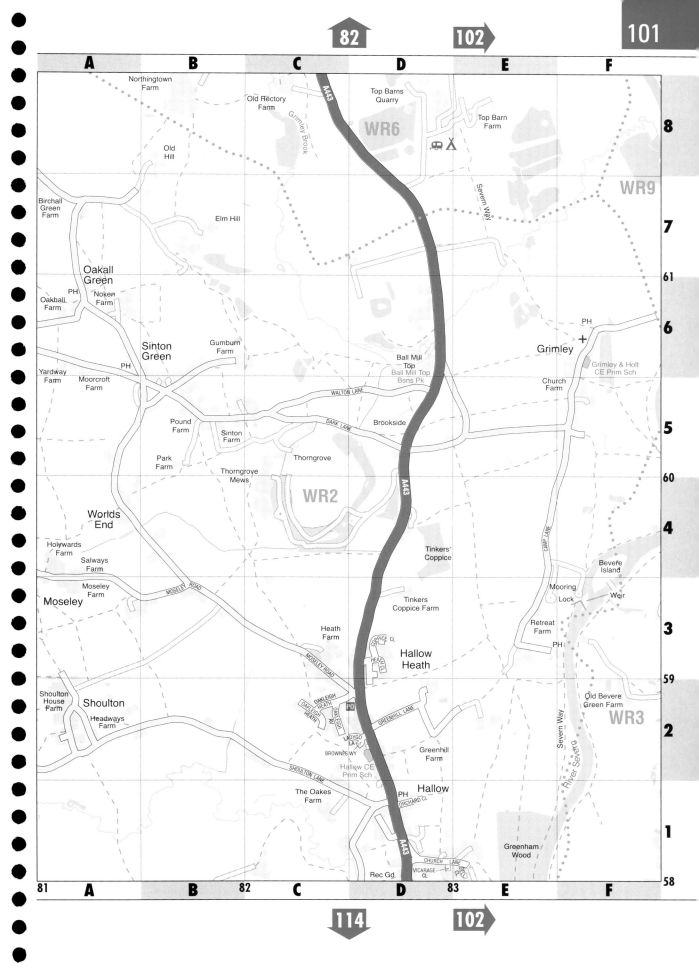

82
102

A   B   C   D   E   F

8

WR6

WR9

7

61

6

5

60

4

3

59

2

1

58

Northingtown
Farm

Old Rectory
Farm

Top Barns
Quarry

Top Barn
Farm

Grimley Brook

A443

Severn Way

Old
Hill

Elm Hill

Birchall
Green
Farm

Oakall
Green

PH

Noken
Farm

Oakhall
Farm

Sinton
Green

Gumburn
Farm

Ball Mill
Top
Ball Mill Top
Bsns Pk

Grimley

PH

Grimley & Holt
CE Prim Sch

Yardway
Farm

PH

Moorcroft
Farm

WALTON LANE

Church
Farm

Pound
Farm

DARK LANE

Brookside

Sinton
Farm

Thorngrove

Park
Farm

Thorngrove
Mews

WR2

A443

Camp Lane

Worlds
End

Tinkers'
Coppice

Holywards
Farm

Salways
Farm

Bevere
Island

Moseley
Farm

MOSELEY ROAD

Mooring
Lock

Weir

Moseley

Tinkers
Coppice Farm

Retreat
Farm

PH

Heath
Farm

COPPICE CL

HEATH CL

Hallow
Heath

Shoulton
House
Farm

Shoulton

Headways
Farm

MOSELEY ROAD

OAKLEIGH
HEATH
OAKLEIGH
AV

OAKLEIGH HEATH

PO

GREENHILL LANE

Greenhill
Farm

Old Bevere
Green Farm

WR3

Severn Way

River Severn

LADYGO
LA

BROWNES WY

Hallow CE
Prim Sch

SHOULTON LANE

The Oakes
Farm

ORCHARD CL

Hallow

PH

A443

Greenham
Wood

Rec Gd

CHURCH
LANE

VICARAGE
CL

81   A   B   82   C   D   83   E   F

114
102

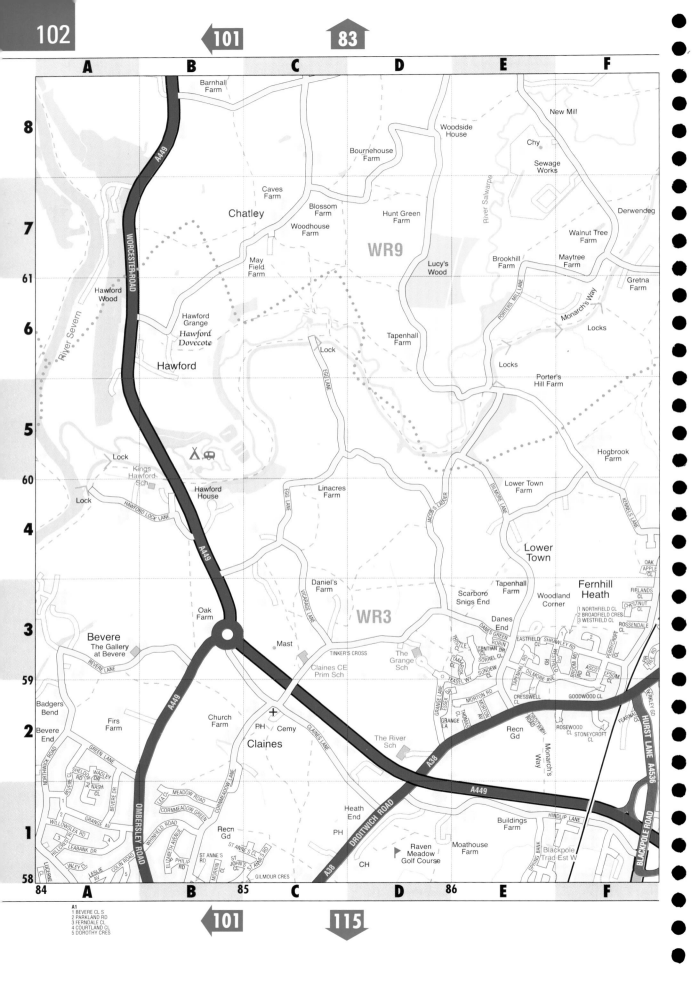

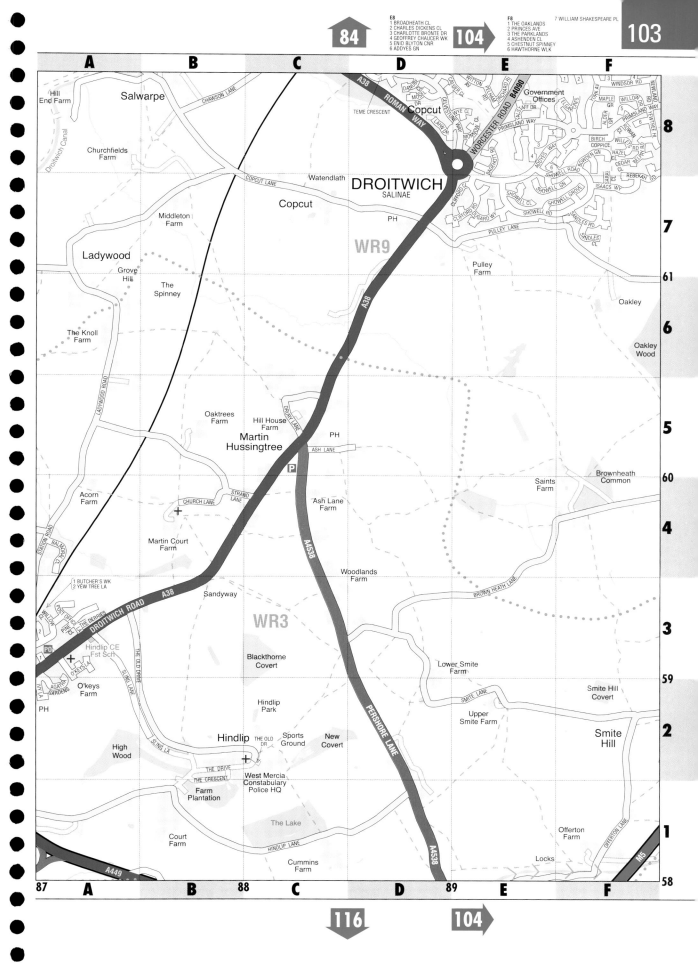

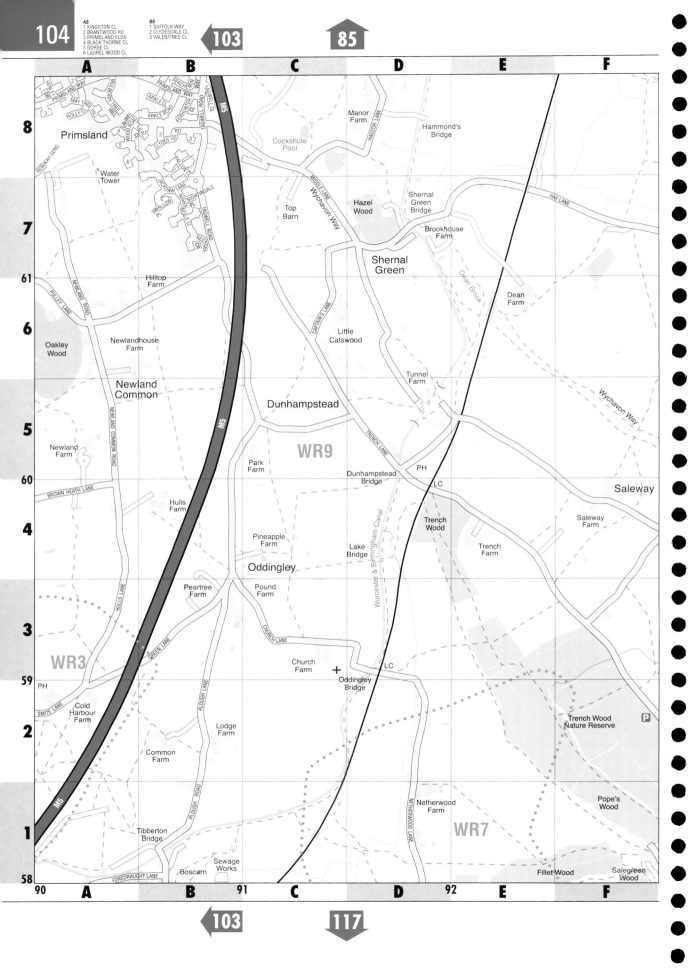

104

A8
1 KINGSTON CL
2 BRANTWOOD RD
3 PRIMSLAND FLDS
4 BLACK THORNE CL
5 GORSE CL
6 LAUREL WOOD CL

B8
1 SUFFOLK WAY
2 CLYDESDALE CL
3 VALENTINES CL

◀ 103

85 ▲

A   B   C   D   E   F

8

7

61

6

5

60

4

3

59

2

1

58

Primsland

Water
Tower

Oakley
Wood

Newland
Common

Newland
Farm

Hilltop
Farm

Newlandhouse
Farm

Hulls
Farm

Park
Farm

Pineapple
Farm

Oddingley

Peartree
Farm

Pound
Farm

Common
Farm

Lodge
Farm

Cold
Harbour
Farm

Tibberton
Bridge

Boscarn

Sewage
Works

WR3

PH

Cockshute
Pool

Top
Barn

Hazel
Wood

Dunhampstead

WR9

Church
Farm

Oddingley
Bridge

Manor
Farm

Hammond's
Bridge

Shernal
Green
Bridge

Brookhouse
Farm

Shernal
Green

Little
Catswood

Tunnel
Farm

Dunhampstead
Bridge

PH

LC

Lake
Bridge

Trench
Wood

LC

Netherwood
Farm

WR7

Dean
Farm

Saleway

Saleway
Farm

Trench
Farm

Trench Wood
Nature Reserve

Pope's
Wood

Fillet Wood

Salegreen
Wood

Hay Lane

Wychavon Way

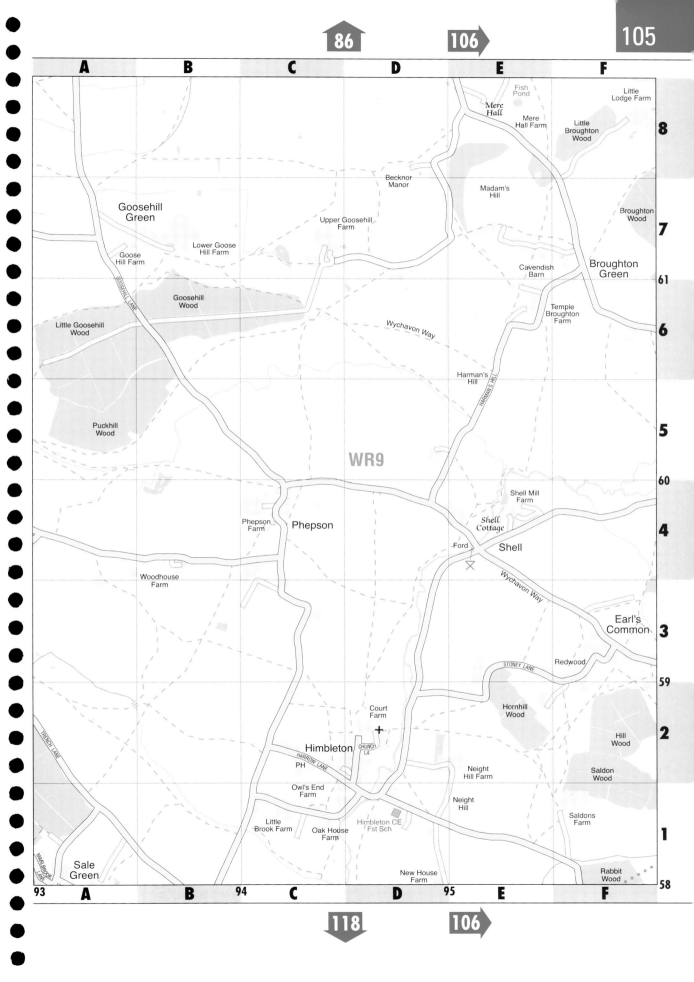

A **B** **C** **D** **E** **F**

Fish Pond

Mere Hall

Mere Hall Farm

Little Lodge Farm

Little Broughton Wood

8

Becknor Manor

Madam's Hill

Goosehill Green

Upper Goosehill Farm

Broughton Wood

7

Lower Goose Hill Farm

Goose Hill Farm

Cavendish Barn

Broughton Green

61

GOOSEHILL LANE

Goosehill Wood

Temple Broughton Farm

6

Little Goosehill Wood

Wychavon Way

Harman's Hill

HARMAN'S HILL

5

Puckhill Wood

WR9

60

Shell Mill Farm

Phepson Farm

Phepson

Shell Cottage

Shell

4

Ford

Woodhouse Farm

Wychavon Way

Earl's Common

3

STONEY LANE

Redwood

59

Court Farm

Hornhill Wood

Hill Wood

2

Himbleton

CHURCH LA

Saldon Wood

PH

HARROW LANE

Neight Hill Farm

Owl's End Farm

Neight Hill

TRENCH LANE

Little Brook Farm

Oak House Farm

Himbleton CE Fst Sch

Saldons Farm

1

MARLBROOK LANE

Sale Green

New House Farm

Rabbit Wood

58

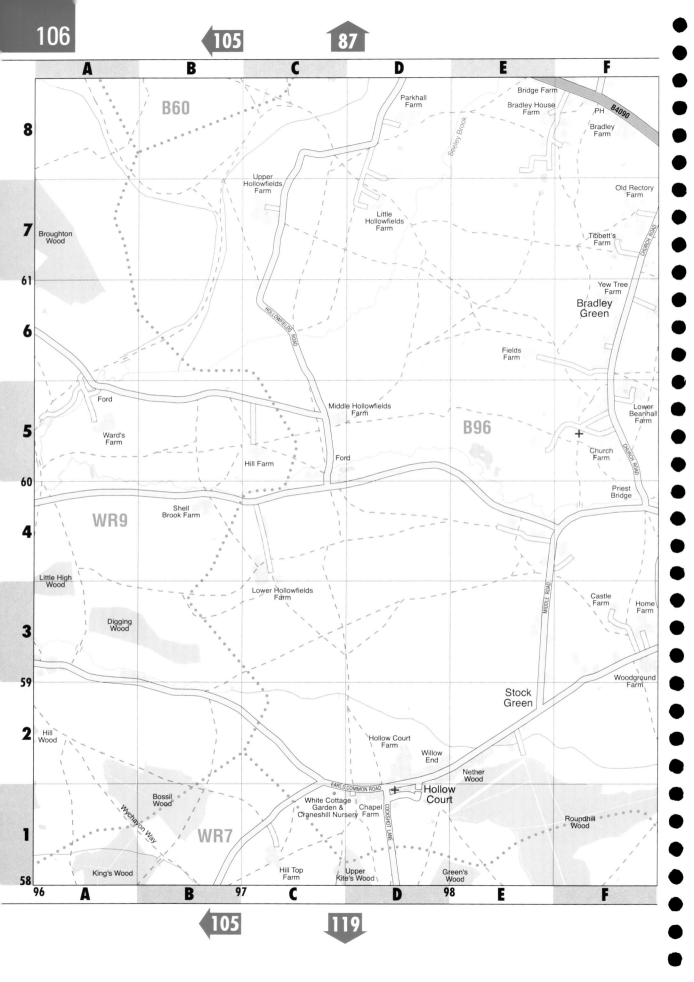

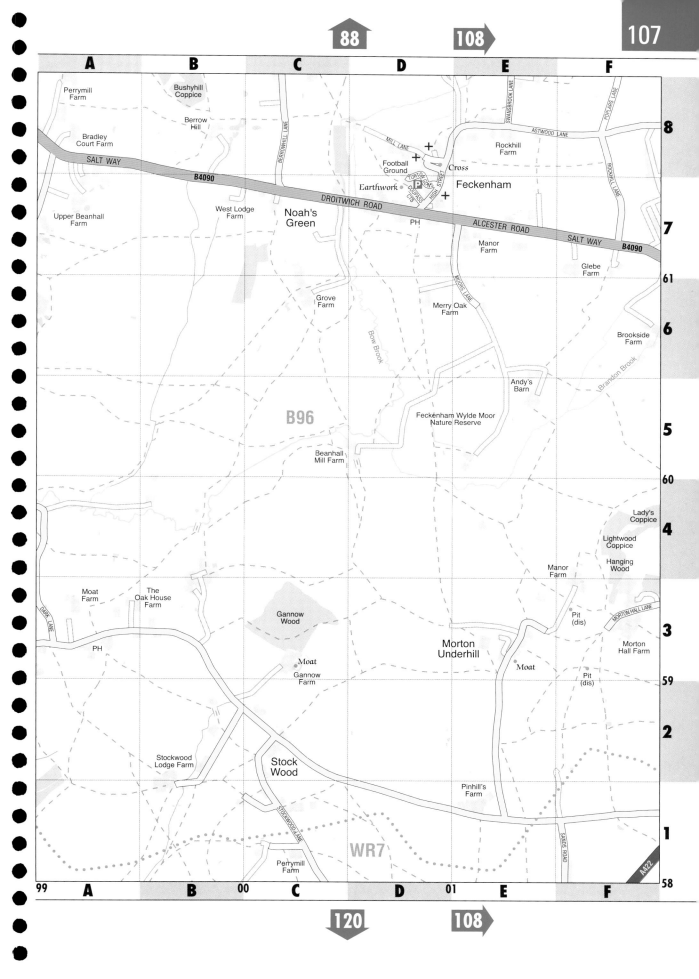

A B C D E F

8

Perrymill Farm

Bushyhill Coppice

Berrow Hill

Bradley Court Farm

SALT WAY

B4090

SWANSBROOK LANE

ASTWOOD LANE

POPLARS LANE

Rockhill Farm

MILL LANE

Football Ground

Cross

Feckenham

ROCKHILL LANE

Earthwork

TURTON CUPASS HIGH STREET

Upper Beanhall Farm

DROITWICH ROAD

West Lodge Farm

BERROWHILL LANE

Noah's Green

PH

ALCESTER ROAD

SALT WAY

B4090

7

Manor Farm

MOORS LANE

Glebe Farm

61

Grove Farm

Merry Oak Farm

6

Brookside Farm

Bow Brook

Brandon Brook

Andy's Barn

B96

Feckenham Wylde Moor Nature Reserve

5

Beanhall Mill Farm

60

Lady's Coppice

4

Lightwood Coppice

Hanging Wood

Moat Farm

The Oak House Farm

DARK LANE

Gannow Wood

Manor Farm

Pit (dis)

MORTON HALL LANE

PH

Morton Hall Farm

3

Moat

Gannow Farm

Morton Underhill

Moat

Pit (dis)

59

Stockwood Lodge Farm

Stock Wood

2

STOCKWOOD LANE

Pinhill's Farm

SANDS ROAD

1

WR7

A422

Perrymill Farm

58

99 A B 00 C D 01 E F

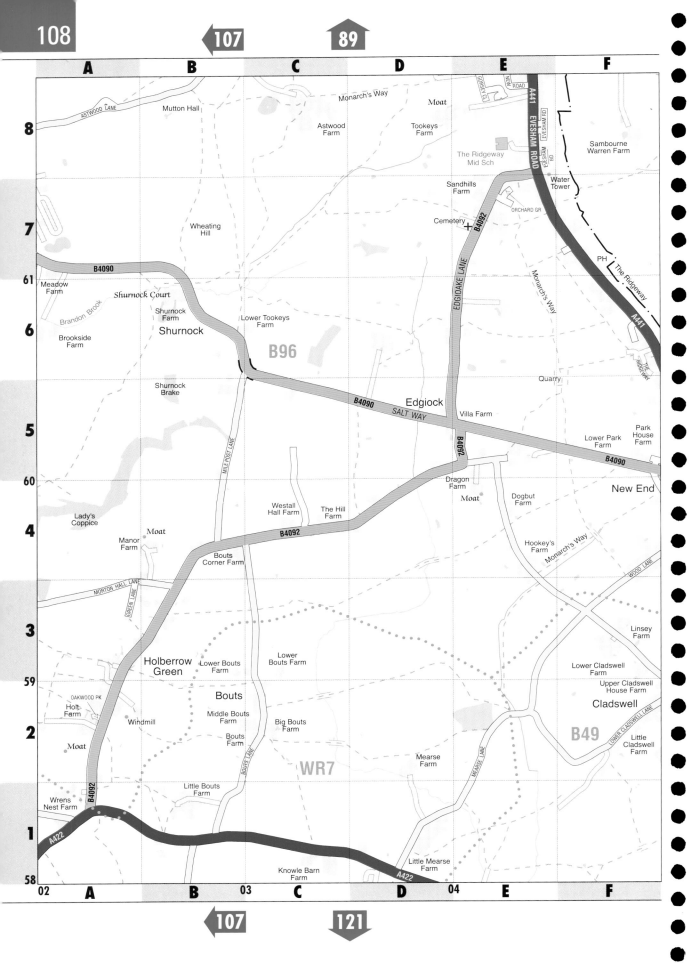

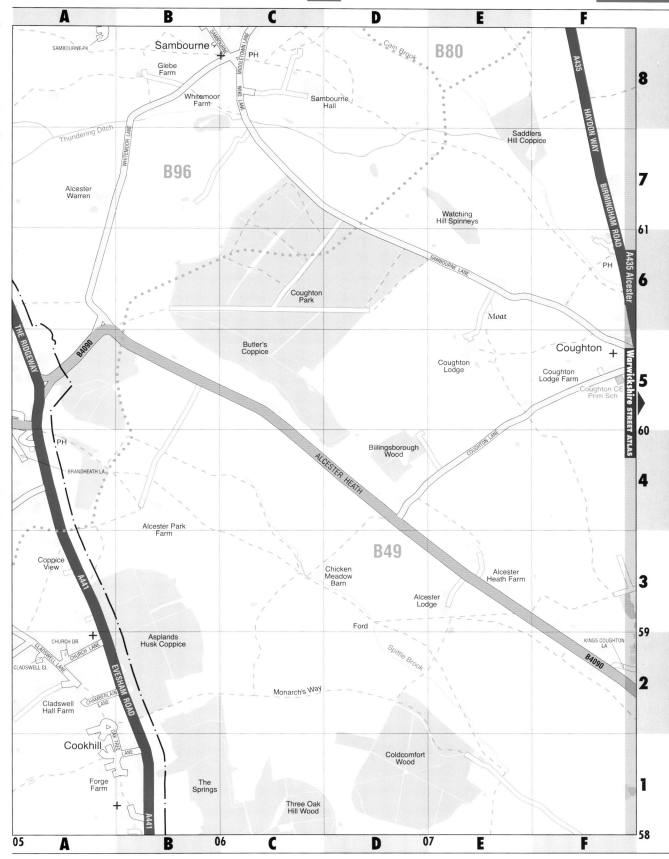

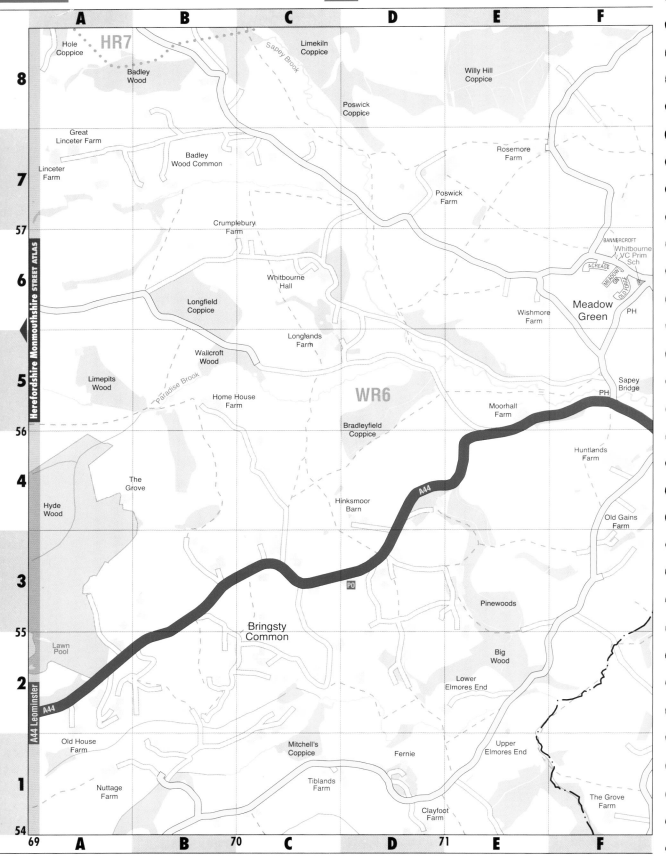

Hole Coppice
HR7
Badley Wood
Limekiln Coppice
Sapey Brook
Willy Hill Coppice
8
Great Linceter Farm
Badley Wood Common
Poswick Coppice
Rosemore Farm
7
Linceter Farm
Poswick Farm
57
Crumplebury Farm
BANNERCROFT
Whitbourne CV Prim Sch
ACREAGE
Whitbourne Hall
MEADOW DRIVE
Meadow Green
6
Longfield Coppice
OLD FORGE
PH
Longlands Farm
Wishmore Farm
Wallcroft Wood
Paradise Brook
Sapey Bridge
Limepits Wood
Home House Farm
WR6
Moorhall Farm
PH
5
56
Bradleyfield Coppice
Huntlands Farm
The Grove
4
Hinksmoor Barn
A44
Hyde Wood
Old Gains Farm
Pinewoods
3
P0
Bringsty Common
Lawn Pool
Big Wood
55
Lower Elmores End
2
A44 Leominster
Old House Farm
Mitchell's Coppice
Fernie
Upper Elmores End
The Grove Farm
A44
1
Nuttage Farm
Tiblands Farm
Clayfoot Farm
54

Herefordshire Monmouthshire Street Atlas

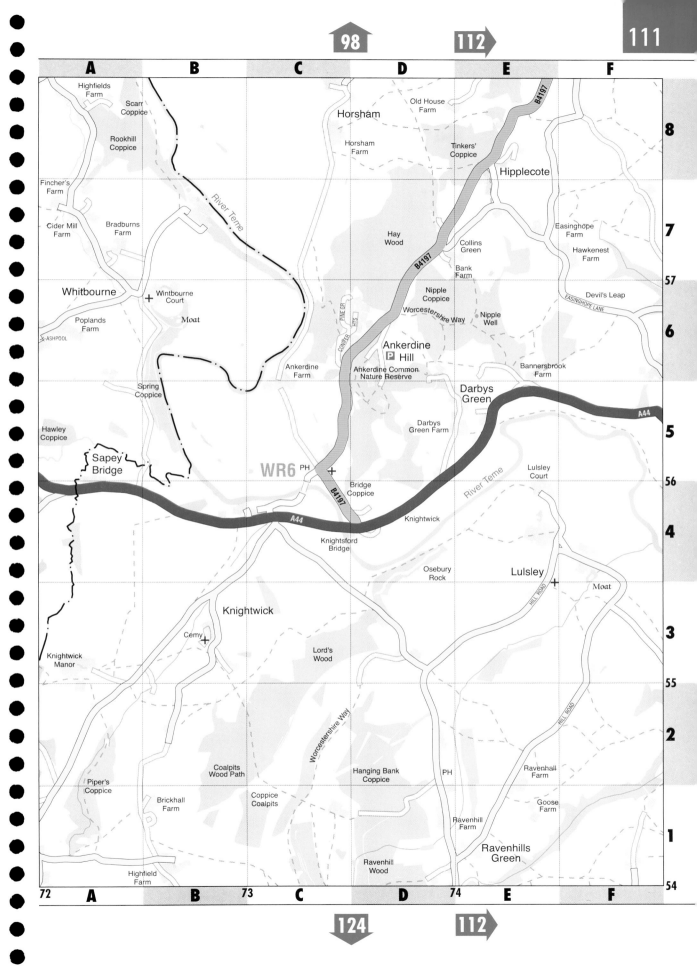

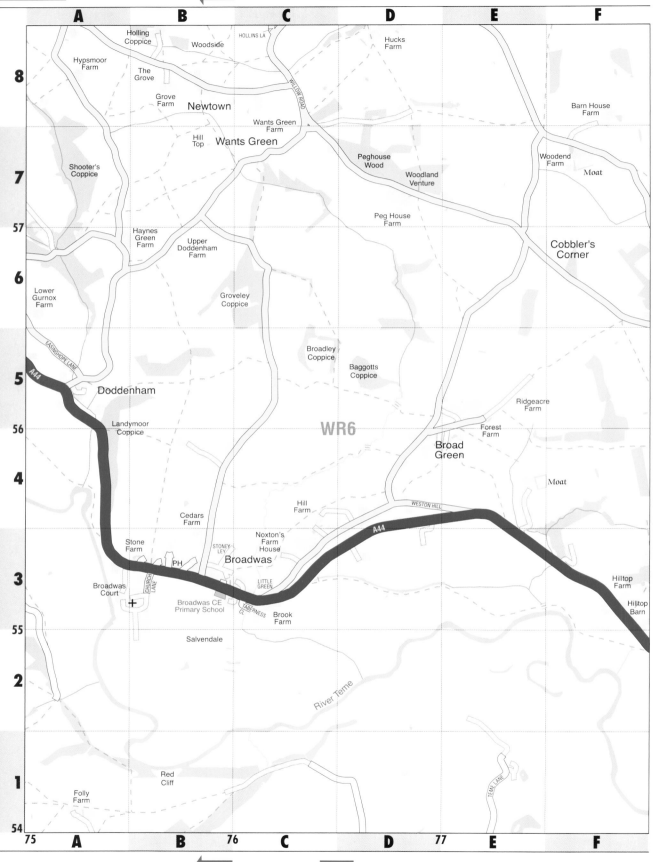

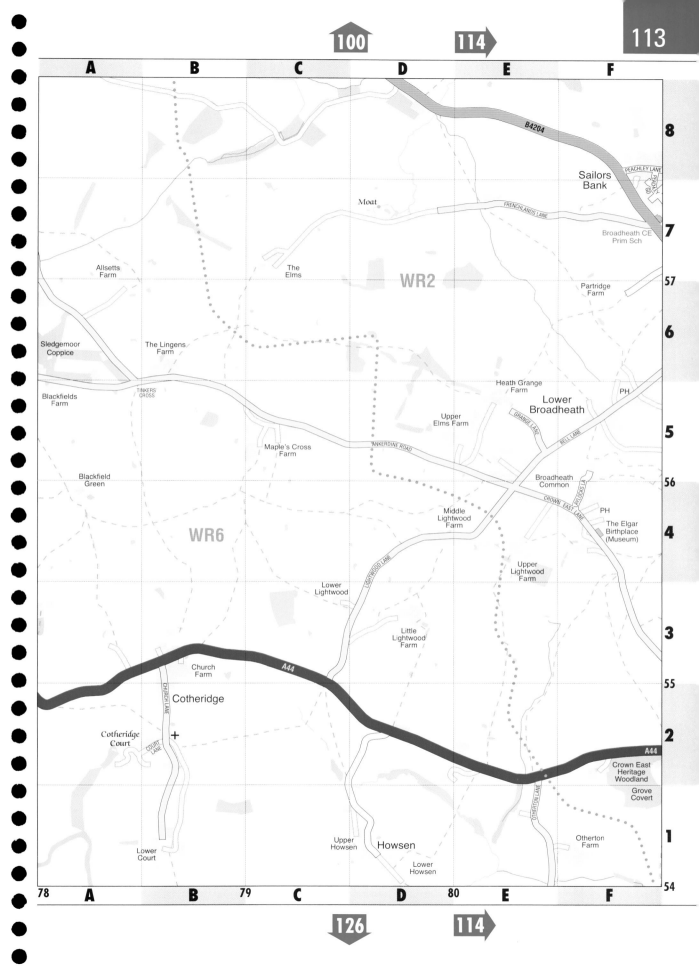

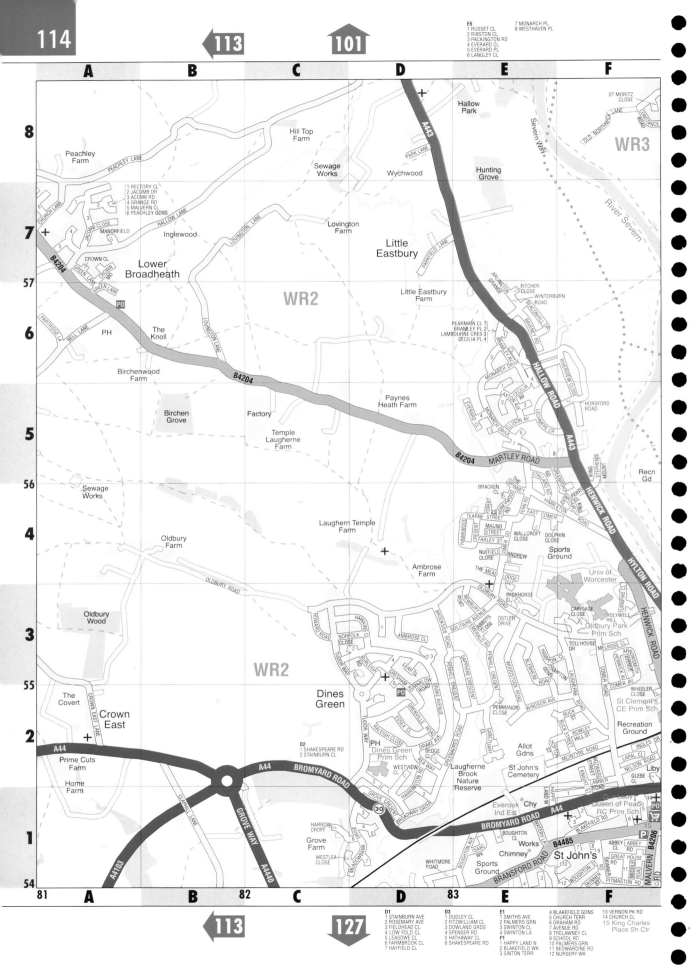

113

101

E5
1 RUSSET CL
2 RIBSTON CL
3 PACKINGTON RD
4 EVERARD CL
5 EVERARD PL
6 LANGLEY CL

7 MONARCH PL
8 WESTHAVEN PL

A B C D E F

8

Peachley
Farm

PEACHLEY LANE

Hill Top
Farm

Sewage
Works

Wychwood

Hallow
Park

PARK LANE

A43

Hunting
Grove

St MORITZ
CLOSE

OLD NORTHWICK
LANE

CONSTANCE
ROAD

WR3

Severn Way

River Severn

7

CHURCH LANE

1 RECTORY CL
2 JACOMB DR
3 ACOMB RD
4 GRANGE RD
5 MALVERN CL
6 PEACHLEY GDNS

HALLOW LANE

CROWN CL

MANORFIELD

JACOMB CLOSE

Inglewood

LOVINGTON LANE

Lovington
Farm

Little
Eastbury

PARKFIELD LANE

ARLINGTON
GRANGE

FITCHER
CLOSE

WINTERBURN
ROAD

B4204

57

GREEN LANE

CROWN
MD

GREEN LANE

PO

Lower
Broadheath

WR2

Little Eastbury
Farm

PEARMAIN CL 1
BRAMLEY PL 2
LAMBOURNE CRES 3
CECILIA PL 4

BEECHMILL DR

BAVERY RD

6

PARTRIDGE LA

BELL LANE

PH

The
Knoll

LOVINGTON LANE

B4204

MONARCH DRIVE

BRAMLEY AV

5

Birchenwood
Farm

Birchen
Grove

Factory

Temple
Laugherne
Farm

Paynes
Heath Farm

B4204

MARTLEY ROAD

LATIN CECILIA
AV

EVERARD PL

ELLISON AV

MONARCH DRIVE

6

HALLOW ROAD

A43

LECHMERE CR

HORSFORD
ROAD

SNIPHTS

KING
STREET

UNTOW

Recn
Gd

56

Sewage
Works

Laughern Temple
Farm

Ambrose
Farm

BRACKEN
CL

THE
SKINNEY

FOREST
CL

STANLEY RD

GREENBANK RD
CRESTS

FERRY
RD

HENWICK ROAD

4

Oldbury
Farm

OLDBURY ROAD

TEARNE STREET

HAWKWOOD
CRESCENT

MAUND
STREET

FARLEY ST

WALLCROFT
CLOSE

DOLPHIN
CLOSE

EAST COMER

HIMBLETON
ROAD

Sports
Ground

HYLTON ROAD

3

Oldbury
Wood

HOWARD ROAD

HARKINS CL

NORFOLK
CLOSE

NUFFIELD
CLOSE

ANDREW
CL

THE MEAD

LODGE
CL

NEWBURN
ROAD

OLDBURY
ROAD

PACKHORSE

Univ of
Worcester

CARRIAGE
CLOSE

HOLYWELL
HILL

Oldbury Park
Prim Sch

TOLLHOUSE
DR

MELROSE RD

ARKWRIGHT
CLOSE

HENWICK ROAD

2

The
Covert

CROWN EAST LANE

Crown
East

A44

A4103

Prime Cuts
Farm

Home
Farm

CAPTILL LANE

GROVE WAY

A4440

A44

BROMYARD ROAD

30

1 SHAKESPEARE RD
2 STAINBURN CL

D2

TUDOR WAY

HARRINGTON

Dines
Green

PO

RALEIGH CLOSE

BURLEIGH
RD

GRESHAM RD

MARLOW
ROAD

GRANVILLE CL

ESSEX CL

DRAKE AVENUE

SOLITAIRE AVENUE

BROOKSIDE ROAD

AMBROSE CL

SAPPHIRE CRESCENT

EMERALD RD

ABBOTS
CLOSE

PENHILL CRESCENT

OSTLER
DRIVE

PENMANOR
ROAD

WOODSTOCK
ROAD

BLENHEIM
GDNS

HAMPTON CL

LAUGHERNE ROAD

BLENHEIM
ROAD

WINDSOR AVE

COMER AV

WHEELER
CLOSE

St Clement's
CE Prim Sch

55

PH

Dines Green
Prim Sch

WESTVIEW
CL

GREENACRES ROAD

SEDGE

REA WAY

BROADWAY GROVE

Laugherne
Brook
Nature
Reserve

St John's
Cemetery

Allot
Gdns

BUCK ST

ROWLEY
HILL ST

McINTYRE ROAD

KNIGHT
STREET

LAMBER
ST

INGLES DR

LAPAL CL

NELSON ROAD

GLEBE
CL

Liby

Recreation
Ground

1

A44103

CROWN EAST LANE

GROVE WAY

A4440

Grove
Farm

HARROW
CROFT

MEADOWBANK

WESTLEA
CLOSE

WHITMORE
ROAD

GROVE CRESCENT

HAPPY
LAND W

Everoak
Ind Est

Chy

BROMYARD ROAD

A44

WATERY LA

Works

Chimney

BOUGHTON AVE

ISAAC
WK

HAPPY
LAND W

BLAKEFIELD RD

B4485

Queen of Peace
RC Prim Sch

PO

ABBEY
CL

ABBEY
RD

GREAT HOUSE
RD

MIDDLE
RD

MALVERN RD

B4206

54

Sports
Ground

BRANSFORD ROAD

St John's

SKINNER ST

PITMASTON RD

BOUGHTON ST

113

127

D1
1 STAINBURN AVE
2 ROSEMARY AVE
3 FIELDHEAD CL
4 LOW FOLD CL
5 LEASOWE CL
6 FARMBROOK CL
7 HAYFIELD CL

D3
1 DUDLEY CL
2 FITZWILLIAM CL
3 DOWLAND GRDS
4 SPENSER RD
5 HATHWAY CL
6 SHAKESPEARE RD

E1
1 SMITHS AVE
2 PALMERS GRN
3 SWINTON CL
4 SWINTON LA
F1
1 HAPPY LAND N
2 BLAKEFIELD WK
3 SINTON TERR

4 BLAKEFIELD GDNS
5 CHURCH TERR
6 GRAHAM RD
7 AVENUE RD
8 TRELAWNEY CL
9 SCHOOL RD
10 PALMERS GRN
11 BEDWARDINE RD
12 NURSERY WK

13 VERNON PK RD
14 CHURCH CL
15 King Charles
   Place Sh Ctr

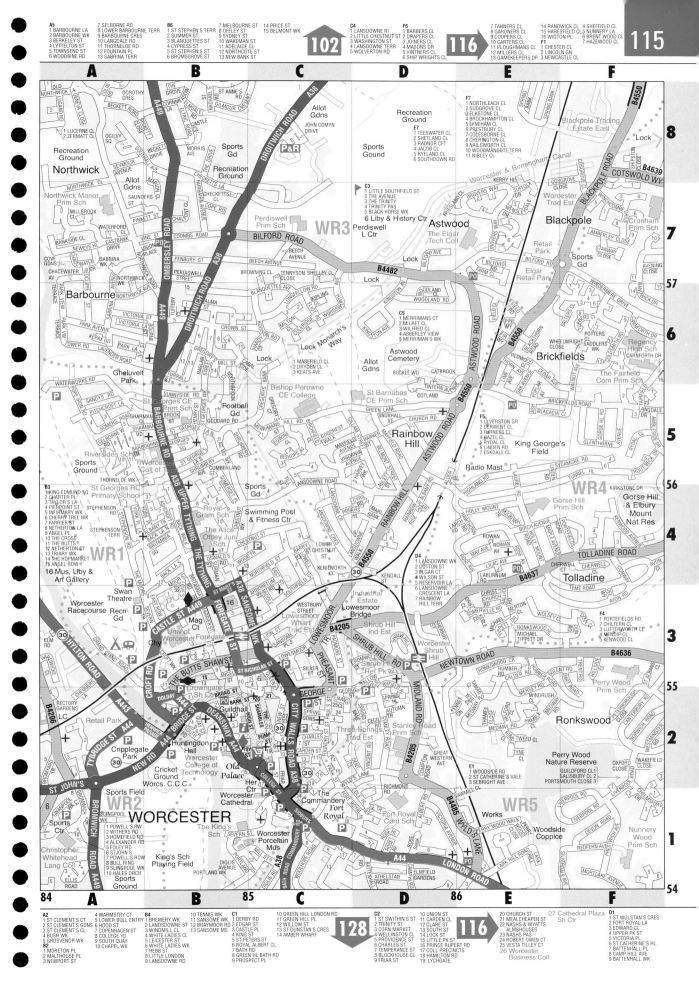

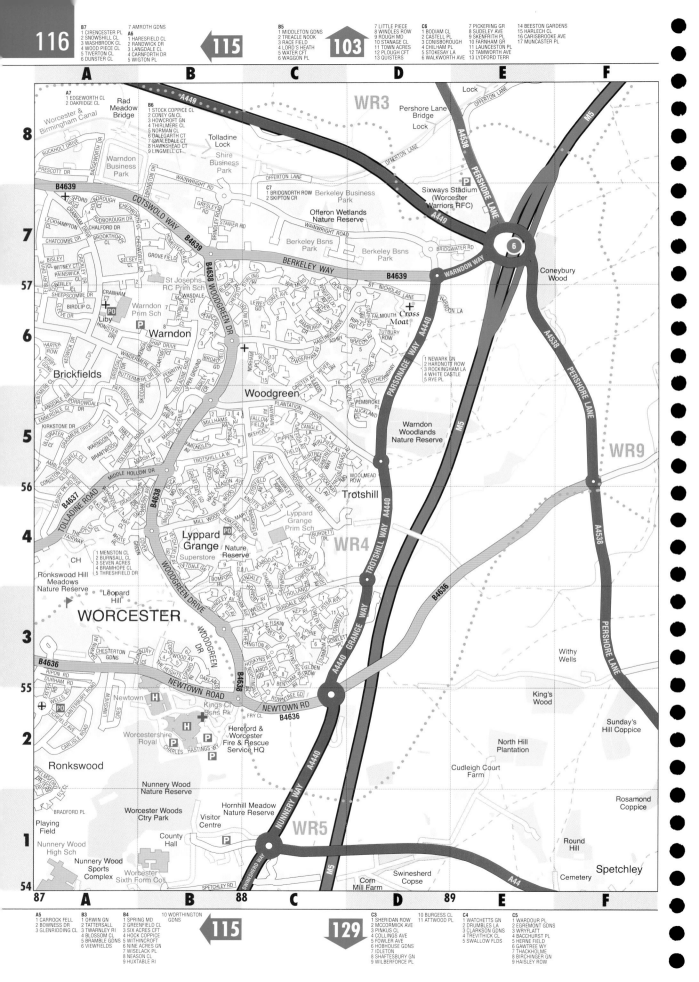

116

B7
1 CIRENCESTER PL
2 SNOWSHILL CL
3 WASHBROOK CL
4 WOOD PIECE CL
5 TIVERTON CL
6 DUNSTER CL

7 AMROTH GDNS
A6
1 HARESFIELD CL
2 RANDWICK DR
3 LANGDALE CL
4 CARNFORTH DR
5 WIGTON PL

◁ **115**

B5
1 MIDDLETON GDNS
2 TREACLE NOOK
3 RACE FIELD
4 LORD'S HEATH
5 WATER CFT
6 WAGGON PL

▽ **103**

7 LITTLE PIECE
8 WINDLES ROW
9 ROUGH MD
10 STANAGE CL
11 TOWN ACRES
12 PLOUGH CFT
13 QUISTERS

C6
1 BODIAM CL
2 CASTELL PL
3 CONISBOROUGH
4 CHILHAM PL
5 STOKESAY LA
6 WALKWORTH AVE

7 PICKERING GR
8 SUDELEY AVE
9 SKENFRITH PL
10 FARNHAM GR
11 LAUNCESTON PL
12 TAMWORTH AVE
13 LYDFORD TERR

14 BEESTON GARDENS
15 HARLECH CL
16 CARISBROOKE AVE
17 MUNCASTER PL

A5
1 CARROCK FELL
2 BOWNESS DR
3 GLENRIDDING CL

B3
1 ORWIN GN
2 TATTERSALL
3 TWARNLEY RI
4 BLOSSOM CL
5 BRAMBLE GDNS
6 VIEWFIELDS

B4
1 SPRING MD
2 GREENFIELD CL
3 SIX ACRES CFT
4 HOCK COPPICE
5 WITHINCROFT
6 NINE ACRES GN
7 WISELACK PL
8 NEASON CL
9 HUXTABLE RI

10 WORTHINGTON GDNS

◁ **115**

▽ **129**

C3
1 SHERIDAN ROW
2 MCCORMICK AVE
3 PINKUS CL
4 COLLINGS AVE
5 FOWLER AVE
6 HOBHOUSE GDNS
7 IDLETON
8 SHAFTESBURY GN
9 WILBERFORCE PL

10 BURGESS CL
11 ATTWOOD PL

C4
1 WATCHETTS GN
2 DRUMBLES LA
3 CLARKSON GDNS
4 TREVITHICK CL
5 SWALLOW FLDS

C5
1 WARDOUR PL
2 EGREMONT GDNS
3 WRYFLATT
4 BACCHURST PL
5 HERNE FIELD
6 GAWTREE WY
7 THACKHOLME
8 BIRCHINGER GN
9 HAISLEY ROW

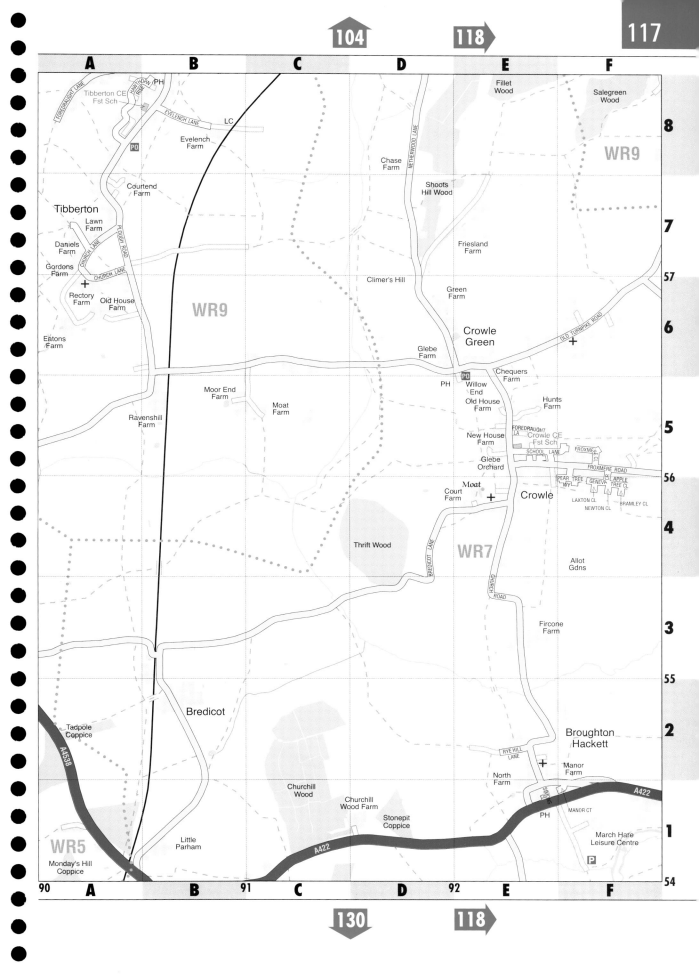

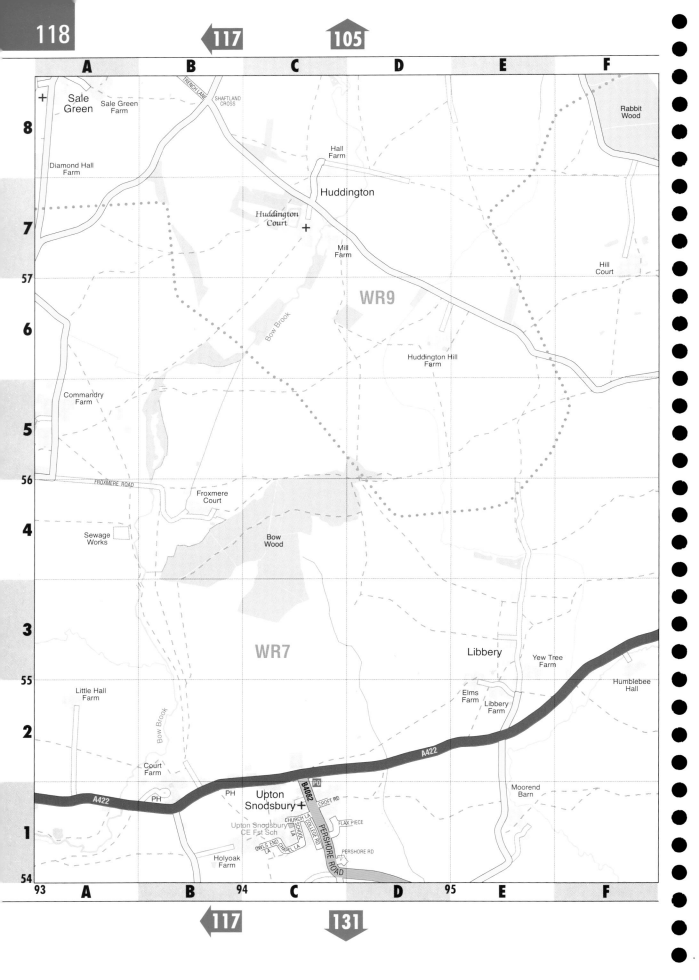

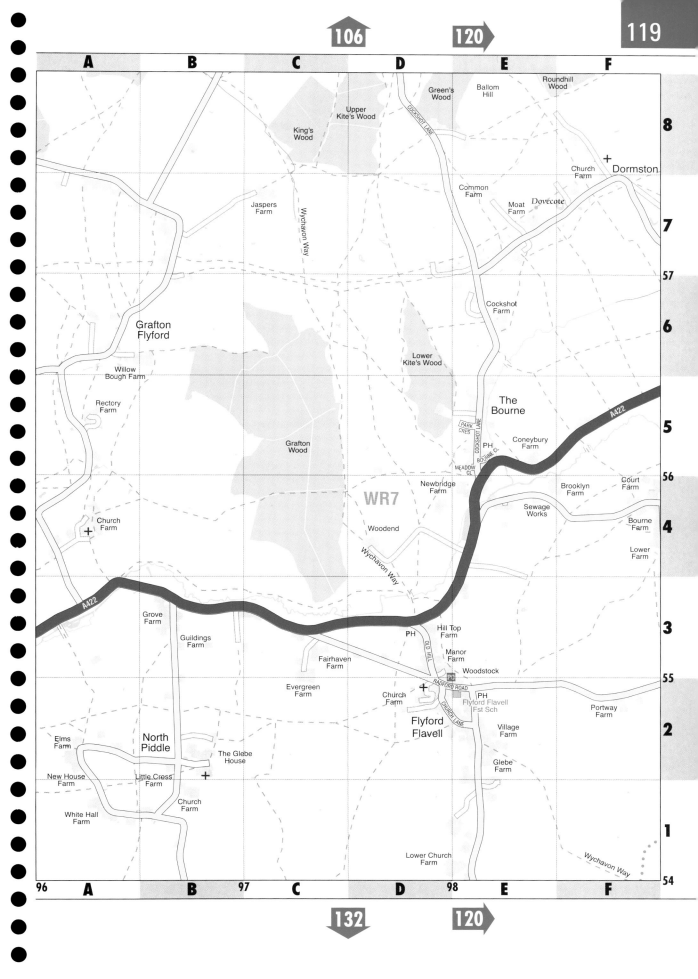

A B C D E F

8
7
57
6
5
56
4
3
55
2
1
54

Green's Wood
Ballom Hill
Roundhill Wood

COCKSHOT LANE

Upper Kite's Wood
King's Wood
Jaspers Farm

Wychavon Way

Church Farm
✛ Dormston

Common Farm
Moat Farm
Dovecote

Cockshot Farm

Grafton Flyford

Willow Bough Farm

Lower Kite's Wood

The Bourne

A422

Rectory Farm

Grafton Wood

PARK CRES
COCKSHOT LANE
PH
BOURNE CL
MEADOW CL

Coneybury Farm

WR7

Newbridge Farm

Brooklyn Farm
Court Farm

Church Farm ✛

Woodend

Sewage Works

Bourne Farm

Wychavon Way

Lower Farm

A422

Grove Farm

PH
Hill Top Farm

OLD HILL

Guildings Farm

Manor Farm
Woodstock

Fairhaven Farm

PO
RADFORD ROAD

PH

Evergreen Farm

Church Farm ✛
Flyford Flavell Fst Sch

Portway Farm

Elms Farm

North Piddle

CHURCH LANE

Flyford Flavell

Village Farm

New House Farm

The Glebe House
✛

Little Cross Farm

Glebe Farm

White Hall Farm

Church Farm

Lower Church Farm

Wychavon Way

A B C D E F

8

Little
Inkberrow

Berrowsfield
Farm

Manor
Farm

Pit (dis)

Recn
Gd

Stonehouse
Farm

All Saints
Farm

STOCKWOOD LANE

Inkberrow
Fst Sch

7

Dormston
Manor

Broadclose
Farm

Pit (dis)

WITHYBED LANE

BREDON CL

THE
PLECK

CHURCHWAY
PIECE

WINDMILL LANE

HIGH
HOUSE DR

HIGH STREET

SANDS RD

A422

Inkberrow

Moat

TUER
WAY

MALTHOUSE
CR

ORCHARD
MD

GREEN CT WY

PH

CHURCH
CL

Perry Fields
Farm

57

Stonepits

STONEPIT LANE

HILL
FARM

PO

Hill
Farm

Littleworth
Farm

DEVON
CL

CHESTNUT LA

CHARFORD

PEPPER ST

RAMBLE CL

DINGLE
END

6

Newhouse
Farm

Hill
Farm

Lower
Farm

Quarry
(dis)

Hillside

BROADCLOSE LANE

Cottage
Farm

BROOKLYN CT

BRECON
CL

ROCK
HL

MIDSUMMER
MD

PEPPER
ST

NODBURY
HL

POPLAR
PIECE

Springfield
Farm

Sewage
Works

5

A422

Quarrypit
Farm

Quarry
(dis)

WR7

56

Earthworks

Piddle Brook

Thorn
Dene

Moat

4

Kington

Redhouse
Farm

Little Ashdene
Farm

Pit (dis)

Thorn
Farm

Tip (dis)

3

Grove
Farm

55

Ridge
Farm

Radford

MILL LANE

2

Radford
Fruit Farm

PH

1

Westol Hall
Farm

RADFORD ROAD

WR11

WR10

54

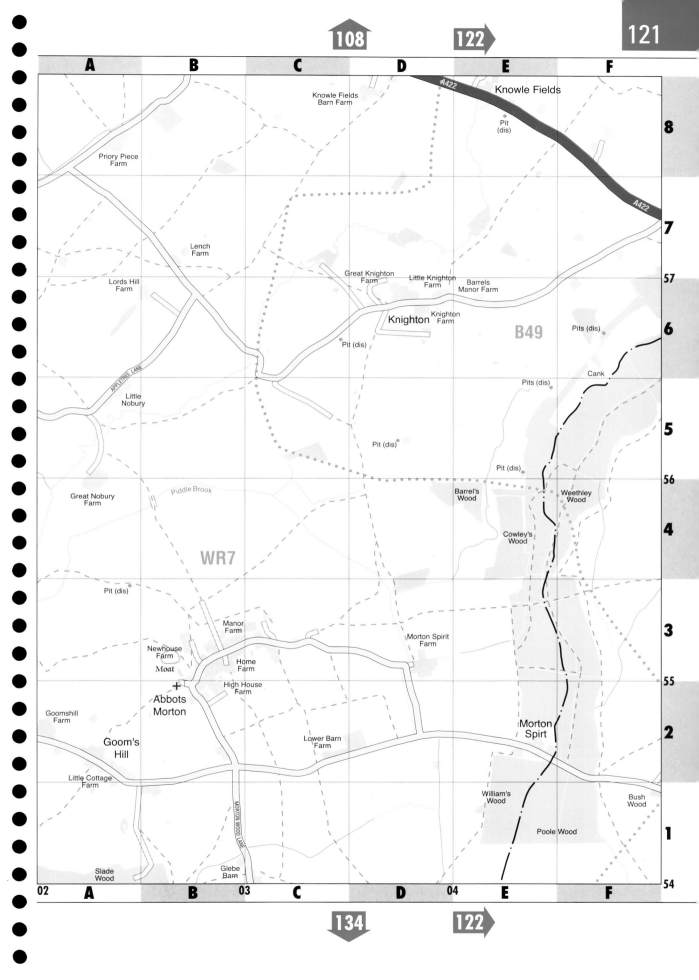

A B C D E F

8

Knowle Fields
Barn Farm

Priory Piece
Farm

Lench
Farm

Lords Hill
Farm

Knowle Fields

Pit
(dis)

A422

A422

7

57

Great Knighton
Farm

Little Knighton
Farm

Barrels
Manor Farm

Knighton

Knighton
Farm

B49

Pits (dis)

6

APPLETREE LANE

Little
Nobury

Pit (dis)

Cank

Pits (dis)

Pits (dis)

5

Pit (dis)

Pit (dis)

Barrel's
Wood

Weethley
Wood

56

Great Nobury
Farm

Piddle Brook

WR7

Cowley's
Wood

4

Pit (dis)

Manor
Farm

Morton Spirit
Farm

3

Newhouse
Farm

Moat

Home
Farm

55

High House
Farm

Goomshill
Farm

Abbots
Morton

Morton
Spirt

2

Goom's
Hill

Lower Barn
Farm

Little Cottage
Farm

MORTON WOOD LANE

William's
Wood

Bush
Wood

1

Slade
Wood

Glebe
Barn

Poole Wood

54

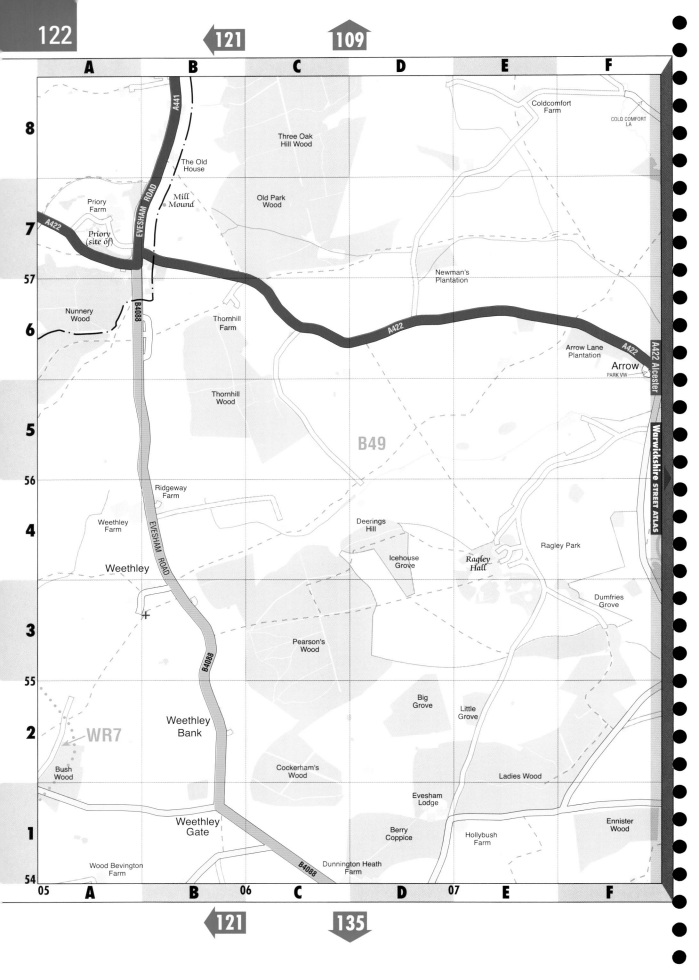

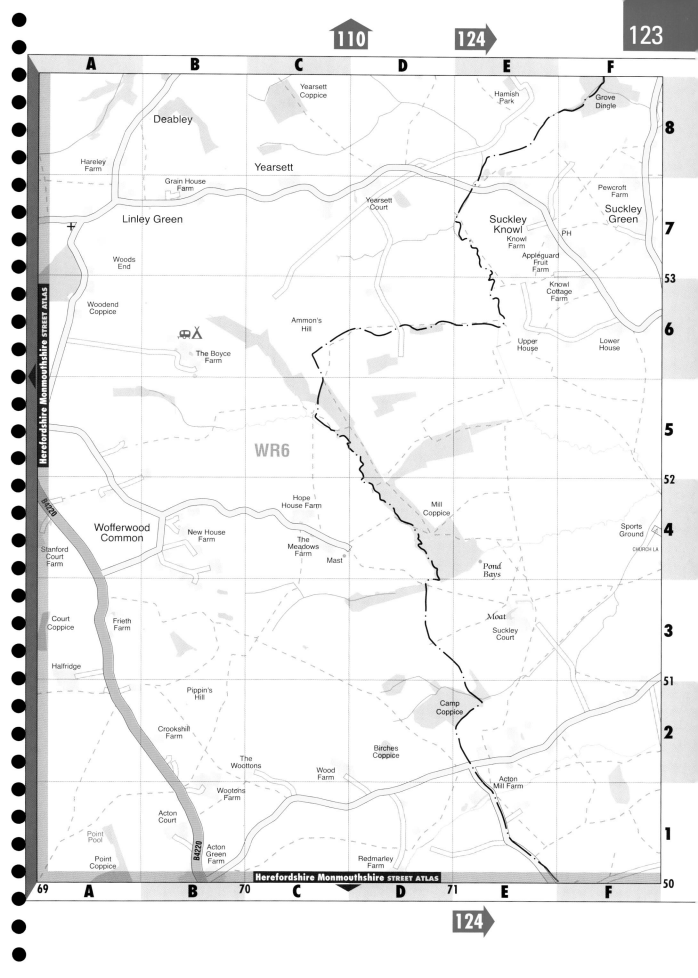

A B C D E F

8

Deabley

Yearsett Coppice

Hamish Park

Grove Dingle

Hareley Farm

Yearsett

Grain House Farm

Yearsett Court

Pewcroft Farm

Suckley Green

7

Linley Green

Suckley Knowl

Knowl Farm

PH

53

Woods End

Appleguard Fruit Farm

Knowl Cottage Farm

Woodend Coppice

Ammon's Hill

Upper House

Lower House

6

The Boyce Farm

WR6

5

52

Hope House Farm

Mill Coppice

Sports Ground

4

Stanford Court Farm

Wofferwood Common

New House Farm

The Meadows Farm

Mast

Pond Bays

CHURCH LA

Court Coppice

Frieth Farm

Moat

Suckley Court

3

Halfridge

51

Pippin's Hill

Camp Coppice

2

Crookshill Farm

Birches Coppice

The Woottons

Wood Farm

Acton Mill Farm

Wootons Farm

1

Point Pool

Acton Court

B4220

Acton Green Farm

Redmarley Farm

50

Point Coppice

Herefordshire Monmouthshire STREET ATLAS

B4220

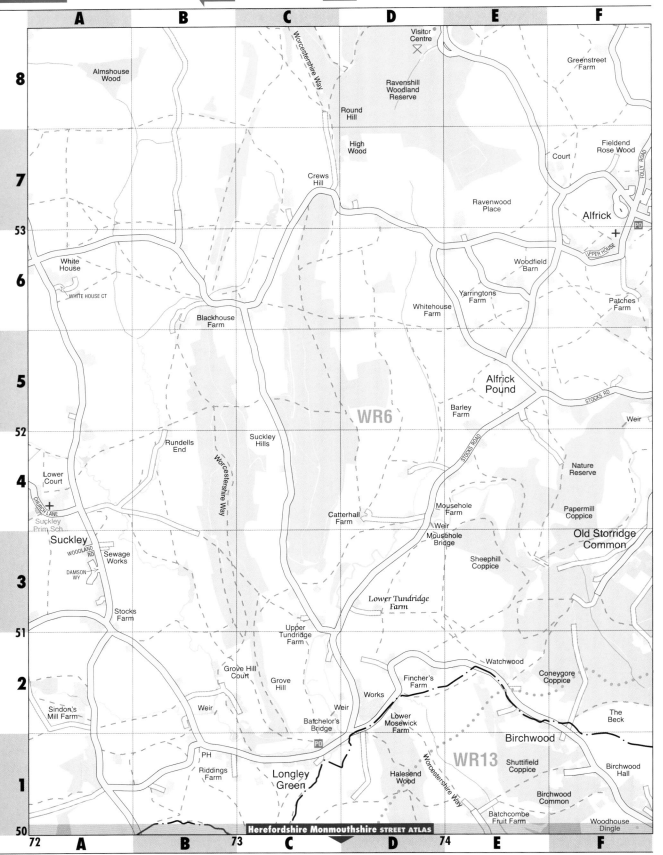

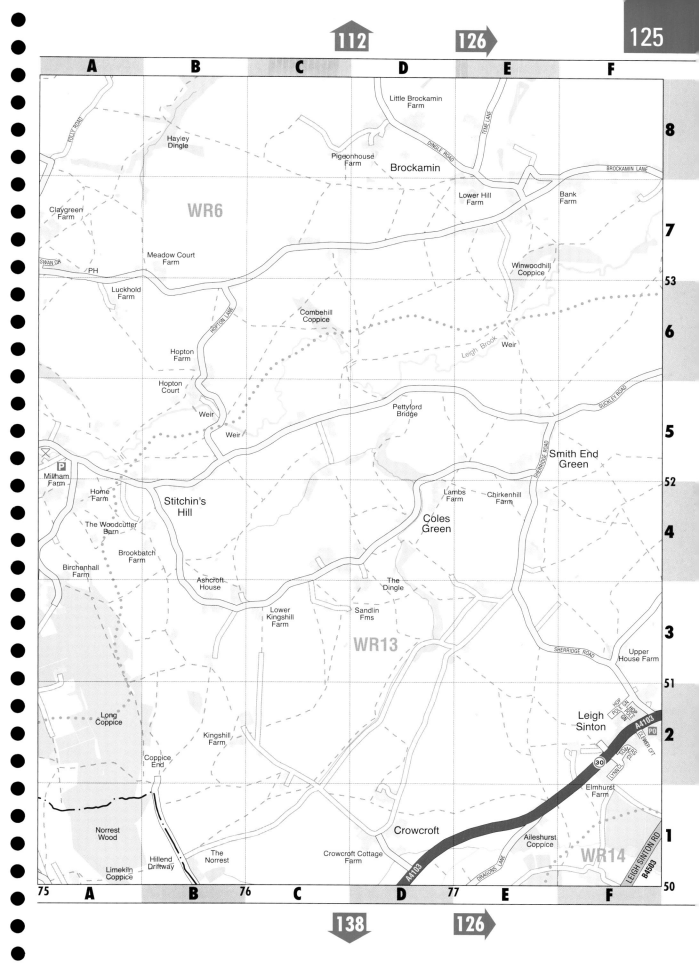

A   B   C   D   E   F

8

Little Brockamin
Farm

Hayley
Dingle

Pigeonhouse
Farm

DINGLE ROAD

TEME LANE

Brockamin

BROCKAMIN LANE

WR6

Lower Hill
Farm

Bank
Farm

7

Claygreen
Farm

Meadow Court
Farm

Winwoodhill
Coppice

53

SWAN DR

PH

Luckhold
Farm

HOPTON LANE

Combehill
Coppice

Leigh Brook

Weir

6

Hopton
Farm

SUCKLEY ROAD

Hopton
Court

Weir

Pettyford
Bridge

5

Weir

Smith End
Green

SHERRIDGE ROAD

Millham
Farm

P

Home
Farm

Lambs
Farm

Chirkenhill
Farm

52

Stitchin's
Hill

Coles
Green

4

The Woodcutter
Barn

Brookbatch
Farm

Ashcroft
House

The
Dingle

Birchenhall
Farm

Lower
Kingshill
Farm

Sandlin
Fms

WR13

SHERRIDGE ROAD

Upper
House Farm

3

51

Long
Coppice

Kingshill
Farm

Leigh
Sinton

HOP
POLE GN
SHOP
PO
FTE
GN

A4103

PO

CLEWER CFT

2

30

LYNFLD

CSMACKS
CTS

Coppice
End

Elmhurst
Farm

Norrest
Wood

Hillend
Driftway

The
Norrest

Crowcroft

Crowcroft Cottage
Farm

Aileshurst
Coppice

WR14

1

A4103

DRAGONS LANE

LEIGH SINTON RD

B4503

Limekiln
Coppice

50

A B C D E F

8

7

53

6

52

5

4

3

51

2

1

50

WR2

Leigh Court Farm

Cross (English Heritage)

Leigh

OLD STATION RD

BROCKAMIN LANE

River Teme

Rockhill Covert

OLD RECTORY GDNS

SUCKLEY ROAD

ORCHARD WAY

BENSFIELD

WR6

Bransford

New House Farm

POST OFFICE LA

Reservoir

Bransford Bridge

PH

P

A4103

Hotel

CH

Whitegate Farm

PH

Cottages Stockend Farm

Middleyard Coppice

Motte

Castle Green

SUFFIELD CL

A4103

Guinness Park Farm

Chapelhill Coppice

CHAPEL LANE

CHAPEL LA

Cemetery

Gilbert's Farm

Stockend Farm

Bush Hill Coppice

Bush Hill Farm

Whitehouse Coppice

NASH GT

Moat

KILN LA

A4103

MALVERN RD

PH

Leigh Sinton

2

1 PEAR TREE DR
2 CHAPEL CL
3 THE CORBETTS

Leigh & Bransford Primary School

SHEALDON

Brook Farm

STOOKS LANE

WR13

Brace's Leigh

Guinness Hop Farm

WR2

Lodge Farm

MONKSFIELD LANE

Monksfield

PH

B4503

LEIGH SINTON RD

LOWER MONKSELL ROAD

Ford

North Wood

Brook Wood

Little Monksfield Farm

WORCESTER ROAD A449

MALVERN RD

HAWTHORN LA

WR14

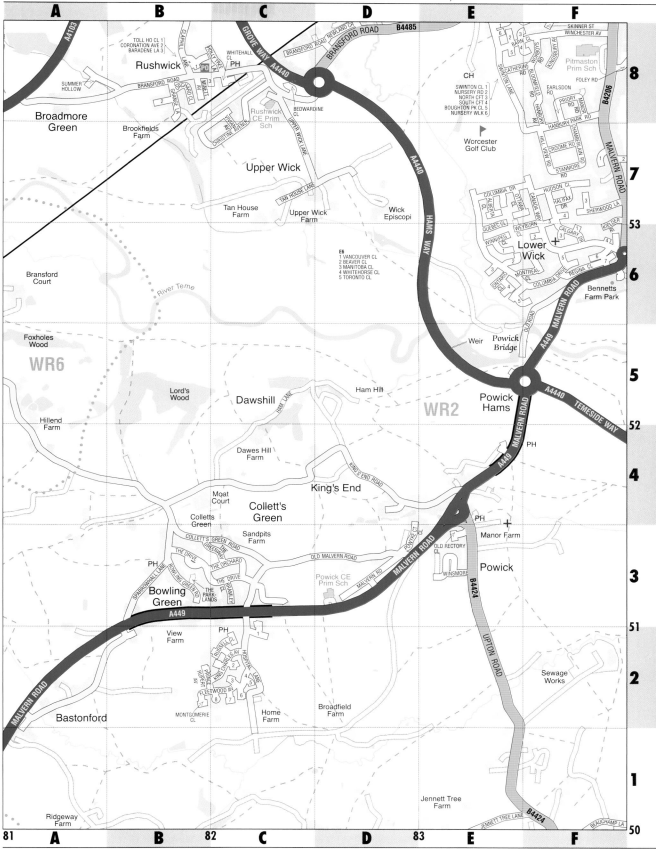

114

128

F7
1 LINKELM CL
2 WHITES RD
3 CHARNWOOD CL
4 ST LAWRENCE CL
5 JASPER RD

F6
1 FRANKLIN CL
2 WESTMOUNT CL
3 DAWSON CL
4 BRUNSWICK CL
5 LABRADOR RD
6 EDMONTON CL

7 BAFFIN RD

SKINNER ST
WINCHESTER AV
Pitmaston Prim Sch
FOLEY RD

CH
SWINTON CL 1
NURSERY RD 2
NORTH CFT 3
SOUTH CFT 4
BOUGHTON PK CL 5
NURSERY WLK 6

EARLSDON
PRIORY
STANMORE RD

Worcester
Golf Club

COLUMBIA DR
ALBERTA
QUEBEC CL
WINNIPEG CL
ONTARIO CL
MONTREAL
HUDSON CL
OTTAWA
CANADA WAY
WEYBURN
HALIFAX DR
SHERWOOD LA
CALGARY
KIELDER
REGINA CL
COLUMBIA DRIVE

Lower
Wick

Bennetts
Farm Park

TOLL HO CL 1
CORONATION AVE 2
BARADENE LA 3

Rushwick
PO
PH
WHITEHALL CL
HOLLY TREE
BRANSFORD ROAD
CLAPHILL LA
GRANGE LA
ORCHARD CL
MINETT AV
VIVIAN
CHRISTINE AVENUE

SUMMER
HOLLOW

Broadmore
Green

Brookfields
Farm

Rushwick
CE Prim
Sch

BEDWARDINE
CL

UPPER WICK LANE

Upper Wick

TAN HOUSE LANE

Tan House
Farm

Upper Wick
Farm

Wick
Episcopi

HAMS WAY

E6
1 VANCOUVER CL
2 BEAVER CL
3 MANITOBA CL
4 WHITEHORSE CL
5 TORONTO CL

A4440

Bransford
Court

River Teme

Foxholes
Wood

WR6

Weir

Powick
Bridge

A449

MALVERN ROAD
B4206

8

7

53

6

Hillend
Farm

Lord's
Wood

Dawshill

HAM LANE

Ham Hill

WR2

Dawes Hill
Farm

KING'S END ROAD

King's End

Moat
Court

Colletts
Green

Collett's
Green

Sandpits
Farm

COLLETT'S GREEN ROAD
GREENWAY
THE DRIVE
THE ORCHARD
THE BRAMLEY
THE PARK-LANDS

PH

SPARROWHALL LANE
BOWLING GREEN RD

Bowling
Green

A449

Powick
Hams

MALVERN ROAD

PH

A4440
TEMESIDE WAY

MALVERN ROAD

PH

PONTEET CT
OLD RECTORY CL

Manor Farm

Powick

OLD MALVERN ROAD

MALVERN RD

Powick CE
Prim Sch

WINSMORE

B4424
UPTON ROAD

5

52

4

3

51

View
Farm

PH

RUSSELL CL
KING CHARLES AV
PRINCE RUPERT AV
FLEETWOOD RD

MALVERN ROAD

Bastonford

MONTGOMERIE
CL

Home
Farm

HOSPITAL LANE

Broadfield
Farm

Sewage
Works

2

1

Ridgeway
Farm

Jennett Tree
Farm

JENNETT TREE LANE
B4424

BEAUCHAMP LA

50

81   A   B   82   C   D   83   E   F

C2
1 HAMILTON CL
2 BYRON CL
3 ESSEX CL
4 CROMWELL CL
5 DEANE CL
6 BERRY CL
7 AUSTEN CL
8 HARRISON CL

140

128

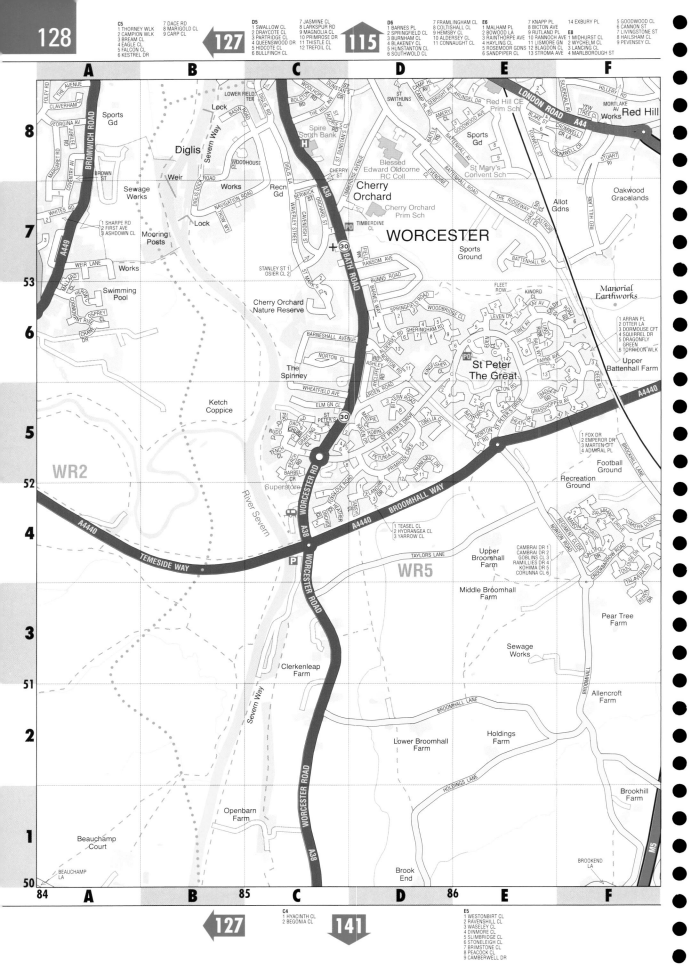

129
117

A B C D E F

8

WR5

Monday's Hill Coppice

A4538

A44

A422

THE CROSSROADS

The Marshes

Churchill Farm

Moat

Churchill

Upper Townsend Farm

7

Sewage Works

PH

Sneachill Farm

Sneachill

Churchill Glebe Farm

53

Aston Court Farm

EDWARDS LANE

6

Brickbarns Farm

Green Farm

White Ladies Aston

EVESHAM ROAD

Lowhill Covert

5

WR7

Sherwood Place

Low Hill

Aston Moat Farm

Moat

52

Lowhill Coppice

A44

4

Spetchley Fruit Farm

Aston Hall Farm

Egdon

Walsgrove Farm

3

Mucknell Farm

B4084

PH

Upper Wolverton Farm

EGDON LANE

51

Lower Wolverton

2

Upper Wolverton

Wolverton Farm

WR10

1

B4084

B4084

Breach Farm

Home Covert

A44

50

90 A 91 B C 91 D 92 E F

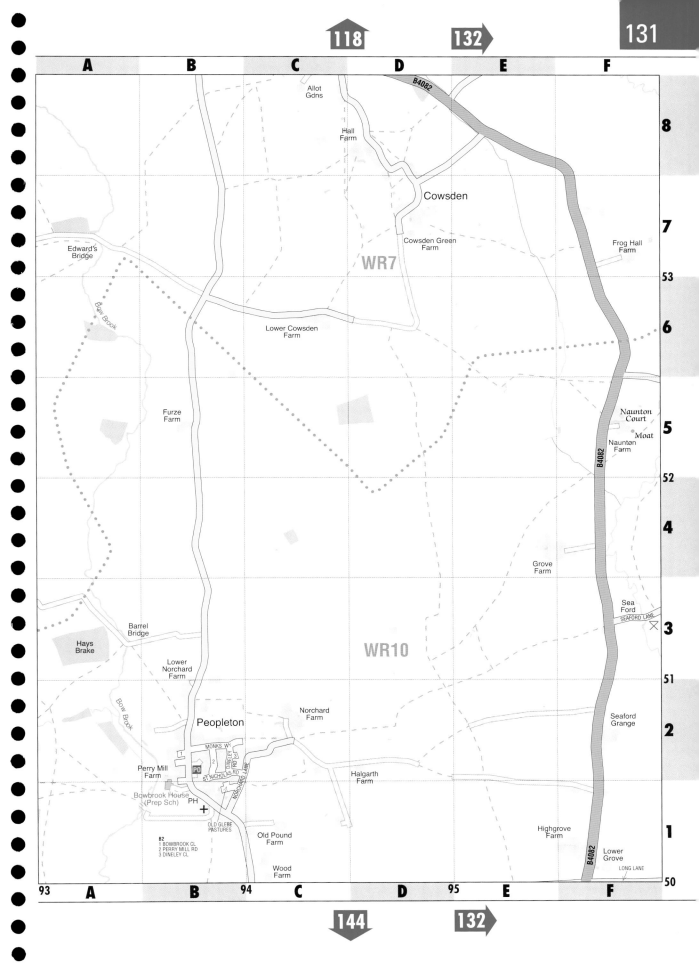

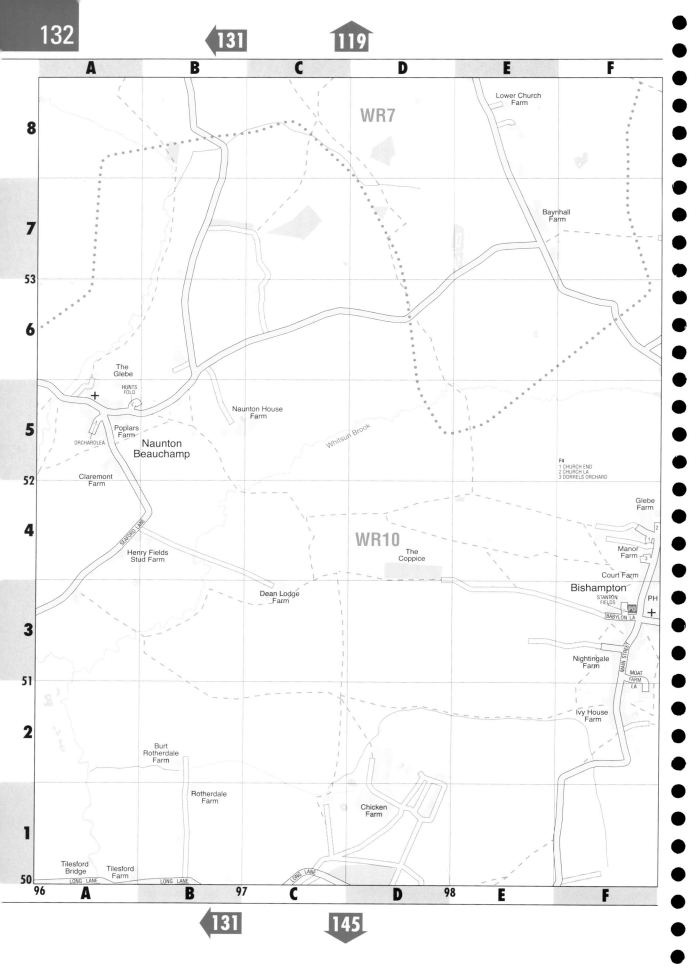

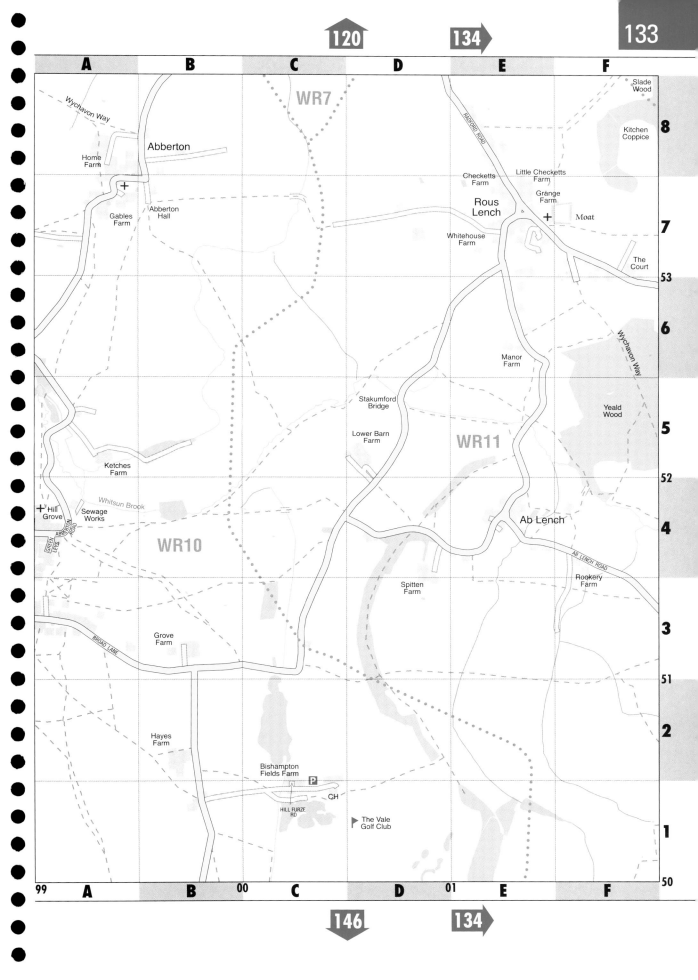

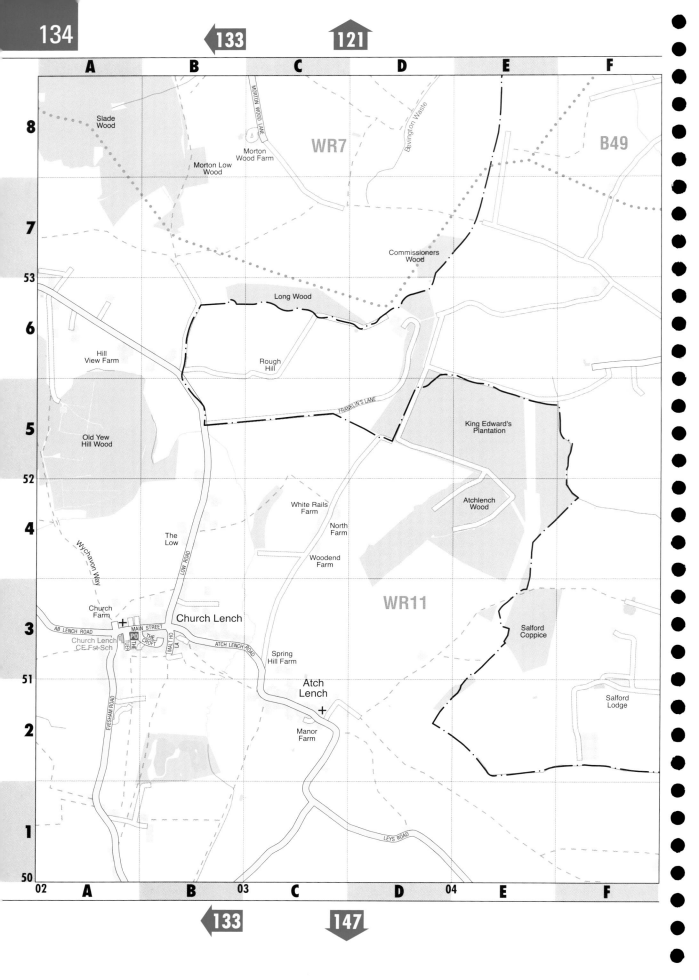

133
121

A   B   C   D   E   F

8

WR7

B49

Slade
Wood

MORTON WOOD LANE

Morton
Wood Farm

Morton Low
Wood

Bevington Waste

7

Commissioners
Wood

53

6

Long Wood

Hill
View Farm

Rough
Hill

FRANKLIN'S LANE

King Edward's
Plantation

5

Old Yew
Hill Wood

52

White Rails
Farm

North
Farm

Atchlench
Wood

4

The
Low

LOW ROAD

Wychavon Way

Woodend
Farm

WR11

Church
Farm

Church Lench

Salford
Coppice

3

AB LENCH ROAD

Church Lench
CE Fst Sch

PO

MAIN STREET

THE CROFT

MALT HO LA

THE

ATCH LENCH ROAD

Spring
Hill Farm

51

Atch
Lench

Salford
Lodge

2

EVESHAM ROAD

Manor
Farm

1

LEYS ROAD

50

02   A   B   03   C   D   04   E   F

133
147

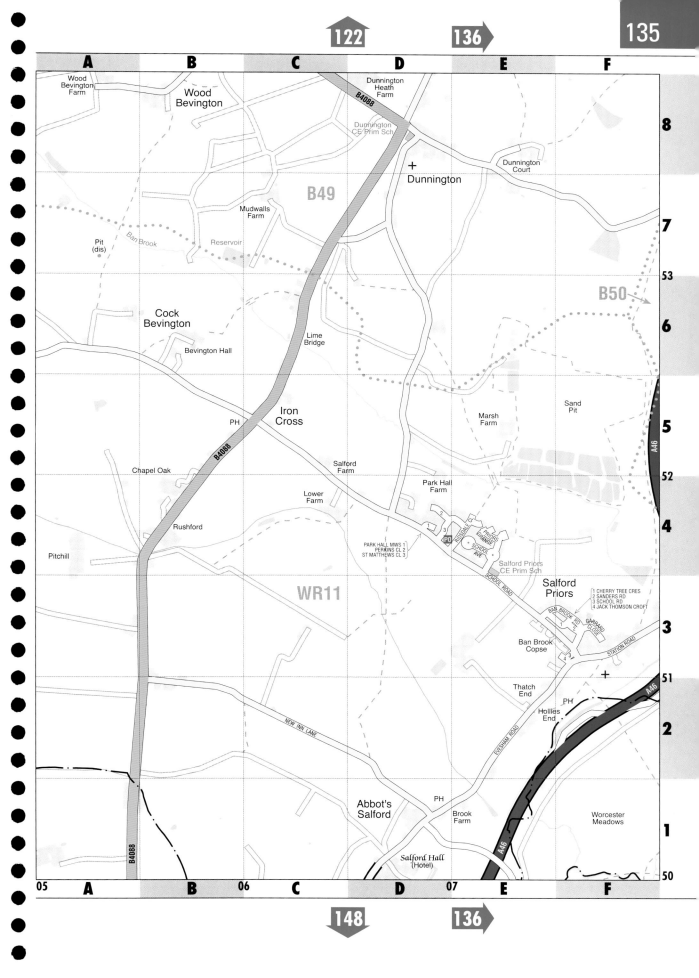

135

149

Warwickshire STREET ATLAS

D5
1 LAMBOURNE CL
2 WADLEYS CL
3 ST LAURENCE WY
4 EBSDORF CL
5 PIPIN CL
6 FRIDAY CL
7 BLENHEIM CL
8 WILKES WY
9 HOLDER CL

A46 Alcester

B49

The Cottage

Moor Hall

Weir Broom

Wixford Lodge

GEORGE'S ELM LANE

MILL CL 1
MILLERS BANK 2
MILL LA 3

MILL LANE

High Street

Famington Farm

GRAFTON LANE

MALT HO CL

ALBION TR

PH

KING'S LANE

River Arrow

Sandhills

Bidavon Industrial Estate

Waterloo Park

Beechtree Park

Wessons Farm

Smallbrook Bsns Ctr

Moat

JACKSONS MD

FRIDAY FURLONG

WATERLOO ROAD

Waterloo Industrial Estate

1 MASON CL
2 JUBILEE CL
3 FALCON CRES
4 TOWER CFT
5 WHARRAD CL

Broom Court

Heart of England Way

THE POPLARS

WATERLOO CR

HILL VIEW ROAD

WESSONS ROAD

B439

B50

STEPPES PIECE

STEPPING STONES

PADDOCK CL

BURNELL

DUGDALE AV

DRATON CL

VICTORIA ROAD

Liby

BRANLEY WAY

BR'LEIGH

CR'LEIGH

CROMPTON AV

THE LEYS

SCOTT

Bidford-on-Avon CE Prim Sch

WESTHOLME ROAD

ELLIOTT CL 1
QUEENSWAY 2

Marriage Hill Farm

THE MEADOWS

GLEB

ORCHARD CL

COURT WAY

TOWER CL

ICKNIELD ST

LONGFORD CLOSE

TOWER HILL

Bidford-on-Avon

Marriage Hill

GABLE MEWS

HARBOUR CL

OLD SCHOOL MD

HOWARD CL

PLECK

THE

HIGH STREET

PO

HIGH STREET

B4085

PH

GRANGE ROAD

SALFORD ROAD

CRAWFORD CLOSE

CHAPEL LA

1 QUINNEYS LA
2 QUINNEYS CT
3 CHURCH ST

Cemy

Recreation Ground

P

ICKNIELD

B439

Station Rd

Salford Bridge

Sewage Works

HONEYBOURNE ROAD

Avon Valley Footpath

Lock

Weir

PH

OWLETS END

Barton

A46

River Avon

Temple Farm

Marlcliff Farm

CLEEVE ROAD

WR11

Weir

Lock

Marlcliff

THE BANK

HONEYBOURNE ROAD

Marlcliff Hill

B4085

BICKMARSH LANE

Staple Hill

135

149

D4
1 TRAFALGAR CT
2 SAXONFIELDS
3 CHAPEL CL
4 HOLLAND CL
5 SALLIEFORTH PL

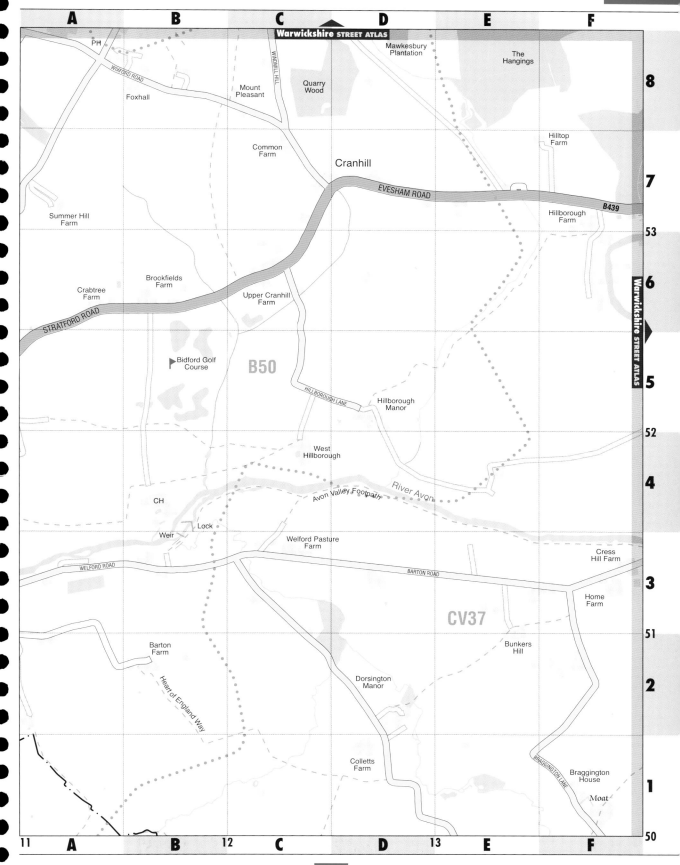

Warwickshire STREET ATLAS

Mawkesbury Plantation

The Hangings

PH

WIXFORD ROAD

Foxhall

Mount Pleasant

Quarry Wood

WINDMILL HILL

Common Farm

Cranhill

Hilltop Farm

8

EVESHAM ROAD

B439

7

Summer Hill Farm

Hillborough Farm

53

Brookfields Farm

Crabtree Farm

STRATFORD ROAD

Upper Cranhill Farm

6

Bidford Golf Course

B50

HILLBOROUGH LANE

Hillborough Manor

5

West Hillborough

52

River Avon

Avon Valley Footpath

4

CH

Lock

Weir

Welford Pasture Farm

Cress Hill Farm

WELFORD ROAD

BARTON ROAD

Home Farm

3

CV37

51

Barton Farm

Bunkers Hill

2

Heart of England Way

Dorsington Manor

Colletts Farm

BRAGGINGTON LANE

Braggington House

Moat

1

50

Warwickshire STREET ATLAS

11 A **B** **12** C **D** **13** E **F**

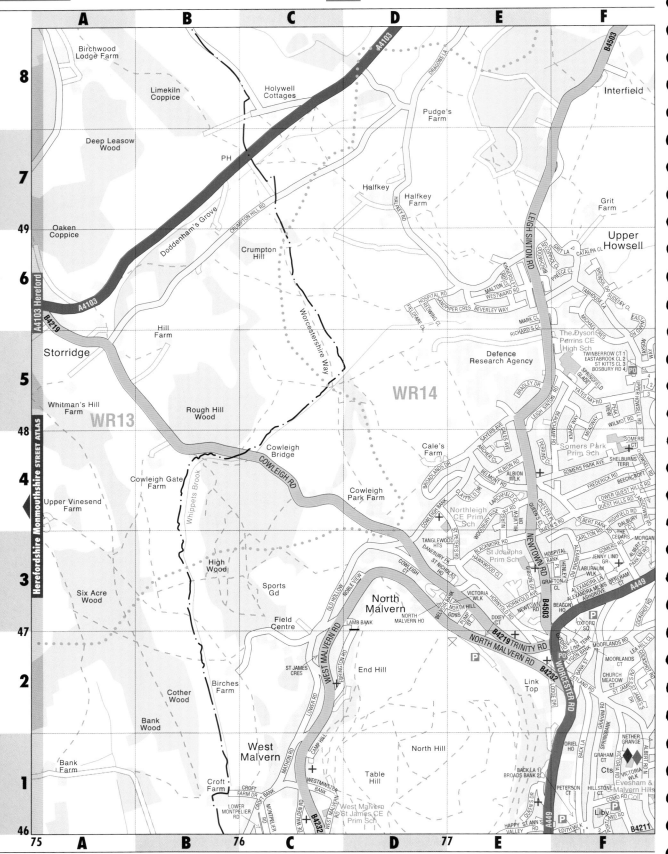

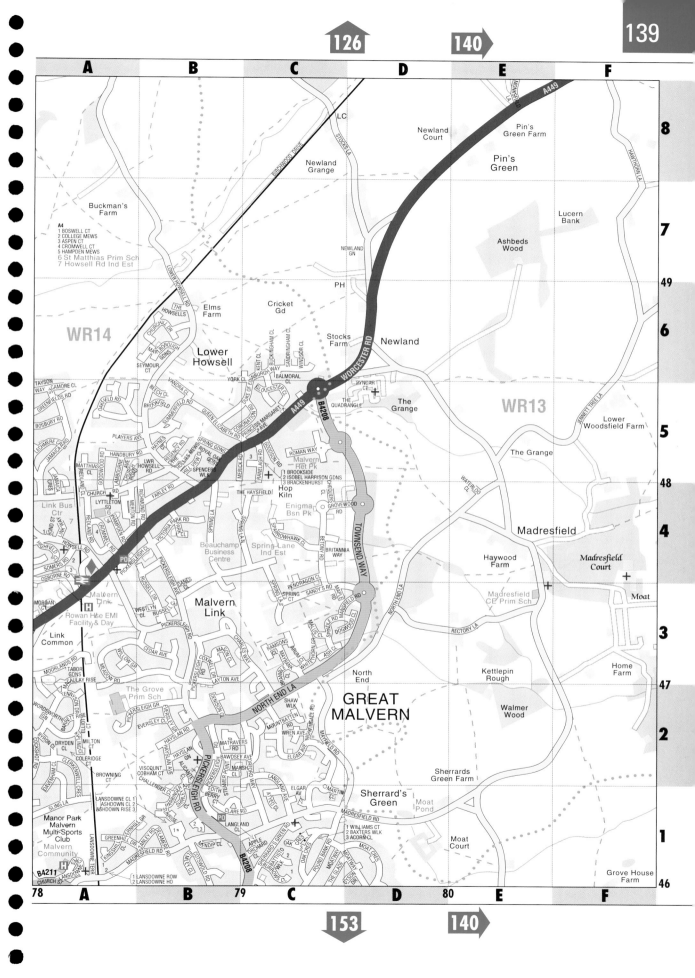

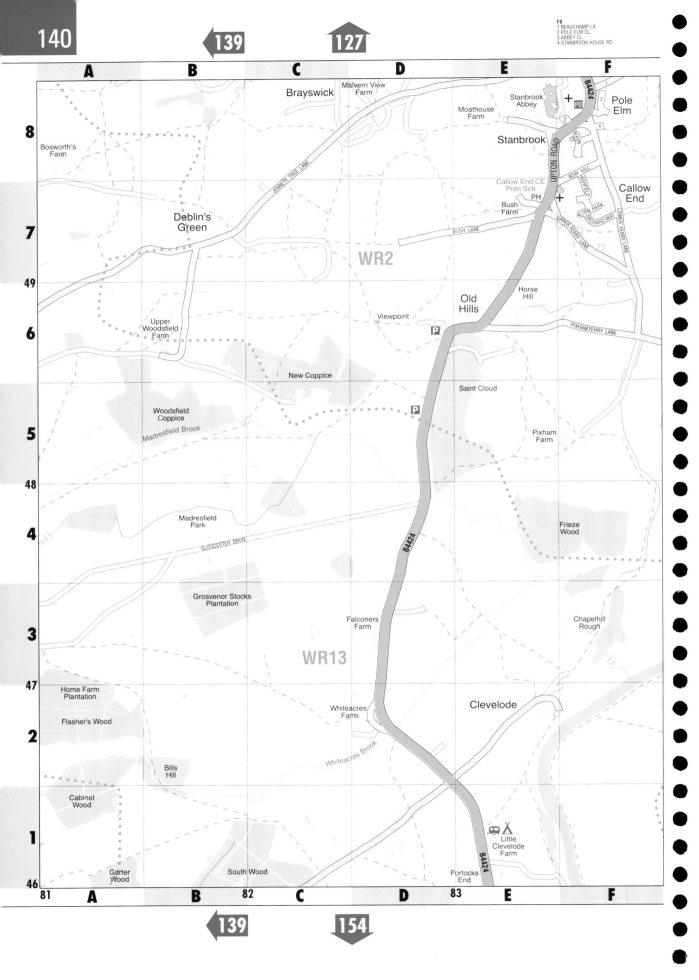

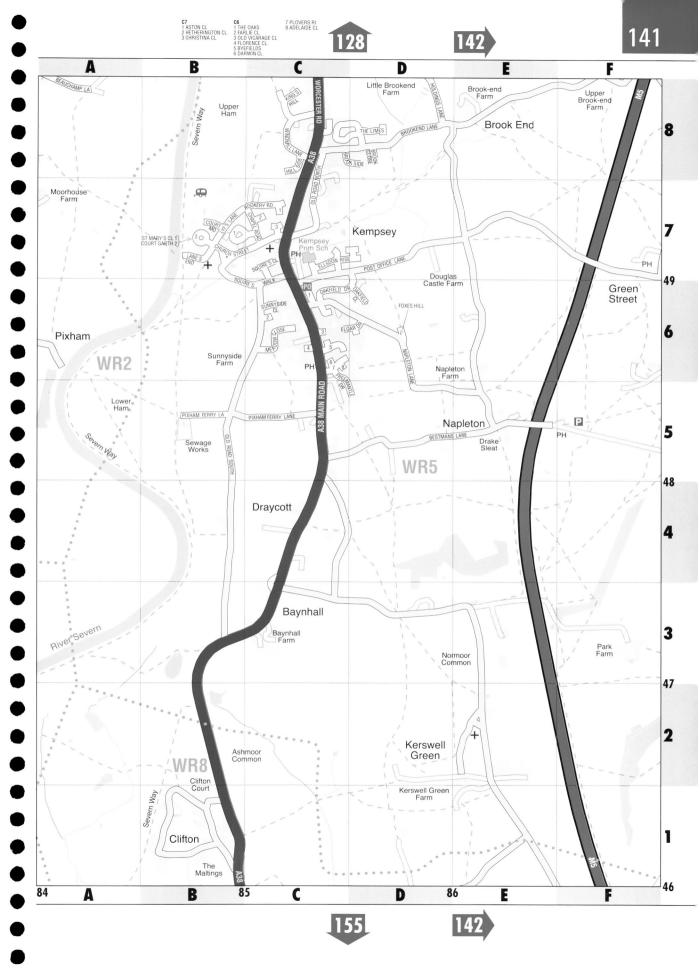

141
129

Littleworth

Allot Gdns

THE HIDAGE

WADBOROUGH ROAD

Abbotswood

FOX LANE

Tadneys Farm

Woodhall Farms

WR5

Abbots Wood

Stonehall Farm

Stonehall Common

Stonehall

PH

Abbots Wood Farm

Moat

Willows Farm

Wadborough Park Farm

Stonehall Farm

Common Farm

Swanbrook Farm

Stonehall Farm

Kempsey Common

Hermitage Farm

Pirton Gorse

Kites Farm

Swanbrook Farm

LC

STATION ROAD

WORCESTER ROAD

Narrow Wood

Pool Covert

Elms Farm

Pirton

WR8

PH

Narrow Wood Farm

Pirton Pool

HILL ROAD

LC

Pirton Siding

Cross

SIDINGS ROAD

Surman's Farm

Pirton Court

Bourne Brook

Moat

The Old Park

Lickmoor Coppice

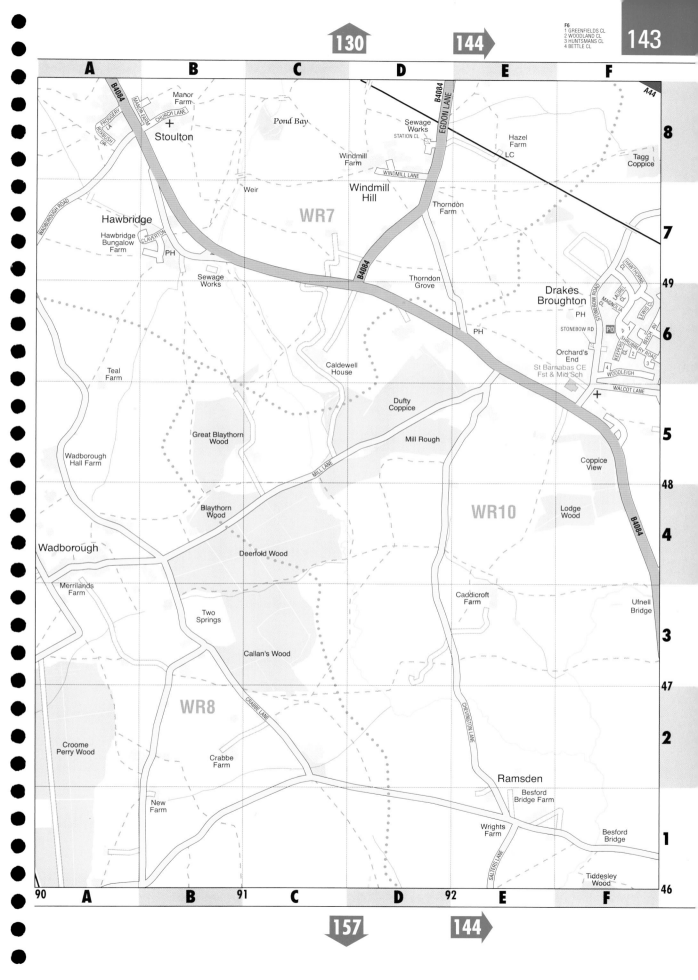

130
144
143

F6
1 GREENFIELDS CL
2 WOODLAND CL
3 HUNTSMANS CL
4 BETTLE CL

A B C D E F

B4084
MANOR FARM
FROGGERY LA
ROYBUSH DR
CHURCH LANE
Manor Farm
+
Stoulton

Pond Bay

B4084
EGDON LANE
A44

Sewage Works
STATION CL

Hazel Farm
LC

Tagg Coppice

8

Windmill Farm

Windmill Lane

Weir

Windmill Hill

Thorndon Farm

WR7

7

Hawbridge

CLAVERTON
PH

Hawbridge Bungalow Farm

Sewage Works

Thorndon Grove

PH

Drakes Broughton

STONEBOW ROAD
HAWTHORNE CL
LAUREL CL
MAGNOLIA CL
KEEPERS CL
SHRUBBERY CL
LEWIS CL
BEECH AV
PH

STONEBOW RD
PO

49

6

WADBOROUGH ROAD

Teal Farm

Caldewell House

Orchard's End
St Barnabas CE Fst & Mid Sch
WOODLEIGH
WALCOT LANE
+

Dufty Coppice

Great Blaythorn Wood

Mill Rough

5

MILL LANE

Coppice View

48

Wadborough Hall Farm

Blaythorn Wood

WR10

Lodge Wood

B4084

4

Wadborough

Deerfold Wood

Merrilands Farm

Two Springs

Caddicroft Farm

Ufnell Bridge

3

Callan's Wood

CRABBE LANE

CHEVINGTON LANE

47

WR8

2

Croome Perry Wood

Crabbe Farm

Ramsden

Besford Bridge Farm

New Farm

Wrights Farm
SALTERS LANE

Besford Bridge

1

Tiddesley Wood

46

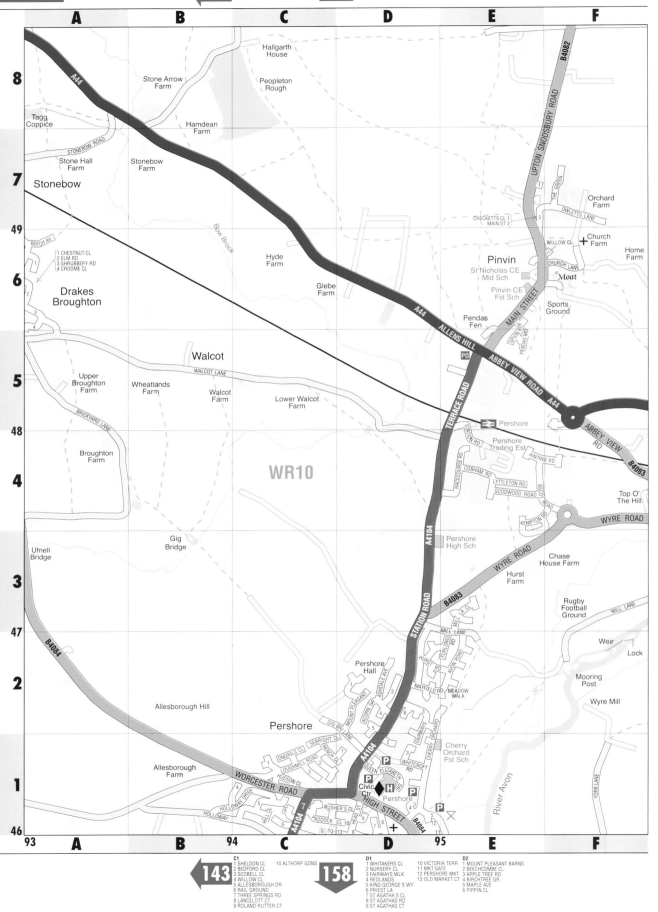

← 143

158

C1
1 SHELDON CL
2 BEDFORD CL
3 SCOBELL CL
4 WILLOW CL
5 ALLESBOROUGH DR
6 RAIL GROUND
7 THREE SPRINGS RD
8 LANCELOTT CT
9 ROLAND RUTTER CT

10 ALTHORP GDNS

D1
1 WHITAKERS CL
2 NURSERY CL
3 FAIRWAYS WLK
4 REDLANDS
5 KING GEORGE'S WY
6 PRIEST LA
7 ST AGATHA S CL
8 ST AGATHAS RD
9 ST AGATHAS CT

10 VICTORIA TERR
11 MKT GATE
12 PERSHORE MKT
13 OLD MARKET CT

D2
1 MOUNT PLEASANT BARNS
2 BEECHCOMBE CL
3 APPLE TREE RD
4 BIRCHTREE GR
5 MAPLE AVE
6 PIPPIN CL

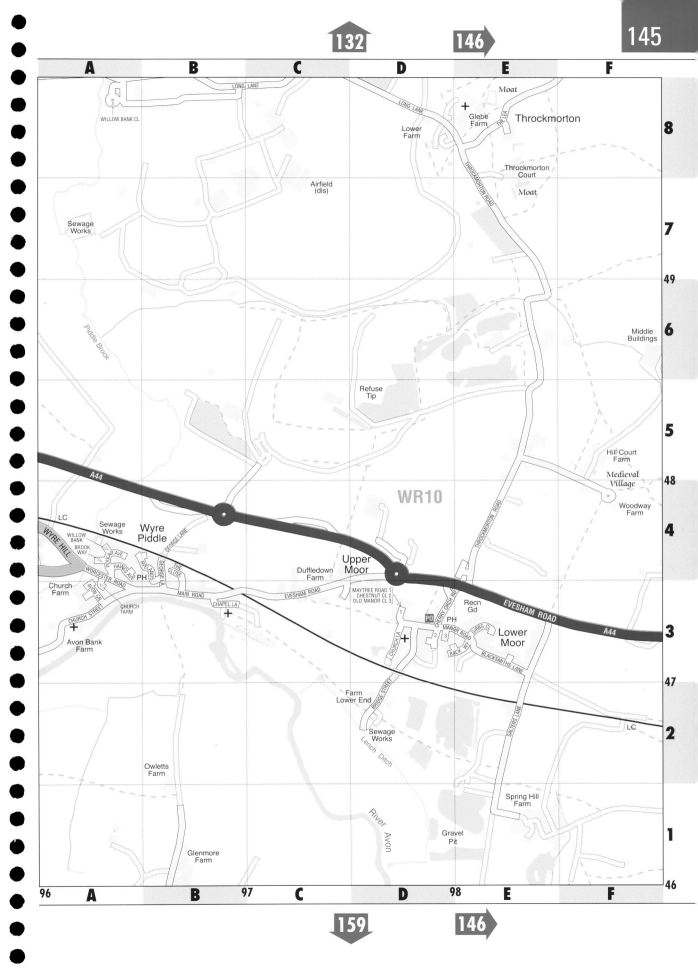

A   B   C   D   E   F

8
7
49
6
5
48
4
3
47
2
1
46

LONG LANE

WILLOW BANK CL

LONG LANE

Moat

Glebe
Farm   +   THE LEA   Throckmorton

Lower
Farm

THROCKMORTON ROAD

Throckmorton
Court

Moat

Airfield
(dis)

Sewage
Works

Piddle Brook

Middle
Buildings

Refuse
Tip

WR10

Hill Court
Farm

Medieval
Village

A44

Woodway
Farm

LC

Wyre
Piddle   GEORGE LANE

Sewage
Works

WILLOW
BANK
BROOK
WAY   R AVE   THE CLOSE   GEORGE LA

HAWC AVE   RYELANDS   PH

THROCKMORTON ROAD

WYRE HILL

WORCESTER ROAD

Duffledown
Farm   Upper
Moor

MAIN ROAD   EVESHAM ROAD

MAYTREE ROAD 1
CHESTNUT CL 2
OLD MANOR CL 3

Recn
Gd

EVESHAM ROAD   A44

AVON GLN   CHAPEL LA   +

Church
Farm   CHURCH
FARM

CHURCH STREET   +

1
PO   2   PH
3

CHURCH LA   +   MANOR ROAD   GIBBS CL   Lower
Moor

CHERRY ORCH RD

BACK WY   BLACKSMITHS LANE

Avon Bank
Farm

Farm
Lower End

BRIDGE STREET

Sewage
Works

SALTERS LANE

LC

Owletts
Farm

Lench Ditch

Spring Hill
Farm

River Avon

Gravel
Pit

Glenmore
Farm

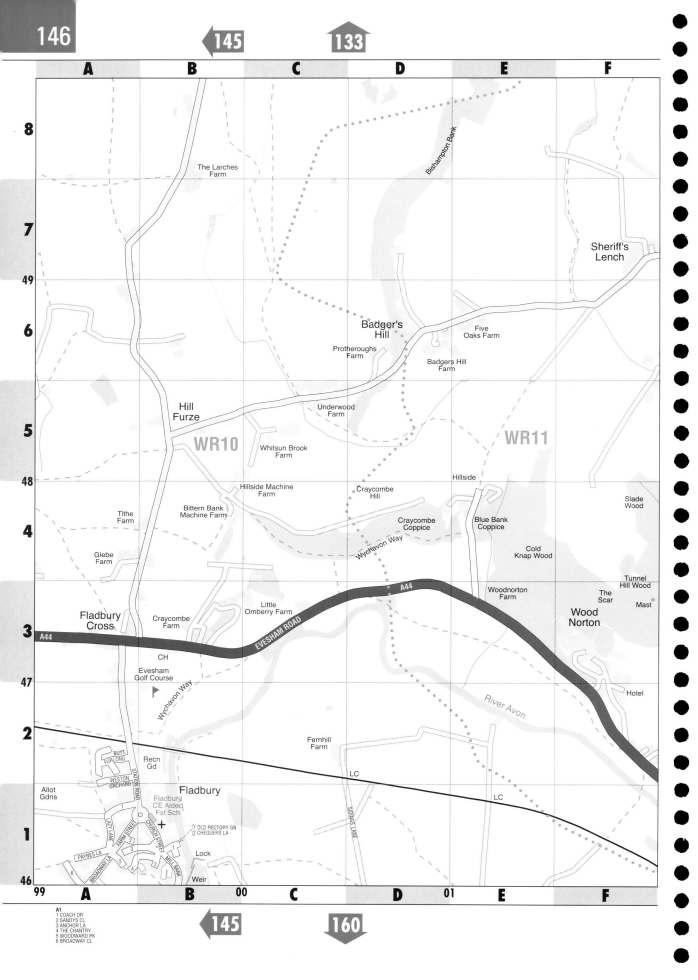

A B C D E F

8
7
49
6
5
48
4
3
47
2
1
46

The Larches Farm

Bishampton Bank

Sheriff's Lench

Badger's Hill

Five Oaks Farm

Protheroughs Farm

Badgers Hill Farm

Hill Furze

Underwood Farm

WR10

WR11

Whitsun Brook Farm

Hillside

Hillside Machine Farm

Craycombe Hill

Slade Wood

Bittern Bank Machine Farm

Craycombe Coppice

Blue Bank Coppice

Tithe Farm

Wychavon Way

Cold Knap Wood

Glebe Farm

A44

Woodnorton Farm

Tunnel Hill Wood

The Scar

Mast

Fladbury Cross

Craycombe Farm

Little Omberry Farm

EVESHAM ROAD

Wood Norton

A44

CH

Evesham Golf Course

Wychavon Way

Hotel

River Avon

BUTT FURLONG

Recn Gd

Fernhill Farm

WESTON ORCHARD

Allot Gdns

STATION ROAD

Fladbury

LC

LC

LAZY LANE

FARM STREET

Fladbury CE Aided Fst Sch

1 OLD RECTORY GN
2 CHEQUERS LA

SIDINGS LANE

PAYNES LA

CHURCH STREET

MILL BANK

Lock

BROADWAY LA

Weir

A1
1 COACH DR
2 SANDYS CL
3 ANCHOR LA
4 THE CHANTRY
5 WOODWARD PK
6 BROADWAY CL

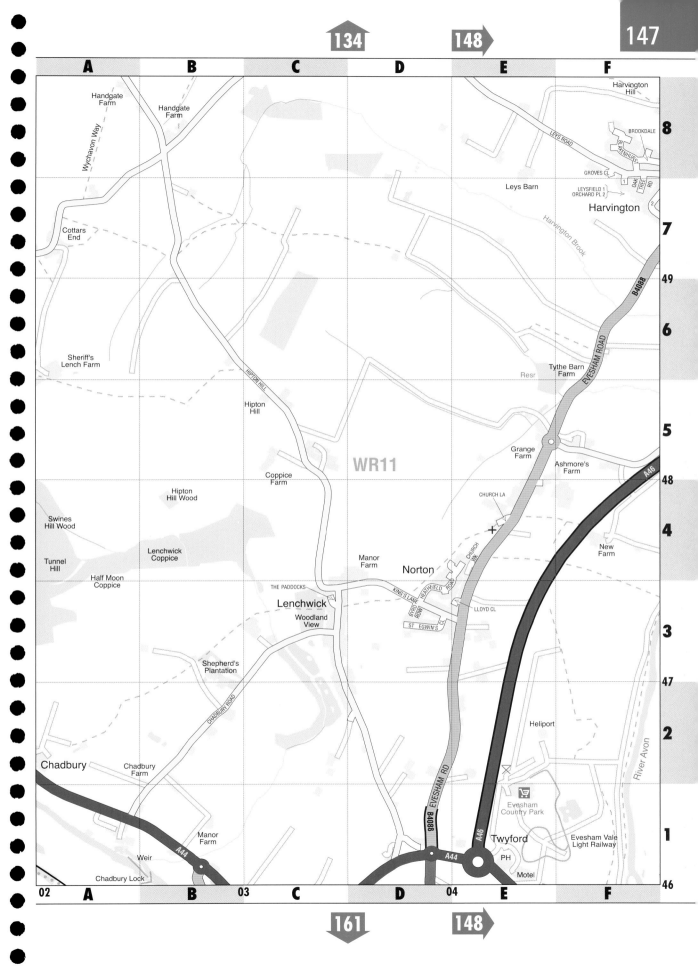

A B C D E F

8 7 49 6 5 48 4 47 2 1 46

02 A B 03 C D 04 E F

Handgate Farm
Handgate Farm
Wychavon Way
Cottars End
Sheriff's Lench Farm
HIPTON HILL
Hipton Hill
Coppice Farm
Hipton Hill Wood
Swines Hill Wood
Tunnel Hill
Lenchwick Coppice
Half Moon Coppice
THE PADDOCKS
Lenchwick
Woodland View
Shepherd's Plantation
CHADBURY ROAD
Chadbury
Chadbury Farm
Manor Farm
A44
Weir
Chadbury Lock
Manor Farm
King's Lane
BYRD ROW
ST EGWIN'S CL
Norton
HEATHFIELD
Lloyd Cl
CHURCH LA
CHURCH RD
WR11
Grange Farm
Ashmore's Farm
Resr
Tythe Barn Farm
EVESHAM ROAD
B4088
A46
A46
New Farm
EVESHAM RD
B4088
A44
A44
Twyford
PH
Motel
Heliport
Evesham Country Park
Evesham Vale Light Railway
River Avon
Harvington Hill
LEYS ROAD
BROOKDALE
BLAKENHURST
GROVES CL
OAK TREE RD
LEYSFIELD 1
ORCHARD PL 2
Leys Barn
Harvington
Harvington Brook

8

Green Street Farm

BROOKDALE

MARSH CL

Salford Spinney

Cleeve Prior Bank Nature Reserve

B4088

EVESHAM ROAD

COPLOW WY

LEYS RD

MYATT'S FIELD

7

PO

Harvington CE Fst Sch

Oak Tree Farm

ORCHARD PL

Harvington

HUGHES LA

HUGHES CL

PAGLEY RD

VILAGE STREET

STATION ROAD

ST JAMES CL

PH

CREST HILL

Lavendon Cott

ANCHOR LANE

Buckthorn Farm

EVESHAM ROAD

49

GRANGE LA

RECTORY CL

CHURCH ST

FINCH LA

1

3

Sports Ground

River Avon

6

WALNUT CL 1
FINCH LA 2
SHAKESPEARE LA 3
MANOR PK 4

STRATFORD ROAD

Harvington Cricket Club

Littleton Coppice

B4085

Sewage Works

ANCHOR LANE

Cleeve Hill

5

A46

WR11

48

Weir

4

Lock

B4510

B4085

ARROW LANE

River Avon

3

The George Billington Lock

Middle Littleton

Tithe Barn

TITHE CT

CROFT RD

CLEEVE ROAD

TITHEWAY

47

Ford

PH

Tumulus

SCHOOL LANE

Manor Orchard Farm

MANOR ROAD

2

Court Farm

Avoncroft Farm

Bennetts Hill Business Park

South Littleton

B4085

Manor House

COURT LA

CHURCH STREET

GIBBS LA

NEWTOWN

FARM LANE

1

Offenham CE Fst Sch

Offenham

THREE COCKS LANE

Church Farm

MAIN STREET

The Littletons Sch

CHERRY CL

MYATT RD

OLD SCHOOL LA

MAIN STREET

The Grove

Recn Gd

1

4

BLACKSMITHS LANE

46

ST MILBURGH CL

MYATT RD

MYATT RD

B4510

MERRY LANE

BENNETTS HILL

LONG HYDE ROAD

ROBERTS LA

2

05 **A** **B** **06** **C** **D** **07** **E** **F**

F1
1 CHURCH LA
2 ST MICHAEL'S CL
3 HATHAWAY CL
4 BLACKSMITHS CL

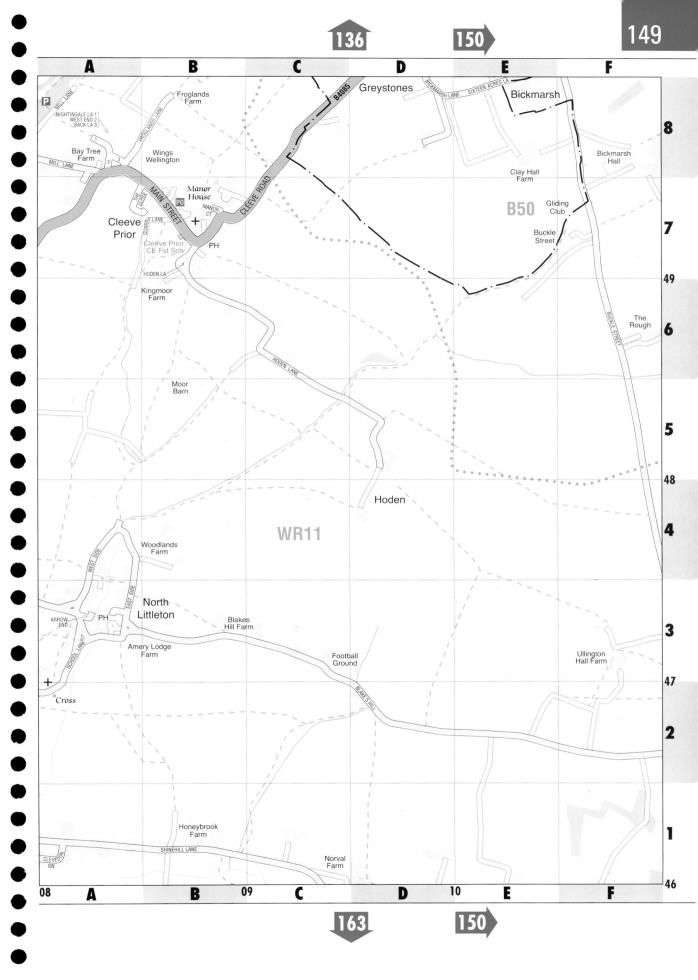

136
150

A B C D E F

8
7
49
6

5
48
4

3
47
2

1
46

Greystones

Bickmarsh Lane   Sixteen Acres La

Bickmarsh

B4085

Froglands Farm

Clay Hall Farm

Bickmarsh Hall

MILL LANE

P

NIGHTINGALE LA 1
WEST END 2
BACK LA 3

Bay Tree Farm

Wings Wellington

FROGLANDS LANE

B50

Gliding Club

MILL LANE

1
2 3

THE CLOSE

MAIN STREET

Manor House

PO

MANOR CT

CLEEVE ROAD

Buckle Street

Cleeve Prior

QUARRY LANE

+

Cleeve Prior CE Fst Sch

PH

HODEN LA

BUCKLE STREET

Kingmoor Farm

The Rough

HODEN LANE

Moor Barn

WR11

Hoden

Woodlands Farm

North Littleton

Blakes Hill Farm

Ullington Hall Farm

WEST SIDE

EAST SIDE

ARROW END

PH

Amery Lodge Farm

Football Ground

SCHOOL LANE

BLAKE'S HILL

+

Cross

Honeybrook Farm

CLEVEDON GN

SHINEHILL LANE

Norval Farm

08   A   B   09   C   D   10   E   F

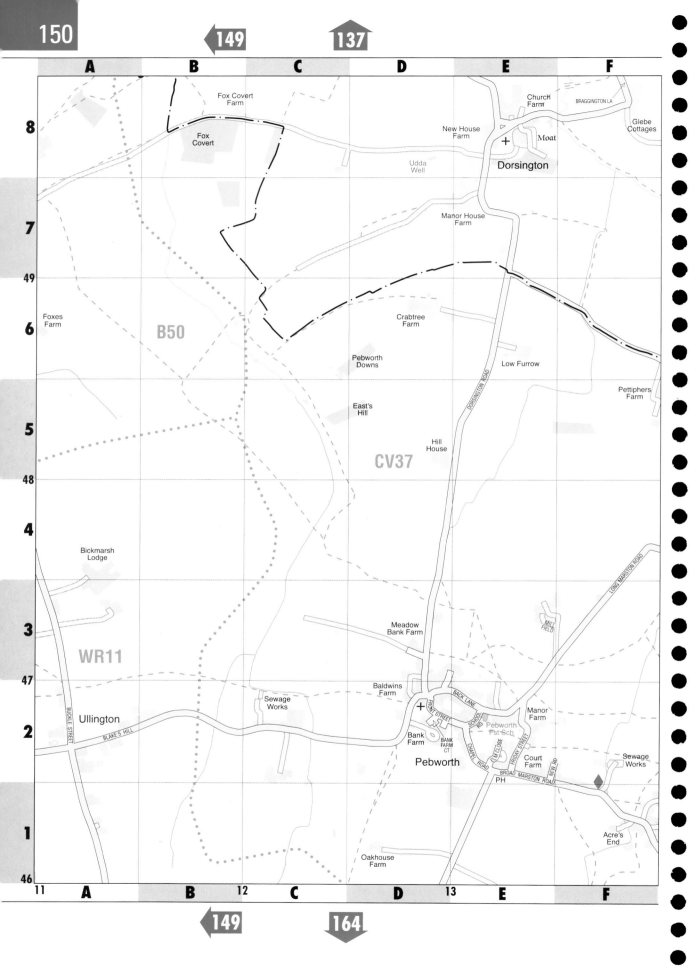

A B C D E F

8

7

49

6

5

48

4

3

47

2

1

46

Fox Covert
Farm

Fox
Covert

Church
Farm

BRAGGINGTON LA

Glebe
Cottages

New House
Farm

Moat

Dorsington

Udda
Well

Manor House
Farm

Foxes
Farm

B50

Crabtree
Farm

Pebworth
Downs

Low Furrow

DORSINGTON ROAD

Pettiphers
Farm

East's
Hill

CV37

Hill
House

Bickmarsh
Lodge

LONG MARSTON ROAD

MILL
FIELD

Meadow
Bank Farm

WR11

Baldwins
Farm

Manor
Farm

Sewage
Works

BACK LANE

FRONT STREET

SCHOOL RD

Pebworth
Fst Sch

Ullington

BUCKLE STREET

BLAKE'S HILL

Bank
Farm

BANK
FARM
CT

CHAPEL ROAD

ELM CLOSE

FRIDAY STREET

NEW RD

Court
Farm

Sewage
Works

Pebworth

PH

BROAD MARSTON ROAD

Acre's
End

Oakhouse
Farm

11 A B 12 C D 13 E F

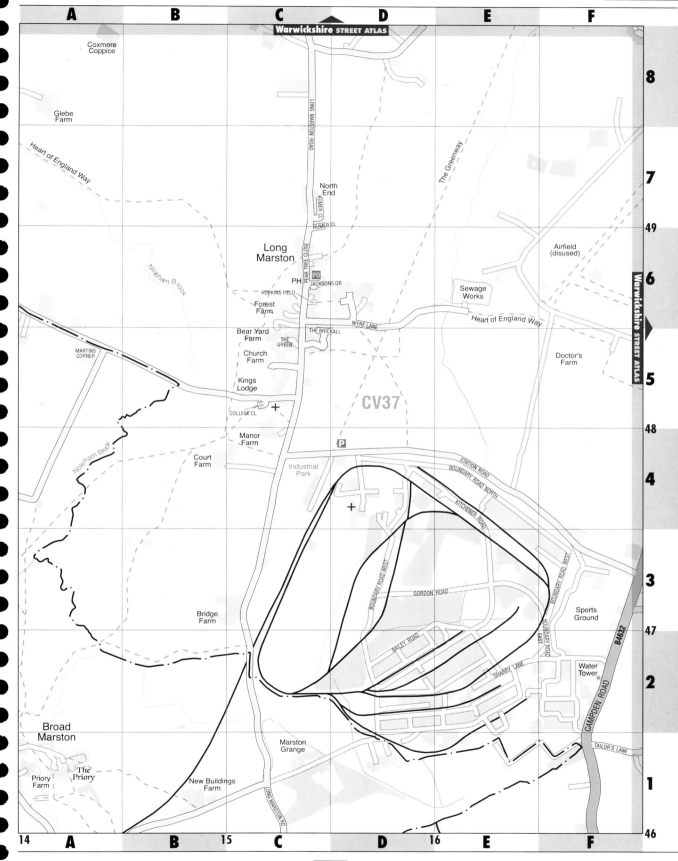

Coxmere
Coppice

Glebe
Farm

Heart of England Way

North
End

Long
Marston

Noleham Brook

The Greenway

Airfield
(disused)

RUMER CL

PEAR TREE CLOSE

PH
PO
JACKSONS OR

HOPKINS FIELD

Forest
Farm

WYRE LANE

Sewage
Works

Heart of England Way

Bear Yard
Farm

THE BRICKALL

THE
GREEN

Church
Farm

Doctor's
Farm

MARTINS
CORNER

Kings
Lodge

CV37

COLLEGE CL

Manor
Farm

Noleham Brook

Court
Farm

Industrial
Park

STATION ROAD

BOUNDARY ROAD NORTH

KITCHENER ROAD

Bridge
Farm

GORDON ROAD

BOUNDARY ROAD WEST

BOUNDARY ROAD EAST

BOUNDARY ROAD WEST

Sports
Ground

B4632

BAILEY ROAD

SHARRY LANE

Water
Tower

Broad
Marston

Marston
Grange

CAMPDEN ROAD

Priory
Farm

The
Priory

New Buildings
Farm

LONG MARSTON RD

TAILOR'S LANE

8
7
49
6
5
48
4
3
47
2
1
46

14   A   B   15   C   D   16   E   F

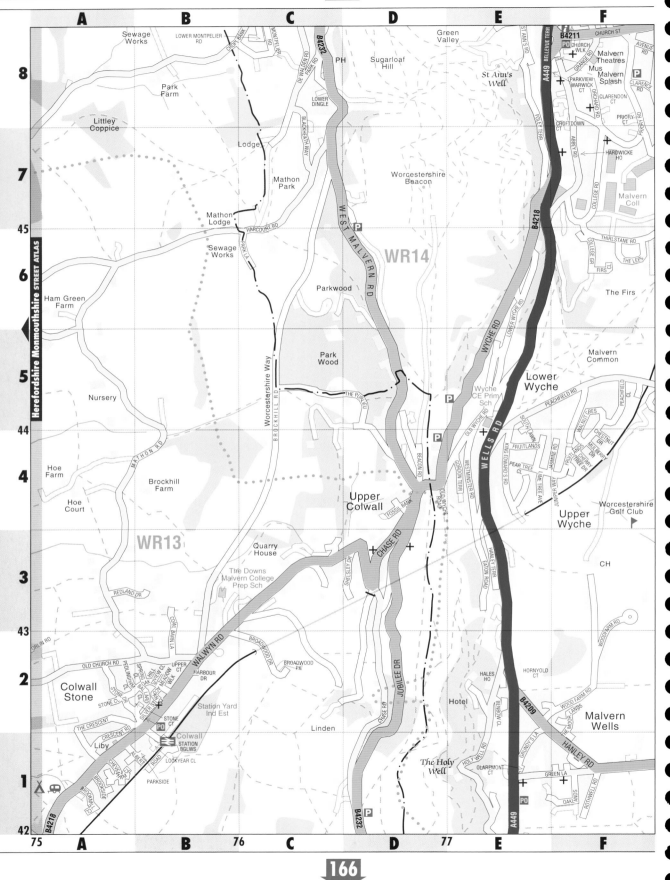

138

A   B   C   D   E   F

8

Sewage Works

LOWER MONTPELIER RD

Park Farm

Littley Coppice

Green Valley

Sugarloaf Hill

St Ann's Well

CHURCH ST

B4211

Malvern Theatres

Mus
Malvern Splash

PARKVIEW WARWICK CT

AVENUE RD

CLARENDON RD

PRIORY CT

DE WALDEN RD

MONTPELIER RD

CROFT BANK

PARK RD

B4232

PH

ST ANN'S RD

BELLEVUE TERR

A449

GRANGE RD

ORCHARD RD

CLARENDON CT

CROFTDOWN CT

7

Lodge

Mathon Park

Worcestershire Beacon

Malvern Coll

HARDWICKE HO

ABBEY RD

COLLEGE RD

FOLEY TERR

45

Mathon Lodge

HARCOURT RD

WEST MALVERN RD

WR14

B4218

THIRLSTANE RD

COLLEGE GR

FIRS CL

THE LEES

The Firs

6

Ham Green Farm

Sewage Works

PARK LA

Parkwood

WYCHE RD

LOWER WYCHE RD

Herefordshire Monmouthshire STREET ATLAS

5

Nursery

Worcestershire Way

BROCKHILL RD

Park Wood

THE PURLIEU

Wyche CE Prim Sch

P

P

OLD WYCHE RD

Lower Wyche

Malvern Common

PEACHFIELD RD

WALNUT CRES

PEACHFIELD CL

CHESTNUT DR

MULBERRY CL

44

Hoe Farm

MATHON RD

Brockhill Farm

WR13

BEACON RD

WELLS RD

GORDON TERR

WESTMINSTER RD

FRUITLANDS

KING EDWARD RD

SOUTH LAWN

JASMINE RD

PEAR TREE CL

LIME TREE AVE

FRUITLANDS

CHERRY TREE DR

4

Hoe Court

Upper Colwall

FOSSIL BANK

OLD WYCHE ROAD

JUNIPER WAY

Worcestershire Golf Club

Upper Wyche

3

REDLAND DR

The Downs Malvern College Prep Sch

Quarry House

SHELSLEY DR

CHASE RD

HANLEY TERR

EATON ROAD

CH

WOODFARM RD

43

CORLIN RD

COWL BARN LA

WALWYN RD

BROADWOOD DR

BROADWOOD PK

JUBILEE DR

CHASE RD

HORNYOLD CT

2

Colwall Stone

OLD CHURCH RD

PEDLINGHAM CT

SPRING HILL

UPPER CT

HARBOUR DR

MEADOW WLK

BROAD VIEW CL

STONE CL

STONE CT

Station Yard Ind Est

Linden

HALES HO

Hotel

BENBOW CL

HOLY WELL RD

B4209

WOOD FARM RD

HE MOOR

Malvern Wells

THE CRESCENT

CRESCENT RD

SILVER TER

STONE CT

PO

Colwall STATION BGLWS

LOCKYEAR CL

The Holy Well

CLAREMONT CT

HANLEY RD

GREEN LA

OAKLANDS

ROTHWELL RD

1

Liby

BROXASH RD

BROOKSIDE

CHEVIDT PK

PARKSIDE

A449

PO

42

B4218

B4232

P

A449

75   A   76   B   C   77   D   E   78   F

166

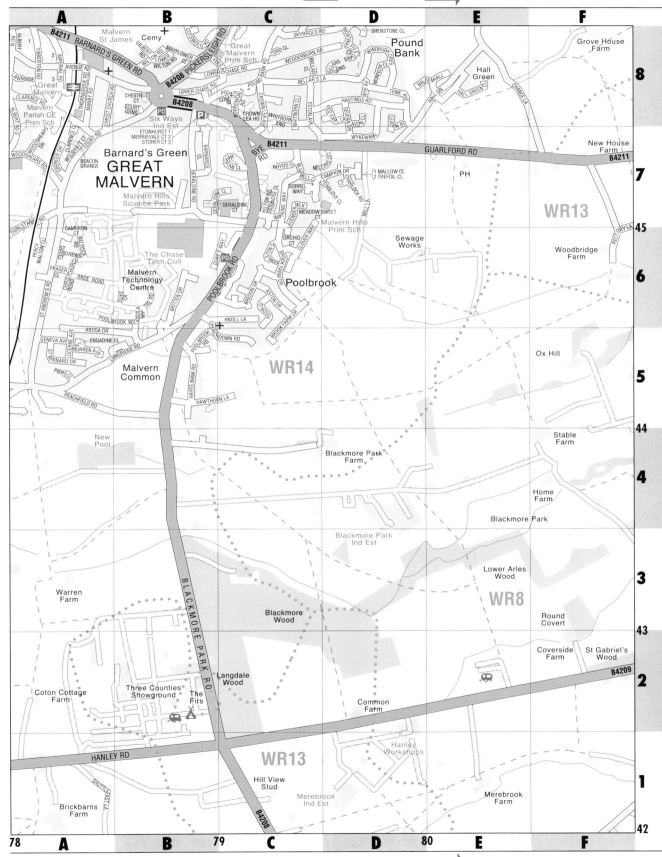

139
154

A8
1 TIBBERTON GRANGE
2 BIRCHWOOD
3 ST MARGARETS

A **B** **C** **D** **E** **F**

8
7
45
6
5
44
4
3
43
2
1
42

Malvern
St James
Cemy

Great
Malvern Prim Sch

BARNARD'S GREEN RD
B4211

Pound
Bank

SHENSTONE CL
SKYRROLD RD

Hall
Green

Grove House
Farm

GUARLFORD RD

New House
Farm
B4211

B4208 PICKERSLEIGH RD

Great
Malvern

Six Ways
Ind Est

ETONHURST 1
MERRIEVALE CT 2
STORER CT 3

Barnard's Green
**GREAT
MALVERN**

Malvern Parish CE
Prim Sch

BEACON
GRANGE

Malvern Hills
Science Park

The Chase
Tech Coll

Malvern
Technology
Centre

Poolbrook

Malvern Hills
Prim Sch

1 MALLOW CL
2 TREFOIL CL

PH

WR13

Sewage
Works

Woodbridge
Farm

B4211

Ox Hill

KNOLL LA

Malvern
Common

WR14

New
Pool

Blackmore Park
Farm

Stable
Farm

Home
Farm

Blackmore Park

Warren
Farm

BLACKMORE PARK RD

Blackmore
Wood

Blackmore Park
Ind Est

Lower Arles
Wood

WR8

Round
Covert

Langdale
Wood

Coton Cottage
Farm

Three Counties
Showground

The
Firs

Common
Farm

Coverside
Farm

St Gabriel's
Wood

B4209

HANLEY RD

WR13

Hill View
Stud

Hanley
Workshops

Merebrook
Farm

Brickbarns
Farm

Merebrook
Ind Est

B4208

78 79 80

A B C D E F

8

Garter Wood

South Wood

White House Farm

BLAKES LANE

Dripshill Wood

The Coppice

River Severn

Guarlford Court Farm

WR13

B4424

Dripshill Farm

7

GUARLFORD ROAD

B4211

Grange Farm

PENNY LANE
BAMFORD CLOSE
PENNY CL

PH

Fowlers Farm

B4211

Rhydd Green

Rhydd

RECTORY LANE

Guarlford

45

Pool Brook

Rhydd Farm

Priestfield Farm

6

Honeypot Farm

Mole End

Priestfield

Jubilee Plantation

Square Plantation

Cliffey Wood

5

Blackmore End

Sink Farm

Water Wheel Covert

Blackmore End Farm

Broadacres Farm

HANGMAN'S LANE

44

Sink Covert

B4211

4

Tickeridge Farm

Northend Farm

Church Covert

Moat

Cross

Shaw Lane Farm

WR8

The Gorse

3

Day's Coppice

Fairway Kingswarden

Mossford Bank

Horton Manor Farm

COVERFIELD

43

B4209

PO

Hanley Swan

Yew Tree Farm

Roberts End Cott

Merevale Farm

2

HANLEY ORCH

THE WALNUTS

Old Parsonage Farm

B4209

WESTMERE

WINNINGTON GDNS

Picken End

PO

Hanley Castle St Gabriel with St Mary CE Prim Sch

Quakers Farm

Chestnuts Farm

Brickwalls Farm

Holloway Farm

GILBERTS END LANE

Hanley Castle

1

Gilbert's End

Sewage Works

Hanley Castle High Sch

Brook Farm

42

81 A B 82 C D 83 E F

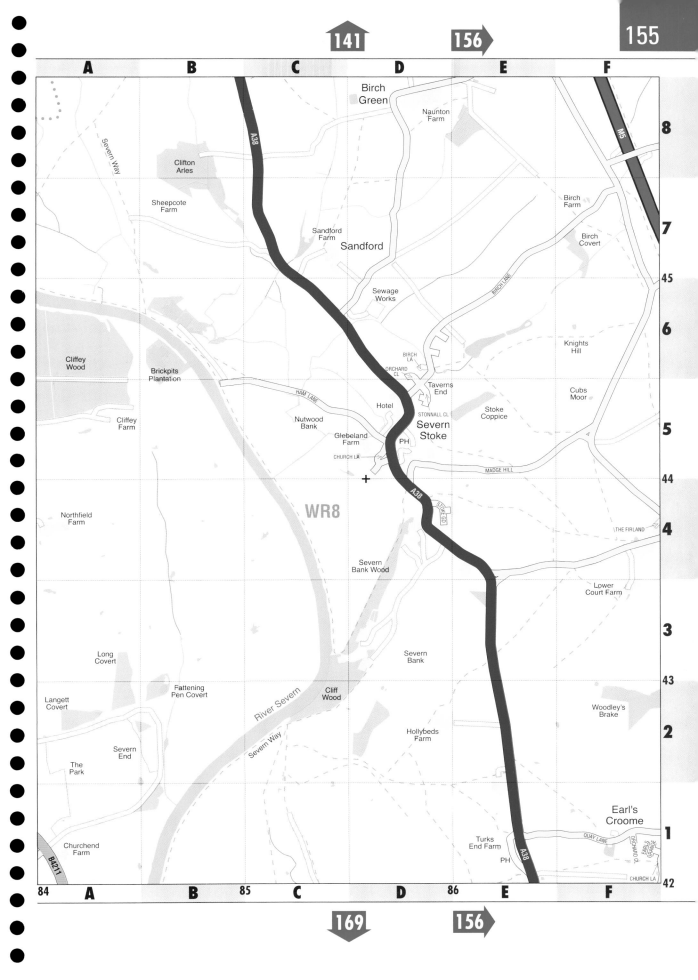

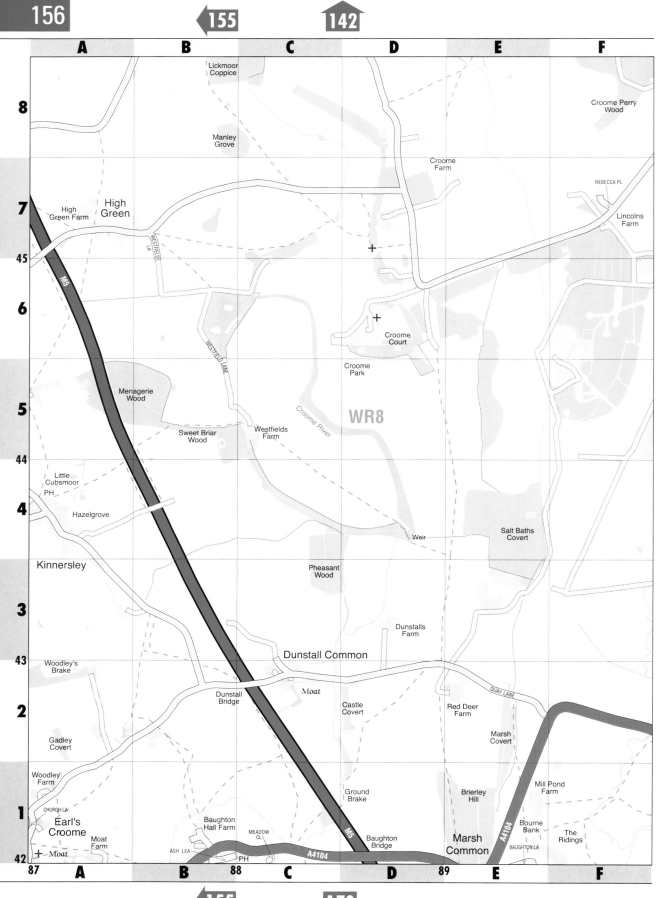

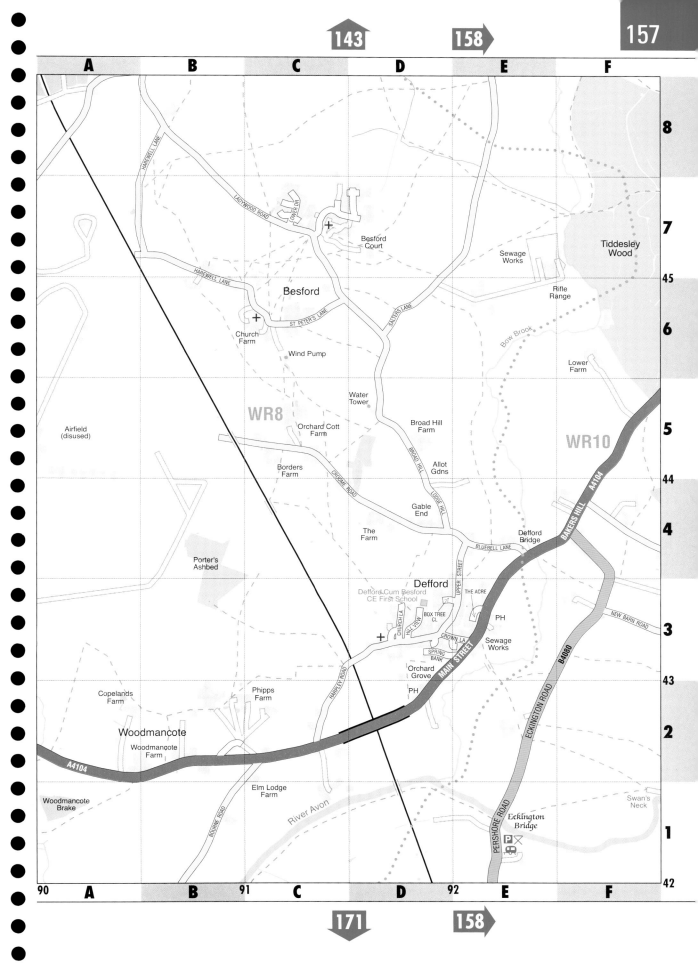

157   144

C8
1 HOLLOWAY
2 ABBOTS GRANGE
3 ORCHARD CL
4 ALTHORP GDNS

D8
1 HEAD ST
2 ST AGATHAS RD
3 ST AGATHA'S CL
4 MONKS CL
5 LITTLE PRIEST LA
6 LOWER PRIEST LA

7 CHURCH ST
8 CHURCH ROW
9 BETJEMAN CL
10 CHURCH WK
11 MASONS RYDE
12 OLD SCHOOL CL
13 THE MILESTONE

14 GANDERTON CT
15 ALMONRY CL

A   B   C   D   E   F

8

Tiddesley Wood

PERSHORE

HUNTER RISE
CONINGSBY DRIVE
AMES RD
ABBEYCROFT
NEW ROAD
NEWLANDS
GD STILES
A4104
NEW ROAD
Liby
Football Ground
Pershore L Ctr
Visitor Ctr
Superstore
The Holy Redeemer RC Prim Sch
Weir
Abbey Park Fst Sch
Pershore Abbey
Abbey Park
HIGH ST
KING GEORGE WY
PO

THREE SPRINGS ROAD

Cemy

LONG HEDGES

ORCHARD ROAD
FARLEIGH ROAD
WOODWARD ROAD
ABBOTS ROAD
WOOD TERR
ST ANDREW'S ROAD
PRIORS WK
ABBEY RD

B4536
WEIR GDNS
AVON MILL PL
Locks
Sports Ground
MANOR GD
B4084

7

Orchard Farm

Cemetery Farm

DEFFORD ROAD

CORNMORE
B4536
FARLEIGH ROAD
BIRLINGHAM CLOSE
FULBERT RD
DEFFORD ROAD
NOGAINS

BRIDGE STREET
Pershore Bridge

York Lane
Wicklands Farm
TIMBER DOWN
WICK HO CL
Wick Farm
TIMBER LANE

45

The Spinney

1 HANSON WY
2 PERSCORAN WY
3 GREAT CALCROFT
4 STONEWELL TERR

6

Tiddesley Wood

A4104

River Avon

C7
1 THREE SPRINGS RD
2 WOODWARD CL
3 FULBERT RD
4 CORNMORE
5 LITTLE PENNYROPE
6 SMITHS WY
7 FARNCOMBE TERR

Allot Gdns

PENSHAM HILL
Pensham Hill Cottages
Avonbank

Pershore Coll
Hazel Wood
Sports Ground

Mary Brook Farm

5

Home Farm

Pensham

WR10

Marybrook Bridge

44

Pensham Farm

Pensham Fields Farm

River Avon

4

Upper End

The Court

Lilworth Farm

The Ridings

NEW BARN RD

THE AVENUE

SHORTHILL

River Avon

3

CHURCH LA
RECTORY LA
PH
CHURCH STREET

Woodfield Farm

WHITEHALL LA

43

BROADWAY

Hall Farm

Kents Farm

QUAY LANE

2

Birlingham

BROADWAY ROAD

Lower End Farm

Great Comberton

GRANGE ROAD

Ringsmere

Tibbetts Farm

1

Lower End Farm

River Avon

Berwick Brook

Joes Farm

CHURCH LANE
RUSSELL STREET
MONGCROFT RD

Blackberry Farm

42

93   A   94   B   C   95   D   E   F

157   172

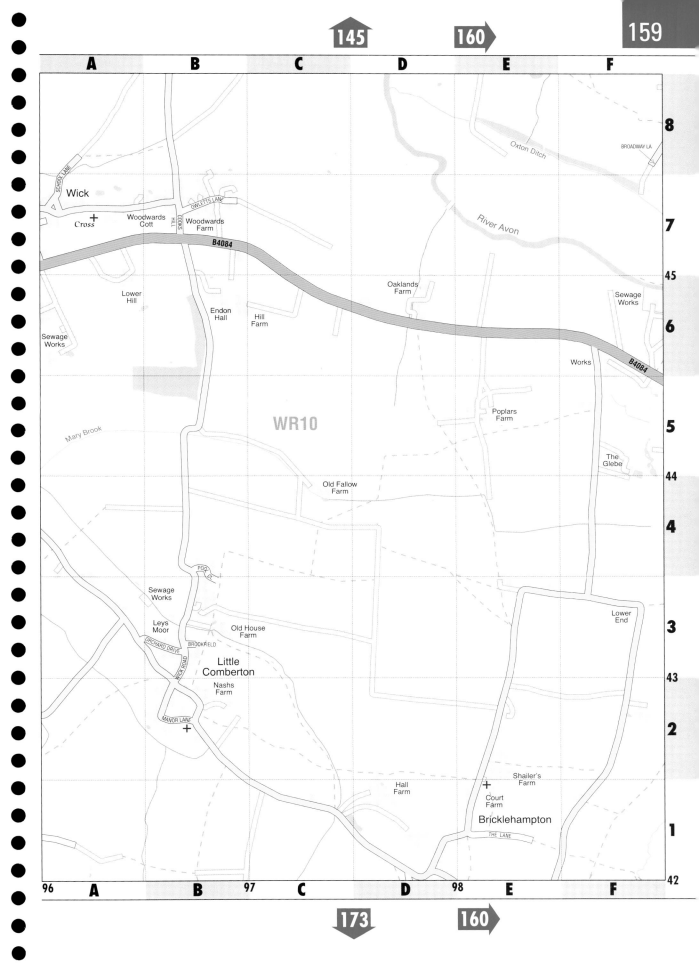

A B C D E F

8

BROADWAY LA

Oxton Ditch

River Avon

7

School Lane

Wick

Cross

Woodwards Cott

Owletts Lane

Woodwards Farm

Cooks Hill

B4084

45

Lower Hill

Endon Hall

Hill Farm

Oaklands Farm

Sewage Works

6

Sewage Works

Works

B4084

WR10

Poplars Farm

5

Mary Brook

The Glebe

44

Old Fallow Farm

4

Poll Cl

Sewage Works

Lower End

3

Leys Moor

Orchard Drive

Wick Road

Brookfield

Old House Farm

Little Comberton

43

Nashs Farm

Manor Lane

Hall Farm

Shailer's Farm

Court Farm

2

Bricklehampton

The Lane

1

42

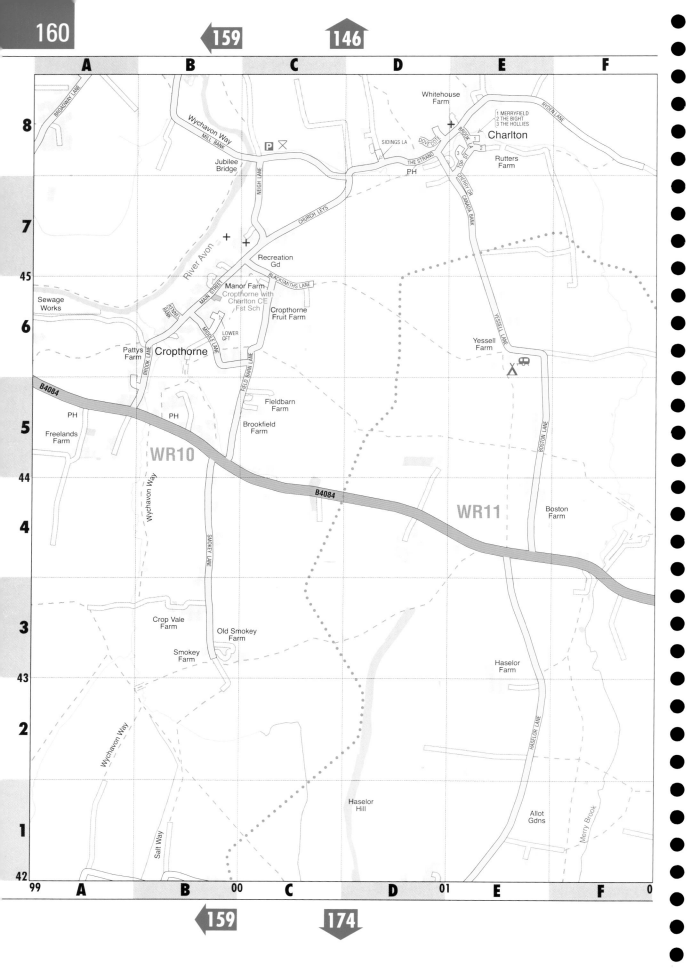

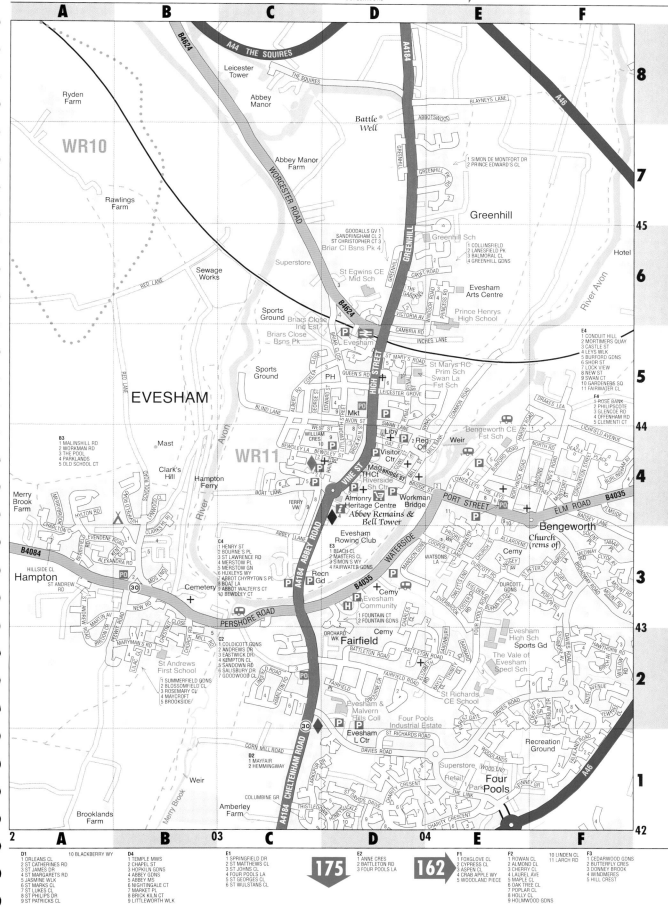

147
162
175
162

A B C D E F

8 7 45 6 5 44 4 3 43 2 1 42

D5
1 SHEPHERDS POOL
2 HENRY FOWLER CL
3 RUDGE RD
4 TERRILL CT
5 RIGHTONS CT
6 ST EGWIN'S RD

7 THE HODGES
8 DE LA BERE CL
9 BURLINGHAM CT

Ryden Farm

WR10

Rawlings Farm

Red Lane

Sewage Works

Leicester Tower

Abbey Manor

Abbey Manor Farm

WORCESTER ROAD

B4624

Battle Well

ABBOTSWOOD

BLAYNEYS LANE

A46

A4184

Greenhill

GREENHILL

Greenhill Sch

1 SIMON DE MONTFORT DR
2 PRINCE EDWARD'S CL

1 COLLINSFIELD
2 LANESFIELD PK
3 BALMORAL CL
4 GREENHILL GDNS

Hotel

River Avon

Superstore

GOODALLS GV 1
SANDRINGHAM CL 2
ST CHRISTOPHER CT 3
Briar Cl Bsns Pk 4

St Egwins CE Mid Sch

THE GARDENS

CROFT ROAD

Evesham Arts Centre

Prince Henrys High School

Sports Ground

Briars Close Ind Est

Briars Close Bsns Pk

B4624

Evesham

P

Victoria Av

CAMBRIA RD

INCHES LANE

COMMON ROAD

E4
1 CONDUIT HILL
2 MORTIMERS QUAY
3 CASTLE ST
4 LEYS WLK
5 BURFORD GDNS
6 SHOR ST
7 LOCK VIEW
8 NEW ST
9 SWAN CT
10 GARDENERS SQ
11 FAIRWATER CL

Sports Ground

River Avon

EVESHAM

WR11

PH

HIGH STREET

ST MARY'S ROAD

St Marys RC Prim Sch Swan La Fst Sch

Leicester Grove

DRAKES LEA

LICHFIELD AVENUE

F4
1 ROSE BANK
2 PHILIPSCOTE
3 GLENCOE RD
4 OFFENHAM RD
5 CLEMENTI CT

B3
1 MALINSHILL RD
2 WORKMAN RD
3 THE POOL
4 PARKLANDS
5 OLD SCHOOL CT

Mast

Clark's Hill

Hampton Ferry

Mkt

PO

Liby

Weir

Reg Off

Bengeworth CE Fst Sch

P

HARVEY ROAD

NORTH RD

Merry Brook Farm

Hampton

Cemetery

SCHOOL ROAD

RED LANE

HYLTON RD

CHARLTON CV

EVENDENE ROAD

BERRYFIELD

ALEXANDRA RD

HILLSIDE CL

ST ANDREW RD

B4084

PO

30

CLARKS LA

Visitor Ctr

BEWDLEY LA

WILLIAM CRES

WEST ST

BLIND LANE

AVON ST

LITTLEWORTH STREET

BRICK KILN ST

BEWDLEY

BOAT LANE

ABBEY LANE

FERRY VW

VINE ST

BRIDGE ST

Mag THCt

Riverside Sh Ctr

Almonry Heritage Centre

Abbey Remains & Bell Tower

Evesham Rowing Club

Workman Bridge

PORT STREET

Bengeworth

Church (rems of)

Cemy

LOWER LEYS

COOPER'S LANE

PRIORS

WATSONS LA

MANSION CL

DURCOTT RD

ST PETER'S LA

ELM ROAD

B4035

MSIDE

TAM46

MEDWAY RD

CLYDE

MOUNT RD

MOUNT RD

C4
1 HENRY ST
2 BOURNE'S PL
3 ST LAWRENCE RD
4 MERSTOW PL
5 MERSTOW GN
6 HUXLEYS WY
7 ABBOT CHYRYTON'S PL
8 BOAT LA
9 ABBOT WALTER'S CT
10 BEWDLEY CT

E3
1 BEACH CL
2 MASTERS CL
3 SIMON'S WY
4 FAIRWATER GDNS

Recn Gd

P

Cemy

P

Evesham Community

H

WATERSIDE

A4184 ABBEY ROAD

B4035

1 FOUNTAIN CT
2 FOUNTAIN GDNS

ORCHARD WK

Fairfield

Cemy

BATTLETON ROAD

Evesham High Sch Sports Gd

The Vale of Evesham Specl Sch

HAWTHORN RD

SCAMBRO ROAD

DAVIES ROAD

BIRCH AV

WILLOW RD

C2
1 COLDICOTT GDNS
2 ANDREWS DR
3 EASTWICK DR
4 KEMPTON CL
5 SANDOWN RD
6 SALISBURY DR
7 GOODWOOD CL

St Andrews First School

MARYMAN'S RD

CHESTNUT CLOSE

NEW RD

PERSHORE ROAD

30

PO

LINGS RD

HAMILTON RD

Fairfield

St Richards CE School

FAIRFIELD ROAD

DAVIES ROAD

CREST GATE

WOODLANDS

HAZEL AVE

YEW TREE

LABURNUM

COLE GR

D2
1 MAYFAIR
2 HEMMINGWAY

1 SUMMERFIELD GDNS
2 BLOSSOMFIELD CL
3 ROSEMARY CL
4 MAYCROFT
5 BROOKSIDE

Evesham & Malvern Hills Coll

Four Pools Industrial Estate

Evesham L Ctr

30

CORN MILL ROAD

CHELTENHAM ROAD

A4184

LARKSLAP DR

Weir

Brooklands Farm

Merry Brook

Amberley Farm

COLUMBINE GR

AMBERLEY

THISTLEDOWN

ST OSVALDS DRIVE

HONEYSUCKLE

Superstore

Retail Park

WOOD END

Four Pools

ST RICHARDS ROAD

DAVIES ROAD

Recreation Ground

THE LINK

SPINNEY GR

FALKLAND ROAD

A46

CHARITY CRESCENT

CRESENT

D1
1 ORLEANS CL
2 ST CATHERINES RD
3 ST JAMES DR
4 ST MARGARETS RD
5 JASMINE WLK
6 ST MARKS CL
7 ST LUKES CL
8 ST PHILIPS DR
9 ST PATRICKS CL

10 BLACKBERRY WY

D4
1 TEMPLE MWS
2 CHAPEL ST
3 HOPKILN GDNS
4 ABBEY GDNS
5 ABBEY MS
6 NIGHTINGALE CT
7 MARKET PL
8 BRICK KILN CT
9 LITTLEWORTH WLK

E1
1 SPRINGFIELD DR
2 ST MATTHEWS CL
3 ST JOHNS CL
4 FOUR POOLS LA
5 ST GEORGES CL
6 ST WULSTANS CL

E2
1 ANNE CRES
2 BATTLETON RD
3 FOUR POOLS LA

F1
1 FOXGLOVE CL
2 CYPRESS CL
3 ASPEN CL
4 CRAB APPLE WY
5 WOODLAND PIECE

F2
1 ROWAN CL
2 ALMOND CL
3 CHERRY CL
4 LAUREL AVE
5 MAPLE CL
6 OAK TREE CL
7 POPLAR CL
8 HOLLY CL
9 HOLMWOOD GDNS

10 LINDEN CL
11 LARCH RD

F3
1 CEDARWOOD GDNS
2 BUTTERFLY CRES
3 DONNEY BROOK
4 WINDMERES
5 HILL CREST

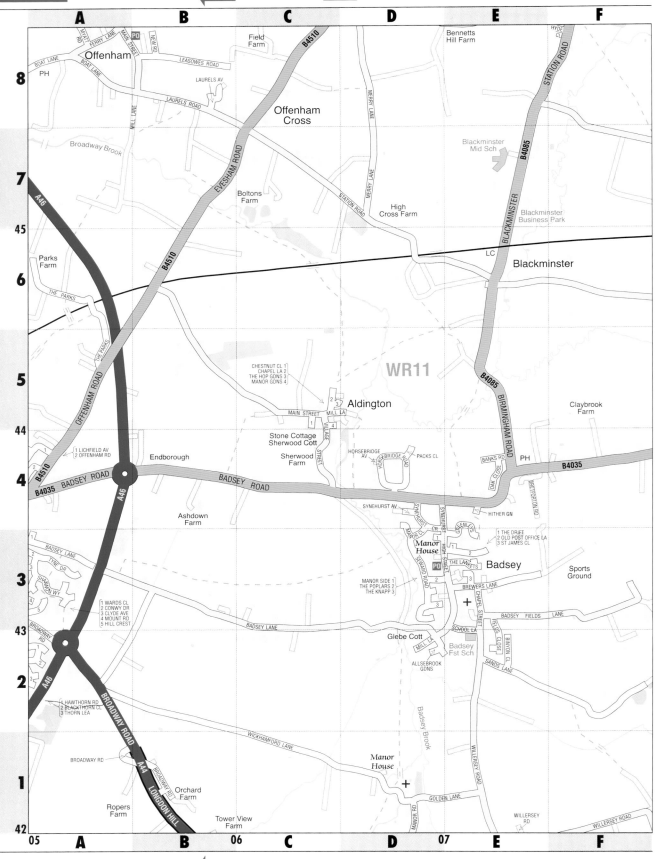

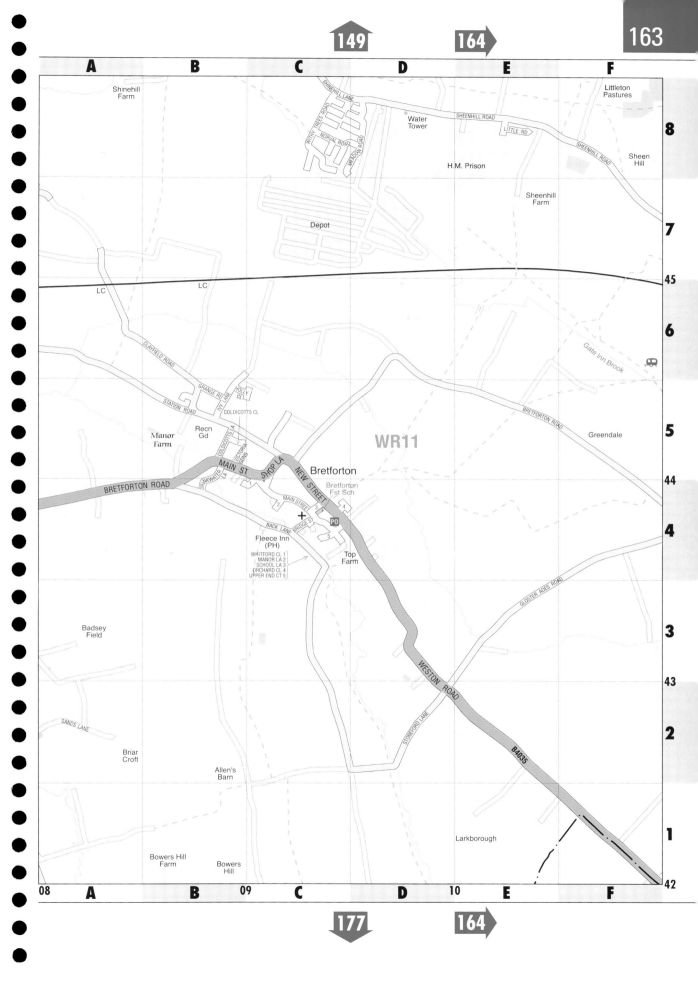

163
150

A **B** **C** **D** **E** **F**

8

Tump Bew Hill

Bew Hill Farm

Pebworth Fields Farm

CV37

7

Blenheim Farm

Baylis's Hill

BUCKLE STREET

SHEENHILL ROAD

Brickworks Trading Estate

Grove Farm

STRATFORD ROAD

45

Peace Egg Farm

Kite's Hill

Honeybourne ⇄

6

BRUNEL WY 1
CHURCHWARD CL 2
GOOCH CL 3

STEPHENSON WAY

Bushy Hill

Bushy Hill Buildings

DUDLEY RD
HARVARD RD
PERRY DR
PENNBOROUGH AV
WESTBOURNE AV
HUDSON RD
WESTBOURNE
GROVE AV

BEAUFORT END

Norton Hall Farm

Domestic Fowl Trust & Honeybourne Rare Breeds

STATION ROAD

5

Cemy

Dairyfield Covert

Honeybourne

STRATFORD ROAD

PH Gate Inn Bridge

Manor Farm

LC

New Hill

44

Corner Farm

HIGH STREET

CORNER FARM DR

GREEN CL
SCHOOL ST
REDDIS
FRESE

MICKLETON ROAD

WR11

PO

BRETFORTON RD
GLOSTER ADES RD

Honeybourne First Sch

CHY CS

4

BRICK WALK

MANOR CL

Mill Mound

PODEN LANE

Manor Farm

The Green Farm

Poden Farm

Weston Fields Farm

3

WESTON ROAD

Far Poden Farm

Moat

43

Long Stretch Farm

GL55

2

Tower Farm

Sewage Works

PODEN LANE

1

HONEYBOURNE ROAD

Honeybourne Airfield Trad Est

Works

42

11 **A** **B** **12** **C** **D** **13** **E** **F**

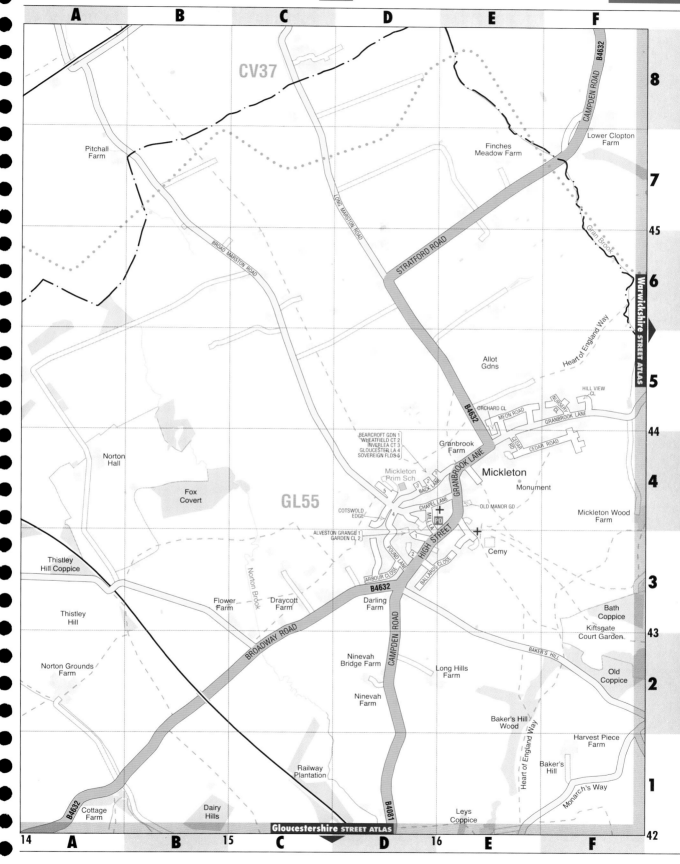

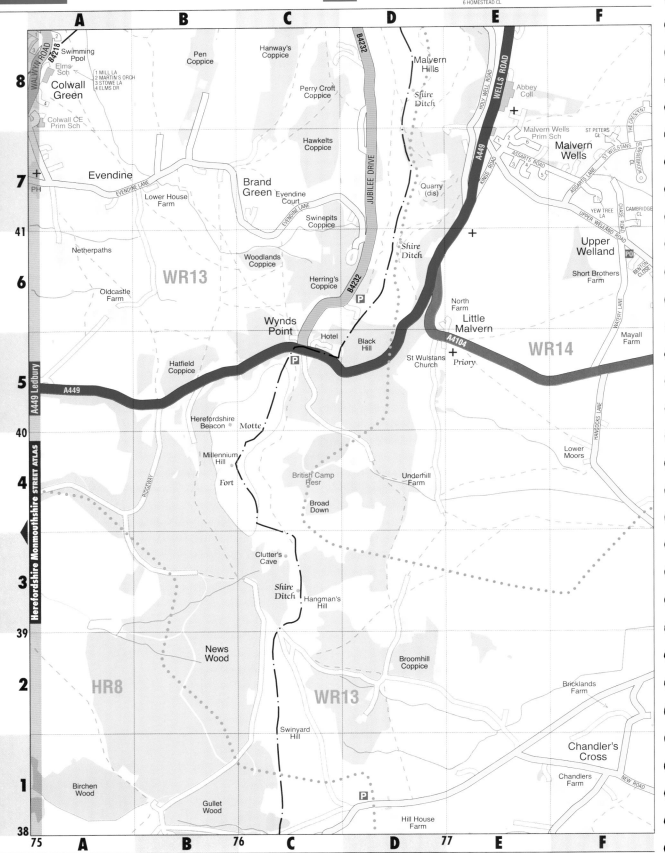

E7
1 RICHMONDS PITCH
2 KINGS RD
3 WOODLANDS CL
4 WELLS CL
5 HEATHLANDS CL
6 HOMESTEAD CL

A B C D E F

8

Swimming Pool

WALWYN ROAD

B4218

Elms Sch

Colwall Green

Colwall CE Prim Sch

1 MILL LA
2 MARTIN'S ORCH
3 STOWE LA
4 ELMS DR

Pen Coppice

Hanway's Coppice

B4232

Malvern Hills

Shire Ditch

Abbey Coll

HOLY WELL ROAD

WELLS ROAD

THE CRESCENT

Perry Croft Coppice

Malvern Wells Prim Sch

ST PETERS CL

Malvern Wells

ST WULSTANS DR

BROMYARD

7

Evendine

PH

Lower House Farm

EVENDINE LANE

Brand Green

Evendine Court

EVENDINE LANE

Hawkelts Coppice

A449

JUBILEE DRIVE

KINGS ROAD

ASSARTS ROAD

ASSARTS LANE

ST WULSTANS LA

YEW TREE LA

CAMBRIDGE CL

41

Swinepits Coppice

Quarry (dis)

UPPER WELLAND ROAD

Upper Welland

PO

BENTON CLOSE

6

WR13

Netherpaths

Woodlands Coppice

Herring's Coppice

B4232

P

Shire Ditch

North Farm

Little Malvern

Short Brothers Farm

WATERY LANE

Oldcastle Farm

Wynds Point

Hotel

Black Hill

A4104

WR14

Mayall Farm

5

A449 Ledbury

A449

Hatfield Coppice

P

St Wulstans Church

Priory

HANDOCKS LANE

40

Herefordshire Beacon

Motte

Lower Moors

Herefordshire Monmouthshire STREET ATLAS

4

Millennium Hill

Fort

RIDGEWAY

British Camp Resr

Underhill Farm

Broad Down

3

Clutter's Cave

Shire Ditch

Hangman's Hill

39

News Wood

Broomhill Coppice

Bricklands Farm

2

HR8

WR13

NEW ROAD

Chandler's Cross

Swinyard Hill

Chandlers Farm

1

Birchen Wood

P

Gullet Wood

Hill House Farm

38

75 A B 76 C D 77 E F

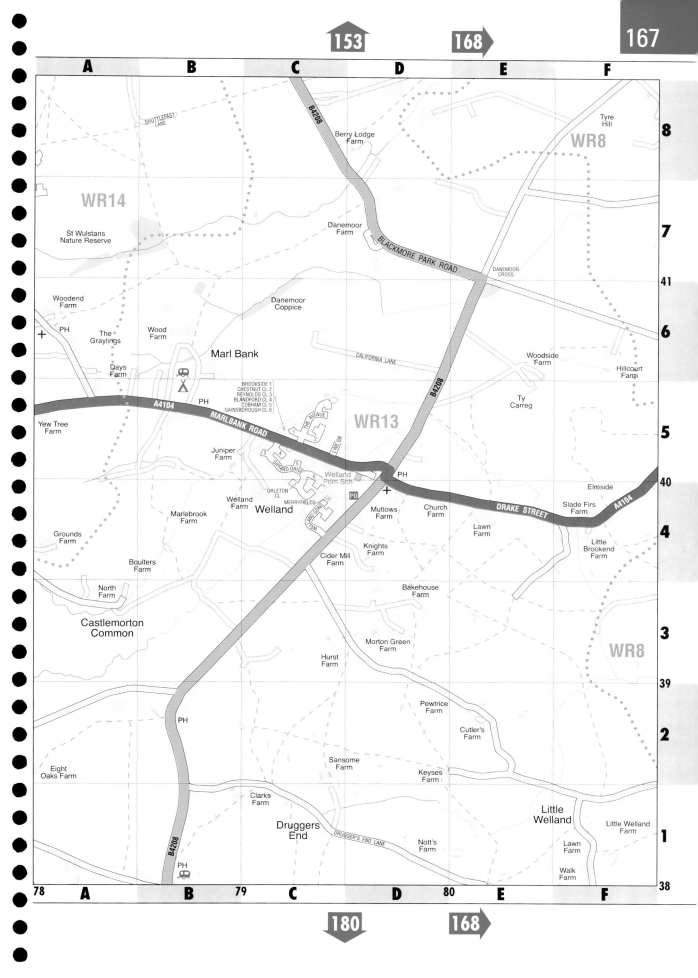

A B C D E F

8 WR8
Tyre Hill

SHUTTLEFAST LANE

Berry Lodge Farm

WR14

7
St Wulstans Nature Reserve

Danemoor Farm

BLACKMORE PARK ROAD

DANEMOOR CROSS

41

6
Woodend Farm

Danemoor Coppice

PH
The Graylings

Wood Farm

Marl Bank

CALIFORNIA LANE

Woodside Farm

Hillcourt Farm

Days Farm

B4208

Ty Carreg

A4104
Yew Tree Farm

MARLBANK ROAD
PH

BROOKSIDE 1
CHESTNUT CL 2
REYNOLDS CL 3
BLANDFORD CL 4
COBHAM CL 5
GAINSBOROUGH CL 6

THE AVENUE

2

WR13

5

Juniper Farm

3

4

5

GIFFARD DRIVE

6

LIME GR

Welland Prim Sch

PH

Elmside

40

Marlebrook Farm

Welland Farm

ORLETON CL

MERRYFIELDS

Welland

PO

Mutlows Farm

Church Farm

DRAKE STREET

Slade Firs Farm

A4104

Grounds Farm

Lawn Farm

Little Brookend Farm

4

Boulters Farm

Cider Mill Farm

Knights Farm

North Farm

Bakehouse Farm

Castlemorton Common

3 WR8

Morton Green Farm

39

Hurst Farm

Pewtrice Farm

2
PH

Cutler's Farm

Eight Oaks Farm

Sansome Farm

Keyses Farm

Clarks Farm

Little Welland

1
Druggers End

DRUGGER'S END LANE

Nott's Farm

Little Welland Farm

Lawn Farm

B4208
PH

Walk Farm

38

A B C D E F

8

Hanley Hall

Gilbert's End Farm

Lodge Farm

Hanley Castle High Sch

Mere Brook

Gilvers' Lane

7

Castle (site of)

Whitehall Farm

Brotheridge Green

Pigeon House Farm

Holyheads Parks

Melrose Farm

41

Clives Fruit Farm

Hook Bank Farm

6

The Hook

Upper Hook Farm

Hook Park Farm

The Boynes

UPPER HOOK ROAD

Tiltridge Farm Vineyard

The Ridings

Hook Bank

The Hyde

HYDE LANE

MULBERRY DR 1
OAKLAND CL 2
PERRINSFIELD 3

Anchor Inn (PH)

5

Lower Hook Farm

WR8

Hyde Farm

DRAKE STREET

A4104

Lower Hook

Tunnel Hill

Sports Ground

MILESTONE RD

Lake Farm

40

Palace Farm

LAWNSIDE CL

Upper Duckswich Farm

Milestone Farm

4

Welland Lodge Farm

Two Acre Covert

WELLAND ROAD

The Hillbee Farm

Duckswich Farm

Duckswich

Malt House Farm

Lockeridge Farm

Round Covert

Young Covert

Smokeacre Covert

LOCKERIDGE LANE

YEWLEIGH LANE

WHEATLEY LANE

Cowhills Farm

3

Welland Court

Big Covert

The Stanks

Highley Brake

39

Long Covert

STANKS LA

Welland Stone

2

Longdon Heath

Longdon Hill End

Mill Bank Farm

Worcestershire Way Link

Hill End Farm

The Reddings

1

Orchard Farm

Eastington Hall

38

81 A B 82 C D 83 E F

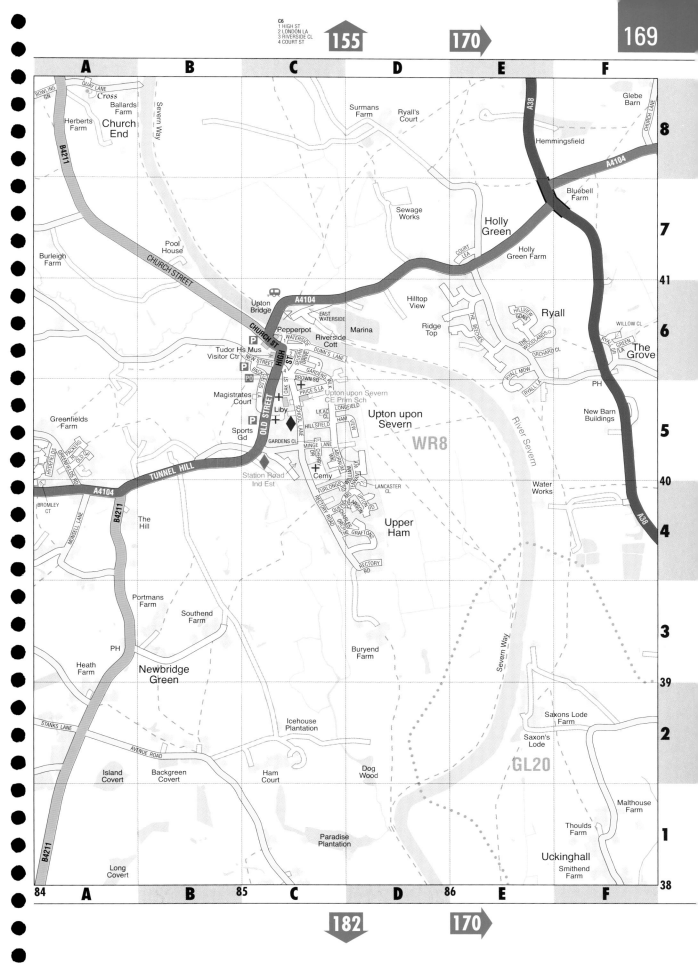

155
170
182
170

C6
1 HIGH ST
2 LONDON LA
3 RIVERSIDE CL
4 COURT ST

A B C D E F

8

Quay Lane
Cross
Ballards Farm
Church End
Herbts Farm
Severn Way
B4211
Glebe Barn
CHURCH LANE
Surmans Farm
Ryall's Court
Hemmingsfield
A38
A4104

7
Pool House
Burleigh Farm
CHURCH STREET
Upton Bridge
A4104
East Waterside
Pepperpot
Waterside
CHURCH ST
Riverside Cott
Marina
Holly Green
Bluebell Farm
Holly Green Farm
Court Lea

41

Hilltop View
Ridge Top
THE BEECHES
HILLVIEW GDNS
HILLVIEW
THE WOODLANDS
ORCHARD CL
Ryall
WILLOW CL
RYALL GR
RYALL GREEN
The Grove

6
Tudor Hs Mus Visitor Ctr
New Street
BACKFIELDS LA
PO
HIGH ST
DUNN'S LANE
GARDENS WLK
BROWN SQ
PRICE S LA
SCHOOL LANE
LILAC CL
HAM VIEW
HILLSFIELD
Upton upon Severn CE Prim Sch
RYALL MDW
RYALL LA
PH
New Barn Buildings

5
Magistrates Court
Liby
Sports Gd
OAK ST
OLD STREET
GARDENS CL
MINGE LANE
CHERRY ORD
LABURNUM WLK
TENNANT WY
Upton upon Severn
WR8
River Severn

40
Greenfields Farm
PACKERS HL OLD CL
GREENFIELDS RD
HYDEFIELDS
TUNNEL HILL
A4104
Station Road Ind Est
Cemy
FURLONGS
QUEENS DR
RECTORY ROAD
CHANNEL CL
MT PLEASANT
WILSON CL
LANCASTER CL
Upper Ham
UPTON GD
Water Works
A38

4
BROMLEY CT
B4211
MONSELL LANE
The Hill
THE GRAFTONS
RECTORY RD

3
Heath Farm
PH
Portmans Farm
Southend Farm
Newbridge Green
Buryend Farm
Severn Way

39
STANKS LANE
AVENUE ROAD
Icehouse Plantation
Saxons Lode Farm

2
Island Covert
Backgreen Covert
Ham Court
Dog Wood
Saxon's Lode
GL20
Malthouse Farm

1
B4211
Long Covert
Paradise Plantation
Uckinghall
Thoulds Farm
Smithend Farm

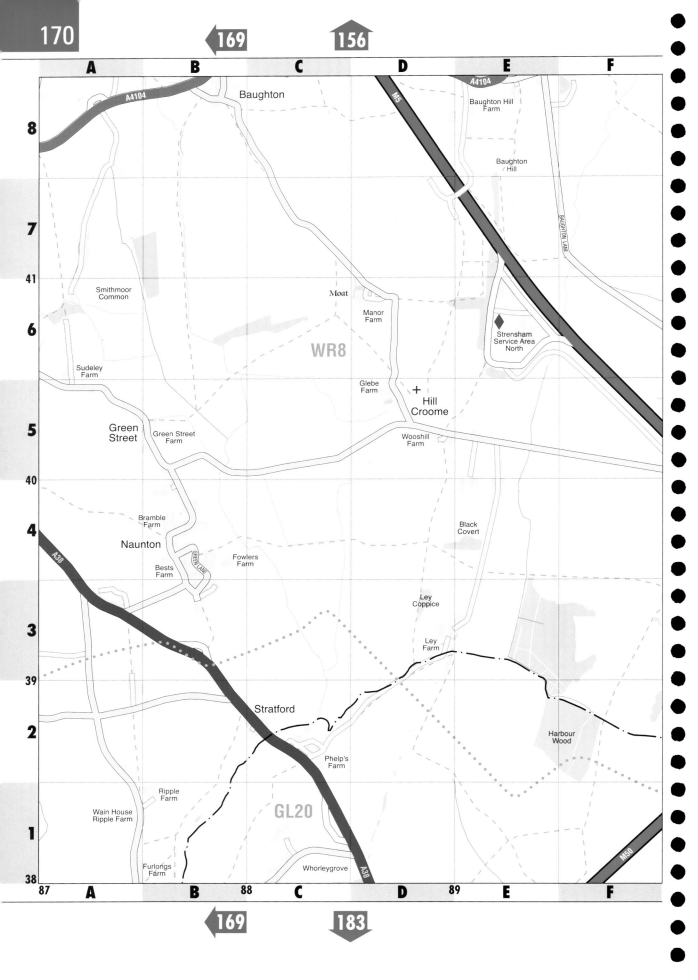

169
156

A   B   C   D   E   F

Baughton

A4104

Baughton Hill Farm

Baughton Hill

M5

8

BAUGHTON LANE

7

41

Smithmoor Common

Moat

Manor Farm

6

Strensham Service Area North

WR8

Sudeley Farm

Glebe Farm

Hill Croome

Green Street

Green Street Farm

Wooshill Farm

5

40

Bramble Farm

GREEN LANE

Black Covert

4

A38

Naunton

Fowlers Farm

Bests Farm

Ley Coppice

3

Ley Farm

39

Stratford

Harbour Wood

2

Phelp's Farm

Ripple Farm

GL20

Wain House Ripple Farm

1

M50

Furlongs Farm

Whorleygrove

A38

38

87   A   B   88   C   D   89   E   F

169
183

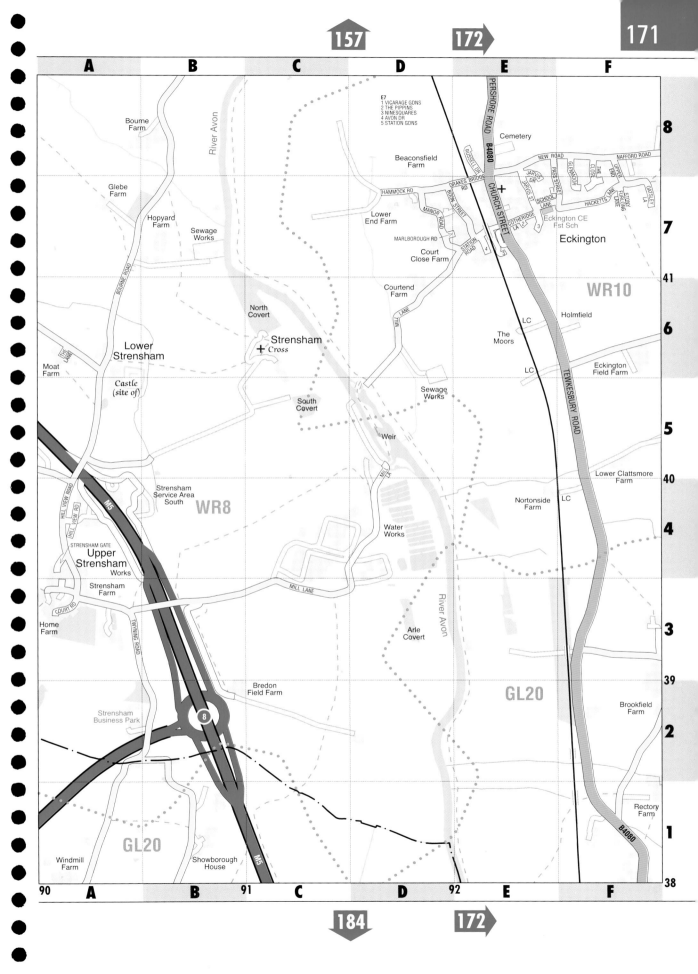

171
158

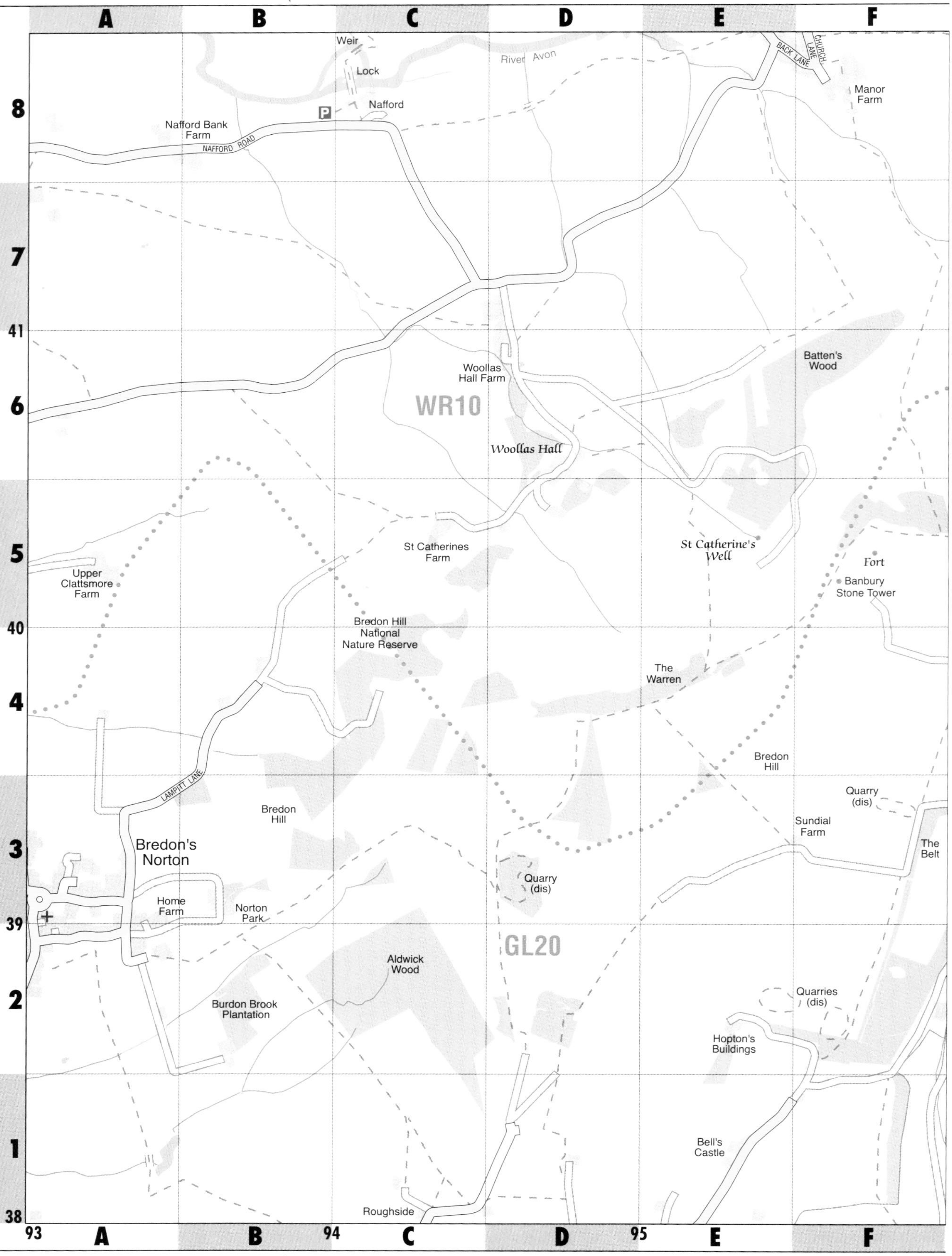

A B C D E F

8

Weir
Lock
Nafford
River Avon
Manor
Farm
P
Nafford Bank
Farm
NAFFORD ROAD
BACK LANE
CHURCH LANE

7

41

Woollas
Hall Farm
Batten's
Wood

6

WR10

Woollas Hall

5

Upper
Clattsmore
Farm
St Catherines
Farm
St Catherine's
Well
Fort
Banbury
Stone Tower

40

Bredon Hill
National
Nature Reserve
The
Warren

4

Bredon
Hill
Quarry
(dis)

3

Bredon
Hill
Sundial
Farm
The
Belt

Bredon's
Norton
Home
Farm
Norton
Park
Quarry
(dis)

39

GL20

2

Burdon Brook
Plantation
Aldwick
Wood
Quarries
(dis)
Hopton's
Buildings

1

Bell's
Castle

38

93 A 94 B C 95 D E F

Roughside

A B C D E F

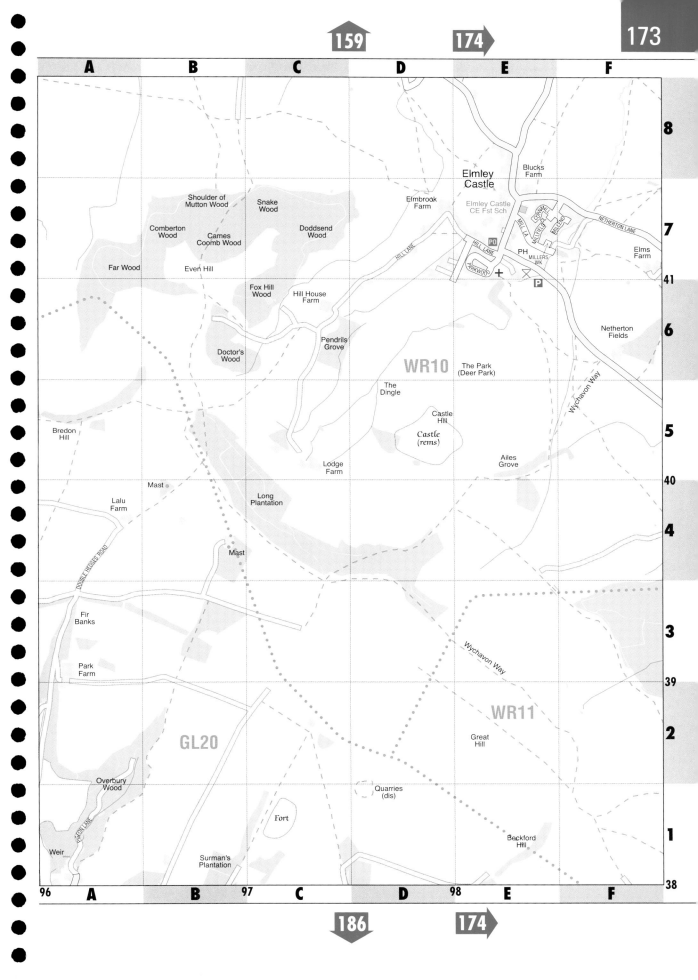

173 160

	A	B	C	D	E	F

Chapel Farm

Netherton

Chapel (remains of)

8

Upper Haselor Farm

Upper Haselor

Coppice Farm

Merry Brook

7

Netherton Lane

Wychavon Way

41

6

WR10

Furzehill Brake

5

Manor Farm

Middle Farm

Kersoe

Furzehill Farm

STATION ROAD

Ballard's Farm

STATION ROAD

Kersoe Farm

40

Furze Hill

WR11

4

Northfield Farm

Sandfield Farm

3

Ashton Wood

39

Holcomb Nap

Nap Coppice

Bredon Hill Mid Sch

CORNFIELD WAY

WOOD LA

GORSE HL

Sandfield Lane

A46

CHELTENHAM ROAD

BRIDEWELL DR

CHURCHILL RD

BARN LA

2

COTTON'S LANE

CHANDLERS END

ELMLEY ROAD

PO +

HILLSIDE

West End Farm

1

BAKER'S LANE

Ashton under Hill

Little Owl Farm

Carrant Brook Farm

38

99 A B 00 C D 01 E F

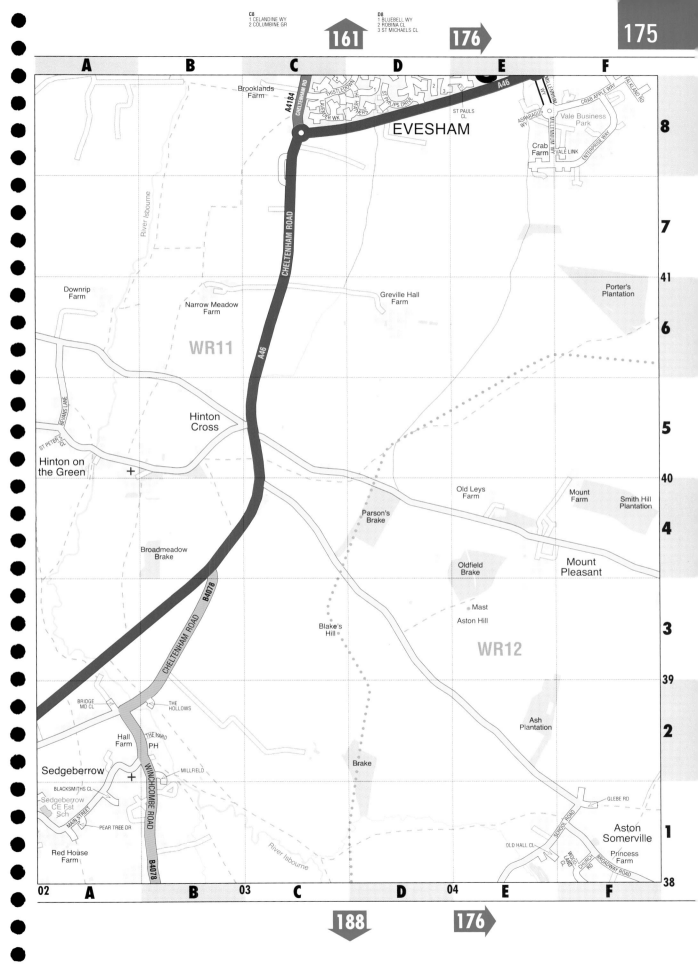

161
176
188
176

C8
1 CELANDINE WY
2 COLUMBINE GR

D8
1 BLUEBELL WY
2 ROBINA CL
3 ST MICHAELS CL

A B C D E F

8
7
41
6
5
40
4
3
39
2
1
38

Brooklands Farm
A4184
CHELTENHAM RD
THISTLEDOWN
THE HEATHERS
LAVENDER WK
ST PHILIPS DRIVE
ST PAULS CL
EVESHAM
A46
MILLENNIUM WY
CRAB APPLE WAY
FALKLAND RD
ASPARAGUS WY
MILLENNIUM WY
VALE LINK
Vale Business Park
Crab Farm
VALE LINK
ENTERPRISE WAY

CHELTENHAM ROAD

River Isbourne

Downrip Farm
Narrow Meadow Farm
Greville Hall Farm
Porter's Plantation

WR11
A46

BEVANS LANE
ST PETER'S CL
Hinton Cross
Hinton on the Green

Old Leys Farm
Mount Farm
Smith Hill Plantation

Parson's Brake
Mount Pleasant

Broadmeadow Brake
B4078
Oldfield Brake

Mast
Aston Hill
WR12

Blake's Hill

Ash Plantation

BRIDGE MD CL
THE HOLLOWS
Brake

Hall Farm
THE YARD
PH
MILLFIELD

Sedgeberrow
WINCHCOMBE ROAD
BLACKSMITHS CL
Sedgeberrow CE Fst Sch
MAIN STREET
PEAR TREE DR
GLEBE RD
SCHOOL ROAD
OLD HALL CL
WOOD LAND CL
CHURCH RD
BROADWAY ROAD
Aston Somerville
Princess Farm

Red House Farm
B4078
River Isbourne

02 A B 03 C D 04 E F

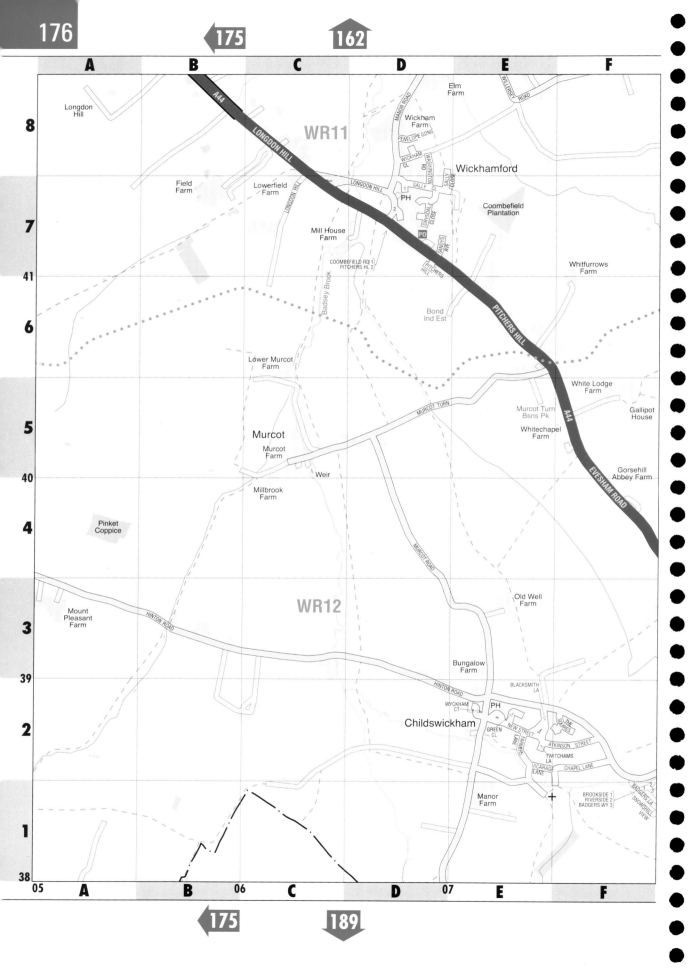

A B C D E F

8

7

41

6

5

40

4

3

39

2

1

38

05 A B 06 C D 07 E F

Longdon
Hill

Field
Farm

Lowerfield
Farm

WR11

A44

LONGDON HILL

Longdon Hill

PH

Mill House
Farm

Elm
Farm

MANOR ROAD

Wickham
Farm

PENELOPE GDNS

WICKHAM
CL

WASHINGTON
RD

SALLY

SALLY CLOSE

Wickhamford

WILLERSEY ROAD

Coombefield
Plantation

DINSDALE CLOSE

PO

SANDYS AVE

COOMBEFIELD RD 1
PITCHERS HL 2

PITCHERS HILL

Bond
Ind Est

PITCHERS HILL

Whitfurrows
Farm

Badsey Brook

Lower Murcot
Farm

MURCOT TURN

White Lodge
Farm

Murcot Turn
Bsns Pk

A44

Gallipot
House

Murcot

Murcot
Farm

Weir

Whitechapel
Farm

Whitechapel

EVESHAM ROAD

Gorsehill
Abbey Farm

Millbrook
Farm

Pinket
Coppice

MURCOT ROAD

Old Well
Farm

WR12

Mount
Pleasant
Farm

HINTON ROAD

HINTON ROAD

Bungalow
Farm

BLACKSMITH
LA

WYCKHAM
CT

PH

THE SQUIRES

Childswickham

GREEN
CL

NEW STREET

FARMERS LANE

ATKINSON STREET

TWITCHAMS
LA

VICARAGE
LANE

CHAPEL LANE

BADGERS LA

SNOWSHILL
VIEW

Manor
Farm

BROOKSIDE 1
RIVERSIDE 2
BADGERS WY 3

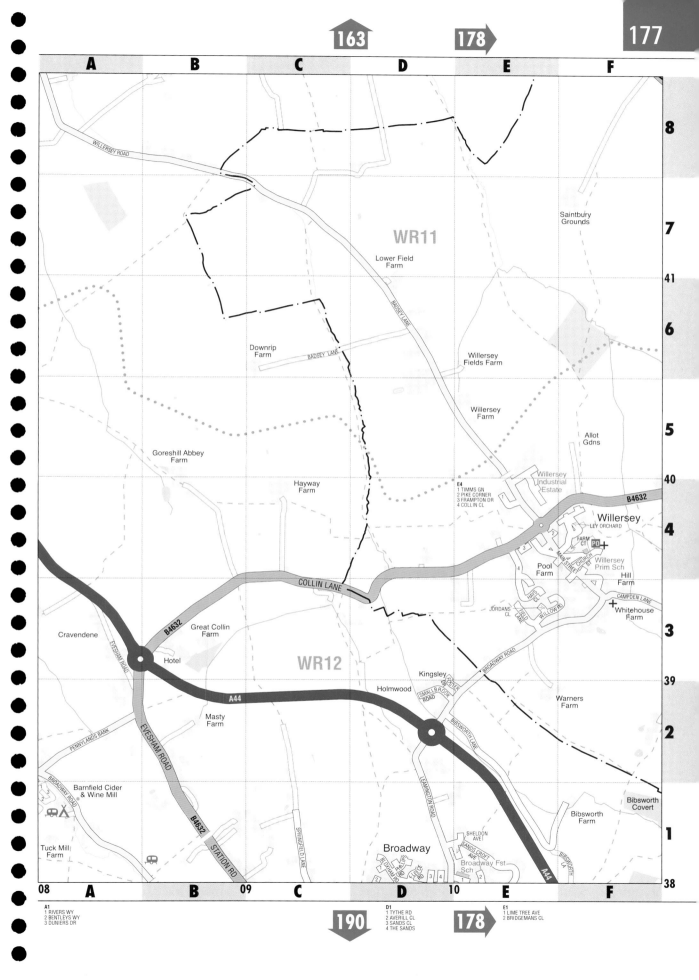

A   B   C   D   E   F

8
7
41
6
5
40
4
3
39
2
1
38

WILLERSEY ROAD

WR11

Lower Field Farm

BADSEY LANE

Saintbury Grounds

Downrip Farm

BADSEY LANE

Willersey Fields Farm

Willersey Farm

Allot Gdns

Goreshill Abbey Farm

Hayway Farm

E4
1 TIMMS GN
2 PIKE CORNER
3 FRAMPTON DR
4 COLLIN CL

Willersey Industrial Estate

B4632

Willersey
LEY ORCHARD

FARM CT
PO
Willersey Prim Sch

MAIN STREET

CHURCH ST

Pool Farm

Hill Farm

CAMPDEN LANE

Whitehouse Farm

JORDANS CL

HAYS CL

FIELD LANE

WILLOW RD

COLLIN LANE

Cravendene

B4632

Great Collin Farm

EVESHAM ROAD

Hotel

WR12

Kingsley

Holmwood

BROADWAY ROAD

FOSTER DR

SMALLBROOK ROAD

Warners Farm

A44

Masty Farm

PENNYLANDS BANK

EVESHAM ROAD

LEAMINGTON ROAD

BIBSWORTH LANE

Bibsworth Covert

Barnfield Cider & Wine Mill

BROADWAY ROAD

B4632 STATION RD

SPRINGFIELD LANE

Broadway

SHELDON AVE

SANDS CROFT AVE

Broadway Fst Sch

Bibsworth Farm

BIBSWORTH LA

A44

Tuck Mill Farm

1 RIVERS WY
2 BENTLEYS WY
3 DUNIERS DR

BLOXHAM RD

PHILLIPS RD

FLEECE RD

08   A   B 09   C   D 10   E   F 38

A1
1 RIVERS WY
2 BENTLEYS WY
3 DUNIERS DR

D1
1 TYTHE RD
2 AVERILL CL
3 SANDS CL
4 THE SANDS

E1
1 LIME TREE AVE
2 BRIDGEMANS CL

A　B　C　D　E　F

B4035

Honeybourne
Airfield Trad Est

Works

Works

Weston
Ind Est

Manor
House

PODER LA

B4632

Glebe
Farm

B4035

Manor
Farm

WR11

B4035

Lower Fields
Farm

HONEYBOURNE ROAD

BUCKLE STREET

Brook
Bend
Merrivale
Fruit Farm

THE ROWS

CIDERMILL
ORCHARD

PH Weston-
sub-Edge

Gardner's
Farm

ASTON RD

Aston
Subedge

8

7

41

6

5

40

4

3

39

2

1

38

PARSONS LANE

CHAPEL LA

DOVER S VW

Middle
Farm

Witt's
End

The Lynches
Wood

Vale
Farm

Cross

Earthwork

Saintbury
Cross
Farm

Manor House
(site of)

Broad
Close Farm

Phillips
Farm

Westwood

Top
Farm

GL55

Oaklands
Farm

B4632

Middle
Hill Farm

Glebe
Farm

Saintbury

Ledge
Plantation

The Lynches
Wood

Dover's
Hill

Upper
Wall Farm

Park
Farm

P

KINGSCOMB LANE

DYER'S LANE

Lane
End

Tumulus

CAMPDEN LANE

Saintbury
Coppice

Weston Park
Farm

Earthwork

Weston Park

Kiftsgate
Stone

Campden
Wood

Weston
Park

Quarry
(dis)

WR12

BUCKLE STREET

THE NARROWS

Cotswold Way
The Mile Drive

Willersey
Hill

Broadway
Golf Course

CH

Saintbury
Hill

Long
Barrow

Saintbury Hill
Barn Farm

Hotel

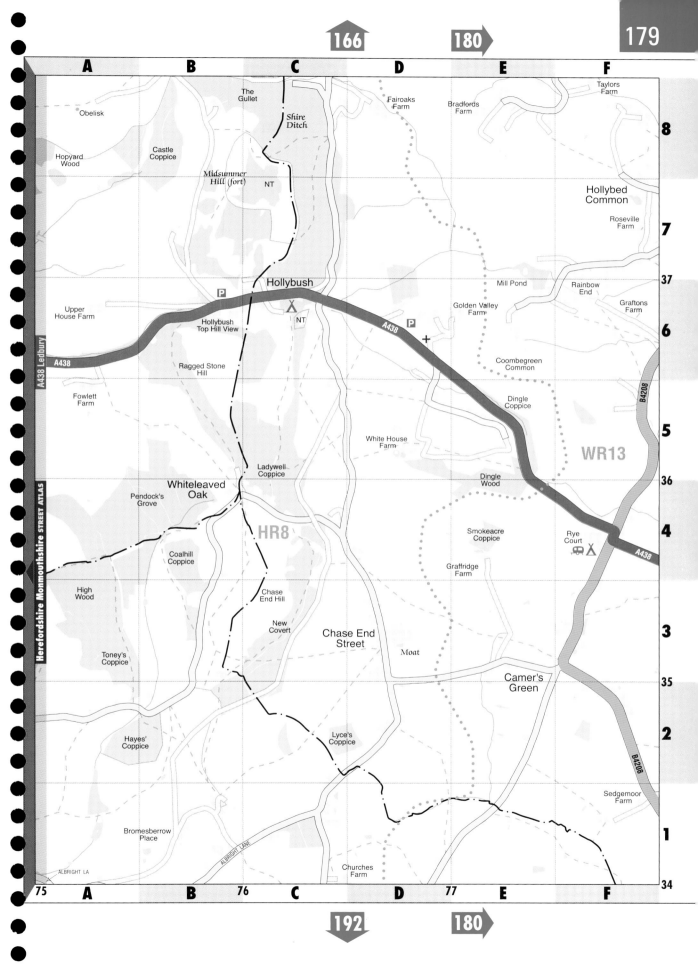

166
180
192
180

A B C D E F

8 7 37 6 5 36 4 3 35 2 1 34

Taylors Farm
Hollybed Common
Roseville Farm
Rainbow End
Graftons Farm

Fairoaks Farm
Bradfords Farm
Mill Pond
Golden Valley Farm
Coombegreen Common
Dingle Coppice
WR13
Dingle Wood
Smokeacre Coppice
Graffridge Farm
Rye Court
B4208
A438
Camer's Green
Sedgemoor Farm

The Gullet
Shire Ditch
Obelisk
Castle Coppice
Hopyard Wood
Midsummer Hill (fort)
NT
Hollybush
P
Upper House Farm
A438 Ledbury
Hollybush Top Hill View
NT
A438
P
Ragged Stone Hill
Fowlett Farm
White House Farm
Ladywell Coppice
Whiteleaved Oak
Pendock's Grove
HR8
Coalhill Coppice
High Wood
Chase End Hill
New Covert
Chase End Street
Moat
Toney's Coppice
Hayes' Coppice
Lyce's Coppice
Bromesberrow Place
ALBRIGHT LANE
ALBRIGHT LA
Churches Farm

Herefordshire Monmouthshire STREET ATLAS

75 76 77

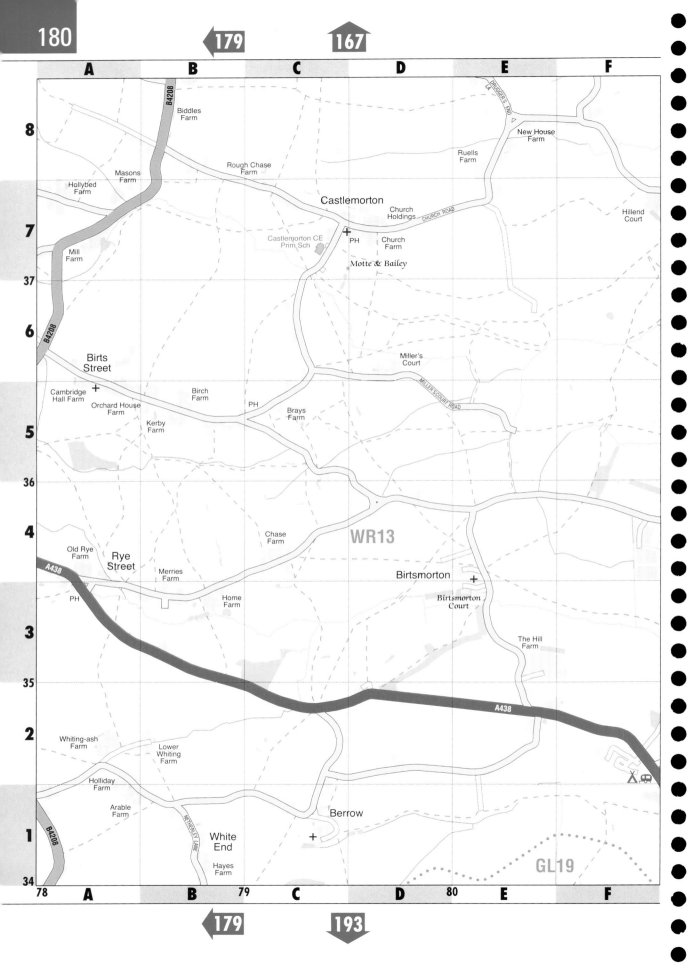

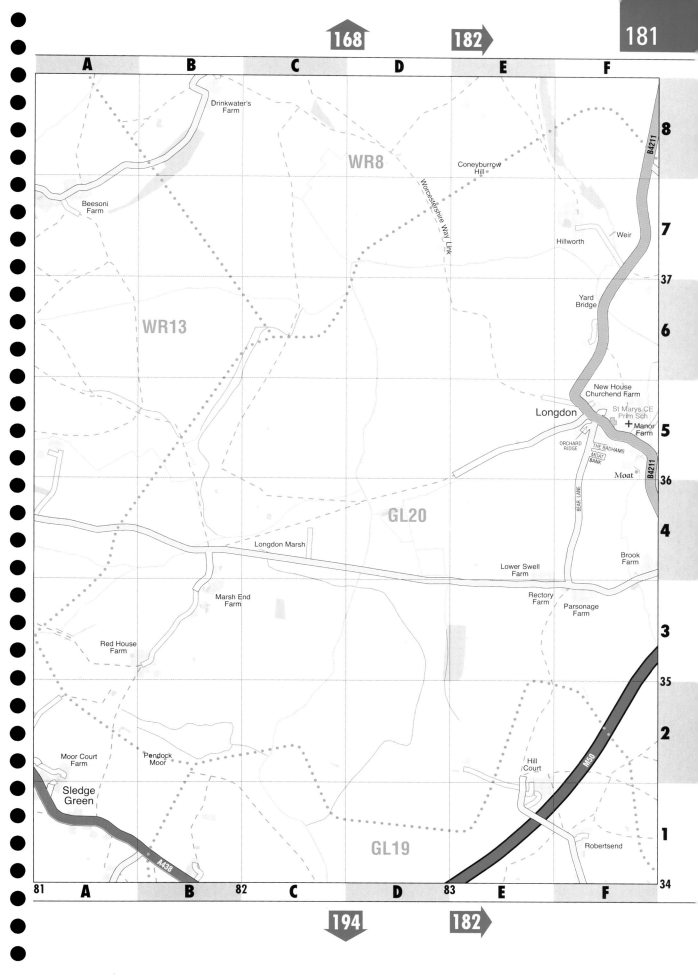

A B C D E F

Drinkwater's Farm

WR8

Coneyburrow Hill

Worcestershire Way Link

Beesoni Farm

WR13

Hillworth

Weir

Yard Bridge

New House
Churchend Farm

St Marys CE Prim Sch

Longdon

Manor Farm

ORCHARD RIDGE

THE BADHAMS

MOAT BANK

BEAR LANE

Moat

B4211

B4211

GL20

Longdon Marsh

Lower Swell Farm

Brook Farm

Marsh End Farm

Rectory Farm

Parsonage Farm

Red House Farm

Moor Court Farm

Pendock Moor

Hill Court

M50

Sledge Green

A438

GL19

Robertsend

81 A B 82 C D 83 E F 34

8 7 37 6 5 36 4 3 35 2 1

181
169

A **B** **C** **D** **E** **F**

B4211

8 Long Covert

Glover Hill Farm

FERRY LANE

Bank Farm

Holdfast

Holdfast Hall

WR8

Green Farm

Manor Farm

7

37 Heath Hill Farm

Hen and Chicken Covert

The Barn Farm

M50

Queenhill

Churchend Farm

6

Bushley Brook

Severn Way

River Severn

Woodend Bridge

5

Bredon Sch (Pull Court)

36

Gunnice Farm

B4211

4 Chambers Court

Gullers End Farm

The Grove

GL20

Pipers End Farm

Guller's End

Weir

Hill House Farm

Mossgreen Shrubbery

3

M50

Slades Green Farm

Broadfield Farm

Windmill Tump

35 Longdon Hall

Piper's End

Aggberrow Wood

Yeandley Farm

Elmwood Barn

2

Slades Green

Orchard Farm

Bushley Green

Green Farm

Tilterdown Farm

GREEN STREET

Wheypools Farm

Hill Wood

WOOD STREET

1 Buckbury Farm

The Rampings

Sarn Hill Wood

Buckbury

B4211

Buckbury End

Upper Green Farm

Wood Street Farm

34

84 **A** **B** **85** **C** **D** **86** **E** **F**

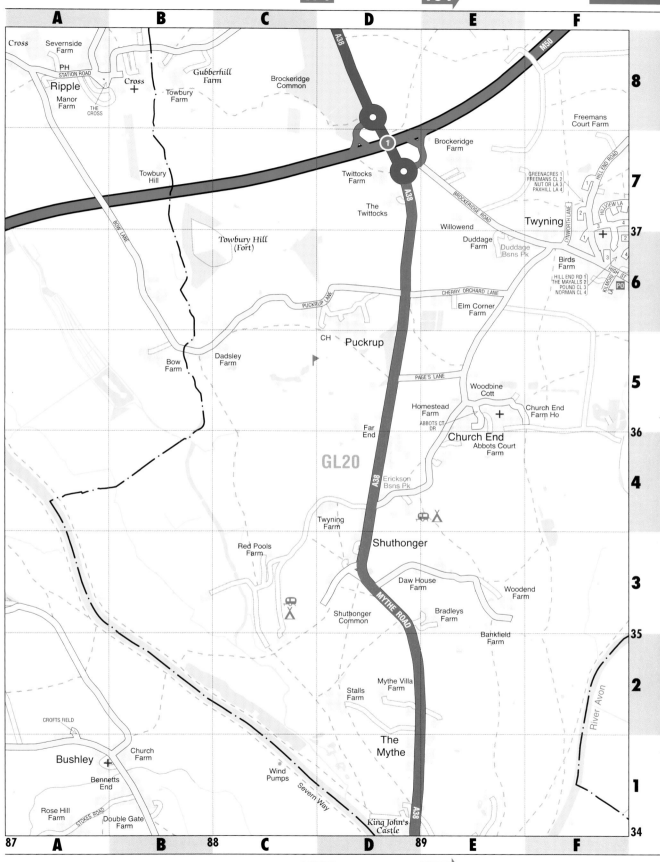

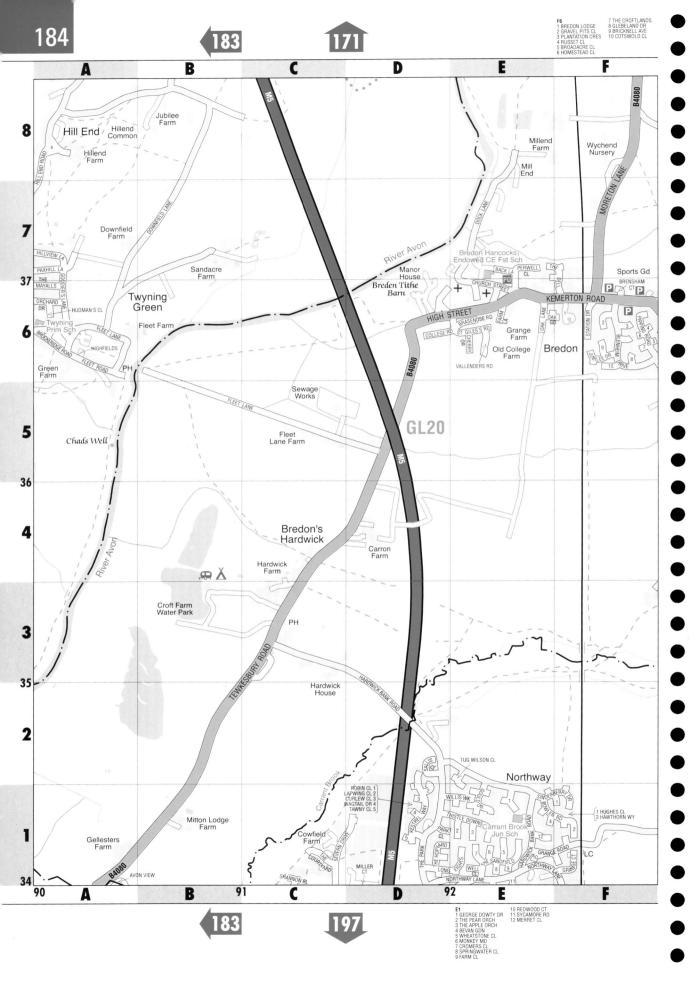

◀ 183
171 ▲

8

7

37

6

5

36

4

3

35

2

1

34

A   B   C   D   E   F

Hill End
Hillend Common
Jubilee Farm
Hillend Farm
HILL END ROAD
Downfield Farm
DOWNFIELD LANE
HILLVIEW LA
PAXHILL LA
THE MAYALLS
GODDIER'S LANE
ORCHARD DR
HUDMAN'S CL
Twyning Green
Sandacre Farm
Fleet Farm
BROCKERIDGE ROAD
Twyning Prim Sch
HIGHFIELDS
FLEET LANE
Green Farm
FLEET ROAD
PH
FLEET LANE
Sewage Works
Chads Well
Fleet Lane Farm
River Avon

River Avon
Breden Tithe Barn
Manor House
BACK LA
PERWELL CL
Bredon Hancocks Endowed CE Fst Sch
CHURCH STREET
PO
THE BELL
HIGH STREET
KEMERTON ROAD
COLLEGE RD
BRASENOSE RD
ST GILES'S RD
GRANGE FARM
Old College Farm
VALLENDERS RD
OAK LA
OAK GD
Bredon
STATION DR
P
BLENHEIM DRIVE
PIPPIN RD
SPILLEE DR CL
Sports Gd
BRENSHAM CT
Wychend Nursery
MORETON LANE
B4080
Millend Farm
Mill End
DOCK LANE
P

GL20

M5

Bredon's Hardwick
Carron Farm
Hardwick Farm
Croft Farm Water Park
PH
TEWKESBURY ROAD
Hardwick House
HARDWICK BANK ROAD
B4080
Mitton Lodge Farm
Gellesters Farm
B4080
AVON VIEW
Cowfield Farm
SHANNON PL
SEVERN DRIVE
THE COURTYARD
Carrant Brook
MILLER CT
ROBIN CL 1
LAPWING CL 2
CURLEW CL 3
WAGTAIL DR 4
TAWNY CL 5
KESTREL WAY
THE PARK
PARK CL
THE HOP
THISTLE DOWNS
LONG LEIGHTS
WILLIS WK
TUG WILSON CL
SALLIS CL
DUCK DR
WILLIS WK
Northway
THISTLE DOWNS
Carrant Brook Jun Sch
THE SANDFIELD
NORTHWAY LANE
WELL CL
SINDERBERRY DR
BOWYER RD
GRANGE ROAD
HARDWICK BANK ROAD
NORTHWAY LANE
GRANGE CT
LC
1 HUGHES CL
2 HAWTHORN WY

90   A   B   91   C   D   92   E   F

◀ 183
197 ▼

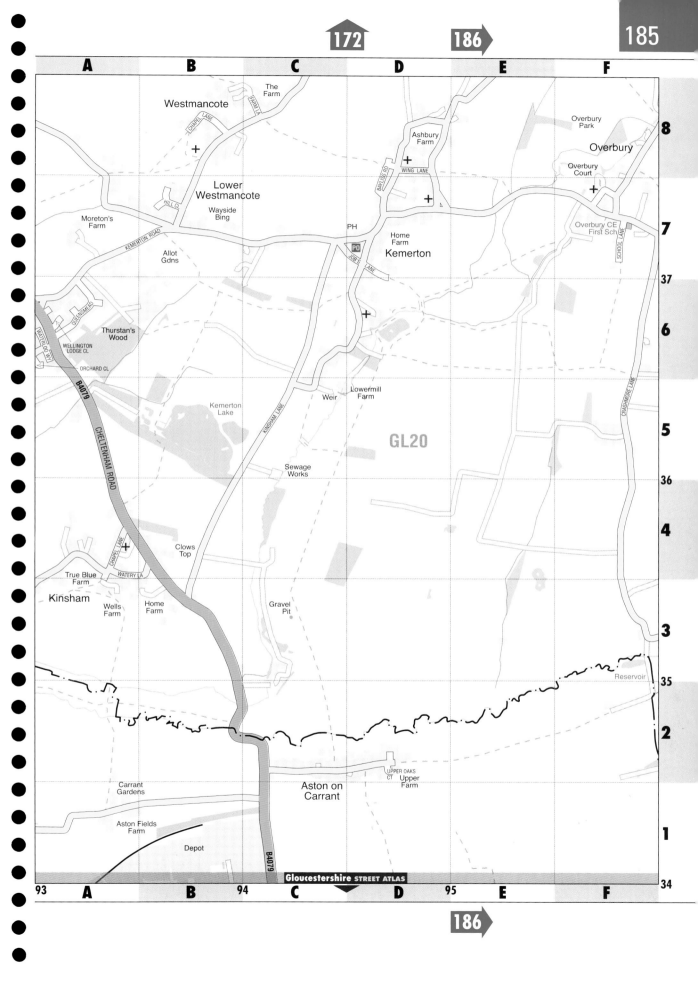

8

7

37

6

5

36

4

3

35

2

1

34

Westmancote

The Farm

FARM LA

CHAPEL LANE

Lower
Westmancote

HILL CL

Wayside
Bing

Moreton's
Farm

KEMERTON ROAD

Allot
Gdns

QUEENSMEAD

WATERLOO RD

WELLINGTON
LODGE CL

ORCHARD CL

Thurstan's
Wood

B4079

CHELTENHAM ROAD

Kemerton
Lake

KINSHAM LANE

Weir

Lowermill
Farm

Sewage
Works

Clows
Top

CHAPEL LANE

WATERY LA

True Blue
Farm

Kinsham

Wells
Farm

Home
Farm

Gravel
Pit

Ashbury
Farm

BAYLISS RD

WING LANE

PH

PO

JOB'S LANE

Home
Farm

Kemerton

GL20

Overbury
Park

Overbury

Overbury
Court

Overbury CE
First Sch

SCHOOL LANE

CRASHMORE LANE

Reservoir

UPPER OAKS
CT

Upper
Farm

Aston on
Carrant

Carrant
Gardens

Aston Fields
Farm

Depot

B4079

A B C D E F

8

Surman's Plantation

Conderton Hill

Ash Coppice

7

WATERGRIP LA

Manor Farm

Conderton Pottery PH

Manor House

Conderton

Beckford Coppice

Lower Coppice

Upper Farm

Middle Farm

Manor Farm

Grafton

37

6

PIGEON LANE

Court Farm

5

Pit (dis)

GL20

ASHTON ROAD

The Silk Printing Centre

Poultey House

36

Beckford Hall & rems of Priory

PO

Aston End

MAIN STREET

4

Home Farm

Mon

Beckford

STATION ROAD

COURTHAM LA

The Manor House

Hotel

BECKFORD CROSS

3

Reservoir

BECKFORD CL

BACK LANE

CHELTENHAM ROAD

Brook Farm

35

Glebe Barns

Glebeland

WESTERN HL RD

BLACKSMITHS CL

SWEDEN LA

BLACKSMITHS LANE

Little Beckford

2

CRASHMORE LANE

CHELTENHAM ROAD

Great Washbourne

Tythe Farm

Perretts Farm

1

Elm Farm

A46

34

96 A B 97 C D 98 E F

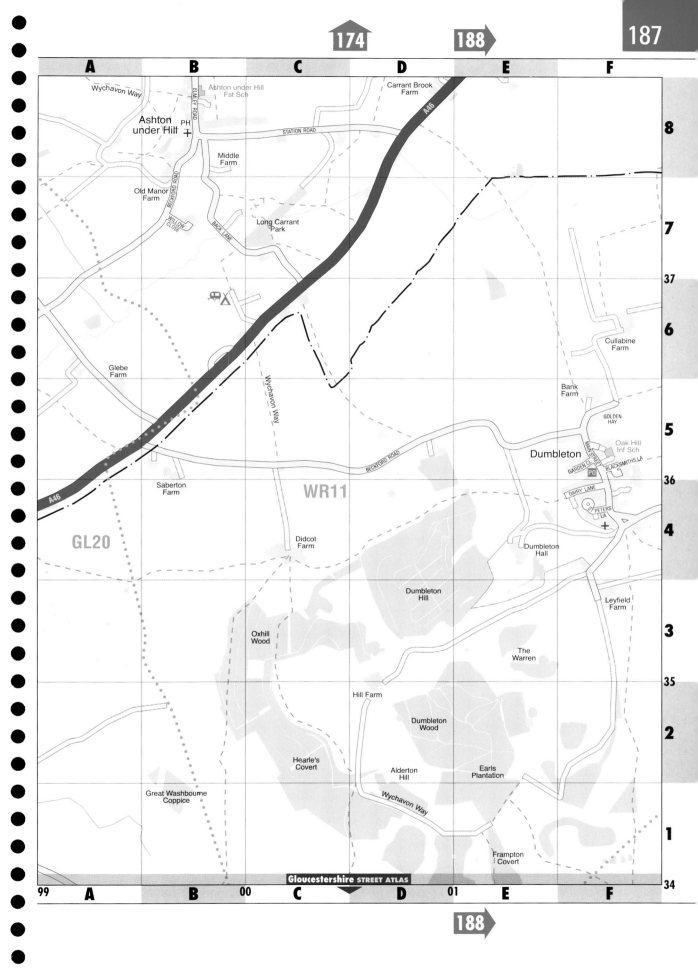

A B C D E F

8

7

37

6

5

36

4

3

35

2

1

34

Wychavon Way

Ashton under Hill Fst Sch

Carrant Brook Farm

A46

Ashton under Hill
PH

STATION ROAD

Middle Farm

ELMLEY ROAD

BECKFORD ROAD

Old Manor Farm

WILLOW CLOSE

BACK LANE

Long Carrant Park

Cullabine Farm

Bank Farm

GOLDEN HAY

Glebe Farm

Wychavon Way

Dumbleton

MAIN STREET

Oak Hill Inf Sch

BLACKSMITHS LA

GARDEN CL
PO

A46

Saberton Farm

BECKFORD ROAD

WR11

DAIRY LANE

ST PETERS LA

GL20

Didcot Farm

Dumbleton Hall

Leyfield Farm

Dumbleton Hill

The Warren

Oxhill Wood

Hill Farm

Dumbleton Wood

Hearle's Covert

Alderton Hill

Earls Plantation

Great Washbourne Coppice

Wychavon Way

Frampton Covert

99 A 00 B C 01 D E F

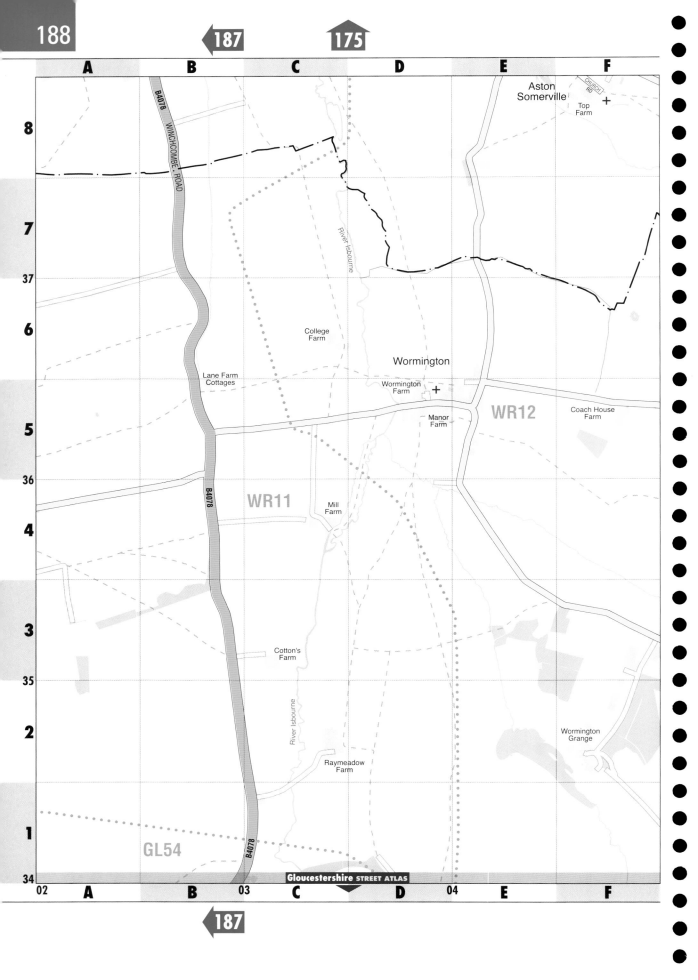

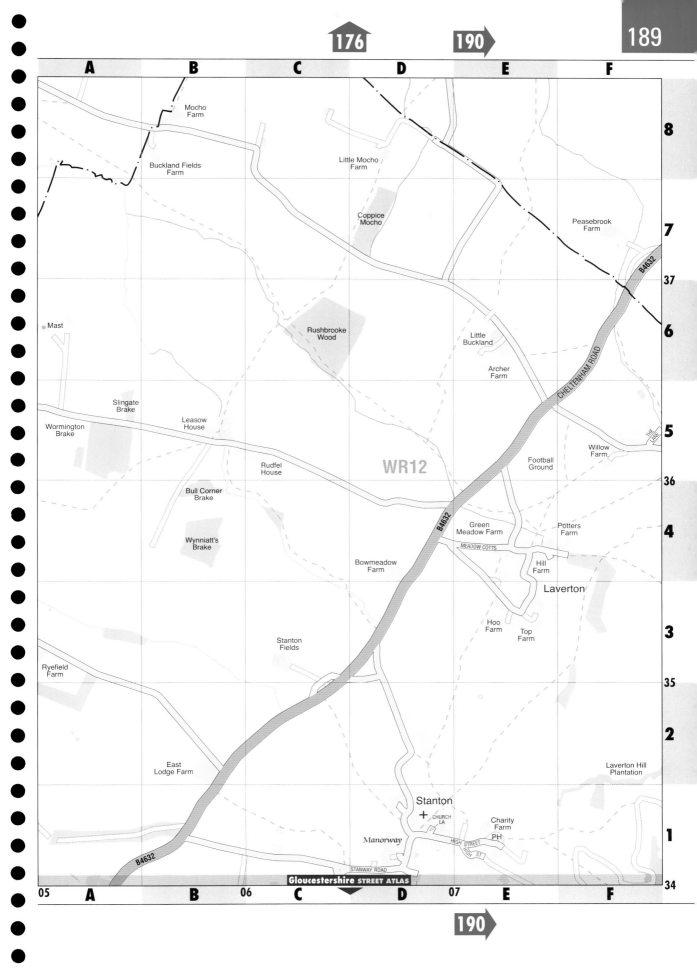

A B C D E F

8

7

37

6

Mast

Mocho Farm

Buckland Fields Farm

Little Mocho Farm

Coppice Mocho

Peasebrook Farm

B4632

Rushbrooke Wood

Little Buckland

Archer Farm

CHELTENHAM ROAD

Slingate Brake

Leasow House

Wormington Brake

Rudfel House

WR12

Football Ground

Willow Farm

THE LANE

5

36

Bull Corner Brake

Green Meadow Farm

Potters Farm

B4632

MEADOW COTTS

4

Wynniatt's Brake

Bowmeadow Farm

Hill Farm

Laverton

Ryefield Farm

Stanton Fields

Hoo Farm

Top Farm

3

35

2

East Lodge Farm

Laverton Hill Plantation

Stanton

CHURCH LA

Charity Farm

PH

Manorway

HIGH STREET

HIGH ST

1

B4632

STANWAY ROAD

34

05 A B 06 C D 07 E F

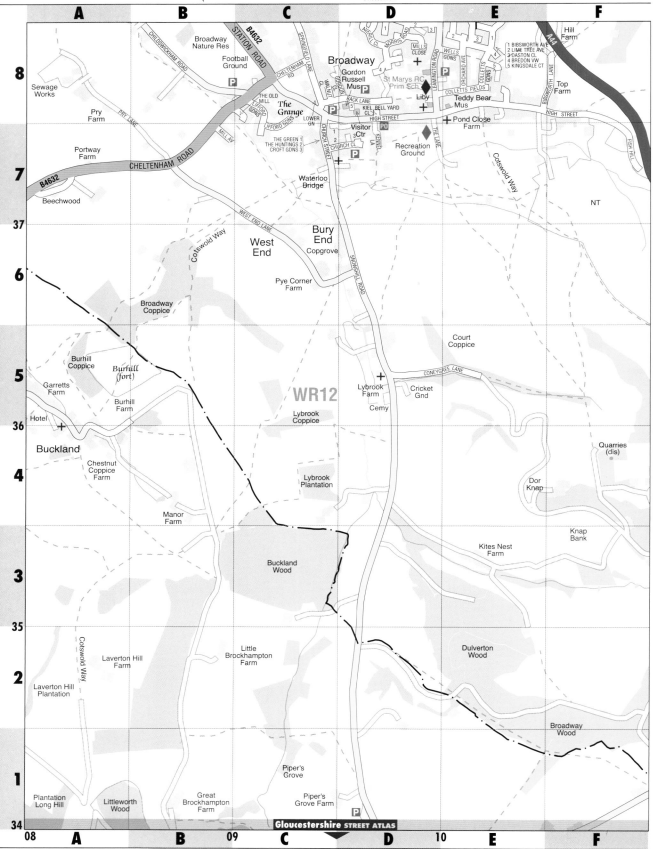

177

D8
1 PARKER PL
2 BLOXHAM RD
3 THE SANDS
4 MEADOW ORCH
5 RUSSELL SQ

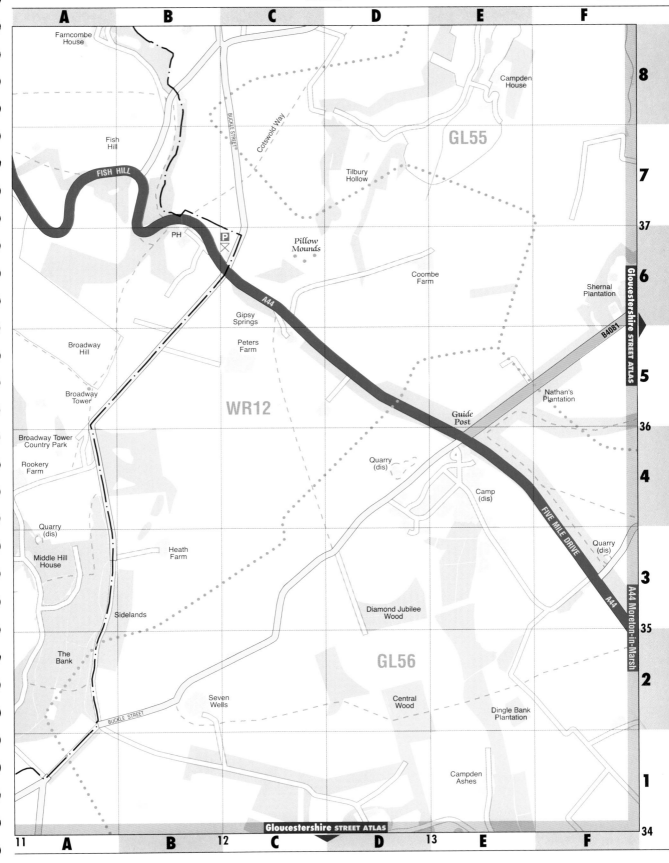

Farncombe House

Fish Hill

FISH HILL

PH

P

Broadway Hill

Broadway Tower

Broadway Tower Country Park

Rookery Farm

Quarry (dis)

Middle Hill House

Sidelands

The Bank

BUCKLE STREET

BUCKLE STREET

Cotswold Way

Tilbury Hollow

Pillow Mounds

Coombe Farm

Gipsy Springs

Peters Farm

WR12

Heath Farm

Seven Wells

GL56

Campden House

GL55

A44

Guide Post

Quarry (dis)

Camp (dis)

Diamond Jubilee Wood

Central Wood

Campden Ashes

Shernal Plantation

B4081

Nathan's Plantation

FIVE MILE DRIVE

Quarry (dis)

A44

A44 Moreton-in-Marsh

Dingle Bank Plantation

Gloucestershire STREET ATLAS

A   B   C   D   E   F

8   7   37   6   5   36   4   3   35   2   1   34

11   12   13

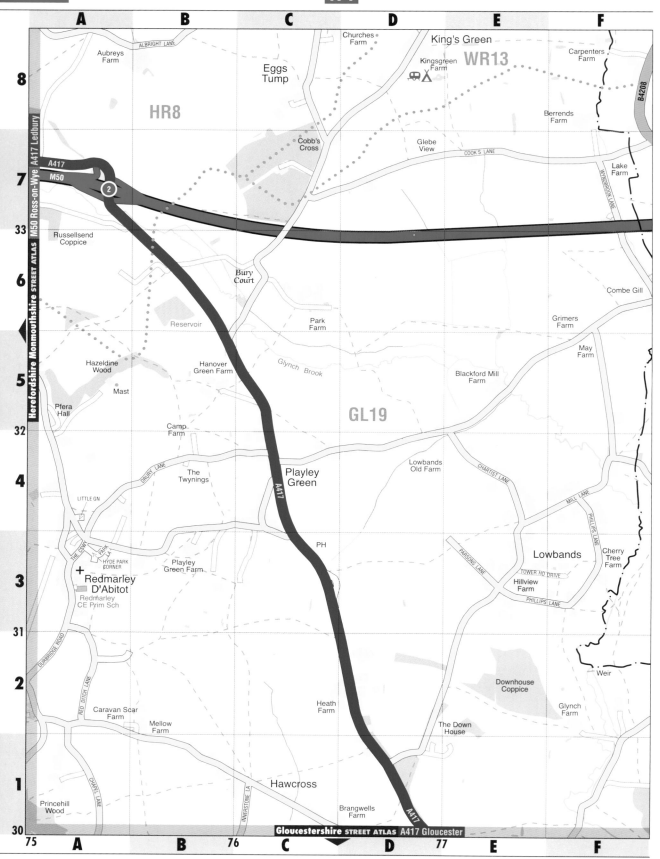

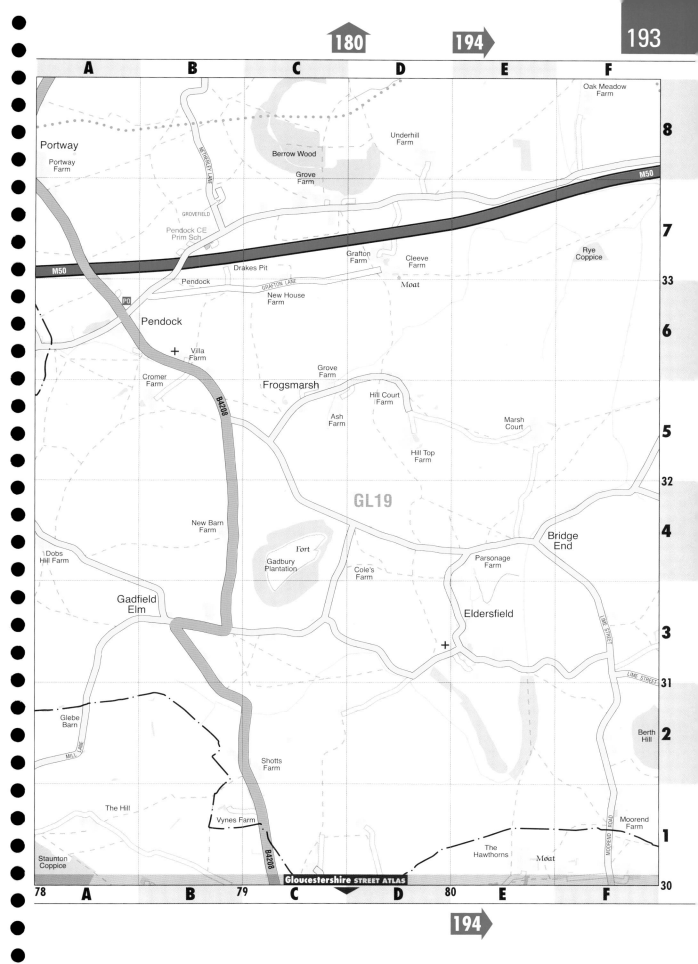

A B C D E F

8

Oak Meadow Farm

Portway

Underhill Farm

Portway Farm

Berrow Wood

Grove Farm

M50

7

GROVEFIELD

Pendock CE Prim Sch

Rye Coppice

Grafton Farm

Cleeve Farm

33

Drakes Pit

M50

Pendock

GRAFTON LANE

Moat

Pendock

New House Farm

6

Villa Farm

Grove Farm

Cromer Farm

Frogsmarsh

Hill Court Farm

Ash Farm

Marsh Court

B4208

5

Hill Top Farm

32

GL19

New Barn Farm

Dobs Hill Farm

Fort

Bridge End

4

Gadbury Plantation

Cole's Farm

Parsonage Farm

Gadfield Elm

Eldersfield

3

LIME STREET

LIME STREET

31

Glebe Barn

Berth Hill

2

MILL LANE

Shotts Farm

The Hill

MOOREND ROAD

Moorend Farm

1

Vynes Farm

B4208

The Hawthorns

Moat

Staunton Coppice

Gloucestershire STREET ATLAS

30

78 A B 79 C D 80 E F

A　B　C　D　E　F

8

WR13

A438

M50

A438

Priors
Court

Downend

Dean
Covert

M50

7

Hillenders

Downend
Coppice

Beech
Coppice

33

6

Hooze
Farm

Hardwick
Green

Hardwick
Farm

Mitre
Farm

Swinley
Green

5

Newbarn

32

Swinley
Court

GL19

Dunshill
Farm

4

Oak
Grove

Nashend
Farm

WAD LANE

Little Dunshill
Farm

3

Moat

Palmers End
Farm

Linkend
Farm

Sports
Gd

Moores
Farm

Pigeon House
Farm

Cranley
Farm

LINKEND ROAD

31

Hardwick Hay
Farm

Linkend

Hillfield
House

Eldersfield Lawn
CE Prim Sch

2

POOLHAY
CL

Corse
Lawn

LIME STREET

Hotel

Lime
Street

PH

Elm
Farm

Stewards
Farm

Hallings
Farm

1

Moat

Plough
Farm

Walnut
Tree Farm

Lucas
Farm

Slad
Farm

Walk
Farm

Wrights
Farm

Villa
Farm

B4211

30

81　A　B　82　C　D　83　E　F

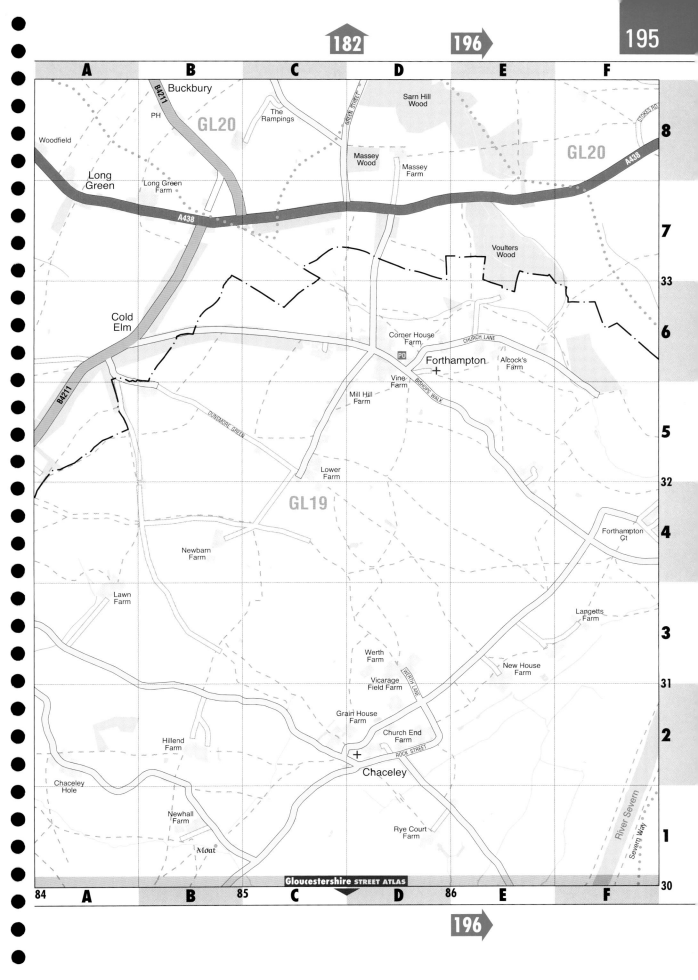

A B C D E F

182
196

B4211
Buckbury
PH
GL20
Woodfield
The Rampings
GREEN STREET
Sarn Hill Wood
STOKES RD
GL20
A438
8
Long Green
Long Green Farm
Massey Wood
Massey Farm
7
A438
Voulters Wood
33
Cold Elm
Corner House Farm
CHURCH LANE
6
PO
Forthampton
Alcock's Farm
Vine Farm
BISHOPS WALK
Mill Hill Farm
DUNSMORE GREEN
5
B4211
Lower Farm
32
GL19
Forthampton Ct
4
Newbarn Farm
Lawn Farm
Langetts Farm
3
Werth Farm
New House Farm
WERTH LANE
31
Vicarage Field Farm
Grain House Farm
Church End Farm
2
Hillend Farm
ROCK STREET
Chaceley Hole
Chaceley
Newhall Farm
Rye Court Farm
River Severn
1
Moat
Severn Way
30

84 A B 85 C D 86 E F

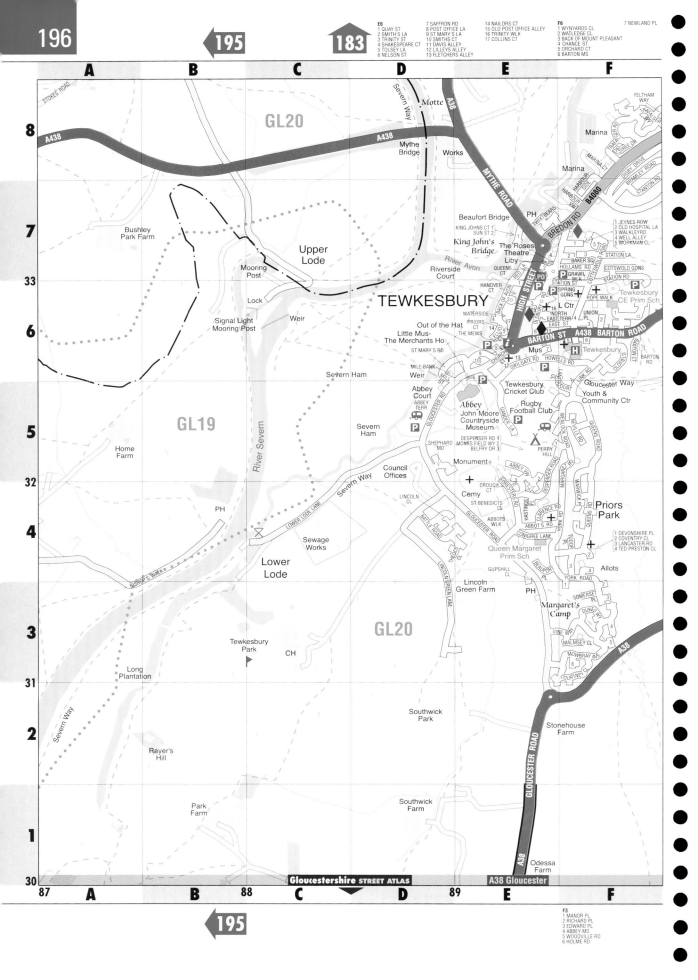

E6
1 QUAY ST
2 SMITH'S LA
3 TRINITY ST
4 SHAKESPEARE CT
5 TOLSEY LA
6 NELSON ST

7 SAFFRON RD
8 POST OFFICE LA
9 ST MARY S LA
10 SMITHS CT
11 DAVIS ALLEY
12 LILLEYS ALLEY
13 FLETCHERS ALLEY

14 NAILORS CT
15 OLD POST OFFICE ALLEY
16 TRINITY WLK
17 COLLINS CT

F6
1 WYNYARDS CL
2 WATLEDGE CL
3 BACK OF MOUNT PLEASANT
4 CHANCE ST
5 ORCHARD CT
6 BARTON MS

7 NEWLAND PL

GL20

A438

Severn Way

Motte

A38

Mythe Bridge

Works

MYTHE ROAD

B4080

BREDON RD

FELTHAM WAY

Marina

Marina

Beaufort Bridge

KING JOHNS CT 1
SUN ST 2

King John's Bridge

The Roses Theatre Liby

River Avon

QUEENS CT

Riverside Court

HANOVER CT

HIGH STREET

PO

P

TEWKESBURY

WATERSIDE

PRIORS CT

THE MEWS

Out of the Hat

Little Mus- The Merchants Ho

ST MARY S RD

Bushley Park Farm

Upper Lode

Mooring Post

Lock

Signal Light Mooring Post

Weir

Severn Ham

MILL-BANK

Weir

Abbey Court

ABBEY TERR

Abbey

John Moore Countryside Museum

SWILGATE RD

GLOUCESTER RD

Tewkesbury Cricket Club

Rugby Football Club

Tewkesbury Youth & Community Ctr

Gloucester Way

GL19

River Severn

Home Farm

Severn Way

Severn Ham

SHEPHARD MD

DESPENSER RD 1
MONKS FIELD WY 2
BELFRY DR 3

Monument

ABBEY VW

Perry Hill

QUEENS ROAD

NEVILLE RD

WENLOCK RD

DESPENSER ROAD

MARGARET RD

WARWICK RD

Priors Park

PH

Council Offices

LINCOLN CL

Cemy

CROUCH CT

ST BENEDICTS CL

ABBOTS WLK

HASTINGS

FORESTERS RD

CLARENCE RD

ABBOT S RD

CON/GREE LANE

1 DEVONSHIRE PL
2 COVENTRY CL
3 LANCASTER RD
4 TED PRESTON CL

32

PH

Sewage Works

Lower Lode

BATTLE ROAD

THE OAKS

GLOUCESTER ROAD

LINCOLN GREEN LANE

Queen Margaret Prim Sch

GUPSHILL CL

Lincoln Green Farm

PH

BEAUFORT PL

YORK ROAD

TUDOR

Allots

SOMERSET

Margaret's Camp

DUKE WY

VINE WK

MALMSEY CL

MOWBRAY AV

COURTNEY CL

A38

GL20

BISHOP'S WALK

Long Plantation

Tewkesbury Park

CH

Rayer's Hill

Park Farm

Southwick Park

Southwick Farm

Stonehouse Farm

GLOUCESTER ROAD

A38

Odessa Farm

F3
1 MANOR PL
2 RICHARD PL
3 EDWARD PL
4 ABBEY MD
5 WOODVILLE RD
6 HOLME RD

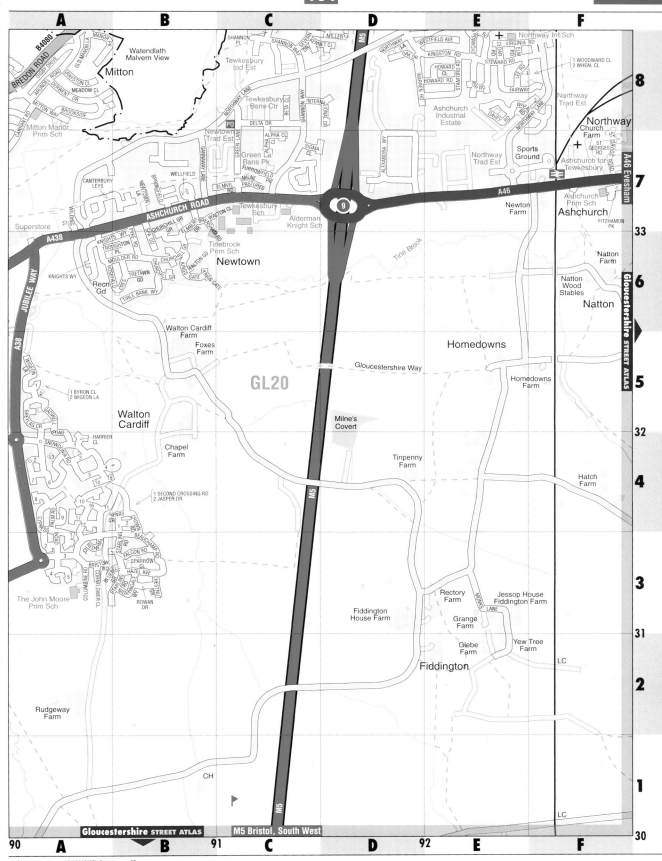

Index

Place name May be abbreviated on the map → **Church Rd** **6** Beckenham BR2..........**53** C6

Location number Present when a number indicates the place's position in a crowded area of mapping

Locality, town or village Shown when more than one place has the same name

Postcode district District for the indexed place

Page and grid square Page number and grid reference for the standard mapping

Cities, towns and villages are listed in Capital Letters

Public and commercial buildings are highlighted in magenta **Places of interest** are highlighted in blue with a star★

Abbreviations used in the index

Acad	Academy	Comm	Common	Gd	Ground	L	Leisure	Prom	Promenade
App	Approach	Cott	Cottage	Gdn	Garden	La	Lane	Rd	Road
Arc	Arcade	Cres	Crescent	Gn	Green	Liby	Library	Recn	Recreation
Ave	Avenue	Cswy	Causeway	Gr	Grove	Mdw	Meadow	Ret	Retail
Bglw	Bungalow	Ct	Court	H	Hall	Meml	Memorial	Sh	Shopping
Bldg	Building	Ctr	Centre	Ho	House	Mkt	Market	Sq	Square
Bsns, Bus	Business	Ctry	Country	Hospl	Hospital	Mus	Museum	St	Street
Bvd	Boulevard	Cty	County	HQ	Headquarters	Orch	Orchard	Sta	Station
Cath	Cathedral	Dr	Drive	Hts	Heights	Pal	Palace	Terr	Terrace
Cir	Circus	Dro	Drove	Ind	Industrial	Par	Parade	TH	Town Hall
Cl	Close	Ed	Education	Inst	Institute	Pas	Passage	Univ	University
Cnr	Corner	Emb	Embankment	Int	International	Pk	Park	Wk, Wlk	Walk
Coll	College	Est	Estate	Intc	Interchange	Pl	Place	Wr	Water
Com	Community	Ex	Exhibition	Junc	Junction	Prec	Precinct	Yd	Yard

Index of towns, villages, streets, hospitals, industrial estates, railway stations, schools, shopping centres, universities and places of interest

ABB–All

A

ABBERLEY............... 60 F4
Abberley Ave DY13....... 43 D1
Abberley Cl
  Halesowen B63 ....7 F2
  Redditch B98 .... 71 C5
Abberley Dr WR9 .... 84 E1
Abberley Hall Sch WR6.. 60 F1
Abberley Parochial Prim Sch
  WR6 .... 60 F4
Abberley Rd B68...........9 B8
Abberley View **4** WR3 . 115 C5
ABBERTON 133 B8
Abberton Cl B63 ....8 C3
Abberton Ho **4** B97.... 70 A4
Abberton Rd WR10....... 133 A4
Abbey Cl
  Bromsgrove B60 .... 49 C2
  3 Callow End WR2 .. 140 F8
  St John's WR2.......... 114 F1
Abbey Coll WR14........ 166 E3
Abbey Cres
  Birmingham B68 .... 9 D8
  Halesowen B63 ....7 D4
Abbeycroft WR10 .... 158 C8
ABBEYDALE 70 F5
Abbeydale Rd B31 ...... 19 A2
Abbey Gdns **4** WR11 . 161 D4
Abbey La WR11 .... 161 C3
Abbey Mdw **4** GL20... 196 F3
Abbey Mews **5** WR11 . 161 D4
Abbey Park Fst Sch
  WR10 .... 158 C8
Abbey Rd
  Evesham WR11 .... 161 C4
  Halesowen B63 ....7 C4
  Kidderminster DY11.... 27 A6
  Malvern WR14......... 152 F7
  Pershore WR10 .... 158 D8
  Redditch B97 .... 70 E4
  Worcester WR2........ 114 F1
Abbey Stadium Sports Ctr
  B97 .... 70 E7
Abbey Terr GL20 .... 196 D5
Abbey Trad Ctr B98 .... 70 E4
Abbey View GL20 ...... 196 E5

Abbey View Rd WR10.... 144 E5
Abbeywood Fst Sch B98.. 71 D6
Abbot Chyrryton's Pl **7**
  WR11................. 161 C4
Abbot Rd B63............ 16 C8
Abbots Cl WR2.......... 114 E3
Abbots Court Dr GL20 . 183 E5
Abbots Grange **2** WR10. 158 C8
ABBOTS MORTON 121 B2
Abbots Rd
  Birmingham B14 .... 20 E7
  Pershore WR10 .... 158 C7
Abbot's Rd GL20 .... 196 E4
ABBOT'S SALFORD 135 D1
Abbots Wlk GL20....... 196 E4
ABBOTSWOOD 142 E7
Abbotswood WR11..... 161 D8
Abbots Wood Cl B98 .... 72 A3
Abbotts Cl DY13........ 44 D6
Abbot Walter's Ct **9**
  WR11................. 161 C4
Abdon Ave B29 .... 19 C7
AB LENCH 133 C4
Ab Lench Rd WR11..... 133 F4
Acacia Ave DY12 ...... 26 C3
Acacia Cl WR4.......... 115 C5
Acacia Ct DY8 ....5 E6
Acacia Rd B30 .... 19 E8
Acanthus Rd B98 ...... 71 F6
Acheson Rd B28, B90... 21 F3
Ackleton Gr B29 ....9 F1
Aconbury Cl WR5 ...... 116 B3
Acorn Cl
  Birmingham, Bournville
    B30................. 19 E8
  Colwall WR13......... 152 B2
  Malvern WR14......... 139 C1
Acorn Ct B45 .... 33 D7
Acorn Gdns B30 .... 20 A7
Acorn Gr WR10 .... 144 D2
Acorn Rd
  Catshill B61 .... 49 B8
  Halesowen B62 ....8 C8
Acorns The B61........ 49 A8
Acreage Rd B45....... 110 F6
Acre La
  3 Droitwich WR9..... 84 E3
  Redditch B97 .... 69 C2
Acres Dr DY5 ....6 E8
Acre The
  Defford WR8 .... 157 E3
  Kinver DY7............ 4 B3
ACTON 64 A3

Acton Cl B98 .... 71 D5
Adam Ct B63 ....7 F4
Adams Brook Dr B32.....9 B1
Adams Ct DY10 .... 28 A7
Adams Hill B32 ....9 B1
Adam's Hill DY9 ...... 15 E4
Adams Ho **3** DY11.... 27 C6
Adam St DY11 .... 27 C5
Addenbrooke Cres WR11.. 27 A1
Addison Rd
  Birmingham, King's Heath
    B14................. 20 F7
  Worcester WR3........ 115 C6
Addyes Gn **6** WR9.... 103 E8
Addyes Way WR9 ...... 103 E8
Adelaide Cl
  8 Kempsey WR5..... 141 C6
  11 Worcester WR3.. 115 B6
Adelaide St B97....... 70 D4
Admiral Pl WR5........ 128 F5
Admiral Wlk DY10..... 27 E8
Adrian Cl **3** WR9..... 85 A1
Adstone Gr B31....... 19 A1
Aerial Way WR9 ...... 85 E8
Agatha Gdns WR3..... 103 A2
Agenoria Dr DY8.........5 F5
AGGBOROUGH 27 F4
Aggborough Cres DY10... 27 E3
Aggborough Stadium
(Kidderminster Harriers
FC) DY10 .... 27 F4
Agmore La B60 .... 50 B3
Agmore Rd B60....... 50 B4
Ainsdale Cl DY8.........5 F2
Ainsdale Gdns B63 ......7 D2
Ainsworth Rd **5** B31... 19 D2
Aintree Cl
  Kidderminster DY11.... 27 D8
  Upper Catshill B61.... 32 A1
Aintree Rd WR10...... 144 E4
Aire Croft B31........ 19 B1
Aintree Way B60 ..... 49 F1
Albany Ct DY10 ...... 28 B6
Albany Rd WR3 ...... 115 D4
Albany Terr WR1..... 115 B4
Albemarle Rd DY8 ......5 F2
Alberta Cl WR2....... 122 E7
Albert Bradbeer Prim Sch
  B31.................. 33 F7
Albert Cl B80 .... 90 E4
Albert Dr B63 ....7 F2
Albert Park Mews WR14. 138 F3
Albert Park Rd WR14.. 138 F4

Albert Rd
  Birmingham, Brandhall B68.. 9 C8
  Birmingham, King's Heath
    B14................ 20 F7
  Bromsgrove B61 ..... 67 E8
  Colwall WR13......... 152 A1
  Evesham WR11 ...... 161 C5
  Halesowen B63 ....7 F3
  Kidderminster DY10... 27 F6
  Worcester WR5........ 115 D1
Albert Road N WR14... 138 F1
Albert Road S WR14... 153 A8
Albert St
  7 Droitwich WR9..... 84 E3
  Redditch B97 .... 70 E5
  Stourbridge DY8 ......5 F5
  Stourbridge, Lye DY9....6 E5
Albion Rd WR14 ...... 138 E4
Albion Terr B50....... 136 C7
Albion Wlk WR14 ..... 138 E4
Alborn Cres B38 ...... 34 D8
Albright La HR8....... 178 A1
Albrighton Rd B63 .....7 F3
Albury Rd B80 .... 90 E4
Alcester Gdns B14 .... 20 F7
Alcester Heath B49 ... 109 C4
Alcester Highway B98.. 89 F8
Alcester Rd
  Feckenham B96....... 107 E2
  Finstall B60 .... 49 F1
  Hollywood B47........ 35 F5
  Lickey End B60....... 49 D5
  Portway B47, B48 .... 52 F7
  Studley B80 .... 90 E3
  Tardebigge B60, B97... 69 B7
Alcester Road S
  Birmingham, Billesley Common
    B14................ 20 E6
  Birmingham, Highter's Heath
    B14................ 20 F2
Alcester St B98....... 70 E4
Aldborough La **4** B97.. 70 B5
Aldbourne Way B38.... 34 E7
Aldbury Rd B14....... 21 A3
Aldeford Dr DY5 ....6 D8
Alder Ave DY10 ...... 27 E8
Alderbrook Cl B97..... 70 B5
Alderbrook Rd **1** WR9.. 84 C1
Alder Carr Cl B98..... 89 F8
Alder Cl
  Hollywood B47........ 36 B6
  Worcester WR4....... 115 D4

Alder Gr
  Droitwich WR9........ 103 F8
  Evesham WR11 ...... 161 F2
  Halesowen B62 ...... 8 E6
Alderhanger La B98.... 72 C6
Alder La B30........... 19 C6
Alderlea Cl DY8.........6 A2
Alderley Rd B61 ...... 67 D8
Alderman Knight Sch
  GL20 .... 197 C7
Aldermans La B97 .... 70 B6
Aldermere Rd DY11.... 27 C8
Alderminster Cl B97... 89 E4
Alderney Gdns B38.... 19 D1
Alders Cl B98......... 71 A3
Alders Dr B98 .... 71 F4
Aldersey Cl **10** WR5 . 128 D6
Aldersey Rd WR5..... 128 D6
Aldersmead Rd B31... 19 C1
Alders The B62 ..... 16 F4
Alder Way B60....... 49 B2
Aldgate Dr DY5 ....6 C7
ALDINGTON 162 D5
Aldington Cl B98..... 70 F1
Aldridge Rd B68.......9 B8
Alexander Ave WR9 .. 84 D1
Alexander Cl B61 .... 32 A1
Alexander Hill DY5.....6 F8
Alexander Rd WR2.... 115 A1
Alexandra Hospl B98... 90 C6
Alexandra La WR14 ... 138 F3
Alexandra Mews WR14. 138 F3
Alexandra Rd
  Birmingham, Stirchley
    B30................ 20 A7
  Evesham WR11 ...... 161 A3
  Halesowen B63 ....7 F4
  Malvern WR14........ 138 F3
Alexandra Way GL20 .. 197 D7
Alford Cl B45 .... 33 C7
Alfreda Ave B47 ..... 36 A8
Alfred Ct B60 .... 67 E2
Alfred St B14 .... 20 F7
Alfreds Well B61...... 48 C6
ALFRICK 124 F7
ALFRICK POUND 124 E5
Alhambra Rd B60 .... 49 C1
Alicante Cl WR14 ... 139 B2
Alice Ottley Jun Sch The
  WR1................ 115 B4
Alison Dr DY8.........5 E3
Alison Rd B62 ....8 F3
Allardene WR11....... 161 E3

Allen Cl B80 . . . . 90 E3
Allendale Ave B80 . . . . 90 E3
Allendale Cres B80. . . . . . . 90 E3
Allendale Ct B80 . . . . 90 E3
Allens Croft Prim Sch
  B14. . . . . 20 C5
Allens Croft Rd B14 . . . . . . 20 C6
Allens Farm Rd B31. . . . . . 18 E3
Allens Hill WR10 . . . . 144 E5
Allensmore Cl B98 . . . . 71 F2
Allesborough Dr **5**
  WR10. . . . . 144 C1
Allesborough Gdns WR11 . . 162 D2
All Saints Ave DY12 . . . . . . 26 C4
All Saints Pl B61 . . . . 49 A4
All Saints Rd B14 . . . . 20 E7
All Saints' Rd B61 . . . . 49 A3
Allsebrook Gdns WR11 . . . 162 D2
Allwell Dr B14 . . . . 20 F7
Allwood Gdns B32 . . . . 9 A2
Allwood Ho B97 . . . . 70 C3
Alma St
  Halesowen B63 . . . . 7 C5
  Worcester WR3 . . . . 115 B6
Almond Ave DY11 . . . . 27 B8
Almond Cl
  Birmingham B29 . . . . 19 A6
  2 Evesham WR11. . . . . 161 F2
Almond Way DY13 . . . . 43 D5
Almonry Cl **15** WR10. . . . . 158 D1
Almonry Her Ctr* WR11 161 D4
Alperton Dr DY9 . . . . 6 E2
Alpha Cl GL20. . . . . 197 C7
Althorp Gdns **10** WR10 . . . 144 C1
Alton Cl B97 . . . . 70 B1
Alton Pk WR2. . . . . 140 F7
Alton Rd WR5. . . . . 128 C5
ALVECHURCH 51 B6
Alvechurch Highway
  Lower Marlbrook B60 . . . . 32 D2
  Redditch B98, B97. . . . . . 70 F3
Alvechurch Ho B60 . . . . . . 49 B3
Alvechurch Rd
  Birmingham B31 . . . . 34 B7
  Halesowen B63 . . . . 7 F2
Alvechurch Sta B48. . . . . . 51 A4
ALVELEY 1 C5
Alveley Cl B98 . . . . 71 D4
Alveley Prim Sch WV15. . . . 1 C5
Alveston Cl B98. . . . . 71 C2
Alveston Grange GL55 . . . 165 D3
Alveston Rd B47. . . . . 36 A7
Alvin Cl B62 . . . . 8 F8
Alwold Ct B29 . . . . 9 F2
Ambergate Cl **8** B97. . . . . 70 B5
Amberley Cl WR4 . . . . 115 F7
Amberley Terr DY10 . . . . . 27 F5
Amber Way B62 . . . . 8 C6
Amber Wharf **14** WR1 . . . 115 C1
AMBLECOTE 5 F7
Amblecote Prim Sch DY8. . . 5 F7
Amblecote Rd
  Brierley Hill DY5 . . . . 6 D8
  Kidderminster DY10. . . . . 28 B5
Ambleside B32 . . . . 9 C1
Ambleside Dr
  Brierley Hill DY5 . . . . 6 C8
  Worcester WR4 . . . . 115 F5
Ambleside Way B60 . . . . . . 49 B1
Ambrose Cl WR2. . . . . 114 D3
Amersham Ct B32. . . . . 9 E5
Amery Cl WR5 . . . . 128 D8
Amos Rd DY9 . . . . 6 F2
Amphlett Ct **2** B60 . . . . . 49 A2
Amphlett Way WR9 . . . . . . 85 E8
Amroth Cl B45. . . . . 33 B7
Amroth Gdns **7** WR4 . . . 116 B7
Amwell Gr B14. . . . . 20 F3
Anchorfields DY10 . . . . 27 F6
Anchor La
  3 Fladbury WR10. . . . . 146 A1
  Harvington WR11. . . . . . 148 B6
Andressy Mews B61. . . . . . 49 A5
Andrew Cl WR2 . . . . 114 E4
Andrew Rd B63 . . . . 8 A3
Andrews Cl DY5. . . . . 6 E8
Andrews Dr **2** WR11. . . . 161 C2
Angelo Rd B13. . . . . 21 D7
Angel Pas DY8. . . . . 6 A5
Angel Pl **9** WR1 . . . . 115 B3
Angel Row **15** WR1 . . . . . 115 B3
Angel St
  Bentley Pauncefoot B97 . . 88 C8
  Upper Bentley B97. . . . . . 69 B1
  Worcester WR1. . . . . 115 B3
Ankadine Rd DY8 . . . . 6 B6
Ankerage Gn WR4 . . . . . . 116 B4
Ankerdine Ave **1** DY13. . . 43 D1
Ankerdine Comm Nature
  Reserve* WR6 . . . . 111 D6
Ankerdine Ct B63 . . . . 8 A3
ANKERDINE HILL 111 D6
Ankerdine Rd WR2. . . . . . 113 D5
Anne Cres **1** WR11 . . . . . 161 E2
Annscroft B38 . . . . 19 D2
Ansley Cl B98. . . . . 71 F1
Anton Cl DY12 . . . . 26 D5
Apley Rd DY8. . . . . 5 E7
Apollo Rd DY9 . . . . 7 A5
Apperley Way B63 . . . . 7 B7
Appian Cl B14 . . . . 20 E5
Appleby Cl B31 . . . . 20 D5
Apple Orchard Cl WR14 . . 139 C1
Apple Orchard The **3**
  GL20. . . . . 184 E1
Appleton Ave DY8. . . . . 6 A2

Appleton Cl B30 . . . . 19 E8
Appleton House B31 . . . . . 18 E5
Appletree Cl B31. . . . . 18 F1
Apple Tree Cl
  Crowle WR7. . . . . 117 F4
  Holt Heath WR6. . . . . 82 B3
  Kidderminster DY10. . . . . 28 B7
Appletree La
  Inkberrow WR7 . . . . 121 A5
  Redditch B97. . . . . 70 B5
Apple Tree Rd **3** WR10 . . 144 D2
Appletrees Cres B61 . . . . . 49 A5
Apple Tree Wlk WR9 . . . . . 83 A4
Apsley Cl B68. . . . . 9 A7
Apsley Croft B38. . . . . 20 B2
Apsley Rd B68 . . . . 9 A7
Aqueduct La B48. . . . . 50 F7
Aqueduct Rd B90 . . . . 21 E1
Aquila Way WR14 . . . . 153 B6
Arboretum Rd WR1 . . . . . 115 C3
Arbour Cl GL55 . . . . 165 D3
Archer Cl
  Malvern WR14. . . . . 138 E4
  Studley B80. . . . . 90 D4
Archer Ct DY9 . . . . 6 E2
Archer Rd
  Birmingham B14 . . . . 21 C4
  Redditch B98. . . . . 70 E4
Archers Cl **8** WR9 . . . . . 84 E3
Archer's Way WR15 . . . . . . 55 E6
Archer Terr B97 . . . . 70 C1
Ardath Rd B38 . . . . 20 A2
Arden Cl DY8 . . . . 5 E7
Ardencote Rd B13 . . . . 21 A6
Arden Leys B94 . . . . 53 D2
Arden Rd
  Birmingham, Rubery B45. . 18 A1
  Hollywood B47. . . . . 36 A6
  Worcester WR5 . . . . 128 D5
Ardens Cl B98 . . . . 72 A2
Arden Way WV15 . . . . 1 C5
Ardingley Wlk DY5 . . . . 6 B7
Ardley Rd B14 . . . . 21 A5
Areley Comm DY13. . . . . . 43 E1
Areley Ct DY13. . . . . 43 E2
ARELEY KINGS 43 E1
Areley La DY13 . . . . 43 E3
Arkle Cl WR9 . . . . 104 B8
Arkle Rd WR9. . . . . 104 B8
Arkwright Rd B32. . . . . 9 C5
Arley Arboretum & Gdn*
  DY12 . . . . 10 C6
Arley Cl
  Kidderminster DY11. . . . . 27 A2
  Redditch B98. . . . . 71 D5
Arley Dr DY8. . . . . 5 E7
Arley La DY12. . . . . 10 F6
Arley Sta DY12 . . . . 10 C5
Arlington Ct DY8 . . . . 6 B4
Arlington Gr B14. . . . . 21 B2
Arlington Grange WR2 . . . 114 E6
Arlington Rd
  Birmingham B14 . . . . 21 B3
  5 Walton Cardiff GL20. 197 A4
Armstrong Cl DY8. . . . . 6 B6
Arnold Gr B30 . . . . 19 D4
Arosa Dr WR14 . . . . 153 A5
Arran Pl WR5 . . . . 128 F6
ARROW 122 F6
Arrow Croft **2** WR9. . . . . 84 E4
Arrowdale Rd B98 . . . . 71 A3
Arrow End WR11 . . . . 149 A3
Arrowfield Gn B38 . . . . . . 34 D7
ARROWFIELD TOP 34 B1
Arrow Ho **1** B68. . . . . 9 B8
Arrow La WR11 . . . . 148 F3
Arrow Road N B98 . . . . . . 71 A4
Arrow Road S B98 . . . . . . 71 A4
Arrowsmith Ave WR2 . . . . 114 F3
Arrow Vale Com High Sch
  B98. . . . . 71 E2
Arrow Vale Sports Ctr
  B98. . . . . 71 E2
Arrow Valley Countryside
  Ctr* B98. . . . . 71 C4
Arrow Valley Pk* B98. . . . . 71 C4
Arrow Wlk B38 . . . . 20 B1
Arthur Dr DY11 . . . . 44 E8
Arthur Dr (Road 2) DY11 . . 27 E1
Arthur St B73 . . . . 71 B3
Artingstall Ho B30 . . . . . . 20 B8
Artrix B60 . . . . 49 B3
Arum Cl WR14 . . . . 139 C3
Arundel Ct **13** B29. . . . . . 19 C7
Arundel Dr WR5 . . . . 128 E8
Arundel Rd
  Birmingham B14 . . . . 21 A1
  Bromsgrove B60 . . . . 49 B1
  Tewkesbury GL20. . . . . . 197 A8
Ascot Cl WR3 . . . . 102 F3
Ascot Ct **11** B29. . . . . . . 19 C7
Ascot Rd WR10 . . . . 144 C4
Ascot Way B61. . . . . 32 B1
Ash Ave WR4 . . . . 115 E5
Ashbourne Ridge B63 . . . . . 7 D5
Ashbridge Ct B45. . . . . . . 33 B6
Ash Bridge Ct B45 . . . . . . 33 B6
Ashbrook Dr B45 . . . . 33 B8
Ashbrook Gr B30 . . . . 20 C8
Ashbrook Rd B30 . . . . 20 C8
Ashburton Rd B14 . . . . . . 20 D5
Ashbury Covert **3** B30 . . 20 D2
Ashby WR4 . . . . 116 C6
ASHCHURCH. 197 F7
Ashchurch for Tewkesbury
  Sta GL20 . . . . 197 F7
Ashchurch Ind Est GL20 . . 197 E8

Ashchurch Prim Sch
  GL20. . . . . 197 F7
Ashchurch Rd GL20 . . . . . 197 B7
Ash Cl WR14 . . . . 139 C3
Ashcott Cl B38. . . . . 19 D2
Ash Cres B47 . . . . 52 F8
Ashcroft Rd WR1 . . . . 115 B4
Ash Ct DY8 . . . . 6 A4
Ashdale Ave WR10 . . . . . . 144 D2
Ashdale Dr B14 . . . . 21 A1
Ashdene Cl
  Hartlebury DY11 . . . . 45 A2
  Kidderminster DY10. . . . . 28 C5
Ashdown Cl
  Birmingham, Frankley B45. 18 A2
  Malvern WR14. . . . . 139 B1
  Worcester WR2 . . . . 128 A7
Ashdown Rise WR14 . . . . . 139 B1
Ash Dr
  Birmingham B31 . . . . 18 C1
  Lower Marlbrook B61 . . . . 32 B1
Ashenden Cl **4** WR9 . . . 103 F8
Ashfield Cres DY9. . . . . 7 A3
Ashfield Ct B38 . . . . 19 E4
Ashfield Gr B63 . . . . 7 E2
Ashfield Ho B28 . . . . 21 E3
Ash Gr
  Evesham WR11 . . . . 161 E2
  Kidderminster DY11. . . . . 27 B7
  Stourbridge DY9 . . . . 6 D3
  14 Stourport-on-Severn
  DY13. . . . . 43 B4
Ashgrove WR14 . . . . 138 F3
Ashgrove Cl B60 . . . . 32 D1
Ashill Rd B45 . . . . 33 B7
Ash La
  Alvechurch B48. . . . . 34 D2
  Martin Hussingtree WR3. . 103 C5
Ash Lea WR8 . . . . 156 B1
Ashley Cl DY8. . . . . 5 D2
Ashley Ct B45. . . . . 33 A1
Ashley Rd
  Kidderminster DY10. . . . . 13 B1
  Worcester WR5 . . . . 128 D6
Ashmead Dr B45. . . . . 33 C4
Ashmead Rise B45 . . . . . . 33 C4
Ashmore Rd B30. . . . . 19 F5
Ashmores Cl B97 . . . . 89 D5
Ashorne Cl B98. . . . . 90 D8
Ashperton Cl B98. . . . . . . 70 E1
Ashpool WR6 . . . . 111 A6
Ash Rd GL20. . . . . 197 E8
Ashton Cl B97 . . . . 70 B1
Ashton Rd GL20. . . . . 186 D5
ASHTON UNDER HILL . . . 174 B1
Ashton under Hill Fst Sch
  WR11 . . . . 187 B8
Ash Tree Rd
  Birmingham B30 . . . . 20 A6
  Redditch B97. . . . . 70 B5
Ashville Dr B63 . . . . 8 A5
Ashwater Dr B14. . . . . 20 D2
Aspall Cl B97 . . . . 70 E3
Aspen Cl **3** WR11. . . . . . 161 F1
Aspen Ct WR14 . . . . 139 A4
Aspen Gr B47 . . . . 36 B5
Aspens Way B61 . . . . 49 A6
Aspen Wlk DY13 . . . . 43 E5
ASPLEY HEATH 53 D2
Aspley Heath B94 . . . . 53 D2
Aspley Heath La B94 . . . . . 53 D2
Assarts La WR14 . . . . 166 F7
Assarts Rd WR14. . . . . . . 166 E7
Astbury Ct **1** B68. . . . . . . 9 B7
Aster Ave DY11 . . . . 12 D1
Astles Rock Wlk DY7 . . . . . . 3 F3
ASTLEY 62 C4
Astley Ave B62. . . . . 8 F6
Astley CE Prim Sch DY13 . . 62 E8
Astley Cl B98 . . . . 90 A7
Astley Cres B62. . . . . 8 F5
ASTLEY CROSS 62 E8
Astley Ct **8** DY13 . . . . . . 62 E8
Astley Gdns DY13. . . . . . . 62 E6
Astley Orch WR15. . . . . . . 58 B5
Astley Rd B60. . . . . 49 C1
Astley Vineyard* DY13 . . . 62 F4
ASTON BANK 37 E1
Aston Cl **1** WR5 . . . . 141 C7
Aston Dr WR14 . . . . 153 C6
ASTON FIELDS 68 B7
Aston Fields Mid Sch B60 . 68 C8
Aston Fields Trad Est **2**
  B60. . . . . 67 F6
ASTON ON CARRANT. . . . 185 C1
Aston Rd
  Aston Subedge GL55 . . . . 178 F4
  Bromsgrove B60 . . . . 67 F6
Astons Cl DY5. . . . . 6 D7
Astons Fold DY5. . . . . 6 D7
ASTON SOMERVILLE 175 F1
ASTON SUBEDGE 178 F4
ASTWOOD
  Dodderhill 86 A7
  Worcester 115 D7
ASTWOOD BANK 89 F1
Astwood Bank Fst Sch
  B96. . . . . 89 E2
Astwood La
  Astwood Bank B96 . . . . . 89 C2
  Dodderhill WR9 . . . . 85 F8
  Feckenham B96. . . . . . . 107 F8
  Inkberrow B96. . . . . 108 A8
Astwood Rd WR3 . . . . 115 D5
Atcham Cl B98. . . . . 71 F3
Atcheson Cl B80. . . . . 90 E4
ATCH LENCH. 134 C2

Atch Lench Rd WR11 . . . . 134 B3
Athelstan Rd WR5. . . . . . . 115 D1
Atherstone Cl
  Redditch B98 . . . . 71 F1
  Solihull B90 . . . . 21 E2
Athol Cl B32 . . . . 18 D8
Atkinson St WR12 . . . . . . 176 E2
Attwood Bsns Ctr **2** DY9. . 6 F5
Attwood Pl **11** WR4 . . . . 116 C3
Attwood St
  Halesowen B63 . . . . 7 F5
  Stourbridge DY9 . . . . 6 F5
Atworth Cl B98 . . . . 90 B5
Atyed Cl WR14 . . . . 139 C1
Aubrey Rd B32. . . . . 9 E7
Auckland Cl WR4 . . . . 116 D5
Auckland Ho B32 . . . . 9 F4
Audley Dr DY11 . . . . 27 A8
Augustine Ave B80. . . . . . . 90 D4
Austcliff Cl B98 . . . . 89 D6
Austcliff Dr B28 . . . . 21 F3
Austcliffe Rd DY10 . . . . . . 13 A5
Austen Cl **7** WR2 . . . . . . 127 C2
Austin Rd B60 . . . . 67 E7
Austin Rise B31 . . . . 33 F7
Austrey Gr B29 . . . . 19 A8
Autumn Terr WR5 . . . . . . 115 D2
Auxerre Ave B98 . . . . 90 B8
Auxerre Ho B98 . . . . 90 B8
Avalon Rd B60 . . . . 49 C2
Avebury Gr B30 . . . . 20 C7
Avebury Rd B30. . . . . 20 C8
Avenbury Cl B98 . . . . 71 F1
Avening Cl WR4. . . . . 115 F7
Avenue Rd
  Astwood Bank B96 . . . . . 89 E1
  Birmingham, King's Heath
  B14. . . . . 20 D8
  Malvern WR14. . . . . 153 A8
  Upton upon Severn WR8 . . 169 A2
  7 Worcester WR2 . . . . 114 F1
Avenue The
  Birlingham WR10. . . . . . 158 A3
  Birmingham B45 . . . . 32 E7
  Blackwell B60 . . . . 50 A6
  Blakedown DY10 . . . . . . 14 B2
  Hartlebury DY11 . . . . 64 A8
  Summerfield DY11. . . . . . 44 F8
  Welland WR13 . . . . 167 C5
  2 Worcester WR1 . . . . 115 C3
  Worcester WR2. . . . . . . 128 A8
Averill Cl **2** WR12 . . . . . 177 D1
Aversley Rd B38 . . . . 34 E8
Avery Dell Ind Est B30 . . . 20 A6
Avill Gr DY11 . . . . 27 C7
Avocet Dr
  Kidderminster DY10. . . . . 28 A2
  4 Stourport-on-Severn
  DY13. . . . . 44 B2
AVONBANK 158 E6
Avonbank Cl B97. . . . . 89 C6
Avon Cl
  Bromsgrove B60 . . . . 67 F6
  Malvern WR14. . . . . 153 D8
  Worcester WR4 . . . . 115 F4
Avoncroft Com Arts Ctr
  B60. . . . . 67 E5
Avoncroft Mus of Historic
  Bldgs* B60 . . . . 67 E5
Avoncroft Rd B60 . . . . 67 D6
Avondale **6** WR9 . . . . . . 84 D1
Avon Dr
  4 Eckington WR10 . . . 171 D2
  Wythall B47. . . . . 35 D2
Avon Gn WR10 . . . . 145 A3
Avon Ho **3** B68. . . . . 9 B8
Avon Mill Pl WR10 . . . . . . 158 E7
Avon Rd
  Halesowen B63 . . . . 7 B5
  Kidderminster DY11. . . . . 27 B3
  Pershore WR10 . . . . 144 E2
  Stourbridge DY8 . . . . 5 F3
  Worcester WR4 . . . . 115 F3
Avon St WR11 . . . . 161 D5
Avon View GL20. . . . . 184 A1
Awford La DY13. . . . . 83 B8
Axborough La DY10 . . . . . . 13 D4
Aycliffe Rd WR5 . . . . 128 C5
Aylesmore Cl B32 . . . . 9 C1

B

Babylon La WR10 . . . . 132 F3
Baccabox La B47. . . . . 35 E7
Bacchurst Pl **4** WR4 . . . . 116 C5
Bach Camp Fort* HR6 . . . . 92 B5
Bach Mill Dr B28. . . . . 21 D3
Backfields La WR8 . . . . . . 169 C6
Back La
  Ashton under Hill WR11 . . 187 B7
  Beckford GL20 . . . . 186 C3
  Bredon GL20 . . . . 184 E7
  Bretforton WR11. . . . . . . 163 C4
  Broadway WR12 . . . . . . 190 D8
  Cleeve Prior WR11 . . . . . 149 A8
  Great Comberton WR10. . . 172 E8
  Malvern WR14. . . . . 138 F1
  Mickleton GL55 . . . . 165 D4
  Pebworth CV37 . . . . 150 F2
  Stone DY10 . . . . 45 F8
Back Lane N WR1 . . . . 115 B4
Back Lane S WR1. . . . . . . 115 B4
Back of Avon GL20 . . . . . . 196 E6
Back Rd B38 . . . . 19 F2
Back Way WR10 . . . . 145 D3

Back Wlk WR1. . . . . 115 B4
Badbury Cl B80 . . . . 90 D4
Badbury Gdns B80 . . . . . . 90 D4
Badge Ct* WR9 . . . . 66 B3
Badger Brook La B96 . . . . . 89 D1
Badger Cl
  Martley WR6 . . . . 99 A4
  Redditch B98 . . . . 71 D3
Badger Gdns WR5 . . . . . . 128 E5
Badgers Croft B62. . . . . 8 B7
BADGER'S HILL 146 D6
Badgers La WR12 . . . . 176 F1
Badger St DY9 . . . . 6 E6
Badgers The B45 . . . . 33 A2
Badgers Way WR12 . . . . . 176 F1
Badgers Wlk **11** DY13. . . 44 A4
Badger Way B60 . . . . 50 B5
Badgeworth Dr WR4 . . . . . 116 A8
Badhams The GL20. . . . . . 181 F5
Badland Ave DY10 . . . . . . 12 F1
BADSEY. 162 E3
Badsey Cl B31. . . . . 19 C4
Badsey Fields La WR11 . . . 162 E3
Badsey Fst Sch WR11 . . . . 162 E2
Badsey La
  Evesham WR11 . . . . 161 F4
  Willersey WR11. . . . . . . 177 D6
Badsey Rd WR11 . . . . 162 A4
Baffin Rd **7** WR2. . . . . . . 127 F6
Bagehott Rd WR9. . . . . . . 103 E8
Bagley's Rd DY5 . . . . 6 D6
Bagley St DY9 . . . . 6 C6
Bagnell Rd B13 . . . . 20 F7
Bailey Rd CV37 . . . . 151 D2
Bainbrigge Ave WR9 . . . . . 85 A2
Bakers Hill WR10 . . . . 157 F4
Baker's Hill GL55 . . . . 165 E2
Baker's La WR11 . . . . 174 B1
Baker Sq GL20 . . . . 196 F7
Balaams Wood Dr B31 . . . . 18 B1
Bala Cl **3** DY13 . . . . 43 F5
Balaclava Rd B14. . . . . . . 20 E8
Bala Way WR5 . . . . 128 E6
Baldenhall WR14. . . . . . . 153 E8
Balden Rd B32 . . . . 9 F7
Baldock Rd WR14 . . . . . . 153 A6
Bald's La DY9. . . . . 6 F5
Baldwin Rd
  Bewdley DY12 . . . . 25 F4
  Birmingham B30 . . . . 20 A3
  Kidderminster DY10. . . . . 28 B7
  Stourport-on-Severn DY13 . 43 B4
Baldwins La B28 . . . . 21 F4
Balholm Rd B62. . . . . 8 D5
Ballarat Wlk DY8. . . . . 5 F5
Ballard Ct WR13 . . . . 152 B2
Ballards Cl GL55 . . . . 165 D3
Balliol Rd WR4. . . . . 115 E3
Ball Mill Top Bsns Pk
  WR2. . . . . 101 D6
Balmoral Cl
  Evesham WR11 . . . . 161 E6
  Fernhill Heath WR3 . . . . . 103 A4
  Halesowen B62. . . . . 8 B7
  Malvern WR14. . . . . 139 C6
Balmoral Ct DY10 . . . . 28 A5
Balmoral Rd B32. . . . . 18 B7
Bamburgh Cres WR4 . . . . . 116 C6
Bamford Cl WR13 . . . . 154 A7
Ban Brook Rd WR11. . . . . 135 E3
Bangham Pit Rd B31. . . . . 18 E6
Bank Farm Cl DY9. . . . . 6 C1
Bank Farm Ct CV37 . . . . . 150 D2
Bank La WR6 . . . . 61 A6
Bank Rd WR6 . . . . 80 E3
Banks Gn B97. . . . . 69 B2
BANK'S GREEN 69 B3
Bankside Cl WR3 . . . . 115 A7
Banks Rd WR11 . . . . 162 E4
Bank St
  Malvern WR14 . . . . 138 F2
  Stourbridge DY9 . . . . 6 F5
  Worcester WR1. . . . . 115 B2
BANK STREET. 76 B2
Bank The B50. . . . . 136 D2
Bannals La WR15 . . . . 76 C2
Bannercroft WR6 . . . . 110 F6
Banners La
  Halesowen B63 . . . . 7 D6
  Redditch B98 . . . . 89 E6
Banners St B63 . . . . 7 D6
Bannut Tree La DY7 . . . . . . 3 C5
Bant Mill Rd B60 . . . . 49 A1
Baradene La WR2. . . . . . . 127 B8
Barass Ave WR4 . . . . 116 C5
Barbara Rd B28. . . . . 21 E4
Barbel Cres WR5. . . . . . . 128 C5
Barberry Ho B38 . . . . 19 F1
Barbers Cl **1** WR4 . . . . . 115 F6
Barbers La WR6. . . . . 99 B5
BARBOURNE 115 A6
Barbourne Cres **9** WR1 . 115 A5
Barbourne La WR1 . . . . . . 115 A5
Barbourne Rd WR1 . . . . . . 115 B5
Barbourne Terr WR1 . . . . . 115 A5
Barbourne Wlk **2** WR1. . . 115 A5
Barbrook Dr DY5. . . . . 6 B7
Bardenholme Gdns DY9 . . . 6 E3
Bardfield Cl B98. . . . . 71 F1
Barford Cres **5** B38. . . . . 20 C2
Barkers La
  Cleobury Mortimer DY14. . . 22 D4
  Wythall B47. . . . . 36 A1
Barker St WR3 . . . . 115 D5

Bark Hill DY12 . . . . 26 A3
Bark Piece B32 . . . . 9 C3
Barley Cres WR4 . . . . 116 B5
Barley Croft B60 . . . . 67 E6
Barley Mow La B61 . . . . . . 49 B8
Barlich Way B98 . . . . 71 A2
Barlow Cl B45 . . . . 17 E2
Barnard Cl WR11 . . . . 161 E2
Barnards Cl WR14 . . . . . . 153 B7
BARNARD'S GREEN 153 B7
Barnard's Green Rd
  WR14 . . . . 153 B8
Barn Cl
  Birmingham B30 . . . . 20 B6
  Cradley Heath B64 . . . . 7 E6
  Halesowen B63 . . . . 7 E2
  Stoke Heath B60 . . . . 67 E6
  Stourbridge DY9 . . . . 6 C4
  Worcester WR2 . . . . 127 E8
Barn Croft B32 . . . . 9 E1
Barneshall Ave WR5 . . . . 128 C6
Barnes Hill B29 . . . . 9 F2
Barnes Pl 1 WR5 . . . . 128 D6
Barnes Way WR5 . . . . 128 D6
BARNETTBROOK 29 D5
Barnetts Cl DY10 . . . . 28 B4
Barnetts Gr DY10 . . . . 28 A4
Barnetts La DY10 . . . . 28 A4
Barnfield Cider & Wine Mill★
  WR12 . . . . 177 A1
Barnfield Rd
  Bromsgrove B61 . . . . 48 E1
  Halesowen B62 . . . . 8 D7
  2 Stourport-on-Severn
    DY13 . . . . 43 F1
Barnfields DY14 . . . . 22 B3
Barn La
  Birmingham, King's Heath
    B13 . . . . 21 A7
  Sedgeberrow WR11 . . . . . 174 F1
Barn Owl Pl DY10 . . . . 28 A2
Barnowl Wlk DY5 . . . . 6 C6
Barnpark Covert 9 B14 . . 20 C2
Barn Piece B32 . . . . 9 B4
Barns Croft Way 6 WR9 . 84 C1
Barnsdale Cres B31 . . . . . . 18 E4
Barnsley Hall Dr B60 . . . . 49 B6
Barnsley Hall Rd B61 . . . . 49 A6
Barnsley Rd B61 . . . . 49 B4
Barnswood Cl B63 . . . . 7 C5
BARNT GREEN 50 A7
Barnt Green Rd B45 . . . . . 33 C5
Barnt Green St Andrews CE
  Fst Sch B45 . . . . 50 B8
Barnt Green Sta B45 . . . . 50 B8
Barnwood Cl B98 . . . . 71 D5
Barnwood Rd B32 . . . . 9 F4
Baron Bsns Ctr DY9 . . . . . 6 E5
Barrack La B63 . . . . 7 B6
Barracks Rd DY13 . . . . . . 44 C1
Barrar Cl DY8 . . . . 5 E8
Barratts Cl 5 DY12 . . . . . 26 A3
Barratts Ho 3 B14 . . . . . . 20 E2
Barratts Rd B38 . . . . 20 A1
Barratts Stile La 4 DY12 . 26 A3
Barrett Cl DY10 . . . . 28 B6
Barrett Rise WR14 . . . . . . 139 A2
Barrie Ave DY10 . . . . 28 C7
Barrington Rd B45 . . . . . . 32 E7
Barron Rd B31 . . . . 19 B3
Barrow Cl B98 . . . . 71 F3
Barrs Cres B64 . . . . 7 F8
Barrs Rd B64 . . . . 7 F8
Barry St WR1 . . . . 115 C4
Barsham Dr DY5 . . . . 6 C8
Barston Rd B68 . . . . 9 B7
Bartestree Cl B98 . . . . 71 F1
Bartholomews La B61 . . . . 48 F5
Bartleet Rd B98 . . . . 90 E8
Bartley Dr B31 . . . . 18 E8
BARTLEY GREEN 18 D7
Bartley Green Sch B32 . . . 9 C1
Bartley Ho B32 . . . . 18 D8
Bartley Mews B31 . . . . 18 E8
Bartley Woods B32 . . . . . . 9 B2
BARTON 136 F3
Barton Croft B28 . . . . 21 F4
Barton Ct GL20 . . . . 196 F6
Barton Lodge Rd B28 . . . . 21 E4
Barton Mews 6 GL20 . . . 196 F6
Barton Rd
  Tewkesbury GL20 . . . . . . 196 F6
  Welford-on-Avon CV37 . . 137 D3
Barton St GL20 . . . . 196 F6
Bascote Cl B97 . . . . 70 B1
Basil Gr B31 . . . . 18 E4
Basil Rd B31 . . . . 18 E4
Basin Rd WR5 . . . . 128 B8
Baskerville Rd DY10 . . . . . 12 F1
Bassett Rd B63 . . . . 7 A6
Bassnage Rd B63 . . . . 7 E2
BASTONFORD 127 A2
Batchelor Cl DY8 . . . . 5 F8
BATCHLEY 70 B3
Batchley Fst Sch B97 . . . . 70 B4
Batchley Rd B97 . . . . 70 C4
BATEMAN'S GREEN 35 E6
Batemans La B47 . . . . 35 E5
Bates Hill B97 . . . . 70 D4
Bates La B94 . . . . 53 F1
Batham Rd DY10 . . . . 28 A8
Bath Ct 4 B29 . . . . 19 B7
Batheaston Cl B38 . . . . . . 34 D7
Bath La DY7 . . . . 3 D5
Bath Mdw B63 . . . . 7 E5

Bath Mews DY8 . . . . 5 F5
Bath Rd
  Kempsey WR5 . . . . 128 C1
  Stourbridge DY8 . . . . 5 F5
  7 Worcester WR5 . . . . . 115 C1
Batsford Cl B98 . . . . 90 B5
Batsford Rd WR5 . . . . 128 E5
Batson Rise DY5 . . . . 6 A8
Battenhall Ave WR5 . . . . 128 D8
Battenhall Pl 7 WR5 . . . . 115 C1
Battenhall Rd WR5 . . . . . 115 D1
Battenhall Rise WR5 . . . . 128 E2
Battenhall Wlk 9 WR5 . . 115 D1
Battens Cl B98 . . . . 70 F3
Battens Dr B98 . . . . 71 D3
BATTENTON GREEN 82 E8
Battisto Wlk WR14 . . . . . 139 C1
Battle Rd
  Tewkesbury GL20 . . . . . . 196 D4
  Worcester WR5 . . . . 128 D8
Battleton Rd 2 WR11 . . . 161 E2
Battle Well★ WR11 . . . . . 161 D8
BAUGHTON 170 B8
Baughton La
  Earl's Croome WR8 . . . . . 156 E1
  Hill Croome WR8 . . . . . . 170 F7
Baveney Rd WR2 . . . . 114 E6
Baverstock Foundation Sch
  & Specialist Sports Coll 6
    B14 . . . . 20 E2
Baverstock Rd B14 . . . . . . 20 E2
Bawdsey Ave WR14 . . . . 139 B2
Baxter Ave DY10 . . . . 27 F7
Baxter Coll DY11 . . . . 27 B6
Baxters Wlk WR14 . . . . . 139 C1
Bayford Ave B31 . . . . 33 E6
Baylie Ct DY8 . . . . 5 F5
Baylie St DY8 . . . . 5 F4
BAYLIS GREEN 53 A1
Bayliss Rd B31 . . . . 19 B5
Bayliss Rd GL20 . . . . 185 D7
Bayly Rd WR11 . . . . 161 E2
BAYNHALL 141 C3
Baynham Dr WR5 . . . . . . 129 A8
Bays Mdw WR9 . . . . 85 A5
Bayston Rd B14 . . . . 20 E3
BAYTON 40 B7
Bayton CE Prim Sch DY14 40 A7
BAYTON COMMON 40 E6
Bay Tree Cl B38 . . . . 34 D8
Beach Cl
  Birmingham B31 . . . . 19 C1
  1 Evesham WR11 . . . . . 161 E3
Beach Dr B63 . . . . 8 A5
BEACH HAY 23 F1
Beach Rd DY13 . . . . 43 E1
Beach St B63 . . . . 8 A5
Beacon Cl B45 . . . . 33 A6
Beacon Grange WR14 . . . 153 A7
Beaconhill Dr WR2 . . . . . 114 E6
Beacon Ho WR14 . . . . . . 138 F3
Beacon La
  Birmingham B60, B45 . . . . 32 E4
  Kinver DY7 . . . . 2 F3
  Upper Arley WV15 . . . . 2 D3
Beacon Rd WR14 . . . . . . 152 D4
Beacon Rise DY9 . . . . 6 E4
Beaconside Prim Sch B45 32 E6
Beacon View B45 . . . . 33 A6
Beaks Hill Rd B38 . . . . . . 19 E2
Beale St DY8 . . . . 5 F5
Bean Croft B32 . . . . 9 C2
Bearcroft Ave WR4 . . . . . 116 B6
Bearcroft Gdn GL55 . . . . 165 D4
Bear Hill B48 . . . . 51 B5
Bear Hill Dr B48 . . . . 51 B6
Bear La GL20 . . . . 181 F4
Beauchamp Ave WR11 . . . 27 D3
Beauchamp Bsns Ctr
  WR14 . . . . 139 B4
Beauchamp Ct DY11 . . . . . 27 D3
Beauchamp Hts DY11 . . . . 27 D3
Beauchamp La
  Callow End WR2 . . . . 127 F1
  Powick WR2 . . . . 128 A1
Beauchamp Rd
  Birmingham B13 . . . . 21 C5
  Malvern WR14 . . . . 138 F4
  Walton Cardiff WR12 . . . . 197 B3
Beaudesert Cl B47 . . . . . . 36 A6
Beaudesert Rd B47 . . . . . 36 A6
Beaufort Ave DY11 . . . . . . 27 A7
Beaufort End WR11 . . . . . 164 C5
Beaufort Pl GL20 . . . . . . 196 E4
Beaufort St B98 . . . . 70 E3
Beaulieu Cl DY11 . . . . 27 D8
Beaumaris House B31 . . . 18 D6
Beaumont Dr DY5 . . . . 6 B7
Beaumont Lawns B60 . . . . 32 D1
Beaumont Pk B30 . . . . 19 F4
Beaumont Rd
  Birmingham B30 . . . . 19 F6
  Halesowen B62 . . . . 8 E8
Beauty Bank B64 . . . . 8 A8
Beauty Bank Cres DY8 . . . . 5 F6
Beaver Cl 2 WR2 . . . . . . 127 E6
Beaver Pk B63 . . . . 7 F6
Beckett Cl
  Redditch B98 . . . . 70 F5
  Worcester WR3 . . . . 115 A8
Beckett Dr WR3 . . . . 115 B8
Beckett Rd WR3 . . . . 115 A8
Beckfield Cl B14 . . . . 20 E2
BECKFORD 186 D4
Beckford Cl GL20 . . . . . . 186 C3
Beckford Cross GL20 . . . 186 E3

Beckford Hall★ GL20 . . . 186 C4
Beckford Rd
  Ashton under Hill WR11 . . 187 B7
  Dumbleton WR11 . . . . . . 187 D5
Beckman Rd DY9 . . . . 6 C2
Becks The B48 . . . . 51 A7
Bedcote Pl DY8 . . . . 6 B4
Bedford Cl 2 WR10 . . . . . 144 C1
Bedlam Wood Rd B31 . . . . 18 C1
Bedwardine Cl WR2 . . . . 127 C8
Bedwardine Rd 11 WR2 . 114 F1
Beech Ave
  Birmingham B32 . . . . 9 D7
  Drakes Broughton WR10 . 143 F6
  Halesowen B62 . . . . 8 C8
  Worcester WR3 . . . . 115 C7
Beech Avenue N WR3 . . . 115 C7
Beech Cl
  Kinver DY7 . . . . 4 B4
  Malvern WR14 . . . . 139 B5
Beechcombe Cl 2
  WR10 . . . . 144 D2
Beechcote Ave DY11 . . . . . 12 D2
Beechcroft WR14 . . . . . . 138 F4
Beechcroft Dr B61 . . . . . . 49 B4
Beechcroft Est B63 . . . . . . 7 C6
Beechcroft Rd DY11 . . . . . 27 A8
Beech Ct
  Birmingham, Bournville
    B30 . . . . 19 E4
  Birmingham, Longbridge
    B45 . . . . 33 D7
Beechdale B68 . . . . 9 B7
Beech Dr DY10 . . . . 64 C8
Beecher Pl B63 . . . . 7 D5
Beecher Rd B63 . . . . 7 D5
Beecher Road E B63 . . . . . 7 D5
Beeches Cl B45 . . . . 32 D8
Beeches Ct B45 . . . . 33 A8
Beeches Farm Dr B31 . . . . 34 A7
Beeches Mews DY9 . . . . . . 14 F4
Beeches Rd DY11 . . . . 12 C1
Beeches The
  Mamble DY14 . . . . 40 A4
  Ryall WR8 . . . . 169 E6
  Upton Warren B61 . . . . . . 67 A4
Beeches View Ave B63 . . . 7 C4
Beeches Way B31 . . . . 34 A7
Beech Farm Croft B31 . . . 19 A3
Beechfield Cl B62 . . . . 8 C8
Beechfield Dr 2 DY11 . . . 12 C1
Beech Gr B14 . . . . 21 A5
Beech Hill Ho B32 . . . . . . 18 C8
Beech Ho B98 . . . . 89 F8
Beech Hurst 1 B38 . . . . . 34 E8
BEECH LANES 9 E6
Beechlawn Dr DY7 . . . . . . 4 E7
Beech Park Dr B45 . . . . . . 50 C8
Beech Rd
  Birmingham, Bournville
    B30 . . . . 19 E6
  Bromsgrove B61 . . . . 48 F4
  Hollywood B47 . . . . 36 B6
  Stourbridge DY9 . . . . 5 F3
Beech Tree Cl B97 . . . . . . 70 B4
Beechtree La DY10 . . . . . . 13 E6
Beechtree Pk B50 . . . . . . 136 E6
Beech Wlk B38 . . . . 34 F8
Beechwood Ct
  1 Birmingham B30 . . . . . 20 C3
  Cradley Heath B64 . . . . . . 8 A7
Beechwood Rd
  Birmingham B67 . . . . 9 F8
  Birmingham, King's Heath
    B14 . . . . 20 F5
Beehive Cl B61 . . . . 32 A1
Beehive Pl WR4 . . . . 116 C5
Beeston Cl DY5 . . . . 6 D8
Beeston Gdns 14 WR4 . . 116 C5
Beeston Rd DY10 . . . . 13 A5
Begonia Cl 2 WR5 . . . . . 128 C4
Beilby Rd B30 . . . . 20 B5
BELBROUGHTON 30 E7
Belbroughton CE Prim Sch
  DY9 . . . . 30 E6
Belbroughton Cl B98 . . . . 70 F2
Belbroughton Rd
  Blakedown DY10 . . . . 14 D1
  Halesowen B63 . . . . 7 F2
  Holy Cross DY9 . . . . 15 E2
  Stourbridge DY8 . . . . 5 E3
Belfont Trad Est B62 . . . . 8 C4
Belfry Dr
  Priors Park GL20 . . . . . . 196 E5
  Stourbridge DY8 . . . . 5 E6
Belfry Rd WR9 . . . . 103 F8
Belgrave Rd B62 . . . . 8 D8
Bellars Cl WR14 . . . . 153 D8
Bellars Gdns WR14 . . . . . 153 D8
Bellar's La WR14 . . . . 153 C8
Bell Cl WR2 . . . . 101 E1
BELL END 31 C7
Belle Orch
  Kidderminster DY11 . . . . . 27 B5
  Tenbury Wells WR15 . . . . 55 F5
BELLE VALE 7 E5
Belle Vale B63 . . . . 7 E5
Belle Vue Cl B60 . . . . 32 C1
Belle Vue Dr B62 . . . . 8 E6
Bellevue Terr WR14 . . . . 152 F8
Bellfield B31 . . . . 18 F4
Bellfield Ho B14 . . . . 20 D1
Bellfield Jun & Inf Schs
  B31 . . . . 18 F4
Bellflower Rd 12 GL20 . . 197 A4
BELL GREEN 35 B5
Bell Green La B38 . . . . . . 35 B5

BELL HEATH 31 E8
Bell Heath Way B32 . . . . . 9 B2
Bell Hill 3 B31 . . . . 19 A4
Bell Holloway B31 . . . . . . 18 F5
Bell La
  Birmingham, Northfield
    B31 . . . . 19 A4
  Broadheath WR2 . . . . . . 113 F5
  Hanley WR15 . . . . 77 A7
  Studley B80 . . . . 90 E4
Bellman's Cross DY12 . . . 11 B7
Bell Mdw WR9 . . . . 15 B8
Bell Mead B80 . . . . 90 E4
Bell Meadow Way B14 . . . 20 E1
Bell Row 6 DY13 . . . . 44 A3
Bells Farm Cl B14 . . . . . . 20 C2
Bells Farm Prim Sch B14 . 20 C2
Bell Sh Ctr The B31 . . . . . 19 A4
Bells La B14 . . . . 20 D2
Bell St B63 . . . . 6 A5
Bellwood Rd B31 . . . . 18 F4
Bell Yd DY13 . . . . 190 D8
Belmont Cl B97 . . . . 70 B1
Belmont Covert B31 . . . . . 19 B6
Belmont Cres B31 . . . . . . 19 B6
Belmont Rd
  Birmingham, Rubery B45 . . 33 A6
  Malvern WR14 . . . . 138 D3
  Stourbridge DY9 . . . . 6 F4
Belmont St WR3 . . . . 115 D5
Belmont Wlk 15 WR3 . . . 115 B6
Belstone Cl B14 . . . . 20 D6
Belton Gr B45 . . . . 33 C8
Belvedere Cl B14 . . . . 20 A5
Belvedere Cres DY12 . . . . 26 C5
Belvedere Dr B61 . . . . 49 A4
Belvide Gr B29 . . . . 19 B8
Belvoir Bank WR14 . . . . . 138 D3
Belvoir Rd B60 . . . . 49 C1
Benbow Cl WR14 . . . . . . 152 E2
BENGEWORTH 161 F3
Bengeworth CE Fst Sch
  WR11 . . . . 161 E4
Bengrove Cl B98 . . . . 90 A7
Bennetts Farm Pk★
  WR2 . . . . 127 F6
Bennetts Hill WR11 . . . . . 148 D1
Bennetts Hill Bsns Pk
  WR11 . . . . 148 D1
Bennett St 2 DY11 . . . . . . 27 C6
Ben Nevis Way DY8 . . . . . . 6 A6
Bensfield WR6 . . . . 126 C5
Benson Rd B14 . . . . 21 B1
Bent Ave B32 . . . . 9 D6
Bentham Ave WR4 . . . . . 116 C3
Bentham Ct B31 . . . . 18 F5
Bentley Cl B97 . . . . 70 D3
Bentley Gr B29 . . . . 18 F6
Bentley La B97 . . . . 88 C7
Bentleys Way 2 WR12 . . 177 A1
Bentmead Gr B38 . . . . 20 A1
Benton Cl WR14 . . . . 166 F6
Benton's Ct DY11 . . . . 27 C6
BEOLEY 71 D7
Beoley Fst Sch B98 . . . . . 71 E8
Beoley Gr B45 . . . . 33 A7
Beoley Hall B98 . . . . 52 C1
Beoley La
  Beoley B98 . . . . 71 F8
  Portway B98 . . . . 53 B1
Beoley Road E B98 . . . . . . 71 A4
Beoley Road W B98 . . . . . 70 F4
Berberry Cl B30 . . . . 19 D6
Berkeley Bsns Pk WR4 . . 116 C7
Berkeley Cl
  Bromsgrove B60 . . . . 68 B8
  Redditch B97 . . . . 72 A3
  Whittington WR5 . . . . . . 129 B7
Berkeley Cres DY13 . . . . . 44 A1
Berkeley Prec B14 . . . . . . 20 F2
Berkeley Rd B90 . . . . 21 F3
Berkeley St 3 WR1 . . . . . 115 A5
Berkeley Way WR1 . . . . . 116 C7
Berkeswell Cl B98 . . . . . . 71 C7
Berkley Gdns WR3 . . . . . 102 F2
Bernie Crossland Wlk
  DY10 . . . . 27 F3
Bernwall Cl DY8 . . . . 5 F4
Berrill Cl WR9 . . . . 85 B1
BERRINGTON 55 B3
Berrington Cl B98 . . . . . . 71 D2
Berrington Gdns WR15 . . . 55 B2
BERRINGTON GREEN 55 C2
Berrington Mews WR15 . . 55 E4
Berrington Rd WR15 . . . . . 55 C4
BERROW 180 C1
BERROW GREEN 98 F1
Berrowhill La B96 . . . . 88 B2
Berrow Hill Rd 3 DY11 . . 12 B1
Berrow View B61 . . . . 67 D7
Berry Cl 6 WR2 . . . . 127 C2
Berry Dr B45 . . . . 33 A1
Berryfield Rd WR11 . . . . . 161 A3
Berry La B61 . . . . 47 C2
Berrymound View B47 . . . 36 C7
Berwick Gr B31 . . . . 18 D3
Berwick St WR5 . . . . 128 C7
BESFORD 157 C6
Besford Gr B31 . . . . 18 D3
Bestmans La WR5 . . . . . . 141 D5
Beta Cl GL20 . . . . 197 C8
Beta Gr B14 . . . . 21 C4
Bethesda Gdns 2 B63 . . . . 7 C7
Betjeman Cl 9 WR10 . . . 158 F9
Betjeman Ct DY10 . . . . . . 28 B5
Betony Rd WR14 . . . . 139 C4
Bettle Cl 4 WR10 . . . . . . 143 F6

Betton Rd B14 . . . . 20 E5
Bevan Gdns 4 GL20 . . . 184 E1
Bevans La WR11 . . . . 175 A5
BEVERE 102 A3
Bevere Cl WR3 . . . . 102 A1
Bevere Close S 1 WR3 . 102 A1
Bevere Dr WR3 . . . . 102 A1
Bevere Rd WR3 . . . . 102 A3
Beverley Cl
  Astwood Bank B96 . . . . . . 89 E2
  Kidderminster DY11 . . . . . 26 F6
Beverley Court Rd B32 . . . 9 C6
Beverley Ct 1 B62 . . . . 9 A6
Beverley Rd B45 . . . . 33 A7
Beverley Way WR14 . . . . 138 E6
BEWDLEY 26 B2
Bewdley Bsns Pk DY12 . . 25 B1
Bewdley Ct 10 WR11 . . . 161 C4
Bewdley Grange DY11 . . . 27 A5
Bewdley Hill DY11 . . . . . . 27 B5
Bewdley La WR11 . . . . . . 161 C4
Bewdley Leisure Ctr DY12 26 C2
Bewdley Mus★ DY12 . . . . 26 B3
Bewdley Prim Sch DY12 . . 26 C5
Bewdley Rd
  Birmingham B30 . . . . 20 B8
  Kidderminster DY11 . . . . . 27 C6
  1 Stourport-on-Severn
    DY13 . . . . 44 A4
Bewdley Road N DY13 . . . 43 D7
Bewdley Sch DY12 . . . . . . 26 C2
Bewdley St WR11 . . . . . . 161 C4
Bewdley Sta DY12 . . . . . . 26 C3
Bewell Cl B61 . . . . 48 F4
Bewell Gdns B61 . . . . 48 F4
Bewell Head B61 . . . . 48 F4
Bewlay Cl DY5 . . . . 6 B7
BGW Bsns Pk 4 B60 . . . . 67 F6
Bibsworth Ave
  Birmingham B13 . . . . 21 D8
  Broadway WR12 . . . . 190 E8
Bibsworth La WR12 . . . . . 177 D2
Bibury Rd B28 . . . . 21 E7
Bickington Rd B32 . . . . 9 D1
BICKLEY 38 B2
BICKMARSH 149 E8
Bickmarsh La B50 . . . . . . 136 D1
Bicknell Croft B14 . . . . . . 20 E2
Bickon Dr DY5 . . . . 6 F8
Bicton Ave 8 WR5 . . . . . 128 E6
Bidavon Ind Est B50 . . . . 136 E6
Biddles Hill B94 . . . . 53 C6
BIDFORD-ON-AVON 136 E4
Bidford-on-Avon CE Prim
  Sch B50 . . . . 136 D5
Bidford Rd
  Bidford-on-Avon B50 . . . 136 C7
  Birmingham B31 . . . . 18 E3
Bigbury La DY13 . . . . 44 D6
Bight The WR10 . . . . 160 E8
Bigwood Dr B32 . . . . 9 D1
Bilberry Cl DY13 . . . . 43 E5
Bilberry Dr B45 . . . . 33 A6
Bilberry Rd B14 . . . . 20 C6
Bilbrook Gr B29 . . . . 9 F2
Bilbury Cl B97 . . . . 89 C6
Bilford Ave WR3 . . . . 115 D7
Bilford Rd WR3 . . . . 115 C7
BILLESLEY 21 C6
BILLESLEY COMMON 21 A5
Billesley La B48 . . . . 52 E6
Billesley Prim Sch B13 . . 21 C6
Billy La B45, B60 . . . . 50 A7
Bilton Ind Est B38 . . . . . . 34 E8
Bine La DY14 . . . . 41 F6
Binswood Rd B62 . . . . 9 A7
Binton Cl B98 . . . . 71 F1
Binton Croft B13 . . . . 20 F8
Binton Rd B90 . . . . 21 F1
Binyon Cl WR11 . . . . 162 E2
BIRCH ACRE 52 D7
Birch Ave
  Birmingham B31 . . . . 18 C1
  Evesham WR11 . . . . 161 F2
  Worcester WR4 . . . . 115 E4
BIRCH BERROW 79 C6
Birch Cl B30 . . . . 19 E6
Birch Coppice WR9 . . . . . 103 C8
Birch Ct B30 . . . . 19 E4
Birch Dr DY8 . . . . 5 E6
BIRCHEN COPPICE 27 B1
Birchen Coppice Prim Sch
  DY11 . . . . 27 B2
BIRCHENSALE 70 A5
Birchensale Farm 10 B97 . 70 B5
Birchensale Mid Sch B97 . 70 C4
Birchensale Rd B97 . . . . . 70 C5
Birches Ho B97 . . . . 70 B2
Birches La B48 . . . . 50 F6
Birches The DY13 . . . . . . 44 B3
Birchfield Cl
  Halesowen B63 . . . . 7 E2
  Worcester WR3 . . . . 115 C5
Birchfield Cres DY9 . . . . . . 6 F3
Birchfield Ct B97 . . . . 70 B2
Birchfield Dr DY13 . . . . . . 43 E5
Birchfield Rd
  Kidderminster DY11 . . . . . 27 B5
  Redditch B97 . . . . 70 B2
  Stourbridge DY9 . . . . 6 F3
Birchgate DY9 . . . . 6 F4
Birch Gr
  Alveley WV15 . . . . 1 C6
  Birmingham B68 . . . . 9 D7
BIRCH GREEN 155 D8
Birch Ho B98 . . . . 89 F8
Birchinger Gn 8 WR4 . . 116 C5

Birch La
Birmingham B68 . . . . 9 D7
Severn Stoke WR8. . . . . . . 155 E6
Birchley Ho B97 . . . . 70 B1
Birch Rd
Rubery B45 . . . . 32 E6
Warley Woods B68 . . . . 9 D7
Birchtree Gr 4 WR10 . . 144 D2
Birch Tree Rd 3 DY12 . . 25 F2
Birch Wlk B68 . . . . 9 D8
BIRCHWOOD 124 E1
Birchwood 2 WR14. . . 153 A8
Birchwood Cl DY11. . . . . . 27 A7
Birchwood Dr WR14. . . . 139 C8
Birchwood Rd WR14 . . . . 138 E6
Birchwoods B32 . . . . 9 B2
Birchy Cl B90 . . . . 36 F6
Birchy Leasowes La B90. . 36 E5
Bird Cage Wlk B38. . . . . . 19 F7
Birdie Cl B38 . . . . 19 D1
Birdlip Cl WR4 . . . . 116 A6
Birdlip Gr B32 . . . . 9 C6
Bird's Barn La DY11 . . . . . 3 C2
BIRDSGREEN 1 D7
Birdwell Croft B13. . . . . . 20 F6
Birkdale Ave B60 . . . . 50 A5
Birkdale Cl DY8. . . . . 5 F2
Birkdale Gr B29. . . . . 20 A8
Birley Gr B63 . . . . 7 C1
BIRLINGHAM 158 B2
Birlingham Cl WR10. . . . 158 C7
Birlingham Ho B60. . . . . . 49 B3
BIRMINGHAM 19 A6
Birmingham Great Pk
B45. . . . . 33 B8
Birmingham Inst of Art &
Design B30. . . . . 19 F7
Birmingham Rd
Alvechurch B48 . . . . 51 B7
Badsey WR11. . . . . 162 E5
Blakedown DY10 . . . . 14 C2
Hagley DY9 . . . . 15 D7
Halesowen B63 . . . . 8 B4
Hopwood B31, B48. . . . . . 34 B4
Kidderminster DY10. . . . . . 28 D7
Lickey End B60, B61 . . . . . 49 B6
Lower Marlbrook B61 . . . . 32 B1
Redditch B97, B98. . . . . . . 70 E1
Rubery B45, B61 . . . . 32 D5
Sambourne B49 . . . . 109 F7
Studley B80, B98. . . . . 90 E7
Birmingham St
Halesowen B63 . . . . 8 B3
Stourbridge DY8 . . . . 6 B5
Birstall Way B38. . . . . 34 C8
BIRTSMORTON 180 D4
BIRTS STREET 180 A6
Bisell Way DY5 . . . . 6 C6
Biset Ave DY10. . . . . 28 B5
BISHAMPTON 132 F3
Bishop Challoner RC Sch
B14. . . . . 20 F8
Bishop Cl B45 . . . . 17 E1
Bishop Hall Cres B60. . . . 67 E7
Bishop Perone CE Coll
WR3. . . . . 115 C5
Bishops Ave WR3 . . . . . . 115 C5
Bishop's Ct B31. . . . . 19 B3
Bishops Gate B31 . . . . 19 A2
Bishop St DY13 . . . . 44 A5
Bishopstone Cl B98 . . . . . 71 F2
Bishops Wlk B64. . . . . 8 A6
Bishops Wood La WR9 . . 63 E4
Bishops Wood Rd WR9 . . 63 D2
Bisley Cl WR4. . . . . 116 A7
Bissell Cl B28. . . . . 21 F6
Bissell St B32. . . . . 9 A6
Bittell Cl B31 . . . . 33 F7
Bittell Ct B31 . . . . 33 F7
Bittell Farm Rd B48. . . . . 34 A2
Bittell La B45 . . . . 50 E8
Bittell Rd
Alvechurch B48 . . . . 51 A8
Barnt Green B45 . . . . 50 E8
Bittern Rd WR5 . . . . 128 D5
Bittern Wlk DY5 . . . . 6 C6
Bittern Wood Rd DY10 . . 28 B3
Blackberry La B63 . . . . 8 A2
Blackberry Way 10
WR11. . . . . 161 D1
Blackburne Rd B28 . . . . . . 21 F6
Blackbushe Cl B17. . . . . . . 9 F7
Blackdown Cl B45 . . . . . . 18 A2
Blackford Cl
Halesowen B63 . . . . 7 D2
Kidderminster DY11. . . . . . 27 A1
Blackfriars Ave WR9 . . . . 84 E2
Black Haynes Rd B29. . . . 19 A6
Blackheath Way WR14 . . 152 C7
Black Horse La 1 DY11 . . 27 E6
Black Horse Wlk 5
WR1. . . . . 115 C3
Black Lake La B60, B97 . . 69 C6
BLACKMINSTER 162 E6
Blackminster WR11 . . . . 162 E6
Blackminster Bsns Pk
WR11. . . . . 162 E7
Blackminster Mid Sch
WR11. . . . . 162 E7
BLACKMORE END 154 B5
Blackmore La B60. . . . . . . 49 A3
Blackmore Park Ind Est
WR8. . . . . 153 D3
Blackmore Park Rd WR14,
WR13. . . . . 153 B2
Blackmore Rd WR14 . . . . 138 E3
BLACKPOLE 115 F7

Blackpole Ind Est WR4 . . 115 F8
Blackpole Rd WR4 . . . . . 102 F1
Blackpole Trading Est E
WR3. . . . . 115 F7
Blackpole Trading Est W
WR3. . . . . 102 E1
Blacksmith Cl GL20 . . . . 186 D2
Blacksmith Dr B60. . . . . . 68 A7
Blacksmiths Bank WR9. . 63 D1
Blacksmiths Cl
Sedgeberrow WR11. . . . . . 175 A1
South Littleton WR11 . . . . 148 F1
Blacksmiths La
Beckford GL20. . . . . 186 D2
Childswickham WR12. . . . 176 E2
Cropthorne WR10 . . . . . . 160 C7
Dumbleton WR11. . . . . . . 187 F5
Hill & Moor WR10 . . . . . . 145 A3
South Littleton WR11. . . . 148 F1
Black Soils Rd B98 . . . . . . 71 F5
Blackstitch La B97. . . . . . 70 A1
BLACKSTONE 26 D1
Blackstone Riverside Pk★
DY12. . . . . 26 C1
Blackthorn Cl
Birmingham B30 . . . . 19 C6
Evesham WR11 . . . . 162 A2
Blackthorn Ct B98. . . . . . . 71 E1
Black Thorne Cl 4 WR9. 104 A8
Blackthorn Rd
Bournville B30. . . . . 19 D6
Worcester WR4. . . . . 115 C6
BLACKWELL 50 B5
Blackwell Fst Sch B60 . . 50 A6
Blackwell La 1 B97. . . . . . 70 B5
Blackwell Rd B45, B60 . . . 50 B5
Blackwell St DY10. . . . . . . 27 E6
Blackwood Rd B60 . . . . . . 49 B2
Blaenwern Dr B63 . . . . 7 B7
Blagdon Cl 12 WR5. . . . . 128 C6
Blagdon Rd B63 . . . . 8 A6
Blair Cl WR4 . . . . 116 B6
Blake Ave WR9 . . . . 84 D1
BLAKEBROOK 27 B6
Blakebrook DY11 . . . . 27 C6
Blakebrook Cl DY11. . . . . 27 C6
Blakebrook Gdns DY11 . . 27 C6
Blakebrook Specl Sch
DY11. . . . . 27 C6
BLAKEDOWN 14 C2
Blakedown CE Fst Sch
DY10. . . . . 14 C1
Blakedown Rd B63. . . . . . . 7 F1
Blakedown Sta DY10 . . . . 14 C2
Blakefield Gdns 4 WR2. 114 F1
Blakefield Rd WR2 . . . . . 114 F1
Blakefield Wlk 2 WR2. . 114 F1
Blake Hall Cl DY5 . . . . 6 C7
Blake Marsh Nature
Reserve★ DY11. . . . . 27 B7
Blakemere Cl B98. . . . . . . 71 F3
Blakemore Cl B32. . . . . . . 9 F3
Blakeney Ave DY8. . . . . . . 5 D6
Blakeney Cl 4 WR5. . . . . 128 D6
Blakenhurst WR11 . . . . . 147 F8
Blake Rd B61 . . . . 49 B8
Blakes Field Dr B45. . . . . 33 A1
BLAKESHALL 12 E7
Blakeshall La DY11. . . . . . 12 D5
Blake's Hill
North & Middle Littleton
WR11. . . . . 149 D2
Pebworth WR11. . . . . 150 A2
Blakes La WR13. . . . . 154 C8
Blake St WR5 . . . . 128 E8
Blandford Cl WR13. . . . . 167 C5
Blandford Rd B32. . . . . 9 F5
Blanquettes Ave WR3 . . 115 B6
Blanquettes St 3 WR3 . 115 B6
Blayneys La WR11. . . . . . 161 E8
Blaze La
Astwood Bank B96, B97. . . 89 A3
Feckenham B96. . . . . 88 F2
Bleachfield La B98. . . . . . 71 F8
Blenheim Cl 7 B50 . . . . 136 D5
Blenheim Cres B60 . . . . . 68 A8
Blenheim Dr GL20. . . . . . 184 F6
Blenheim Rd WR2. . . . . . 114 E3
Blessed Edward Oldcorne RC
Coll WR5 . . . . 128 D8
Blind La
Evesham WR11 . . . . 161 C5
Tanworth-in-A B94. . . . . . . 53 D1
BLISS GATE. 41 F6
Blissgate Rd DY14. . . . . . 41 F7
Blithe Cl DY8 . . . . 6 A8
Blithfield Dr DY5. . . . . 6 B7
Blockhouse Cl 8 WR1 . . 115 C2
Blockley Cl B97. . . . . 69 E2
Bloomfield Rd WR2. . . . . 127 F8
Bloomfield Street N B63 . . 7 F5
Bloomfield Street W B63 . 7 F4
Bloomsbury Gr B14 . . . . . 20 C7
Blossom Cl 4 WR5 . . . . . 116 B3
Blossom Dr B61 . . . . 49 A6
Blossomfield Cl
1 Birmingham B38. . . . . . 34 D8
Evesham WR11 . . . . 161 D1
Blossomfield Ct 2 B38. . . 34 D8
Blount Ho WR11 . . . . 27 B8
Blount Terr DY11 . . . . 27 D3
Bloxham Rd WR12 . . . . . 177 D1
Blue Ball La B63 . . . . 7 C7
Blue Bell Cl WR14. . . . . . 153 C7
Bluebell Croft B31 . . . . . . 18 F4
Bluebell Gr GL20. . . . . . . 197 A3
Bluebell La WR8 . . . . 157 E4
Bluebell Way 1 WR11. . . 175 D8

Blue Bird Pk B62 . . . . 17 B7
Blue Cedars DY8 . . . . 5 C6
BLUNTINGTON 29 E1
Blythe Cl B97. . . . . 89 D7
Blythesway B48. . . . . 51 A6
BMI Droitwich Spa WR9. . 84 F3
Boat La
8 Evesham WR11. . . . . . 161 C4
Offenham WR11. . . . . 162 A8
Boatmans Reach B14 . . . . 20 C4
Bobs Coppice Wlk DY5. . . 6 F7
BOCKLETON. 93 E7
Bockleton Rd
Bockleton WR15 . . . . 93 E8
Tenbury WR15 . . . . 55 E1
Bodenham Cl B98. . . . . . . 71 D3
Bodenham Rd
Brandhall B68. . . . . 9 B8
Frankley B31. . . . . 18 E1
Bodiam Cl 1 WR4 . . . . . 116 C6
Bog La 2 WR15. . . . . 55 E4
Boleyn Rd B45. . . . . 17 E2
Bolney Rd B32. . . . . 9 E4
Bolston Rd WR5 . . . . 128 C3
Bolton Ave WR4 . . . . 116 C5
Bomers Field B45. . . . . . . 33 C7
Bomford Hill WR4. . . . . . 116 B4
Bondfield Rd B13. . . . . . . 21 B6
Bond Ind Est WR11. . . . . 175 D6
Bond St
Malvern WR14. . . . . 139 A4
Stirchley B30. . . . . 20 A7
Bonfire Hill DY9. . . . . 31 E6
Boon St WR10 . . . . 171 D7
Booton Ct DY10 . . . . 13 A1
Boot Piece La B97 . . . . . . 70 B5
BORASTON 37 D1
Boraston Bank WR15. . . . 56 A7
BORASTON DALE. 37 C1
Boraston Dr WR15 . . . . . . 56 A6
Boraston La
Burford WR15 . . . . 56 A7
Tenbury Wells WR15 . . . . . 55 F6
Boraston Rd DY14. . . . . . . 41 F5
Bordenham Arboretum &
Visitor Ctr★ WR11 . . . . . 11 F7
Borderway WR15 . . . . 55 F6
BORDESLEY 51 D1
Bordesley Abbey★ B98. . . 70 F6
Bordesley Abbey Visitor Ctr★
B98. . . . . 70 F6
Bordesley La B98 . . . . 70 E6
BORELEY 82 C7
Boreley La WR9. . . . . 63 D1
Borough Cres DY8 . . . . 5 E5
Borough Ct B63. . . . . 8 B4
Borrington Gdns DY10. . . 28 B4
Borrington Rd DY10. . . . . 28 B5
Borrowdale Cl DY5. . . . . . . 6 B8
Borrowdale Dr WR4. . . . . 116 A5
Borrowdale Gr B31 . . . . . . 18 D3
Borrowdale Rd
Birmingham B31 . . . . 18 C3
Malvern WR14. . . . . 153 C8
Bosbury Rd WR14. . . . . . 139 A5
Bosbury Terr B30. . . . . . . 20 B7
Bosmere Ct B31. . . . . 18 F3
Boston La WR11 . . . . 160 E5
Boswell St WR14. . . . . . . 139 A4
Bott La DY9. . . . . 6 E6
Boughton Ave WR2 . . . . . 114 E1
Boughton Ct WR2. . . . . . 114 E1
Boughton Park Cl WR2. . 127 E8
Boughton St WR2. . . . . . 114 F1
Boultons La B97. . . . . 89 D6
Boundary Road E CV37 . . 151 F2
Boundary Road N CV37. . 151 E4
Boundary Road W CV37. 151 D3
Bourlay Cl B45. . . . . 17 E2
Bourne Ave
Fairfield B61 . . . . 31 F1
Halesowen B62 . . . . 8 F4
Bournebrook Cres B62 . . . 9 A4
Bourne Cl
Birmingham B13 . . . . 21 D6
6 Droitwich WR9 . . . . . . 84 F1
The Bourne WR7. . . . . . . 119 E5
Bourne Gn B32 . . . . 9 E6
Bourne Rd
Defford WR8. . . . . 157 D7
Strensham WR8. . . . . 171 A6
Bournes Cl B63 . . . . 7 F3
Bournes Cres B63. . . . . . . 7 F4
BOURNES GREEN. 30 C2
Bournes Hill B63. . . . . 7 F4
Bourne's Pl 2 WR11. . . . 161 C4
Bourne St WR3 . . . . 115 B6
BOURNE THE. 119 E5
Bourne Way Gdns B29 . . 20 A8
BOURNHEATH 48 D8
Bournheath Rd B61. . . . . . 31 D2
BOURNVILLE. 19 E7
Bournville Coll of FE B31. 19 C7
Bournville Inf Sch B30 . . 19 E7
Bournville Jun Sch B30. . 19 E6
Bournville La B30. . . . . . . 19 E6
Bournville Mews B30. . . . 19 E5
Bournville Sch B30 . . . . . 19 C6
Bournville Sta B30 . . . . . . 20 A7
BOUTS 108 B2
Bouts La WR7. . . . . 108 B2
Bowbrook Cl 1 WR10. . . 131 B2
Bowbrook House
(Preparatory Sch)
WR10 . . . . 131 B1
Bowden Gn WR9 . . . . 103 F8
Bower Bank 2 DY13. . . . . 43 E2
Bower Hill WR9 . . . . 84 D1

Bower Hill Dr 4 DY13. . . 43 E2
Bower La DY5 . . . . 7 A8
Bowes Rd B45 . . . . 32 E7
Bow Hill WR2. . . . . 140 F7
Bow La GL20. . . . . 183 B7
Bowler Rd GL20 . . . . 184 E1
BOWLING GREEN 127 B3
Bowling Green La WR8. . 169 A8
Bowling Green Rd
Bowling Green WR2. . . . . 127 B3
Stourbridge DY8 . . . . 5 E5
Bowmore Rd B60. . . . . 49 B1
Bowness Dr 2 WR4 . . . . 116 A5
Bowood Cres B31. . . . . . . 19 B2
Bowood Ct B97 . . . . 70 D4
Bowood La 4 WR5 . . . . . 128 E6
Bowpatch Cl DY13. . . . . . 62 D8
Bowpatch Rd DY13. . . . . . 43 D1
Boxbush Dr WR7. . . . . . . 143 A8
Boxnott Cl B97. . . . . 70 A2
Box Tree Cl WR8. . . . . . . 157 D3
Bozward St WR2. . . . . . . 114 F2
Bozzards Bank WR9. . . . . 63 C1
Brabham Cl DY11 . . . . 12 D1
Braceby Ave B13. . . . . 21 C6
Braces La B60. . . . . 32 C1
Bracken Cl WR2 . . . . 114 E4
Brackendale Way DY9. . . . 6 D4
Brackenfield Rd B63 . . . . . 7 E3
Bracken Gr B61. . . . . 32 A1
Brackenhurst WR14 . . . . 139 C5
Bracken Way B38. . . . . . . 34 C6
Brades Cl B63 . . . . 7 B7
Bradford La B97 . . . . 30 D5
Bradford Pl WR5. . . . . . . 116 A1
Bradley Dr WR14. . . . . . . 138 E5
BRADLEY GREEN 106 F6
Bradley Rd DY8 . . . . 5 F6
Bradleys Cl B64. . . . . 7 E7
Bradley Thursfield Ct
DY11 . . . . 27 C7
Bradmore Gr B29 . . . . 19 A8
Bradnock Cl B13 . . . . 21 C7
Bradshaw Ave B38 . . . . . . 19 D1
Bradshawe Cl B28 . . . . . . 21 D3
Bradstock Rd B30. . . . . . . 20 C4
Bradwell House B31. . . . . 18 D5
Braggington La CV37 . . . 137 E1
Braid Cl B38. . . . . 19 D1
Brake Cl B38 . . . . 14 E6
Brake The DY8. . . . . 14 F6
Bramber Way DY8 . . . . 5 F2
Bramble Cl
Malvern WR14. . . . . 139 C3
Shenley Fields B31 . . . . . . 18 F6
Bramble Gdns 5 WR5. . . 116 B3
Bramble Ho B98 . . . . 89 F8
Brambles The
Catshill B61 . . . . 49 A8
Stourbridge DY9 . . . . 6 D3
Brambling Rise B98. . . . . . 28 B1
Brambling Wlk DY5 . . . . . . 6 C6
Bramcote Rd B32 . . . . 9 C5
Bramhope Cl WR4 . . . . . . 116 A4
Bramley Ave WR2. . . . . . 114 E6
Bramley Cl
Bowling Green WR2. . . . . 127 C3
Crowle WR7. . . . . 117 F6
Bramley Dr B47. . . . . 36 B6
Bramley Pl WR2 . . . . 114 E6
Bramley Rd GL20. . . . . . . 196 F7
Bramley Way
1 Bewdley DY12 . . . . 25 F3
Bidford-on-Avon B50 . . . . 136 D5
Brampton Ct DY10 . . . . . . 13 B4
Bramshaw Cl B14 . . . . 20 F2
Branches Cl 2 DY12. . . . . 25 F2
Branch Rd B38. . . . . 34 E8
Branden Rd B48 . . . . 51 A5
BRAND GREEN 166 C7
Brandhall Prim Sch B68. . . 9 B8
Brandheath La B96. . . . . . 109 A4
Brandon Ct B31. . . . . 19 B1
Brandon Gr B31. . . . . 33 F7
Brandon Way DY5. . . . . . . 6 B8
BRANDWOOD END. 20 E4
Brandwood Gr B14. . . . . . 20 D5
Brandwood Ho B14 . . . . . 20 D7
Brandwood Park Rd B14 . 20 D4
Brandwood Rd B14. . . . . . 20 D5
Branscombe Cl B14 . . . . . 20 D5
BRANSFORD 126 C6
Bransford Rd WR2 . . . . . 114 E1
BRANSON'S CROSS 53 C1
Brantwood Ave B14 . . . . . 116 A5
Brantwood Cl 6 WR9. . . . 85 A1
Brantwood Rd 2 WR9 . . 104 A8
Brasenose Rd GL20 . . . . . 184 E6
Brassie Cl B38 . . . . 19 D1
Brayford Ave DY5. . . . . 6 B7
Braymoor Rd 12 WR1. . . 115 B4
BRAYSWICK 140 C8
Breaches La B98. . . . . 90 D8
Breakback Rd B61. . . . . . . 67 D8
Bream Cl 3 WR5 . . . . 128 C5
Brecknell Rise DY10. . . . . 27 F8
Brecon Ave
Bromsgrove B61 . . . . 49 A5
Warndon WR4 . . . . 116 A6
Brecon Cl
5 Droitwich WR9 . . . . . . 84 C1
Inkberrow WR7 . . . . 120 F6
Brecon Dr DY8. . . . . 6 B6

BREDON 184 F6
Bredon Ave
Kidderminster DY11. . . . . . 27 A1
Stourbridge DY9 . . . . 6 C5
Bredon Cl WR7 . . . . 120 E8
Bredon Cres WR11. . . . . . 161 A2
Bredon Ct B63 . . . . 8 A3
Bredon Gr WR14 . . . . 153 C6
Bredon Hancocks Endowed
CE Fst Sch WR11 . . . . . 184 E7
Bredon Hill Mid Sch
WR11 . . . . 174 C2
Bredon Hill National Nature
Reserve★ WR10 . . . . . . 172 C5
Bredon Ho B98 . . . . 90 B7
Bredon Lodge 1 GL20 . . 184 F6
Bredon Rd
Bromsgrove B61 . . . . 67 D7
Stourbridge DY8 . . . . 6 B6
Tewkesbury GL20 . . . . . . 196 E7
Bredon Sch (Pull Court)
GL20 . . . . 182 E5
BREDON'S HARDWICK . . 184 C4
BREDON'S NORTON. 172 A3
Bredon View
Broadway WR12 . . . . 190 E8
Redditch B97. . . . . 89 D8
Bredon Way 4 DY13. . . . . 43 D1
BREEDON CROSS. 20 B6
Breedon Ct B30. . . . . 20 A5
Breedon Gdns B98. . . . . . 71 A3
Breedon Rd B30. . . . . 20 A5
Breme Lodge B60. . . . . . . 68 A7
Brennand Cl B68. . . . . 9 C8
Brennand Rd B68. . . . . 9 B8
Brensham Ct GL20 . . . . . 184 F6
Brensham Rd GL20 . . . . . 197 B7
Brentford Rd B14 . . . . 21 A5
Brent Rd B30. . . . . 20 D8
Brent Wood Cl 6 WR5 . . 115 F1
BRETFORTON 163 C5
Bretforton Fst Sch
WR11 . . . . 163 C4
Bretforton Rd WR11. . . . . 162 E4
Brett Dr B32. . . . . 18 C8
Brettell La DY8. . . . . 5 F8
Brett Young Cl DY10 . . . . 28 B5
Brewers La WR11. . . . . . . 162 E3
Brewery Wlk 1 WR1. . . . 115 B4
Briar Cl
Evesham WR11 . . . . 161 D5
Lickey End B60. . . . . 49 C6
Briar Close Bsns Pk
WR11 . . . . 161 D6
Briar Hill
Bluntington DY10 . . . . 29 E1
Chaddesley Corbett DY10 . 46 E8
Briar Mill WR9. . . . . 84 D3
Briars Hollow WR9. . . . . . 84 D3
Briars The DY9 . . . . 14 F4
Briar Way
Hawkesley B38. . . . . 35 A8
16 Stourport-on-Severn
DY13. . . . . 43 E4
Brickall The CV37. . . . . . . 151 C5
BRICKFIELDS. 115 F6
Brickfields Rd WR4 . . . . . 115 E5
Brickhouse La B60. . . . . . . 67 C4
Brick Kiln Ct 8 WR11 . . . 161 D4
Brick Kiln La B47 . . . . 35 F4
Brick-Kiln St WR11 . . . . . 161 D4
Brick Kiln St DY5 . . . . 7 A8
BRICKLEHAMPTON 159 E1
Bricknell Ave 9 GL20 . . . 184 F6
Brickworks Trad Est
WR11 . . . . 162 B7
Brickyard La
Drakes Broughton &
Wadborough WR10 . . . . 144 A5
Studley B80. . . . . 90 C4
Bridewell Dr WR11 . . . . . 174 F1
Bridgeburn Rd B31 . . . . . 18 E2
BRIDGE END 193 F4
Bridgemans Cl WR12. . . . 177 E1
Bridge Meadow Cl
WR11 . . . . 175 A2
Bridge Piece B31. . . . . . . 19 B2
Bridge Rd
Alveley WV15. . . . . 1 D6
Aston Fields B60 . . . . 68 A6
Cookley DY10 . . . . 13 A6
Bridge St
Bretforton WR11. . . . . . . 163 C4
Evesham WR11 . . . . 161 D4
Halesowen B63 . . . . 7 C7
Hill & Moor WR10 . . . . . . 145 D2
1 Kidderminster DY10. . . 27 E5
Pershore WR10 . . . . 158 E7
Redditch B97. . . . . 70 D4
Stourport-on-Severn DY13. 43 F3
Worcester WR1. . . . . 115 B2
Bridge Trad Ctr B64 . . . . . 7 D8
Bridgnorth Rd
Kidderminster Foreign
DY11. . . . . 11 F4
Kinver DY7. . . . . 4 B7
Stourbridge DY7, DY8. . . . . 5 C6
Bridgnorth Row 1 WR4. 116 C7
Bridgwater Cl WR11. . . . . 116 D7
Bridle Mead B38. . . . . 34 D8
Bridle Rd DY8. . . . . 5 D6
Bridley Moor Rd B97. . . . 70 C5
Bridport Ho B31. . . . . 18 E7
BRIERLEY HILL. 6 F8

Brierley Rd B60 . . . . 49 C1
Brier Mill Rd B63 . . . . 8 C3
Briery Cl B64 . . . . .7 F7
Briery Rd B63 . . . . .7 E3
Brigadoon Gdns DY9 . . . . . . 6 C2
Brigfield Cres B13 . . . . 21 B5
Brigfield Rd B13 . . . . 21 B5
Bright Ave WR4 . . . . 116 C4
Bright St DY8 . . . . .5 D6
Brightstone Rd B45 . . . . . . 18 B2
Brimstone Cl **7** WR5 . . . . 128 C5
Brimstone La B61 . . . . 48 D7
Brindley Brae DY7 . . . . 4 C5
Brindley Heath Jun Sch
DY7 . . . . 4 A5
Brindley Rd WR4 . . . . 116 B7
Brindley St DY13 . . . . 43 F5
Brine Pits La WR9 . . . . 66 C1
Bringewood Gr B32 . . . . . . 18 B8
BRINGSTY COMMON 110 C3
Brinklow Cl B98 . . . . 90 D8
Brinklow Rd B29 . . . . .9 F2
Brinton Cl DY11 . . . . 27 C3
Brinton Cres DY11 . . . . . . 27 C3
Briseley Cl DY5 . . . . .6 D8
Bristol Ct **15** B29 . . . . 19 C7
Bristol Rd B29 . . . . 19 D8
Bristol Road S
Birmingham B31 . . . . 18 F2
Bournville B29, B30, B31 . . 19 C7
Longbridge B31, B45 . . . . 33 C8
Briston Cl DY5 . . . . .6 C8
Bristow Rd GL20 . . . . 197 A3
Britannia Cl B98 . . . . 70 F3
Britannia Gdns **1** DY13 . . 44 B1
Britannia Rd B14 . . . . 115 B4
Britannia Sq WR1 . . . . . . 115 B6
Britannia Way WR14 . . . . 139 C4
Britford Cl B14 . . . . 20 F3
Britten Dr WR14 . . . . 153 B6
Britten St B97 . . . . 70 D4
Broach Rd DY13 . . . . 44 B1
Broadacre Cl **5** GL20 . . . 184 F6
Broad Acres B31 . . . . 18 E6
BROAD ALLEY 65 D3
Broad Alley WR9 . . . . 65 D3
Broadclose La WR7 . . . . . 120 C7
BROAD COMMON 65 B4
Broadcott Ind Est B64 . . . . . 8 A8
Broadfield Cres WR3 . . . . 102 F3
Broadfield Gdns WR4 . . . 116 B6
BROADFIELDS 55 A5
Broadfields DY9 . . . . 15 A6
Broad Gd Rd B98 . . . . 71 B2
BROAD GREEN
Alvechurch 50 B1
Broadwas 112 E4
BROAD HEATH 77 A7
Broadheath CE Prim Sch
WR2 . . . . 113 F7
Broadheath Cl **1** WR9 . . 103 E8
Broad Heath Cl B97 . . . . . 70 B5
Broadhidley Dr B32 . . . . . . .9 B1
Broad Hill WR8 . . . . 157 D5
Broad La
Birmingham B14 . . . . 20 E4
Bishampton WR10 . . . . . 133 A3
Tanworth-in-A B98 . . . . . . 53 E3
Broadlands Dr WR14 . . . . 138 D4
BROAD MARSTON 151 A2
Broad Marston Rd
Mickleton GL55 . . . . 165 B6
Pebworth CV37 . . . . 150 E2
Broadmeadow WR9 . . . . . 84 E1
Broadmeadow B30 . . . . . . 20 B3
Broadmeadow Ho B32 . . . 18 D8
Broadmeadow Inf Sch
B30 . . . . 20 B2
Broadmeadow Jun Sch
B30 . . . . 20 B2
Broad Meadow La B30 . . . 20 B3
BROADMORE GREEN . . . 127 A8
Broads Bank WR14 . . . . . 138 F1
Broad St
Bromsgrove B61 . . . . 48 F4
Kidderminster DY10 . . . . . 27 E7
Worcester WR1 . . . . 115 B2
Broadstone Ave B63 . . . . . .7 B4
BROADWAS 112 C3
Broadwas CE Prim Sch
WR6 . . . . 112 B3
Broadwas Cl B98 . . . . 71 C5
BROADWATERS 13 B1
Broadwaters Dr
Kidderminster DY10 . . . . . 28 A8
West Hagley DY9 . . . . . . 15 B4
BROADWAY 190 D8
Broadway Ave B8 . . . . 8 A2
Broadway Cl **6** WR10 . . 146 A1
Broadway Fst Sch WR12 . 177 E1
Broadway Gr WR2 . . . . . 114 D1
Broadway La WR10 . . . . . 146 A1
Broadway Nature Reserve★
WR12 . . . . 190 B8
Broadway Rd
Aston Somerville WR12 . . 175 F1
Birlingham WR10 . . . . . . 158 B2
Broadway WR12 . . . . . . 177 A2
Evesham WR10 . . . . 161 F3
Weston-sub-Edge GL55 . . 165 C2
Willersey WR12 . . . . . . 177 E3
Broadway Teddy Bear Mus★
WR12 . . . . 190 E8
Broadway The DY8 . . . . . . 5 D3

Broadway Twr Ctry Pk★
WR12 . . . . 191 A4
Broadwood Dr WR13 . . . . 152 C2
Broadwood Pk WR13 . . . . 152 C2
Brochan Way B31 . . . . 18 E6
BROCKAMIN 125 D8
Brockamin La WR6 . . . . . 125 F8
Brock Cl B45 . . . . 18 A1
BROCKENCOTE 46 D8
Brockeridge Rd GL20 . . . . 183 C1
Brocket Cl **6** DY13 . . . . . 43 E6
Brockhampton Cl **4**
WR4 . . . . 115 F7
Brockhampton Est★
WR6 . . . . 110 A3
Brockhill Dr B97 . . . . 70 A5
Brockhill La
Alvechurch B48 . . . . 35 B2
Beoley B98 . . . . 53 A4
Norton Juxta Kempsey
WR5 . . . . 128 C1
Tardebigge B97 . . . . 69 E8
Brockhill Rd WR13 . . . . . 152 C5
Brockley's Wlk DY7 . . . . . . 4 C3
BROCKMANTON 92 B4
Brockmoor Cl DY9 . . . . 6 C2
Brockton Pl **2** DY13 . . . . 43 E1
Brockworth Rd B14 . . . . . 20 C2
Bromfield Rd B97 . . . . 70 D2
Bromford Dell B31 . . . . . . 19 C4
Bromley St DY9 . . . . .9 F6
Brompton Dr DY5 . . . . .6 B7
Brompton Pool Rd B28 . . . 21 E3
BROMSGROVE 48 E2
Bromsgrove Highway
Bromsgrove B60 . . . . 49 D1
Redditch B97 . . . . 69 C6
Tardebigge B60, B97 . . . . 69 C6
Bromsgrove Lower Sch
B60 . . . . 48 F1
Bromsgrove Mus★ B61 . . 49 A3
Bromsgrove Rd
Clent DY9 . . . . 15 D4
Dodford B61 . . . . 48 D6
Droitwich WR9 . . . . 85 A4
Halesowen B63 . . . . 8 C4
Mustow Green DY10 . . . . 28 F2
Redditch B97 . . . . 70 B3
Romsley B62 . . . . 17 A5
Studley B80 . . . . 90 D2
Bromsgrove Ret Pk B60 . . 49 A3
Bromsgrove Sch-Housman
Hall B61 . . . . 48 F2
Bromsgrove Sch-Senior
Campus B60 . . . . 48 F1
Bromsgrove St
Halesowen B63 . . . . 8 C4
Kidderminster DY10 . . . . . 27 E6
Worcester WR3 . . . . . . 115 B6
Bromsgrove Sta B60 . . . . . 68 B7
Bromwall Rd B13 . . . . 21 B6
Bromwich La
Stourbridge DY9 . . . . 15 B8
Worcester WR2 . . . . . . 115 A1
Bromwich Rd WR2 . . . . . 115 A1
Bromyard Rd
Kyre WR15 . . . . 75 E6
Stoke Bliss WR15 . . . . . . 76 A3
Tenbury Wells WR15 . . . . 55 F4
Tenbury WR15 . . . . 56 B2
Worcester WR2 . . . . . . 114 E1
Bromyard Terr WR2 . . . . 115 A2
Bronsil Cl WR5 . . . . 129 A8
Bronsil Dr WR14 . . . . 138 F6
Bronte Dr DY10 . . . . 28 C6
Bronweningham Ct DY10 . 27 E7
Brook Cl
Kempsey WR5 . . . . 141 D8
Solihull B90 . . . . 21 F1
Brook Cres
Stourbridge DY9 . . . . .6 F3
West Hagley DY9 . . . . . . 15 B5
Brook Ct B60 . . . . 49 B3
Brookdale
Harvington WR11 . . . . . 147 F8
Kidderminster DY10 . . . . . 27 F8
Brookdale Cl B45 . . . . 18 A1
Brook Dr B32 . . . . .9 D1
BROOK END 141 B8
Brookend Dr B45 . . . . 32 F7
Brookend La WR5 . . . . . . 128 F1
Brook Farm Dr WR14 . . . 153 C6
Brookfield
Little Comberton WR10 . . 159 B3
Malvern WR14 . . . . 139 B5
Brookfield Cl B97 . . . . 89 D4
Brookfield Ho DY9 . . . . . . 30 C7
Brookfield Rd B30 . . . . . . 20 D3
Brook Fields Rd B60 . . . . . 32 C1
Brook Holloway DY9 . . . . . .6 F4
Brookhouse La B97 . . . . . 88 E4
Brookhouse Rd B45 . . . . . 49 F7
Brook La
Birmingham B32 . . . . .9 F5
Birmingham, Billesley B13 . 21 B7
Charlton WR10 . . . . 160 E8
Cropthorne WR10 . . . . . 160 B6
Brookland Rd DY9 . . . . . . 15 A4
Brooklands Dr
Birmingham B14 . . . . 20 E5
Kidderminster DY11 . . . . . 12 D1
Brooklands La B98 . . . . . . 71 B5
Brooklands Pk B98 . . . . . . 71 F5
Brooklea Gr B38 . . . . 20 A1
Brooklyn Ct WR7 . . . . . . 120 E6
Brookmans Ave B32 . . . . . .9 D4
Brookmeadow Ct B28 . . . . 21 D6

Brookmill Cl WR13 . . . . . 152 A1
Brook Park Ind Est **4** DY9 . .6 F5
Brookpiece Ho **4** B14 . . . . 20 E2
Brook Rd
Birmingham, Rubery B45 . . 32 E7
Bromsgrove B61 . . . . 48 E1
Fairfield B61 . . . . 31 C2
Stourbridge DY8 . . . . .6 B3
Brookside
Birmingham, Northfield
B31 . . . . 18 F5
Childswickham WR12 . . . 176 F1
Colwall WR13 . . . . 152 A1
Hampton WR11 . . . . 161 B2
Malvern WR14 . . . . 139 C5
Tewkesbury GL20 . . . . . . 197 A8
Welland WR13 . . . . 167 C5
Brook Side WR5 . . . . 141 C8
Brookside Ave B13 . . . . . . 21 B7
Brookside Cl
Alvechurch B48 . . . . 51 B6
Halesowen B63 . . . . 7 D3
Brookside Dr B61 . . . . 48 F8
Brookside Rd WR2 . . . . . 114 D3
Brookside Way DY10 . . . . 14 B2
Brook St
Brierley Hill DY5 . . . . 7 A8
Kidderminster DY11 . . . . . 27 C6
Redditch B98 . . . .+. 71 A4
Stourbridge DY8 . . . . .5 E5
Stourbridge, Lye DY9 . . . . .6 F5
Worcester WR1 . . . . . . 115 B5
Brookthorpe Cl WR4 . . . . 116 A7
Brook Vale **4** DY12 . . . . 26 C3
Brookvale Cl B61 . . . . 49 B4
Brookwillow Rd B63 . . . . . .7 E1
Brook Wlk B32 . . . . .9 D2
Brookwood Ave B28 . . . . . 21 D5
Brookwood Dr B45 . . . . . . 50 C8
BROOM 136 B8
BROOMBANK 39 C1
Broom Cl B60 . . . . 49 B2
Broom Cres DY10 . . . . 28 A6
Broom Dr B14 . . . . 20 E4
BROOME 15 A2
Broome Cl **5** B63 . . . . 8 A3
Broomehill Cl DY5 . . . . 6 C7
Broome La DY9 . . . . 15 B2
Broomfield Cl DY11 . . . . . 27 C7
Broomfield Gn DY11 . . . . . 27 C7
Broomfield Rd DY11 . . . . . 27 C7
Broomhall WR5 . . . . 128 E5
Broomhall Gn **10** WR5 . . 128 E5
Broomhall La WR5 . . . . . 128 D2
Broomhall Way WR5 . . . . 128 D4
BROOM HILL 30 D3
Broom Meadow Rd WR3 . 102 F3
Broom Rise DY10 . . . . 28 A6
Broomy Cl DY13 . . . . 43 D5
Broseley Ave B31 . . . . 34 B8
BROTHERIDGE GREEN . . 168 C1
Brotherton Ave B97 . . . . . 69 F2
Broughton Cres B31 . . . . . 33 D8
BROUGHTON GREEN 105 F7
BROUGHTON HACKETT . . 117 F2
Broughton Rd DY9 . . . . . . .6 D3
Brownes Way WR2 . . . . . 101 C2
Browning Cl
Kidderminster DY10 . . . . . 28 B6
Worcester WR3 . . . . . . 115 B7
Browning Rd WR14 . . . . . 139 A2
Browning Twr B31 . . . . . . 19 C3
Brownsea Cl B45 . . . . 17 F1
Brown Sq WR8 . . . . 169 C6
Brown St WR2 . . . . 128 A8
Brown Westhead Pk DY10 12 F3
Bruce Rd DY10 . . . . 28 B7
Brueton Ave B60 . . . . 68 A8
Brueton Dr B98 . . . . 71 A3
Brunel Cl **4** DY13 . . . . . . 44 A5
Brunel Way WR11 . . . . . . 164 A6
Brunswick Cl **4** WR2 . . . 127 F6
Brunswick Gate DY8 . . . . . 6 A1
BRYAN'S GREEN 65 D5
Bryher Wlk B45 . . . . 17 E1
Bryndale Ave B14 . . . . . . 20 C4
Brynside Cl B14 . . . . 20 D2
Bryony Rd B29 . . . . 19 B7
BUCKBURY 182 A1
Buckbury Cl DY9 . . . . .6 D2
Buckfast Cl B61 . . . . 48 D1
Buckholt Dr WR4 . . . . . . 116 A8
Buckingham Cl
Malvern WR14 . . . . 139 C6
3 Walton Cardiff GL20 . 197 A4
BUCKLAND 190 A4
Buckle St
Bickmarsh B50 . . . . 149 F6
Chipping Campden WR12 . 191 A2
Honeybourne WR11 . . . . 164 A7
Pebworth WR11 . . . . . . 150 A2
Saintbury GL55 . . . . 178 C7
Willersey WR12 . . . . . . 178 B2
Buck Wood Wlk WR3 . . . 115 D6
Buckley Cl B14 . . . . 20 F8
Buckleys Gn B48 . . . . 51 A6
Buckleys The B48 . . . . 51 A6
Bucknall Cres B32 . . . . . . 18 A8
Bucknall Ho B31 . . . . 20 E6
BUCKRIDGE 24 A1
Buckridge Cl B38 . . . . 34 D7
Buck St WR2 . . . . 114 F2
BUGLE GATE 63 C4
Bulford Cl B14 . . . . 20 F2
Bullfinch Cl **6** WR5 . . . . 128 D5

Bull Ring
4 Halesowen B63 . . . . . 8 B3
Kidderminster DY10 . . . . . 27 E6
St John's WR2 . . . . 115 A1
Bullus Rd **3** DY13 . . . . . . 44 A4
Bumble Hole La B61 . . . . . 48 E7
Bunbury Gdns B30 . . . . . . 19 D4
Bunbury Rd B30, B31 . . . . 19 C4
Bundle Hill B63 . . . . 8 A4
Bungay Lake La B61 . . . . . 47 F3
Bunns Rd WR5 . . . . 128 D6
Buntsford Hill Bsns Ctr **5**
B60 . . . . 67 F5
Buntsford Dr B60 . . . . 67 F6
Buntsford Gate Bsns Pk
B60 . . . . 67 F6
Buntsford Hill B60 . . . . . . 67 F5
Buntsford Park Rd B60 . . . 67 F6
Burcher Gn DY10 . . . . 28 B5
BURCOT 49 C4
Burcot Ave B60 . . . . 49 B4
Burcot Ho B60 . . . . 49 B3
Burcot La Burcot 49 B3
Burdett Pl WR4 . . . . 116 C4
Burdock Ho B38 . . . . 19 F1
Burdock Rd B29 . . . . 19 A6
Burfield Rd B63 . . . . .7 C6
BURFORD 55 E6
Burford CE Prim Sch
WR15 . . . . 55 F6
Burford Cl WR4 . . . . 116 A7
Burford Ct DY9 . . . . .6 A8
Burford Gdns **5** WR11 . 161 E4
Burford House Gdns★
WR15 . . . . 55 C5
Burford La B98 . . . . 91 E1
Burford Park Rd B38 . . . . 34 E1
Burford Rd
Evesham WR11 . . . . 161 E4
Hollywood B47 . . . . 36 A6
BURF THE 62 F4
Burgess Cl **10** WR4 . . . . 116 C3
Burgesses The DY7 . . . . . .4 B3
Burghley Dr DY11 . . . . . . 27 C5
Burghley Wlk DY5 . . . . . . 6 B8
Burleigh Cl **5** WR15 . . . . 55 E4
Burleigh Rd WR2 . . . . . . 114 D3
Burley Cl B90 . . . . 21 F2
Burley Way B38 . . . . 34 C8
Burlingham Ave WR11 . . 161 F4
Burlingham Ct **9** WR11 . 161 D5
Burlington Cl DY10 . . . . . 28 B4
Burlish Cl DY13 . . . . 43 F6
Burlish Crossing DY13 . . . 43 F7
BURLISH PARK 43 F6
Burlish Park Prim Sch
DY13 . . . . 43 F6
Burlish Top Nature Reserve★
DY13 . . . . 43 F6
Burma Cl WR11 . . . . 161 E3
Burnell Cl B50 . . . . 136 C5
Burnham Cl **3** WR5 . . . . 128 D6
Burnhill Gr B29 . . . . 19 A8
Burnlea Gr B31 . . . . 19 C1
Burnsall Cl WR4 . . . . 116 A4
Burns Cl
Kidderminster DY10 . . . . . 28 B6
Redditch B97 . . . . 89 C8
Stourbridge DY8 . . . . .6 A8
Burnside Way B31 . . . . . . 33 F7
Burnthorne La WR13 . . . . 43 C1
Burnthorn La DY13 . . . . . 62 B8
Burnt Meadow Rd B98 . . . 71 F6
Burnt Oak Dr DY8 . . . . .6 B5
Burrington Rd B32 . . . . . . 18 A8
Burrish St WR9 . . . . 84 F3
Burrows Cl WR14 . . . . . . 139 C1
Burton Gr B64 . . . . .7 F8
Burton La B98 . . . . 70 F3
Burtree Ave WR4 . . . . . . 116 C5
BURY END 190 C6
Bury Mound Ct B90 . . . . . 21 C2
Bush La WR2 . . . . 140 D7
BUSHLEY 183 A1
Bushley Cl B98 . . . . 90 A7
BUSHLEY GREEN 182 E2
Bush Wlk **4** WR2 . . . . . 115 A2
Butchers La B63 . . . . 7 C7
Butcher's Wlk WR3 . . . . 103 A3
Bute Cl B45 . . . . 17 E1
Butler's Hill La B97 . . . . . 70 B5
Butler St B96 . . . . 89 E1
Buttercup Cl DY10 . . . . . . 27 E8
Buttercup Dr B61 . . . . 48 E2
Butterfly Cres **2** WR11 . 161 F3
Buttermere Cl DY5 . . . . . .6 B7
Buttermere Dr
Birmingham B32 . . . . .9 F3
Worcester WR4 . . . . . . 116 A6
Buttermere Rd DY13 . . . . 43 F6
Butter Wlk B38 . . . . 34 C8
Butt Furlong WR10 . . . . . 146 A2
Button Bridge La DY12 . . . 10 A6
Button Dr B61 . . . . 48 E2
BUTTONOAK 10 A1
Butts La DY10 . . . . 28 D1
Butts The WR9 . . . . 84 D2
Byefields **5** WR5 . . . . . . 141 C6
Bye Rd WR14 . . . . 153 C7
Byfield Rise WR5 . . . . . . 115 D2
Byford Cl B98 . . . . 70 E2
Bylands Cl B61 . . . . 48 E1
Byrd Row WR11 . . . . 147 D3
Byron Cl
2 Bowling Green WR2 . 127 C2
Kidderminster DY10 . . . . . 28 B5
Malvern WR14 . . . . 139 A2
Walton Cardiff GL20 . . . . 197 A5

Byron Rd B97 . . . . 89 D8
Byron Way B61 . . . . 49 A8

C

Caban Cl B31 . . . . 18 E5
Cadbury Sixth Form Coll
B38 . . . . 19 F1
Cadbury World★ B30 . . . . 19 F7
Cairndhu Dr DY10 . . . . . . 28 B7
Caister Ave WR4 . . . . . . 116 C5
CAKEBOLE 46 B5
Cakebole La DY10 . . . . . . 46 B5
Calder Cl **8** WR9 . . . . . . 84 D1
Calder Rd
Stourport-on-Severn DY13 . 43 E7
Worcester WR5 . . . . . . 115 E3
Caldwall Cres DY11 . . . . . 27 D5
Caldy Ave WR5 . . . . 128 E6
Caldy Wlk
5 Birmingham B45 . . . . 17 F1
7 Stourport-on-Severn
DY13 . . . . 43 E6
Caledonia DY5 . . . . .6 D7
Cales Ave WR14 . . . . 138 E4
Calewood Rd DY5 . . . . . . .6 D7
Calgary Dr WR2 . . . . 127 F6
CALIFORNIA 9 F2
California Ho B32 . . . . .9 E2
California La WR13 . . . . . 167 D6
California Way B32 . . . . . . .9 F2
Callcott Dr DY5 . . . . .6 D7
Callowbridge Rd B45 . . . . 32 F7
Callowbrook La B45 . . . . . 32 F7
Callow Cl **7** DY13 . . . . . . 43 D1
CALLOW END 140 F7
Callow End CE Prim Sch
WR2 . . . . 140 E7
CALLOW HILL
Callow Hill 89 A7
Rock 41 E8
Callow Hill La
Feckenham B97 . . . . 88 F6
Redditch B97 . . . . 89 B6
Callow Hill Rd B48 . . . . . . 51 A6
Callows La **2** DY10 . . . . . 27 E6
Callows Mdw WR15 . . . . . 55 E2
Calverley Rd B38 . . . . 34 D8
Camberwell Dr **9** WR5 . 128 E5
Cambrai Dr
Birmingham B28 . . . . 21 F8
Worcester Norton WR5 . . 128 F4
Cambria Dr B90 . . . . 36 E7
Cambrian Rd
11 Walton Cardiff GL20 . 197 A4
1 Walton Cardiff GL20 . 197 A4
Cambria Rd WR11 . . . . . 161 D5
Cambridge Cl WR14 . . . . 166 F7
Camel Cotts DY9 . . . . 15 E2
Cameo Dr DY5 . . . . .5 F8
Cameron Ct WR14 . . . . . 153 A6
CAMER'S GREEN 179 E3
Camford Gr B14 . . . . 20 F3
Camino Rd B32 . . . . .9 F3
Campden Cl B97 . . . . 89 D6
Campden La WR12 . . . . . 177 F3
Campden Rd
Mickleton GL55 . . . . 165 D2
Quinton CV37 . . . . 151 F2
Camp Furlong **10** WR9 . . 84 D1
Camp Hill
Malvern WR14 . . . . 138 C1
Witton WR9 . . . . 84 D1
Camp Hill Ave
8 Worcester WR5 . . . . 115 D1
Worcester WR5 . . . . . . 128 D8
Camp Hill Rd WR5 . . . . . 115 D1
Campion Cl **3** B38 . . . . . 34 F8
Campion Dr WR14 . . . . . 153 A6
Campion Gr B63 . . . . .7 D3
Campion Ho **2** B38 . . . . 34 E8
Campion Way DY12 . . . . . 26 D5
Camp La
Birmingham, King's Norton
B38 . . . . 19 F3
Grimley WR2 . . . . 101 E4
Shelsley Beauchamp WR6 . 60 E1
Camp Wood Cl B30 . . . . . 19 F8
Canada Bank WR10 . . . . . 160 E7
Canada Way WR2 . . . . . . 127 F7
Canal Side
Hopwood B48 . . . . 34 B2
Worcester WR3 . . . . . . 115 B6
Canal Side Dr B38 . . . . . . 20 A1
Canal St DY8 . . . . .5 F6
Cangle La WR4 . . . . 116 C5
Can La WR11 . . . . 135 A3
Cannon St WR5 . . . . 128 E8
Canterbury Cl B80 . . . . . . 90 C4
Canterbury Leys GL20 . . . 197 A7
Canterbury Rd
Kidderminster DY11 . . . . . 27 A6
Worcester WR5 . . . . . . 115 F2
Cantlow Rd B13 . . . . 21 A6
Canvey Cl B45 . . . . 17 E1
Capcroft Rd B13 . . . . 21 B6
Capern Gr B32 . . . . .9 F5
Captain's La WR9 . . . . . . 104 C6
Captain's Pool Rd DY10 . . 28 B2
Carden Cl **11** WR11 . . . . 115 C2
Carden St WR1 . . . . 115 C2
Cardinal Cres B61 . . . . . . 48 D1
Cardinal Dr DY10 . . . . 28 B3
Cardington Cl B98 . . . . . . 71 F3
Cardy Cl B97 . . . . 70 B4
Careless Gn DY9 . . . . .6 F4

Carisbrooke Ave 16
WR4 . . . . 116 C6
Carisbrooke Dr B62 . . . . 8 D3
Carlisle Rd WR5 . . . . 116 A2
Carlton Ave DY9 . . . . 6 E3
Carlton Cl
Kidderminster DY11 . . . . . . 27 A8
Redditch B97 . . . . 70 B1
Carlton Rd WR14 . . . . 138 F3
Carlyle Ave DY10 . . . . 28 B6
Carlyle Rd B60 . . . . 68 B8
Carmel Gr B32 . . . . .9 B1
Carnforth Dr WR4 . . . . . . 115 F6
Carnforth Rd B60 . . . . 49 B1
Carnoustie Cl B61 . . . . 67 D8
Carol Ave B61 . . . . 48 D3
Carol Cres B63 . . . . .7 F5
Carol Gdns DY8 . . . . .5 E8
Carp Cl 9 WR5 . . . . 128 C5
Carpenter Glade B63 . . . . . . 7 D5
CARPENTER'S HILL 52 F1
Carpenters Hill B98 . . . . . 52 F2
Carpet Trades Way DY11 . 27 D7
Carrant Brook Jun Sch
GL20 . . . . 184 E1
Carrant Rd GL20 . . . . 197 A7
Carriage Cl WR2 . . . . 114 F3
Carrock Fell 1 WR4 . . . . . 116 A5
Carroll Wlk DY10 . . . . 28 C5
Carter Ave DY11 . . . . 27 B4
Carter Ct DY11 . . . . 27 C4
Carters Cl
Bromsgrove B61 . . . . 67 D7
10 Worcester WR4 . . . . . 115 F6
Carter's La
Birmingham B62 . . . . 9 A3
Halesowen B62 . . . . .8 A7
Carthorse La B97 . . . . 70 B5
Cartland Rd B14, B30 . . . . 20 C7
Cartmel Cl WR4 . . . . 116 B6
Cartwright Ave WR4 . . . . 116 C3
Cartwright Rd B60 . . . . . . 67 D2
Carver Gdns DY8 . . . . .5 E2
Cascades Leisure Ctr
GL20 . . . . 196 E6
Caslon Cres DY8 . . . . 5 D4
Caslon Flats B63 . . . . 7 C4
Caslon Prim Sch B63 . . . . 7 C4
Caslon Rd B63 . . . . 7 C6
Castell Pl 2 WR4 . . . . . . 116 C6
Castillo Ct B14 . . . . 21 A5
Castle Cl
Burford WR15 . . . . 56 A6
Northwick WR3 . . . . 115 B8
Castle Croft B68 . . . . .9 D8
Castleditch La B98 . . . . . . 89 E7
Castle Gr DY8 . . . . .6 B3
CASTLE HILL 99 E3
Castle Hts B64 . . . . .8 B8
Castle La DY12 . . . . 26 C4
CASTLEMORTON 180 C7
Castlemorton CE Prim Sch
WR13 . . . . 180 C7
CASTLEMORTON
COMMON 167 A3
Castle Pl 3 WR1 . . . . 115 C1
Castle Rd
Birmingham, King's Norton
B30 . . . . 19 F4
Cookley DY10 . . . . 13 A4
Kidderminster DY11 . . . . . 27 E5
Studley B80 . . . . 90 F4
Castle Road E B68 . . . . . . .9 D8
Castle Road W B68 . . . . . . 9 C8
Castle St
Astwood Bank B96 . . . . . . 89 E2
3 Evesham WR11 . . . . . 161 E4
Kinver DY7 . . . . 4 A4
Worcester WR1 . . . . 115 B3
Castle The DY8 . . . . .6 B3
Castle Toot ★ DY14 . . . . . 22 E5
Catalpa Cl WR14 . . . . 138 F6
Catbrook WR3 . . . . 115 D6
CATCHEMS END 26 C5
Catesby Pk B38 . . . . 19 E3
Cathcart Rd DY8 . . . . .5 E5
Cathedral Ave DY11 . . . . . 27 A6
Cathedral Plaza Sh Ctr **27**
WR1 . . . . 115 C2
Catherine Cl B60 . . . . 67 F8
Catherine Rd WR2 . . . . . . 127 C6
Catherton Cl DY14 . . . . . . 22 B4
Catherton Rd DY14 . . . . . . 22 B5
CATSHILL 49 A8
Catshill Fst Sch B61 . . . . 49 A8
Catshill Mid Sch B61 . . . 48 F8
CAUNSALL 13 B7
Caunsall Rd DY11 . . . . 13 B6
Causeway The GL19 . . . . 192 A3
Causey Farm Rd B63 . . . . 16 C8
Cavalier Dr B63 . . . . 8 A3
Cavendish Cl
Birmingham B38 . . . . 20 B1
Lower Marlbrook B60 . . . . 32 C1
Cavendish Dr
Kidderminster DY10 . . . . . 28 B7
West Hagley DY9 . . . . 14 F4
Cavendish Rd B62 . . . . .8 F4
Cavendish St WR5 . . . . . . 128 C2
Caynham Cl B98 . . . . 71 D4
Caynham Rd B32 . . . . 18 B8
Cecilia Ave WR2 . . . . 114 E5
Cecilia Pl WR2 . . . . 114 E6
Cecil Rd WR5 . . . . 115 D2
Cecil St DY8 . . . . .5 F5
Cedar Ave
Malvern WR14 . . . . 139 B3
Worcester WR4 . . . . 115 E6

Cedar Cl
Alveley WV15 . . . . 1 C6
Birmingham, Bournville B30 **19** E6
Birmingham, Brandhall B68. . . 9 C8
Droitwich WR9 . . . . 103 F8
Stourbridge DY8 . . . . 5 D2
Stourport-on-Severn DY13 . 43 F2
Cedar Cres DY11 . . . . 27 C6
Cedar Dr
Birmingham, West Heath
B31 . . . . 34 B7
Bromsgrove B60 . . . . 49 A1
Kidderminster DY11 . . . . . 27 C7
Cedar Gdns DY7 . . . . 3 F8
Cedar Gr DY9 . . . . 15 A6
Cedar Park Rd B97 . . . . . . 70 D4
Cedar Rd
Birmingham B30 . . . . 19 E6
Mickleton GL55 . . . . 165 E4
Northway GL20 . . . . 197 E8
Redditch B97 . . . . 70 D4
Cedar Rise **15** DY13 . . . . 43 E4
Cedars The WR14 . . . . . . 138 F3
Cedar Terr B60 . . . . 49 A1
Cedar View B97 . . . . 70 C4
Cedar Way B31 . . . . 18 F1
Cedarwood Gdns 1
WR11 . . . . 161 F3
Celandine Dr WR5 . . . . . . 128 D4
Celandine Way WR11 . . . 175 C8
Celestine Way WR9 . . . . 84 C2
Celeste Rd B60 . . . . 49 C1
Celvestune Way WR9. . . . 84 B7
Cemetery La B63 . . . . 8 B3
Cemetery Rd DY9 . . . . .6 E5
Centenary Cl 1 B31 . . . . . 19 A1
Central Ave
Birmingham B31 . . . . 33 F8
Cradley Heath B64 . . . . . . .7 D7
Stourbridge DY9 . . . . 6 E3
Central Rd B60 . . . . 49 A2
Centre Cl B63 . . . . .8 B3
Centre La B63 . . . . .8 B3
Centre Pl WV15 . . . . 1 C5
Centreway The B14 . . . . . 21 D4
Century Way B63 . . . . 7 D6
CHACELEY 195 D2
Chaceley Dr B97 . . . . 89 D8
Chacewater Ave WR3 . . . 115 A7
Chacewater Cres WR3 . . 115 A7
CHADBURY 147 A2
Chadbury Rd
Halesowen B63 . . . . 8 C3
Norton & Lenchwick WR11 147 B2
Chadcote Way B61 . . . . . . 31 F1
Chaddersley Cl 2 B45 . . . 17 F1
Chaddesley Cl B97 . . . . . . 70 F1
CHADDESLEY CORBETT . . 46 E8
*Chaddesley Corbett Endowed
Prim Sch* DY10 . . . . 46 E8
Chaddesley Dr DY9 . . . . . .6 B1
Chaddesley Gdns 2 DY10 28 A5
Chaddesley Rd
Birmingham B31 . . . . 19 D2
Halesowen B63 . . . . .7 F2
Kidderminster DY10 . . . . . 28 A5
*Chaddesley Woods National
Nature Reserve* ★ WR10. . 47 B7
Chadsgrove Specl Sch
B61 . . . . 48 F8
Chadwick La DY9 . . . . 31 F7
CHADWICK 63 E7
Chadwick WR4 . . . . 116 C4
Chadwick Ave B45 . . . . . . 33 B6
Chadwick Bsns Pk DY13 . . 63 D8
Chadwick Ind Est DY13. . . 63 D8
Chadwick La
Chapman's Hill DY9 . . . . . 32 A7
Hartlebury DY11 . . . . 44 E2
Chadwick Mews B98 . . . . 90 A7
Chaffinch Dr DY10 . . . . . . 27 F2
Chaffinch Rd DY9 . . . . 6 D3
Chale Gr B14 . . . . 21 A3
Chalfont Cl WR3 . . . . 115 B7
Chalfont Pl DY9 . . . . .6 E2
Chalford Dr WR4 . . . . . . 116 A7
Chalgrove Ave B38 . . . . . . 19 E1
Challenger Cl WR14 . . . . 139 B1
Chalverton Ct 9 WR9 . . . . 84 C1
Chalybeate Cl B45 . . . . . . 17 F1
Chamberlain La B49 . . . . 109 A2
Chamberlain Rd
Birmingham B13 . . . . 21 A6
Worcester WR2 . . . . 127 F7
Champney DY10 . . . . 27 E2
Chance Croft B68 . . . . .9 B8
Chance La WR14 . . . . 153 E8
Chancel Way B62 . . . . 8 C6
Chancery Mews 1 B61 . . 48 F1
Chance St 4 GL20 . . . . . 196 F6
Chandler Ave DY7 . . . . . . .3 F5
Chandlers Cl B97 . . . . 89 D7
CHANDLER'S CROSS . . . 166 F1
Chandlers End WR11 . . . 174 B1
Channon Dr DY5 . . . . 6 D8
Chanston Ave B14 . . . . . . 20 E4
Chantry Cl
Hollywood B47 . . . . 36 A7
7 Tenbury Wells WR15. . . 55 E5
Chantry Dr B62 . . . . .9 A6
Chantry High Sch The
WR6 . . . . 99 B5
Chantry Rd DY7 . . . . .3 F5
Chantry The 1 WR10 . . . 146 A1
Chapel Cl
3 Bidford-on-Avon B50 . 136 D4
Cradley Heath B64 . . . . . . 8 B8
Leigh WR13 . . . . 126 A4

Chapel Ct
Astwood Bank B96 . . . . . . 89 E1
Kidderminster DY10. . . . . . 13 A1
Chapel Dr B47 . . . . 35 F3
Chapelfield Mews
Birmingham B45 . . . . 32 F6
Chapelfield Rd B45 . . . . . . 33 A7
Chapel Hill DY10 . . . . 13 A1
Chapel House La B63 . . . . . 7 C6
Chapel La
Aldington WR11 . . . . 162 C5
Beoley B98 . . . . 71 F8
Bidford-on-Avon B50 . . . 136 D4
Bransford WR6 . . . . 126 D4
Bredon GL20 . . . . 185 A4
Childswickham WR12 . . . 176 F2
Lindridge WR6 . . . . 59 D7
Madeley Heath DY9 . . . . . 31 D7
Mickleton GL55 . . . . 165 D4
Ombersley WR9 . . . . 83 A4
Redmarley D'abitot GL19. 192 A1
Rock WR14 . . . . 24 E1
Romsley B62 . . . . 16 C6
Rowney Green B48 . . . . . . 51 F4
5 Stourport-on-Severn
DY13 . . . . 62 E8
Upton Snodsbury WR7 . . 131 C8
Weston-sub-Edge GL55 . . 178 D6
Wyre Piddle WR10 . . . . . 145 B3
Wythall B47 . . . . 35 E2
Chapel Mews WR9 . . . . . 85 E8
Chapel Mill Apartments
B62 . . . . 8 C8
Chapel Pl DY11 . . . . 27 D6
Chapel Rd
Alveley WV15 . . . . 1 C5
Astwood Bank B96 . . . . . . 89 E1
Kempsey WR5 . . . . 141 C7
Pebworth CV37 . . . . 150 E2
Chapel St
Astwood Bank B96 . . . . . . 89 E1
Badsey WR11. . . . . 162 E3
2 Brierley Hill, Quarry Bank
DY5 . . . . 7 A8
Bromsgrove B60 . . . . 49 A2
2 Evesham WR11. . . . . . 161 D4
Halesowen B63 . . . . 8 A3
Kidderminster DY11. . . . . 27 D6
Redditch B97 . . . . 70 D1
Stourbridge, Lye DY9. . . . . 6 E5
Stourbridge, Wollaston DY8. . 6 A4
West Hagley DY9. . . . . . . 15 A5
Chapel Street Prec 1
B60 . . . . 49 A2
Chapel Wlk
Birmingham B30 . . . . 20 A2
Bromsgrove B60 . . . . 49 A2
10 Worcester WR1 . . . . . 115 B2
CHAPMAN'S HILL 32 B8
Chapman's Hill B62 . . . . . 17 B1
Charfield Cl B30 . . . . 19 D7
CHARFORD 67 F7
Charford Fst Sch B60 . . . 67 F7
Charford Rd B60 . . . . 67 F8
Charity Cres WR11 . . . . . 161 D1
Charland Ct 10 WR9 . . . . 84 D5
Charlecote Cl B98 . . . . . . 71 D2
Charlecot Rd WR9 . . . . . . 85 A1
Charlecott Cl B13 . . . . . . 21 D7
Charles Ave
Evesham WR11 . . . . 161 D3
15 Walton Cardiff GL20. 197 A4
Charles Dickens Cl 2
WR9 . . . . 103 E8
Charles Hastings Way
WR5 . . . . 116 B2
Charles Henry Rd WR9 . . 85 A3
Charles Orch WR8 . . . . . 169 C4
Charles Rd
Halesowen B63 . . . . .7 F4
Stourbridge DY8 . . . . 5 E4
Charles St
Kidderminster DY10 . . . . . 27 F6
Redditch B97 . . . . 70 C1
6 Worcester WR1 . . . . . 115 C2
Charles Way WR14 . . . . . 139 C3
Charlock Rd WR14 . . . . . 153 D7
Charlotte Bronte Dr 3
WR9. . . . . 103 E8
Charlotte Rd B30 . . . . . . 20 A6
CHARLTON
Charlton 160 E8
Hartlebury 44 E3
Charlton Cl WR11 . . . . . . 161 A3
Charlton Dr B64 . . . . .7 D7
Charlton La DY13 . . . . 44 F4
Charnwood Cl
Birmingham B45 . . . . 18 B3
Brierley Hill DY5 . . . . 6 B8
3 Worcester WR2 . . . . . 127 F7
Charnwood Dr DY9 . . . . . .6 E2
Charter Cres B64 . . . . .8 B8
Charter Pl 2 WR1 . . . . . . 115 B3
Chartist La GL19 . . . . 192 E4
Chartwell Grange B64 . . . 8 A7
Chase End Cl WR5 . . . . . 128 C7
CHASE END STREET . . . 179 D3
Chase Rd
Colwall WR13. . . . . 152 D2
Great Malvern WR14 . . . 166 F7
Chase Tech Coll The
WR14 . . . . 153 B6
Chaston Cl WR7 . . . . 120 E6
Chatcombe Dr WR4 . . . . 116 A7
Chatham Rd B31 . . . . 19 A3
CHATLEY 102 C7

Chatsworth Rd B62 . . . . . . 8 A7
Chatterton Wlk 4 DY10. . 28 B6
Chaucer Cl WR5 . . . . 6 A8
Chaucer Cres DY10 . . . . . 28 C5
Chaucer Ho B63 . . . . .7 B5
Chaucer Rd B60 . . . . 68 B8
Chawn Hill WR5 . . . . 6 C3
Chawnhill Cl DY9 . . . . 6 C3
Chawn Park Dr DY9 . . . . . 6 C3
CHAWSON 84 E1
Chawson Fst Sch WR9 . . . 84 E1
Chawson La WR9 . . . . 84 C1
Chawson Pleck WR9 . . . . 84 E2
Chawson Rd WR9 . . . . 84 E2
Cheapside 1 DY13 . . . . . 44 A2
Checketts Cl
Pershore/Pinvin WR10 . . 144 E7
Worcester WR3 . . . . 115 B7
Checketts La WR3 . . . . . . 115 B8
Chedworth Cl
Birmingham B29 . . . . 19 B6
Redditch B98 . . . . 71 C5
Worcester WR4 . . . . 116 A7
Chedworth Dr WR4 . . . . . 116 A7
Chells Gr B13 . . . . 21 B5
Chelmarsh Cl B98 . . . . . . 71 C7
Chelmsford Dr WR5 . . . . 115 F1
Chelsea Cl B32 . . . . .9 F4
Chelsea Ct **6** B29 . . . . . 19 B5
Chelston Rd B31 . . . . 18 E2
Cheltenham Ave B61 . . . . 32 B1
Cheltenham Rd
Beckford GL20 . . . . 186 C2
Bredon GL20 . . . . 185 A5
Broadway WR12 . . . . 190 A5
Buckland WR12 . . . . 189 F5
Evesham WR11 . . . . 161 C1
Hinton on the Green WR11 175 B3
Sedgeberrow WR11 . . . . 174 F1
Chelworth Rd B38 . . . . . . 20 B2
Chepstow Ave WR4 . . . . . 116 B6
Chepstow Dr B61 . . . . 32 B1
Chepstow Rd B45 . . . . . . 33 B4
Chequers Cl
Malvern WR14 . . . . 139 C4
3 Stourport-on-Severn
DY13 . . . . 62 F8
Chequers La
1 Dodderhill WR9 . . . . . 66 E1
Fladbury WR10 . . . . 146 B1
Worcester WR2 . . . . 115 A2
Cherhill Covert **7** B14 . . 20 C2
Cherington Cl
Redditch B98 . . . . 71 F1
8 Worcester WR4 . . . . . 115 F7
Cherington Rd B29 . . . . . . 20 A8
Cherrington Cl B31 . . . . . 18 F7
Cherrington Gdns DY9 . . 15 C7
Cherry Cl
16 Bewdley DY12 . . . . . . 25 F3
2 Droitwich WR9 . . . . . . 85 B1
3 Evesham WR11. . . . . . 161 F2
Offenham WR11 . . . . 148 A1
Cherry Cres B61 . . . . 48 E2
Cherry Gr
Barnt Green B45 . . . . 50 C8
Stourbridge DY9 . . . . 5 E4
Cherry Hill Ave B45 . . . . . 50 C8
Cherry Hill Dr B45 . . . . . . 50 C8
Cherry Hill Rd B45 . . . . . . 50 C8
Cherry Orch
Bredon GL20 . . . . 184 E6
Charlton WR10. . . . . 160 E7
Holt WR6 . . . . 82 B3
Kidderminster DY10. . . . . . 27 F6
Pershore WR10 . . . . 144 D1
Upton upon Severn WR8 . 169 C5
CHERRY ORCHARD 128 D7
Cherry Orchard Ave B63. . .7 F5
Cherry Orchard Cres B63. .7 F6
Cherry Orchard Dr B61 . . 48 E3
Cherry Orchard Fst Sch
WR10 . . . . 128 D7
Cherry Orchard La GL20. 183 E6
*Cherry Orchard Nature
Reserve* ★ WR5. . . . . . . 128 C6
Cherry Orchard Prim Sch
WR5 . . . . 128 D7
Cherry Orchard Rd
WR10. . . . . 145 D3
Cherry Pit La B98 . . . . 53 A1
Cherry St
Halesowen B63 . . . . .7 F5
Stourbridge DY8 . . . . 5 E4
Worcester WR5 . . . . 128 C8
Cherry Tree Cres WR11. . 135 F3
Cherrytree Ct DY9 . . . . . . .6 E3
Cherry Tree Dr WR14 . . . 152 F4
Cherry Tree La B63 . . . . . . 7 D1
Cherry Tree Wlk
Astley & Dunley DY13 . . . 62 E7
Redditch B97 . . . . 70 B4
6 Worcester WR1 . . . . . 115 B3
Cherry Wlk B47 . . . . 36 B5
Cherwell Cl WR4 . . . . 115 F4
Cherwell Ct WR4 . . . . . . 115 F4
Cheshire Cl DY8 . . . . 5 D8
Cheshire Gr DY11 . . . . . . 27 A7
Cheslyn Gr B14 . . . . 21 A3
Chessetts Gr B13 . . . . . . 21 A6
Chesshire Cl 4 DY13. . . . 62 E8
Chester Cl 1 WR5 . . . . . 115 F1
Chester Ct **5** B23 . . . . . . 19 B7
Chesterfield Cl B31 . . . . . 19 B2
Chesterfield Ct B38 . . . . . 19 E4
Chester Pl WR14 . . . . 138 E4

Chester Rd
Cradley Heath B64. . . . . . . 7 C8
Kinver DY7 . . . . .3 F7
Chester Rise B68 . . . . .9 B8
Chester Road N DY10 . . . 28 A7
Chester Road S DY10 . . . . 27 F4
Chesterton Cl B97 . . . . . . 89 D4
Chesterton Gdns WR5 . . 116 A3
Chesterwood B47. . . . . . . 36 A6
Chesterwood Rd B13. . . . 20 F6
Chestnut Cl
Aldington WR11. . . . . 162 C5
Drakes Broughton WR10. . 144 A6
Evesham WR11 . . . . 161 B2
Hill & Moor WR10 . . . . . . 145 D3
Stourbridge DY8 . . . . 5 D3
Welland WR13. . . . . 167 C5
Chestnut Ct
Kidderminster DY11. . . . . . 27 B8
Malvern WR14. . . . . 153 B8
Chestnut Dr
Birmingham, Rednal B45. . .33 D4
Malvern WR14. . . . . 152 F4
West Hagley DY9 . . . . 14 F4
Chestnut Gr
Kidderminster DY11. . . . . . 27 B8
Kinver DY7. . . . . 3 F5
Tewkesbury GL20 . . . . . . 197 B3
Chestnut La WR7 . . . . . . 120 E7
Chestnut Pl B14 . . . . 20 E8
Chestnut Rd
Astwood Bank B96 . . . . . . 89 E1
Birmingham, Brandhall B68. . .9 C7
Bromsgrove B61 . . . . 48 F4
Chestnut Spinney 5
WR9. . . . . 103 F8
Chestnut St WR1. . . . . . . 115 C4
Chestnuts The DY11. . . . . 27 C3
Chestnut Wlk
Ombersley WR9. . . . . 83 A5
Worcester WR1 . . . . 115 B4
Cheswick Cl B98 . . . . 72 A3
Chesworth Rd B60 . . . . . . 49 B1
Cheveley Ave B45 . . . . . . 33 B7
Chevenham Cl WR13 . . . 152 A1
Cheverton Rd B31 . . . . . . 18 E4
Chevington La WR10 . . . 143 E2
Cheviot Cl
Stourport-on-Severn
DY13 . . . . 62 D8
Worcester WR4 . . . . 115 F4
Cheviot Rd DY8 . . . . 6 A6
Cheviot Way B63 . . . . .7 D2
Cheyne Gdns B28 . . . . . . 21 E3
Cheyne Wlk DY5 . . . . 6 C7
Chichester Ave DY11 . . . . 12 C1
Chichester Dr B32 . . . . . . .9 A5
Chilcote Cl B28 . . . . 21 F4
Chilcote Prim Sch B28 . . 21 F4
Childe Rd DY14 . . . . 22 C4
CHILDSWICKHAM 176 E2
Childswickham Rd WR12 190 B8
Chilham Pl 4 WR4. . . . . . 116 C6
Chiltern Cl
Great Witley WR6 . . . . . . 61 A1
Halesowen B63 . . . . .7 D1
Stourport-on-Severn DY13 . 62 D8
2 Worcester WR4 . . . . . 115 F4
Chiltern Ho B71 . . . . 71 E1
Chiltern Rd DY8. . . . . .6 B6
Chilton Rd B14 . . . . 21 D4
China Cnr WR11 . . . . 164 A4
Chinn Brook Ho B14 . . . . 21 B4
Chinn Brook Rd B13. . . . . 21 C5
Chip Cl B38. . . . . 19 D2
Chirbury Gr B31 . . . . 19 B1
Chirk Cl DY10 . . . . 27 E2
Chirton Gr B14 . . . . 20 D6
Chiseldon Croft B14 . . . . 21 A3
Chorley Rd 2 WR9 . . . . . . 84 F3
Christ Church Rd WR14 . 153 A6
Christ Church Rd
Malvern WR14. . . . . 153 A8
Worcester WR5 . . . . 115 E3
Christina Cl 3 WR5 . . . . . 141 C7
Christine Ave WR2 . . . . . 127 C7
*Christopher Cadbury Reserve
The* ★ B61. . . . . 67 B3
Christopher Rd B62 . . . . . 8 F8
*Christopher Whitehead Lang
Coll* WR2 . . . . 115 A1
Chubb Cl WR5 . . . . 128 C5
Church Ave
Clent DY9 . . . . 15 F3
Stourbridge DY8 . . . . 6 A7
Stourport-on-Severn DY13 . 44 A4
Church Cl
Broadway WR12 . . . . 190 C7
Inkberrow WR7 . . . . 120 C2
14 St John's WR2 . . . . . 114 F1
Upper Sapey WR6 . . . . . . 77 D1
Wythall B47 . . . . 35 F3
Church Croft B63 . . . . 8 A4
Church Ct
Astwood Bank B96 . . . . . . 89 E2
Stourbridge DY8 . . . . 6 A5
Church Down Cl B97 . . . . 89 D6
Churchdown Rd WR14 . . 153 C5
Church Dr
Birmingham B30 . . . . 20 B7
Cookhill B49. . . . . 109 A2
10 Stourport-on-Severn
DY13. . . . . 44 A4
CHURCH END
Hanley Castle 169 A8

CHURCH END continued
Twyning 183 E4
Church End **1** WR10 . . . . 132 F4
Church Farm
Wick WR10 . . . . 145 A3
Wyre Piddle WR10 . . . . . . 145 A4
Church Farm Barn & Cotts
DY10 . . . . 14 B3
Churchfields
Bromsgrove B61 . . . . 48 F3
Kidderminster DY10 . . . . . 27 E7
Churchfield's Bsns Pk
DY10 . . . . 27 E7
Churchfields Cl B61 . . . . 48 F3
Churchfields Gdns B61 . . . . 48 F3
Churchfields Rd B61 . . . . 48 F3
Churchfield Terr WR6 . . . . 60 F4
Church Gr B13 . . . . 21 C5
Church Green E B98 . . . . . 70 E4
Church Green W B97 . . . . . 70 E4
CHURCH HILL 71 C6
Church Hill
Belbroughton DY9 . . . . 30 D6
Beoley B98 . . . . 71 D8
Birmingham, Northfield B31 19 B3
Frankley B32 . . . . 18 B6
Kinver DY7 . . . . 4 B2
Rushock WR9 . . . . 46 C3
Church Hill Mid Sch B98 . . 71 D6
Church Hill Way B98 . . . . . 71 D6
CHURCHILL
Blakedown 14 C3
Crowle 130 E7
Churchill Ave WR9 . . . . 84 E1
Churchill Dr
Malvern WR14 . . . . 139 B6
Stourbridge DY8 . . . . 6 A7
Churchill Gr GL20 . . . . 197 B6
Churchill La DY10 . . . . 14 B3
Churchill Rd
Halesowen B63 . . . . 7 F2
Sedgeberrow WR11 . . . . . . 174 F1
Upper Catshill B61 . . . . . . 32 A1
Church La
Birlingham WR10 . . . . 158 A3
2 Bishampton WR10 . . . 132 F4
Broadheath WR2 . . . . 114 A7
Broadwas WR6 . . . . 112 B3
Bromsgrove B61 . . . . 48 F2
Cookhill B49 . . . . 109 A2
Cotheridge WR6 . . . . 113 B2
Defford WR8 . . . . 157 D3
Dodderhill WR9 . . . . 66 E1
Earl's Croome WR8 . . . . . . 156 A1
Flyford Flavell WR7 . . . . . 119 D1
Forthampton GL19 . . . . 195 E6
Great Comberton WR10 . . . 158 F1
Hallow WR2 . . . . 101 D1
Hill & Moor WR10 . . . . 145 D2
Himbleton WR9 . . . . 105 D2
Little Witley WR6 . . . . . . 81 A4
Long Bank DY12 . . . . 25 C1
Mamble DY9 . . . . 39 F4
Martin Hussingtree WR3 . . 103 B3
Norton Juxta Kempsey
WR5 . . . . 129 B3
Norton & Lenchwick WR11 147 E4
Oddingley WR9 . . . . 104 C3
Ombersley WR9 . . . . 83 A3
Pershore/Pinvin WR10 . . . 144 F6
Rock DY14 . . . . 24 B2
Severn Stoke WR8 . . . . . . 155 D5
1 South Littleton WR11 . 148 A1
Stanton WR12 . . . . 189 D1
Stoulton WR7 . . . . 143 B8
Suckley WR6 . . . . 123 F4
Tibberton WR9 . . . . 117 A6
Upper Sapey WR6 . . . . 77 E4
Upton Snodsbury WR7 . . . . 131 C8
Whittington WR5 . . . . 129 B6
CHURCH LENCH 134 B3
Church Lench CE Fst Sch
WR11 . . . . 134 A3
Church Leys WR10 . . . . 160 C7
Church Meadow Ct
WR14 . . . . 138 F2
Church Rd
Alveley WV15 . . . . 1 C5
Aston Somerville WR12 . . 175 F1
Astwood Bank B96 . . . . 89 C2
Belbroughton DY9 . . . . 30 D6
Birmingham, Northfield B31 19 A4
Bromsgrove B61 . . . . 48 F2
Castlemorton WR13 . . . . . . 180 D7
Catshill B61 . . . . 48 F8
Crowle WR7 . . . . 117 E4
Dodford B61 . . . . 48 A7
Evesham WR11 . . . . 161 B2
Halesowen B63 . . . . 7 C7
Kinver DY7 . . . . 3 F2
Lower Howsell WR14 . . . . . 139 A5
Redditch, St George's B97 . . 70 E4
Redditch, Webheath B97 . 69 F2
Stock & Bradley B96 . . . . 106 F1
Stourbridge, Lye DY9 . . . 6 E5
Stourbridge, Old Swinford
DY8 . . . . 6 B3
Worcester WR3 . . . . 115 D5
Church Row **8** WR10 . . . . . 158 D8
Church Row Cotts DY9 . . . 15 F3
Church St
Bidford-on-Avon B50 . . . . 136 E4
Birlingham WR10 . . . . 158 A3
Bredon GL20 . . . . 184 E6

Church St continued
Broadway WR12 . . . . 190 C7
Bromsgrove B61 . . . . 48 F2
Cleobury Mortimer DY14 . . 22 C4
Eckington WR10 . . . . 171 E7
Evesham WR11 . . . . 161 E3
Fladbury WR10 . . . . 146 B1
Hanley Castle WR8 . . . . . . 169 B7
Harvington WR11 . . . . 148 B6
Kempsey WR5 . . . . 141 B7
Kidderminster DY10 . . . . . 27 E6
Malvern WR14 . . . . 152 F8
Offenham WR11 . . . . 148 A1
7 Pershore WR10 . . . . . 158 D8
Stourbridge DY8 . . . . 6 A5
Studley B80 . . . . 90 E3
2 Tenbury Wells WR15 . . 55 E5
Tewkesbury GL20 . . . . 196 E6
Upton upon Severn WR8 . . 169 C6
West Hagley DY9 . . . . 15 A1
Willersey WR12 . . . . 177 F4
20 Worcester WR1 . . . . . 115 C2
Wyre Piddle WR10 . . . . . . 145 A3
Churchstone Cl B61 . . . . . 48 F8
Church Terr **5** WR2 . . . . . 114 F1
Church View
Bewdley DY12 . . . . 26 A3
Wythall B47 . . . . 35 E2
Church View Gdns **2** DY7 . . 4 A4
Churchward Cl
Honeybourne WR11 . . . . . . 164 A6
Stourbridge DY8 . . . . 6 B6
Churchway Piece WR7 . . . . . 120 E7
Churchwell Ct B63 . . . . 8 B2
Church Wlk
Great Malvern WR14 . . . . . 152 F8
Kidderminster DY11 . . . . . 27 C6
Little Hereford SY8 . . . . 54 C5
Malvern WR14 . . . . 152 F8
Norton WR11 . . . . 147 E4
10 Pershore WR10 . . . . . 158 D8
Stourport-on-Severn DY13 . 43 E2
Cider Ave DY5 . . . . 6 E8
Cidermill Orch GL55 . . . . . 178 D7
Cinders La WR15 . . . . 74 D6
Cinders Rd WR15 . . . . 55 D1
Cirencester Cl B60 . . . . . 49 B2
Cirencester Pl **1** WR4 . . . 116 B7
City Est B64 . . . . 7 D8
City Walls Rd WR1 . . . . 115 C2
CLADSWELL 108 F2
Cladswell Cl B49 . . . . 109 A2
Cladswell La B49 . . . . 109 A2
Cladsworth Ho **1** B97 . . . . 70 A4
Claerwen Ave DY13 . . . . 43 E7
Claerwen Gr B31 . . . . 18 E5
CLAINES 102 C2
Claines CE Prim Sch
WR3 . . . . 102 C3
Claines Cres DY10 . . . . 28 B5
Claines La WR3 . . . . 102 C2
Claines Rd
Birmingham B31 . . . . 19 C4
Halesowen B63 . . . . 7 D5
CLANBROOK 4 A7
Clanbrook Rd DY7 . . . . 3 F7
Clandon Cl B14 . . . . 20 C2
Clapgate La B32 . . . . 9 C2
Claphill La
Rushwick WR2 . . . . 114 B1
Worcester WR2 . . . . 127 B8
Clarage Ho B62 . . . . 8 D8
Clare Cl B90 . . . . 21 D2
Claremont Ct WR14 . . . . 152 E1
Claremont Way B63 . . . . 8 A3
Clarence Cl WR14 . . . . 153 A7
Clarence Rd
Malvern WR14 . . . . 153 A8
Tewkesbury GL20 . . . . 196 E4
Clarence St DY10 . . . . 27 F6
Clarence Way DY12 . . . . 26 B4
Clarendon Cl B97 . . . . 70 B5
Clarendon Ct WR14 . . . . . . 152 F8
Clarendon Pl B62 . . . . 9 A6
Clare Rd WR14 . . . . 139 B1
Clare St B97 . . . . 115 C2
Clare Witnell Cl DY11 . . . . 27 B8
Clarke St **1** B97 . . . . 70 E3
Clarks Hill Rise WR11 . . . . 161 B3
Clarkson Gdns **3** WR4 . . . . 116 C4
Clark St DY8 . . . . 5 E4
Clatterbach La DY9 . . . . 16 A4
Clattercut La WR9 . . . . 46 E3
Claughton Ct DY11 . . . . 27 C5
Claughton St DY11 . . . . 27 C5
Claverdon Cl B31 . . . . 18 E7
Claverdon Cl B97 . . . . 89 D4
Claverdon Ho B13 . . . . 21 A7
Claverham Cl WR2 . . . . 128 A8
Claverton WR7 . . . . 143 B7
Claybrook Dr B98 . . . . 90 F7
Claycroft Pl DY9 . . . . 6 E5
Claydon Gr **3** B14 . . . . . . 21 A3
Clay Dr B32 . . . . 9 A5
Clayfield Dr WR14 . . . . 138 E4
Clayfield Rd WR11 . . . . . . 163 B6
Clayfields B96 . . . . 88 F3
Clayhall Rd **8** WR9 . . . . . 85 A1
Claypit La B61 . . . . 31 E1
Clayton Dr B60 . . . . 68 B7
Clayton Gdns B45 . . . . 33 A2
Clearwell Rd B98 . . . . 71 C3
Clee Ave DY11 . . . . 27 C2
Clee Hill Rd
Burford WR15 . . . . 55 E8
Nash SY8 . . . . 37 A6

Clee Rd
Birmingham B31 . . . . 34 A8
Cookley DY10 . . . . 13 B5
Stourbridge DY8 . . . . 6 A6
Cleeve Cl
Redditch B98 . . . . 71 D5
Stourport-on-Severn DY13 . 62 D8
Cleeve Dr WR4 . . . . 116 A6
CLEEVE PRIOR 149 A7
Cleeve Prior Bank Nature
Reserve★ WR11 . . . . 148 F8
Cleeve Prior CE Fst Sch
WR11 . . . . 149 B7
Cleeve Rd
Bidford-on-Avon B50 . . . . 136 D2
Birmingham B14 . . . . 21 C4
Cleeve Prior WR11 . . . . . . 149 B7
South Littleton WR11 . . . 148 F3
Clee View WR9 . . . . 84 E2
Clementi Ct **5** WR11 . . . . 161 F4
Clensmore St DY10 . . . . 27 D7
CLENT 15 F3
Clent Ave
Kidderminster DY11 . . . . . 27 B1
Redditch B97 . . . . 89 D7
Clent Cott DY9 . . . . 15 F3
Clent Dr DY9 . . . . 15 D6
Clent Hills Ctry Pk★ DY9 . 16 A4
Clent Ho B63 . . . . 8 A2
Clent Parochial Prim Sch
DY9 . . . . 15 F2
Clent Rd
Birmingham B45 . . . . 32 E8
Birmingham, Brandhall B68 . 9 C8
Stourbridge DY8 . . . . 6 A6
Clent View Rd
Birmingham B32 . . . . 9 A1
Halesowen B63 . . . . 7 C5
Stourbridge DY8 . . . . 5 C2
Clent Way B32 . . . . 18 A8
Cleobury Cl B97 . . . . 70 B5
Cleobury Mdws DY14 . . . . . . 22 B4
CLEOBURY MORTIMER 22 C4
Cleobury Mortimer Prim Sch
DY14 . . . . 22 B4
Cleobury Rd
Bewdley DY12 . . . . 25 E3
Fingerpost DY14 . . . . 24 C1
Clerkenwell Cres WR14 . . . 139 A2
Clevedon Gn WR11 . . . . 149 A1
Cleveland Dr B45 . . . . 33 A2
Cleveland St DY8 . . . . 5 E4
CLEVELODE 140 E2
Cleves Dr B45 . . . . 32 E7
Cleves Rd B45 . . . . 32 E8
Clewer Croft WR13 . . . . . . 125 F2
Clewley Gr B32 . . . . 9 B5
Clewshaw La B38 . . . . 35 C4
Clews Rd B98 . . . . 89 F7
Clifford Ave **6** GL20 . . . . 197 A4
Clifford Cl WR9 . . . . 103 E7
Clifford Cl B97 . . . . 103 E7
Cliff Rock Rd B45 . . . . 33 B7
Cliff The DY7 . . . . 4 A3
CLIFTON 141 B1
Clifton Cl B98 . . . . 90 E8
CLIFTON HILL 98 B6
Clifton Rd
Halesowen B63 . . . . 8 E8
Kidderminster DY11 . . . . . 27 A1
Wolverley & Cookley DY10 . 13 C3
Clifton St DY8 . . . . 5 F4
CLIFTON UPON TEME 97 E8
Clifton upon Teme Prim Sch
WR6 . . . . 97 E7
Clinic Dr DY9 . . . . 6 E5
Clivedon Way B62 . . . . 8 B7
Clive Rd
Birmingham B32 . . . . 9 D7
Bromsgrove B60 . . . . 68 B8
Redditch B97 . . . . 70 D5
Cloister Dr B62 . . . . 8 D3
Cloisters The B80 . . . . 90 D4
Clonmel Rd B30 . . . . 20 A6
Close The
Birmingham B17 . . . . 9 F7
Birmingham, Griffin's Hill
B29 . . . . 19 D8
Cleeve Prior WR11 . . . . . . 149 A7
Eckington WR10 . . . . 171 F8
Halesowen B63 . . . . 7 D6
Hollywood B47 . . . . 36 A5
Hunnington B62 . . . . 17 A7
Wyre Piddle WR10 . . . . . . 145 B4
Clover Ct B38 . . . . 19 D2
Cloverdale B60 . . . . 67 C3
Clover Dr B32 . . . . 9 D2
Clover Rd B29 . . . . 19 A7
Clover Way WR14 . . . . 153 C6
Cloweswood La B94 . . . . . . 53 F8
Clows Top Rd
Abberley WR6 . . . . 60 E5
Bayton DY14 . . . . 40 C6
Club View B38 . . . . 19 D2
Clunbury Rd B31 . . . . 34 A8
Clun Rd B31 . . . . 18 F6
Clusters The DY9 . . . . 6 E5
Clyde Ave
Evesham WR11 . . . . 161 F3
Halesowen B62 . . . . 7 F3
Clydesdale Cl **2** WR9 . . . 104 B8
Clydesdale Rd B32 . . . . 9 B6
Clydes Dale Rd WR9 . . . . . . 104 B8
Coach Cotts B45 . . . . 50 D8
Coalash La B60 . . . . 68 C2
Coalbourne Gdns B63 . . . . . 7 C5
Coalbourn La DY8 . . . . 5 F7
Coates Rd DY10 . . . . 28 B7

COBBLER'S CORNER 112 F6
Cobden Ave WR4 . . . . 116 C4
Cobden St
Kidderminster DY11 . . . . . 27 D5
Stourbridge DY8 . . . . 5 E5
Cobham Cl
Bromsgrove B60 . . . . 67 F7
Welland WR13 . . . . 167 C5
Cobham Court Mews DY9 . . 15 D6
Cobham Cres DY12 . . . . 26 A3
Cobham Ct **11** WR9 . . . . . 84 F3
Cobham Rd
Halesowen B63 . . . . 8 B4
Kidderminster DY10 . . . . . 27 E4
Pershore/Pinvin WR10 . . . 144 E4
Stourbridge DY8 . . . . 6 B2
Cob La B30 . . . . 19 C6
COBLEY HILL 50 A4
Cobley Hill B48 . . . . 50 A4
Cobnall Rd B61 . . . . 32 A2
Cobs Field B30 . . . . 19 C6
Cochrane Cl DY9 . . . . 15 C8
COCK BEVINGTON 135 B6
Cock Hill La B45 . . . . 32 F8
Cocksheds La B62 . . . . 8 C8
Cockshot La B96 . . . . 106 D1
Cockshot Rd WR14 . . . . . . 138 F2
Cockshute Hill WR9 . . . . . . 85 B2
Cockshutt La B61 . . . . 48 D7
Cocksmead Croft B14 . . . . . 20 D5
Cocksmoor Ho B14 . . . . 20 D7
Cocks Moors Woods Leisure
Ctr B14 . . . . 20 D7
Cockthorpe Cl B17 . . . . 9 F7
Codsall Rd B64 . . . . 7 E8
COFT COMMON 33 F6
COFTEN HACKETT 33 C3
Cofton Ave DY10 . . . . 28 B5
Cofton Church La B45 . . . . 33 B3
Cofton Cl B97 . . . . 70 B5
Cofton Ct B45 . . . . 33 D7
Cofton Gr B31 . . . . 33 E6
Cofton Lake Rd B45 . . . . . . 33 C3
Cofton Prim Sch B31 . . . . . 34 A6
Cofton Rd B31 . . . . 34 B7
Cokeland Pl B64 . . . . 7 D8
Coldbath Rd B13 . . . . 21 B8
Cold Comfort La B49 . . . . 122 F4
COLD ELM 195 A6
Coldfield Dr B98 . . . . 89 E7
COLDHEART 125 A3
Coldicott Gdns **1** WR11 . 161 C2
Coldicotts Cl WR11 . . . . . . 163 B5
Coldicotts La WR11 . . . . . . 163 B5
Cole Bank Rd B28 . . . . 21 E8
Colebourne Rd B13 . . . . . . 21 D6
Colebrook Croft B90 . . . . . 21 F2
Colebrook Rd B90 . . . . 21 F2
Coleford Cl B97 . . . . 70 A2
Cole Gn B90 . . . . 21 F2
Cole Hill WR5 . . . . 115 D1
Colemeadow Rd
Birmingham B13 . . . . 21 B6
Redditch B98 . . . . 71 F6
Coleridge Cl
Redditch B97 . . . . 89 C8
Worcester WR14 . . . . 115 C6
Colesborne Ct **7** WR4 . . . 115 F7
Colesbourne Ave B14 . . . . . 20 C7
COLES GREEN 125 D4
Coleshill Ct B97 . . . . 89 C5
Coleside Ave B13 . . . . 21 D6
Cole Valley Rd B28 . . . . . . 21 D6
Coley Pits La WR9 . . . . 66 E3
Coleys La B31 . . . . 19 A2
Colford Cl **3** WR9 . . . . . 84 C1
Colin Rd WR3 . . . . 102 A1
Colleen Ave B30 . . . . 20 B3
College Cl
Cleobury Mortimer DY14 . . 22 C5
Long Marston CV37 . . . . . . 151 C5
College Ct **1** WR15 . . . . 55 E4
College Gdns **9** WR15 . . . 55 E5
College Gn WR9 . . . . 84 E1
College Gr WR14 . . . . 152 F6
College Mews WR14 . . . . . . 139 A4
College Precincts **17**
WR1 . . . . 115 C2
College Rd
Birmingham B32 . . . . 9 A6
Bredon GL20 . . . . 184 D6
Bromsgrove B60 . . . . 49 A2
Kidderminster DY10 . . . . . 27 E4
Malvern WR14 . . . . 152 F7
Stourbridge DY9 . . . . 6 A4
Upton Snodsbury WR7 . . . . 131 C8
College St WR1 . . . . 115 C2
College Wlk
Birmingham B29 . . . . 19 D8
Bromsgrove B60 . . . . 49 A2
Kidderminster DY10 . . . . . 27 E4
Tenbury WR15 . . . . 74 C8
College Yd **8** WR1 . . . . . 115 B2
Collett Cl DY8 . . . . 6 A6
Colletts Fields WR12 . . . . 190 E8
Colletts Gdns WR12 . . . . . 190 E8
COLLETT'S GREEN 127 C4
Collett's Green Rd WR2 . . 127 B3
Colley Gate B63 . . . . 7 C6
Colley La B63 . . . . 7 C6
Colley La Prim Sch B63 . . 7 C6
Colley Orch B63 . . . . 7 C6
Collin Cl **4** WR12 . . . . . 177 E4
Collings Ave **4** WR4 . . . . 116 C3
COLLINGTON 95 E5
Collingwood Rd B30 . . . . . 20 D3
Collin La WR12 . . . . 177 C3

Collins Cl B32 . . . . 9 A5
Collins Ct **17** GL20 . . . . 196 E6
Collinsfield WR11 . . . . . . 161 E6
Collinson Cl B98 . . . . 71 A1
Collis Cl B60 . . . . 67 E7
Collis St DY8 . . . . 5 F8
Colman Hill B63 . . . . 7 D5
Colman Hill Ave B63 . . . . . 7 D6
Colmers Farm Inf Sch
B45 . . . . 33 B8
Colmers Farm Jun Sch
B45 . . . . 33 B8
Colmers Sch & Sports Coll
B45 . . . . 33 B8
Colmers Wlk B31 . . . . 18 D1
Colmore Ave B14 . . . . 20 D7
Colmore Jun Sch B14 . . . . . 20 D7
Colmore Rd B14 . . . . 20 D7
Coln Cl B31 . . . . 18 F6
Colshaw Rd DY8 . . . . 5 E4
Coltishall Cl **8** WR5 . . . 128 D6
Colts La B98 . . . . 71 D3
Columbia Dr WR2 . . . . 127 E7
Columbine Gr WR11 . . . . . . 161 C1
Columbine Rd GL20 . . . . . . 197 A3
COLWALL 152 D4
Colwall CE Prim Sch
WR13 . . . . 166 A8
COLWALL GREEN 166 A8
Colwall Sta WR13 . . . . . . 152 B1
COLWALL STONE 152 A2
Colworth Rd B31 . . . . 18 F4
Comber Croft B13 . . . . 21 D4
Comber Gr DY7 . . . . 4 A3
Comber Rd DY7 . . . . 3 F2
COMBERTON 28 B5
Comberton Ave DY10 . . . . . 28 B6
Comberton Ct **5** DY10 . . 28 A5
Comberton Gdns DY10 . . . . 28 B5
Comberton Hill DY10 . . . . 27 F5
Comberton Mans **4** DY10 . 28 A5
Comberton Mid Sch DY10 . 28 B4
Comberton Park Rd DY10 . 28 B4
Comberton Pl DY10 . . . . . . 27 F5
Comberton Prim Sch
DY10 . . . . 28 B4
Comberton Rd DY10 . . . . . . 28 B4
Comberton Terr DY10 . . . . 27 F5
Comer Ave WR2 . . . . 114 F2
Comer Gdns WR2 . . . . 114 E4
Comer Rd WR2 . . . . 114 F3
COMHAMPTON 63 F2
Comhampton La DY13 . . . . . 63 F2
Commandery Rd WR5 . . . . . 115 C1
Commandery The★
WR1 . . . . 115 C1
Common Barn La DY10 . . . . 13 D5
Common La
Mappleborough Green
B80 . . . . 72 B3
Neen Savage DY14 . . . . . . 22 A7
Common Rd WR11 . . . . 161 E5
Common The WR6 . . . . 60 E3
Como Rd WR14 . . . . 138 F1
Compass Way B60 . . . . 68 A7
Compa The DY7 . . . . 4 A3
COMPTON 3 B6
Compton Cl
Kinver DY7 . . . . 3 F4
Redditch B98 . . . . 70 E2
Compton Gdns DY7 . . . . 3 F4
Compton Gr B63 . . . . 7 C4
Compton Grange B64 . . . . . 7 C8
Compton Rd
Halesowen B62 . . . . 8 F5
Kinver DY7 . . . . 3 E4
Stourbridge DY9 . . . . 6 D2
Worcester WR5 . . . . 115 D2
CONDERTON 186 A7
Conderton Pottery★
GL20 . . . . 186 A7
Condover Rd B31 . . . . 34 B8
Conduit Hill **1** WR11 . . . 161 E4
Coney Dr DY8 . . . . 6 B5
Coneygree La WR12 . . . . . . 190 D5
Coney Green Cl **2** WR4 . 116 B6
Coney Green Dr B31 . . . . . 33 F8
Congleton Cl B97 . . . . 70 B5
Conifer Cl DY5 . . . . 6 C8
Conifer Dr B31 . . . . 19 B3
Conifer Gr B61 . . . . 48 F3
Conifer Hts WR6 . . . . 111 C6
Conifer Paddock B62 . . . . . 8 E8
Conigree La GL20 . . . . 196 E4
Coningsby Dr WR11 . . . . . . 27 A8
Coningsby Dr WR10 . . . . . . 158 B8
Conisborough **3** WR4 . . . 116 C6
Coniston Cl
Birmingham B28 . . . . 21 F6
Bromsgrove B60 . . . . 49 B1
Malvern WR14 . . . . 153 C6
Worcester WR4 . . . . 116 A5
Coniston Cres DY13 . . . . . 43 F6
Coniston Ho DY10 . . . . 27 E7
Coniston Way DY12 . . . . . . 25 E3
Connaught Ave DY11 . . . . . 27 C4
Connaught Cl **11** WR5 . . 128 D6
Connaught Rd B60 . . . . 49 C1
Conningsby Dr WR10 . . . . . 158 B8
Connops Way DY9 . . . . 6 E5
Conolly Dr B45 . . . . 18 B1
Consort Gdns B61 . . . . 49 A3
Consort Rd B30 . . . . 20 A3
Constance Rd WR3 . . . . . . 114 F8
Constitution Hill Ringway
DY10 . . . . 27 E5
Conway WR4 . . . . 115 F4
Conway Ave B32 . . . . 9 B6

Conway House B31 . . . . . . 18 D6
Conway Rd B60 . . . . 48 F1
Conwy Dr WR11 . . . . 162 A3
Cookes Croft B31 . . . . 19 B2
COOKHILL 109 A1
COOKLEY. 13 A6
Cookley Cl B63 . . . . .7 F2
Cookley La DY7 . . . . .4 B1
Cookley Sebright Endowed
  Fst Sch DY11 . . . . 13 A5
Cooks Cross WV15 . . . . 1 C6
COOKSEY CORNER 66 C5
COOKSEY GREEN 66 B8
Cooksey Green La
  Elmbridge WR9 . . . . 65 F6
  Upton Warren WR9 . . . . . 66 A7
Cooks Hill WR10 . . . . 159 B7
Cook's La GL19 . . . . 192 E7
Coombefield Rd WR11 . . 176 D2
Coombe Hill B64 . . . . .8 B8
Coombes La B31 . . . . 33 F7
Coombes Rd B62 . . . . .8 B7
COOMBESWOOD 8 C7
Coombs Rd
  Halesowen B62 . . . . 8 B7
  Worcester WR3 . . . . 115 B7
Coombswood Way B65 . . . .8 B8
Cooper Cl B60 . . . . 67 E6
Coopers Cl 9 WR4. . . . . . 115 F6
Coopers Hill B48. . . . . 50 E6
Cooper's La WR11 . . . . . . 161 E6
COPCUT
  Droitwich 103 D8
  Salwarpe 103 C7
Copcut La WR9 . . . . 84 A1
Copelands The DY7 . . . . . . 4 A3
Copenhagen St 7 WR1 . 115 B2
Cope Rd WR3. . . . . 115 B7
Copes La DY11. . . . . 12 A5
Copperbeech Cl B32 . . . . . .9 F5
Coppice Ave DY9 . . . . .6 F3
Coppice
  Birmingham B45 . . . . 32 F7
  Droitwich Spa WR9 . . . . . 84 C5
  Hallow WR2 . . . . 101 D3
  Malvern WR14. . . . . 138 E6
  Redditch B97 . . . . 70 C3
Coppice Gdns B47 . . . . . . 36 A7
Coppice Hollow B32 . . . . . .9 B1
Coppice Hts DY11 . . . . 27 B1
Coppice Prim Sch The
  B47. . . . . 36 A6
Coppice Rd B64. . . . . .7 E7
Coppice The
  Birmingham, Frankley B31 . 18 C2
  West Hagley DY8. . . . . . . 14 F5
Coppice Trad Est DY11 . . 44 B8
Coppice Way WR9 . . . . 84 C5
Copse Cl B31 . . . . 19 A2
Copsewood Ave WR5. . . . 116 B3
Copston Gr B29. . . . . 19 B8
Copyholt La
  Stoke Prior B60. . . . . 68 D3
  Upper Bentley B60, B97. . . 69 A3
Corbett Cl B60. . . . . 68 B8
Corbett Cres DY8 . . . . .6 C1
Corbett Dr B60 . . . . 67 C1
Corbett Ho 1 DY8 . . . . . . .5 F8
Corbett Hospl DY8 . . . . . . .5 F7
Corbett Rd
  Hollywood B47. . . . . 36 A7
  Kidderminster DY11. . . . . 27 A8
Corbett St WR9 . . . . 84 F2
Corbetts The WR13 . . . . . 126 A2
Corbizum Ave B80 . . . . . . 90 D4
Cordle Marsh Rd DY12 . . 26 C5
CORELEY. 37 D8
Corfe Ave WR4 . . . . 116 C6
Corfe Cl B32. . . . . .9 F5
Coriander Cl
  Birmingham B45 . . . . 18 B2
  Stoke Prior B60. . . . . 67 C1
Corinne Cl B45 . . . . 33 A6
Corley Ave B31 . . . . 19 B3
Corley Cl B90. . . . . 21 C1
Cormorant Gr DY10 . . . . . 28 B3
Cormorant Rise WR2. . . . 128 A6
Cornbow Sh Ctr B63. . . . . .8 B3
Cornbrook Rd B29 . . . . . . 18 F7
Corndon Cl DY11. . . . . 27 B2
Corner Farm Dr WR11. . . 164 A4
Corner La B97 . . . . 69 E2
Cornerway B38 . . . . 34 F7
Cornfield Ave B60 . . . . . . 67 D6
Cornfield Rd B31 . . . . 19 B4
Cornfield Way WR11 . . . . 174 B2
Cornflower Cl GL20 . . . . . 197 A3
Corngreaves Rd B64 . . . . . .7 C7
Corngreaves Trad Est B64 . 7 D7
Corngreaves Wlk B64 . . . . .7 E7
Cornhampton Cl 7 B97 . 70 B5
Cornhill Gr B30. . . . . 20 C7
Cornmeadow Gn WR3. . . 102 B1
Cornmeadow La WR3 . . . 102 B1
Cornmill Cl WR10 . . . . . . 173 E7
Cornmill Gdns B60. . . . . . 50 A5
Corn Mill Rd WR11. . . . . 161 C1
Corn Mkt 3 WR1 . . . . . . 115 C2
Cornmore WR10 . . . . 158 B7
Cornwall Ave
  Birmingham B68 . . . . .9 B8
  Kidderminster DY11. . . . . 12 C1
Cornwall Gdns 5 WR15 . . 55 E5
Cornwall Rd
  Birmingham, Rubery B45. . . 17 E1
  Stourbridge DY8 . . . . .5 D8

Cornwell Cl B98 . . . . 90 B5
Coronation Ave WR2. . . . 127 B8
Coronation Cotts WR5 . . 129 C1
Coronation Rd WR14. . . . 139 C5
Coronation St WR11 . . . . 161 F4
Coronation Terr B60 . . . . 68 B7
Coronation Way DY10 . . . 28 B5
Corporation St DY10 . . . . 27 E5
Corrie Croft B32 . . . . 18 B7
Corron Hill 2 B63 . . . . . . .8 A4
CORSE LAWN 194 E2
Corser St DY8 . . . . .6 A3
Corunna Cl WR5 . . . . 128 F4
Corvedale Rd B29. . . . . . . 19 A6
Corven Croft B31. . . . . . . 18 E6
Cosford Cl B98. . . . . 71 F1
Cosgrove Cl WR3 . . . . . . 115 F8
Costers La B98 . . . . 71 F2
Cote La
  Enville DY7 . . . . .3 F8
  Kinver DY7. . . . . 4 A7
Cotford Rd B14. . . . . 21 A2
COTHERIDGE 113 B2
Cotheridge Ct* WR6. . . 113 A2
Cotheridge La WR10 . . . . 171 C7
Cotland WR3 . . . . 115 C5
Coton Gr B90 . . . . 21 E2
Cotswold Ave 6 DY13 . . . 43 D1
Cotswold Cl
  Birmingham B45 . . . . 18 B2
  10 Bredon GL20 . . . . . . 184 F6
  Kidderminster DY11. . . . . 27 C2
Cotswold Croft B63 . . . . . .7 C1
Cotswold Edge GL55 . . . . 165 D4
Cotswold Gdns GL20 . . . 196 F7
Cotswold Rd
  Malvern WR14. . . . . 139 B1
  Stourbridge DY8 . . . . 6 B6
Cotswold Way
  Bromsgrove B61 . . . . 49 A5
  Worcester WR4 . . . . 115 F8
Cottage Dr B60 . . . . 32 D1
Cottage Farm La B60. . . . 32 C1
Cottage Gdns B45. . . . . . 32 F6
Cottage La B60 . . . . 32 C1
Cottages The B63 . . . . . . .7 E6
COTTERIDGE 19 E5
Cotteridge Prim Sch B30. 20 A5
Cotteridge Rd B30 . . . . . . 20 A4
Cotteswold Rd GL20. . . . 196 F6
Cotton Pool Rd B61 . . . . . 48 E2
Cotton's La WR11 . . . . . . 174 A1
Cottrells Cl B14. . . . . 21 C4
COUGHTON 109 F5
Coughton CE Prim Sch
  B49. . . . . 109 F5
Coughton La B49 . . . . . . 109 E4
Countinghouse Way 2
  B60 . . . . 67 E6
County Cl
  Birmingham B32 . . . . 9 D3
  Birmingham, Stirchley B30 . 20 C6
County La DY8 . . . . 14 D8
County Park Ave B62. . . . 8 D3
Coupass Cotts B96. . . . . 107 D7
Court Cl WR11. . . . . 12 B1
Court Dr 3 DY13 . . . . . . 43 F4
Courtfarm La GL20. . . . . 186 C4
Court Farm Way B29 . . . . 18 F7
Court Gdns WR14 . . . . . . 153 B8
Court La
  Cotheridge WR6. . . . . . . 113 B2
  Offenham WR11. . . . . . . 148 A2
Courtland Cl 4 WR3 . . . 102 A1
Court Lea WR8 . . . . 169 E7
Courtney DY10. . . . . 27 E2
Courtney Cl GL20 . . . . . . 196 F3
Court Rd
  Malvern WR14. . . . . 153 A7
  Strensham WR8. . . . . . . 171 A3
Court St
  9 Stourbridge DY8. . . . . . 6 A5
  4 Upton upon Severn
    WR8 . . . . 169 C6
Court Way B50. . . . . 136 D4
Courtway Ave B14 . . . . . . 21 B1
Courtyard Bsns Pk The 5
  B60 . . . . 67 F6
Courtyard The
  Northway GL20 . . . . 184 C1
  Stoke Prior B60. . . . . 67 D2
Cove Gdns WR3. . . . . 115 A7
Coventry Ave WR4 . . . . . 128 A7
Coventry Cl GL20. . . . . . 196 F4
Coventry Highway B98 . . 71 C4
Coventry St
  Kidderminster DY10. . . . . 27 F6
  Stourbridge DY8 . . . . .6 A5
Covercroft 3 WR9 . . . . . 84 F3
Coverfield WR8 . . . . 154 A2
Cover Gn WR4 . . . . 116 B4
Covers The B80 . . . . 90 E6
Covert La DY8 . . . . .5 D2
Cow La WR13 . . . . 64 B1
Cowl Barn La WR13 . . . . 152 B2
Cowleigh Bank WR14 . . . 138 D4
Cowleigh Ct WR14 . . . . . 138 D3
Cowleigh Rd WR13,
  WR14. . . . . 138 C4
Cowl St WR11 . . . . 161 D4
Cowper Wlk DY10 . . . . . . 28 C6
COWSDEN. 131 D7
Cowslip Cl
  1 Birmingham, Hawkesley
    B38. . . . . 34 F8
  Birmingham, Selly Oak B29. 19 A7

Cowslip Wlk DY5. . . . . 6 C6
Cox Cl B50 . . . . 136 E5
Coxcroft Ave DY5 . . . . .6 F8
Coxlea Cl WR11. . . . . 161 C5
Coxwell Dr WR14 . . . . . . 139 B3
Crab Apple Way
  4 Evesham WR11. . . . . . 161 F1
  Evesham WR11 . . . . 175 F8
Crabbe La WR8 . . . . 143 C2
Crabbe St DY9 . . . . .6 F5
CRABBS CROSS 89 E6
Crabbs Cross La B97 . . . . 89 E5
Crabmill Cl B38. . . . . 34 E7
Crabmill La B38. . . . . 35 D8
Crabtree Cl
  Birmingham B31 . . . . 19 C2
  Redditch B98 . . . . 71 A2
  West Hagley DY9. . . . . . . 15 B6
Crabtree Dr B61 . . . . 48 E3
Crabtree La B61 . . . . 48 E3
CRADLEY 7 D6
Cradley CE Prim Sch B63. .7 C7
Cradley Cl B98. . . . . 71 C1
Cradley Fields DY9 . . . . . . 7 D5
Cradley Forge DY5. . . . . . .7 A8
CRADLEY HEATH 7 D8
Cradley Heath Factory Ctr
  B64. . . . . .7 B8
Cradley Heath Sta B64 . . .7 B8
Cradley Rd B64 . . . . .7 C8
Cralves Mead WR15. . . . . 55 D8
Cranberry Dr 3 DY13 . . . 43 E4
Cranbourne Cl B45. . . . . . 18 B2
Cranbourne Rd DY8. . . . . .6 B4
Crane Dr 128 A6
Cranesbill Dr WR5 . . . . . 128 D5
Cranesbill Rd B29. . . . . . . 19 A6
Crane St DY11 . . . . 27 C6
Cranham Cl B97 . . . . 70 B1
Cranham Ct WR4 . . . . . . 116 A6
Cranham Dr WR4 . . . . . . 116 A7
Cranham Prim Sch WR4. 116 A7
CRANHILL. 137 D7
Cranmoor Cres B63 . . . . . .8 A5
Crashmore La
  Beckford GL20. . . . . 186 A2
  Overbury GL20. . . . . 185 F5
Craufurd Ct DY8 . . . . .6 A3
Craufurd St DY8 . . . . .6 A3
Crawford Cl B50 . . . . 136 C4
Crendon Cl B80. . . . . 90 E5
Crescent Grange Rd The
  DY9 . . . . .6 C4
Crescent Ho B97 . . . . 70 D2
Crescent Pl WR15 . . . . . . 55 F3
Crescent Rd
  Colwall WR13. . . . . 152 A1
  Kidderminster DY11. . . . . 27 C5
Crescent The
  2 Bromsgrove B60 . . . . . 48 F1
  Colwall WR13. . . . . 152 A2
  Cradley Heath B64. . . . . . 8 A7
  Great Malvern WR14. . . . 166 F7
  Hindlip WR3. . . . . 103 B1
  Tenbury Wells WR15 . . . . 55 F3
  West Hagley DY8. . . . . . . 14 F5
  Wolverley & Cookley DY10 . 13 B4
Cressage Ave B31. . . . . . . 19 A1
Cresswell WR3 . . . . 102 E2
Crest Hill WR11 . . . . 148 B6
Crest The
  Birmingham B31 . . . . 34 C7
  Edwyn Ralph HR7 . . . . . . 95 C1
Crest View B14 . . . . 21 B4
Crestwood Ave DY11 . . . . 27 A5
Creswick Gr B45. . . . . 33 C7
Cricketers Mdw B64 . . . . .7 F7
Cricklewood Dr B62. . . . . 8 D3
Crickley Dr WR4 . . . . 116 A7
Crimmond Rise B63. . . . . .7 E5
Croft Bank WR14. . . . . . . 138 C1
Croft Cl B98 . . . . 71 D3
Crofters Cl
  Stourbridge DY8 . . . . 6 B4
  Westlands WR9 . . . . 84 D5
Crofters End WR9 . . . . . . 84 D6
Crofters Gn WR9. . . . . 84 D6
Crofters Hill WR9 . . . . . . 84 D6
Crofters Way WR9 . . . . . . 84 D6
Croft Farm Dr WR14 . . . 138 C1
Croft Farm Waterpark*
  GL20. . . . . 184 B3
Croft Gdns WR12. . . . . . 190 D7
Croftlands The 7 GL20. . 184 F6
Croft Rd
  Evesham WR11 . . . . 161 D6
  South Littleton WR11. . . 148 F2
  Upton Snodsbury WR7. . . 131 C8
  Worcester WR1 . . . . 115 C2
Crofts Field GL20 . . . . . . 183 A2
Crofts La
  Astwood Bank B96 . . . . . 89 B2
  Feckenham B96. . . . . 88 F2
Croft The
  Birmingham B31 . . . . 19 B2
  Blakedown DY10 . . . . 14 C2
Croft The B60. . . . . 67 E6
Croft The
  Church Lench WR11. . . . 134 A3
  Kidderminster DY11. . . . . 27 A4
Croft Wlk WR1. . . . . 115 B3
Croftwood Rd DY9 . . . . . . 6 D4
Cromdale Dr B63 . . . . 7 D3
Cromers Cl 7 GL20 . . . . 184 E1
Crompton Ave B50. . . . . . 136 E5
Crompton Rd B45. . . . . . . 17 D1
Cromwell Cres WR5. . . . 128 E8

Cromwell Crescent La
  WR5. . . . . 128 E8
Cromwell Ct WR14 . . . . . 139 A4
Cromwell La B31 . . . . 18 E8
Cromwell Rd
  4 Bowling Green WR2. . 127 C2
  Malvern WR14. . . . . 139 A4
Cromwell St WR4 . . . . . . 115 D3
Crookbarrow Rd WR5 . . . 128 F4
Crookbarrow Way WR5. . 129 A5
Crookham Cl B17. . . . . . . .9 F7
Crooks La B80 . . . . 90 D3
Croome Cl
  Drakes Broughton WR10. 144 A6
  Redditch B98 . . . . 71 F1
Croome Rd
  Defford WR8 . . . . 157 C5
  Worcester WR2 . . . . 127 F7
Cropredy Rd B31. . . . . . . 34 B8
CROPTHORNE 160 B6
Cropthorne Dr B47. . . . . . 36 B7
Cropthorne Dr B47. . . . . . 36 B7
Cropthorne Ho B60 . . . . . 49 B3
Cropthorne with Charlton CE
  Fst Sch WR10. . . . . 160 C6
CROSS BANK 42 A7
Cross Farms La B45. . . . . 17 C1
Crossgate B98 . . . . 90 C7
Cross St
  Halesowen B63 . . . . 8 A3
  Stourbridge DY8 . . . . 5 E5
  Tenbury Wells WR15 . . . . 55 E4
Cross The
  Ripple GL20. . . . . 183 A8
  Stourbridge DY9 . . . . 6 E6
  10 Worcester WR1 . . . . 115 B3
CROSSWAY GREEN 63 F6
Cross Wlks DY9 . . . . .6 E5
Crouch Ct GL20. . . . . 196 E4
CROWCROFT 125 D1
Crowhurst Rd B31. . . . . . 33 E7
CROWLE 117 E4
Crowle CE Fst Sch WR7 . 117 E5
Crowle Dr DY9. . . . . 6 C5
CROWLE GREEN 117 E6
Crown Cl
  Broadheath WR2 . . . . . . 114 A7
  Bromsgrove B61 . . . . 48 F2
Crown Ctr The 3 DY8. . . .6 A5
CROWN EAST 114 A4
Crown East Heritage
  Woodland* WR2 . . . . . . 113 F2
Crown East La
  Broadheath WR2 . . . . . . 113 E4
  Rushwick WR2. . . . . 114 A2
Crowngate Sh Ctr 11
  WR1 . . . . 115 B2
Crownhill Mdw B61 . . . . . 48 F7
Crown La
  Defford WR8 . . . . 157 D3
  Dodderhill WR9 . . . . 66 C2
  Hartlebury DY13 . . . . 63 E8
  Iverley DY8 . . . . 14 C7
  Kidderminster DY10. . . . . 27 E6
  Stourbridge DY8 . . . . 5 F5
Crown Lea Ave WR14. . . . 153 C8
Crown Lea Ho WR14 . . . . 153 C8
Crown Mdw
  Alvechurch B48 . . . . 51 A7
  Broadheath WR2 . . . . . . 114 A7
Crown Meadow Fst Sch
  B48. . . . . 51 B6
Crown Rd
  Birmingham, King's Norton
    B30. . . . . 20 A4
  Walton Cardiff GL20 . . . 197 B4
Crown St WR3 . . . . 115 B6
Crowther Gdns B63 . . . . . 7 C7
Crowther St DY11 . . . . . . 27 C6
Croydon Ct 20 B29 . . . . 19 C7
CRUISE HILL 88 D4
Cruisehill La B97 . . . . . . 88 D5
Crumpfields La
  Feckenham B97 . . . . 88 E8
  Redditch B97 . . . . 69 F1
CRUMPFILED 88 E8
Crumpton Hill Rd WR13,
  WR14. . . . . 138 C7
Crundalls La DY12 . . . . . . 26 B5
Crundelend La WR6. . . . . 60 B2
Crutch La
  Dodderhill WR9 . . . . 85 A7
  Droitwich WR9 . . . . 85 A4
  Upton Warren WR9 . . . . . 66 B4
Crychan Cl B45 . . . . 18 B2
Crystal Gdns DY7 . . . . 4 A3
Culford Dr B32 . . . . 18 C8
Culmington Rd B31 . . . . . 33 F8
Cumberland Rd B68. . . . . .9 B7
Cumberland St WR11 . . . 115 B5
Cumbrian Croft B63. . . . . 7 D2
Curdale Cl DY14 . . . . 22 B4
Curdale Rd B32. . . . . 18 B8
Cur La B97 . . . . 69 D3
Curlew Cl
  Kidderminster DY10. . . . . 28 B2
  Northway GL20 . . . . 184 D1
Curslow La
  Chaddesley Corbett DY10 . 45 F5
  Mustow Green DY10 . . . . 28 F1
  Stone DY10 . . . . 45 F8
Curtis Cl B60 . . . . 68 F8
Cutlers Rough Cl B31. . . . 18 F5
Cutmill Bridge WR15 . . . . 59 B5
CUTNALL GREEN 65 C5

Cutnall Green CE Fst Sch
  WR9 . . . . 65 B5
Cutsdean Cl B31. . . . . 18 F6
Cutts Pool WR7. . . . . 131 C8
Cutty Sark Dr 2 DY13 . . . 44 B2
Cygnet Cl B48. . . . . 51 A7
Cygnet Ct DY10 . . . . 28 A1
Cypress Cl 2 WR11 . . . . 161 F1
Cypress Ct DY10 . . . . 28 A4
Cypress Gr B31 . . . . 18 E1
Cypress Rd GL20 . . . . . . 197 A4
Cypress St WR3. . . . . 115 B6
Cypress Way B31 . . . . 33 F8
Cyprus Ave B96. . . . . 89 D2
Cyprus Cl B29 . . . . 19 A7
Cyril Rd WR3 . . . . 115 D4

D

Dacer Cl B30 . . . . 20 B5
Dace Rd 7 WR5 . . . . 128 C5
Daddlebrook Rd WV15 . . . 1 C6
Daffodil Way B31 . . . . 33 E8
Dagnell End Rd B98. . . . . 71 B7
DAGTAIL END 89 E3
Dagtail La B97 . . . . 89 D3
Daimler Rd B14. . . . . 21 D3
Dainton Gr B32 . . . . .9 C1
Dairy Ct B68. . . . . .9 D7
Dairy La
  Dumbleton WR11. . . . . . 187 F4
  Redditch B97 . . . . 70 A5
Daisy Farm Rd B14. . . . . . 21 B3
Dalbury Cl WR14 . . . . . . 138 F4
Dalbury Rd B28. . . . . 21 E5
Dale Cl B61. . . . . 48 F7
Dalegarth Ct 6 WR4 . . . 116 B6
Dale Hill B60 . . . . 49 F6
Dale Rd
  Halesowen B62 . . . . .8 F8
  Redditch B98 . . . . 70 F5
  Stourbridge DY8 . . . . .5 F2
Daleswood Pk B62. . . . . . 16 F2
Dale The WR9 . . . . 84 D2
Daleview Rd B14. . . . . . . 21 C4
Damar Croft B14. . . . . . . 20 D4
Damaskfield WR4. . . . . . 116 C4
Dame Elizabeth Cadbury
  Tech Coll B30 . . . . 19 D7
Dame Ellen Pinsent Sch
  B13. . . . . 21 A7
Damson Cl B97 . . . . 89 C6
Damson Way
  Bewdley DY12 . . . . 26 C4
  Suckley WR6. . . . . 124 A3
Danebury Pk WR14. . . . . 138 E3
Dane Gr B13. . . . . 20 D8
Danemoor Cross WR13. . 167 E7
Danes Cl WR14 . . . . 139 B3
Danescroft 4 DY13 . . . . 43 F4
Danes Gn WR3 . . . . 102 E3
Danford Cl DY8 . . . . .6 A4
Danford Rd B47. . . . . 35 F6
Danube Rd WR9 . . . . 103 D8
Danzey Cl B98 . . . . 90 B5
Danzey Gr B14. . . . . 20 C3
DARBYS GREEN 111 E5
Dark La
  Astley & Dunley DY13 . . . 62 C6
  Astwood Bank B96 . . . . . 89 D1
  Belbroughton DY9 . . . . . . 30 F8
  Grimley WR2 . . . . 101 C5
  Hollywood B38, B47 . . . . 35 E7
  Kinver DY7. . . . . 4 B3
  Ombersley DY9 . . . . 63 F1
  Rock DY14 . . . . 41 E7
  Romsley B62 . . . . 16 F4
  Stock & Bradley B96. . . . 107 A3
  Stoke Heath B60 . . . . 67 D6
Dark Orch WR15 . . . . 55 E3
Darris Rd B29. . . . . 20 A8
Dartmoor Cl B45. . . . . . . 18 A2
Dart Rd WR5. . . . . 115 F3
Darwin Ave WR5 . . . . . . 116 A3
Darwin Cl 6 WR5. . . . . . 141 C6
Daston Cl WR12. . . . . . . 190 E8
Dauntsey Covert B14. . . . 20 D2
Davena Dr B29. . . . . .9 E2
Davenham Cl WR14 . . . . 139 A4
Davenham Rd B60 . . . . . . 49 C1
Davenport Dr B60. . . . . . . 49 B1
Daventry Gr B32 . . . . .9 D6
Davey Rd GL20. . . . . 197 B8
Davids The B31 . . . . 19 C5
Davids Cl B97. . . . . 70 D2
Davies Rd WR11 . . . . 161 D1
Davis Alley 11 GL20 . . . 196 E6
Dawberry Cl B14. . . . . . . 20 D5
Dawberry Fields Rd B14. . 20 D5
Dawberry Rd B14. . . . . . . 20 C6
Dawn Rd B31 . . . . 18 E6
DAWSHILL. 127 C5
Dawson Cl 3 WR2. . . . . 127 B8
Dawson Rd B61. . . . . 48 E2
Daybrook Cl B97. . . . . . . 70 B5
DAYHOUSE BANK 17 A1
Dayhouse Bank B62. . . . . 17 B1
DEABLEY. 123 B8
Deacle Pl WR11. . . . . 161 C4
Deal Cres WR4. . . . . 116 C7
Deal Gr B31 . . . . 19 A3
Dean Cl
  Stourbridge DY8 . . . . .6 B6
  1 Tenbury Wells WR15. . 55 F6

Deane Cl 5 WR2 . . . . 127 C2
Deans CI B98 . . . . 71 D5
Deanscroft Dr B60 . . . . . . 49 C6
Deansford La DY10 . . . . . . 29 B6
Deansway
 Bromsgrove B61 . . . . 48 E2
 Worcester WR1 . . . . 115 B2
Deansway Ho DY10 . . . . . . 28 A7
Deansway The DY10 . . . . . . 28 A7
Dearmont Rd B31 . . . . 33 E7
Debdale Ave WR4 . . . . . . 116 B5
DEBLIN'S GREEN 140 B7
Dee Gr B38 . . . . 34 E8
Deelands Rd B45 . . . . 32 F8
Deeley Cl B64 . . . . 7 E7
Deepwood Gr B32 . . . . . . 18 B8
Deer Ave WR5 . . . . 128 F6
Deer Barn Hill B98 . . . . . . 71 A1
Deerhurst Cl B98 . . . . 71 C7
Dee Way WR4 . . . . 115 F3
DEFFORD 157 D3
Defford Cl B97 . . . . 69 E1
Defford cum Besford CE Fst
 Sch WR8 . . . . 157 D3
Defford Rd WR10 . . . . . . 158 A7
De La Bere Cl 8 WR11 . . 161 D5
Delamere Rd
 Bewdley DY12 . . . . 26 C4
 Birmingham B28 . . . . 21 F7
 Malvern WR14 . . . . 139 B1
 Tedstone Delamere HR7 . . 96 E2
Delingpole Wlk 2 B64 . . . . 7 E8
Della Dr B32 . . . . 18 D8
Dellow Gr B48 . . . . 51 A5
Dellows Cl B38 . . . . 34 D7
Dell Rd B30 . . . . 20 A5
Dells Farm B47 . . . . 35 F6
Dell The
 Birmingham, Shenley Fields
  B31 . . . . 18 D6
 Bredon GL20 . . . . 184 E7
 Stourbridge DY8 . . . . 5 E6
 Stourport-on-Severn DY13 . 44 B4
Dellway Ct DY8 . . . . 5 E5
Delph Dr DY5 . . . . 6 E7
Delphinium Cl 3 DY11 . . . 12 C1
Delph La DY5 . . . . 6 D8
Delrene Rd B28, B90 . . . . . 21 F3
Delta Dr GL20 . . . . 197 C8
Denaby Gr B14 . . . . 21 D4
Denbigh Ct 3 B29 . . . . . . 19 C7
Dencer Cl B45 . . . . 33 A8
Dencil Cl B63 . . . . 7 D5
Dene Hollow B13 . . . . 21 C7
Denehurst Cl B45 . . . . . . 33 A1
Dene Rd DY8 . . . . 5 F3
Denford Gr B14 . . . . 20 D5
Denholme Gr B14 . . . . . . 21 A3
Denison Cl WR14 . . . . . . 139 B2
Dennis Hall 2 DY8 . . . . 5 E8
Dennis Hall Rd DY8 . . . . . . 6 A8
Dennis St DY8 . . . . 5 E8
Denshaw Rd B14 . . . . 20 D6
Dent Cl WR5 . . . . 115 D2
Denton Rd DY9 . . . . 7 A4
Denver Rd B14 . . . . 21 A2
Derby Rd 1 WR1 . . . . . . 115 C1
Dereham Ct WR14 . . . . . 138 F3
Derick Burcher's Mall 5
 DY10 . . . . 27 E6
Derries The WR3 . . . . . . 103 A3
Derwent Ave DY13 . . . . . . 43 F5
Derwent Cl 2 WR4 . . . . . 115 F5
Derwent Dr
 6 Bewdley DY12 . . . . . . 25 F4
 Tewkesbury GL20 . . . . . 197 A8
Derwent Gr 8 WR9 . . . . . 84 C1
Derwent Ho DY10 . . . . 27 F7
Derwent Rd B30 . . . . 20 C8
Derwent Way B60 . . . . . . 49 B1
De Salis Dr WR9 . . . . 84 D7
De Salls Ct WR9 . . . . 84 D7
Design Cl B60 . . . . 68 A7
Desiree Dr GL20 . . . . . . 196 F8
Despenser Rd GL20 . . . . 196 E4
Dettonford Rd B32 . . . . . . 18 B8
Devil's Spittleful Nature
 Reserve★ DY12 . . . . 26 E3
Devon Cl
 Inkberrow WR7 . . . . 120 F6
 Kidderminster DY11 . . . . . 12 C1
Devon Ct 3 B29 . . . . 19 B7
Devonport Cl 3 B97 . . . . . 70 B5
Devon Rd
 Birmingham B45 . . . . 17 F1
 Smethwick B67 . . . . 9 E7
 Stourbridge DY8 . . . . 5 E7
 Worcester WR5 . . . . 115 F1
Devonshire Pl GL20 . . . . 196 F4
Devon Way B31 . . . . 33 E8
De Walden Rd WR14 . . . . 152 C8
Dewberry Cl 9 DY13 . . . . 43 E4
Dewsbury Cl B96 . . . . 89 E1
De Wyche Cl WR9 . . . . . . 85 E8
De Wyche Rd WR9 . . . . . . 85 E8
Dial Cl B14 . . . . 20 E2
Dial La DY8 . . . . 4 E8
Dice Pleck B31 . . . . 19 C2
Didcot Cl B97 . . . . 89 C5
Digby Dr GL20 . . . . 196 F7
Digby Rd WR11 . . . . 161 F3
DIGLIS 128 E8
Diglis Ave WR1 . . . . 115 B1
Diglis Dock Rd WR5 . . . . 128 B7
Diglis La WR5 . . . . 128 C8

Diglis Rd WR5 . . . . 115 C1
Dilmore Ave WR3 . . . . . . 102 E3
Dilmore La WR3 . . . . 102 E4
Dilwyn Cl B98 . . . . 71 F1
Dimmingsdale Bank B32 . . 9 C4
Dimsdale Gr B31 . . . . 18 E3
Dimsdale Rd B31 . . . . 18 D3
Dinchall Rd WR5 . . . . . . 129 A8
Dinedor Cl B98 . . . . 71 D3
Dineley Cl 3 B98 . . . . . . 131 B2
Dineley Rd WR10 . . . . . . 131 B2
DINES GREEN 114 C2
Dines Green Prim Sch
 WR2 . . . . 114 D2
Dingle Ave B64 . . . . 7 E8
Dingle Cl B30 . . . . 19 D7
Dingle End WR7 . . . . 120 F6
Dingle Rd
 Leigh WR6 . . . . 125 D8
 Stourbridge DY9 . . . . 6 C2
Dingleside B98 . . . . 70 E2
Dinmore Ave B31 . . . . . . 19 B4
Dinmore Cl
 Redditch B98 . . . . 71 D3
 4 Worcester WR5 . . . . 128 E5
DITCHFORD BANK 87 E5
Ditchford Cl B97 . . . . 89 D4
Ditton Gr B31 . . . . 33 F6
Dixey Ct WR14 . . . . 138 E2
Dixon Ct DY10 . . . . 28 C8
Dixon St DY10 . . . . 27 C5
Dobbins Oak Rd DY9 . . . . . 6 C7
Dobes La DY10 . . . . 46 C7
Dockar Rd B31 . . . . 18 E2
Dockeray Ave WR4 . . . . . 116 C5
Dock La GL20 . . . . 184 E7
Dock The
 Catshill B61 . . . . 49 A8
 Stourbridge DY9 . . . . 6 F5
Doctors Hill
 Bournheath B61 . . . . 48 D8
 Stourbridge DY9 . . . . 6 C3
DODDENHAM 112 A5
Dodderhill Rd WR9 . . . . . 85 A5
Dodderhill Sch WR9 . . . . 85 A4
Doddington Gr B32 . . . . . 18 B8
DODFORD 48 A7
Dodford Cl B45 . . . . 32 F7
Dodford Ct B61 . . . . 48 C6
Dodford Fst Sch B61 . . . . 48 A5
Dodford Ho B60 . . . . 49 B3
Dodford Rd B61 . . . . 31 D1
Dogkennel La B63 . . . . 8 B3
Dog La
 Bewdley DY12 . . . . 26 B3
 Ombersley DY13 . . . . 63 F4
 Upton Warren B61 . . . . . . 66 C6
Dogwood Cl WR14 . . . . . 139 D3
Dolan Park Hospl (Private)
 B60 . . . . 50 B1
Dolben La B98 . . . . 71 D3
Dolday WR1 . . . . 115 B2
Dolphin Cl WR2 . . . . 114 E4
Dolphin Ctr The B60 . . . . 49 A2
Dolphin Rd B98 . . . . 71 A5
Domar Cl DY11 . . . . 27 B7
Domestic Fowl Trust &
 Honeybourne Rare
 Breeds★ WR11 . . . . . . 164 A5
Dominic Dr B30 . . . . 19 D4
Donney Brook 3 WR11 . . 161 F3
Donnington Cl B98 . . . . . . 71 C5
Don Rd WR4 . . . . 115 F3
Doran Cl B31 . . . . 18 D5
Dorchester Rd DY9 . . . . . . 6 D2
Dordale Cl B31 . . . . 18 C1
Dordale Rd DY9 . . . . 30 E2
Dordon Cl B90 . . . . 21 E1
Dormie Cl B38 . . . . 19 D1
Dormouse Croft WR5 . . . . 128 F7
DORMSTON 119 F8
Dormston Cl B98 . . . . 70 F1
Dormston Dr B29 . . . . 9 F2
Dormy Dr B31 . . . . 34 A7
Dornie Dr B38 . . . . 19 F1
Dornton Rd B30 . . . . 20 C8
Dorothy Adams Cl 3 B64 . . 7 E8
Dorothy Cres 5 WR3 . . . 102 A1
Dorrels Orch 3 WR10 . . . 132 F4
Dorridge Cl B97 . . . . 70 B1
Dorset Cl B45 . . . . 17 F2
Dorset Cotts B30 . . . . . . 20 A6
Dorset Ct 2 B29 . . . . 19 B7
Dorset Dr DY8 . . . . 5 D8
Dorsett Rd 3 DY13 . . . . . 43 F5
DORSINGTON 150 E8
Dorsington Rd CV37 . . . . 150 E5
Dorstone Covert B14 . . . . 20 C2
Dorville Cl B38 . . . . 34 D8
Dotterel Pl DY10 . . . . 27 A8
Double Hedges Rd GL20 . 173 A3
Douglas Rd B47 . . . . 36 A7
Doulton Cl B32 . . . . 9 F3
Dove Cl
 Kidderminster DY10 . . . . . 28 B2
 Worcester WR4 . . . . 115 F3
Dovecote WR10 . . . . 160 D8
Dovecote Rd
 Bromsgrove B61 . . . . 48 E1
 Droitwich WR9 . . . . 85 A1
Dovedale Cl 19 B29 . . . . . 19 C7
Dovedale Dr B28 . . . . 21 F5
Dove Dr DY8 . . . . 6 A8
Dove Gdns B38 . . . . 20 B2
Dove Ave WR4 . . . . 116 C6
Dover Ct B32 . . . . 18 A7
DOVERDALE 64 E1

Doverdale Ave DY10 . . . . . 28 B5
Doverdale Cl
 Droitwich WR9 . . . . 84 E2
 Halesowen B63 . . . . 7 E5
 Redditch B98 . . . . 90 B7
Doverdale La
 Hampton Lovett WR9 . . . . 83 F8
 Ombersley WR9 . . . . 64 D1
Doverdale Pk WR9 . . . . . . 84 D7
Dove Ridge DY8 . . . . 6 A7
Doveridge Rd B28 . . . . . . 21 E5
Doversley Rd B14 . . . . . . 20 C5
Dover's View GL55 . . . . . 178 D7
Doveton Ho DY8 . . . . 6 A3
Dowar Rd B45 . . . . 33 C7
Doweries The B45 . . . . . . 32 F8
Dowland Gdns 3 WR2 . . 114 D3
Dowler's Hill Cres B98 . . . 90 A8
DOWLES 25 F6
Dowles Cl B29 . . . . 19 B6
Dowles Croft 2 WR9 . . . . 84 E3
Dowles Manor★ DY12 . . . 25 E5
Dowles Rd
 Bewdley DY12 . . . . 26 A4
 Kidderminster DY11 . . . . . 27 B2
 Upper Arley DY12 . . . . . . 25 F5
Downcroft Ave B38 . . . . . 19 E2
Downfield La GL20 . . . . . 184 B7
Downing Ct 2 B68 . . . . . . 9 B7
Downing St B63 . . . . 8 A5
Downland Cl B38 . . . . 19 F1
Downsell Ho B97 . . . . 70 A2
Downsell Rd B97 . . . . 70 A2
Downs Malvern Coll Prep
 Sch The WR13 . . . . 152 B3
Dragonfly Gn WR5 . . . . . 128 F6
Dragons La WR13 . . . . . . 125 E1
Dragoon Fields B60 . . . . . 68 B8
Drake Ave WR2 . . . . 114 D3
Drake Cres DY11 . . . . 27 A7
DRAKELOW 12 B5
Drakelow La DY11 . . . . . . 12 C5
Drakes Bridge Rd WR10 . 171 D7
DRAKES BROUGHTON . . 144 A6
Drakes Cl
 Redditch B97 . . . . 89 C6
 Silver Street B47 . . . . 35 F5
DRAKES CROSS 36 A6
Drakes Cross Par B47 . . . . 36 A5
Drakes Hill Cl DY8 . . . . . . 5 C4
Drakes Lea WR11 . . . . . . 161 F5
Drake St WR13 . . . . 167 E4
Drapers Cl WR4 . . . . 115 F6
Drawbridge Rd B90 . . . . . 36 E8
Draycote Cl 2 WR5 . . . . 128 D5
DRAYCOTT 141 C4
Draycott Cl 9 B97 . . . . . . 70 B5
Draycott Dr B31 . . . . 18 E7
DRAYTON 30 B4
Drayton Cl
 Bidford-on-Avon B50 . . . 136 C5
 Redditch B98 . . . . 90 D8
Drayton Ct B60 . . . . 68 B8
Drayton Rd
 Belbroughton DY9 . . . . . . 30 B5
 Birmingham B14 . . . . 20 F8
Drew Cres DY9 . . . . 6 D2
Drew Rd DY9 . . . . 6 D3
Drews Ho B14 . . . . 20 D1
Drews Holloway B63 . . . . . 7 D5
Drews Holloway S B63 . . . . 7 D5
Drews Meadow Cl 1 B14 . 20 C2
Driffield Cl B98 . . . . 71 D2
Drift The WR11 . . . . 162 E3
Driftwood Cl B38 . . . . 34 D7
Drinkwater La WR11 . . . . 163 B4
Drive The
 Bowling Green WR2 . . . . 127 B3
 Halesowen, Cradley B63 . . 7 D5
 Halesowen, Hasbury B63 . . 8 A3
 Hindlip WR3 . . . . 103 B2
 Hopwood B48 . . . . 34 B3
 Redditch B97 . . . . 69 C7
 Worcester WR3 . . . . 115 B8
Droitwich Rd
 Feckenham B96 . . . . 107 C7
 Fernhill Heath WR3 . . . . . 103 A3
 Hartlebury DY10 . . . . 45 A6
 Worcester WR3 . . . . 115 C8
DROITWICH SPA 84 C4
Droitwich Spa Brine Baths
 Complex The WR9 . . . . . 84 F3
Droitwich Spa High Sch
 WR9 . . . . 84 D3
Droitwich Spa Leisure Ctr
 WR9 . . . . 84 D3
Droitwich Spa Lido Pk★
 WR9 . . . . 85 A3
Droitwich Spa Sta WR9 . . . 84 E5
Drovers Gn 1 WR9 . . . . . 84 E5
Drovers Pl 3 WR9 . . . . . . 84 E5
Drovers Way
 Bromsgrove B60 . . . . 67 E6
 2 Droitwich WR9 . . . . . . 84 D5
 Worcester WR3 . . . . 115 E7
Drovers Wlk DY10 . . . . . . 27 E5
DRUGGERS END 167 C1
Drugger's End La WR13 . 167 C1
Druids Cl B14 . . . . 20 D1
Drumbles La 2 WR4 . . . . 116 C4
Drummond Rd
 Bromsgrove B60 . . . . 68 B8
 Stourbridge DY9 . . . . 6 F4
Drury La
 Martin Hussingtree WR3 . 103 C5
 Redmarley D'abitot GL19 . 192 B4
 Stourbridge DY8 . . . . 6 A5
Drybrook Cl B38 . . . . 34 E8

Dryden Cl
 Malvern WR14 . . . . 139 A2
 Worcester WR5 . . . . 115 C6
Dry Mill La DY12 . . . . 25 E4
Drysdale Cl WR11 . . . . . 176 D7
Duck Mdw WR4 . . . . 116 B4
DUCKSWICH 168 E4
Duddage Bsns Pk GL20 . . 183 E6
Dudley Cl 1 WR2 . . . . . . 114 D3
Dudley Rd
 Halesowen B63 . . . . 8 B5
 Honeybourne WR11 . . . . 164 B5
 Stourbridge DY9 . . . . 6 E6
Dudley St DY10 . . . . 27 E7
Dudnill Gr B32 . . . . 18 A8
Dufton Rd B32 . . . . 9 E4
Dugard Way WR9 . . . . . . 103 C2
Dugdale Ave B50 . . . . . . 136 C5
Dugdale Dr WR4 . . . . . . 116 C3
Duke Cres WR14 . . . . . . 153 B6
Duke of Edinburgh Way
 WR14 . . . . 139 C6
Dukes Rd B30 . . . . 20 A3
Duke St DY8 . . . . 6 A6
Dukes Way GL20 . . . . . . 196 F3
Duke's Way WR14 . . . . . 153 C6
Dulais Cl B98 . . . . 70 E1
Dulvern Gr B14 . . . . 20 D5
Dumble Pit La B47, B48 . . 52 F7
DUMBLETON 187 F5
Dumbleton La WR15 . . . . 59 B6
Dumphouse La B48 . . . . . 52 C3
Dunard Rd B90 . . . . 21 F3
Dunbar Cl
 Birmingham B32 . . . . 9 D1
 Kidderminster DY10 . . . . . 28 C6
Dunchurch Cl B98 . . . . . . 71 F1
Dunchurch Dr B31 . . . . . 18 E7
Dunclent Cres DY10 . . . . 28 B5
Dunclent La DY10 . . . . . . 28 E3
Duncombe St DY8 . . . . 5 D5
Dunedin Dr B45 . . . . 33 B1
Dunedin Ho B32 . . . . 9 F4
DUNHAMPSTEAD 104 C2
DUNHAMPTON 64 A1
Dunhampton Dr DY10 . . . 13 B1
Duniers St 3 WR12 . . . . 177 A1
Dunkirk Dr WR5 . . . . 129 A4
DUNLEY 62 B7
Dunley Rd
 Astley & Dunley DY13 . . . 61 F8
 Rock DY12 . . . . 42 F2
Dunlin Dr DY10 . . . . 27 F2
Dunlop Rd B97 . . . . 89 D5
Dunmore Rd DY12 . . . . . . 26 D5
Dunmow Ave WR4 . . . . . 116 C3
Dunnigan Rd B32 . . . . 9 F3
DUNNINGTON 135 D7
Dunnington Ave B13 . . . . 13 A1
Dunnington CE Prim Sch
 B49 . . . . 135 D8
Dunns Bank DY5 . . . . 6 F7
Dunn's La WR8 . . . . 169 C6
Dunsford Cl DY5 . . . . 6 B7
Dunslade Cres DY5 . . . . . . 6 F7
DUNSLEY 4 C4
Dunsley Dr DY7 . . . . 4 C4
Dunsley Rd
 Kinver DY7 . . . . 4 B4
 Stourbridge DY9 . . . . 5 C4
Dunsmore Dr DY5 . . . . . . 6 F8
Dunsmore Gn GL19 . . . . 195 B5
Dunstall Cl B97 . . . . 70 B2
DUNSTALL COMMON . . . 156 C3
Dunstall Gr B29 . . . . 18 F8
Dunstall Rd B63 . . . . 7 D3
Dunster Cl
 Birmingham B30 . . . . 20 C4
 6 Worcester WR4 . . . . 116 B7
Durant Cl B45 . . . . 17 D1
Durbridge Rd GL19 . . . . 192 A2
Durcott Cl WR11 . . . . 161 F3
Durcott Gdns WR11 . . . . 161 E3
Durcott Rd WR11 . . . . . . 161 E3
Durham Cl B61 . . . . 48 E4
Durham Rd
 Stourbridge DY8 . . . . 5 D8
 Worcester WR5 . . . . 116 A3
Durnford Croft B14 . . . . . 20 E1
Dursley La B98 . . . . 72 A3
Dusthouse La B60 . . . . . . 68 D7
Dutton St 2 WR3 . . . . . . 115 D4
Duxford Cl B97 . . . . 89 B8
Dwellings La B32 . . . . 9 B5
Dyas Rd B47 . . . . 36 A7
Dyer's La GL55 . . . . 178 F3
Dyson Dr WR14 . . . . 139 D1
Dyson Perrins CE High Sch
 WR14 . . . . 138 F5

E

EACHWAY 32 F6
Eachway B45 . . . . 32 F6
Eachway Farm Cl B45 . . . 33 A6
Eachway La B45 . . . . 33 A6
Eadie Mews B97 . . . . 70 D1
Eagle Cl 4 WR5 . . . . 128 C5
Eagle Croft B14 . . . . 20 E2
Eagle La DY14 . . . . 22 C4
Eagle Rd B98 . . . . 71 E5
Eagle Trad Est B63 . . . . . . 8 A4
Eardisley Cl B98 . . . . 71 F1
EARDISTON 59 B5
Earls Cl B97 . . . . 69 F2
EARL'S COMMON 105 F3
Earls Comm Rd WR9 . . . 106 C1

EARL'S CROOME 155 F1
Earlsdon Rd WR2 . . . . . . 127 F8
Earls Ferry Gdns B32 . . . . 18 B7
Earls Grange WR8 . . . . . 155 F1
Earls High Sch B63 . . . . . . 8 A4
Earls Way B63 . . . . 8 B4
Earlswood Lakes Craft Ctr★
 B94 . . . . 36 F2
Earlswood Rd B30 . . . . . . 20 D3
Earlswood Sta B94 . . . . . . 36 D1
Earlswood Trad Est B94 . . 53 C6
Early River Pl 5 DY12 . . . 25 F3
Easemore Rd B98 . . . . . . 70 F5
Easenhall La B98 . . . . . . 71 E1
Easinghope La WR6 . . . . 111 F6
Easmore Cl B14 . . . . 20 D2
Eastabrook Cl WR14 . . . . 138 F5
Eastbank Dr WR3 . . . . . . 115 A7
East Cl WR9 . . . . 85 E8
East Comer WR2 . . . . . . 114 E4
EASTERN HILL 89 F3
Eastern Hill B96 . . . . 89 F2
Easterton Croft B14 . . . . . 20 E2
Eastfield Cl WR3 . . . . . . 102 E3
EASTHAM 57 F6
Eastham Rd B13 . . . . 21 C6
Eastleigh Dr B62 . . . . 17 A4
East Moons Moat B98 . . . . 71 E4
Eastnor Cl
 Kidderminster DY10 . . . . . 27 C2
 Redditch B98 . . . . 70 E1
 Worcester WR5 . . . . 128 E2
Easton Gr B47 . . . . 36 B7
East Park Dr WR9 . . . . . . 84 D4
East Rd
 Bromsgrove B60 . . . . 49 A1
 Stourport-on-Severn DY13 . 44 B5
East Side WR11 . . . . 149 A3
East St
 Brierley Hill DY5 . . . . 7 A8
 Kidderminster DY10 . . . . . 27 F6
 Tewkesbury GL20 . . . . . 196 E6
 Worcester WR1 . . . . 115 C4
Eastville B31 . . . . 19 B3
Eastward Rd WR14 . . . . . 138 F6
East Waterside WR8 . . . . 169 C6
Eastwick Dr 3 WR11 . . . 161 C2
Eastwood Ct B96 . . . . 89 E1
Eastwood Dr DY10 . . . . . . 28 B5
Easy Row WR1 . . . . 115 B3
Eathorpe Cl B98 . . . . 71 E1
Eaton Rd WR14 . . . . 152 E3
Ebmore Dr B14 . . . . 20 D2
Ebrington Cl B14 . . . . 20 D4
Ebrington Dr WR4 . . . . . 116 B7
Ebrington Rd WR14 . . . . 138 C2
Ebsdorf Cl 4 B50 . . . . . . 136 D5
Ebury Rd B30 . . . . 20 B4
Echells Cl B61 . . . . 48 D2
Eckersall Rd B38 . . . . 19 E3
ECKINGTON 171 F7
Eckington CE Fst Sch
 WR10 . . . . 171 F7
Eckington Cl B98 . . . . 90 B8
Eckington Rd WR10 . . . . 157 E2
Eckington Wlk B38 . . . . . 34 E7
Eddy Rd DY10 . . . . 27 E7
Eden Cl
 Birmingham B31 . . . . 33 E8
 St Peter the Great WR5 . . 128 E6
 Studley B80 . . . . 90 D3
Edenfield Cl B97 . . . . 70 A5
Edenhall Rd B32 . . . . 9 B6
Eden Ho 2 DY8 . . . . 6 A5
Edenhurst Rd B31 . . . . . . 33 F7
Edgar St 2 WR1 . . . . . . 115 C1
Edgecliff High Sch DY7 . . . 4 B5
Edge Hill DY7 . . . . 3 F4
Edgehill Rd B31 . . . . 19 B1
Edge View Cl DY7 . . . . . . 3 F5
Edge View Wlk DY7 . . . . . 3 F5
Edgewood Cl 2 B64 . . . . . 7 F8
Edgewood Dr B45 . . . . . . 33 B1
Edgewood Rd
 Birmingham, King's Norton
  B38 . . . . 34 F7
 Birmingham, Rednal B45 . . 33 B6
Edgeworth Cl
 Redditch B98 . . . . 71 C5
 1 Worcester WR4 . . . . 116 A7
Edgioake La B96 . . . . . . 108 E6
EDGIOCK 108 D5
Edgmond Cl B98 . . . . 71 D4
Edinburgh Cl DY10 . . . . . 27 E8
Edinburgh Rd
 Birmingham B68 . . . . 9 B8
 Birmingham, Brandhall B68 . 9 C8
Edison Gr B32 . . . . 9 D5
Edith Berry Ct WR14 . . . . 139 B1
Edith Wlk WR14 . . . . 138 F1
Edmonton Cl 6 WR2 . . . 127 F6
Ednall La B60 . . . . 48 F1
EDVIN LOACH 96 B1
Edward Cl 3 WR5 . . . . . 115 D1
Edward Pl 3 GL20 . . . . . 196 F3
Edward Rd
 Birmingham B68 . . . . 9 C8
 Birmingham, Highter's Heath
  B14 . . . . 21 A1
 Halesowen B63 . . . . 7 F4
Edwards La WR7 . . . . . . 130 C6
Edward St
 Evesham WR11 . . . . 161 D5
 Redditch B97 . . . . 70 D4
Edwin Ave (Road 4) DY10 . 27 C1
Edwin Cres B60 . . . . 67 F7

Edwin Ct B60 . . . . 67 F8
Edwin Rd B30 . . . . 20 B7
EDWYN RALPH 95 C1
Effingham Rd B13 . . . . 21 C7
EGDON 130 D4
Egdon La WR7 . . . . 130 D2
Egghill La B31, B45 . . . . . . 18 B3
Eggington Rd DY8 . . . . 5 D6
Egginton Rd B28 . . . . 21 E5
Egg La
  Belbroughton DY9, DY10 . . . 30 A5
  North Claines WR3 . . . . . 102 C6
EGGS TUMP 192 C8
Egremont Gdns 2 WR4 116 C5
Egret Ct DY10 . . . . 28 A1
Eider Ct DY10 . . . . 28 B1
Elan Ave DY13 . . . . 43 E7
Elan Cl
  Bewdley DY12 . . . . 25 F4
  Cookley DY10 . . . . 13 B4
Elan Rd B31 . . . . 18 C2
Elbury Park Rd WR4 . . . . . 116 A4
ELCOCK'S BROOK 88 E5
Elderberry Cl
  Stourbridge DY8 . . . . 5 C3
  6 Stourport-on-Severn
  DY13 . . . . 43 E4
Elderfield Rd B30 . . . . 20 B3
ELDERSFIELD 193 E3
Eldersfield Cl B98 . . . . 71 E7
Eldersfield Lawn CE Prim
  Sch GL19 . . . . 194 E2
Eldon Rd
  Birmingham B32 . . . . 9 A3
  Halesowen B62 . . . . 8 F3
Eldorado Cl B80 . . . . 90 D4
Eleanor Harrison Dr DY10 13 B5
Elford Cl B14 . . . . 20 E5
Elgar Ave WR14 . . . . 139 C1
Elgar Birthplace (Mus) The★
  WR2 . . . . 113 F4
Elgar Cl B97 . . . . 89 C8
Elgar Cres WR9 . . . . 103 F8
Elgar Ct 3 WR3 . . . . 115 D4
Elgar Dr WR5 . . . . 141 C6
Elgar Mews 2 B60 . . . . . . 48 F2
Elgar Ret Pk WR5 . . . . . . 115 E7
Elgar Tech Coll The
  WR3 . . . . 115 D7
Elgin Cl DY8 . . . . 6 A7
Eliot Rd WR3 . . . . 115 C6
Eliot Wlk DY10 . . . . 28 C6
Elizabeth Ave
  Droitwich WR9 . . . . 85 A3
  Worcester WR3 . . . . 102 B1
Elizabeth Ct WR9 . . . . 85 A3
Elizabeth Ho DY9 . . . . 6 E5
Elizabeth Rd
  Evesham WR11 . . . . 161 D2
  Halesowen B63 . . . . 7 F3
Elizabeth Way B97 . . . . . . 70 D5
Eliza Gdns B61 . . . . 32 B1
Elkstone Cl 3 WR4 . . . . . 115 F7
Elkstone Covert B14 . . . . . 20 C2
Ellen Brook Cl 6 B97 . . . . 70 B5
Ellerdene Cl B98 . . . . 89 D8
Ellerside Gr B31 . . . . 18 F2
Ellerslie Cl DY5 . . . . 6 D8
Ellerslie Rd B13 . . . . 21 C7
Elliot Ct
  Malvern WR14 . . . . 139 A2
  Tewkesbury GL20 . . . . . 196 E6
Elliot Gdns B45 . . . . 33 B5
Elliott Cl 1 B50 . . . . 136 C5
Ellison Ave WR2 . . . . 114 E5
Ellis Rd WR2 . . . . 115 A1
Ellsdon Rise WR5 . . . . . . 141 C7
ELMBRIDGE 65 F4
Elmbridge Cl B63 . . . . 7 D5
Elmbridge La
  Elmbridge WR9 . . . . 66 A4
  Rushock WR9 . . . . 46 D1
Elmbridge Way 7 B31 . . . . 19 D2
Elmbury Dr GL20 . . . . 197 B6
Elm Cl
  Cookley DY10 . . . . 13 B4
  Pebworth CV37 . . . . 150 E2
  Stourbridge DY8 . . . . 5 D2
Elm Croft B68 . . . . 9 C7
Elmcroft Ave B32 . . . . 9 A1
Elm Ct B97 . . . . 70 D4
Elmdale B62 . . . . 9 A7
Elmdale Cres B31 . . . . 18 E4
Elmdale Dr DY10 . . . . 28 C5
Elmdale Gr B31 . . . . 18 E4
Elmdale Rd WR3 . . . . 115 B8
Elm Dr
  Birmingham, Frankley B31 . 18 C1
  Blakedown DY10 . . . . 14 B2
  Frankley B31 . . . . 18 C1
  Hartlebury DY10 . . . . 64 D8
Elmfield Gdns WR5 . . . . . 115 D1
Elmfield Rd 2 WR11 . . . . 45 A1
Elmfield Rudolf Steiner Sch
  DY8 . . . . 6 A3
Elmfield Wlk 1 DY13 . . . . 43 E4
Elm Gr
  Bromsgrove B61 . . . . 49 A4
  Kinver DY7 . . . . 4 C3
  Stourport-on-Severn DY13 . 62 D8
Elm Green Cl WR5 . . . . . . 128 C5
Elmhurst Cl B97 . . . . 89 D4
ELMLEY CASTLE 173 E7
Elmley Castle CE Fst Sch
  WR10 . . . . 173 E7
Elmley Cl
  Elmley Lovett WR9 . . . . . 65 B6
  Kidderminster DY11 . . . . . 27 B3

Elmley Cl continued
  Malvern WR14 . . . . 139 B1
Elmley Gr B30 . . . . 20 B2
Elmley Ho 9 B97 . . . . 70 A4
Elmley La WR9 . . . . 65 B6
ELMLEY LOVETT 65 A8
Elmley Rd WR11 . . . . 174 B1
Elm Pl
  Cookley DY10 . . . . 13 B4
  Harvington DY10 . . . . 29 B3
Elm Rd
  Birmingham, Bournville
  B30 . . . . 19 F8
  Drakes Broughton WR10 . 144 A6
  Evesham WR11 . . . . 161 F4
  Kidderminster DY10 . . . . . 28 A6
  Northway GL20 . . . . 197 D6
  Redditch B97 . . . . 70 D4
  Worcester WR2 . . . . 115 A3
Elms Cl B38 . . . . 34 C8
Elms Dr WR13 . . . . 166 A8
ELMS GREEN 60 B2
Elmside WR11 . . . . 161 F4
Elms Sch WR13 . . . . 166 A8
Elmstone Cl B97 . . . . 89 C5
Elm Tree Gr B63 . . . . 7 D6
Elm Tree Rd B30 . . . . 20 A6
Elmvil Rd GL20 . . . . 197 C7
Elmwood Gr B47 . . . . 36 A6
Elmwoods B32 . . . . 9 B2
Elsma Rd B68 . . . . 9 C8
Elsworth Rd 6 B31 . . . . . 19 D2
Elton Rd 6 DY12 . . . . 25 F3
Eltric Rd WR3 . . . . 115 B8
Elvaston Way B90 . . . . . . 36 F5
Ely Cl
  Kidderminster DY11 . . . . . 27 A6
  Worcester WR5 . . . . 116 A1
Ely Gr B32 . . . . 9 F4
Embassy Ind Est 1 DY9 . . . 6 F5
Emerald Rd WR2 . . . . 114 E3
Emery Ct DY10 . . . . 27 E7
Emes Ct WR10 . . . . 158 C8
Emperor Dr WR5 . . . . 128 C5
Emperor Pl DY10 . . . . 27 E8
Empire Ct B97 . . . . 70 E5
Emsworth Gr B14 . . . . 20 D6
Endeavour Pl DY13 . . . . . . 44 A2
ENFIELD 70 D5
Enfield Cl B60 . . . . 67 E7
Enfield Ind Est B97 . . . . . . 70 D5
Enfield Rd B97 . . . . 89 D5
Engadine Cl WR14 . . . . . . 153 A6
Engadine Rd B60 . . . . 49 C1
Engine La
  Stourbridge DY9 . . . . 6 D6
  7 Stourport-on-Severn
  DY13 . . . . 44 A3
Enid Blyton Cnr 5 WR9 . 103 F8
Enigma Bsns Pk WR14 . . . 139 C4
Ennerdale Cl WR4 . . . . . . 116 A5
Ennerdale Dr B63 . . . . 7 D2
Ennerdale Rd DY13 . . . . . . 43 F6
Enterprise Dr DY9 . . . . 6 F6
Enterprise Way WR11 . . . 175 F8
Enville Pl DY8 . . . . 5 E5
Enville Rd DY7 . . . . 3 F6
Enville St DY8 . . . . 5 E5
Epping Cl B45 . . . . 18 B2
Epsom Cl
  Fernhill Heath WR3 . . . . 102 F3
  Redditch B97 . . . . 89 C8
Epsom Ct 16 B29 . . . . 19 C7
Epsom Rd B61 . . . . 32 A1
Erica Cl
  Birmingham B29 . . . . 19 A8
  Kidderminster DY11 . . . . . 12 D1
Erickson Bsns Pk GL20 . . 183 D4
Erneley Cl 1 DY13 . . . . . . 43 F1
Ernest St B38 . . . . 20 A1
Erwood Cl B97 . . . . 70 B2
Eskdale Cl 7 WR4 . . . . . 115 F5
Eskdale Wlk DY5 . . . . 6 B8
Esmond Cl B30 . . . . 19 D5
Essex Cl
  3 Bowling Green WR2 . . 127 C2
  Worcester WR2 . . . . 114 D2
Essex Ct 5 B29 . . . . 19 C7
Essex Dr WR3 . . . . 102 D2
Essex Gdns 5 D7
Eston Ave WR14 . . . . 153 C8
Eton Dr DY8 . . . . 6 A3
Etonhurst WR14 . . . . 153 B8
Eton Wlk DY10 . . . . 15 A6
Ettingley Cl B98 . . . . 90 B5
Etwall Rd B28 . . . . 21 E6
Eunal Ct B97 . . . . 89 E5
Evans Cl DY11 . . . . 12 C3
Evelench La WR9 . . . . 117 B8
Evendene Rd WR11 . . . . . 161 A3
EVENDINE 166 A4
Evendine Cl WR5 . . . . 128 D8
Evendine La WR13 . . . . . . 166 A7
Evenlode Cl B98 . . . . 70 F1
Everard Cl 4 WR2 . . . . . . 114 E5
Everard Pl 5 WR2 . . . . . 114 E5
Evergreen Way DY13 . . . . . 44 B4
Everoak Ind Est WR2 . . . . 114 E1
Eversley Gr WR14 . . . . . . 139 B2
Eversley Gr WR14 . . . . . . 139 B2
Evers St DY5 . . . . 7 A8
Evertons Cl WR9 . . . . 84 E1
Eves Croft B32 . . . . 9 C1
EVESHAM 161 B5
Evesham Arts Ctr★
  WR11 . . . . 161 E6
Evesham Com Hospl
  WR11 . . . . 161 D3

Evesham Ct DY11 . . . . 27 D5
Evesham Ctry Pk★
  WR11 . . . . 147 E1
Evesham High Sch
  WR11 . . . . 161 E2
Evesham Ho B60 . . . . 49 B3
Evesham Leisure Ctr
  WR11 . . . . 161 D1
Evesham & Malvern Hills Coll
  (Evesham Campus)
  WR11 . . . . 161 D2
Evesham & Malvern Hills Coll
  (Malvern Hills Campus)
  WR14 . . . . 138 F1
Evesham Mews 8 B97 . . . 70 E3
Evesham Rd
  Astwood Bank B96 . . . . . 108 E8
  Broadway WR12 . . . . . . 177 B2
  Childswickham WR12 . . . 176 F5
  Church Lench WR11 . . . . 134 A2
  Cleeve Prior WR11 . . . . . 148 F5
  Cookhill B49 . . . . 122 B7
  Fladbury WR10 . . . . 146 C3
  Harvington WR11 . . . . . . 148 A7
  Hill & Moor WR10 . . . . . 145 D3
  Norton & Lenchwick WR11 147 F5
  Redditch B96, B97 . . . . . . 89 E3
  Salford Priors WR11 . . . . 135 E2
  Stoulton WR7 . . . . 130 C6
  Temple Grafton B50 . . . . 137 D7
  Weethley B49 . . . . 122 B4
Evesham Sq 3 B97 . . . . . 70 E3
Evesham Sta WR11 . . . . . 161 D5
Evesham Vale Light Rly★
  WR11 . . . . 147 F1
Evesham Wlk 2 B97 . . . . 70 E4
Eveson Cl DY8 . . . . 5 E5
Eveson Rd DY8 . . . . 5 E2
Ewloe Cl DY10 . . . . 27 E1
Exbury Pl 14 WR5 . . . . . . 128 E6
Exchange St DY10 . . . . . . 27 E6
Exe Croft B31 . . . . 34 B8
Exeter Ct DY11 . . . . 27 A6
Exeter Rd WR5 . . . . 116 A2
Exford Cl DY5 . . . . 6 B7
Exhall Cl B98 . . . . 71 D5
Exmoor Ct B61 . . . . 49 A4
Exmoor Dr B61 . . . . 49 A4
Eymore Cl B29 . . . . 19 B6
Eyton Cl B98 . . . . 71 D3

F

Fabian Cl B45 . . . . 18 A2
Fabricius Ave WR9 . . . . . . 84 F2
Facet Rd B38 . . . . 20 A2
Factory La B61 . . . . 48 F1
Fairbairn Ave WR3 . . . . . . 115 B8
Fairbourne Gdns B97 . . . . 89 C7
Fairfax Dr B31 . . . . 34 B8
Fairfax Rd B31 . . . . 34 A8
FAIRFIELD
  Evesham 161 D2
  Fairfield 31 D3
  Wolverley and Cookley . . . 12 B3
Fairfield Cl WR4 . . . . 115 F5
Fairfield Dr DY7 . . . . 4 A3
Fairfield Fst Sch B61 . . . . . 31 D3
Fairfield Ho B60 . . . . 49 B3
Fairfield La DY11 . . . . 12 B3
Fairfield Pl WR11 . . . . . . 161 D2
Fairfield Rd
  Birmingham B14 . . . . 20 E8
  Evesham WR11 . . . . 161 D2
  Fairfield B61 . . . . 31 D1
  Halesowen B63 . . . . 8 A2
Fairfield Rise DY8 . . . . 5 D5
Fairford Cl B98 . . . . 71 E7
Fairlie Cres B38 . . . . 19 D1
Fairlight Dr B45 . . . . 33 A1
Fairmead Rise B38 . . . . . . 19 E1
Fairmile Rd B63 . . . . 8 A6
Fairmont Rd B60 . . . . 68 B8
Fairoak Dr B60 . . . . 67 F6
Fairwater Cl 11 WR11 . . . 161 E4
Fairwater Gdns 4 WR11 161 E3
Fairway
  Birmingham B31 . . . . 18 E3
  Northway GL20 . . . . 197 E8
Fairway Dr B45 . . . . 32 F6
Fairway Prim Sch B38 . . . . 19 D1
Fairways WR10 . . . . 144 D1
Fairways Ave DY8 . . . . 5 E2
Fairways Cl DY8 . . . . 5 E2
Fairways Dr B60 . . . . 50 B5
Fairways Wlk 3 WR10 . . . 144 D1
Fairway The
  Birmingham B38 . . . . 19 D2
  Worcester WR4 . . . . 116 A4
Fakenham Croft B17 . . . . . . 9 F7
Falcon Cl
  Droitwich Spa WR9 . . . . 104 B8
  Kidderminster DY10 . . . . . 27 E2
  5 Worcester WR5 . . . . . 128 C5
Falcon Cres B50 . . . . 136 E5
Falcon Rd GL20 . . . . 197 B3
Falcon Rise DY8 . . . . 5 C6
Falcon View B30 . . . . 20 A4
Falfield Gr B31 . . . . 33 F7
Falkland Croft B30 . . . . . . 20 B6
Falkland Rd WR11 . . . . . . 161 F1
Fallow Field WR4 . . . . . . 116 C5
Fallowfield Ave B28 . . . . . 21 F5
Fallowfield Rd B63 . . . . 7 D3

Fallowfields Cl B61 . . . . . . 48 E3
Fallow Wlk B32 . . . . 9 A2
Falmouth WR4 . . . . 116 D6
Falstaff Ave B47 . . . . 36 A6
Falstaff Dr WR9 . . . . 103 E8
Falstaff Ho B13 . . . . 21 D7
Fancott Rd B31 . . . . 19 A5
Faraday Ave B32 . . . . 9 D5
Faraday Ct B32 . . . . 9 D5
Farfield
  Kidderminster DY10 . . . . . 27 F5
  Stoke Prior B60 . . . . 67 F4
Farfield Cl B31 . . . . 19 B2
Farfield Cl WR11 . . . . 27 F5
Farfield Studios DY10 . . . . 27 F5
FAR FOREST 24 B2
Far Forest Lea Meml CE Prim
  Sch DY14 . . . . 24 C2
Farlands Dr DY8 . . . . 6 A3
Farlands Rd DY8 . . . . 6 A3
Farleigh Rd WR10 . . . . . . 158 C8
Farley La WR14 . . . . 139 B4
Farley St WR2 . . . . 114 E4
Farlie Cl 2 WR5 . . . . 141 C6
Farlow Cl B60 . . . . 71 D3
Farlow Rd B31 . . . . 19 C3
Farm Bank Rd WR9 . . . . . 84 B7
Farmbrook Cl 6 WR2 . . . 114 D1
Farm Cl
  Kidderminster DY11 . . . . . 27 B2
  9 Northway GL20 . . . . . 184 E1
  Worcester WR3 . . . . 115 E1
Farmcote Cl B97 . . . . 89 D4
Farmcroft Rd DY9 . . . . 6 E2
Farm Ct WR12 . . . . 177 F4
Farmdale Gr B45 . . . . 33 A6
Farmers Ct
  6 Droitwich WR9 . . . . . . 84 D5
  Halesowen B63 . . . . 7 F4
Farmers Gn 17 WR9 . . . . 84 D5
Farmers La WR12 . . . . . . 176 E2
Farmers Piece 16 WR9 . . . 84 D5
Farmers Rd B60 . . . . 67 E2
Farmers Way WR9 . . . . . . 84 D5
Farm La
  Bredon GL20 . . . . 184 E6
  South Littleton WR11 . . . 148 F1
Far Moor La B98 . . . . 72 A3
Farm Rd
  Redditch B98 . . . . 71 A3
  Stourport-on-Severn DY13 . 44 B4
Farmside Cl DY9 . . . . 7 A3
Farm St WR10 . . . . 146 A1
Farnborough Cl B98 . . . . . 71 F1
Farnbury Croft B38 . . . . . . 20 B2
Farncombe Terr 7
  WR10 . . . . 158 C7
Farndale Cl DY5 . . . . 6 B6
Farne Ave WR5 . . . . 128 E6
Farnham Gn 10 WR4 . . . . 116 C6
Farren Rd B31 . . . . 18 D1
Farrier Cl B60 . . . . 67 E6
Farriers Cl 8 WR9 . . . . . . 84 D4
Farriers Sq 7 WR9 . . . . . 84 D4
Farrier St 7 WR1 . . . . . . 115 B3
Farriers Way WR9 . . . . . . 84 D4
Farthing La B97 . . . . 70 B5
Farundles Ave WR4 . . . . . 116 B5
Far Wood Rd B31 . . . . 18 E8
Fastlea Rd B32 . . . . 9 D1
Fatherless Barn Cres B63 . . 7 D5
Faulkner Cl DY8 . . . . 5 F4
Fawley Gr B14 . . . . 20 B5
Fearnal Ct WR3 . . . . 102 F2
Fearnings Cotts B97 . . . . . 89 D5
Featherbed La B97 . . . . . . 89 C5
Featherstone Rd B14 . . . . . 20 E6
FECKENHAM 107 E7
Feckenham CE Fst Sch
  B96 . . . . 88 E1
Feckenham Ho B60 . . . . . . 49 B3
Feckenham Rd
  Astwood Bank B96 . . . . . 89 C2
  Redditch, Headless Cross
  B97 . . . . 89 C8
  Redditch, Hunt End B97 . . 89 C4
Feckenham Wylde Moor
  Nature Reserve★ B96 . . 107 C5
Felbrigg Cl DY5 . . . . 6 D8
Feldon La B62 . . . . 8 E7
Fels Ave WR4 . . . . 116 C3
Feltham Way GL20 . . . . . . 196 F8
Felton Cl B98 . . . . 71 E1
Fen Cl DY10 . . . . 27 E8
Fennel Rd DY5 . . . . 6 C7
FENN GREEN 1 E3
Fenton Rd B47 . . . . 36 A4
Fenwick Cl B97 . . . . 70 B1
Ferguson Dr DY11 . . . . . . 27 A1
Fernbank Cl B63 . . . . 7 E2
Ferndale Cl
  Hartlebury DY13 . . . . 44 C3
  Upper Catshill B61 . . . . . 32 A1
  West Hagley DY9 . . . . . . 15 A5
  3 Worcester WR3 . . . . . 102 A1
Ferndale Cres DY11 . . . . . 27 B8
Ferndale Pk DY9 . . . . 15 C8
Ferndale Rd B28 . . . . 21 F8
Ferney Hill Ave B97 . . . . . 70 C3
Fernhill Gr WR14 . . . . . . 139 A1
FERNHILL HEATH 102 F3
Fernihough Ave WR11 . . . 164 B5
Fernleigh B60 . . . . 49 A1
Fern Rd WR2 . . . . 114 E4
Fernwood Cl B98 . . . . 90 B5
Fernwood Croft B14 . . . . . 20 E6
Fernwoods B32 . . . . 9 B2
Ferry Cl WR2 . . . . 114 F4

Ferry La
  Offenham WR11 . . . . 162 A8
  Ripple GL20 . . . . 182 F8
Ferry View WR11 . . . . 161 C4
FIDDINGTON 197 C2
Field Ave B31 . . . . 18 F5
Field Barn La WR10 . . . . . 160 C5
Field Cl
  Bromsgrove B60 . . . . 67 E6
  Worcester WR4 . . . . 115 E6
Field Cottage Dr DY8 . . . . . 6 B3
Fielden Cl WR11 . . . . 161 E3
Field End 7 B13 . . . . 43 E4
Fielden Row WR4 . . . . . . 116 C3
Fieldfare Cl WR14 . . . . . . 138 D6
Fieldfare Ct DY10 . . . . 28 A1
Fieldfare Rd DY9 . . . . 6 D4
Field Farm La B98 . . . . . . 71 D2
Fieldhead Cl 3 WR2 . . . . 114 D1
Fieldhouse La B62 . . . . . . 16 E4
Field La
  Birmingham B32 . . . . 18 B8
  Clent DY9 . . . . 15 D4
  Stourbridge DY8 . . . . 6 A3
  Tenbury SY8 . . . . 54 D2
Field Rd WR4 . . . . 115 E6
Fields Cl WR11 . . . . 162 E2
Fields La WR12 . . . . 177 E3
Fieldways Cl B47 . . . . 36 A7
Field Wlk WR5 . . . . 128 D7
Fiery Hill Dr B45 . . . . 50 C8
Fiery Hill Rd B45 . . . . 50 C8
Fimbrell Cl DY5 . . . . 6 A8
Finchfield Cl DY8 . . . . 5 C4
Finch La WR11 . . . . 148 B6
Findon Cl B97 . . . . 70 A5
Findon St DY10 . . . . 27 F6
FINGERPOST 24 D1
Finmere Rd B28 . . . . 21 F8
Finsbury Dr DY5 . . . . 6 C7
FINSTALL 49 D1
Finstall Fst Sch B60 . . . . . 49 B1
Finstall Rd
  Bromsgrove B60 . . . . 68 C8
  Finstall B60 . . . . 49 D1
Firbank Cl B30 . . . . 19 E7
Fircroft B31 . . . . 18 F8
Fir Croft DY5 . . . . 6 C8
Fircroft Cl B60 . . . . 67 D6
Firecrest Way DY10 . . . . . 28 B1
Firenze Rd B60 . . . . 49 C1
Fire Sta Flats B30 . . . . . . 19 F4
Fir Gr
  Birmingham B14 . . . . 20 F5
  Stourbridge DY8 . . . . 5 D6
Firhill Croft B14 . . . . 20 D2
Firlands Cl WR3 . . . . 102 F3
Firland The WR8 . . . . 155 F4
Firmstone Ct DY8 . . . . 5 E7
Firmstone St DY8 . . . . 5 E7
Firsby Rd B32 . . . . 9 E5
Firs Cl
  Lower Marlbrook B60 . . . . 32 D1
  Malvern WR14 . . . . 152 F6
Firs Cl The DY10 . . . . 28 A5
Firs Ind Est DY11 . . . . 44 B7
First Ave WR2 . . . . 128 A7
First Meadow Piece B32 . . . 9 E4
Firs The
  Kidderminster DY10 . . . . . 28 A5
  Westacre WR9 . . . . 84 D3
Firth Dr
  Birmingham B14 . . . . 21 B5
  Halesowen B62 . . . . 8 B3
Firth Park Cres B62 . . . . . . 8 E8
Fir Tree Cl B97 . . . . 70 D4
Fir Tree Rd WR3 . . . . 102 F3
Fir Way WR4 . . . . 115 E6
Fisher Cl B45 . . . . 17 E2
Fishers Dr B90 . . . . 36 F5
Fishers La DY10 . . . . 46 E8
Fish Hill
  Broadway WR12 . . . . . . 190 F7
  Redditch B97 . . . . 70 E4
Fish House La B60 . . . . . . 67 E4
Fishing Line Rd B97 . . . . . 70 E5
Fish St WR1 . . . . 115 B2
Fiskin La WR4 . . . . 116 C3
Fitcher Cl WR2 . . . . 114 E6
Fitzgerald Pl DY5 . . . . 6 B6
Fitzhamon Pk GL20 . . . . . 197 F7
Fitz Roy Ave B17 . . . . 9 F7
Fitzroy Rd B31 . . . . 18 E8
Fitzwilliam Cl 2 WR2 . . . 114 D3
Five Mile Dr GL56 . . . . . . 191 F4
Five Oaks Cl WR14 . . . . . 153 D8
Five Ways
  Churchill DY10 . . . . 14 A5
  Cradley Heath B64 . . . . . . 7 C8
FLADBURY 146 B2
Fladbury CE Aided Fst Sch
  WR10 . . . . 146 B1
Fladbury Cl B98 . . . . 90 B8
FLADBURY CROSS 146 A3
Flag Meadow Wlk WR1 . . 115 B5
Flanders Cl B98 . . . . 71 D5
Flatlea B31 . . . . 18 F4
Flats The B61 . . . . 48 F3
Flavell Cl B32 . . . . 9 B1
Flavel Rd B60 . . . . 67 E2
Flax Cl B47 . . . . 36 A5
Flax Gdns B38 . . . . 34 C8
Flaxley Cl B98 . . . . 72 A4
Flax Piece WR7 . . . . 131 C8
Fleece Inn The★ WR11 . . 163 C4

Fleece Rd WR12 . . . . 177 D1
Fleet La GL20 . . . . 184 B5
Fleet Rd GL20 . . . . 184 A6
Fleet Row WR5 . . . . 128 E6
Fleetwood Ave WR2 . . . . . 127 B2
Fleming Rd B32 . . . . 9 D5
Fletchers Alley **13** GL20 . . 196 E6
Fletcher St DY9 . . . . 6 F5
Fletton Gr B14 . . . . 21 A3
Flint Cl DY10 . . . . 27 E2
Florence Ave WR9 . . . . 84 E1
Florence Cl **4** WR5 . . . . . 141 C6
Florence Rd B14 . . . . 20 F8
Flyford Cl B98 . . . . 70 F1
Flyford Croft B29 . . . . 9 F2
FLYFORD FLAVELL 119 D2
Flyford Flavell Fst Sch
  WR7 . . . . 119 E1
Fockbury Mill La B61 . . . . . 48 E5
Fockbury Rd B61 . . . . 48 B5
Foel Gr B31 . . . . 18 E6
Fold The B38 . . . . 20 A1
Foley Ave DY11 . . . . 44 C8
Foley Bsns Pk DY11 . . . . . . 44 C8
Foley Dr DY11 . . . . 44 B8
Foley Gdns B60 . . . . 67 E3
Foley Gr DY11 . . . . 44 B8
Foley Inf Sch DY7 . . . . 4 A3
FOLEY PARK 27 C2
Foley Park Com Prim Sch
  DY11 . . . . 27 D3
Foley Rd
  Stourbridge DY9 . . . . 6 C2
  Worcester WR2 . . . . 115 A1
Foley St DY7 . . . . 4 A4
Foley Terr WR14 . . . . 152 E7
Foley Wlk **3** WR2 . . . . . . 128 A8
Folkes Rd DY9 . . . . 7 A6
Folly Rd WR6 . . . . 124 F7
Folly The B97 . . . . 89 D8
FOOTRID 39 E2
Ford Abbey HR6 . . . . 92 E1
Fordbridge Cl B97 . . . . 70 C1
Ford Cl WR14 . . . . 153 C8
Forde Hall La B94 . . . . 72 F8
Forder Gr B14 . . . . 21 A2
Forde Way Gdns B38 . . . . . 34 D7
Fordhouse La B30 . . . . 20 B6
Fordhouse Rd B60 . . . . 49 B1
Ford La WR9 . . . . 85 B6
Fordraught La B62 . . . . 17 B1
Ford Rd B61 . . . . 48 E1
Fordrough The
  Birmingham B31 . . . . 19 C1
  Hollywood B90 . . . . 36 C7
Fords Rd B90 . . . . 36 E7
Foredraft Cl B32 . . . . 9 C2
Foredraft St B63 . . . . 7 D5
Foredraught **1** B80 . . . . . . 90 E4
Foredraught La
  Crowle WR7 . . . . 117 E5
  Tibberton WR9 . . . . 104 A1
Foredrift Cl B98 . . . . 70 E2
Foregate St Sta WR1 . . . . . 115 B3
Foregate St
  Astwood Bank B96 . . . . . . 89 E1
  Worcester WR1 . . . . 115 B3
Forelands Gr B61 . . . . 67 D8
Forest Cl
  10 Bewdley DY12 . . . . 25 F3
  3 Bewdley DY12 . . . . 26 A3
  Lickey End B60 . . . . 49 B6
  Worcester WR2 . . . . 114 E4
Forest Dale B45 . . . . 33 B6
Forestdale Prim Sch B45 . 18 B2
Forest Dr DY7 . . . . 3 F3
Foresters Rd GL20 . . . . 196 E5
Forester Way DY10 . . . . . . 27 E5
Forest Gate WR11 . . . . . . 161 E2
Forest La B60 . . . . 87 D5
Forest Rd B68 . . . . 9 C7
Forest The WR9 . . . . 84 D8
Forest View B97 . . . . 89 E6
Forest Way B47 . . . . 36 B6
Forfar Wlk B38 . . . . 19 D2
Forge Ave B60 . . . . 68 B7
Forge Dr B61 . . . . 48 F3
Forge La
  Belbroughton DY9 . . . . 30 D7
  Blakedown DY10 . . . . 14 B1
  Cradley Heath B64 . . . . 7 B8
  Halesowen B62 . . . . 8 C5
Forge Mdws WR6 . . . . 97 E7
Forge Mill Needle Mus★
  B98 . . . . 70 F6
Forge Mill Rd B98 . . . . 70 F6
Forge Rd DY8 . . . . 5 F6
Forge The B60 . . . . 7 B8
Forge Trad Est B62 . . . . 8 C5
Forhill Ho B38 . . . . 34 F3
Forrell Gr B31 . . . . 34 B7
Forresters Rd WR15 . . . . . 55 F6
FORSHAW HEATH 53 C7
Forshaw Heath La B94 . . . . 53 A7
Forshaw Heath Rd B94 . . . 36 C1
Forsythia Cl B31 . . . . 18 F8
FORTHAMPTON 195 E6
Forth Gr B38 . . . . 34 E8
Forth Way B62 . . . . 8 E8
Fort-Mahon Pl **8** DY12 . 25 F3
Fort Royal★ WR5 . . . . 115 C1
Fort Royal Com Sch
  WR5 . . . . 115 D1
Fort Royal Hill WR5 . . . . . 115 C1
Fort Royal La **2** WR5 . . . 115 D1

Forward Cotts B48 . . . . 50 F6
Fossil Bank WR13 . . . . 152 D4
Fossil Dr B45 . . . . 33 A7
Foster Ave B80 . . . . 90 E3
Foster Cres **3** DY7 . . . . . . 4 A4
Foster Dr
  Broadway WR12 . . . . 177 D2
  Elmley Lovett WR9 . . . . . . 65 B5
Foster Pl DY8 . . . . 5 E6
Foster Rd WR11 . . . . 161 E1
Fosters Gn B60 . . . . 87 D7
FOSTER'S GREEN 87 D7
Foster's Green National
  Nature Reserve★ B60 . . . 87 D7
Foster St
  Kinver DY7 . . . . 4 A4
  8 Stourbridge DY8 . . . . . . 6 A5
Foster Street E DY8 . . . . 6 A5
Fotheringay WR4 . . . . 116 D6
Foundry St
  9 Stourport-on-Severn
    DY13 . . . . 44 A4
  Worcester WR1 . . . . 115 C2
Fountain Cl B31 . . . . 33 E6
Fountain Ct **1** WR11 . . . . 161 D3
Fountain Gdns **2** WR11 . 161 D3
Fountain Pl **12** WR1 . . . . . 115 A5
Four Acres B32 . . . . 9 C4
Four Dwellings High Sch
  B32 . . . . 9 B5
Four Dwellings Prim Sch
  B32 . . . . 9 B5
Fourlands Rd B31 . . . . 18 E6
Four Oaks Cl B98 . . . . 89 D8
Four Oaks Dr B61 . . . . 32 B1
FOUR POOLS 161 E1
Four Pools Ind Est
  WR11 . . . . 161 D2
Four Pools La **3** WR11 . . 161 E1
Four Pools Rd WR11 . . . . . 161 E2
Fowler Ave **5** WR4 . . . . . 116 C3
Fowler Pl **2** DY13 . . . . 44 A5
Fownhope Cl B98 . . . . 71 E3
Foxcote Cl B98 . . . . 71 F4
Foxcote La B63, DY9 . . . . . . 7 F4
Fox Covert DY8 . . . . 5 E5
Fox Dr WR5 . . . . 128 F5
Foxes Cl B60 . . . . 50 B5
Foxes Hill WR5 . . . . 141 D6
Foxes Mdw B30 . . . . 19 F4
Foxes Ridge B64 . . . . 7 E8
Foxfield B31 . . . . 18 F4
Foxfield Dr DY8 . . . . 6 A3
Foxglove Cl
  1 Evesham WR11 . . . . . . 161 F1
  Malvern WR14 . . . . 153 D7
Foxglove Rd WR5 . . . . 128 C4
Foxglove Way B60 . . . . 49 C6
Fox Hill B29 . . . . 19 C8
Foxhill Barns B48 . . . . 50 E5
Fox Hill B29 . . . . 19 C8
Foxhill La B48 . . . . 50 E5
Foxholes La
  Feckenham B97 . . . . 88 F6
  Redditch B97 . . . . 89 A6
Foxholes The DY10 . . . . . . 27 F8
Foxhollies Dr B63 . . . . 7 E4
Foxhollow B61 . . . . 67 D8
Fox Hollow Cl B45 . . . . 33 C7
Foxhope Cl B38 . . . . 20 B2
Foxhunter Cl WR9 . . . . . . 104 B8
Foxhunt Rd B63 . . . . 7 E2
Fox La
  Bromsgrove B61 . . . . 67 E8
  Chaddesley Corbett DY10 . 46 D6
  Kempsey WR5 . . . . 142 A8
  Lindridge WR6 . . . . 59 D7
  Norton Juxta Kempsey
    WR5 . . . . 129 A1
Foxland Ave B45 . . . . 33 C7
Foxlea Rd B63 . . . . 7 D1
FOXLYDIATE 69 F3
Foxlydiate Cres B97 . . . . . . 70 A4
Foxlydiate La B97 . . . . 69 F3
Foxlydiate Mews **3** B97 . 70 A4
Foxlydiate Wood Nature
  Reserve★ B97 . . . . 70 A3
Foxtail Pl B61 . . . . 49 B8
Foxwalks Ave B61 . . . . 67 D8
Foxwell St WR5 . . . . 128 E8
Foyle Rd B38 . . . . 19 F1
Fradley Cl B30 . . . . 19 D4
Framlingham Cl **7** WR5 . 128 D6
Frampton Cl B30 . . . . 7 B8
Frampton Dr **3** WR12 . . . 177 E4
Frances Rd B30 . . . . 20 A5
FRANCHE
  Kidderminster 27 B8
  Wolverley and Cookley . . . 12 C1
Franchecourt Dr DY11 . . . 12 B1
Franche Prim Sch DY11 . . . 27 B8
Franche Rd DY11 . . . . 27 C8
Franchise St DY11 . . . . 27 C5
Francis Rd
  Bromsgrove B60 . . . . 67 F7
  Stourbridge DY8 . . . . 5 C5
  3 Stourport-on-Severn
    DY13 . . . . 43 E6
Francis Wlk B31 . . . . 34 A7
Frank Freeman Ct DY10 . . 27 F8
FRANKLEY
  Birmingham 18 B2
  Frankley Green 18 B5
Frankley Beeches Rd B31 . 18 A2
Frankley Beeches Rd B31 . 18 D3
Frankley Com High Sch
  B45 . . . . 17 F1
Frankley Gn B32 . . . . 17 D5

FRANKLEY GREEN 18 A5
Frankley Green La B32 . . . . 17 E5
FRANKLEY HILL 17 F3
Frankley Hill La B32 . . . . . . 18 A4
Frankley Ind Pk B45 . . . . . . 18 B1
Frankley La B31, B32 . . . . . . 18 D6
Frankley Lodge Rd B31 . . . . 18 D4
Frankley Mid Sch B45 . . . . 18 B2
Frankley Rd B68 . . . . 9 B8
Franklin Cl **1** WR2 . . . . . 127 F6
Franklin Rd B30 . . . . 19 F5
Franklin's La WR11 . . . . . . 134 C5
Franklin Way B30 . . . . 19 F6
Frankton Cl B98 . . . . 90 E8
Fraser Cl WR14 . . . . 153 A6
Freda Eddy Ct **3** DY10 . . 27 E6
Frederick Eary Ho B98 . . . . 90 B7
Frederick Rd
  Birmingham, Beech Lanes
    B68 . . . . 9 D7
  Malvern WR14 . . . . 138 F4
Frederick Rd (Road 1)
  DY10 . . . . 27 F1
Fredericks Cl DY8 . . . . 5 E4
Freeman Ct DY11 . . . . 27 B3
Freemans Cl GL20 . . . . . . 183 F7
Freemantle Dr WR5 . . . . . 141 C6
French Cl WR10 . . . . 144 C1
Frenchlands La B62 . . . . . 113 E7
Freshwater Dr DY5 . . . . 6 B8
Friars Gorse DY7 . . . . 5 C8
Friar St
  Droitwich WR9 . . . . 84 F3
  9 Worcester WR1 . . . . . 115 C2
Friary Wlk **13** WR1 . . . . . 115 B3
Friday Cl **6** B50 . . . . 136 D5
Friday Furlong B50 . . . . . . 136 D5
Fridays Acre WR9 . . . . 84 D1
Friday St CV37 . . . . 150 E4
Friesland Dr DY13 . . . . . . 115 D7
Fringe Green Cl B60 . . . . . . 68 A7
Fringe Meadow Rd B98 . . . 71 F6
FRITH COMMON 59 A8
Froggery La WR7 . . . . 143 A8
Froglands La WR11 . . . . . 149 B8
Frogmill Rd B45 . . . . 18 B2
FROG POOL 81 E8
FROGSMARSH 193 C5
Frome Way B14 . . . . 20 D6
Front Cotts B48 . . . . 50 F6
Front St CV37 . . . . 150 D2
Froxmere Cl WR7 . . . . 117 F5
Froxmere Rd WR7 . . . . . . 117 F5
Fruitlands WR14 . . . . 152 F4
Fry Cl WR5 . . . . 116 C2
Fryer Rd B31 . . . . 34 B7
Fryers Cl DY14 . . . . 22 B4
Fugelmere Cl B17 . . . . 9 F7
Fulbert Rd WR10 . . . . 158 C5
Fulbrook Cl B98 . . . . 71 C5
Fulbrook Gr B29 . . . . 18 F8
Fulford Cl B47 . . . . 36 C3
Fulford Hall Rd B90, B94 . . 36 D3
FULFORD HEATH 36 D2
Fulmar Cres DY10 . . . . 28 B2
Fulton Cl B60 . . . . 49 B1
Fulwood Ave B62 . . . . 8 F8
Furlong Cl B63 . . . . 7 C6
Furlong La B63 . . . . 7 D6
Furlong Mdw B31 . . . . 19 C2
Furlongs Cl **1** DY14 . . . . . 22 D5
Furlongs Rd
  Cleobury Mortimer DY14 . . 22 C5
  Pershore WR10 . . . . 144 E2
  Upton upon Severn WR8 . 169 C4
Furlongs The DY8 . . . . 6 B3
Furlong The WR9 . . . . 84 F5
Furnace Hill B63 . . . . 8 B5
Furnace La B63 . . . . 8 B5
Furness Cl **3** WR4 . . . . . 115 F5
Furrowfield Pk GL20 . . . . . 197 C7
Furrows The B60 . . . . 67 D6
Furze La B98 . . . . 72 A4

G

Gable Mews B50 . . . . 136 C4
Gaddesby Rd B14 . . . . 20 F8
GADFIELD ELM 193 B3
Gadwell Rd GL20 . . . . 197 A5
Gainsborough Cl WR13 . . 167 C5
Gainsborough Hill DY8 . . . . 6 A3
Gainsborough Mews
  DY11 . . . . 27 B5
Gainsborough Trad Est
  DY9 . . . . 6 C4
Gainsford Dr B62 . . . . 8 B6
Galahad Way DY13 . . . . . . 43 F4
Gall at Bevere The★
  WR3 . . . . 102 A3
Gallipoli Dr WR5 . . . . 128 F4
GALLOWS GREEN 86 B2
Gallows Hill DY7 . . . . 3 F6
GALLOWSTREE ELM 4 A6
Galtons La DY9 . . . . 31 A7
Galton Way WR9 . . . . 85 C2
Gamekeepers Dr **13**
  WR4 . . . . 115 F6
Gamson Cl DY10 . . . . 27 E4
Ganborough Cl B98 . . . . . . 71 E1
Gander La GL20 . . . . 196 E5
Ganderton Ct **14** WR10 . 158 D8
Gannaway La GL20 . . . . . . 197 B7
GANNOW GREEN 17 C1
Gannow Green La B45 . . . . 17 C1
Gannow Manor Cres B45 . 17 E2
Gannow Manor Gdns B45 17 F1

Gannow Rd B45 . . . . 32 E7
Gannow Wlk B45 . . . . 32 E7
Garden Cl
  Birmingham, Frankley B45 . 18 A2
  Dumbleton WR11 . . . . . . 187 F5
  Mickleton GL55 . . . . 165 D3
Gardeners Cl DY11 . . . . 27 C8
Gardeners Sq **10** WR11 . 161 E4
Gardens Cl WR8 . . . . 169 C5
Gardens The WR11 . . . . . . 161 D6
Garden Stiles WR10 . . . . . 158 C8
Gardens Wlk WR8 . . . . . . 169 C6
Gardners Cl **8** WR4 . . . . 115 F6
Gardners Mdw DY12 . . . . . 26 B3
Garganey Ct DY10 . . . . 27 F1
Garibaldi Terr B60 . . . . 49 A1
Garland Cres B62 . . . . 8 E8
Garland Rd DY13 . . . . 43 D6
Garland Way B31 . . . . 19 C4
Garrard Cl WR11 . . . . 135 F3
Garratts Wlk B14 . . . . 20 E1
Garrick Rd B60 . . . . 49 C1
Garrington Rd B60 . . . . 68 B7
Garth Ct WR5 . . . . 141 B7
Garth The B14 . . . . 21 D4
Garway Cl B98 . . . . 71 E1
Gas Sq B61 . . . . 48 F1
Gate House La B60 . . . . 68 A7
Gateley Cl B98 . . . . 72 A4
Gateley Rd B68 . . . . 9 D7
Gauden Rd DY9 . . . . 6 D2
Gaunts The B48 . . . . 51 B6
Gawtree Way **6** WR4 . . . 116 C5
Gaydon Cl B98 . . . . 70 F1
Gay Hill La B38 . . . . 35 B8
Gaymore Rd DY10 . . . . 13 B5
Gazala Dr WR5 . . . . 129 A4
Gedney Cl B90 . . . . 21 C3
Geneva Ave WR14 . . . . . . 153 A4
Geneva Cl WR3 . . . . 115 A8
Geneva Cres WR7 . . . . 117 F4
Genners App B31 . . . . 18 D8
Genners La B31 . . . . 18 D7
Gentian Cl
  Birmingham B31 . . . . 18 F6
  Fernhill Heath WR3 . . . . 102 E3
Geoffrey Chaucer Wlk **4**
  WR9 . . . . 103 E8
Geoffrey Rd B90 . . . . 21 F3
George Baylis Rd WR9 . . . . 84 E5
George Dance Cl **2** DY10 . 28 B6
George Dowty Dr **1**
  GL20 . . . . 184 E1
George La WR10 . . . . 145 B4
George Law Ct DY10 . . . . . 27 F5
George Rd
  Alvechurch B48 . . . . 51 A5
  Halesowen B63 . . . . 7 F4
George's Elm La B50 . . . . . 136 E8
George St
  1 Bromsgrove B61 . . . . . 48 F2
  Evesham WR11 . . . . 161 C5
  Kidderminster DY10 . . . . . 27 F6
  Worcester WR1 . . . . 115 C2
George Wlk **5** B97 . . . . . . 70 E3
Georgina Ave B97 . . . . . . 128 A8
Geraldine Cl WR14 . . . . . . 153 B7
Geraldine Ct WR14 . . . . . . 153 B7
Geraldine Rd WR14 . . . . . 153 B7
Gerald Rd DY8 . . . . 5 E7
Gheluvelt Ave DY10 . . . . . . 27 F7
Gheluvelt Ct **6** DY13 . . . . 43 F4
Gheluvelt Pk WR3 . . . . . . 115 A6
Gibbet La
  Kinver DY7 . . . . 4 E5
  Stourbridge DY7 . . . . 5 B4
Gibb La B61 . . . . 49 A8
Gibbons Cres **1** DY13 . . . 43 F4
Gibbs Cl WR8 . . . . 145 E3
Gibbs Hill Rd B31 . . . . 34 C7
Gibbs La WR11 . . . . 148 A1
Gibbs Rd
  Redditch B98 . . . . 71 A5
  Stourbridge DY9 . . . . 7 A5
Gibraltar DY7 . . . . 4 B4
Gibson Gr WR14 . . . . 138 E3
Giffard Dr WR13 . . . . 167 C5
Gig Bridge La WR10 . . . . . 144 C2
Gig Mill Prim Sch DY8 . . . . 5 E4
Gigmill Way DY8 . . . . 5 E4
Gilbanks Rd DY8 . . . . 5 D7
Gilbert Rd
  Bromsgrove B60 . . . . 67 E7
  Malvern WR14 . . . . 153 B8
Gilbert Scott Way DY10 . . . 27 F7
GILBERT'S END 154 C1
Gilberts End La WR8 . . . . 154 F1
GILBERT'S GREEN 53 E3
Gilbertstone Cl B98 . . . . . . 70 E1
Gildas Ave B38 . . . . 20 A1
Gilgal DY13 . . . . 44 A4
Gillam St WR3 . . . . 115 C5
Gilmour Cres B45 . . . . 102 C1
Gilt Edge Club Leisure Ctr
  DY11 . . . . 44 A8
GILVERS' LANE 168 B7
Gimble Wlk **2** B17 . . . . 9 F7
Gipsy La
  Kinver DY11 . . . . 4 A1
  Wolverley & Cookley DY11 . . 3 F1
Gisburn Cl **5** B97 . . . . 70 B5
GK Davies Trad Est DY9 . . . 7 A6
Glade The
  Malvern WR14 . . . . 139 C1
  Stourbridge DY9 . . . . 6 E5
Gladstone Dr DY8 . . . . 5 D6
Gladstone Rd DY8 . . . . 5 D6
Glasbury Croft B38 . . . . . . 34 C7

Glasshouse Coll DY8 . . . . . 5 F7
Glasshouse Hill DY8 . . . . . . 6 B3
Glastonbury Cl DY11 . . . . . 27 A6
Glastonbury Rd B14 . . . . . . 21 C5
Gleads Croft B62 . . . . 9 A3
Glebe Cl
  Bidford-on-Avon B50 . . . . 136 D4
  Redditch B98 . . . . 71 D2
  Worcester WR2 . . . . 114 F2
Glebe Fields DY9 . . . . 30 E6
Glebe La DY9 . . . . 5 E4
Glebeland Dr **8** GL20 . . . 184 F6
Glebe Rd
  Alvechurch B48 . . . . 51 A7
  Aston Somerville WR12 . . 175 F1
Glebe The
  Belbroughton DY9 . . . . 30 E6
  Beoley B98 . . . . 71 F7
  Great Witley WR6 . . . . 61 B1
Glenavon Rd B14 . . . . 21 A3
Glencoe Rd **3** WR11 . . . . 161 F4
Glendale **3** WR9 . . . . 84 D1
Glendale Cl B63 . . . . 8 B4
Glendene Cres B38 . . . . . . 34 C7
Glen Devon Cl B45 . . . . 18 A2
Gleneagles Dr B60 . . . . 50 A5
Glenelg Dr DY8 . . . . 6 B2
Glenfield Cl B97 . . . . 89 D6
Glengarry Cl B32 . . . . 18 B7
Glenhill Dr B38 . . . . 35 A8
Glenmoor WR10 . . . . 171 F8
Glenmore Dr B38 . . . . 19 D2
Glen Rd DY8 . . . . 5 F3
Glenridding Cl **3** WR4 . . 116 A5
Glen Rise B13 . . . . 21 C6
Glenroyde B38 . . . . 34 E7
Glen Side B32 . . . . 9 D2
Glen The B60 . . . . 50 A5
Glenthorne Ave WR4 . . . . 115 F5
Glenwood Cl DY5 . . . . 6 D8
Glenwood Rd B38 . . . . 34 D8
Gloster Ades Rd WR11 . . . 163 E3
Gloucester Cl
  Malvern WR14 . . . . 139 C5
  Redditch B97 . . . . 70 D4
Gloucester Dr WR13 . . . . 140 D4
Gloucester La GL55 . . . . . 165 D4
Gloucester Rd GL20 . . . . . 196 D5
Gloucester Way DY12 . . . . 26 B4
Glover Cl B28 . . . . 21 F6
Glover St B98 . . . . 70 E3
Glyn Farm Rd B32 . . . . 9 C6
Glynn Cres B63 . . . . 7 B7
Glyn Rd B32 . . . . 9 D6
Glynside Ave B32 . . . . 9 D6
Goblins Cl WR5 . . . . 128 F4
Goddard Rd WR1 . . . . 115 B5
Godson Cres DY11 . . . . 27 C3
Godson Pl DY11 . . . . 27 C3
Godson's Cl WR15 . . . . 55 F5
Goffs Cl B32 . . . . 9 F3
Goldcrest Dr DY10 . . . . 28 B2
Golden Acres WV15 . . . . . . 1 C5
Golden Cross La B61 . . . . . 32 B1
Golden Hind Dr DY13 . . . . 44 A2
Golden La WR11 . . . . 162 D1
GOLDER FIELD 92 F6
GOLDFINCH FIELD 19 D8
Goldfinch Rd DY9 . . . . 6 C3
Goldsmith Rd
  Birmingham B14 . . . . 20 F8
  Worcester WR4 . . . . 115 F6
Goldsmith Wlk DY10 . . . . . 28 C5
Goldthorne Cl B97 . . . . 70 C1
Goldthorne Wlk DY5 . . . . . . 6 D8
Goldthorn Mews DY11 . . . 27 C2
Goldthorn Pl DY11 . . . . 27 C2
Goldthorn Rd DY11 . . . . . . 27 C2
Gomeldon Ave B14 . . . . . . 20 F3
Gooch Cl DY8 . . . . 6 B6
Goodalls Gr WR11 . . . . . . 161 D6
Goodier's La GL20 . . . . . . 184 A7
Goodleigh Ave B45 . . . . . . 33 E6
Goodman Cl B28 . . . . 21 F6
Goodrest Ave B62 . . . . 9 A5
Goodrest Croft B14 . . . . . . 21 C4
Goodrest La B38 . . . . 34 F6
Goodrest Wlk WR3 . . . . . 115 C5
Goodrich Cl B98 . . . . 71 F2
Goodrich Covert **10** B14 . 20 C2
GOOD'S GREEN 11 A7
Goodson Rd WR14 . . . . . . 139 C5
Goodwin Cl DY11 . . . . 27 C7
Goodwood Ave WR5 . . . . 128 E8
Goodwood Cl
  7 Evesham WR11 . . . . . 161 C2
  Fernhill Heath WR3 . . . . 102 F2
  5 Worcester WR5 . . . . 128 E8
Goodwood Rd
  Lower Marlbrook B61 . . . . 32 B1
  Malvern WR14 . . . . 139 A5
  Pershore/Pinvin WR10 . . 144 E4
Goodwyn Ave B68 . . . . 9 C7
GOOM'S HILL 121 A2
Goosehill Cl B98 . . . . 71 E1
GOOSEHILL GREEN 105 B7
Goosehill La WR9 . . . . 86 A2
Gorcott Hill B98 . . . . 72 C5
Gordon Cl WR12 . . . . 190 C8
Gordon Rd CV37 . . . . 151 D3
Gordon Russell Mus★
  WR12 . . . . 190 D8
Gordon Terr WR14 . . . . . . 152 E4
Gorleston Gr B14 . . . . 21 B2
Gorleston Rd B14 . . . . 21 B2
Gorse Cl
  Birmingham, Selly Oak
    B29 . . . . 19 A8

Gorse Cl *continued*
5 Droitwich WR9 . . . . 104 A8
Gorse Green La DY9 . . . . . . 31 C8
Gorse Hill WR11 . . . . 174 B2
Gorse Hill & Elbury Mount Nature Reserve★ WR4 . 115 F4
Gorse Hill Prim Sch WR4 . . . . 115 F4
Gorse Hill Rd WR4 . . . . . . 115 F5
Gorse Meadow Dr B45 . . . 50 B8
Gorsey Cl B96 . . . . 108 E8
Gorsey La B47 . . . . 36 A3
Gorsly Piece B32 . . . . 9 C4
GORST HILL 41 E7
Gorsty Hill Rd B65 . . . . .8 B8
Gorsymead Gr B31 . . . . 18 C2
Gorsy Rd B32 . . . . 9 D5
Goscote Cl B97 . . . . 70 A5
Gould Avenue E DY11 . . . . 27 A2
Gould Avenue W DY11 . . . . 27 A1
Gould Dr GL20 . . . . 184 E1
Gower Ho B62 . . . . .8 F6
Gower Rd B62 . . . . .8 F6
Gracemere Cres B28 . . . . . 21 E3
Gracewell Homes B13 . . . . 21 D8
Grafson Pl WR9 . . . . 84 D1
GRAFTON 186 E7
Grafton Cl
Malvern WR14 . . . . 138 F3
Redditch B98 . . . . 90 B7
Grafton Cres B60 . . . . 67 E8
GRAFTON FLYFORD 119 B5
Grafton Ho B60 . . . . 49 B3
Grafton La
Bidford-on-Avon B50 . . . . . 136 F6
Bromsgrove B61 . . . . 67 C7
Pendock GL19 . . . . 193 C6
Grafton Manor House★ B61 . . . . 67 B7
Grafton Rd B90 . . . . 21 C2
Graftons The WR8 . . . . . . 169 C4
Graham Cres B45 . . . . 33 A7
Graham Ct WR14 . . . . 138 F1
Graham Rd
Halesowen B62 . . . . 8 C8
Malvern WR14 . . . . 138 F2
6 Worcester WR2 . . . . 114 F1
Grainger's La B64 . . . . 7 D8
Graith Cl B28 . . . . 21 E3
Grammar School La 1 B63 . . . . 8 A4
Grampian Rd DY8 . . . . 6 A6
Granary Rd B60 . . . . 67 E6
Granbrook La GL55 . . . . . . 165 E4
Granby Cl B98 . . . . 71 F4
Grand Stand Rd WR1 . . . . 115 A3
Grange Ave WR3 . . . . 102 A1
Grange Cres
Birmingham B45 . . . . 32 F8
Halesowen B63 . . . . 8 B3
Grange Ct
Northway GL20 . . . . 184 F1
1 Redditch B98 . . . . 70 F4
Stourbridge DY9 . . . . 6 C3
Grange Farm Dr B38 . . . . . 34 D8
Grange Hill B62 . . . . 8 C2
Grange Hill Rd B38 . . . . 19 E1
Grange La
Alvechurch B48 . . . . 51 B3
Broadheath WR2 . . . . 113 E5
Fernhill Heath WR3 . . . . . . 102 D2
Harvington WR11 . . . . 148 A6
Stourbridge DY9 . . . . 6 D4
Worcester WR2 . . . . 127 B8
Grange Rd
Bidford-on-Avon B50 . . . . . 136 E4
Birlingham WR10 . . . . 158 B1
Birmingham, King's Heath B14 . . . . 20 E8
Bretforton WR11 . . . . 163 B5
Broadheath WR2 . . . . 114 A7
Cradley Heath B64 . . . . 8 B8
Halesowen B63 . . . . 8 C3
Kidderminster DY11 . . . . . . 27 B7
Malvern WR14 . . . . 152 F8
Northway GL20 . . . . 184 E1
2 Redditch B98 . . . . 70 F4
Stourbridge DY9 . . . . 6 C4
Grange Rise B38 . . . . 34 F7
Grangers La B98 . . . . 89 F5
Grange The B62 . . . . .8 F6
Grange Way WR4 . . . . 116 D3
Grange Wlk B31 . . . . 34 C7
Granhill Cl B98 . . . . 90 A8
Granshaw Cl B38 . . . . 19 F1
Grant Ct B30 . . . . 20 A5
Granton Cl B14 . . . . 20 D5
Granton Rd B14 . . . . 20 D5
Granville Cl B60 . . . . 49 B1
Granville Crest DY10 . . . . . 28 B6
Granville Rd B64 . . . . .8 B8
Grasmere Cl DY10 . . . . 27 E7
Grasmere Dr WR4 . . . . 116 A5
Grasmere Gr DY13 . . . . 43 F6
Grasshopper Ave WR5 . . 128 E5
Grassington Dr WR4 . . . . 116 A4
Grassmere Dr DY8 . . . . .5 F3
Grassmoor Rd B38 . . . . 19 E2
Gratham Cl DY5 . . . . .6 B7
Gravel Bank B32 . . . . 9 D2
Gravel Pit La B48 . . . . 51 E3
Gravel Pits Cl 2 GL20 . . . 184 F6
Gravel Wlk GL20 . . . . 196 F7
Gray Cl DY10 . . . . 28 B6
Grayling Cl WR5 . . . . 128 C5
Grayling Rd DY9 . . . . 6 C6
Grayshott Cl B61 . . . . 48 E3
Grayston Cl GL20 . . . . 197 A8
Grayswood Park Rd B32 . . . 9 C6
Grayswood Rd B31 . . . . 33 F7
Grazebrook Croft B32 . . . . 18 D8
Grazing La B97 . . . . 69 F2
Grazings The DY7 . . . . 4 C3
Great Barn La B97 . . . . 70 B1
Great Calcroft WR10 . . . . 158 D7
GREAT COMBERTON 158 F1
Great Cornbow 5 B63 . . . . .8 B3
Great Farley Dr B31 . . . . . . 18 C1
Greatfield Rd DY11 . . . . . . 27 B4
Great Hockings La B97 . . . 69 E2
Great House Rd WR2 . . . . 114 F1
GREAT MALVERN 139 D2
Great Malvern Prim Sch WR14 . . . . 153 C8
Great Malvern Sta WR14 153 A8
Great Oaty Gdns WR4 . . . 116 B5
Great Stone Rd B31 . . . . . . 19 A3
GREAT WASHBOURNE . . . 186 E2
Great Western Ave WR5 115 D2
Great Western Way DY13 . 44 A5
GREAT WITLEY 61 B1
Great Witley CE Prim Sch WR6 . . . . 80 B8
Greaves Gdns DY11 . . . . . . 12 B1
Greaves Sq B38 . . . . 20 B1
Greenacres
Birmingham B32 . . . . 9 E2
Twyning GL20 . . . . 183 F7
Greenacres La DY12 . . . . . . 26 A4
Greenacres Rd
Bromsgrove B61 . . . . 48 E3
Worcester WR2 . . . . 114 D2
Green Acres Rd B38 . . . . . . 34 D8
Greenaleigh Rd B14 . . . . . . 21 D3
Greenbank
Barnt Green B45 . . . . 50 D8
2 Droitwich WR9 . . . . 85 B2
Greenbank Rd DY12 . . . . . . 25 E2
Green Bower Dr B61 . . . . . 49 A5
Greenbush Dr B63 . . . . 8 A5
Green Cl
Childswickham WR12 . . . . 176 E2
Honeybourne WR11 . . . . . . 164 A4
Studley B80 . . . . 90 E3
Wythall B47 . . . . 36 A3
Green Ct B28 . . . . 21 F8
Greendale Cl B61 . . . . 49 B8
Green Dr B32 . . . . 9 C1
Greenfield Ave
Lower Marlbrook B60 . . . . . 32 D1
Stourbridge DY8 . . . . .5 F5
Greenfield Cl 2 WR4 . . . . 116 B4
Greenfield Cotts B48 . . . . . 51 A5
Greenfield Prim Sch DY8 . . .5 F5
Greenfields B98 . . . . 70 E2
Greenfields Cl 1 WR10 . . 143 F6
Greenfields Rd
Kinver DY7 . . . . 3 C3
Malvern WR14 . . . . 139 A5
Tunnel Hill WR8 . . . . 169 A5
Greenfinch Cl DY10 . . . . . . 28 B3
Greenfinch Rd DY9 . . . . 6 D3
Greenford Cl B97 . . . . 70 B5
Greenford Gdns WR2 . . . . 114 E5
Greenford Rd B14 . . . . 21 C3
Green Gables B47 . . . . 36 A7
GREENHILL
Evesham 161 E7
Kidderminster 28 A8
Greenhill
Blackwell B60 . . . . 49 F4
Evesham WR11 . . . . 161 D6
Greenhill Ave DY10 . . . . . . 27 F7
Green Hill Bath Rd 8 WR5 . . . . 115 C1
Greenhill Cl WR15 . . . . 55 F5
Green Hill Cl B60 . . . . 49 D6
Greenhill Ct B62 . . . . .8 E7
Greenhill Dr WR14 . . . . . . 139 A1
Greenhill Gdns
Greenhill WR11 . . . . 161 E6
Halesowen B62 . . . . 8 D6
Tenbury Wells WR15 . . . . . . 55 F5
Greenhill Ind Est DY10 . . . 28 A7
Greenhill La WR2 . . . . 101 D2
Green Hill London Rd 10 WR5 . . . . 115 C1
Greenhill Oak DY10 . . . . . . 27 F7
Greenhill Park Rd WR11 161 D7
Green Hill Pl 11 WR5 . . . . 115 C1
Greenhill Rd B62 . . . . 8 D7
Greenhill Sch WR11 . . . . . 161 E6
Greenhurst Dr B45 . . . . 33 A1
Green La
Birmingham B32 . . . . 9 C6
Birmingham, Hawkesley B38 . . . . 34 E8
Broadheath WR2 . . . . 114 A6
Feckenham B97 . . . . 88 F6
Hadzor WR9 . . . . 85 C1
Inkberrow B96 . . . . 108 A3
Malvern WR14 . . . . 152 F1
Redditch B97 . . . . 89 A7
Ripple WR8 . . . . 170 B4
Ryall WR8 . . . . 169 F6
Solihull B90 . . . . 21 E1
Stourbridge DY9 . . . . 6 E5
Studley B80 . . . . 90 B5
Tewkesbury GL20 . . . . 197 C7
Tibberton WR9 . . . . 104 B3
Upper Catshill B61 . . . . 32 A1
Worcester WR3 . . . . 102 A2
GREENLANDS 90 A8
Greenlands Ave B98 . . . . . . 71 A1
Greenlands Bsns Ctr B98 . 71 B1
Greenlands Dr B98 . . . . 89 F8
GREEN LANE 90 C6
Green Lane Bsns Pk GL20 . . . . 197 C7
Greenleas Gdns B63 . . . . . . 8 C3
Greenleys WR11 . . . . 162 E3
Green Leys WR10 . . . . 133 A4
Green Leys Cres WV15 . . . . 1 C5
Green Mdw DY9 . . . . 15 B7
Green Meadow Prim Sch B29 . . . . 18 F7
Green Meadow Rd B29 . . . 19 A7
Greenoak Cres B30 . . . . . . 20 C8
Green Park Rd
Birmingham B31 . . . . 18 E2
Bromsgrove B60 . . . . 49 B2
Greenroyde DY9 . . . . .6 B1
Greens Croft Way WR7 . . 120 E7
Greensforge La DY7 . . . . 4 C7
Greenside B60 . . . . 67 C2
Green Slade Cres B60 . . . . 32 C1
Greenslade Croft B31 . . . . 19 A2
Greenslade Rd B90 . . . . . . 21 C2
Green St
Bushley GL20 . . . . 182 D1
Kidderminster DY10 . . . . . . 27 E5
Stourbridge DY8 . . . . .5 F5
GREEN STREET
Kempsey 141 F6
Ripple 170 A5
Green Sward La B98 . . . . . 71 D1
Green The
Birmingham, Frankley B31 . 18 C2
Birmingham, King's Norton B38 . . . . 19 F2
4 Birmingham, Quinton B32 9 A6
Bluntington DY10 . . . . 29 E1
Broadway WR12 . . . . 190 C7
Long Marston CV37 . . . . . 151 C5
Pershore/Pinvin WR10 . . . 144 F7
West Hagley DY9 . . . . 14 F4
Greenvale B31 . . . . 18 F5
GREENWAY 41 E2
Greenway Ave WV15 . . . . . . 1 C5
Greenway Gdns B38 . . . . . . 34 E7
Greenways
Birmingham B31 . . . . 18 F8
Halesowen B63 . . . . 7 C6
Greenway The
Bowling Green WR2 . . . . . 127 C3
Rock DY14 . . . . 41 D2
West Hagley DY9 . . . . 14 F5
Green Wickets B13 . . . . 20 E6
Green Wlk 4 B17 . . . . .9 F7
Greenwood Cl B14 . . . . 20 E5
Greenwoods The DY8 . . . . . .5 E5
Gregory Ave B29 . . . . 19 A8
Gregory Rd DY8 . . . . 5 D5
Gregorys Bank WR3 . . . . . 115 C5
Gregory's Ct WR3 . . . . 115 C5
Gregory's Mill St WR3 . . . 115 B6
Grendon Cl B98 . . . . 71 D1
Grendon Prim Sch B14 . . . 21 A3
Grendon Rd B14 . . . . 21 A3
Grenville Rd WR2 . . . . 114 D2
Gresham Rd
Birmingham B28 . . . . 21 F6
Worcester WR2 . . . . 114 D3
Gresley Rd WR4 . . . . 116 B7
Greyfriars Dr B61 . . . . 48 D2
Grey Green La DY12 . . . . . . 26 B5
Greyhound La DY8 . . . . 5 D2
Greylag Cres GL20 . . . . . . 197 A5
Grey's Rd B80 . . . . 90 E3
Greystone Cl B98 . . . . 71 C5
GREYSTONES 149 D8
Griffin Ave DY10 . . . . 27 E4
Griffin Cl B31 . . . . 19 B6
Griffins Brook Cl B30 . . . . 19 D7
Griffins Brook La B30 . . . . 19 D6
GRIFFIN'S HILL 19 D8
Grigg Gr B31 . . . . 18 E1
GRIMES HILL 36 B4
GRIMLEY 101 F6
Grimley Cl B98 . . . . 70 F1
Grimley & Holt CE Prim Sch WR2 . . . . 101 F6
Grimley La B60 . . . . 68 E6
Grimley Rd 2 B31 . . . . 19 D2
Grimpits La B38 . . . . 35 A7
Grisedale Dr WR4 . . . . 116 A6
Gristhorpe Rd B29 . . . . 20 A8
Grit La WR14 . . . . 138 F6
Grizedale Cl B45 . . . . 18 B2
Grosmont Ave WR4 . . . . . 116 D6
Grosvenor Ave DY10 . . . . . 28 A6
Grosvenor Cl 6 WR9 . . . . . 85 B1
Grosvenor Cres 5 WR9 . . . 85 A1
Grosvenor Ct DY9 . . . . .6 B1
Grosvenor Gdns B61 . . . . . 49 B5
Grosvenor Ho B97 . . . . 70 E4
Grosvenor Sh Ctr B31 . . . . 19 A4
Grosvenor Sq B28 . . . . 21 F5
Grosvenor Way
Brierley Hill DY5 . . . . 6 E7
Droitwich WR9 . . . . 85 A1
Grosvenor Wlk 5 WR2 . . 115 A2
Grosvenor Wood 12 DY12 . 25 F3
Grove Ave
Halesowen B63 . . . . .7 F3
Honeybourne WR11 . . . . . . 164 B5
Grove Cres WR2 . . . . 114 D1
Grovefield GL19 . . . . 193 B7
Grove Field WR4 . . . . 116 B7
Grove Gdns B61 . . . . 49 A6
Grove Inf Sch The WR14 139 A2
Groveley La B31, B45 . . . . . 33 E5
Grove Mdw 4 DY14 . . . . . . 22 D5
Grove Mews B31 . . . . 34 B8
Grove Prim Sch The WR14 . . . . 139 A2
Grove Rd
Birmingham, King's Heath B14 . . . . 20 D6
Stourbridge DY9 . . . . .6 F3
Groves Cl WR11 . . . . 147 F8
Grove St B98 . . . . 70 E4
GROVE THE 169 F6
Grove The
Birmingham, Rednal B45 . . . 33 D4
Birmingham, West Heath B31 . . . . 34 B8
Stourport-on-Severn DY13 . 44 B2
Studley B80 . . . . 90 D3
Worcester WR3 . . . . 115 B8
Grove Villas B64 . . . . 7 D7
Grove Way WR2 . . . . 114 B1
Grovewood Dr 2 B38 . . . . . 19 E1
Grovewood Rd WR14 . . . . 139 C4
Grundy's La WR14 . . . . . . 152 E1
Guardian Ct
Birmingham, Frankley B31 . 18 D3
4 Bromsgrove B60 . . . . 49 A2
Guardian Ho B68 . . . . 9 C7
Guardians Way B31 . . . . . . 18 E8
GUARLFORD 154 A7
Guarlford Rd
Guarlford WR13 . . . . 154 A7
Malvern WR14 . . . . 153 E7
Guild Ct 4 B60 . . . . 48 F2
Guildford Cl
Kidderminster DY11 . . . . . . 27 A6
Worcester WR5 . . . . 115 F2
Guildford Ct 12 B29 . . . . . 19 C7
Guild Rd B60 . . . . 48 F1
Guinness Cl B98 . . . . 89 D8
Guiting Cl B97 . . . . 70 B1
Guiting Rd B29 . . . . 19 A7
Gullane Cl B38 . . . . 19 D1
GULLER'S END 182 C3
Gullswood Cl B14 . . . . 20 D2
Gun Barrel Ind Ctr B63 . . . . .7 F6
Gunner La B45 . . . . 32 D7
Gunners La B80 . . . . 90 E4
Gunnings La WR10 . . . . . . 132 E4
Gupshill Cl GL20 . . . . 196 E4
Gurneys La 5 WR9 . . . . 85 A3
Gutter The DY9 . . . . 31 E7
Guy's Wlk B61 . . . . 49 A5
Gypsy La B97 . . . . 69 C5

H

HABBERLEY 27 A6
Habberley La DY11 . . . . 27 A8
Habberley Rd
Bewdley DY12 . . . . 26 E5
Kidderminster DY11 . . . . . . 27 B7
Habberley St 1 DY11 . . . . . 27 C6
Habberley Valley Nature Reserve★ DY11 . . . . 26 E8
Hacketts La WR10 . . . . . . 171 F7
HACKMAN'S GATE 14 F1
Hackmans Gate La DY9 . . . 30 B7
Hadcroft Grange DY9 . . . . . 6 D4
Hadcroft Rd DY9 . . . . 6 C4
Haddon Croft B63 . . . . 7 C1
Haden Arch Ct B64 . . . . 8 A7
Haden Cl B64 . . . . 8 A7
HADEN CROSS 8 A8
Haden Cross Dr B64 . . . . . . 8 A7
Hadendale B64 . . . . 8 A7
Haden Hill Rd B63 . . . . .8 B6
Haden Park Rd B64 . . . . 7 F7
HADLEY 83 E4
Hadley Cl B47 . . . . 36 A5
HADZOR 85 D1
Hadzor Ho 5 B97 . . . . 70 A4
Hadzor La WR9 . . . . 85 C2
Hadzor Rd B68 . . . . 9 D8
Hafren Cl B45 . . . . 18 B2
Hafren Way DY13 . . . . 43 E4
Haggs Mdw WR4 . . . . 116 C5
HAGLEY 15 D6
Hagley Cl DY9 . . . . 15 C6
Hagley Cswy DY9 . . . . 16 B8
Hagley Grange DY9 . . . . . . 15 B6
Hagley Hall★ DY9 . . . . 15 D6
Hagley Hall Gdns DY9 . . . . 15 D6
Hagley Hill DY9 . . . . 15 E7
Hagley Ho B60 . . . . 49 B3
Hagley Mews DY9 . . . . 15 D6
Hagley Park Dr B45 . . . . . . 33 A6
Hagley Prim Sch DY9 . . . . . 15 B5
Hagley RC High Sch DY8 . 14 F6
Hagley Rd
Halesowen B63 . . . . 7 E2
Stourbridge DY8 . . . . 6 B3
Hagley Road W B32, B68 . . . 9 D7
Hagley St 3 B63 . . . . .8 B3
Hagley Sta DY9 . . . . 15 A6
Hagley Wood La DY9, B62 . 16 B7
Haig Pl B13 . . . . 21 A7
Hailsham Cl 8 WR5 . . . . . 128 E8
Haines Ave
Worcester WR4 . . . . 116 C3
Wyre Piddle WR10 . . . . . . 145 A4
Haines Pl WR11 . . . . 161 D4
Haisley Row 9 WR4 . . . . . 116 C5
Halas Ind Est B62 . . . . 8 C5
Haldon Gr B31 . . . . 33 E7
Halesbury Ct B63 . . . . .7 F2
Halesbury Specl Sch B62 . . .8 E7
Halescroft Sq B31 . . . . 18 E6
Hales Ho WR14 . . . . 152 E2
Halesmere Way B63 . . . . 8 C3
Hales Orch WR2 . . . . 115 A1
HALESOWEN 8 D4
Halesowen CE Prim Sch 3 B63 .8 B4
Halesowen Coll (E-Business Ctr) B62 . . . . 8 C8
Halesowen Coll (Shenstone House) B63 . . . . .8 B4
Halesowen Coll (Whittingham Road Campus) B63 . . . . .8 B5
Halesowen Ind Pk B62 . . . . .8 B6
Halesowen Rd
Halesowen B62 . . . . .8 F6
Lower Marlbrook B61 . . . . . 32 C3
HALES PARK 25 F3
Hales Pk 14 DY12 . . . . 25 F3
Hales Rd B63 . . . . 8 A4
Halfcot Ave DY9 . . . . 6 C3
Halfkey Rd WR14 . . . . 138 D7
Halfshire La DY10 . . . . 14 B1
Halifax Ct DY11 . . . . 27 B8
Halifax Dr WR2 . . . . 127 F7
Halladale B38 . . . . 19 F1
Hall Cl WR4 . . . . 116 A5
Hall Dale Cl B28 . . . . 21 F5
Hall Dr DY9 . . . . 15 D6
HALL FLAT 49 C7
Hall Gn WR14 . . . . 153 E8
Hall Green Cl WR14 . . . . . 153 E8
Hall Green Inf Sch B28 . . . 21 F7
Hall Green Jun Sch B28 . . . 21 F7
Hall Green Sch B28 . . . . 21 E8
Hall La DY9 . . . . 15 D6
Hall Mdw DY9 . . . . 15 D7
HALLOW 101 D1
Hallow CE Prim Sch WR2 . . . . 101 D2
Hallow Cl 3 B31 . . . . 19 D2
Hallowfields Cl B98 . . . . . . 70 E1
HALLOW HEATH 101 D3
Hallow La WR2 . . . . 114 B7
Hallow Rd WR2 . . . . 114 E6
Halls Farm La DY12 . . . . . . 11 C1
Hall St DY8 . . . . 6 A3
Hallstead Rd B13 . . . . 21 B5
Hamble Cl WR5 . . . . 115 E2
Hambleton Rd B63 . . . . 7 D2
Hambury Dr B14 . . . . 20 D7
Ham Dingle Prim Sch DY9 . 6 C2
HAM GREEN 88 E4
Ham Green La B97 . . . . 88 E5
Hamilton Ave
Halesowen B62 . . . . 8 C3
Stourbridge DY8 . . . . 5 D6
Hamilton Cl
1 Bowling Green WR2 . . . 127 C2
Lickey End B60 . . . . 49 C6
Hamilton Dr
Birmingham B29 . . . . 19 D8
Studley B80 . . . . 90 D3
Hamilton Rd
Evesham WR11 . . . . 161 C2
Kidderminster DY11 . . . . . . 27 B3
Redditch B97 . . . . 89 C8
18 Worcester WR5 . . . . . . 115 C2
Ham La
Dawshill WR2 . . . . 127 C5
Severn Stoke WR8 . . . . 155 C5
Stourbridge DY9 . . . . 6 C2
Hamlet Gdns B28 . . . . 21 F8
Hamlet Rd B28 . . . . 21 F8
Hammer Bank DY5 . . . . 7 A8
Hammersley Cl B63 . . . . 7 C7
Hammock Rd WR10 . . . . . 171 D7
Hammond Cl 9 WR9 . . . . . 85 A1
Hammond Way DY8 . . . . 6 A7
Hampden Cl 3 DY5 . . . . 7 A8
Hampden Mews WR14 . . . 139 A4
Hampden Rd WR14 . . . . . . 139 A4
Hampshire Ct 1 B29 . . . . . 19 B7
Hampstall La DY13 . . . . 63 A4
Hampstead Glade B63 . . . . . 8 C2
HAMPTON 161 A3
Hampton Ave B60 . . . . 68 A8
Hampton Cl
Redditch B98 . . . . 90 B7
Worcester WR2 . . . . 114 E3
Hampton Gdns
Dines Green WR2 . . . . 114 E3
Stourbridge DY9 . . . . 6 D3
Hampton Gr DY7 . . . . .4 B4
HAMPTON LOVETT 84 D7
Hampton Lovett Ind Est WR9 . . . . 84 C7
Hampton Rd WR9 . . . . 84 F4
Hams Way WR2 . . . . 127 E7
Ham View WR8 . . . . 169 C5
HANBURY 87 A4
Hanbury Ave WR2 . . . . 127 F8
Hanbury CE Fst Sch B60 . 86 F5
Hanbury Cl
Bromsgrove B60 . . . . 68 A8
Halesowen B63 . . . . .7 F2
Hanbury Croft B60 . . . . 87 A3
Hanbury Ct DY8 . . . . 6 A4
Hanbury Hall★ B60 . . . . . . 86 C4
Hanbury Hill DY8 . . . . 6 A4
Hanbury Ho B97 . . . . 70 B4
Hanbury Park Rd WR2 . . . 127 F7
Hanbury Pk★ B60 . . . . 86 C4
Hanbury Rd
Hadzor WR9 . . . . 85 C3
Hanbury B60 . . . . 87 A6
Stoke Heath B60 . . . . 67 D4

Hanbury St WR9 . . . . 85 A3
Hancocks La
  Castlemorton WR13. . . . . 167 B3
  Welland WR14. . . . . 166 F4
Handbury Rd WR14 . . . . . . 139 A5
Handley Gr B31. . . . . 18 C2
Hanging La B31. . . . . 18 E2
Hangman's La WR8 . . . . . . 154 E4
HANLEY CASTLE 154 F1
Hanley Castle High Sch
  WR8 . . . . 154 F1
HANLEY CHILD 76 E7
Hanley Cl B63 . . . . 7 E4
Hanley Orch WR8 . . . . 154 A4
Hanley Rd WR14 . . . . 152 F1
HANLEY SWAN 154 E4
Hanley Swan St Gabriel with
  St Mary CE Prim Sch
  WR8 . . . . 154 A1
Hanley Terr WR14. . . . . . . 152 E3
HANLEY WILLIAM 77 C8
Hanley Workshops WR8 153 D1
Hannon Rd B14. . . . . 20 E5
Hanover Ct
  Redditch B97 . . . . 89 D8
  Tewkesbury GL20. . . . . . 196 E6
Hanover Pl **3** B60 . . . . 48 F1
Hanover St B61. . . . . 48 F1
Hansom Rd B32. . . . . 9 C5
Hanson Way WR10 . . . . . . 158 D7
Hanstone Rd DY13 . . . . 43 F1
Happy Land N **1** WR2. . . . 114 C1
Happy Land W WR2. . . . . . 114 C1
Happy Valley WR14 . . . . . . 138 C1
Harberrow Cl DY9. . . . . 15 A6
Harbinger Ave WR14 . . . . . 139 B1
Harbinger Rd B38. . . . . 20 B2
Harborne Rd B68. . . . . 9 E8
Harborough Wlk DY9. . . . . . 6 B2
Harbour Cl B50. . . . . 136 C4
Harbour Dr WR13 . . . . 152 B2
Harbours Cl B61 . . . . 67 D7
HARBOURS HILL 86 F8
Harbours Hill WR9. . . . . . . 31 E6
Harbourside GL20. . . . . . . 196 F7
Harbour View GL20 . . . . . . 196 F7
Harbury Cl B98. . . . . 71 D1
Harcourt Rd
  Cradley Heath B64. . . . . . . 7 F4
  Malvern WR14. . . . . 152 C6
Harden Cl B31. . . . . 18 E1
Harden Manor Ct B63. . . . . 8 C3
Harden Vale B63. . . . . 7 E5
Hardnott Row WR4 . . . . . . 116 C6
Hardwick Bank Rd GL20 184 D3
Hardwick Ct DY9. . . . . 6 D5
Hardwick Dr B62. . . . . 8 A7
Hardwicke Cl WR2 . . . . . . 115 A3
Hardwicke Ho WR14 . . . . . 152 F7
Hardwicke Way DY9 . . . . . . 6 D5
HARDWICK GREEN 194 A6
Hardwick La B80. . . . . 91 B6
Hardiwke Wlk B14 . . . . 20 D2
Hardy Ave DY10. . . . . 28 A6
Hardy Ct WR3 . . . . 115 C4
Harebell Gdns B38. . . . . . . 34 F8
Hare Gr B31. . . . . 18 D3
Haresfield Cl
  Redditch B97 . . . . 70 D3
  15 Worcester WR4 . . . . . . 115 F6
Harewell La WR8 . . . . 157 B8
Harewood Cl B28. . . . . 21 E5
Hargrave Rd B90. . . . . 21 D1
Hargreaves Ct DY11. . . . . . 27 C3
Harland Cl B61 . . . . 48 D3
Harlech Cl
  Birmingham B32. . . . . 18 A7
  15 Worcester WR4 . . . . . . 116 C6
Harlech Way DY10 . . . . 27 E2
Harlestones Ho DY8. . . . . . . 5 F7
Harlstones Cl DY8. . . . . 6 A8
Harman's Hill WR9. . . . . . . 105 E5
Harmon Rd DY8. . . . . 5 C5
Harold Davies Dr **1** DY13 43 F2
Harold Evers Way DY10 . . . 27 F7
Harpers Rd
  Birmingham, Highter's Heath
  B14 . . . . 21 A1
  Birmingham, Northfield B31 19 A2
HARPLEY 96 F7
Harpley Rd B14 . . . . 157 C2
Harport Rd B98. . . . . 71 A1
Harrier Cl GL20 . . . . 197 A4
Harriers Gn DY10 . . . . 28 B8
Harriers Trade Ctre DY10 . 27 F5
Harringay Dr DY8 . . . . 5 E3
Harrington Rd WR2 . . . . . . 114 D1
Harris Bsns Pk B60 . . . . . . 67 E2
Harris Cl
  6 Droitwich WR9 . . . . . . 84 E3
  Redditch B98 . . . . 89 F8
Harrison Cl **8** WR2. . . . . 127 C2
Harrison Ho B14. . . . . 20 F3
Harrison Rd B97 . . . . 89 C8
Harrop Way DY8. . . . . 5 E8
Harrow Cl
  Stoke Heath B60 . . . . 67 E6
  West Hagley DY9. . . . . . . 15 A6
Harrow Croft B97 . . . . 114 C1
Harrow La WR9 . . . . 105 C2
Harry Taylor Fst Sch The
  B97 . . . . 89 E6
Harry Taylor Ho B98 . . . . . 71 A4
Harter Row WR14 . . . . 116 A6
Hartford Rd B60 . . . . 49 B1

Hartland Rd B31 . . . . 33 E6
HARTLE. 30 F6
HARTLEBURY 45 A2
Hartlebury Castle ★ DY11 . 44 F3
Hartlebury CE Fst Sch
  DY11 . . . . 44 F3
Hartlebury Cl B98. . . . . 71 E7
Hartlebury Comm/Hillditch
  Pool Nature Reserve ★
  DY13 . . . . 44 C2
HARTLEBURY COMMON . . 44 C2
Hartlebury Ind Sch DY11 . 45 A2
Hartlebury Rd
  Halesowen B63 . . . . 7 F2
  Stourport-on-Severn DY13 . 44 C3
Hartlebury Sta DY11 . . . . . 45 B2
Hartlebury Trad Est DY10 . 64 D8
Hartle La DY9. . . . . 30 F6
Hartmann Cl **7** DY14. . . . . 22 C4
Harton Way B14 . . . . 20 C5
Hartsbourne Dr B62. . . . . . . 8 D4
HARTSGREEN 2 C4
Hartside Cl B63. . . . . 7 D2
Hartswell Dr B13 . . . . 20 F6
Harvard Ave WR11 . . . . . . 164 B6
Harvest Cl
  Birmingham B30 . . . . 20 B6
  Stoke Heath B60 . . . . 67 E6
Harvey Mews B30. . . . . . . 19 D7
Harvey Rd WR11 . . . . 161 E4
Harvey Wlk WR3 . . . . 115 D5
Harvey Works Ind Est B63 . 7 F6
Harvine Wlk DY8. . . . . 5 E3
HARVINGTON
  Evesham 148 A7
  Stone 29 B2
Harvington CE Fst Sch
  WR11 . . . . 148 B7
Harvington Cl
  Kidderminster DY11. . . . . . 12 A1
  Redditch B97 . . . . 70 B5
Harvington Hall ★ DY10 . . 29 B1
Harvington Hall La
  Chaddesley Corbett DY10 . 46 C8
  Harvington DY10 . . . . 29 B1
Harvington Rd
  Birmingham, Brandhall B68. . 9 A8
  Birmingham, Weoley Castle
  B29 . . . . 19 A8
  Bromsgrove B60 . . . . 68 A8
  Halesowen B63 . . . . 7 E2
HASBURY 7 E3
Hasbury CE Prim Sch B63 . 7 F2
Hasbury Rd B32. . . . . 18 B8
Haseley Cl B98 . . . . 71 E1
Haselor La WR11. . . . . . . 160 E2
Haselwell Dr B30 . . . . 20 D3
HASLUCK'S GREEN 21 F2
Haslucks Green Rd B90 . . . 36 E7
Hastings Cl WR6 . . . . 99 A3
Hastings Dr WR4. . . . . 116 C6
Hastings Pl GL20. . . . . 196 E4
Hastings Rd
  Bromsgrove B60 . . . . 67 E7
  Malvern WR14. . . . . 153 D8
Haswell Rd B63. . . . . 7 D4
HATFIELD
  Hatfield and Newhampton. . 93 E4
  Norton Juxta Kempsey . . . 129 B1
Hatfield Bank WR5. . . . . . 129 A1
Hatfield Cl B98. . . . . 71 E1
Hatfield La WR5 . . . . 129 B2
Hatfield Rd DY9. . . . . 6 C4
Hathaway Cl
  3 South Littleton WR11. . 148 F1
  5 Worcester WR2 . . . . . . 114 D3
Hatherton Gr B29. . . . . 9 F1
Haunch La B13 . . . . 21 A5
Haven The
  Barnt Green B45 . . . . 50 A8
  Birmingham B14. . . . . 21 D4
Haverford Dr B45. . . . . 33 B6
Havergal Wlk B63. . . . . 7 B4
HAWBRIDGE 143 A4
Hawcross 192 C1
Hawfinch Rise DY10. . . . . . 28 A2
HAWFORD. 102 B6
Hawford Ave DY10 . . . . 28 B6
Hawford Dovecote ★
  WR3 . . . . 102 B6
Hawford Lock La WR3. . . . 102 A6
Hawford Pl WR9 . . . . 84 D1
Hawkesbury Rd B90. . . . . . 21 F1
Hawkes Cl B30. . . . . 20 A7
HAWKESLEY 34 F8
Hawkesley Church Prim Sch
  B38. . . . . 34 E7
Hawkesley Cres B31. . . . . . 19 A1
Hawkesley Dr B31. . . . . . . 33 F8
Hawkesley End B38. . . . . . . 34 E7
Hawkesley Mill La B31. . . . 18 F2
Hawkesley Sq B38. . . . . . . 34 E7
Hawkestone Rd B29. . . . . . 19 A7
Hawkhurst Rd B14 . . . . . . 20 F2
Hawkins Cl WR2 . . . . 114 D3
Hawkley Row WR4. . . . . . 116 C5
Hawkmoor Gdns B38. . . . . 35 A8
Hawkmoth Cl **10** GL20 . 197 A4
Hawksbury Cl B98. . . . . . . 71 D5
Hawkshead Ct **8** WR4 . 116 B6
Hawkstone Cl DY11 . . . . . . 27 D8
Hawkswood Gr B14 . . . . . . 21 B3
Hawkwood Cl WR14. . . . . . 138 E3
Hawkwood Cres WR2 . . . . 114 E4
HAWNE 8 A6
Hawne Cl B63 . . . . 7 F6
Hawne La B63 . . . . 7 F6

Hawnelands The B63. . . . . . 7 F5
Hawthorn Coppice DY9. . . 15 A6
Hawthorn Cres DY12 . . . . . 25 E2
Hawthorn Croft B68. . . . . . . 9 D7
Hawthorne Cl WR10. . . . . . 143 F7
Hawthorne Croft B30 . . . . . 19 D5
Hawthorne Dr B47. . . . . . . 36 B6
Hawthorne Rd
  Birmingham, King's Norton
  B30. . . . . 19 D5
  Halesowen B63 . . . . 7 E2
Hawthorne Way DY7 . . . . . . 4 C3
Hawthorne Wlk **6** WR9 . 103 F8
Hawthorn Gr DY11 . . . . 27 A6
Hawthorn La
  Madresfield WR13. . . . . . 139 F8
  Malvern WR14. . . . . 153 B5
  Powick WR2. . . . . 126 F1
Hawthorn Rd
  Brierley Hill DY5 . . . . 6 E8
  Bromsgrove B61 . . . . 49 B4
  Evesham WR11 . . . . 161 F2
  Redditch B97 . . . . 70 A4
  Worcester WR4 . . . . 115 E4
Hawthorn Rise WR9. . . . . . 117 A8
Hawthorns The
  Birmingham, Warley Woods
  B68. . . . . 9 D7
  1 Kidderminster DY10. . . 28 A5
  West Hagley DY9. . . . . . . 14 F4
Hawthorn Way GL20 . . . . . 184 F1
HAYBRIDGE 38 C8
Haybridge Ave DY8 . . . . . . 14 F5
Haybridge High Sch & Sixth
  Form DY8 . . . . 14 F6
Haybridge Mews DY9 . . . . 15 A6
Hay Cl
  Kidderminster DY11. . . . . . 27 C7
  Worcester WR4 . . . . 116 A4
Haydock Rd B61. . . . . 32 B1
Haydon Way B49. . . . . 109 F8
Haye La
  Mappleborough Green
  B80. . . . . 72 B1
  Ombersley WR9. . . . . 83 C5
Hayes Bank Rd WR14. . . . . 153 B5
Hayes Croft B38 . . . . 34 F7
Hayes La
  Stourbridge DY9 . . . . 7 A6
  Tenbury WR15 . . . . 54 F3
Hayes Rd DY11. . . . . 12 C3
Hayes The
  Birmingham B31. . . . . 34 C7
  Stourbridge DY9 . . . . 7 A5
Hayes Trad Est The DY9. . . . 7 A6
Hayfield Cl **1** WR2. . . . . . 114 D1
Hayford Cl B98. . . . . 71 A5
Hay Gn DY9. . . . . 6 D5
Hay Green Cl B30. . . . . 19 D6
Hay Green La B30. . . . . 19 D6
Hay La WR9 . . . . 104 E7
Hayle Cl B38. . . . . 20 B2
HAYLEY GREEN 7 C1
Hayley Green Rd B32. . . . . 18 B8
Hayley Park Rd B63. . . . . . 16 C8
Hayling Cl
  Birmingham B45 . . . . 17 F1
  4 St Peter the Great County
  WR5 . . . . 128 E6
Hayloft Cl B60. . . . . 67 E6
Haylofts The B63 . . . . 7 C1
Haynall La SY8. . . . . 54 A3
Haynes Cl B61 . . . . 49 B8
Haynes Ct WR14 . . . . 139 B5
Haynes Ho B98. . . . . 70 D2
Hays Cl WR12. . . . . 177 E3
Hayseech B64. . . . . 8 A7
Hayseech Rd B63 . . . . 7 F6
Haysfield The WR14. . . . . . 139 C4
Hayslan Ave WR14 . . . . . . 139 B2
Hayslan Gn WR14 . . . . . . 139 B2
Hayslan Gn WR14 . . . . . . 139 B2
Hayslan Rd WR14 . . . . . . 139 B2
Haytor Ave B14 . . . . 20 D5
Haywain Ave WR4. . . . . . . 116 C5
Haywood Dr B62. . . . . 8 C8
Haze Croft WR4. . . . . 116 B4
Hazel Ave
  Evesham WR11 . . . . 161 F2
  Walton Cardiff GL20 . . . . 197 B3
Hazelbank B38. . . . . 19 E2
Hazel Cl
  Droitwich Spa WR9 . . . . . 103 F8
  4 Worcester WR4 . . . . . 115 F5
Hazel Croft B31. . . . . 19 A3
Hazeldene DY13 . . . . 44 C3
Hazeldene Rd B63 . . . . 7 E2
Hazel Dr
  Hollywood B47. . . . . 36 B5
  Weoley Castle B29 . . . . . . 19 A7
Hazel Gr DY8 . . . . 5 C3
Hazelgrove WV15 . . . . 1 D6
Hazelhurst Rd B14. . . . . . . 20 E7
Hazelmere Rd B28 . . . . . . 21 F8
Hazel Rd
  Birmingham B45 . . . . 32 F6
  Redditch B97 . . . . 70 C5
Hazels The DY9. . . . . 14 F5
Hazelton Cl B61. . . . . 49 C8
Hazelton Rd B61. . . . . 32 C1
Hazelwell Cres B31. . . . . . . 20 B6
Hazelwell Dr B14. . . . . 20 D6
Hazelwell Fordrough B30 20 B6
Hazelwell La B30. . . . . 20 B7
Hazelwell Rd B30 . . . . 20 A6
Hazelwell St B30. . . . . 20 A7
Hazelwood Cl DY11 . . . . . . 27 B4
Hazelwood Cl **7** WR5. . . 115 F1
Hazlitt Gr B30 . . . . 19 D4

HEADLESS CROSS 89 D8
Headless Cross Dr B97. . . . 70 D1
Headley Croft B38 . . . . 34 D8
Headley Ct B97 . . . . 89 D8
HEADLEY HEATH 35 C6
Headley Heath La B38. . . . . 35 B6
Head St **1** WR10. . . . . . . 158 D8
Heale Cl B63 . . . . 7 A7
Heath Cl
  Birmingham B30. . . . . 19 D5
  Bromsgrove B60 . . . . 67 E6
  Cleobury Mortimer DY14. . . 22 B4
  Hallow WR2. . . . . 101 D3
Heathcote Rd B30 . . . . 20 A5
Heath Croft B31. . . . . 34 A7
Heath Dr
  Kidderminster DY10. . . . . . 13 B1
  Worcester WR5 . . . . 128 C5
Heath End Rd DY9 . . . . 31 D7
Heather Cl WR5. . . . . 128 C4
Heather Dr
  Birmingham B45 . . . . 32 F6
  Kinver DY7. . . . . 3 F4
Heather Ho B38. . . . . 19 F1
Heathermount Grange DY7 3 F6
Heathers The WR11 . . . . . . 175 D8
Heath Farm Rd DY8 . . . . . . 5 B3
Heathfield Cres DY11 . . . . . 27 B4
Heathfield Gdns DY8. . . . . . 5 F4
Heathfield Rd
  Bewdley DY12 . . . . 26 C4
  Birmingham, King's Heath
  B14. . . . . 20 F8
  Halesowen B63 . . . . 7 E3
  Hartlebury DY13 . . . . 44 C1
  Norton & Lenchwick WR11 147 D3
  Redditch B97 . . . . 70 A1
Heathfield Sch DY10 . . . . . 12 F2
HEATH GREEN 52 F3
Heath Ho B14. . . . . 20 F2
Heath La
  Kidderminster DY10. . . . . . 28 C1
  Stone DY10 . . . . 45 D8
  Stourbridge DY8 . . . . 6 A4
Heathlands Cl **5** WR14. . 166 E7
Heathlands Gr **5** B31. . . 19 A1
Heathlands The
  Stourbridge DY9 . . . . 6 B4
  Stourport-on-Severn DY13 . 44 B8
Heathleigh Rd B38. . . . . . . 34 C8
Heath Rd
  Birmingham B30. . . . . 19 D5
  Hollywood B47. . . . . 36 A7
Heath Rise B14 . . . . 21 A1
Heath Road S B31. . . . . . . 19 B4
Heathside Dr B38 . . . . 20 B2
Heath The WR6. . . . . 82 B3
Heathy Farm Cl B32. . . . . . . 9 B1
Heathy Rise B32 . . . . 9 A2
Hebb St **7** WR1 . . . . 115 B4
Hebden Gr B28. . . . . 21 E3
Hedera Rd B98. . . . . 71 F6
Hedgefield Gr B63. . . . . 7 C1
Hedgerow Cl B98. . . . . 89 F8
Hedgerows The B62. . . . . . 16 F4
Hedges Way B60. . . . . 49 B1
HEIGHTINGTON. 25 E1
Heightington Pl DY13. . . . . 43 E1
Heightington Rd
  Ribbesford DY12 . . . . 25 F1
  Rock DY14 . . . . 41 F6
Heights The WR5. . . . . . . 116 B3
Helford Cl WR5 . . . . 115 E2
Helmsley Cl DY5 . . . . 6 C8
Heming Rd B98. . . . . 90 E8
Hemmings Cl DY8. . . . . 5 F5
Hemming St DY11. . . . . . . 27 C4
Hemmingway **2** WR11 . 161 D2
Hemming Way DY10 . . . . . 46 E8
Hemplands Rd DY8 . . . . 5 F5
Hemsby Cl **9** WR5. . . . . 128 D6
Hemyock Rd B29. . . . . 19 B8
Henderson Ct **7** B68. . . . 9 B8
Henley Dr WR9 . . . . 104 A8
Henley Pl WR14. . . . . 138 F3
Henley Rd B80 . . . . 72 C2
Henlow Rd B14 . . . . 21 A2
Hennals Ave B97. . . . . 69 F2
Henry Cres GL20. . . . . 197 B4
Henry Fowler Cl **2**
  WR11 . . . . 161 D5
Henry St
  1 Evesham WR11. . . . . . 161 C4
  Worcester WR1 . . . . 115 B5
Henry Wlk B60. . . . . 67 E7
Hentland Cl B98. . . . . 71 D4
Henwick Ave WR2 . . . . . . 114 F4
Henwick Par WR1. . . . . . . 115 B2
Henwick Rd WR2 . . . . 114 F3
Herbert Austin Dr B60. . . . . 32 E1
Herbert St B98. . . . . 70 E4
Hereford Cl
  Birmingham B45 . . . . 18 A2
  Kidderminster DY11. . . . . . 27 A5
Hereford Rd B45. . . . . 18 A2
Hereward Rise B62 . . . . 8 C5
Heriotts Ct **7** WR9 . . . . . 84 F3
Heritage Way **7** WR9 . . . 84 F3
Hermitage Way **2** DY13. . 62 F8
Herne Field **5** WR4. . . . 116 C5
Hernehurst B32. . . . . 9 C6
Herne's Nest DY12 . . . . . . 26 A2
Hern Rd DY5. . . . . 6 C6
Heron Cl
  Alvechurch B48. . . . . 51 A7
  Worcester WR2 . . . . 128 A6
Herondale Cres DY8 . . . . . . 5 C4
Herondale Rd DY8 . . . . 5 C4

HEADLESS CROSS 89 D8
Heronfield Cl B98 . . . . 71 C5
Heronfield Dr B31 . . . . 33 F6
Heron Pl WR9 . . . . 85 B3
Herons Gate Rd DY7 . . . . . . 2 F5
Heronswood Prim Sch
  DY10 . . . . 28 A2
Heronswood Rd
  Birmingham B45 . . . . 33 B6
  Kidderminster DY10. . . . . . 28 A2
Heron Way B45. . . . . 32 F7
Hestia Dr B29. . . . . 19 C8
Hetherington Cl **2** WR5. 141 C7
Hetherington Rise WR4 . . 116 C3
Hever Ave WR4 . . . . 116 C6
Hever Cl **13** GL20 . . . . . . 197 A4
Hewell Ave B60. . . . . 67 F7
Hewell Cl
  Birmingham B31 . . . . 33 F7
  Redditch B97 . . . . 69 C6
Hewell La
  Barnt Green B45 . . . . 50 D8
  Redditch B60, B97. . . . . . . 69 D6
Hewell Rd
  Barnt Green B45 . . . . 50 D8
  Redditch B97 . . . . 70 D4
Hewell Rd Swimming Pool
  B97 . . . . 70 C5
Hexton Cl B90. . . . . 21 D2
Heycott Gr B38 . . . . 20 C2
Heydon Rd B60. . . . . 49 D1
Heythrop Gr B13. . . . . 21 D8
Hickmans Cl **2** B62. . . . . . 9 A6
Hickman St DY9 . . . . 6 C6
Hidage The WR5. . . . . 142 D8
Hidcote Cl **5** WR5 . . . . . 128 D5
Higgins La B32 . . . . 9 C5
High Ave B64. . . . . 7 F8
Highbury Ct B13 . . . . 20 E7
Highbury Rd B14. . . . . 20 D8
Highclere WR12 . . . . 26 A2
High Clere B64 . . . . 8 A7
Highclere Dr DY12 . . . . 26 A2
Highcrest Cl B31. . . . . 34 A7
High Elms La
  Bentley Pauncefoot B60 . . 87 E8
  Upper Bentley B60. . . . . . 68 E1
High Farm Rd
  Halesowen, Hasbury B63. . . 7 F3
  Halesowen, Hurst Green B62 .8 F8
Highfield WR2 . . . . 140 F3
Highfield Ave B97. . . . . 89 D8
Highfield Cl
  Birmingham B28 . . . . 21 D5
  Droitwich WR9 . . . . 84 F2
  Malvern WR14. . . . . 139 A4
Highfield Cres
  Cradley Heath B65. . . . . . . 8 B8
  Halesowen B63 . . . . 7 D6
Highfield La
  Birmingham B32 . . . . 9 B4
  Clent DY9 . . . . 16 A3
  1 Halesowen B63 . . . . . . 8 A3
Highfield Mews B63. . . . . . . 7 D6
Highfield Pl B14 . . . . 21 D5
Highfield Rd
  Birmingham, Yardley Wood B14,
  B28 . . . . 21 D5
  Bromsgrove B61 . . . . 67 E8
  Cookley DY10 . . . . 13 A5
  Evesham WR11 . . . . 161 B4
  Halesowen B63 . . . . 7 D5
  Kidderminster DY10. . . . . . 28 A8
  Malvern WR14. . . . . 138 F4
  Redditch B97 . . . . 89 D8
  Studley B80 . . . . 90 D4
Highfields
  Bromsgrove B61 . . . . 48 E1
  Twyning GL20. . . . . 184 A6
Highfields Prim Sch B65 . . . 8 C8
Highgate Cl DY11 . . . . 27 A4
HIGH GREEN 156 A7
Highgrove Ct DY10 . . . . . . 13 A1
High Haden Cres B64 . . . . . 8 A8
High Haden Rd B64 . . . . . . 8 A8
High Heath Cl B30 . . . . . . 19 D5
High House Dr
  Inkberrow WR7 . . . . 120 E7
  Lower Marlbrook B45 . . . . 32 F3
High House La B60. . . . . . . 69 A6
High La HR7 . . . . 96 D5
Highland Ho B62. . . . . 8 C8
Highland Rd WR4 . . . . 115 E4
Highland Ridge B62. . . . . . . 8 E5
Highlands Cl DY11 . . . . . . 27 A5
Highland Way B98 . . . . 90 A7
HIGH LANE 96 D6
High Leasowes B63 . . . . 8 A4
Highley Cl
  Kidderminster DY11. . . . . . 27 B2
  Redditch B98. . . . . 71 E4
Highlow Ave DY11 . . . . 12 C1
High Mdws B60. . . . . 67 D7
High Meadow Rd B38 . . . . . 20 A2
Highmoor Dr B32. . . . . 18 C8
Highpark Ave DY8 . . . . 5 D5
High Park Rd B63 . . . . 7 C5
High St
  Astwood Bank B96 . . . . . . 89 E1
  Badsey WR11. . . . . 162 D3
  Belbroughton DY9 . . . . . . 30 E7
  Bewdley DY12 . . . . 26 B3
  Bidford-on-Avon B50 . . . . 136 C7
  Birmingham, King's Heath
  B14. . . . . 20 E8
  Birmingham, Quinton B32. . . 9 A6
  Bredon GL20 . . . . 184 D6
  Brierley Hill, Quarry Bank
  DY5. . . . . 7 A8

High St continued
Broadway WR12 . . . . **190** D8
Bromsgrove B61 . . . . **49** A2
Cleobury Mortimer DY14 . . . **22** B4
Cradley Heath B64 . . . . **7** C8
Droitwich WR9 . . . . **85** A3
Evesham WR11 . . . . **161** D5
Feckenham B96 . . . . **107** F3
1 Halesowen B63 . . . . **8** B3
Honeybourne WR11 . . . . . **164** B4
Inkberrow WR7 . . . . **120** E7
Kidderminster DY10 . . . . . . **27** E6
Kinver DY7 . . . . **4** B3
Mickleton GL55 . . . . **165** D3
Pershore WR10 . . . . **144** D1
Solihull, Shirley B90 . . . . . . **21** D2
Stanton WR12 . . . . **189** D1
Stourbridge, Amblecote DY8 . . **5** F7
Stourbridge DY8 . . . . **6** A5
Stourbridge, Lye DY9 . . . . **6** E5
Stourbridge, Wollaston DY8 . . **5** F7
Stourport-on-Severn DY13 . . **44** A3
Studley B80 . . . . **90** E4
Tewkesbury GL20 . . . . **196** E6
Twyning GL20 . . . . **183** F6
1 Upton upon Severn
  WR8 . . . . **169** C6
Worcester WR1 . . . . **115** C3
Highters CI B14 . . . . **21** B2
HIGHTER'S HEATH **21** B2
Highter's Heath La B14 . . . **21** A2
Highters Heath Prim Sch
  B14 . . . . **21** B3
Highters Rd B14 . . . . **21** A3
High Timbers B45 . . . . . . **17** F1
Hightown B63 . . . . **7** C6
Hightree CI B32 . . . . **9** B1
High Trees CI B98 . . . . . . **89** E7
HIGHWOOD **57** F3
Highwood Croft B38 . . . . . **19** D1
Hilary Gr B31 . . . . **18** F4
Hilda Peers Way DY12 . . . **26** A3
Hillaire CI B38 . . . . **20** C2
HILL AND CAKEMORE **8** D7
Hillary Rd DY13 . . . . **44** D7
Hill Ave The WR5 . . . . . . **128** C8
Hill Bank B63 . . . . **6** F5
Hill Bank Rd
  Birmingham B38 . . . . **20** A2
  Halesowen B63 . . . . **7** D6
Hillboro Rise DY7 . . . . **4** A5
Hillborough La B50 . . . . . **137** C5
Hillbrow Cres B62 . . . . **8** F8
Hill CI
  Birmingham B31 . . . . **19** C1
  Bredon GL20 . . . . **185** B7
  Pershore WR10 . . . . **144** C1
Hill Crest 5 WR11 . . . . . **161** F3
Hillcrest Ave B63 . . . . **7** B7
Hillcrest Ind Est B64 . . . . . . **7** D8
Hillcrest Pk B47 . . . . **52** F8
Hillcrest Rd B62 . . . . **17** A4
Hillcrest Rise WR3 . . . . . **102** A1
Hillcrest Sch & Sixth Form
  Ctr B32 . . . . **29** E3
Hillcroft Ho B14 . . . . **20** E2
Hill Croft Rd B14 . . . . **20** C6
HILL CROOME **170** D5
Hillditch La DY11 . . . . . . **44** E2
HILL END
  Droitwich Spa **85** B4
  Twyning **184** A8
Hill End Rd GL20 . . . . . . **183** F6
Hillery Rd WR5 . . . . **128** F8
Hill Farm WR7 . . . . **120** E7
Hillfields Rd DY5 . . . . **6** F5
HILL FURZE **146** B5
Hill Furze Rd WR10 . . . . **133** C1
Hill Grove Cres DY10 . . . . **28** A4
Hillgrove Gdns DY10 . . . . **28** A4
Hill La
  Alvechurch B47, B48 . . . . . **35** D1
  Bentley Pauncefoot B60 . . . **87** E6
  Bromsgrove B60 . . . . **48** F1
  Clent DY9 . . . . **15** E4
  Elmley Castle WR10 . . . . . **173** D7
Hillmeads Rd B38 . . . . **20** A1
Hillmorton CI B98 . . . . . . **71** E6
HILLPOOL **29** E5
Hill Rd
  Lulsley WR6 . . . . **111** E3
  Pirton WR8 . . . . **142** D3
Hill Rise View B60 . . . . . . **49** C6
Hillsfield WR8 . . . . **169** C5
HILL SIDE **99** B7
Hillside
  Ashton under Hill WR11 . . **174** B1
  Redditch B98 . . . . **70** D2
Hill Side WR5 . . . . **141** C8
Hillside Ave
  Brierley Hill DY5 . . . . **7** A8
  Cradley Heath B65 . . . . **8** B8
  Halesowen B63 . . . . **7** D6
Hillside CI
  Birmingham B32 . . . . **18** A8
  Evesham WR11 . . . . **161** A3
  Kidderminster DY11 . . . . . **27** A7
  6 Stourport-on-Severn
    DY13 . . . . **62** E8
  Upton Snodsbury WR7 . . . **131** C8
  Worcester WR5 . . . . **115** F3
Hillside Dr
  Kidderminster DY11 . . . . . **27** A7
  Lickey End B61 . . . . **49** B6
Hillside Gr DY10 . . . . **13** C3
Hill St
  Brierley Hill, Quarry Bank
    DY5 . . . . **7** A8

Hill St continued
Halesowen B63 . . . . **8** A3
Kidderminster DY11 . . . . . . **27** D6
Stourbridge, Amblecote DY8 . . **5** F8
Stourbridge DY8 . . . . **7** C8
Stourbridge, Lye DY9 . . . . **6** F5
Worcester WR5 . . . . **115** D3
Hillstone Ct WR14 . . . . . . **138** F1
Hill The B32 . . . . **9** E2
Hilltop DY9 . . . . **6** F3
Hill Top B97 . . . . **69** F1
Hilltop Ave DY12 . . . . **26** D4
Hill Top Ave B62 . . . . **8** E7
Hill Top La WR9 . . . . **83** B4
Hill Top Rd B31 . . . . **18** F3
Hill View WR8 . . . . **157** D3
Hillview CI
  Halesowen B63 . . . . **7** E6
  Lickey End B60 . . . . **49** C6
Hill View CI
  Colwall WR13 . . . . **152** B2
  Malvern WR14 . . . . **139** B5
  Mickleton GL55 . . . . **165** F5
Hillview Dr WR14 . . . . . . **138** E4
Hillview Gdns WR28 . . . . **169** E6
Hillview La GL20 . . . . . . **183** F7
Hillview Rd
  Birmingham B45 . . . . **32** E8
  Lickey End B60 . . . . **49** C6
Hill View Rd
  Bidford-on-Avon B50 . . . . **136** E5
  Strensham WR8 . . . . **171** A4
  Worcester WR2 . . . . **127** F7
Hillville Gdns DY8 . . . . **6** B3
Hill Wood Cl WR4 . . . . . . **116** B4
Hillwood Rd
  Birmingham B31 . . . . **18** E7
  Halesowen B62 . . . . **8** C7
Hilston Ave B63 . . . . **7** F4
Hilton Ave B28 . . . . **21** F4
Hilton Rd WR14 . . . . **153** C7
HIMBLETON **105** C2
Himbleton CE Fst Sch
  WR9 . . . . **105** D1
Himbleton CI B98 . . . . **70** F1
Himbleton Rd WR2 . . . . . **114** E4
Himley Gr B45 . . . . **33** B6
Hindhead Rd B14 . . . . **21** C4
HINDLIP **103** B2
Hindlip CE Fst Sch WR3 **103** A3
Hindlip CI
  Halesowen B63 . . . . **7** F2
  Redditch B98 . . . . **72** A3
Hindlip La WR3 . . . . **103** C1
Hindon Wlk B32 . . . . **9** C2
Hingley Ave WR4 . . . . . . **116** B3
Hingley Rd DY9 . . . . **7** A6
Hinton Ave B48 . . . . **51** A6
HINTON CROSS **175** B5
Hinton Fields B61 . . . . **48** E7
HINTON ON THE
  GREEN **175** A5
Hinton Rd WR12 . . . . **176** D2
Hipkiss Gdns 3 WR9 . . . . **84** E4
Hiplands Rd B62 . . . . **8** F4
HIPPLECOTE **111** E8
Hipton Hill WR11 . . . . **147** C5
Hither Gn WR11 . . . . **162** E4
Hither Green La B98 . . . . . **70** F7
Hoarstone DY8 . . . . **14** F5
Hoarstone CI DY12 . . . . . . **26** C5
Hoarstone La DY12 . . . . . . **26** C6
Hobacre CI B45 . . . . **33** A8
Hobbis Ho B38 . . . . **34** C7
Hobden Hall Farm Ind Units
  B60 . . . . **67** B3
Hob Green Prim Sch DY9 . . **6** E2
Hob Green Rd DY9 . . . . **6** E2
Hobhouse Gdns 6 WR4 . . **116** C3
Hock Coppice 4 WR4 . . . **116** B4
Hockham's La WR6 . . . . . . **80** D2
Hockley Brook La DY9 . . . . **30** F3
HODEN **149** D4
Hoden La WR11 . . . . **149** B7
Hodfar Rd DY13 . . . . **44** B1
Hodge Hill Ave DY9 . . . . **6** F3
Hodge Hill Cotts DY10 . . . . **28** E7
Hodges The 7 WR11 . . . . **161** D5
Hodgetts Dr B63 . . . . **16** C8
Hoggs La B31 . . . . **18** E4
HOLBEACHE **11** A2
HOLBERROW GREEN **108** B3
Holcroft Rd
  Halesowen B63 . . . . **7** C5
  Stourbridge DY9 . . . . **6** C4
Holdens The B28 . . . . **21** E6
Holder CI 5 B50 . . . . **136** D5
Holdgate Rd B29 . . . . **19** C7
Holdings La WR5 . . . . . . **128** D1
Hole Farm Rd B31 . . . . . . **19** C5
Hole Farm Way B38 . . . . . **34** F7
Hole La B31 . . . . **19** C5
Hollams Rd GL20 . . . . . . **196** F7
Holland CI 4 B50 . . . . . . **136** D4
Holland Gn WR4 . . . . **116** C3
Hollaway Ct B63 . . . . **7** D5
Hollie Lucas Rd B13 . . . . . **20** F7
Hollies Dr B62 . . . . **8** E6
Hollies La
  Enville DY7 . . . . **2** F7
  Kidderminster Foreign DY11 **11** F3
Hollies Mews The WR14 . **139** B5
Hollies Rd B64 . . . . **7** F8
Hollies The
  Barnt Green B45 . . . . **33** A1
  Charlton WR10 . . . . **160** E8

Hollies The continued
2 Stourport-on-Severn
    DY13 . . . . **43** E6
Hollins La WR6 . . . . **99** A3
Hollister Dr B32 . . . . **9** F3
Holloway
  Birmingham B31 . . . . **18** E5
  1 Pershore WR10 . . . . . **158** C8
Holloway Dr
  Pershore WR10 . . . . **144** B1
  Redditch B98 . . . . **71** B3
Holloway La B98 . . . . **70** F3
Holloway Pk B98 . . . . **71** A3
Holloway The
  Alvechurch B48 . . . . **51** D3
  Bluntington DY10 . . . . **29** E2
  Chaddesley Corbett DY10 . . **46** E8
  Droitwich WR9 . . . . **85** A2
  Stourbridge DY8 . . . . **5** F7
HOLLOW COURT **106** D1
Hollow Croft B31 . . . . **19** B3
Hollowfields Rd B96 . . . . **106** C6
Hollows The WR11 . . . . . **175** B2
Hollowtree La B60 . . . . . . **50** A3
Hollybank Gr B63 . . . . **7** D1
Hollybank Rd B13 . . . . **21** A6
HOLLYBED COMMON **179** F7
Hollyberry CI
  8 Halesowen B63 . . . . **8** A3
  Redditch B98 . . . . **72** A4
Hollybrow B29 . . . . **19** B7
HOLLYBUSH **179** C6
Holly Bush Gr B32 . . . . **9** D7
Hollybush La DY8 . . . . **5** F7
Holly Bush La WR6 . . . . . . **97** A7
Holly CI
  Bretforton WR11 . . . . **163** B5
  Droitwich WR9 . . . . **104** A8
  8 Evesham WR11 . . . . . **161** F2
  Kinver DY7 . . . . **3** F5
Holly Ct DY10 . . . . **27** D8
Holly Dell B38 . . . . **20** B2
Holly Dr B47 . . . . **36** B7
Hollyfield Dr B45 . . . . **33** A1
Holly Gr
  Birmingham, Bournville
    B30 . . . . **19** F8
  Bromsgrove B61 . . . . **48** F3
  Stourbridge DY8 . . . . **5** F5
HOLLY GREEN **169** E7
Hollyhedge CI B31 . . . . . . **18** D6
Holly Hill 4 B45 . . . . **17** F1
Holly Hill Meth CE Inf Sch
  B45 . . . . **17** F2
Holly Hill Rd B45 . . . . **18** A2
Hollyhurst Farm Cvn Site
  B62 . . . . **17** B6
Holly La B48 . . . . **52** F5
Hollymoor Way B31 . . . . . **18** B1
Hollymount B62 . . . . **9** A7
Holly Mount WR4 . . . . . . **115** E4
Holly Mount Rd WR4 . . . . **115** E4
Hollyoak Croft B31 . . . . . . **34** B8
Holly Rd
  Birmingham B68 . . . . **9** C8
  Birmingham, King's Norton
    B30 . . . . **20** A4
  Bromsgrove B61 . . . . **48** F4
  Stourport-on-Severn DY13 . . **44** B4
  Tenbury Wells WR15 . . . . . **55** F6
Holly Tree La WR2 . . . . . . **127** B8
Holly Well La DY14 . . . . . . **40** E6
HOLLYWOOD **36** B8
Hollywood By-Pass B38,
  B47 . . . . **35** E6
Hollywood Gdns B47 . . . . . **36** A8
Hollywood La B47 . . . . **36** B7
Hollywood Motor Pk B47 . **36** A8
Hollywood Prim Sch B14 . . **21** A1
Hollyword Dr B47 . . . . **36** A8
Holman St DY11 . . . . **27** C5
Holmcroft Rd DY10 . . . . . . **28** A5
Holme Rd 6 GL20 . . . . . . **196** F3
Holmes Dr B45 . . . . **32** F6
Holmes La
  Hanbury B60 . . . . **87** A7
  Stoke Prior B60 . . . . **68** B1
Holmes Orch WV15 . . . . **1** C6
Holmoak CI 8 GL20 . . . . . **197** A4
Holmwood Ave DY11 . . . . . **27** A6
Holmwood Dr B97 . . . . **70** C3
Holmwood Gdns 9
  WR11 . . . . **161** F2
Holmwood Ho B97 . . . . . . **70** C3
HOLT **82** D2
HOLT END **71** F8
Holt Fleet B82 . . . . **82** C4
Holt Fleet Rd WR9 . . . . . . **82** E4
Holt Gdns B80 . . . . **90** E2
HOLT HEATH **82** B3
Holt Hill B98 . . . . **71** F8
Holt Ho B61 . . . . **49** A3
Holt La B62 . . . . **16** D4
Holt Rd B80 . . . . **90** E2
Holy Austin Rock Houses*
  DY7 . . . . **3** F4
HOLY CROSS **15** E2
Holy Cross Gn DY9 . . . . . . **15** E2
Holy Cross La DY9 . . . . . . **30** E8
Holy Oaks CI B98 . . . . **71** E2
Holy Redeemer RC Prim Sch
  The WR10 . . . . **158** D8
Holy Trinity Sch DY10 . . . . **27** F6
Holywell La B45 . . . . **32** D6
Holywell Prim Sch B45 . . . **32** D7

Holy Well Rd WR14 . . . . . **166** E8
Home CI B28 . . . . **21** F6
Homedene Rd B31 . . . . . . **18** E7
HOMEDOWNS **197** E5
Homefield Rd WR2 . . . . . **115** A1
Home Meadow Ct B13 . . . . **21** A5
Home Meadow La B98 . . . **71** E6
Home Peal Ho B14 . . . . . . **20** E6
Home Piece WR9 . . . . **84** D2
HOMER HILL **7** B6
Homer Hill Rd B63 . . . . **7** C7
Homestead 12 WR9 . . . . . **84** D1
Homestead Ave WR4 . . . . **116** B7
Homestead CI
  6 Bredon GL20 . . . . . . **184** F6
  6 Malvern Wells WR14 . **166** E3
Homfray Rd DY10 . . . . **12** F1
HONEYBOURNE **164** A5
Honeybourne Airfield Ind Est
  WR11 . . . . **164** B1
Honeybourne CI 3 B63 . . . . **8** A3
Honeybourne Fst Sch
  WR11 . . . . **164** A4
Honeybourne Rd
  Alveley WV15 . . . . **1** C6
  Bidford-on-Avon B50 . . . . **136** E2
  Halesowen B63 . . . . **8** C3
  Weston-sub-Edge WR11 . . **164** B1
Honeybourne Sta WR11 . . **164** A6
Honeybrook CI DY11 . . . . . **12** D2
Honeybrook La DY11 . . . . **12** B1
Honeybrook Terr DY11 . . . **12** B1
Honeychurch CI B98 . . . . . **70** F3
Honeycomb Way B31 . . . . **18** E3
Honeymans Gdns WR9 . . . **84** E4
Honeysuckle CI
  Birmingham B32 . . . . **9** B5
  Evesham WR11 . . . . **161** D4
Honeywood Rd WR2 . . . . **114** E4
Honister Dr WR4 . . . . **116** A6
Honiton CI B31 . . . . **18** E4
Honiton Cres B31 . . . . **18** E4
Honnington Ct 2 B29 . . . . . . **9** F1
HOOBROOK **27** F2
Hoobrook Ind Est DY10 . . . **27** E2
Hood Gr B30 . . . . **19** D4
Hood St 6 WR1 . . . . **115** B2
Hoo Farm Ind Est DY10 . . . **27** F1
HOOK BANK **168** A5
HOOK THE **168** C6
Hoopers CI WR13 . . . . . . **126** A2
Hoopers La B96 . . . . **89** E1
Hoo Rd DY10 . . . . **27** E4
Hoosen CI B62 . . . . **9** A6
Hopedale Rd B32 . . . . **9** C5
Hopehouse La WR6 . . . . . . **99** B3
Hope La WR6 . . . . **97** C6
Hope St B62 . . . . **8** D8
Hopgardens Ave B60 . . . . . **49** B2
Hop Gardens The WR11 . . **162** C5
Hopkiln Gdns 3 WR11 . . . **161** D4
Hopkins Field CV37 . . . . . **151** C6
Hopmarket The 14 WR1 . . **115** B3
Hop Pole Gn WR5 . . . . . . **125** F2
Hop Pole La DY12 . . . . **25** E4
Hopton Dr DY10 . . . . **27** E1
Hopton Gr B13 . . . . **21** C5
Hopton La WR6 . . . . **125** B6
Hopton St WR2 . . . . **114** C2
HOPWOOD **34** B3
Hopwood CI B63 . . . . **8** A2
Hopwood Gr B31 . . . . **33** E6
Hopyard La B98 . . . . **71** D4
Hopyard The GL20 . . . . . . **184** D1
Hordern Cres DY5 . . . . **6** D8
Hornbeam CI
  15 Bewdley DY12 . . . . **25** F3
  Birmingham B29 . . . . **19** B7
Hornby Gr B14 . . . . **21** C4
Hornhill Meadow Nature
  Reserve* WR5 . . . . . . **116** C1
Horn La WR9 . . . . **99** B7
Hornsby Ave WR4 . . . . . . **116** C3
Hornyold Ave WR14 . . . . . **138** E3
Hornyold Ct WR14 . . . . . . **152** E2
Hornyold Rd WR14 . . . . . **138** E3
Horrell Rd B90 . . . . **21** F2
Horsebridge Ave WR11 . . **162** D4
Horse Bridge La DY7 . . . . . . **4** C2
Horse Fair DY10 . . . . **27** E7
Horsford Rd WR2 . . . . . . **114** F5
HORSHAM **111** C8
Horton La WR9 . . . . **65** A2
Horton Dr DY7 . . . . **3** F5
Hoskyns Ave WR4 . . . . . . **116** C3
Hospital Bank WR14 . . . . **138** F3
Hospital La WR2 . . . . **127** C2
Hospital Rd WR14 . . . . . . **138** D6
Hossil La
  Belbroughton DY9 . . . . . . **30** C8
  Clent DY9 . . . . **15** D1
Hough Rd B14 . . . . **20** D6
Houghton Ct B28 . . . . **21** D4
Houldey Rd B31 . . . . **19** B1
Houndsfield CI B47 . . . . . . **36** C6
Houndsfield Farm B47 . . . **36** B5
Houndsfield Gr B47 . . . . . . **36** A5
Houndsfield La B47 . . . . . . **36** C6
Housman CI B60 . . . . **67** E8
Housman Ct B60 . . . . **49** A3
Housman Pk B60 . . . . **49** A2
Housman Wlk DY10 . . . . . . **28** C6
Houx The DY8 . . . . **5** E8
Hoveton B98 . . . . **71** B2
Howard Ave B61 . . . . **48** E3
Howard CI
  Bidford-on-Avon B50 . . . . **136** C4

Howard CI continued
  Northway GL20 . . . . **197** E8
Howard Rd
  Birmingham, King's Heath
    B14 . . . . **20** E7
  Northway GL20 . . . . **197** D8
  Redditch B98 . . . . **90** C8
  Worcester WR2 . . . . **114** C3
Howard Road E B13 . . . . . **20** F7
Howcroft Gn 3 WR4 . . . . **116** B6
Howells Rd GL20 . . . . **196** E6
Howlett Pl WR4 . . . . **116** C3
Howley Grange Prim Sch
  B62 . . . . **8** F5
Howley Grange Rd B62 . . . . **9** A4
Howsell Rd WR14 . . . . . . **139** A4
Howsell Road Ind Est 7
  WR14 . . . . **139** A4
Howsells The WR14 . . . . . **139** B6
HOWSEN **113** D1
Hoyland Way B30 . . . . **19** E8
Huband CI B98 . . . . **71** A5
HUDDINGTON **118** C7
Huddington Ct* WR7 . . . **118** C7
Hudman's CI GL20 . . . . . . **184** A6
Hudson CI
  Honeybourne WR11 . . . . . **164** B5
  Pershore WR10 . . . . **144** C1
  Worcester WR2 . . . . **127** C4
Hudson's Dr B30 . . . . **20** A4
Hudswell Dr DY5 . . . . **6** D8
Hughes CI
  Harvington WR11 . . . . . . **148** A3
  Northway GL20 . . . . **184** F1
Hughes La WR11 . . . . **148** A7
Huins CI B98 . . . . **71** A4
Hullbrook Rd B13 . . . . **21** C6
Hulls La WR9 . . . . **104** A3
Humber Gdns B63 . . . . **7** C5
Humber Rd WR5 . . . . **115** C3
Hume St DY11 . . . . **27** C5
Humphrey Ave B60 . . . . . . **67** F7
Humphries Dr DY10 . . . . . **27** F2
Hungary CI DY9 . . . . **6** C5
Hungary Hill DY9 . . . . **6** C5
Hungerford Rd DY9 . . . . **5** E2
Hungerpit Wlk WR3 . . . . . **115** B6
HUNNINGTON **17** B8
Hunnington CI B32 . . . . **9** A1
Hunnington Cres B63 . . . . . . **8** B2
Hunscote CI B90 . . . . **21** F1
Hunscote Ho B90 . . . . **21** F1
Hunslet CI B32 . . . . **9** F4
Hunslet Rd B32 . . . . **9** F4
Hunstanton Ave B17 . . . . . . **9** F8
Hunstanton CI
  Brierley Hill DY5 . . . . **6** C7
  5 Worcester WR5 . . . . **128** D6
Hunt Ave WR4 . . . . **116** C4
HUNT END **89** C5
Hunt End Ind Est B97 . . . . **89** C5
Hunt End La B97 . . . . **89** C5
Hunter Rise WR10 . . . . . . **158** C8
Hunters CI 2 WR9 . . . . . . **84** D4
Hunters End 3 WR9 . . . . . **84** D4
Hunters Gn 4 WR9 . . . . . . **84** D4
Hunters Hill Sch B60 . . . . . **49** F6
Hunters Pl 1 WR9 . . . . . . **84** D4
Hunters Rise B63 . . . . **7** D1
Hunters Way WR9 . . . . . . **84** D4
Huntingdon CI B98 . . . . . . **71** F2
Huntings The WR12 . . . . . **190** C7
Huntingtree Prim Sch B63 . . **7** E3
Huntingtree Rd B63 . . . . **7** E3
Huntlands Rd B63 . . . . **7** F2
Hunts Fold WR10 . . . . **132** A5
Huntsmans CI 3 WR10 . . **143** F6
Huntsmans Dr DY7 . . . . **3** F5
Hunts Rd B30 . . . . **20** B7
Hunts Rise DY12 . . . . **26** C3
HURCOTT **28** C8
Hurcott Ct DY10 . . . . **28** A8
Hurcott La DY10 . . . . **28** C8
Hurcott Pools & Wood
  Nature Reserve* DY10 . . **13** D1
Hurcott Rd DY10 . . . . **28** B8
Hurst Ct DY9 . . . . **6** F5
HURST GREEN **8** F8
Hurst Green Prim Sch B62 . . **8** E8
Hurst Green Rd B62 . . . . . . **8** F8
Hurst La WR3 . . . . **102** F2
Hurst Rd WR10 . . . . **144** D2
Hurst The
  Birmingham B13 . . . . **21** D7
  2 Cleobury Mortimer DY14 **22** C4
  Hollywood B47 . . . . **36** A6
Husum Way DY10 . . . . **28** C7
Huxleys Way 6 WR11 . . . **161** C4
Huxtable Rise WR4 . . . . . **116** B4
Hyacinth CI 1 WR5 . . . . . **128** C4
Hyatt Sq DY5 . . . . **6** C7
Hyde CI
  Bromsgrove B60 . . . . **49** B2
  Kinver DY7 . . . . **4** A5
Hydefields WR8 . . . . **169** A5
Hyde La
  Kinver DY7 . . . . **4** A6
  Upton upon Severn WR8 . . **168** E5
Hyde Park Cnr GL19 . . . . **192** A3
HYDE THE **168** F5
Hyde The DY9 . . . . **6** D2
Hydrangea CI WR5 . . . . . **128** D4
Hylton Rd
  Evesham WR11 . . . . **161** A4
  Worcester WR2 . . . . **114** F4

Hyperion Rd DY7.......... 5 C7
Hytall Rd B90 .... 21 C2

I

Ibberton Rd B14 .... 21 B3
Ibis Cl B98 .... 28 B3
Ibstock Cl B98 .... 71 E4
Ibstock Dr DY8 .... 6 A4
Ibstock Ho B98 .... 71 E4
Icknield Cl B50 .... 136 E4
Icknield St Dr B98 ...... 90 D7
Icknield St
  Alvechurch B38 .... 35 B2
  Bell Green B38 .... 35 B6
  Beoley B48, B98 ...... 52 C2
  Bidford-on-Avon B50 .. 136 E4
  Redditch, Church Hill B98 . 71 C7
  Redditch, Ipsley B98 ... 71 D2
  Rowney Green B48 ..... 52 B6
Ideal Bldgs **7** DY11 ...... 27 D6
Ideal Wks DY9 .... 7 A6
Idleton **7** WR4 .... 116 C3
Idmiston Croft B14....... 20 F2
Ikon Ind Est DY10 .... 45 D6
Ilkley Cl WR4 .... 116 A4
ILLEY 17 E8
Illeybrook Sq B32........ 9 D2
Illey Cl B31 .... 18 C1
Illey La
  Birmingham B32 .... 18 A7
  Halesowen B62 .... 17 E8
Illshaw Cl B98 .... 72 A4
Ilmington Cl B98........ 71 D1
Ilmington Rd B29......... 9 F1
Ilsham Gr B31 .... 33 E6
Imber Rd DY10........... 28 A1
Imex Bsns Ctr B98 .... 71 E4
Imperial Ave DY10 .... 27 F8
Imperial Ct DY10........ 27 F8
Imperial Gr DY10........ 27 F8
Imperial Rd WR14....... 153 A8
Impey Rd B31........... 18 F1
Impney Cl B98 .... 71 E6
Impney Gn WR9.......... 85 B3
Impney Way WR9 .... 85 C3
Inches La WR11......... 161 D5
Inett Way WR9 .... 84 C3
Infield The B63 .... 7 D7
Infirmary Wlk **6** WR1 .. 115 B3
Ingeva Dr B45 .... 33 A1
Inglemere Gr B29........ 18 F7
Ingles Dr WR2 .... 114 E3
Ingoldsby Rd B31........ 19 C3
INKBERROW 120 F7
Inkberrow Fst Sch WR7 . 120 F8
Inkberrow Rd B63......... 7 F2
INKFORD 35 F1
Innage Rd B31.......... 19 B4
Innage The B47......... 36 A5
Innerstone La GL19 .... 192 C1
Innisfree Cl B47 .... 36 C4
Inn La DY11............ 45 A2
Insetton Cl B98 .... 71 D4
Institute Rd B14 .... 20 F8
Instone Rd B63 .... 8 A3
Insull Ave B14 .... 21 B1
Intended St B63 .... 7 C7
INTERFIELD.......... 138 F8
International Dr GL20 ... 197 C8
Inverlea Ct GL55 ...... 165 D4
Inverness Rd B31....... 18 F3
IO Ctr The B98......... 71 C1
IPSLEY 71 C2
Ipsley Alders Marsh Nature
  Reserve ★ B98 .... 71 F4
Ipsley CE Mid Sch **1** B98 71 E3
Ipsley Church La B98..... 71 C1
Ipsley La B98 .... 71 C2
Ipsley St B98 .... 70 E3
Iris Cl B29 .... 19 B8
Iris Dr B14............. 20 D3
Iron Bridge Wlk DY9 .... 15 B8
IRON CROSS.......... 135 C5
Ironside Cl **17** DY12 ..... 25 F3
Iron Way B60........... 68 B7
Irwin Ave B45.......... 33 C7
Isaacs Way WR9 .... 103 F7
Isaac Wlk WR2......... 114 E1
Isbourne Cres WR11 .... 161 D2
Island Dr DY10.......... 27 E4
Islington Dr B14 .... 8 A4
Ismere Way DY10 ...... 12 F1
Isobel Harrison Gdns
  WR14.............. 139 C5
Ithon Gr B38........... 34 E8
IVERLEY............. 14 C8
Iverley Ct **6** WR15 ..... 55 F6
Iverley La DY10, DY8 ... 14 C5
Iverley Rd B63 .... 8 C4
Iverley Wlk DY9......... 6 C2
Ivor Rd B97............ 70 D2
Ivyhouse Rd B38........ 34 C8
Ivy La
  Bretforton WR11...... 163 B5
  Fernhill Heath WR3 ... 103 A2
  Romsley B62 .... 16 D5
Ivy Rd B30............ 20 A6
Ivy St WR3............ 115 A6
Izod St B97............ 70 D4

J

Jackdaw La WR9........ 104 B7
Jackfield Cl B98 .... 71 E1
Jackson Cres DY13...... 43 E1
Jacksons Mdw B50 ..... 136 C6
Jacksons Orch CV37 .... 151 C6
Jackson St DY9.......... 6 E6
Jackson Way B32........ 9 A5
Jack Thomson Croft
  WR11.............. 135 F3
Jacob Cl **4** WR3........ 115 E7
Jacob's Ladder WR3 .... 102 D4
Jacomb Cl WR2........ 114 A7
Jacomb Dr WR2 .... 114 A7
Jacomb Rd WR2 .... 114 A7
Jakeman Cl B98 .... 71 E4
Jamaica Cres WR14..... 139 A4
Jamaica Rd WR14...... 139 A5
James Cl WR1 .... 115 C7
James Ct B38.......... 19 F2
James Lloyd Trust Flats
  B30 .... 19 C5
James Rd DY10........ 28 A8
James Scott Rd B63...... 7 A6
James St DY7........... 4 A4
Janice Gr B14 .... 21 B4
Jardine Cl **4** DY8....... 6 A6
Jarvis Dr DY10......... 171 E8
Jarvis St WR10........ 171 E7
Jasmin Croft B14....... 20 E3
Jasmine Cl **7** WR5..... 128 D5
Jasmine Cl B98 .... 71 E4
Jasmine Gr B61........ 48 F4
Jasmine Rd WR14...... 152 F4
Jasmine Wlk **5** WR11 .. 161 D1
Jason Rd DY9........... 6 F4
Jasper Dr GL20 .... 197 B4
Jasper Rd **5** WR2 ...... 127 F7
Jay Park Cres DY10 ..... 28 B2
Jays Cl B98 .... 72 A3
Jays Cres B48 .... 34 B1
Jeal Cl B47 .... 35 E2
Jelleyman Cl DY11...... 27 C6
Jenks Ave DY11.......... 3 F5
Jennett Tree La
  Madresfield WR13 .... 139 F5
  Powick WR2.......... 127 C1
Jennings Wood La DY13.. 43 A2
Jenny Lind Gr WR14.... 138 F3
Jersey Cl B98.......... 71 D7
Jerusalem Ct DY10...... 27 E7
Jervoise Dr B31......... 19 B5
Jeynes Row GL20 ...... 196 F7
Jiggins La B32......... 9 D1
Jill La B96............. 90 B2
Jinnah Rd B98......... 70 E2
Jinney Ring Craft Ctr★
  B60 .... 87 A5
Job's La GL20......... 185 D7
John Comyn Dr WR3 ... 115 C8
John Moore Countryside
  Mus★ GL20......... 196 E5
John Moore Prim Sch The
  GL20 .... 197 A3
John Rd B62............ 8 F3
Johns Cl B80.......... 90 C4
Johnson Cl B98........ 71 A5
Johnsons Gr B68........ 9 D8
Joiners Cl **3** WR4 ...... 115 F6
Jordan Cl DY11......... 27 A6
Jordans Cl
  Redditch B97......... 89 D6
  Willersey WR12....... 177 E3
Jorden's Wlk DY12...... 26 D4
Joseph Perkins Cl B96 .. 89 E2
Josiah Rd B31.......... 18 D2
Joyberry Dr DY8......... 6 A3
Jubilee Ave B97........ 89 D7
Jubilee Bsns Pk DY9 ..... 7 A5
Jubilee Cl
  Bidford-on-Avon B50 .. 136 E5
  Stoke Prior B60....... 67 C1
Jubilee Ct B31......... 19 B1
Jubilee Dr
  Bredon GL20......... 184 F6
  Colwall WR13........ 152 D2
Jubilee Drive N DY11.... 27 B2
Jubilee Drive S DY11.... 27 B2
Jubilee Ho B98........ 70 E2
Jubilee Rd
  Birmingham B45 ...... 17 E2
  Littleworth WR5...... 129 C1
  Worcester WR2....... 128 A8
Jubilee Terr B60....... 67 C1
Jubilee Way GL20 ...... 197 A6
Judge Rd DY5.......... 6 F7
Juggins La B94......... 53 B7
Julian Cl B61 .... 49 A8
Juliet Rd B62........... 8 F3
Junction Rd
  Bromsgrove B61....... 48 E3
  Stourbridge DY5 .... 5 E8
  Stourbridge DY8....... 6 B4
Juniper Ct DY10 .... 28 A4
Juniper Rise B63........ 7 C5
Juniper Way WR14..... 152 F4
Jury La WR6........... 99 A4
Jury Rd DY5............ 6 F7
Jutland Rd B13........ 21 B8

K

Karen Way DY5 .... 6 D8
Kateshill DY12......... 26 B2
Katmandu Rd B60...... 49 C1
Katrine Rd DY13 .... 43 E6

Keats Ave WR3 .... 115 C6
Keats Cl DY8........... 6 A8
Keats Ho B97 .... 89 C8
Keats Pl DY10......... 28 B6
Keble Cl WR4 .... 115 E3
Kedleston Ct B28....... 21 F4
Kedleston Rd B28....... 21 F5
Keele Cl B98 .... 71 E6
Keepers Cl WR10 ...... 143 F6
Keir Pl DY8............ 5 E8
Keith Winter Cl B61..... 48 F6
Kelby Cl B98.......... 18 E4
Kelby Rd B31 .... 18 F4
Kelling Cl DY5 .... 6 C8
Kelverdale Gr B14...... 20 C4
Kelvin Cl DY11........ 27 A8
Kelvin Rd B31.......... 19 B1
Kelwood Dr B63........ 8 B5
Kemelstowe Cres B63.. 16 C8
KEMERTON 185 D7
Kemerton Ho B97....... 70 B4
Kemerton Rd GL20 ..... 184 E6
KEMPSEY 141 D7
Kempsey Cl
  Halesowen B63 .... 7 E4
  Redditch B98.......... 90 B7
Kempsey Covert B38 .... 34 E7
Kempsey Ho B32........ 18 A8
Kempsey Prim Sch WR5 141 C7
Kempsford Cl B98 ...... 89 F6
Kempton Cl **4** WR11 ... 161 C2
Kempton Ct B61........ 32 A1
Kempton Rd WR10 ..... 144 E4
Kempton Way DY9....... 5 C3
Kemshead Ave B31..... 33 E8
Kemsley Rd B14....... 20 F2
Kenchester Cl B98 ..... 71 F2
Kendal Ave B45........ 33 B7
Kendal Cl
  Bromsgrove B60...... 49 B1
  Redditch B98......... 72 A3
Kendal Ct **14** B29 .... 19 C7
Kendal Dr B45......... 33 D1
Kendal End Rd B45..... 33 D1
Kendal Gn WR4....... 116 B6
Kendall St WR3........ 115 D4
Kendal Rise Rd B45..... 33 B7
Kendlewood Rd DY10 .. 13 B1
Kenelm Cl WR6........ 97 E8
Kenelm Ct B62......... 17 A4
Kenelm Rd WR6........ 97 E8
Kenilworth Cl
  Redditch B97......... 89 D6
  Worcester WR1....... 115 C4
Kenilworth Dr DY10..... 27 E2
Kenilworth Ho B13...... 21 A6
Kenilworth Rd B68..... 9 B3
Kenley Gr B30......... 20 B3
Kennedy Cl DY10....... 27 F3
Kennedy Cl DY8......... 5 F5
Kennedy Gr B30....... 20 B6
Kennel Bank WR10 ... 160 B6
Kennel La WR12....... 190 D7
Kennels La WR3....... 102 F4
Kennet Cl GL20........ 197 C8
Kennet Gn WR5........ 115 D2
Kenneth Vincent Cl B97.. 89 E4
Kenrose Mill DY7........ 4 B3
Ken Somner Gdns B98 . 71 A3
Kenswick Dr B63 .... 8 A2
Kent Cl
  Evesham WR11....... 161 A3
  Kidderminster DY10... 27 E2
  Malvern WR14........ 139 C6
Kentmere Cl WR4...... 116 A5
Kentmere Rd B60....... 49 C1
Kent Rd
  Birmingham B45 ...... 17 F1
  Halesowen B63......... 8 F5
  Stourbridge DY8....... 5 D7
Kenward Croft B17....... 9 F7
Kenway B47........... 36 A7
Kenwood Ave WR4..... 115 F4
Kenwood Cl **5** WR4.... 115 F4
Kenyon Cl
  Bromsgrove B60...... 49 A1
  Stourbridge DY8....... 6 A7
Kepax Gdns WR3...... 115 A6
Keren Dr WR5......... 128 F3
Keresley Gr B29........ 9 F2
Kernthorpe Rd B14..... 20 D4
Kerry Cl B31........... 18 F6
Kerry Croft Cl B97..... 89 E5
Kerry Hill
  3 Bromsgrove B60 ... 67 E6
  Worcester WR3....... 115 E8
KERSOE............ 174 A5
Kerswell Cl **2** B97..... 70 B5
KERSWELL GREEN ... 141 D2
Kestrel Cl DY10........ 27 E3
Kestrel Cres WR9 ..... 104 B7
Kestrel Dr **6** WR5 ..... 128 C5
Kestrel Gr B30......... 19 D8
Kestrel Rd B63.......... 7 B7
Kestrel View B60....... 49 C7
Kestrel Way GL20 ..... 184 D1
Keswick Dr WR4....... 116 A6
Kettles Wood Dr B32... 9 C2
Kewstoke Croft B31..... 18 E6
Key Ave WR4.......... 116 C3
Keynell Covert B30..... 20 C2
KIDDERMINSTER 27 D4
Kidderminster Coll **4**
  DY10 .... 27 E5
Kidderminster Hospl
  DY11 .... 27 C5

Kidderminster Rd
  Bewdley DY12........ 26 C4
  Bromsgrove B61...... 48 C3
  Chaddesley Corbett DY10. 47 A6
  Droitwich WR9....... 84 A4
  Iverley DY8.......... 14 C7
  West Hagley DY9..... 15 B5
Kidderminster Rd S DY9.. 14 F3
Kidderminster Rly Mus★
  DY10 .... 27 F5
Kidderminster Sta DY10.. 27 F5
Kidderminster Town Sta★
  DY10 .... 27 F5
Kiel Cl WR12.......... 190 D8
Kielder Gdns DY9....... 6 B1
Kielder Rise WR2 ..... 127 F6
Kiftsgate Stone★ GL55 .. 178 E2
Kilbury Dr WR5........ 129 A8
Kilcote Rd B90........ 21 C2
Kilmore La GL20....... 183 F6
Kiln Cl B80............ 90 C4
Kiln La B98........... 126 A2
Kilpeck Cl B98 .... 71 F2
Kimberley Ave DY10.... 13 B4
Kimberley Cl B98 ...... 71 B7
Kimbolton Dr B60...... 50 A5
Kimpton Cl B14........ 20 E2
Kineton Cl B98 .... 71 D1
Kineton Croft B32...... 18 D8
Kineton Ho B13........ 21 A6
Kineton Rd B45........ 32 E7
King Arthur's Cl WR2 .. 114 F4
King Charles Ave WR2 . 127 C2
King Charles Cl B61.... 48 F5
King Charles I Sch DY10.. 28 A5
King Charles Pl Sh Ctr **15**
  WR2............... 114 F1
King Charles Rd B63..... 8 F4
King Charles Sq **4** DY10. 27 E6
Kingcomb La GL55 .... 178 F3
King Edmund Sq **1**
  WR1............... 115 B3
King Edward Ave B61 ... 48 F5
King Edward Rd B61 ... 48 F5
King Edward's Rd WR14. 152 E4
King Edward VI Camp Hill
  Sch For Boys B13 .... 20 D7
King Edward VI Camp Hill
  Sch For Girls B13 .... 20 D8
King Edward VI Coll DY8 . 6 A6
King Edward VI Five Ways
  Sch B32............. 18 C8
Kingfield Rd B90....... 21 C2
Kingfisher Cl WR5 .... 128 D6
Kingfisher Ct B48...... 51 A7
Kingfisher Dr DY8....... 5 F7
Kingfisher Ent Pk B98... 71 A3
Kingfisher Gr DY10..... 28 B3
Kingfisher Sch The **1**
  B98 .... 71 D1
Kingfisher Sh Ctr **2** B97. 70 E3
Kingfisher Sq B97....... 70 D4
Kingfisher Way B30 .... 19 D8
Kingfisher Wlk B97..... 70 D4
King George Ave
  Bromsgrove B61...... 48 F4
  Droitwich WR9....... 84 F1
King George Cl B61..... 48 F4
King George's Way **5**
  WR10.............. 144 D1
Kingham Cl B98........ 72 A4
Kingham Covert B14.... 20 D2
King Johns Ct GL20 ... 196 E7
Kingmead Ho B14...... 20 D4
Kings Arms La DY13.... 62 E8
Kingsbridge Rd B32..... 9 D1
Kingsbury Ave WR2 ... 127 D4
Kings Cl B43.......... 19 D4
Kingscote Cl B98....... 71 D7
Kings Coughton La B49 . 109 F2
Kings Ct DY5........... 5 E5
Kingsdale Ct WR12 .... 190 E8
Kingsdown Rd B31..... 9 F1
KING'S END.......... 127 D4
King's End Rd WR2 .... 127 D4
Kingsfield Rd B14...... 20 E8
KINGSFORD 12 B8
Kingsford Forest Pk Nature
  Reserve★ DY11...... 3 D2
Kingsford La
  Kinver DY11 .... 3 C1
  Wolverley & Cookley DY11. 12 C7
Kings Gate GL20 ...... 197 B6
Kings Gdn B30......... 19 E4
KING'S GREEN 192 D8
Kings Green Ave B38.... 19 F2
Kings Hawford Sch WR3 102 A5
KING'S HEATH 20 F7
Kings Heath Boys'
  Mathematics & Computing
  Coll B13............ 21 A6
King's Hill WR5....... 141 C8
Kingshill Cl WR14..... 139 A1
Kingshill Dr B38....... 19 F2
Kingshurst Rd
  Birmingham B31 ..... 19 A3
  Solihull B90......... 21 F1
King's La
  Bidford-on-Avon B50 .. 136 B6
  Norton & Lenchwick WR11 147 D3
Kingsley Ave B98...... 71 A3
Kingsley Coll B98...... 90 C6
Kingsley Rd B30........ 19 D8
Kingsley Sports Ctr B98. 90 C6
King's Mdw DY9....... 15 E3
KING'S NORTON....... 19 E2

King's Norton Boys Sch
  B30 .... 19 E4
King's Norton Bsns Ctr
  B30 .... 20 A4
King's Norton Girls Sch &
  Lang Coll B30....... 19 F5
King's Norton High Sch
  B38 .... 34 F8
King's Norton Prim Sch
  B30 .... 20 A3
King's Norton Sta B30 .. 19 F4
Kings Rd
  Birmingham, Stirchley
    .... 20 C6
  2 Great Malvern WR14. 166 E7
King's Rd
  Evesham WR11....... 161 F4
  Kidderminster DY11... 27 C6
King's Sch The WR1.... 115 B1
King St
  Brierley Hill DY5 .... 7 A8
  Halesowen B63 .... 8 A4
  Stourbridge DY8 .... 5 E6
  Stourbridge, Lye DY9... 6 F5
  4 Worcester WR1 .... 115 C1
King Stephen's Mount
  WR2............... 114 F5
Kings Terr B14........ 20 D6
Kingsthorpe Rd B14.... 21 A3
Kingston Ave B31...... 33 D6
Kingston Cl **1** WR9 ... 104 A8
Kingston Ct **17** B29..... 19 C7
Kingston Rd GL20 ..... 197 E8
King Street Pas DY5.... 7 A8
Kingsway
  Birmingham B68 ...... 9 B7
  Stourbridge DY8 .... 5 E8
  Stourport-on-Severn DY13. 43 F7
Kingsway Dr B38....... 19 F2
KING'S WOOD........ 20 D1
KINGSWOOD CL B30 .. 20 E3
Kingswood Dr B30..... 20 C3
Kingswood Ho **1** B14 .. 20 E2
KINGSWOOD LOWER ... 24 C7
Kingswood Rd
  Birmingham, Coft Common
    B31............... 33 F7
  Hampton Lovett WR9.. 84 C7
KINGTON 120 A4
King William St DY8..... 5 F8
Kinlet Cl B98 .... 71 E3
Kinlet Gr B31......... 19 C2
Kinlet Rd DY14........ 24 A5
KINNERSLEY 156 A3
Kinnersley Cl B98...... 71 E3
Kinnersley Rd WR14... 138 C6
Kinnerton Cres B29..... 9 F2
Kinord Cl WR5........ 128 C6
Kinsey Gr B14......... 20 F4
KINSHAM 185 A3
Kinsham La GL20...... 185 C5
Kinthall La WR15...... 77 B6
Kintore Croft B32...... 18 B7
Kintyre Cl B45......... 17 E1
KINVER 3 F4
Kinver Ave DY11....... 27 A1
Kinverdale DY11....... 12 B6
Kinver Dr DY9......... 15 C7
Kinver Edge★ DY7 ..... 3 E2
Kinver Cl DY11........ 13 B7
Kinver Leisure Ctr DY7.. 4 A5
Kinver Rd
  Birmingham B31 ..... 19 D2
  Enville DY7.......... 3 E8
Kipling Cl
  Malvern WR14....... 139 A2
  Worcester WR3....... 115 C6
Kipling Rd B30........ 19 C4
Kipling Wlk **3** DY10.... 28 B6
Kirby Gdns WR4...... 116 A6
Kirkstone Ct DY5....... 6 B8
Kirkstone Dr WR4..... 115 F4
Kirkstone Way DY5...... 6 B8
Kirkwall Rd B32....... 9 D1
Kitchener Rd CV37 .... 151 E4
Kitebrook Cl B98...... 71 E4
Kite La B97........... 70 A5
Kitswell Gdns B32..... 18 A8
Kittiwake Dr
  Brierley Hill DY5 ...... 6 D7
  Kidderminster DY10.. 28 B3
KITWELL............ 18 A7
Kitwell La B32......... 18 A8
Kitwell Prim Sch B32 ... 18 A7
Knapp Pl WR5........ 128 E6
Knapp The WR11..... 162 D3
Knapp Way WR14..... 138 F5
Knaresdale Cl DY5..... 6 C8
Knight Ho B13........ 21 D7
KNIGHTON 121 D6
KNIGHTON ON TEME ... 57 A8
Knighton Rd B31...... 19 C4
Knight Rd DY11....... 12 C3
Knightsford Cl B97..... 69 F2
Knight St WR14....... 114 F2
Knights Way GL20..... 197 A6
KNIGHTWICK 111 B3
Knoll La B14.......... 153 C6
Knoll Sch The DY11.... 27 A7
Knoll The B32......... 9 C1
Knottesford Cl B80..... 90 C3
Knotts Ave WR4....... 116 C4
Knowesley Cl B60..... 49 B2
Knowle Cl
  Birmingham B45 ..... 33 D7
  Redditch B98......... 71 C6
KNOWLE FIELDS 121 E8
Knoyle Ct **1** DY8...... 5 E6

Knutswood Cl B13 . . . . 21 D7
Kohima Dr
  Stourbridge DY8 . . . . 5 E5
  Worcester Norton WR5 . . 128 F4
Kylemilne Way WR13 . . 44 C3
Kyles Way B32 . . . . 18 B7
KYRE 75 F3
KYRE GREEN 75 C2
Kyre Park Gdns★ WR15 . . 75 F3
Kyreside WR15 . . . . 55 F5
KYREWOOD 56 B4
Kyrewood Rd WR15 . . . . . 55 F5

L

Labrador Rd 5 WR2 . . 127 F6
Laburnum Cl
  Hollywood B47 . . . . 36 A5
  Kinver DY7 . . . . .3 F5
  Redditch B98 . . . . 70 E2
  Stourbridge DY8 . . . . 5 E1
Laburnum Dr WR11 . . . . 161 F1
Laburnum Gr
  Bromsgrove B61 . . . . 48 F4
  Kidderminster DY11 . . . . . 27 B8
Laburnum Rd
  Birmingham B30 . . . . 19 F8
  Worcester WR4 . . . . 115 E4
  Stourbridge DY8 . . . . 5 E7
Laburnum Trees B47 . . . 35 F7
Laburnum Way B31 . . . . 19 A1
Laburnum Wlk
  Malvern WR14 . . . . 138 F3
  Upton upon Severn WR8 . 169 C5
Lacon Childe Sch DY14 . . 22 C4
Lacon Cl DY14 . . . . 22 B4
Ladbrook Cl B98 . . . . 89 E7
Lady Bank B32 . . . . 18 B7
Lady Bracknell Mews B31 19 C4
Ladygo Cl WR2 . . . . 101 C2
Lady Grey's Wlk DY8 . . . . 5 D5
Ladygrove Cl B98 . . . . . . 90 A8
Lady Harriet's La B98 . . 70 F4
Ladypool Cl B62 . . . . 8 C4
Ladysmith Rd B63 . . . . . . 7 C6
LADYWOOD 103 A7
Ladywood Rd
  Besford WR8 . . . . 157 B7
  Martin Hussingtree WR3 . . 103 A3
Lahn Dr WR9 . . . . 103 D8
Lakedown Cl B14 . . . . . . 20 E1
Lakefield B31 . . . . 18 F4
Lakehouse Dr B38 . . . . . 19 D3
Laker Cl DY8 . . . . 6 A7
Lakes Cl DY11 . . . . 27 C7
Lakes Ct DY12 . . . . 25 F3
LAKESIDE 71 B3
Lakeside B97 . . . . 69 D7
Lakeside Ct DY5 . . . . .6 B8
Lakeside Ctre The B30 . . 20 A4
Lakeside Ind Est B98 . . . 71 B3
Lakes Rd The DY12 . . . . 25 F3
Lakes Sta The B94 . . . . . 53 F8
LAKES THE 25 F4
Lake View Cl B30 . . . . . . 19 E5
Lakewood Dr B45 . . . . . . 18 B1
Lamb Bank WR14 . . . . . . 138 D3
Lambert Rd WR2 . . . . . . 114 F2
Lambourne Ave WR14 . . 139 A5
Lambourne Cl 1 B50 . . 136 D5
Lambourne Cres WR2 . . 114 E6
Lambourne Dr 2 DY12 . . 25 F4
Lambourne Orch WR6 . . 82 B3
Lambourne Way DY5 . . . .6 B8
Lambscote Cl B90 . . . . . . 21 C2
Lamont Ave B32 . . . . .9 F3
Lampitt La GL20 . . . . . . 172 A3
Lancaster Ave B45 . . . . . 33 A8
Lancaster Cl
  Birmingham B30 . . . . 20 A6
  Upper Ham WR8 . . . . . . 169 D4
Lancaster Rd 3 DY12 . . 25 F3
Lancelot Ho DY10 . . . . . . 28 C8
Lancelott Ct 8 WR10 . . 144 C1
Lanchester Rd B38 . . . . . 20 A1
Lancing Cl 3 WR5 . . . . . 128 E8
Lander Cl B45 . . . . 33 A6
Land Oak Dr DY10 . . . . . 28 B7
Landor Rd B98 . . . . 71 A1
Landsdowne St 2 WR1 . 115 B4
Landsgate DY8 . . . . 6 A1
Lanescourt Cl GL20 . . . . 196 F6
Lane's End WR5 . . . . 141 B7
Lanesfield Pk WR11 . . . . 161 E6
Lane The
  Bricklehampton WR10 . . 159 E1
  Broadway WR12 . . . . . . 190 D7
  Buckland WR12 . . . . 189 F5
  Elmley Castle WR10 . . . 159 E1
  Strensham WR8 . . . . . . 171 A6
Langdale Cl WR4 . . . . . . 116 A6
Langdale Dr WR4 . . . . . . 115 F5
Langdale Rd
  3 Stourport-on-Severn
    DY13 . . . . 43 D1
  10 Worcester WR1 . . . . 115 A5
Langdale Way DY9 . . . . . . 6 D1
Langland Ave WR14 . . . . 139 C1
Langland Cl WR14 . . . . . 139 C1
Langland Rd DY14 . . . . . 22 C5
Langley Cl
  Redditch B98 . . . . 71 D1
  6 Worcester WR4 . . . . 114 E5
Langley Rd 4 WR9 . . . . 85 A1
Langleys Rd B29 . . . . . . 19 E8
Langstone Rd B14 . . . . . 21 B3
Lankets The WR11 . . . . . 162 E1

Lannacombe Rd B31 . . . 33 E6
Lansbury Gn B64 . . . . . . .8 B8
Lansbury Rd B64 . . . . . . .8 B8
Lansdown Cl WR14 . . . . 139 B1
Lansdowne Cres
  Malvern WR14 . . . . 139 A1
  Studley B80 . . . . 90 D3
  Worcester WR3 . . . . 115 C4
Lansdowne Cres La 6
    WR3 . . . . 115 D4
Lansdowne Ct DY9 . . . . . 6 C1
Lansdowne Ho WR14 . . 139 A1
Lansdowne Rd
  Halesowen, Hasbury B63 . . 7 D2
  Malvern WR14 . . . . 138 F4
  Studley B80 . . . . 90 D3
  9 Worcester WR1 . . . . 115 B4
Lansdowne Rise 1 WR3 . 115 C4
Lansdowne Row WR14 . 139 A1
Lansdowne Terr
  Malvern WR14 . . . . 139 A1
  4 Rainbow Hill WR1 . . . 115 C4
Lansdowne Wlk 1 WR3 . 115 D4
Lansdown Gn DY11 . . . . 27 C5
LAPAL 8 F3
Lapal Cl WR2 . . . . 114 F2
Lapal La B62 . . . . 9 A2
Lapal Lane N B62 . . . . . . .8 E3
Lapal Lane S B32, B62 . . .8 F2
Lapal Prim Sch B62 . . . . .8 F4
Lappath Ho B32 . . . . 18 D8
Lapwing Cl
  Kidderminster DY10 . . . . 28 B1
  Northway GL20 . . . . 184 D1
Lapworth Cl B98 . . . . . . 89 F7
Larch Cl DY7 . . . . 4 C3
Larch Dr B31 . . . . 18 C1
Larches Cottage Gdns
    DY11 . . . . 27 C3
Larches La WR11 . . . . . . 27 D4
Larches The WR9 . . . . . . 84 F2
Larchfield Cl WR14 . . . . 138 E4
Larch Ho DY8 . . . . 5 C6
Larchmere Dr
  Birmingham B28 . . . . 21 F8
  Bromsgrove B61 . . . . 48 E3
Larch Rd
  11 Evesham WR11 . . . . . 161 F2
  Worcester WR4 . . . . 115 D4
Larford Wlk DY13 . . . . . 43 F1
Lark Cl B14 . . . . 21 A2
Larkfield Rd B98 . . . . . . 71 A1
Larkhill DY10 . . . . 27 E7
Lark Hill WR5 . . . . 115 C1
Larkhill Rd DY8 . . . . 5 C4
Lark Hill Rd WR5 . . . . . . 115 E1
Larkhill Wlk B14 . . . . . . 20 D1
Larksfield Mews DY5 . . . . 6 C7
Larkspur Ct B62 . . . . .8 F7
Larkspur Cl WR11 . . . . . 161 C1
Larkspur Rd 8 WR5 . . . 128 D5
Larks Rise DY14 . . . . 22 B4
Lashbrooke Ho B45 . . . . 32 F7
Laslett St WR3 . . . . 115 D4
Lassington Cl B98 . . . . . . 71 E4
Latchford Cl WR14 . . . . . 71 E6
Latimer Rd B48 . . . . 51 A5
Laugherne Brook Nature
  Reserve★ WR2 . . . . . . 114 E2
Laugherne Rd WR2 . . . . 114 F3
LAUGHERN HILL 99 E2
Laughton Cl B31 . . . . . . 34 B7
Launceston Pl 11 WR4 . 116 C6
Launde The B28 . . . . 21 E3
Laurel Ave
  4 Evesham WR11 . . . . . 161 F2
  9 Walton Cardiff GL20 . 197 A4
Laurel Bank Mews B60 . 49 F4
Laurel Cl
  Drakes Broughton WR10 . 143 F6
  Redditch B98 . . . . 70 E2
Laurel Gdns B45 . . . . . . 50 E8
Laurel Gr
  Birmingham B30 . . . . 19 E6
  Bromsgrove B61 . . . . 48 F4
Laurel La B63 . . . . .8 B3
Laurel Rd
  Birmingham, King's Norton
    B30 . . . . 20 A4
  Worcester WR4 . . . . 115 C5
Laurels Ave WR11 . . . . . 162 B8
Laurels Rd WR11 . . . . . . 162 B8
Laurels The
  Birch Acre B47 . . . . 52 F8
  Birmingham B68 . . . . .9 B6
  Portway B47 . . . . 52 F8
Laurel Wood Cl 6 WR9 . 104 A8
Laurel Wood Rd WR9 . . 104 A8
Laurence Ct B31 . . . . . . 19 B5
Lavender Ho B38 . . . . . . 34 F8
Lavender La WR9 . . . . . . 5 D3
Lavender Rd WR3 . . . . . 115 A6
Lavender Wlk
  Evesham WR11 . . . . 175 C8
  Malvern WR14 . . . . 153 C7
LAVERTON 189 E3
Lavinia Rd B62 . . . . .8 E3
Lawford Gr B90 . . . . 21 D2
Lawley The B63 . . . . 7 D1
Lawn Ave DY8 . . . . 5 E4
Lawnsdown Rd DY5 . . . . .6 F2
Lawnside WR14 . . . . 153 A8
Lawn St DY8 . . . . .5 E4
Lawns The B47 . . . . 52 F7
Lawrence Ct 6 B68 . . . . .9 B8
Lawrence St WR9 . . . . . . 6 C6
Lawson Cl WR8 . . . . 169 D4
Lax La DY12 . . . . 26 B3

Laxton Ave WR2 . . . . . . 114 E5
Laxton Cl WR7 . . . . 117 F4
Laxton Dr 3 DY12 . . . . 25 F4
Layamon Wlk DY13 . . . . 43 F2
Laylocks La WR2 . . . . . . 113 F4
Layton Ave WR14 . . . . . 139 B3
Lazy Hill B38 . . . . 20 B2
Lazy La WR10 . . . . 146 A1
Lea Bank Ave DY11 . . . . 27 B5
Leabank Dr WR3 . . . . . . 102 A1
Lea Castle Cl DY10 . . . . 12 F1
Lea Castle Dr DY10 . . . . 13 C2
Leach Green La B45 . . . . 33 B6
Leach Heath La B45 . . . . 33 A7
Lea Cl WR3 . . . . 102 B1
Lea Croft Rd B97 . . . . . . 89 D5
Lea Cswy The DY11 . . . . 27 A4
Leadbetter Dr B61 . . . . . 48 D2
Leadon Rd WR14 . . . . . . 153 D7
LEA END 34 F3
Lea End La B48 . . . . 34 D3
Leafield Gdns B62 . . . . . .8 D8
Lea Green Dr B47 . . . . . . 36 C4
Lea Green La B47 . . . . . . 36 C5
Lea Hill Cl WR14 . . . . . . 138 F2
Leaholme Gdns DY9 . . . . .6 B2
Lea House Rd B30 . . . . . 20 A7
Leamington Rd WR12 . . 177 D2
Leander Gdns B14 . . . . . 20 F5
Leander Rd DY9 . . . . .6 F4
Lea Park Rise B61 . . . . . 48 F5
Leasowe Cl 5 WR2 . . . 114 D1
Leasowe Rd B45 . . . . . . 32 F8
Leasowes DY14 . . . . 40 B7
Leasowes Com Coll B62 . .8 E6
Leasowes Ct
  Halesowen B63 . . . . .7 F3
  9 Hasbury B63 . . . . 8 A3
Leasowes La B62 . . . . 8 D4
Leasowes Rd WR11 . . . . 162 B8
Lea St DY10 . . . . 27 F6
Lea The
  Alveley WV15 . . . . 1 C6
  Kidderminster DY11 . . . . . 27 A6
  Throckmorton WR10 . . . 145 E8
Lea Vale Rd DY8 . . . . . . .5 F3
Lea View DY14 . . . . 22 B4
Lea Wlk B45 . . . . 32 F8
Lea Wood Gr DY11 . . . . 27 A5
Lea Yield Cl B30 . . . . 20 A7
Lechlade Cl B98 . . . . 71 B7
Lechmere Cres
  Malvern WR14 . . . . 139 A5
  Worcester WR2 . . . . 114 E5
Leckhampton Cl
  Crabbs Cross B97 . . . . . . 89 E6
  Worcester WR4 . . . . 116 A4
Ledbury Cl B98 . . . . 71 F2
Ledbury Ho B97 . . . . 70 B4
Ledsam Gr B32 . . . . .9 F6
Ledwych Cl WR9 . . . . . . 84 D3
Ledwych Gdns WR9 . . . . 84 E3
Ledwych Rd 1 WR9 . . . 84 E3
Leebank Rd B63 . . . . .7 E2
Leeds Ave WR4 . . . . 116 C6
Lee Rd
  Cradley Heath B64 . . . . . .7 F8
  Hollywood B47 . . . . 36 A7
  Northway GL20 . . . . 197 E8
Lees The WR14 . . . . 152 F6
Legion Rd B45 . . . . 32 E7
Leicester Cl WR11 . . . . . 161 D5
Leicester St 5 WR1 . . . 115 B4
Leicester Twr★ WR11 . . 161 C8
LEIGH 126 A7
Leigh & Bransford Prim Sch
  WR13 . . . . 126 A7
Leigh Court Barn★ WR6 126 A7
Leigh Gr WR9 . . . . 84 E4
LEIGH SINTON 125 F2
Leigh Sinton Rd
  Leigh WR13 . . . . 126 A1
  Malvern WR14 . . . . 125 F1
Leith Gr B38 . . . . 34 E8
LEM HILL 24 A2
Lench Cl B97 . . . . 70 A5
Lenchville DY10 . . . . 13 A1
Lenwade Rd B68 . . . . . . .9 D8
Leominster Ct B45 . . . . . 32 F8
Leominster Wlk B45 . . . 32 F8
Leonard Ave WR10 . . . . 13 A1
Leonard Rd DY8 . . . . 5 C5
Leopard Rise WR5 . . . . . 116 B3
Leslie Ave WR3 . . . . 102 A1
Leswell Gr DY10 . . . . . . 27 F6
Leswell La DY10 . . . . . . 27 F6
Leswell St DY10 . . . . . . 27 F6
Leven Dr WR5 . . . . 128 E6
Lewes Gdns WR4 . . . . . . 116 C6
Lewis Cl WR10 . . . . 143 F6
Lewis Rd
  Birmingham, Brandhall B68 . .9 B7
  Birmingham, Stirchley B30 . 20 C7
  Stourbridge DY9 . . . . 6 D5
Lewkner Almshouses The
  B48 . . . . 51 A5
Lexington Cl 4 GL20 . . 197 A4
Lexington Gn DY5 . . . . . . .6 F2
Leybrook Rd B45 . . . . . . 33 B8
Leycester Cl B31 . . . . . . 34 A7

Leycroft 4 WR9 . . . . . . 85 B1
Leydon Croft B38 . . . . . 20 B2
Ley Hill Farm Rd B31 . . 18 E5
Ley Hill Jun & Inf Sch
  B31 . . . . 18 E5
Leylan Croft B13 . . . . . . 21 D7
Leyman Cl B14 . . . . 21 C4
Ley Orch WR12 . . . . 177 F4
Leys Cl
  Hinton on the Green
    WR11 . . . . 175 A5
  Stourbridge DY9 . . . . 6 C2
Leysfield WR11 . . . . 147 F2
Leys Rd WR11 . . . . 134 D1
LEYSTERS 73 E4
Leysters Cl WR11 . . . . . 71 E3
Leys The
  Bidford-on-Avon B50 . . . 136 E5
  Birmingham B31 . . . . 19 B5
  Evesham WR11 . . . . 161 E4
Leys Wlk 4 WR11 . . . . . 161 E4
Leyton Cl DY5 . . . . .6 D8
LIBBERY 118 E3
Library Way B45 . . . . . . 32 F7
Lichen Gdns B38 . . . . . . 34 D7
Lichfield Ave
  Evesham WR11 . . . . 161 F4
  Kidderminster DY11 . . . . . 26 F6
  Worcester WR5 . . . . 116 A2
Lichfield Ct B90 . . . . 21 D2
Lichfield St DY13 . . . . . . 44 A3
LICKEY 33 A3
Lickey Coppice B45 . . . . 33 C4
LICKEY END 49 C6
Lickey End Fst Sch B60 . 49 C6
Lickey Gr DY11 . . . . 27 B2
Lickey Grange B60 . . . . . 32 E1
Lickey Grange Dr B60 . . 32 E1
Lickey Hills Ctry Pk & Visitor
  Ctr★ B45 . . . . 33 A3
Lickey Hills Prim Sch B45 32 F3
Lickey Rd
  Birmingham B45 . . . . 33 C6
  Stourbridge DY8 . . . . 6 B6
Lickey Rock B60 . . . . . . 32 D1
Lickey Sq B45 . . . . 33 A2
LICKHILL 43 E5
Lickhill Fst Sch DY13 . . 43 D5
Lickhill Rd DY13 . . . . . . 43 F4
Lickhill Road N DY13 . . 43 D6
Liddiard Ct DY8 . . . . .5 E6
LIFFORD 20 B5
Lifford Cl B14 . . . . 20 C4
Lifford Gdns WR12 . . . . 190 C7
Lifford La B30 . . . . 20 B4
Lightning Way B31 . . . . 34 B7
Lightoak Cl B97 . . . . 89 C6
Lightwood La WR6 . . . . 113 D3
Lightwoods Hill B67 . . . .9 E8
Lightwoods Prim Sch B68 . 9 D8
Lightwoods Rd DY9 . . . . .6 C1
Lilac Ave WR4 . . . . 115 E4
Lilac Cl
  Droitwich WR9 . . . . 104 A8
  Evesham WR11 . . . . 161 B2
  Redditch B98 . . . . 70 E2
  Upton upon Severn WR8 . 169 C5
Lilac Gr 17 DY13 . . . . . . 43 E4
Lilac Way B62 . . . . .8 F8
Lilleshall Cl B98 . . . . 71 E3
Lilley Green Rd B48 . . . . 52 D5
Lilley La B31 . . . . 34 B8
Lilleys Alley 12 GL20 . . 196 E6
Lilycroft La B38 . . . . 35 A7
Lily Green La B97 . . . . . . 70 A4
Limbrick Cl B90 . . . . 21 F2
Lime Ave WR4 . . . . 115 E6
Lime Cl
  Alveley WV15 . . . . 1 D6
  Hollywood B47 . . . . 36 A5
Lime Ct DY10 . . . . 28 A4
Lime Gr
  Bromsgrove B61 . . . . 48 F4
  Kinver DY7 . . . . 4 C3
  Welland WR13 . . . . 167 C5
Lime Kiln Cl B38 . . . . . . 34 D7
Limekiln La B14 . . . . 21 A4
Lime Rd 2 GL20 . . . . . . 197 A3
Lime St
  Eldersfield GL19 . . . . . . 193 F3
  Evesham WR11 . . . . 161 E4
Limes The WR5 . . . . 141 D8
LIME STREET 194 A1
Lime Tree Ave
  Broadway WR12 . . . . . . 177 E1
  Malvern WR14 . . . . 152 E4
Lime Tree Cres B97 . . . . 70 B4
Lime Tree Gr B31 . . . . . . 19 C2
Lime Tree Wlk DY13 . . . 43 E5
Lincoln Cl GL20 . . . . 196 D4
Lincoln Cres DY11 . . . . . 26 F6
Lincoln Ct 9 B29 . . . . . . 19 C7
Lincoln Gn 2 WR5 . . . . 115 F1
Lincoln Gn La GL20 . . . 196 D4
Lincoln Rd B61 . . . . 48 E4
LINCOMB 63 C6
Lincomb La DY13 . . . . . 63 D7
Lindale Cres DY5 . . . . . . .6 B6
Linden Ave
  Halesowen B62 . . . . 8 E7
  Kidderminster DY10 . . . . . 28 A7
  5 Stourport-on-Severn
    DY13 . . . . 43 E1
Linden Cl 10 WR11 . . . 161 F2
Linden Dr DY8 . . . . 6 A3
Linden Gdns DY10 . . . . . 28 A7
Linden Glade B63 . . . . . . 8 A4
Linden Gr DY10 . . . . 28 A7

Linden Rd
  Birmingham B30 . . . . 19 E7
  6 Worcester WR4 . . . . 115 F5
Lindens The B32 . . . . . . .9 E7
Lindford Way B38 . . . . . 20 B2
LINDRIDGE 58 D7
Lindridge CE Prim Sch
  WR15 . . . . 58 D6
Lindridge Cl B98 . . . . . . 72 A3
Lindridge Rd B90 . . . . . . 21 F1
Lindsey Ave
  Birmingham B31 . . . . 19 C4
  Evesham WR11 . . . . 161 E3
Lindsworth App B30 . . . 20 C3
Lindsworth Ct 2 B30 . . 20 C3
Lindsworth Rd B30 . . . . 20 C3
Lindsworth Sch (South)
  B30 . . . . 20 C3
Lineage Ct WR15 . . . . . . 55 E6
LINEHOLT 63 D1
Lineholt Cl B98 . . . . 90 A6
LINEHOLT COMMON . . 63 E3
Lineholt La WR9 . . . . . . 63 E1
Linehouse La
  Catshill B60 . . . . 49 D8
  Lower Marlbrook B60 . . . . 32 D1
Lingen Cl B98 . . . . 71 E3
Lingfield Rd
  Bewdley DY12 . . . . 26 D5
  Evesham WR11 . . . . 161 C2
Lingfield Wlk B61 . . . . . . 32 B1
Lingmell Cl 9 WR4 . . . 116 B6
Link Bus Ctr WR14 . . . . 139 A4
Linkelm Cl 1 WR2 . . . . 127 C4
LINKEND 194 D2
Linkend Rd GL19 . . . . . . 194 E3
Link Rd
  Evesham WR11 . . . . 161 E1
  Tewkesbury GL20 . . . . . 196 F5
Links Cres B68 . . . . .9 B8
Links Dr
  Birmingham B45 . . . . 33 A5
  Stourbridge DY8 . . . . 5 E2
Links Rd
  Birmingham, Brandhall B68 . . 9 B8
  Birmingham, Highter's Heath
    B14 . . . . 21 A1
Links The DY10 . . . . 28 A4
Links View B62 . . . . .8 D4
Linksview Cres WR5 . . . 116 A2
Link Terr WR14 . . . . 138 F2
Link Way WR14 . . . . 139 A4
Linkwood Ind Est DY8 . . .5 F6
Linley Cl WR3 . . . . 102 A1
Linley Gr B14 . . . . 20 C6
LINLEY GREEN 123 A7
Linnet Cl
  Birmingham B30 . . . . 19 E8
  Halesowen B62 . . . . 8 B6
Linnet Rise DY10 . . . . . . 27 F1
Linpole Wlk B14 . . . . . . 20 D2
LINTHURST 50 A6
Linthurst Newtown B60 . 50 B5
Linthurst Rd B45, B60 . . 50 A7
Lint Mdw B47 . . . . 36 B7
Linton Cl
  Halesowen B63 . . . . .7 D5
  Redditch B98 . . . . 71 F2
Linton Mews B98 . . . . . . 71 F2
Lion Ct WR1 . . . . 115 C3
Lionfields Cl DY10 . . . . . 13 A5
Lionfields Rd DY10 . . . . 13 A4
Lion Hill DY13 . . . . 44 A3
Lion La DY14 . . . . 22 D4
Lion Pas DY8 . . . . .5 F5
Lion Sq DY10 . . . . 27 E6
Lion St
  Kidderminster DY10 . . . . . 27 E6
  Stourbridge DY8 . . . . .5 F5
Lisko Cl DY5 . . . . .6 A8
Lisle Ave DY11 . . . . 27 D3
Lisle & Foley Ind Est
  DY11 . . . . 27 D3
Lismore Cl B45 . . . . 17 E1
Lismore Gn 11 WR5 . . . 128 E6
Lister Ave WR4 . . . . 116 C3
Lister Rd DY11 . . . . 27 B4
Listowel Rd B14 . . . . . . 20 D6
Little Acre B97 . . . . 89 D6
Little Battenton WR9 . . . 63 D1
LITTLE BECKFORD 186 D2
Little Boughton St WR2 . 114 E1
Little Chestnut St 2
  WR1 . . . . 115 C4
LITTLE COMBERTON . . 159 B3
Little Cornbow B63 . . . . .8 B3
Littlecote Croft 1 B14 . . 21 A3
LITTLE EASTBURY 114 D7
Little Forge Rd B98 . . . . 90 C8
Little Gn
  Broadwas WR6 . . . . 112 C3
  Redmarley D'abitot GL19 . 192 A4
Little Grebe Rd DY10 . . . 28 B3
Little Hayes DY11 . . . . . 12 C3
Little Heath La B60 . . . . 49 D6
LITTLE HEREFORD 54 C6
Little Hill WR9 . . . . 84 C2
Littlehill Cres 3 B64 . . . .7 C7
Little Hill Ct WR9 . . . . . 84 D2
Little Hill Gn WR9 . . . . . 84 D2
Little Hill Rd B38 . . . . . . 20 A1
Little Hill Way B32 . . . . . 9 D2
LITTLE INKBERROW . . 120 C8
LITTLE LONDON 38 A3
Little London 8 WR1 . . 115 B4

LITTLE MALVERN 166 E6
Littlemead Ave B31 ...... 19 C1
Little Meadow Croft B31 .. 18 F4
Littlemead Rd B90 .... 36 E8
Little Mus-The Merchants
House★ GL20 .... 196 E6
Little Orch WR9 .... 84 E2
Littleover Ave B28 .... 21 F6
Little Park St **15** WR5 ... 115 C2
Little Pennyrope WR10 .. 158 C7
Little Piece **7** WR4 ..... 116 B5
Little Pk
  Birmingham B32 .... 9 B4
  Chawson WR9 .... 84 D2
Little Priest La **5** WR10 . 158 D8
Little Rd WR11 .... 163 E8
Littleshaw Croft B47 ..... 36 C4
Littleshaw La B47 .... 36 C4
Little Southfield St **1**
  WR1 .... 115 C3
Littletons Sch The WR11 . 148 F1
LITTLE WELLAND 167 F1
LITTLE WITLEY 81 A4
Littlewood Gn B80 .... 90 D3
LITTLEWOOD GREEN 90 D2
Little Woods B97 .... 89 E6
LITTLEWORTH
  Feckenham 88 B1
  Norton Juxta Kempsey .. 129 D1
Littleworth La B96 .... 88 B1
Littleworth St WR11 ..... 161 D4
Littleworth Wlk **9**
  WR11 .... 161 D4
Liverpool Rd WR5 .... 115 F1
Livingstone Rd B14 ...... 20 E6
Livingstone St **7** WR5 .. 128 E8
Llangorse Cl DY13 .... 43 E7
Llewellyn Cl DY13 .... 63 C8
Lloyd Cl WR11 .... 147 E3
Lloyds Rd B62 .... 8 C8
Load St DY12 .... 26 B3
Lobelia Cl
  Kidderminster DY11 ..... 12 C1
  Worcester WR5 .... 128 D5
Lock Cl B97 .... 70 A4
Lockeridge La WR8 ...... 168 B3
Lockington Croft B62 ...... 8 E4
Lock Keepers Reach B48 . 50 F6
Lockside Dr DY7 .... 4 B4
Lock St **14** WR5 .... 115 C2
Lockton Rd B30 .... 20 C8
Lock View **7** WR11 .... 161 E4
Lockwood Rd B31 .... 18 F4
Lockyear Cl WR13 .... 152 B1
Lodge Bank WR9 .... 63 C3
Lodge Cl
  Bewdley DY12 .... 26 D4
  Halesowen B62 .... 8 E8
  Worcester WR2 .... 114 E4
Lodge Cres DY9 .... 15 B5
Lodge Croft B31 .... 18 E6
Lodge Dr WR14 .... 138 F2
Lodgefield Rd B62 .... 8 B7
Lodge Forge Trad Est B64 . 7 C7
Lodge Hill WR8 .... 157 D6
LODGE PARK 70 F2
Lodge Pool Dr B98 ...... 70 F1
Lodge Rd
  Redditch B98 .... 70 E3
  5 Stourport-on-Severn
  DY13 .... 44 A3
Lofthouse Cres B31 ..... 18 F3
Lofthouse Gr B31 .... 18 F3
Loftus Cl B29 .... 18 F8
Lomaine Dr B30 .... 19 E4
Lomas Dr B31 .... 18 E3
Lombard St DY13 .... 44 A3
Lombardy Croft **3** B62 .. 9 A6
London La
  Bromsgrove B60 .... 68 F7
  Tardebigge B60 .... 69 A6
  2 Upton upon Severn
  WR8 .... 169 C6
London Rd WR5 .... 115 D1
LONG BANK 25 C1
Long Bank
  Bewdley DY12 .... 25 C1
  Westlands WR9 .... 84 E6
Longboat La DY13 ...... 44 A4
Longborough Cl B97 .... 89 B6
Longbow Rd B29 .... 18 F7
LONGBRIDGE 33 D7
Longbridge La B31 ..... 33 E8
Longbridge Sta B31 .... 33 E8
Long Cl DY9 .... 15 A4
Long Compton Dr DY9 .. 15 A6
Longcroft The B63 .... 7 E4
Longdales Rd B38 ...... 34 E7
LONGDON 181 F5
Longdon Cl B98 .... 90 B7
LONGDON HEATH 168 F2
Longdon Hill
  Evesham WR11 .... 162 B1
  Wickhamford WR11 .... 176 D8
LONGDON HILL END 168 C2
Long Eights GL20 ...... 184 D1
Longfellow Cl B97 ...... 89 C7
Longfellow Gn DY10 .... 28 C6
Longfellow Rd
  Birmingham B30 .... 19 D4
  Worcester WR3 .... 115 C6
Longfield WR8 .... 169 C5
Longfield B28 .... 21 F6

Longfield Rd
  Birmingham B31 .... 18 E8
  Stourbridge DY9 .... 6 D5
Longford Cl
  Bidford-on-Avon B50 .. 136 F5
  Birmingham B32 .... 18 A7
LONG GREEN 195 A8
Long Green Cl B31 ..... 19 A2
Longham Croft B32 ...... 9 F4
Longheadland WR9 ..... 83 A5
Long Hedges WR10 .... 158 B7
Longhope Cl B98 .... 72 B4
Longhurst Croft B31 .... 34 B7
Long Hyde Rd WR11 ... 148 E1
Long Innage B63 .... 7 B6
Long La
  Halesowen B62 .... 8 E8
  Peopleton WR10 ...... 131 F1
  Pinvin WR10 .... 132 A1
  Throckmorton WR10 .. 145 B8
Longlands Cl **2** B38 .. 34 C8
Longlands Rd B62 .... 8 E3
Longlands The B45 ..... 50 D7
Long Leasow B29 ...... 19 B7
LONGLEY GREEN 124 C1
LONG MARSTON 151 C6
Long Marston Rd
  Mickleton GL55 ...... 165 C7
  Pebworth CV37 ...... 150 F3
  Welford-on-Avon CV37 . 151 C8
Longmeadow Dr **5** WR5 55 F6
Longmeadow Gr B31 ... 34 A6
Long Meadow Rd B60 .. 49 C6
Longmoor Cl B97 ...... 70 B5
Longmoor Rd B63 .... 7 E3
Longmore Hill DY13 .... 62 F6
Long Mynd B63 .... 7 D1
Longmynd Rd B31 ..... 18 F6
Longmynd Way DY13 ... 43 D1
Long Nuke Rd B31 .... 18 E7
Longridge Rd WR14 ... 153 B5
Long Saw Dr B31 ..... 18 D1
Long Sling WR9 .... 84 D1
Longtown Rd **7** GL20 . 197 A4
Longwill Specl Sch B31 . 19 A5
Long Wood B30 .... 19 E5
Longwood Rd B45 ...... 33 A7
Lord Austin Dr B60 .... 32 E1
Lord's Heath **4** WR4 . 116 B5
Lords La B80 .... 90 E2
Lordswood Cl B97 ..... 69 F2
Lorne Gr DY10 .... 28 A6
Lorne St
  Kidderminster DY10 ... 28 A5
  Stourport-on-Severn DY13 . 44 A5
Lorrainer Ave DY5 ...... 6 A8
Loughmill Rd WR10 ... 144 C1
Loughton Gr B63 .... 7 F4
Louise Croft B14 ...... 20 E2
Lovage Rd B98 .... 71 F6
Love La
  Cleobury Mortimer DY14 . 22 C4
  Hollywood B47 .... 35 F7
  Stourbridge, Lye DY9 ... 6 F5
  Stourbridge, Old Swinford
  DY8 .... 6 A3
Lovell Cl B29 .... 19 B6
Love Lyne
  Feckenham B97 .... 88 F6
  Redditch B97 .... 88 F6
Love's Gr WR1 .... 115 B4
Lovett Pl WR4 .... 116 C4
Lovett Rd WR9 .... 84 D7
Lovington La WR2 .... 114 B7
Lowans Hill Cotts B97 .. 70 C5
Lowans Hill View B97 .. 70 C4
LOWBANDS 192 E3
Lowbrook La B90 ..... 36 D4
Lowe La
  Alveley WV15 .... 1 D2
  Wolverley & Cookley DY11 . 12 B2
Lowell St WR1 .... 115 C4
LOWER BACH 92 A7
Lower Barbourne Terr **8**
  WR1 .... 115 B3
Lower Beeches Rd B31 . 18 C2
LOWER BENTLEY 87 E8
Lower Bentley La B60 .. 68 F1
LOWER BROADHEATH ... 113 E5
Lower Bull Entry **5**
  WR1 .... 115 B2
Lower Chase Rd WR14 . 153 C8
Lower Chestnut St WR1 . 115 C4
Lower Cladswell La B49 . 108 F2
LOWER CLENT 15 D4
Lower Comm La B97 ... 70 B2
Lower Croft WR10 .... 160 B6
Lower Dingle WR14 ... 152 C8
Lower Dr WR8 .... 157 C7
Lower Ferry La WR2 ... 140 F7
Lower Field Terr WR5 .. 128 C8
Lower Gambolds La B60. 68 B6
Lower Gn WR12 ...... 190 C8
Lower Grinsty La B97 .. 89 A8
Lower High St
  Cradley Heath B64 ...... 7 C8
  Stourbridge DY8 .... 5 F6
Lower Higley Cl B32 ..... 9 E4
LOWER HOOK 168 B5
LOWER HOWSELL 139 B6
Lower Howsell Rd
  Leigh WR14 .... 126 A1
  Malvern WR14 .... 139 B6
LOWER ILLEY 17 D7
Lower Inhedge **5** DY14 . 22 D5
Lower Leys WR11 ..... 161 E4
Lower Lickhill Rd DY13 . 43 E5
LOWER LODE 196 C4

Lower Lode La GL20 ... 196 C4
LOWER MARLBROOK 32 C1
Lower Mdw WR9 ...... 84 D2
Lower Mill St **8** DY11 . 27 D6
Lower Montpelier Rd
  WR14 .... 138 C1
LOWER MOOR 145 E3
Lower Moor B30 ...... 19 E8
Lower Parklands DY11 .. 27 C5
Lower Pk DY12 .... 26 B3
Lower Priest La **6**
  WR10 .... 158 D8
Lower Quest Hills Rd
  WR14 .... 138 F4
Lower Rd WR14 ...... 138 C2
LOWER SAPEY 97 B5
Lower Shepley La B60 .. 49 E6
Lower St DY14 .... 22 D4
LOWER STRENSHAM ... 171 A6
Lower Teme Bsns Pk
  WR15 .... 55 D6
LOWER TOWN 102 E4
LOWER
  WESTMANCOTE 185 B7
Lower White Rd B32 .... 9 D5
LOWER WICK 127 F6
Lower Wilton Rd WR14 . 153 B8
LOWER WOLVERTON ... 130 F2
LOWER WYCHE 152 E5
Lower Wyche Rd WR14 . 152 E6
Lowesmoor WR1 ...... 115 C3
Lowesmoor Terr WR1 .. 115 C3
Lowes Moor Wharf WR1 115 C3
Loweswater Ho B38 .... 20 B1
Loweswater Rd DY13 ... 43 E7
Lowfield Cl B62 .... 9 A3
Lowfield La B97 .... 70 B5
Low Fold Cl **4** WR21 .. 114 D1
Lowhill La B45 .... 33 D6
Lowlands La B98 .... 71 D3
Lowndes Rd DY8 .... 5 E6
Low Rd WR11 .... 134 B4
Low Thatch B38 .... 34 E7
Loxley Ave
  Birmingham B14 .... 21 C3
  Solihull B90 .... 21 F1
Loxley Cl
  Birmingham B31 ...... 18 E8
  Redditch B98 .... 71 D6
Loynells Rd B45 .... 33 B7
Lucerne Ave WR14 .... 153 A5
Lucerne Cl **1** WR3 ... 115 A8
Lucy Baldwin Unit DY13 . 43 F5
Lucy Edwards Ct DY11 .. 27 C5
Ludford Rd B32 .... 9 A1
Ludgate Ave DY11 ..... 27 A4
Ludlow Ave WR4 ..... 116 B6
Ludlow Ho B13 .... 21 A6
Ludlow Rd
  Cleobury Mortimer DY14 . 22 A4
  Kidderminster DY10 .... 27 E3
  Redditch B97 .... 70 E3
Ludstone Rd B29 .... 9 F1
Lugano Rd WR3 .... 115 A8
LULSLEY 111 E4
Lulworth Cl B63 .... 7 C6
Lundy Row WR5 ...... 128 E6
Lunnon La WR9 .... 46 C2
Lunt Gr B32 .... 9 D5
Lupton Cl B60 .... 49 A1
Lusbridge Cl B63 .... 7 B4
LUTLEY 7 C3
Lutley Ave B63 .... 7 E4
Lutley Dr DY9 .... 6 C3
Lutley Gr B32 .... 9 B1
Lutley La B63 .... 7 C2
Lutley Mill Rd B63 ...... 7 E4
Lutley Prim Sch B63 .... 7 D1
Lutterworth Cl **3** WR4 . 115 F4
Lyall Gdns B45 .... 17 E1
Lychgate **19** WR1 .... 115 C2
Lychgate Ave DY9 ...... 6 C1
Lydate Rd B62 .... 8 F4
Lydbrook Covert **5** B38 . 34 E8
Lyddington Dr B62 ...... 8 B7
Lyde Gn B63 .... 7 B7
Lydes Rd WR14 ...... 153 C8
Lydford Terr **13** WR4 . 116 B6
Lydham Cl B98 .... 70 E5
LYDIATE ASH 32 C3
Lydiate Ash Rd B60 ... 32 C3
Lydiate Ave B31 ...... 18 D1
Lydney Cl B98 .... 71 D7
Lydney Gr B31 .... 18 F3
LYE 6 E6
Lye Ave B32 .... 9 A2
Lye Bsns Ctr DY9 .... 6 F6
Lye By-Pass DY9 .... 6 E6
Lye Close La B32 .... 9 A2
LYE HEAD 42 B7
Lye Sta DY9 .... 6 E6
Lye Valley Ind Est DY9 ... 6 F6
Lyf's La WR5 .... 141 B7
Lygon Bank WR14 .... 138 F2
Lygon Cl B98 .... 71 A5
Lygon Gr B32 .... 9 B3
Lynbrook Cl B47 ...... 36 A7
Lynch La
  Brimfield SY8 .... 54 B4
  Middleton on the Hill SY8 . 73 B8
Lyncourt Gr B32 .... 9 B6
Lynden Cl B61 .... 48 E3
Lyndenwood B97 ..... 70 A2
Lyndholm Rd DY10 .... 28 A6
Lyndhurst Dr DY10 .... 27 E8
Lyndon Cl B63 .... 7 F4
Lyndon Ho B31 .... 19 B3

Lyndon Rd B45 .... 32 E7
Lyndworth Rd B30 .... 20 C8
Lyneham Cl **5** WR4 . 115 F7
Lynfield Cl B38 .... 34 F7
Lynn Cl WR13 .... 125 F2
Lynval Rd DY5 .... 6 F7
Lynwood Cl WR11 .... 161 B4
Lynwood Dr DY10 .... 14 C2
Lynwood Way WR5 .... 33 A3
Lynworth La GL20 .... 183 F6
LYPPARD GRANGE 116 B4
Lyppard Grange Nature
  Reserve★ WR4 ...... 116 B4
Lyppard Grange Prim Sch
  WR4 .... 116 C4
Lysander Rd B45 ..... 18 A2
Lytham Cl DY8 .... 5 F2
Lyth La WR9 .... 63 B2
Lythwood Dr DY5 ...... 6 C8
Lyttelton Pl DY9 ..... 15 C6
Lyttelton Rd
  Bewdley DY12 .... 26 A4
  Droitwich WR9 .... 84 F1
  Stourbridge DY9 .... 5 D5
Lyttelton St **4** WR1 . 115 A5
Lyttleton Ave
  Bromsgrove B60 ...... 67 E7
  Halesowen B62 .... 8 E7
Lyttleton Ct WR9 ..... 85 A2
Lyttleton Ho B63 .... 8 A2
Lyttleton Rd WR10 ... 144 E4
Lyttleton Sq WR14 ... 139 A4
Lytton La B32 .... 9 F3

M

Maas Rd B31 .... 19 A4
Mabey Ave B98 .... 70 F5
MacArthur Rd B64 ...... 7 C8
McArthur Way **4** DY13 . 44 A4
MacAulay Rise WR14 .. 139 A2
McConnell Cl B60 ..... 68 B7
McCormick Ave **2** WR4 . 116 C3
McIntyre Rd WR2 .... 114 F2
MADELEY HEATH 31 E7
Madeley Rd
  Madeley Heath DY9 .... 31 D6
  Redditch B98 .... 71 F5
Madge Hill WR8 ...... 155 E5
Madinatul Uloom Al Islamiya
  Sch DY10 .... 28 D1
Madley Cl B45 .... 32 E8
MADRESFIELD 139 E4
Madresfield CE Prim Sch
  WR13 .... 139 E3
Madresfield Ct★ WR13 . 139 F3
Madresfield Dr B63 ..... 8 B2
Madresfield Rd WR13,
  WR14 .... 139 D1
Mafeking Villas B62 ..... 8 B7
Magnolia Cl
  Birmingham B29 ...... 19 A7
  Drakes Broughton WR10 . 143 F6
  9 Worcester WR5 .. 128 D5
Magpie Cl WR5 ...... 128 D5
Magpie Way WR10 .... 28 B2
Maiden Way B60 ..... 68 A6
Main Rd
  Kempsey WR5 .... 141 C5
  Wyre Piddle WR10 ... 145 B3
Main St
  Aldington WR11 ..... 162 C5
  Beckford GL20 ...... 186 D4
  Bishampton WR10 ... 132 F3
  Bretforton WR11 .... 163 B5
  Church Lench WR11 .. 134 A3
  Cleeve Prior WR11 ... 149 B7
  Cropthorne WR10 ... 160 B6
  Defford WR8 .... 157 D3
  Dumbleton WR11 ... 187 F5
  Offenham WR11 ..... 148 A1
  Pershore/Pinvin WR10 . 144 E6
  Sedgeberrow WR11 .. 175 A1
  South Littleton WR11 . 148 B1
  Willersey WR12 ..... 177 E4
Mainstone Cl B98 ..... 71 E3
Maisemore Cl B98 .... 71 D6
MAJOR'S GREEN 36 D8
Malcolm Ave B61 .... 48 E3
Malcolm Gr B45 ..... 33 A7
Malfield Ave B97 ..... 69 F3
Malham Pl **1** WR5 . 128 E6
Malham Rd B13 ...... 43 E7
Malinshill Rd WR11 .. 161 B3
Mallard Ave DY10 .... 28 B3
Mallard Cl
  Brierley Hill DY5 .... 6 C7
  Redditch B98 .... 70 F5
  Worcester WR2 ..... 128 A6
Mallard Pl WR9 .... 85 B3
Mallard Rd B80 ...... 90 F4
Mallards Cl WV15 ...... 1 D5
Mallory Dr DY11 .... 12 D1
Mallow Cl WR14 ..... 153 D7
Mallow Cres DY10 .... 27 F4
Mallow Dr B61 .... 48 F6
Malmsey Cl GL20 .... 196 F3
Malpas Dr B32 .... 18 C8
Malpass Rd DY5 .... 6 F7
Malt House Cl B50 ... 136 C7
Malthouse Cres WR7 . 120 E7
Malthouse La B94 ..... 53 E7
Malt House La WR11 .. 134 B8
Malt House Mews WR15 . 55 F5
Malthouse Pl **2** WR1 . 115 B2
Maltings The B80 ..... 90 D4
Malt Mill La B62 .... 8 D8

Malt Mill La Trad Est B62 . 8 D8
Malton Cl WR14 ...... 138 E6
Malton Gr B13 .... 21 B7
Malus Cl WR14 ...... 139 C3
Malvern Ave DY9 ...... 6 C5
Malvern Cl
  Broadheath WR2 ..... 114 A7
  Stourport-on-Severn DY13 . 62 D8
Malvern Coll WR14 ... 152 F7
Malvern Com Hospl
  WR14 .... 139 A1
Malvern Dr DY10 ...... 27 E3
Malvern Hills Prim Sch
  WR14 .... 153 D7
Malvern Hills Science Pk
  WR14 .... 153 B7
Malvern Ho
  7 Halesowen B63 .... 8 A3
  Redditch B97 .... 70 C1
MALVERN LINK 139 B3
Malvern Link Sta WR14. 139 A3
Malvern Mus★ WR14 .. 152 F8
Malvern Parish CE Prim Sch
  WR14 .... 153 A8
Malvern Rd
  Barnt Green B45 ..... 33 A2
  Birmingham B68 .... 9 B8
  Bromsgrove B61 ..... 67 D7
  Leigh Sinton WR13 .. 126 A2
  Newland WR2 ...... 126 F1
  Powick WR2 .... 127 D3
  Redditch B97 .... 89 D8
  Worcester WR2 ..... 114 F1
Malvern Ret Pk WR14 . 139 C5
Malvern St James WR14 153 A8
Malvern Splash Leisure
  Complex WR14 ..... 152 F8
Malvern Theatres★
  WR14 .... 152 F8
Malvern View
  Bluntington DY10 ..... 29 E1
  Kidderminster DY11 ... 27 B1
  Mamble DY14 .... 40 E4
MALVERN WELLS 152 F2
Malvern Wells Prim Sch
  WR14 .... 166 E7
MAMBLE 39 F3
Mamble Rd DY8 .... 5 E5
Manby Rd WR14 ..... 153 A8
Mandalay Dr WR5 .... 128 F4
Mandarin Ave DY10 ... 28 B3
Manders Cl B96 ...... 89 D1
Mandeville Way B61 .. 48 F5
Manitoba Cl **3** WR2 . 127 E6
Manitoba Croft **2** B38 . 34 F8
Manningford Ct B14 ... 20 F3
Manningford Rd B14 .. 20 E3
Manning Rd WR9 ..... 84 E2
Manor Abbey Rd B62 ... 8 E4
Manor Ave DY11 ..... 27 A7
Manor Ave S DY11 ... 27 A6
Manor Cl
  Badsey WR11 .... 162 D3
  Droitwich WR9 ...... 85 A2
  Honeybourne WR11 .. 164 A4
  Kidderminster DY11 ... 27 A6
  Stourport-on-Severn DY13 . 44 B5
  Wickhamford WR11 . 176 D8
Manor Court Rd B60 .. 67 F8
Manor Ct
  5 Birmingham, Hurst Green
  B62 .... 9 A7
  Birmingham, King's Norton
  B30 .... 20 A2
  Broughton Hackett WR7 . 117 E1
  Cleeve Prior WR11 ... 149 B7
Manor Dr B80 .... 91 F7
Manor Farm WR7 .... 143 A8
Manorfield WR2 ...... 114 A7
Manor Gdns
  Aldington WR11 ..... 162 C5
  Pershore WR10 ..... 158 E7
Manor House Cl B29 .... 9 F1
Manor House Dr B29 .. 19 B7
Manor House La B96 .. 89 E3
Manor La
  Bretforton WR11 .... 163 C4
  Halesowen B62 .... 8 E4
  Hartlebury DY11 ..... 64 B8
  Little Comberton WR10 . 159 B2
  Lower Marlbrook B61 .. 32 C4
  Stourbridge DY8 .... 5 D3
Manor Mews B80 ..... 90 E4
Manor Park Gr B31 ... 18 C1
Manor Park Malvern Multi
  Sports Club WR14 .. 139 A1
Manor Pk
  Harvington WR11 .... 148 B6
  Tewkesbury GL20 ... 197 D3
Manor Pl **1** GL20 .. 196 F3
Manor Rd
  Clifton upon Teme WR6 . 97 E8
  Eckington WR10 ..... 171 D7
  Hill & Moor WR10 ... 145 D3
  South Littleton WR11 . 148 A3
  Stourport-on-Severn DY13 . 44 A5
  Studley B80 .... 90 E4
  Upper Bentley B97 ... 69 B1
  Wickhamford WR11 . 162 D1
  Worcester WR2 ..... 127 F8
  Wythall B47 .... 36 A3
Manor Side WR11 .... 162 D3
Manor Side Ind Est B98 . 71 E6
Manor Way B62, B63 ... 8 C3
Manor Way Prim Sch B63 . 8 C3
Manse Gdns B80 ..... 90 E3
Mansell Cl B63 .... 7 B7
Mansell Rd B97 ...... 89 D7

Mansfield Rd WR14 . . . . . 139 D3
Mansion Ct B62 . . . . .8 E7
Mansion Gdns WR11 . . . . 161 D3
Mapit Pl WR4 . . . . 116 C4
Maple Ave
  5 Pershore WR10 . . . . 144 D2
  Worcester WR4 . . . . . . 115 B4
Maple Cl
  5 Evesham WR11 . . . . . 161 F2
  Kidderminster DY11 . . . . . 27 B8
  Kinver DY7 . . . . 4 A5
  Stourbridge DY8 . . . . 5 D2
  11 Stourport-on-Severn
    DY13 . . . . 43 E4
Maple Cres WV15 . . . . 1 C6
Maple Croft B13 . . . . 20 F5
Maple Gr WR9 . . . . 103 F8
Maple Ho
  Redditch, Greenlands B98 . . 89 F8
  Redditch, Webheath B97 . . 70 B2
Maple Rd
  Birmingham B45 . . . . 32 F6
  Birmingham, Selly Oak B30 . 19 E8
  Halesowen B62 . . . . 8 D8
  Malvern WR14 . . . . 139 C3
Maple Tree La B63 . . . . 7 C6
Maple Way B31 . . . . 18 F1
Mappleborough Cl B97 . . 70 B5
MAPPLEBOROUGH
  GREEN 72 A1
Mappleborough Green CE
  Jun & Inf Sch B98 . . . . 72 B2
Mappleborough Rd B90 . . 21 E1
Mapps Cl B63 . . . . 7 C6
Marans Croft B38 . . . . 34 D7
Marble Alley B80 . . . . 90 E4
Marbury Cl B38 . . . . 19 D2
March Gr DY12 . . . . 26 B4
March Hare Leisure Ctr
  WR7 . . . . 117 F1
Marchwood Cl B97 . . . . . . 70 A5
Marcliff Cres B90 . . . . 21 C2
Marden Gr B31 . . . . 34 A7
Margaret Ave B63 . . . . .7 F4
Margaret Cl DY5 . . . . .6 E8
Margaret Dr DY8 . . . . .6 B4
Margaret Llewlyn Davies Ct
  B98 . . . . 71 A3
Margaret Rd
  Tewkesbury GL20 . . . . . . 196 F4
  Worcester WR2 . . . . 128 A8
Margesson Dr B45 . . . . . . 33 D1
Marhon Cl 5 WR9 . . . . . . 85 B1
Marigold Cl 8 WR5 . . . . 128 C5
Marina Cl GL20 . . . . 196 F8
Marion Cl WR3 . . . . 115 B8
Marion Way B28 . . . . 21 E7
Marjoram Cl B38 . . . . 34 F8
Marjorie Ave B30 . . . . 20 B3
Mark Cl
  Malvern WR14 . . . . 138 E6
  Redditch B98 . . . . 70 E2
Market Gate 11 WR10 . . . 144 D1
Market Pl
  Bromsgrove B61 . . . . 48 F2
  7 Evesham WR11 . . . . . 161 D4
  Redditch B98 . . . . 70 E4
Market Sq B64 . . . . 7 C8
Market St
  Bromsgrove B61 . . . . 48 F2
  Kidderminster DY10 . . . . . 27 E5
  Stourbridge DY8 . . . . 6 A5
  Tenbury Wells WR15 . . . . . 55 F5
Market Way DY9 . . . . 15 C6
Market Wlk 4 B98 . . . . . . 70 E4
MARL BANK 167 B6
Marl Bank WR3 . . . . 115 C4
Marlbank Rd WR3 . . . . . . 167 B5
Marlborough Ave B60 . . . 68 A8
Marlborough Ct B60 . . . . 68 B8
Marlborough Dr
  Astley & Dunley DY13 . . . 62 F8
  Stourbridge DY8 . . . . 6 A3
Marlborough Gdns
  WR14 . . . . 139 B6
Marlborough Mews B80 . . 90 E4
Marlborough Rd WR10 . . 171 D2
Marlborough St
  2 Kidderminster DY10 . . . 27 E5
  4 Worcester WR5 . . . . . 128 E3
Marlbrook Gdns B61 . . . . 32 B1
Marlbrook La
  Crowle WR9 . . . . 105 A1
  Lower Marlbrook B60 . . . . 32 D2
MARLCLIFF 136 C2
Marlcliff Gr B13 . . . . 21 A6
Marldon Rd B14 . . . . 20 E6
Marleigh Rd B50 . . . . 136 E5
Marlfield La B98 . . . . 71 B4
Marlgrove Ct B61 . . . . 49 B8
Marlowe Cl DY10 . . . . 28 B6
Marlow Rd WR2 . . . . 114 D2
Marlpit La B97 . . . . 70 C1
Marlpool Cl 4 DY11 . . . . . 12 B1
Marlpool Ct DY11 . . . . 27 C8
Marlpool Dr B97 . . . . 70 C3
Marlpool La DY11 . . . . 12 B1
Marlpool Pl DY11 . . . . 27 C8
Marl Top B62 . . . . 19 F2
Marquis Dr B62 . . . . 8 A7
Marsden Rd B98 . . . . 70 E3
Marsham Rd B14 . . . . 20 F3
Marsh Ave WR4 . . . . 116 A5
Marsh Cl
  Harvington WR11 . . . . . . 148 A8
  Malvern WR14 . . . . 139 B2
MARSH COMMON 156 E1
Marsh End B38 . . . . 35 A8

Marshfield Cl B98 . . . . 71 B7
Marsh Gr DY10 . . . . 27 E8
Marsh Way B61 . . . . 31 F1
Marshwood Croft B62 . . . . 9 A3
Marston Cl DY8 . . . . 5 D4
Marston Rd B29 . . . . 18 F8
Marten Croft WR5 . . . . . . 128 F5
Martin Ave WR11 . . . . . . 161 A2
Martin Cl
  Bromsgrove B61 . . . . 48 E1
  Malvern WR14 . . . . 139 C1
Martindale Cl WR4 . . . . . 116 B6
Martindale Wlk DY5 . . . . . . 6 B6
Martingale Cl 4 B60 . . . . 67 E6
MARTIN HUSSINGTREE . 103 C5
Martins Cnr CV37 . . . . . . 151 A5
Martin's Orch WR13 . . . . 166 A8
Martins Way DY13 . . . . . . 43 F3
Mart La DY13 . . . . 44 A3
MARTLEY 99 A4
Martley CE Prim Sch WR6 99 B4
Martley Cl B98 . . . . 90 B7
Martley Croft B32 . . . . .9 C4
Martley Dr DY9 . . . . 6 C4
Martley Rd
  Broadheath WR2 . . . . . . 114 C5
  Great Witley WR6 . . . . 80 B7
  Stourport-on-Severn DY13 . 62 D8
Mary Draper La DY14 . . . . 41 F7
Maryland Dr B31 . . . . 19 B5
Maryland Rd DY5 . . . . 6 D7
Marylebone Cl DY8 . . . . . . 6 A7
Maryman's Rd WR11 . . . . 161 B2
Maryvale WR15 . . . . 55 D4
Mary Vale Rd B30 . . . . 19 F6
Marywell Cl B32 . . . . 18 B7
Masefield Cl WR3 . . . . . . 115 C6
Masefield Gdns 1 DY10 . . 28 B6
Masefield Rise B62 . . . . . . 8 D3
Masefield Sq B31 . . . . 19 C4
Mashie Gdns B38 . . . . 19 D1
Maslen Pl B63 . . . . .8 B3
Mason Cl
  Bidford-on-Avon B50 . . . 136 E5
  Malvern WR14 . . . . 139 B3
  Redditch B97 . . . . 89 D7
Mason La B94 . . . . 36 F1
Masonleys Rd B31 . . . . . . 18 D3
Mason Rd
  Kidderminster DY11 . . . . . 27 C6
  Redditch B97 . . . . 89 D8
Masons Cl B63 . . . . 7 C6
Masons Ct WR11 . . . . 161 F4
Masons Dr WR4 . . . . 115 F6
Masons Ryde 11 WR10 . . 158 D8
Masons Yd DY11 . . . . 27 D6
Masters Cl 2 WR11 . . . . 161 E3
MATCHBOROUGH 71 E1
Matchborough Ctr B98 . . 71 E1
Matchborough Fst Sch
  B98 . . . . 71 E1
Matchborough Way B98 . . 71 E1
Math Mdw B32 . . . . .9 F5
Mathon Rd
  Colwall WR13 . . . . 152 B4
  Malvern WR14 . . . . 138 C1
Matravers Rd WR14 . . . . 139 B2
Matthew La (Road 3)
  DY10 . . . . 27 F1
Matthias St WR14 . . . . . . 139 A5
Maughan St DY5 . . . . 7 A8
Maund Cl B60 . . . . 67 E7
Maund St WR2 . . . . 114 C4
Maurice Rd B14 . . . . 20 E5
Mavis Gdns B68 . . . . .9 B8
Mavis Rd B31 . . . . 18 E1
Maxstoke Cl
  Birmingham B32 . . . . 18 A7
  Redditch B98 . . . . 71 D1
Mayalls The GL20 . . . . . . 183 F4
May Ave WR4 . . . . 115 E4
Maybank WR14 . . . . 139 C3
Mayberry Cl
  Birmingham B14 . . . . 21 B2
  5 Stourport-on-Severn
    DY13 . . . . 43 E4
Maycroft WR11 . . . . 161 B2
Mayfair
  1 Evesham WR11 . . . . . 161 D2
  Stourbridge DY8 . . . . 6 D2
May Farm Cl B47 . . . . 36 A6
Mayfield Ave WR3 . . . . . . 115 C5
Mayfield Cl
  Fairfield B61 . . . . 31 F1
  Kidderminster DY11 . . . . . 27 A8
  Tenbury Wells DY11 . . . . . 27 C7
Mayfield Rd
  Birmingham, Stirchley
    B30 . . . . 20 A6
  Halesowen, Hasbury B63 . . 7 E2
  Malvern, Sherrards Green WR13,
    WR14 . . . . 139 C2
  Pershore WR10 . . . . 144 D2
  Worcester WR3 . . . . 115 D5
Mayfields B98 . . . . 70 E2
Mayflower Cl
  Malvern WR14 . . . . 153 B8
  2 Stourport-on-Severn
    DY13 . . . . 44 A2
Mayflower Rd WR9 . . . . . 85 B2
Mayford Gr B13 . . . . 21 B6
Mayhurst Cl B47 . . . . 36 C6
Mayhurst Rd B47 . . . . 36 B6
May La
  Birmingham B14 . . . . 20 F5

May La continued
  Hollywood B47 . . . . 36 A7
Maynard Ave DY8 . . . . 5 D3
Maypole Cl
  Bewdley DY12 . . . . 26 C3
  Cradley Heath B64 . . . . . . 7 B8
Maypole Dr DY8 . . . . .5 E5
Maypole Gr B14 . . . . 21 B2
Maypole Fields B63 . . . . . . 7 A7
Maypole Hill B63 . . . . 7 A7
Maypole La B14 . . . . 21 A2
Mayswood Gr B32 . . . . 9 D4
May Tree Hill WR9 . . . . . 104 A8
Maytree Rd WR10 . . . . . . 145 D3
May Trees B47 . . . . 35 F6
Meaburn Cl B29 . . . . 19 A7
Meadfoot Ave B14 . . . . . . 20 F3
Meadowbank Dr WR2 . . 114 D1
Meadowbrook Cl WV15 . . . 1 C5
Meadowbrook Rd B63 . . . . .7 E3
Meadow Brook Rd B31 . . 18 F5
Meadow Cl
  Kempsey WR5 . . . . 141 C6
  Kington WR7 . . . . 119 E4
  Marsh Common WR8 . . . 156 C1
  Tewkesbury GL20 . . . . . . 197 A8
  4 Westlands WR9 . . . . . 84 E5
Meadow Cotts WR12 . . . 189 E4
Meadow Croft
  West Hagley DY9 . . . . . . 14 F4
  Wythall B47 . . . . 36 A3
Meadow Ct
  Kempsey WR5 . . . . 141 B7
  20 Westlands WR9 . . . . . 84 E5
Meadowfield Rd WR5 . . . 33 A6
Meadow Gate B31 . . . . . . 18 E2
Meadow Gn
  Droitwich Spa WR9 . . . . . 84 D5
  Whitbourne WR6 . . . . . . 110 F6
MEADOW GREEN 110 F6
Meadow Green Prim Sch
  B47 . . . . 47 D7
Meadow Hill Cl DY11 . . . . 27 A5
Meadowhill Cres B98 . . . . 70 F5
Meadowhill Rd B98 . . . . . 70 F5
Meadow Hill Rd B38 . . . . 19 E2
Meadow La B48 . . . . 51 B6
Meadow Mill WR15 . . . . . 55 F3
Meadow Mill Ind Est
  DY10 . . . . 27 E5
Meadow Orch 4 WR12 . . 190 D8
Meadowpark Rd DY8 . . . . 5 D8
Meadow Piece 19 WR9 . . 84 D5
Meadow Pl 8 WR9 . . . . . 84 D5
Meadow Rd
  Birmingham B32 . . . . 9 A6
  Catshill B61 . . . . 48 F8
  Droitwich WR9 . . . . 84 E4
  Halesowen B62 . . . . 8 C8
  Honeybourne WR11 . . . . 163 D8
  Malvern WR14 . . . . 139 A3
  Worcester WR3 . . . . 102 B1
  Wythall B47 . . . . 36 A3
Meadow Rise
  Bewdley DY12 . . . . 26 D5
  Birmingham B30 . . . . 20 A7
  2 Tenbury Wells WR15 . . 55 F6
Meadows End WR11 . . . . 161 B3
Meadows Fst Sch B45 . . . 33 A3
Meadows Prim Sch B31 . 18 E1
Meadows The
  Bidford-on-Avon B50 . . . 136 C4
  Catshill B61 . . . . 48 F8
  Stourbridge DY9 . . . . 15 B7
Meadowsweet Ave B38 . . 34 F4
Meadowsweet Ct WR14 . 153 C7
Meadowsweet Pl DY10 . . 27 D8
Meadowvale Rd B60 . . . . 49 C6
Meadow View
  Birmingham B13 . . . . 21 C8
  9 Stourport-on-Severn
    DY13 . . . . 44 A2
Meadow View Ct B80 . . . 90 E3
Meadow Way WR9 . . . . . . 84 D5
Meadow Wlk
  Birmingham B14 . . . . 20 E1
  Colwall WR13 . . . . 152 B2
  Cradley Heath B64 . . . . . . 7 D8
  Pershore WR10 . . . . 144 E2
Mead The WR2 . . . . 114 E4
Meadvale Rd B45 . . . . 33 B6
Meadway WR14 . . . . 138 F5
Meadway The B97 . . . . . . 70 C1
Mealcheapen St 21 WR1 . 115 C2
Mears Coppice DY5 . . . . . .6 E6
Mearse La
  Barnt Green B45 . . . . 33 A1
  Cookhill WR7 . . . . 108 E2
  Madeley Heath DY9 . . . . . 31 B6
Meaton Gr B32 . . . . 18 B8
Meaton La DY14 . . . . 23 E8
Meddins Cl 1 DY7 . . . . . . 4 A4
Meddins La DY7 . . . . .3 F4
Meddins Rise DY7 . . . . . . .3 F4
Medici Rd B31 . . . . 18 E2
Medway Gr B38 . . . . 34 E4
Medway Rd
  Evesham WR11 . . . . 161 F3
  Worcester WR5 . . . . 115 E2
Meer End B38 . . . . 34 D7
Meeting House La B31 . . 19 A4
Meir Rd B98 . . . . 90 C8
Melbourne Ave B61 . . . . . 48 E4
Melbourne Cl B61 . . . . . . 48 E3
Melbourne Rd
  Bromsgrove B61 . . . . 48 E3
  Halesowen B63 . . . . 8 B5
Melbourne St 7 WR3 . . . 115 B6

Melbury Gr B14 . . . . 20 E5
Melchett Rd B30 . . . . 20 A4
Melen St B97 . . . . 70 D4
Melfort Gr B14 . . . . 21 A3
Melrose Ave DY8 . . . . 6 A2
Melrose Cl
  Birmingham B38 . . . . 19 F1
  Worcester WR2 . . . . 114 F3
Melstock Rd B14 . . . . 20 D7
Melton Rd B14 . . . . 20 E8
Melzer Ho DY10 . . . . 27 E7
Mendip Cl
  Bromsgrove B61 . . . . 49 A5
  Malvern WR14 . . . . 139 B1
  4 Worcester WR4 . . . . . 115 F4
Mendip Ho B98 . . . . 71 D6
Mendip Rd
  Halesowen B63 . . . . 7 D1
  Stourbridge DY8 . . . . 6 B6
Menin Cres B13 . . . . 21 B7
Menin Rd B13 . . . . 21 B8
MENITHWOOD 59 D7
Menston Cl WR4 . . . . 116 A4
Menteith Cl DY13 . . . . 43 E7
Meon Rd GL55 . . . . 165 E5
Meon Rise DY9 . . . . 6 C3
Mercia Cl B60 . . . . 67 F7
Mercia Dr
  Birmingham B14 . . . . 20 D6
  Hampton Lovett WR9 . . . . 84 C7
Mercot Cl B98 . . . . 90 A6
Merebrook WR14 . . . . . . 166 F7
Merebrook Ind Est
  WR13 . . . . 153 D1
Meredith Gn DY11 . . . . . . 27 A1
MERE GREEN 86 D1
Mere Hall* WR9 . . . . 105 E8
Mere Rd DY8 . . . . .5 E3
Meres Rd B63 . . . . 7 C5
Merevale Cl B98 . . . . 90 D8
Merick Rd WR14 . . . . 139 B5
Meriden Ave DY8 . . . . 5 D6
Meriden Cl
  Redditch B98 . . . . 72 A3
  Stourbridge DY8 . . . . 5 D6
Meridian Pl B60 . . . . 49 A1
Merino Ave B31 . . . . 34 A8
Merlin Dr B30 . . . . 28 B3
Merret Cl 12 GL20 . . . . . 184 E1
Merrick Cl B63 . . . . 7 D2
Merricks Cl 11 DY12 . . . . 25 F3
Merricks La 7 DY12 . . . . . 25 F3
Merriemont Dr B45 . . . . . 33 A1
Merrievale Ct WR14 . . . . 153 B8
Merrill Gdns B60 . . . . 32 D2
Merriman's Ct 1 WR3 . . 115 C5
Merrimans Hill Rd WR3 . 115 C5
Merriman's Wlk 5 WR3 . 115 C5
Merrishaw Rd B31 . . . . . . 34 A8
Merritts Brook Cl B29 . . . 19 A5
Merritt's Brook La B31 . . 18 E5
Merritt's Hill B31 . . . . 18 E6
Merrivale Rd B62 . . . . .8 F8
Merrybrook WR11 . . . . . . 161 A4
Merryfield WR10 . . . . 160 E8
Merryfields WR13 . . . . . . 167 C4
Merry La WR11 . . . . 148 D1
Merse Rd B98 . . . . 71 E6
Mersey Gr B38 . . . . 34 E8
Mersey Rd WR5 . . . . 115 E2
Merstow Gn 5 WR11 . . . 161 C4
Merstow Pl 4 WR11 . . . . 161 C4
Merton Cl
  4 Bewdley DY12 . . . . . . 25 F4
  Kidderminster DY10 . . . . . 28 B7
  Worcester WR4 . . . . 115 E3
Merton Rd WR14 . . . . 139 A4
Michael Cres WR14 . . . . 138 F6
Michael Tippett Dr WR4 . 115 E3
Michaelwood Cl B97 . . . . 69 D7
Michelle Cl B13 . . . . 21 A5
MICKLETON 165 E4
Mickleton Cl B98 . . . . 89 E7
Mickleton Prim Sch
  GL55 . . . . 165 D4
Mickleton Rd WR11 . . . . 164 D5
Middle Acre Rd B32 . . . . . .9 E2
Middle Dr B45 . . . . 33 D4
Middlefield Gdns B62 . . . .8 F8
Middlefield Ho B14 . . . . . 20 F3
Middlefield La DY9 . . . . . . 15 B6
Middlefield Rd B60 . . . . . 68 B7
Middle Field Rd B31 . . . . 19 D2
Middlehill Rise B32 . . . . . . 9 D3
Middle Hollow Dr WR4 . 116 A5
Middle House Dr B60 . . . 32 D1
Middlehouse La B97 . . . . 70 E6
Middle La
  Cropthorne WR10 . . . . . . 160 B6
  Hadzor WR9 . . . . 104 C7
  Wythall B38 . . . . 35 D5
Middle Leasowe B32 . . . . .9 D4
MIDDLE LITTLETON . . . 148 F3
Middle Meadow Ave B32 . .9 F5
Middlemore Cl B80 . . . . . 90 D3
Middlemore Rd B31 . . . . . 19 B8
Middle Park Cl B29 . . . . . 19 B8
Middlepark Dr B31 . . . . . . 19 B8
Middle Park Rd B29 . . . . . 19 C8
Middle Piece Dr B97 . . . . 70 B1
Middle St
  Fairfield B61 . . . . 31 F4
  Stock & Bradley B96 . . . 106 E3
  Upper Bentley B60 . . . . . . 69 A2
  Worcester WR2 . . . . 114 F1
Middles Ave WR4 . . . . . . 116 B4
Middle St WR1 . . . . 115 C3

MIDDLETON 54 B8
Middleton Cl B98 . . . . 71 F2
Middleton Gdns
  Birmingham B30 . . . . 19 D4
  1 Worcester WR4 . . . . . 116 B5
Middleton Grange B31 . . 19 C4
Middleton Hall B30 . . . . . 19 E4
Middleton Hall Rd B30 . . 19 E4
Middleton Mews B98 . . . 71 F2
MIDDLETON ON THE
  HILL 73 A6
Middleton Rd
  Birmingham B14 . . . . 20 F7
  Bromsgrove B61 . . . . 48 F4
  Kidderminster DY11 . . . . . 12 C1
MIDDLETOWN 90 D1
Middletown B80 . . . . 90 D1
Middletown La B96, B80 . . 90 D1
Middletree Rd B63 . . . . . . 7 C7
Midhurst Cl 1 WR5 . . . . 128 E8
Midhurst Rd B30 . . . . 20 B3
Midland Rd
  Birmingham B30 . . . . 19 F5
  Worcester WR5 . . . . 115 D3
Midsummer Mdw WR7 . 120 F6
Midvale Dr B14 . . . . 20 D2
Mikado Rd B60 . . . . 49 D1
Milcote Cl B98 . . . . 90 A7
Milcote Rd B29 . . . . 19 A8
Milebrook Gr B32 . . . . . . 18 B8
Mile Post La B96 . . . . . . 108 B5
Milestone Dr DY9 . . . . . . 14 F4
Milestone Rd WR8 . . . . . 168 F4
Milestone The 13 WR10 . 158 D8
Milford Ave 4 DY13 . . . . 43 E6
Milford St B97 . . . . 89 C6
Milford Pl B14 . . . . 20 E8
Milhill Rd B98 . . . . 71 E1
Mill Ave WR12 . . . . 190 B7
Mill Bank
  Evesham WR11 . . . . 161 E4
  Fladbury WR10 . . . . 146 B1
  Tewkesbury GL20 . . . . . . 196 D6
Mill Bank Cotts DY11 . . . 27 D6
Millbrook Cl WR3 . . . . . . 115 A7
Millbrook Ct B62 . . . . .8 A7
Mill Brook Dr B31 . . . . . . 33 E8
Millbrook Rd B14 . . . . 20 C6
Millbrook Way DY5 . . . . . .6 B8
Mill Cl
  Bidford-on-Avon B50 . . . 136 B7
  Blakedown DY10 . . . . 14 B2
  Bromsgrove B60 . . . . 67 F6
  Hollywood B47 . . . . 36 A7
  4 Stourport-on-Severn
    DY13 . . . . 44 B4
Millcroft B32 . . . . .9 E2
Mill Ct B48 . . . . 51 C6
Milldale Cl DY10 . . . . 27 E8
Millend WR10 . . . . 173 E7
Millennium Way WR11 . . 173 E7
Millennium Cl 2 GL20 . . 197 A4
Miller Cl B60 . . . . 67 E6
Miller Ct GL20 . . . . 197 D8
Millers Bank B50 . . . . . . 136 B7
Millers Cl 12 WR4 . . . . . 115 F6
Miller's Court Rd WR13 . 180 D5
Millers Croft WR14 . . . . . 153 D7
Millers Ct
  1 Kidderminster DY11 . . . 27 D6
  Solihull B90 . . . . 21 F2
Millers Gn WR6 . . . . 60 F4
Miller St WR9 . . . . 84 F3
Millers Wlk WR10 . . . . . . 173 E7
Millfield
  Birmingham B31 . . . . 19 A4
  Elmley Castle WR10 . . . . 173 E7
  Hinton on the Green WR11 175 B2
Mill Field CV37 . . . . 150 E3
Millfield Gdns 2 DY11 . . . 27 D6
Millfield Rd B61 . . . . 48 E1
Mill Fields DY7 . . . . 4 B3
Millfields Dr DY13 . . . . . . 44 B4
Millfields Fst Sch 1 B61 . 48 E1
Millfields View B97 . . . . . .7 E4
Millgate Cl 5 DY13 . . . . . 44 B4
Mill Gdns B14 . . . . 21 D5
Millhams Ave WR4 . . . . . 116 B5
Millhaven Ave B30 . . . . . . 20 B6
Mill La
  Aldington WR11 . . . . . . 162 C5
  Badsey WR11 . . . . 162 D2
  Bidford-on-Avon B50 . . . 136 B7
  Birmingham B32 . . . . 9 E2
  Birmingham, Northfield B31 19 A2
  Blakedown DY10 . . . . 14 B2
  Bromsgrove B61 . . . . 48 F2
  Cleeve Prior WR11 . . . . . 149 A8
  Colwall Stone WR13 . . . . 166 A8
  Dodderhill WR9 . . . . 66 E1
  Drakes Broughton &
    Wadborough WR10 . . . 143 C5
  Earlswood B94 . . . . 53 B8
  Eckington WR10 . . . . . . 171 D6
  Elmley Castle WR10 . . . . 173 E7
  Fairfield B61 . . . . 31 F3
  Feckenham B96 . . . . 107 D8
  Halesowen B63 . . . . 8 C4
  Kidderminster, Blakebrook
    DY11 . . . . 27 D6
  Kidderminster, Hoobrook
    DY10 . . . . 27 F2
  Kinver DY7 . . . . 4 B3
  Knighton on Teme WR15 . 57 C7
  Lindridge WR15 . . . . 59 A4

Mill La *continued*
Malvern WR14 . . . . **153** D7
Mickleton GL55 . . . . **165** D4
Offenham WR11 . . . . **162** B7
Pershore WR10 . . . . **144** D2
Redmarley D'abitot GL19 . . **192** F4
Rous Lench WR7 . . . . **120** D3
Staunton GL19 . . . . **193** A2
Stourport-on-Severn DY13 . . **44** B4
Strensham WR8 . . . . **171** C3
Wolverley & Cookley DY11 . **12** D2
Wythall B47, B94 . . . . **36** B1
Mill Lane Cl WR10 . . . . . . **144** E3
Mill Lodge Prim Sch B90 . **21** E2
Millmead Lodge B13 . . . . **21** D8
Millmead Rd B32 . . . .**9** E1
Mill Mound ★ WR11 . . . . **164** A4
Mill Pleck B80 . . . . **90** E3
Mill Pool Cl DY9 . . . . **15** A4
Millpool Gdns B14 . . . . . **20** F3
Millpool Hill B14 . . . . **20** F4
Mill Pool Pl DY14 . . . . **22** D5
Mill Race La DY8 . . . . **6** A6
Millrace Rd B98 . . . . **70** E5
Mill Rd
Cradley Heath B64 . . . .**7** E7
Evesham WR11 . . . . **161** B2
Stourport-on-Severn DY13 . . **44** B4
Millridge Way DY11 . . . . . **64** A8
Millsborough Rd B98 . . . . **70** F3
Mills Cl WR12 . . . . **190** D8
Millside B28 . . . . **21** E3
Millside Cl DY12 . . . . **26** B3
Mill St
Evesham WR11 . . . . **161** D4
Halesowen B63 . . . .**7** C7
Kidderminster DY11 . . . . . . **27** D6
Redditch B97 . . . . **70** D4
Tewkesbury GL20 . . . . **196** D6
Worcester WR1 . . . . **115** C1
Mill Wlk The B31 . . . . **18** F1
Mill Wood Dr WR4 . . . . . **116** B4
Milne Pastures GL20 . . . . **197** C7
Milner Way B13 . . . . **21** D8
Milret Cl ❷ WR3 . . . . **115** C5
MILSON **38** C6
Milston Cl B14 . . . . **20** E1
Milton Cl
Kidderminster DY11 . . . . . . **27** A6
Redditch B97 . . . . **89** C8
Stourbridge DY8 . . . .**6** A7
Worcester WR3 . . . . **115** C6
Milton Ct WR14 . . . . **139** A2
Milton Dr DY9 . . . . **15** D7
Milton Ho B63 . . . .**7** B5
Milton Rd B61 . . . . **49** A8
Milverton Cl B63 . . . . **8** A6
Milverton Ct ❸ B62 . . . . . .**9** A7
Milward Sq ❼ B97 . . . . . **70** E3
Mimosa Cl B29 . . . . **19** B7
Minett Ave WR2 . . . . **127** B8
Minge La WR8 . . . . **169** C5
Minley Ave B17 . . . .**9** F7
Minster Mews B60 . . . . . . **68** B8
Minter Ave WR9 . . . . **84** F2
Minton Mews B60 . . . . . . **68** B8
Minton Rd B32 . . . .**9** F4
Minworth Cl B97 . . . . **70** B2
Miranda Cl B45 . . . . **18** A2
Mitcheldean Cl B98 . . . . . **89** E7
Mitcheldean Covert B14 . **20** D2
Mitre Ct B61 . . . . **49** A3
Mitre Rd DY9 . . . .**6** E5
Mitten Ave B45 . . . . **18** A1
MITTON **197** B6
Mitton Cl DY13 . . . . **44** A4
Mitton Gdns DY13 . . . . . . **44** A3
Mitton Manor Prim Sch
GL20 . . . . **197** A8
Mitton St DY13 . . . . **44** A3
Mitton Way GL20 . . . . . . **197** A8
Mitton Wlk ❽ DY13 . . . . . **44** A3
Moat Bank GL20 . . . . **181** F5
Moat Coppice B62 . . . .**9** A1
Moat Cres WR14 . . . . **139** D1
Moat Farm Dr B32 . . . .**9** A1
Moat Farm La WR10 . . . . **132** F3
Moat Mdws B32 . . . .**9** E4
Moatway WR14 . . . . **139** D1
Moatway The B38 . . . . **34** E7
Modbury Ave B32 . . . .**9** D1
Moffit Way ❿ DY13 . . . . . **43** E4
Mogul La B63 . . . .**7** A7
Moira Cres B14 . . . . **21** C4
Monarch Dr WR2 . . . . . . **114** E6
Monarch Pl ❼ WR2 . . . . **114** C5
Monarch Works ★ DY9 . . . .**6** F5
Monckton Rd B68 . . . .**9** A7
Mondrian Rd B60 . . . . . . **49** C1
Money La B61 . . . . **32** A7
Mongcroft Rd WR10 . . . . **158** F1
Monkey Mdw ❻ GL20 . . . **184** E1
Monks Cl ❹ WR10 . . . . . **158** D3
Monks Dr B80 . . . . **90** D4
Monksfield La WR13 . . . . **126** E1
Monks Field Way GL20 . . **196** E5
Monks Path B97 . . . . **69** F4
Monksway B38 . . . . **20** B1
Monks Way WR10 . . . . . . **131** B2
Monkswood Rd B31 . . . . . **19** C2
MONKWOOD GREEN . . . **100** E5
Monkwood Nature Reserve ★
WR2 . . . . **100** E6

Monmouth Rd
Birmingham, Bartley Green
B32 . . . . **18** D8
Birmingham, Warley Woods
B67 . . . .**9** E8
Monnow Cl
Droitwich WR9 . . . . **103** E8
Malvern WR14 . . . . **153** D8
Monsell Rd WR14 . . . . . . **169** A4
Monsieurs Hall La B61 . . **48** B3
Monterey Rd ❸ GL20 . . . **197** A3
Montfort St WR11 . . . . . . **161** F4
Montfort Wlk B32 . . . .**9** A2
Montgomery Cl WR2 . . . . **127** B2
Montgomery Cl B61 . . . . . **32** A1
Montgomery Cres DY5 . . . .**6** F7
Montpelier Rd WR14 . . . . **138** C1
Montreal Cl WR2 . . . . **127** E6
Monument Ave DY9 . . . .**6** E4
Monument La
Birmingham B45 . . . . **32** F4
Hagley DY9 . . . . **15** D7
Monyhull Hall Rd B30 . . . **20** C3
MOONS MOAT **71** F5
Moons Moat Dr B98 . . . . . **71** E5
Moons Moat Fst Sch B98 . **71** D5
Moons Moat North Ind Est
B98 . . . . **71** E6
Moons Moat South Ind Est
B98 . . . . **71** D4
Moons Pk B98 . . . . **71** E6
Moorcroft Cl B97 . . . . **89** B6
Moorcroft Gdns B97 . . . . **89** B6
Moorend Rd GL19 . . . . . . **193** F1
Moorfield Dr
Bromsgrove B61 . . . . **48** F3
Halesowen B63 . . . .**8** A5
Moorfoot Ave B63 . . . .**7** C1
Moorgate Cl B98 . . . . **71** E6
Moorgate Rd B60 . . . . **68** A2
Moor Hall Dr DY9 . . . . **16** A1
Moorhall La DY13 . . . . . . **43** E3
Moor Hill Dr ❺ DY13 . . . . **43** F4
Moor Ho B14 . . . . **20** C2
Moorlands Ct WR14 . . . . **138** F2
Moorlands Rd WR14 . . . . **138** F2
Moorlands The WR14 . . . **152** F2
Moor Leasow B31 . . . . . . **19** C2
Moorpark Rd B31 . . . . **19** A1
Moors Ave DY11 . . . . **45** B2
Moors Croft B32 . . . .**9** A4
Moors La
Birmingham B31 . . . . **18** E7
Feckenham B96 . . . . **107** E7
Moorsom Way B60 . . . . . . **68** B7
Moor St WR1 . . . . **115** B3
Moors The WR1 . . . . **115** A4
Moray Cl B62 . . . .**8** E8
Mordiford Cl B98 . . . . **71** E4
Moreland Pl B31 . . . . **18** F1
Moreland Rd WR9 . . . . . . **84** E2
Morelands The B31 . . . . . **19** B1
Morella Cl ❶❸ DY12 . . . . **25** F3
Moreton La GL20 . . . . **184** F7
Moreton Pl ❶ WR1 . . . . . **115** B2
Morgan Cl
❶ Cradley Heath B64 . . . . . .**7** E8
Studley B80 . . . . **90** F2
Morgan Ct WR14 . . . . **138** F3
Morillon Ct DY10 . . . . **28** A1
Morlich Rise DY5 . . . .**6** B8
Morning Pines DY8 . . . .**5** A4
Morningside WR15 . . . . . . **55** E4
Morrin Cl WR3 . . . . **102** B1
Morris Ave WR3 . . . . **115** B8
Morris Field Croft B28 . . **21** E4
Morris Rd WR1 . . . . **190** D8
Morris Wlk B60 . . . . **67** E8
Morsefield La B98 . . . . . . **71** D1
Mortimer Gdns ❺ DY14 . . **22** C4
Mortimer Dr DY12 . . . . . . **26** C4
Mortimers Cl B14 . . . . . . **21** B1
Mortimers Quay ❷
WR11 . . . . **161** E4
Mortlake Ave WR5 . . . . . **128** F8
Mortlake Dr WR6 . . . . **99** A4
Morton Ave WR3 . . . . . . **102** E2
Morton Hall La B96 . . . . **107** F3
Morton Ho B97 . . . . **70** A3
Morton La B97 . . . . **89** B7
Morton Rd
Brierley Hill DY5 . . . .**6** D7
Fernhill Heath WR3 . . . . . **102** E2
Harvington DY10 . . . . **29** B2
MORTON SPIRT **121** E2
MORTON UNDERHILL . . . **107** E3
Morton Wood La WR7 . . **121** B1
Morvale Ct DY9 . . . .**6** E5
Morvale Gdns DY9 . . . .**6** E5
Morvale St DY9 . . . .**6** E5
Mosel Dr WR9 . . . . **103** D8
MOSELEY **101** A3
Moseley Rd WR2 . . . . . . **101** B3
Mossfield Rd B14 . . . . **20** F7
Moss Gr B14 . . . . **20** D6
Moss La
Beoley B98 . . . . **71** F8
Mappleborough Green B98 . **72** A7
Moss La Cl B98 . . . . **71** F8
Mostyn Rd DY13 . . . . **43** E6
Moulder Rd GL20 . . . . . . **197** A6
Moule Cl DY11 . . . . **27** B3
Moundsley Gr B14 . . . . . . **21** A3
Moundsley Ho B14 . . . . . . **20** F2
Mounds The B38 . . . . **34** E8
Mountain Ash Dr DY9 . . . . .**6** C2

Mountbatten Rd WR14 . . **139** C2
Mountfield Cl B14 . . . . . . **21** A2
Mountford Rd B90 . . . . . . **21** D1
Mount La DY9 . . . . **15** E4
Mount Orch ❹ WR15 . . . . **55** E4
MOUNT PLEASANT **88** D5
Mount Pleasant
Pershore WR10 . . . . **144** D2
Redditch B97 . . . . **70** D2
❸ Tenbury Wells WR15 . . . **55** E4
Mount Pleasant Barns ❶
WR10 . . . . **144** D2
Mount Pleasant La DY13 . . **63** F4
Mount Rd
Evesham WR11 . . . . **161** F3
Fairfield B61 . . . . **31** E2
Stourbridge, Stambermill DY8 .**6** B5
Mountserrat Rd B60 . . . . . **49** B1
Mount St
Halesowen B63 . . . .**8** A3
Redditch B98 . . . . **70** D3
Stourbridge DY8 . . . .**6** B5
Mount Vernon Dr B61 . . . **49** A5
Mousehall Farm Rd DY5 . . .**6** D7
Mouse La DY11 . . . . **27** B8
Mousesweet Wlk B64 . . . . .**7** B8
Mowbray Ave GL20 . . . . **196** F3
Mowbray Cl B45 . . . . **18** A2
Moyle Dr B63 . . . .**7** B7
Mr B's Sh Ctr ❶ B45 . . . . **32** F7
MUCKLOW HILL **8** D6
Mucklow Hill B62 . . . .**8** D5
Mucklow Hill Trad Est B62 .**8** C5
Muirfield Gdns B38 . . . . . **19** D1
Mulberry Dr
Malvern WR14 . . . . **152** F4
Upton upon Severn WR8 . . **168** F5
Mulberry Rd B30 . . . . **19** C5
Mulberry Terr WR4 . . . . . **115** E4
Mulberry Tree Hill WR9 . **104** A8
Mull Cl B45 . . . . **17** E1
Mullion Croft B38 . . . . . . **19** E1
Muncaster Pl ❶❼ WR4 . . **116** C6
Munches La B62 . . . . **31** C8
Munro Cl DY10 . . . . **28** C6
Munsley Cl B98 . . . . **71** F2
Munslow Gr B31 . . . . **33** F8
MURCOT **176** C5
Murcot Rd WR12 . . . . **176** D4
Murcot Turn WR12 . . . . . **176** D5
Murcot Turn Bsns Pk
WR12 . . . . **176** E5
Murcroft Rd DY9 . . . .**6** E1
Murren Ave WR14 . . . . . . **153** A5
Musket Cl ❶❹ GL20 . . . . **197** A4
Musketts Ct B97 . . . . **70** B2
Muskoka DY12 . . . . **25** F3
MUSTOW GREEN **28** F1
Myatt Rd WR11 . . . . **148** A1
Myatt's Field WR11 . . . . . **148** A7
Mynors Cres B47 . . . . **36** A6
Myrtle Ave
Birmingham, Highter's Heath
B14 . . . . **20** F2
Redditch B98 . . . . **70** E2
Mythe Rd GL20 . . . . **196** E8
MYTHE THE **183** D1
Myton Dr B90 . . . . **21** D1
Mytton Rd B30 . . . . **19** C5

N

Nafford Gr B14 . . . . **20** F2
Nafford Rd WR10 . . . . . . **171** F8
Nailers Cl
Birmingham B32 . . . .**8** F2
Stoke Heath B60 . . . . **67** E6
Nailers Ct ❸ B60 . . . . **48** F2
Nailors Ct ❶❹ GL20 . . . . **196** E6
Nailsworth Cl ❾ WR4 . . . **115** F7
Nailsworth Rd B98 . . . . . . **70** F2
Nairn Cl
Birmingham B28 . . . . **21** F5
Redditch B98 . . . . **71** E4
Nantmel Gr B32 . . . . **18** C8
NAPLETON **141** E5
Napleton La WR5 . . . . . . **141** D6
Napton Cl B98 . . . . **71** D1
Napton Gr B29 . . . .**9** F2
Narrow La B62 . . . .**8** E8
Narrows The GL55 . . . . . **178** E2
Naseby Cl B98 . . . . **71** D6
Naseby Dr B63 . . . .**7** D2
NASH **37** A4
Nash Cl
Martley WR6 . . . . **99** A4
Worcester WR3 . . . . **102** A1
Nashe Cl DY10 . . . . **28** C5
NASH END **10** E8
Nash Gn WR13 . . . . **126** A2
Nash La DY9 . . . . **30** D7
Nash Rd B98 . . . . **71** B1
Nashs Pas ❷❸ WR1 . . . . **115** C2
Nashs & Wyatts Almshouses
❷❷ WR1 . . . . **115** C2
NATTON **197** F6
NAUNTON **170** B4
**NAUNTON
BEAUCHAMP** **132** B5
Naunton Cl B29 . . . . **19** A7
Navenby Cl B90 . . . . **21** C3
Navigation Rd WR5 . . . . **128** B7
Naylor Cl DY11 . . . . **27** B3
Nearhill Rd B38 . . . . **34** C8
Near Lands Cl B32 . . . .**9** A3
Near Oak Ho B32 . . . . **18** D8
Neason Cl ❽ WR4 . . . . . . **116** B4

Needle Cl B80 . . . . **90** E4
Needle Mill La B98 . . . . . . **70** E6
NEEN SAVAGE **22** D7
NEEN SOLLARS **39** A5
NEEN SOLLARS **39** A5
Neighbrook Cl B97 . . . . . . **69** F2
Neigh La WR10 . . . . **160** C7
Nelson Rd
Stourport-on-Severn DY13 . . **44** B1
Worcester WR2 . . . . **114** F2
Nelson St ❻ GL20 . . . . . . **196** E6
Nene Cl DY8 . . . .**6** A5
Nesfield Cl B38 . . . . **19** C1
Nestor Ho B13 . . . . **21** D7
Netheravon Cl B14 . . . . . . **20** D1
Nethercote Gdns B90 . . . **21** E3
Netherdale Rd B14 . . . . . . **21** A1
Netherend Cl B63 . . . .**7** A7
Netherend La B63 . . . .**7** B7
Netherend Sq B63 . . . .**7** A7
Netherfield B98 . . . . **90** A8
Nether Grange WR14 . . . **138** F1
Netherley La
Berrow WR13 . . . . **180** B1
Pendock GL19 . . . . **193** B8
NETHERTON **174** A8
Netherton Ct ❶❷ WR1 . . **115** B3
Netherton La
Bewdley DY12 . . . . **26** C2
Netherton WR10 . . . . **173** F7
❽ Worcester WR1 . . . . . . **115** B3
Netherton Rd
Astley & Dunley DY13 . . . . . **62** A8
Rock DY13 . . . . **61** E7
Netherwich Gdns ❹ WR9 . **84** E4
Netherwood La
Crowle WR9 . . . . **117** D8
Oddingley WR7 . . . . **104** D1
Netley Ho B32 . . . .**9** F5
Neville Ave WR11 . . . . **27** D3
Neville Cl B98 . . . . **71** A5
Neville Ct
Birmingham B13 . . . . **20** F6
Kidderminster DY11 . . . . . . **27** D3
Neville Rd
Solihull B90 . . . . **21** F1
Tewkesbury GL20 . . . . **196** F5
Newall Ho B97 . . . . **70** D2
Newark Gn WR4 . . . . **116** D6
New Bank St WR3 . . . . . . **115** B6
New Barn Rd
Birlingham WR10 . . . . **158** A3
Defford WR10 . . . . **157** F3
Newbold Ct B63 . . . .**8** B3
Newborough Gr B28, B90,
105 . . . . **21** F3
Newborough Rd B28 . . . . **21** F4
Newbourne Hill B48 . . . . . **51** E4
NEWBRIDGE GREEN **169** B3
Newbrook Farm ★ B32 . . **17** D4
Newburn Croft B32 . . . .**9** B5
Newbury Cl
Halesowen B62 . . . .**8** D3
Lower Marlbrook B61 . . . . . **32** B1
Newbury Rd WR2 . . . . . . **114** E3
Newcastle Cl ❸ WR5 . . . **115** F1
New Chawson La WR9 . . . **84** C1
New Coll (Britten Ho)
B98 . . . . **70** D4
**New Coll (Bromsgrove
Campus)** B60 . . . . **70** E5
New Coll (IT Ctr) B98 . . . **70** E5
**New Coll (Redditch Main
Campus)** B98 . . . . **70** E4
New Coll Worcester
WR5 . . . . **129** A7
New Coppice Ct B97 . . . . **89** E6
NEW END **108** F4
New England B62 . . . .**8** E7
Newent Cl B98 . . . . **72** A3
Newent Rd B31 . . . . **19** C4
Newey Cl B45 . . . . **33** A6
Newey Rd B28 . . . . **21** F6
Neweys Hill WR3 . . . . **115** A7
New Farm Rd DY9 . . . .**6** C4
Newfield Cres B63 . . . .**8** A5
Newfield Gdns DY9 . . . . . **15** A4
Newfield La B63 . . . .**8** B5
Newfield Park Prim Sch
B63 . . . .**8** A5
Newfield Pl DY9 . . . . **15** A4
Newfield Rd DY9 . . . . **15** A4
New Forest Cl DY14 . . . . . **24** C2
Newhouse Farm Dr B31 . . **19** C6
Newhouse La B61 . . . . **66** D8
Newick Gr B14 . . . . **20** C4
New Inn La
Salford Priors WR11 . . . . . **135** C2
Shrawley WR6 . . . . **62** D1
New Inns La B45 . . . . **17** E1
New John St B62 . . . .**8** D8
NEWLAND **139** D6
Newland Cl B98 . . . . **90** B7
NEWLAND COMMON . . . **104** A5
Newland Common Rd
WR9 . . . . **104** A5
Newland Cres WR2 . . . . . **127** D8
Newland Dr WR9 . . . . **84** F1
Newland Gdns B64 . . . .**7** E7
Newland Gn WR13 . . . . . **139** D7
Newland Pl ❼ GL20 . . . . **196** F6
Newland Rd WR9 . . . . **84** F1
Newlands WR10 . . . . **158** C7
Newlands Cl
Hagley DY9 . . . . **15** C6
Kidderminster DY11 . . . . . . **27** C7
Newlands Dr B62 . . . .**8** E7

Newlands Rd B30 . . . . **20** C7
Newlands The B80 . . . . . . **90** D3
Newlyn Rd
Birmingham B31 . . . . **18** F3
Cradley Heath B64 . . . .**7** D8
Newman Coll Cl B32 . . . . **18** C8
Newman University Coll
Birmingham B32 . . . . **18** C8
Newman Way B45 . . . . . . **33** A6
New Meadow Cl B31 . . . . **19** B2
New Meadow Rd B98 . . . . **71** B3
NEWNHAM BRIDGE **57** D7
New Pool Rd B64 . . . .**7** B8
Newport Cl B97 . . . . **89** B6
Newport St ❸ WR1 . . . . **115** B2
New Rd
Bewdley DY12 . . . . **26** D5
Birmingham B45 . . . . **32** F7
Bromsgrove B60 . . . . **49** A1
Bromsgrove, Sidemoor B61 . **48** E3
Castlemorton WR13 . . . . . **166** F1
Cleobury Mortimer DY14 . . **22** D5
Doverdale WR9 . . . . **64** F3
Eckington WR10 . . . . **171** E8
Evesham WR11 . . . . **161** B3
Fairfield B61 . . . . **31** E2
Halesowen B63 . . . .**8** B4
Hanley WR15 . . . . **58** C1
Hollywood B47 . . . . **36** A8
Kidderminster DY10 . . . . . . **27** E5
Offenham WR11 . . . . **162** B8
Pebworth CV37 . . . . **150** E2
Pershore WR10 . . . . **158** C8
Rock DY14 . . . . **24** B2
Stourbridge DY8 . . . .**6** A5
Studley B80 . . . . **90** E3
Wolverley & Cookley DY11 . **13** B7
Worcester WR2 . . . . **115** A2
New Road Gdns ❻ DY14 . . **22** D5
New St
Birmingham, Frankley B45 . . **18** A1
Bretforton WR11 . . . . **163** C5
Childswickham WR12 . . . . **176** E2
❽ Evesham WR11 . . . . . . **161** E4
Stourbridge DY8 . . . .**5** F5
Stourport-on-Severn DY13 . . **43** F3
Upton upon Severn WR8 . . **169** C6
Worcester WR1 . . . . **115** C2
New Swinford Hall DY9 . . . .**6** C4
Newton Cl
❺ Bewdley DY12 . . . . **25** F4
Crowle WR7 . . . . **117** F4
Redditch B98 . . . . **90** A6
Newton Rd B60 . . . . **68** A7
Newton Sq B60 . . . . **68** A7
Newton Works B60 . . . . . . **68** A6
NEWTOWN
Aschchurch **197** C6
Bronsgrove **31** D8
Droitwich **84** E4
Madeley Heath **131** D8
Martley **112** B8
Newtown Hospl WR5 . . . **116** B2
Newtown La
Madeley Heath B62 . . . . . . **31** D8
Romsley B62 . . . . **17** D2
Newtown Rd
Malvern WR14 . . . . **138** E3
Worcester WR4 . . . . **115** D3
Newtown Trad Est GL20 . **197** B7
New Wharf Cotts B60 . . . . **69** B7
New Wlk ❸ B97 . . . . **70** E4
New Wood Cl DY7 . . . .**5** C8
New Wood Dr B31 . . . . . . **18** D1
New Wood La DY10 . . . . . **29** B8
Niblett's Hill B61 . . . . **48** B7
Nibley Cl ❶❶ WR4 . . . . . **115** F7
Nigel Ave B31 . . . . **19** A5
Nightingale Ave WR4 . . . **116** C3
Nightingale Cl WR9 . . . . **104** B7
Nightingale Cres DY5 . . . . .**6** D7
Nightingale Ct ❻ WR11 . **161** D4
Nightingale Dr DY10 . . . . **28** B2
Nightingale La WR11 . . . **149** A8
Nightingale Pl WR9 . . . . **104** B7
Nightingale Rd WR14 . . . **139** C2
Nightingale Way GL20 . . **197** B3
Nimmings Cl B31 . . . . **33** F6
Nimmings Rd B62 . . . .**8** D8
Nimmings Visitor Ctr ★
B62 . . . . **16** B6
Nina Cl DY13 . . . . **44** B3
Nine Acres Gn ❻ WR4 . . **116** B4
Nine Days La B98 . . . . **90** B6
Ninesquares ❸ WR10 . . **171** E7
NINEVEH
Bayton **39** E8
Kyre **75** E6
Nixon Ct WR2 . . . . **140** F8
NOAH'S GREEN **107** C7
Noble View WR14 . . . . . . **138** D3
Nodbury Hill WR7 . . . . . . **120** F6
Node Hill B80 . . . . **90** D3
Node Hill Cl B80 . . . . **90** D3
Noel Ct B97 . . . . **89** C8
Nogains WR10 . . . . **158** D7
No Man's Green La DY7 . . . .**2** F6
Nonsuch Prim Sch B32 . . . .**9** D2
Noonan Cl B97 . . . . **70** B2
Norbury Cl B98 . . . . **71** B7
NORCHARD **64** A6
Norchard La WR10 . . . . . **131** B1
Norfolk Cl
Birmingham B30 . . . . **20** B6
Worcester WR2 . . . . **114** C3
Norfolk Ct ❻ B29 . . . . . . **19** C7
Norfolk Ho B30 . . . . **20** A3

Norfolk Rd
Birmingham, Brandhall B68. . **9** B7
Birmingham, Frankley B45 . **17** F2
Stourbridge DY8 . . . . **5** D8
Norgrove La B97. . . . . **88** D6
Norham Pl WR4. . . . . **116** C6
Norlan Dr B14 . . . . **20** F3
Norley Gr B13 . . . . **21** C7
Norman Ave B32. . . . .**9** E7
Norman Cl
Twyning GL20. . . . . **183** F6
5 Worcester WR4. . . . . **116** B6
Norman Rd B31. . . . . **19** B3
Norrington Gr B31. . . . . . . **18** C3
Norrington Rd B31. . . . . . . **18** D3
Northampton La WR9 . . . . **82** F7
North Bank WR9. . . . . **84** E6
North Bromsgrove High Sch
B60. **49** B3
Northbrook Cl WR3 . . . . . **115** B6
Northcliffe Hts DY11. . . . . . **27** C7
Northcote St [2] WR3 . . . . **115** B6
North Croft WR2. . . . . **127** E4
North East Terr GL20. . . . **196** F6
North End La WR13 . . . . . **139** D3
NORTHFIELD. **19** B4
Northfield Children's Farm★
B31. **18** C4
Northfield Cl
Fernhill Heath WR3 . . . . . . **102** F3
Redditch B98. . . . . **71** D6
Northfield Manor Prim Sch
B29. **19** B7
Northfield Rd B30. . . . . **19** E4
Northfield St WR1. . . . . . . **115** C4
Northfield Sta B31. . . . . . . **19** A2
Northgate B64. . . . . **7** D8
Northgate Cl DY11. . . . . **27** A4
North Hill Gdns WR14. . . **138** E3
Northleach Ave B14. . . . . . **20** D2
Northleach Cl
Redditch B98. . . . . **71** B5
1 Worcester WR4. . . . . . **115** E5
Northleigh CE Prim Sch
WR14 . . . . **138** E4
NORTH LITTLETON **149** B3
NORTH MALVERN **138** D4
North Malvern Ho WR14 . **138** D3
North Malvern Rd WR14. . **138** E2
NORTH PIDDLE. **119** B2
North Rd
Bromsgrove B60. . . . . **49** A2
Evesham WR11 . . . . **161** F4
Stourport-on-Severn DY13 . . **44** A5
Northside Cl B98. . . . . **89** E7
North St WR9. . . . . **84** F3
North Street Ind Est [10]
WR9 . . . . **84** E3
Northumberland Ave
DY11 . . . . **27** D3
NORTHWAY **184** E2
Northway Infants Sch
GL20. . . . . **197** E8
Northway La GL20. . . . . . . **184** D1
Northway Trad Est GL20 . **197** E7
NORTHWICK. **115** A8
Northwick Ave WR3. . . . . . **115** A6
Northwick Cl WR3 . . . . **115** A7
Northwick Manor Prim Sch
WR3 . . . . **115** A7
Northwick Rd
Evesham WR11 . . . . **161** E4
Worcester WR3 . . . . **102** A1
Northwick Wlk WR3. . . . . **115** A7
North Wlk B31. . . . . **19** C1
Northwood Halt Sta DY12 **25** F7
Northwood La DY12. . . . . . . **10** F1
Northwood Way DY5 . . . . . .**6** B8
NORTON
Norton and Lenchwick. . . . **147** D4
Norton Juxta Kempsey **129** C2
Stourbridge **5** D2
Norton Cl
Birmingham B31 . . . . **19** A3
Redditch B98. . . . . **71** F2
Worcester WR5 . . . . **128** C6
Norton Dr B47. . . . . **36** C4
Norton Gate B38. . . . . **19** F1
Norton Juxta Kempsey Sch
WR5 . . . . **129** C1
Norton La B47, B90, B94. . . **36** E3
Norton Mews B61. . . . . **49** A4
Norton Rd
Kempsey WR5 . . . . **128** C4
Kidderminster DY10. . . . . . . **28** B6
Stourbridge DY8 . . . . **5** E2
Norton Terr B30. . . . . **20** B6
Norton View
Birmingham B14 . . . . **20** D7
Mickleton GL55. . . . . **165** D3
Nortune Cl B38. . . . . **19** D2
Norval Rd WR11. . . . . **163** C8
Norwich Ave DY11 . . . . **26** F6
Norwich Dr B17. . . . .**9** F8
Norwich Rd WR5. . . . . **115** F2
Norwood Ave B64. . . . .**7** E7
NOUTARD'S GREEN **62** E2
Nuffield Cl WR2. . . . . **114** E4
Nuffield Dr WR9 . . . . **84** C3
Nunnery Ave WR9. . . . . **84** E2
Nunnery La
5 Worcester WR5 . . . . . **115** F1
Worcester WR5. . . . . **129** A8
Nunnery Way WR5 . . . . . . **116** C1
Nunnery Wood High Sch
WR5 . . . . **116** A1
*Nunnery Wood Nature
Reserve*★ WR5. . . . . . . **116** B2

Nunnery Wood Prim Sch
WR5 . . . . **115** F1
*Nunnery Wood Sports
Complex* WR5. . . . . **116** A1
Nursery Cl
Birmingham B30 . . . . **19** F5
Kidderminster DY11. . . . . . . **27** B8
Mickleton GL55. . . . . **165** F5
2 Pershore WR10 . . . . . **144** D1
West Hagley DY9. . . . . **15** A4
Nursery Dr B30 . . . . **19** F5
Nursery Gdns B90. . . . . **36** E8
Nursery Gr
5 Kidderminster DY11. . . **12** B1
Kidderminster DY11. . . . . . . **27** B8
Nursery Rd
Bewdley DY12 . . . . **26** B4
Birmingham, Cotteridge B30 **19** E5
Malvern WR14 . . . . **138** E4
Worcester WR2 . . . . **127** E8
Nursery Wlk
Wick Episcopi WR2 . . . . . **127** E8
12 Worcester WR2 . . . . **114** F1
Nutbush Dr B31. . . . . **18** D6
Nutfield Wlk B32. . . . .**9** F5
Nutgrove Cl B14. . . . . **20** F7
Nuthatch Dr DY5. . . . .**6** C7
Nuthurst Gr B14. . . . . **20** F2
Nuthurst Rd B31. . . . . **33** F6
Nut Orchard La GL20. . . . **183** F7

O

OAKALL GREEN **101** A6
Oakalls Ave B60 . . . . **49** B2
Oak Apple Cl
Fernhill Heath WR3 . . . . . . **102** F4
Stourport-on-Severn DY13 . . **62** E7
Oak Apple Rd B61. . . . . **49** B8
Oak Ave WR4 . . . . **115** E5
Oak Barn Rd B62. . . . .**8** E8
Oak Bridge Ct WR15 . . . . . **55** F3
Oak Cl
Badsey WR11. . . . . **162** E4
Kinver DY7. . . . . **4** C3
Oak Cotts B14 . . . . **21** C2
Oak Cres WR14 . . . . **139** C1
Oakcroft Rd B13 . . . . **21** C7
Oak Ct
Halesowen B63 . . . .**7** F2
Stourbridge DY8 . . . .**6** A4
Oakdene DY13. . . . . **44** B3
Oakdene Dr B45. . . . . **50** C8
Oak Dr
Colwall WR13. . . . . **152** B2
Hartlebury WR9. . . . . **64** E8
Northway GL20 . . . . **197** D8
Oaken Pl DY11. . . . . **27** C7
OAKENSHAW. **89** E6
Oakenshaw Rd B98. . . . . . . **71** A1
Oak Farm Rd B30 . . . . **19** E5
Oakfield Cl WR5 . . . . **141** D6
Oakfield Dr
Birmingham B45 . . . . **33** D4
Kempsey WR5 . . . . **141** C6
Oakfield Rd
Kidderminster DY11. . . . . . . **27** B5
Malvern WR14 . . . . **139** A5
Ombersley WR9. . . . . **83** A5
Stourbridge, Wollescote DY9. .**6** F2
Oak Gdns GL20 . . . . **184** F6
Oak Gr
Birmingham B31 . . . . **18** E1
Kidderminster DY10. . . . . . . **28** A5
Oakham Cl B98 . . . . **90** A5
Oakham Dr WR9 . . . . **84** C2
Oakham Gn WR9. . . . . **84** D2
Oakham Pl WR9 . . . . **84** C2
Oakhampton Rd DY13 . . . . **62** E7
Oakhill Ave DY10. . . . . **27** E4
Oakhill Dr DY5. . . . .**6** B7
Oakhill Fst Sch B98. . . . . . . **71** A2
Oak Hill Infants Sch
WR11 . . . . **187** F5
Oakhurst Dr B60. . . . . **49** A3
Oak La GL20 . . . . **184** E6
Oakland Ave WR9. . . . . **84** E1
Oakland Cl WR8 . . . . **168** F5
Oakland Gr B61. . . . . **49** B4
Oaklands
Birmingham B62 . . . .**9** A4
Birmingham, Northfield B31 **18** F4
Malvern WR14 . . . . **152** F1
Worcester WR5 . . . . **116** B3
Oaklands Ct B61. . . . . **67** D6
Oaklands The
1 Droitwich WR9 . . . . . . **103** F8
Greenhill DY10. . . . . **28** A7
Halesowen B62 . . . .**8** F6
Kidderminster DY10. . . . . . . **28** A7
Tenbury Wells WR15 . . . . . . **55** F3
Oaklands Way B31. . . . . **18** C1
Oakleaf Cl B32. . . . .**9** C2
Oakleaf Rise DY14 . . . . **24** C2
Oak Leasow B32. . . . .**9** B4
Oakleigh B31. . . . . **19** C2
Oakleigh Ave WR2. . . . . . . **101** C2
Oakleigh Heath WR2. . . . . **101** C2
Oakleigh Rd
2 Droitwich WR9 . . . . . . **84** C1
Stourbridge DY8 . . . .**6** B2
Oakley Ho B60. . . . . **49** A1
Oakley Rd B30. . . . . **20** B5
Oakly Rd B97. . . . . **70** D3
Oak Rd
Birmingham B68. . . . .**9** C7
Catshill B61. . . . . **49** B8

Oakridge Cl
Redditch B98. . . . . **71** C7
2 Worcester WR4. . . . . **116** A7
Oakridge Rd B31. . . . . **19** D2
Oaks Prim Sch The B14 . . . **20** D2
Oak St WR8. . . . . **169** C5
Oaks The
Birch Acre B47. . . . . **52** F8
Birmingham, Hawkesley B38 **34** F7
1 Kempsey WR5 . . . . . . **141** C6
Redditch B98 . . . . **89** F7
Stoke Bliss WR15 . . . . **75** F3
Oak Tree Ave B97. . . . . **70** B4
Oaktree Cl B48. . . . . **51** A7
Oak Tree Cl
6 Evesham WR11. . . . . . **161** F2
4 Tenbury Wells WR15. . . **55** F6
Oak Tree Cres B62. . . . .**8** F6
Oak Tree Dr WR9 . . . . **65** B5
*Oaktree Farm Mobile Homes
Pk* B94. . . . . **53** B7
Oak Tree Gdns B28 . . . . . . **21** E3
Oak Tree Ho B30. . . . . **19** E7
Oak Tree La
Birmingham B30 . . . . **19** E8
Cookhill B49. . . . . **109** A2
Hollywood B47. . . . . **36** B6
Sambourne B96. . . . . **90** B2
Oak Tree Pk B98. . . . . **71** F6
Oak Tree Rd WR11. . . . . . **147** F7
Oak Trees B47. . . . . **36** A7
Oak Turn Dr [3] B38. . . . . . . **34** D8
Oak Wlk The B31 . . . . **19** A1
Oakwood Ct B63. . . . . **8** A4
Oakwood Dr B14. . . . . **20** D4
Oakwood Rd
2 Bewdley DY12 . . . . **26** A3
Hollywood B47. . . . . **36** A6
Oasis The DY9 . . . . **14** F5
Oasthouse Cl B60. . . . . **67** D6
Oatlands Wlk [3] B14. . . . . . **20** C2
Oatsley La WR10 . . . . **171** F7
Oat St WR11. . . . . **161** D4
Oberon Cl B45. . . . . **18** A2
Ockam Croft B31 . . . . **19** C2
OCKERIDGE. **80** F1
ODDINGLEY. **104** C4
Oddingley Rd B31. . . . . **19** C2
Odnall La DY9 . . . . **15** F3
OFFENHAM. **148** A1
Offenham CE Fst Sch
WR11 . . . . **148** A1
Offenham Cl B98. . . . . **71** B6
Offenham Covert B38 . . . . **34** E8
OFFENHAM CROSS **162** C8
Offenham Rd [4] WR11. . . . **161** F4
Offerton La WR3 . . . . **103** F1
*Offerton Wetlands Nature
Reserve*★ WR4 . . . . **116** C7
Offley St WR3. . . . . **115** B6
Offmoor Rd B32. . . . . **18** B8
Offmore Ct DY10. . . . . **28** C6
OFFMORE FARM **28** A6
Offmore Farm Cl DY10 . . . **28** C6
Offmore Fst Sch The
DY10. . . . . **28** B6
Offmore La DY10. . . . . **28** A6
Offmore Rd DY10 . . . . **27** F6
Offwell Rd B98 . . . . **71** D1
Ogbury Cl B14. . . . . **20** C2
Ogilvy Sq WR3. . . . . **115** A8
O'Key's La WR3. . . . . **103** A3
Oldacre Rd B68. . . . . **9** A7
Old Bakery Ct DY9 . . . . **15** A5
Old Bank Top B31. . . . . **19** B2
Old Barn Rd B30. . . . . **19** D6
Old Birmingham Rd
Alvechurch B48 . . . . **51** B8
Catshill B60 . . . . **49** C8
Lower Marlbrook B60, B45 . **32** E1
Old Bowling Gn Cl WR15 . . **55** E6
Old Burcot La B60 . . . . **49** C4
Oldbury Cl B98. . . . . **71** B6
Oldbury Park Prim Sch
WR2 . . . . **114** F3
Oldbury Rd
Broadheath WR2 . . . . **114** B4
Tewkesbury GL20 . . . . **196** E6
Worcester WR2 . . . . **114** B3
Old Chawson La [4] WR9. . **84** C1
Old Chester Rd S DY10 . . . **27** E2
Old Church Rd WR13. . . . . **152** A2
Old Coach Rd WR9. . . . . . . **84** E2
Old Crescent Ct [8] B68. . . .**9** B8
Old Crest Ave B98. . . . . **70** E2
Old Crown Cl B32. . . . .**9** B1
Old Dr The WR3 . . . . **103** C2
Old Farm Gr B14. . . . . **21** D5
OLDFIELD. **83** B6
Oldfield GL20 . . . . **196** F6
Oldfield Dr DY9 . . . .**6** A3
Oldfield La WR9 . . . . **83** C7
Oldfields
Cradley Heath B64. . . . .**7** D8
West Hagley DY9. . . . . **15** B6
Old Fold Yard Ct The
WR6. . . . . **77** E4
Old Forge WR6 . . . . **110** F6
Old Forge Bsns Ctr B98 . . **90** C8
Old Forge Dr B98. . . . . **90** C8
Old Forge Gdns [4] DY11. . **45** B2
Old Forge Trad Est DY9. . . . .**6** E2
Old Glebe Pastures
WR10. . . . . **131** B1
Old Grove Gdns DY9 . . . . . . **6** D3
Old Hall Cl
Aston Somerville WR12. . . **175** E1
Stourbridge DY8 . . . .**6** A8

Old Ham La DY9 . . . . **6** D2
Old Hawne La B63 . . . . **8** A5
Old Hill WR7. . . . . **119** D2
OLD HILLS. **140** E6
Old Hill Sta B64. . . . . **8** A8
Old Hollow WR14. . . . . **138** C3
Old Hospital La GL20 . . . . **196** F7
Old House La B62. . . . . **17** B1
Old La B48. . . . . **52** D4
Old Lime Gdns B38. . . . . . . **34** E8
Old Malvern Rd WR2. . . . . **127** C3
Old Manor Cl WR10 . . . . . **145** D3
Old Manor Gdns GL55 . . . **165** E4
Old Manor La GL20. . . . . . **197** A8
Old Market Ct [13] WR10 . . **144** D1
Old Meadow Rd B31. . . . . . **34** C7
Old Mill Cl WR9 . . . . **21** D2
Old Moat Dr B31. . . . . **19** B3
Oldnall Cl DY9 . . . .**6** F4
Oldnall Rd
Kidderminster DY10. . . . . . . **28** A4
Stourbridge B63, DY9 . . . . . .**7** A4
Old Northwick La WR3 . . . **114** F8
Old Oak Rd B38. . . . . **20** A2
Old Orch WR8 . . . . **169** A5
Old Pk B29 . . . . **19** A5
Old Portway B38. . . . . **34** E7
Old Post Office Alley [15]
GL20. . . . . **196** E6
Old Post Office La WR11. . **162** E3
Old Quarry Cl B45. . . . . **32** F8
Old Rd
Clifton upon Teme WR6 . . . **97** F7
Powick WR2. . . . . **127** F5
Old Rectory Cl WR2. . . . . . **127** E3
Old Rectory Gdns WR6. . . **126** C6
Old Rectory Gn WR10 . . . . **146** B1
Old Rectory La B48. . . . . . . **51** B7
Old Road N WR5. . . . . **141** C7
Old Road S WR5. . . . . **141** B5
Old School Cl
Offenham WR11. . . . . **148** A1
12 Pershore WR10 . . . . . **158** D8
Old School Ct [5] WR11. . . **161** B3
Old School La WR15. . . . . . **55** F6
Old School Mead B50 . . . . **136** C4
Old St WR8. . . . . **169** C5
Old Station Rd
Bromsgrove B60. . . . . **49** A1
Leigh WR6 . . . . **126** A8
Old Stone Cl B45. . . . . **17** F1
**OLD STORRIDGE
COMMON**. **124** F3
Old Stratford Rd B60. . . . . **49** C2
OLD SWINFORD. **6** A2
Oldswinford CE Prim Sch
DY8. . . . .**6** A3
Old Swinford Hospl Sch
DY8. . . . .**6** A4
Old Town Cl B38. . . . . **19** F2
Old Town Sta Bsns Pk
DY14. . . . . **22** E7
Old Turnpike Rd WR7 . . . . **117** F6
Old Vicarage Cl
Aston Fields B60 . . . . **68** B6
3 Kempsey WR5 . . . . . . **141** C6
Old Vicarage Gdns B80. . . **90** E4
Old Wharf Rd DY8. . . . .**5** F6
OLDWOOD. **55** E2
Oldwood Rd WR15 . . . . **55** D1
Old Woodyard The DY9. . . **15** D6
Old Wyche Rd WR14. . . . . **152** E5
Olive Dr B62. . . . .**8** C8
Olive Gr DY13. . . . . **43** F4
Olive Hill Rd B62. . . . .**8** D8
Olive La B62. . . . .**8** D8
Olive Pl B14. . . . . **20** E7
Olliver Cl B62. . . . .**9** A3
Olympus Gdns DY13. . . . . **44** C3
OMBERSLEY. **83** A4
Ombersley Cl B98. . . . . **90** C7
Ombersley Endowed Fst Sch
WR9 . . . . **83** B4
Ombersley Pk★ WR9. . . . . **83** A3
Ombersley Rd
Droitwich WR9. . . . . **84** E3
Halesowen B63 . . . .**7** F2
Worcester WR3 . . . . **102** A1
Ombersley Street E [4]
WR9 . . . . **84** F3
Ombersley Street W WR9. **84** E3
Ombersley Way
4 Birmingham B31. . . . . . **19** D2
Droitwich WR9. . . . . **84** D2
Ongrils Cl WR10 . . . . **144** C1
Ontario Cl
Birmingham B38 . . . . **35** A8
Worcester WR2 . . . . **127** E6
Open Field Cl B31. . . . . **19** C2
Orangery The DY9 . . . . **15** D7
Orchard Ave WR12. . . . . . **190** E8
Orchard Cl
Bidford-on-Avon B50 . . . . **136** D5
Bredon GL20 . . . . **185** A6
Bretforton WR11. . . . . **163** C4
Earl's Croome WR8 . . . . . . **155** F1
Halesowen B63 . . . .**7** C6
Hallow WR2. . . . . **101** D1
Mickleton GL55. . . . . **165** A5
3 Pershore WR10 . . . . . **158** C8
Rock DY14 . . . . **41** F6
Ryall WR8 . . . . **169** E6
Severn Stoke WR8 . . . . . . **155** D6

Orchard Cl *continued*
3 Stourport-on-Severn
DY13. . . . . **44** B4
West Hagley DY9. . . . . **15** B4
Worcester WR2 . . . . **127** B8
Orchard Cres B60. . . . . **67** C3
Orchard Croft B45. . . . . **50** D8
Orchard Ct
8 Tenbury Wells WR15 . . . **55** E5
5 Tewkesbury GL20 . . . . **196** F6
Orchard Dr
Birmingham B31 . . . . **33** F7
Little Comberton WR10 . . . **159** A3
Twyning GL20. . . . . **184** A6
Orchard End DY14 . . . . **22** C5
Orchard Gdns WR6. . . . . . . **77** E3
Orchard Gr
Cookhill B96. . . . . **108** E7
Cookley DY11. . . . . **13** A6
Kinver DY7. . . . .**4** B4
Norton Juxta Kempsey
WR5. . . . . **129** D1
Orchardlea WR10 . . . . **132** A5
Orchard Lea The [1] WR9 . **85** A1
Orchard Mead WR7 . . . . . . **120** E7
Orchard Pl
Harvington WR11. . . . . **147** F7
Redditch B80 . . . . **90** F8
Orchard Rd
Bromsgrove B61. . . . . **48** F4
Malvern WR14 . . . . **152** F5
Pershore WR10 . . . . **158** C8
Wolverley & Cookley DY10 . **13** C4
Orchard Ridge GL20. . . . . **181** F5
Orchard Rise
Bewdley DY12 . . . . **26** A3
Droitwich WR9. . . . . **103** E8
Orchard St
Kidderminster DY10. . . . . . . **27** E6
Redditch B98. . . . . **70** E3
Worcester WR5 . . . . **128** C7
Orchards The
Astwood Bank B96 . . . . **89** D1
Hollywood B47. . . . . **36** A7
2 Kidderminster DY11. . . **12** B1
Orchard The
Bewdley DY12 . . . . **25** E3
Bowling Green WR2. . . . . . **127** C3
Bromsgrove B61. . . . . **48** E4
Orchard Villas
Fairfield B61. . . . . **31** D2
Wythall B47. . . . . **35** F1
Orchard Way
Bransford WR6 . . . . **126** C5
Callow End WR2 . . . . **140** F7
Hollywood B47. . . . . **36** A8
Studley B80. . . . . **90** E2
Orchard Wlk WR11. . . . . . **161** D2
Orcheston Wlk B14 . . . . **20** D2
Orchid Cl WR5. . . . . **128** C4
Orchid Ct WR14. . . . . **153** C6
Orford Way WR14. . . . . . . **139** C2
Oriel Cl WR4. . . . . **115** E3
Oriel Ho WR14. . . . . **138** F1
Oriole Gr DY10. . . . . **28** B2
Orleans Cl [1] WR11 . . . . . **161** D1
ORLETON. **59** B2
Orleton Cl WR13. . . . . **167** C4
Orleton La WR15. . . . . **58** F4
Ormande Cl B63. . . . .**7** B7
Orme Cl DY5. . . . .**6** B8
Ormond Rd B45. . . . . **17** F1
Ormscliffe Rd B45 . . . . **33** B6
Orwell Cl DY8. . . . .**5** D4
Orwell Dr B38 . . . . **34** C8
Orwin Gn [1] WR4 . . . . **116** B3
Osborne Cl
Brierley Hill DY5 . . . .**6** F8
Kidderminster DY10. . . . . . . **28** B6
Osborne Rd
Bromsgrove B60. . . . . **49** C1
Malvern WR14 . . . . **139** A4
Osier Cl WR5 . . . . **128** C7
Osmaston Rd DY8. . . . .**5** F2
Osmington Gr B63. . . . .**7** D6
Osnor Ct B60. . . . . **68** B7
Osprey Cl WR2. . . . . **128** A6
Osprey Ho B80. . . . . **90** D4
Osprey Park Dr DY10. . . . . **28** B3
Ostler Dr WR2. . . . . **114** E3
Oswald St B98. . . . . **70** E3
Oswestry Cl B97. . . . . **89** C7
Other Rd B98. . . . . **70** E4
Otherton La WR6. . . . . **113** E1
Otley Cl WR4 . . . . **116** A4
Ottawa Cl WR2. . . . . **127** E7
Otter Cl B98. . . . . **72** A3
Otter La WR5. . . . . **128** F6
Oulton Cl DY11. . . . . **12** D1
Ounty John La DY8. . . . .**6** A1
*Our Lady of Fatima RC Prim
Sch* B17. . . . . **21** D5
*Our Lady of Lourdes RC Prim
Sch* B13. . . . . **21** D5
*Our Lady of Mount Carmel
RC Fst Sch* [2] B97. . . . . . **70** A2
*Our Lady Queen of Peace RC
Prim Sch* WR2. . . . . **114** F1
*Our Lady & St Kenelm RC
Prim Sch* [5] B63. . . . . **8** A4
*Our Lady & St George of Lima
RC Prim Sch* [1] B29. . . . **19** B8
Outfields B13. . . . . **20** E6
OUTHILL. **72** E1
Out of the Hat★ GL20. . . . **196** E6

OUTWOOD............47 B5
Outwood Cl B98.........89 E7
Out Wood Dr B31.......18 D1
Overbrook WR11.......161 E3
Over Brunton Cl B31....19 B2
OVERBURY...........185 F8
Overbury CE Fst Sch
  GL20...............185 F7
Overbury Cl
  Birmingham B31......19 C3
  Halesowen B63.......8 B2
Overbury Rd B31.......19 C3
Overdale B96..........89 E1
Overdale Rd B32.......9 E5
OVEREND.............7 E6
Overend Rd B63, B64...7 D7
Overfield Rd B32......9 F1
Overman Cl DY9.......6 D5
Oversley Cl B97.......70 C5
Owens Croft B38.......20 A1
Owlets End B50........136 F3
Owletts End WR11.....161 E3
Owletts La
  Pershore/Pinvin WR10..144 F7
  Wick WR10..........159 B7
Owlhill La WR13.......63 E2
Owls End La WR7......118 C1
Ox Bow Way DY10.....27 E8
Oxenshaw Wood Nature
  Reserve★ B98........89 E8
Oxenton Croft B63.....7 D2
Oxford Cl WR5.........115 F2
Oxford Ct 8 B29.......19 C7
Oxford Dr DY8.........5 F4
Oxford Rd WR14.......138 F2
Oxford Sq WR14.......138 F2
Oxford St
  Birmingham, Stirchley
  B30...............20 A7
  Kidderminster DY10...27 E5
Oxhill Cl B98..........71 E1
Oxhill Rd B90.........21 C2
Ox Leasow B32........9 C2
Oxleasow Rd B98......71 E4
Oxley Gr B29..........19 A8
Oxwood La B32........17 D4

P

Packers Hill WR8......169 A5
Packhorse Cl WR2.....114 E3
Packhorse La B38, B47...35 E6
Packington Rd
  Droitwich WR9.......84 E2
  3 Worcester WR2....114 E5
Packs Cl WR11........162 D4
Packwood Cl B97......69 F1
Packwood Ct 8 B29....9 F1
Padbury Ho B31.......18 D5
Padbury House B31....18 D5
Paddock Cl
  Bidford-on-Avon B50..136 C5
  Pershore WR10.......144 C5
  Westlands WR9.......84 D5
Paddock Hill 15 WR9...84 D5
Paddock La B98........89 E7
Paddocks Rd B47......35 F6
Paddocks The
  Cleobury Mortimer DY14..22 C5
  Norton & Lenchwick WR11..147 C3
Paddock The
  Birmingham B31......19 C4
  Stoke Heath B60......67 D6
  Stourbridge DY9......15 C8
  Stourport-on-Severn DY13..43 D6
Paddock Way WR9.....84 D5
Padgets La B98........71 D4
Padgewell Hill 1 WR9..84 D1
Padmore Cl WR1.......115 C3
Padua Rd B60.........49 C1
Page's La GL20........183 D5
Paget Cl B61..........48 E2
Pagnell Gr B13........21 C6
Painswick Cl
  Redditch B98.........89 E6
  Worcester WR4.......116 A7
Painswick Rd B28......21 F7
Pakefield Rd B30......20 C3
Palace Theatre★ B98...70 E3
Pale La B17...........9 F8
Palfrey Rd DY8........5 D5
Palmcourt Ave B28....21 E7
Palm Croft DY5.......6 C8
Palmers Gn 10 WR2....114 F1
Palmers Rd B98.......71 F5
Palm Rd GL20.........197 A4
Palmyra Rd B60.......49 C2
Pamela Rd B31........19 A3
Paper Mill Cotts B97...69 E5
Paper Mill Dr B98......71 B5
Paper Mill La WR9.....66 E2
Papworth Dr B61......48 F5
Parade The B64.......7 E8
Paradise Ct B28.......21 D6
Paradise La B28.......21 E6
Paradise Row B60.....48 F2
Pargeter St DY8.......5 F4
Par Gn B38...........19 D1
Parish Gdns DY9......6 C1
Parish Hill B61........31 D1
Park Ave
  Birmingham, King's Norton
  B30...............20 A5
  Stourport-on-Severn DY13..43 F4

Park Ave continued
  Studley B80.........90 E3
  Worcester WR3......115 A6
Parkbrook Ind Est 5 DY9..6 F5
Park Butts Ringway DY11.27 D6
Park Cl
  Bewdley DY12.......26 B3
  Malvern WR14.......139 B4
  Northway GL20.......184 D1
Park Cres
  Stourport-on-Severn DY13..43 F4
  The Bourne WR7.....119 C5
Park Croft
  Hollywood B47.......36 A5
  Upper Rochford WR15..56 F3
Park Ct
  Kidderminster DY11...27 D5
  Redditch B98........71 A4
Parkdale Dr B31.......34 A7
Park Dingle DY12......25 E2
PARK END............42 D7
Park End Dr B32.......9 D1
Parker Ho B14........20 F3
Parker Pl
  Broadway WR12......190 D8
  Kidderminster DY13...44 C7
Parkes Pas 2 DY13....44 A3
Parkes Quay 3 DY13...44 A3
PARK FARM..........90 C8
Park Farm Ind Est B98..90 C7
Parkfield B32.........9 A2
Parkfield Cl
  Birmingham, Quinton B62..9 A5
  Hartlebury DY11......45 A2
  Redditch B98........71 B6
Parkfield La WR2......114 D7
Parkfield Rd DY8......6 B5
Park Gate Rd DY10....13 B2
Park Hall Mews WR11..135 D4
Park Ho DY11.........27 C3
Park La
  Bewdley DY12.......25 F2
  Halesowen B63.......7 B6
  Hallow WR2.........114 D8
  Harvington DY10.....29 A2
  Kidderminster DY11...27 D6
  Malvern WR14.......152 C6
  Redmarley D'abitot GL19..192 A3
  Rushock WR9........46 D2
  Upper Sapey WR6....78 C5
  Worcester WR3......115 A6
Parkland Ave DY11....27 B5
Parkland Rd 2 WR3...102 A1
Parklands 4 WR11....161 B3
Parklands B97........70 A5
Parklands The
  Bowling Green WR2...127 B3
  3 Droitwich WR9....103 F8
  Stourbridge DY9......6 D3
Park Rd
  Brierley Hill DY5.....6 F8
  Halesowen B63.......7 B5
  Malvern WR14.......152 C6
  Stourbridge DY8......5 D5
  West Hagley DY9.....15 B6
Park Ridge Dr B63.....7 B6
Park Rise DY11........27 D5
Park Road W DY8......5 D5
Parkside
  Birmingham B32......9 C2
  Colwall WR13........152 B1
Parkside Mid Sch B61..49 A3
Parkside Rd B63.......7 D5
Parkside Way B31......18 C1
Park St
  Kidderminster DY11...27 D5
  Stourbridge DY8......5 F8
  Stourbridge, Lye DY9..6 A5
  Stourbridge, Stambermill DY8..6 A5
  Worcester WR5......115 C2
Parks The WR11.......162 A6
Parkstone Ave B61....67 D8
Park Street Gdns DY11..27 D6
Park The
  Northway GL20......184 D1
  Redditch B97........69 C7
Parkview WR14.......152 F8
Park View B49........122 F6
Park View Rd
  Birmingham B31......18 F3
  Stourbridge DY9......6 F4
Park View Terr WR3...115 A6
Park Way
  Birmingham B45......33 B8
  Droitwich WR9.......84 D4
  Redditch B98........71 A5
Park Wlk
  Brierley Hill DY5.....6 F8
  4 Redditch B97......70 E3
Parkwood WR10.......173 E7
Parkwood Rd B61......48 E3
Parlows End B38......34 D7
Parmington Cl B97....89 B6
Parry Rd DY11........27 B3
Parsonage Dr
  Birmingham B45......33 D4
  Halesowen B63.......7 A7
Parsonage La WR9....82 F4
Parsonage Way WR4...116 C5
Parsons Cnr 11 WR9...84 D1
Parsons Ct DY13......44 C4
Parson's Hill B30.....20 B2
Parsons La
  Hartlebury DY11......44 F1
  Redmarley D'abitot GL19..192 E3
  Weston-sub-Edge GL55..178 D6
Parsons Rd B98.......70 E2

Partons Rd B14........20 D6
Partridge Cl 3 WR5...128 D5
Partridge Gr DY10.....28 A2
Partridge Ho B97......70 D2
Partridge La
  Broadheath WR2.....114 A6
  Redditch B97........89 A7
Partridge Rd DY8......5 C4
Pass St WR10.........171 E8
Pastorale Rd B60......49 C1
Pastoreale Rd B60.....49 C1
Pastures Wlk B38......34 D7
Patch La B98..........89 F6
Pat Davis Ct DY10.....27 E7
Paternoster Row 4 DY11.27 D6
Pathway The B14......20 C5
Patina Cl DY5.........6 F8
Patios The DY11.......27 C7
Patricia Ave B14......21 C4
Patterdale Dr WR4....116 A5
Patterdale Way DY5...6 A8
Pavilion Gdns B61.....48 F5
Paxford Cl B98........71 B6
Paxford Way B31......18 F6
Paxhill La GL20.......183 F7
Paxton Cl B60.........49 B1
Paxton Rd DY9........7 A4
Paynes La WR10......146 A1
Peabody Ave WR4.....116 C4
Peach Cl 1 GL20......197 A3
Peachfield Cl WR14...152 F5
Peachfield Rd WR14...152 F5
Peachley Cl 8 B63....8 B3
Peachley Gdns WR2...113 F8
Peachley La WR2......113 F8
Peach Ley Rd B29.....18 F7
Peacock Cl 8 WR5....128 E5
Peacock Mews DY10...27 E8
Peacock Rd B13.......20 F6
Peakman Cl B45.......33 A6
Peakman St B98......70 E4
Peak View WR14......138 F5
Pearl La DY13.........43 D1
Pearmain Cl WR2.....114 E6
Pearman Rd B45......17 D1
Pearmans Croft B47...36 A6
Pear Orch The 2 GL20..184 E1
Pearson St DY9.......6 F4
Peart Dr B80..........90 C4
Pear Tree Cl
  Kidderminster DY10...28 B7
  Long Marston CV37...151 C6
  Malvern WR14.......152 E4
  Solihull B90.........21 D2
Pear Tree Cres B90...21 C2
Peartree Dr DY8.......6 A2
Pear Tree Dr
  Leigh WR13.........126 A2
  Sedgeberrow WR11...175 A1
Pear Tree Gr B90.....21 D2
Pear Tree Way
  Crowle WR7.........117 E4
  2 Dodderhill WR9...66 E1
Peason La WR10......171 D4
Pebble Cl DY8.........6 B5
PEBWORTH..........150 D2
Pebworth Cl B98......71 C7
Pebworth Fst Sch CV37..150 E2
Peckingham St 2 B63..8 B3
Peckinghall Cl WR13..152 A2
PEDMORE............6 B1
Pedmore CE Prim Sch DY9..6 C1
Pedmore Cl B98.......90 B7
Pedmore Ct Rd DY9....6 B1
Pedmore Hall La DY9..15 C8
Pedmore La
  Hagley DY9.........15 F8
  Stourbridge DY9......6 E1
Pedmore Rd DY9......6 F6
Pedmore Tech Coll & Com
  Sch DY9............6 D4
Peel St DY11..........27 D5
Peel Wlk 3 B17.......9 F7
Peewit Rd WR11......161 B2
Pegasus Ct B62........8 F5
Pegleg Wlk 2 B14.....20 C2
Pelham Lodge DY10...28 A5
Pelham Rd WR9......103 E8
Pemberton Cres DY10..13 C3
Pembridge Cl
  Birmingham B32......18 A7
  Redditch B98........71 D2
Pembroke Ave WR15...55 F5
Pembroke Pl WR4.....116 D5
Pembroke Way DY13...43 E6
Penbury St WR3.......115 B7
Pendas Mdw WR10....144 E5
Pendeen Rd B14......21 C4
Pendennis Cl B30.....19 D5
PENDOCK............193 B6
Pendock CE Prim Sch
  GL19...............193 B7
Pendragon Cl WR14...139 C4
Penelope Gdns WR11..176 D8
Penfields Rd DY9......6 B6
Penhill Cres WR2.....114 D3
Peninsula Rd B45.....129 A4
Penlu Rd 7 WR15.....55 F6
Penmanor B60........68 D8
Penmanor Cl WR2....114 E2
Pennard Gr B32.......9 F4
Penn Hall La WR6.....59 E7
Penn La B94..........53 C4
Pennyacre Rd B14....20 D2

Penny Cl WR13.......154 A7
Pennyford Cl B97.....70 A5
Penny La WR13.......154 A7
Pennylands Bank WR12.177 E4
Penrice Rd WR9......84 E1
Penrith Cl
  Brierley Hill DY5.....6 B8
  Worcester WR4......116 B6
Penrith Croft B32......18 D8
PENSAX.............60 B6
Pensax Rd
  Pensax WR6.........60 A5
  Stockton on Teme WR6..59 F3
Pensby Cl B13.........21 D8
Pensby Rd B31........19 C3
PENSHAM...........158 C5
Pensham Hill WR10...158 C6
Penshurst Rd B60.....49 C1
Penstock Ct DY10.....28 C8
Penzer Dr B45........50 D8
PEOPLETON..........131 B2
Peplins Way B30......20 B3
Pepper Hill DY8.......6 A4
Pepperpot The★ WR8..169 C6
Pepper St WR7.......120 F6
Pepperwood Cl B61...31 C3
Pepper Wood Dr B31..18 C1
Percheron Way
  7 Droitwich WR9....85 B1
  Droitwich WR9.......104 B8
Perch Rd WR5........128 C5
Percy Walton Cl WR14..153 A6
Perdiswell Leisure Ctr
  WR3...............115 D7
Perdiswell Prim Sch
  WR3...............115 C7
Perdiswell St WR3.....115 B7
Perivale Way DY8......6 A8
Perkins Cl WR11......135 D4
Peregrine Gr DY10....28 A2
Perrett Wlk 5 DY11...27 D6
Perrie Dr WR11.......164 B5
Perrin Ave DY11......27 B4
Perrins Cl WR14......138 E4
Perrins Field WR8....168 F5
Perrins La DY9.......6 F4
Perrins Rise DY9.....6 F4
Perrycroft Cl WR3....102 F3
Perry Ct B68.........9 B7
PERRYFIELDS........48 E4
Perryfields Cl B98....89 F6
Perryfields Cres B61..48 F5
Perryfields High Sch B68..9 A7
Perryfields Prim Sch B68..9 A7
Perryfields Rd B61....48 D4
Perry Hill GL20.......196 F5
Perry Hill Cres B68...9 B7
Perry Hill Ho B68.....9 C8
Perry Hill La B68.....9 B7
Perry Hill Rd B68.....9 B7
Perry La
  Bromsgrove B61......48 F2
  Hartlebury DY10.....45 B5
Perrymill La B96......90 B1
Perry Mill Rd 2 WR10..131 B2
Perry Wood Cl WR5...115 E1
Perry Wood Nature
  Reserve★ WR5......115 E2
Perry Wood Prim Sch
  WR5...............115 F3
Perry Wood Wlk WR5..115 E1
Perscoran Way WR10..158 D2
PERSHORE..........144 C2
Pershore Abbey★ WR10.158 D8
Pershore Coll WR10...158 F6
Pershore High Sch
  WR10..............144 A3
Pershore Hospl WR10..144 D1
Pershore La WR3......103 D2
Pershore Leisure Ctr
  WR10..............158 E8
Pershore Mkt 12 WR10..144 D1
Pershore Rd
  Birmingham, Breedon Cross
  B30...............20 A5
  Birmingham, Ten Acres B30..20 B8
  Eckington WR10......157 E1
  Evesham WR11.......161 C3
  Halesowen B63.......8 A2
  Kidderminster DY11...27 A6
  Upton Snodsbury WR7..131 C8
Pershore Road S B30..19 F3
Pershore Sta WR10....144 E5
Pershore Trad Est WR10..144 E4
Perton Gr B29........19 A8
Perwell Cl GL20......184 C2
Pestilence La B48.....51 D8
Peterborough Ct WR5..115 F2
Peterbrook Cl B98....89 F7
Peterbrook Prim Sch B90..21 D1
Peterbrook Rd B90....21 D1
Peterbrook Rise B90..21 D1
Peters Ave B31.......18 F2
Petersbourne Ct B28..21 F8
Petersfield Ct B28....21 F8
Petersfield Rd B28....21 E7
Peter's Finger B60....48 F1
Peter's Hill Prim Sch DY5..6 C6
Peter's Hill Rd DY5...6 C6
Peterson Ct WR14....138 F1
Pettitt Cl B14.........20 E2
Petton Cl B98.........71 F3
Petunia Cl WR5......128 D5
Pevensey Cl 9 WR5...128 E8
Pevensey Rd B60.....49 C1
Peverell Dr B28......21 F7
Pewterers Alley DY12..26 B3

Pheasant Cl DY10.....28 A2
Pheasant La B98......89 F7
Pheasant St WR1.....115 C3
PHEPSON...........105 C4
Philip Rd
  Halesowen B63......7 F3
  Worcester WR3......102 B1
Philipscote 2 WR11...161 F4
Phillips La GL19......192 E3
Phillips Rd WR12.....177 D1
Phillips Terr B98......70 F4
PICKEN END........154 B2
Pickenham Rd B14....21 A1
Pickering Croft B32...9 D1
Pickering Gn 7 WR4...116 C6
Pickersleigh Ave WR14..139 B4
Pickersleigh Cl
  6 Halesowen B63....8 A3
  Malvern WR14.......139 B4
Pickersleigh Gr WR14..139 B2
Pickersleigh Rd WR14..139 B2
Picton Gr B13.........21 B6
PIE CORNER.........95 D7
Pierpoint St 4 WR1...115 B3
Piers Cl WR14........153 A5
Pigeon La GL20.......186 A8
Pike Cl WR5..........128 C5
Pike Cnr 2 WR12.....177 E4
Pike Hill B60.........50 A7
Pikes Pool La B60....49 E2
Pikes The B45........32 F8
Pilgrim Rd WR9.......85 B2
Pinchers Cl DY9......30 E7
Pineapple Cl B14.....20 C6
Pineapple Gr B30.....20 C8
Pineapple Pl B14......20 D6
Pineapple Rd B30....20 C7
Pine Cl
  Fernhill Heath WR3..103 A3
  Kinver DY7.........4 C3
Pine Ct DY9..........6 B1
Pinedene DY13.......44 C3
Pine Gr
  Ankerdine Hill WR6..111 C6
  Birmingham B14.....21 A5
  Lower Marlbrook B45..32 C2
Pinehurst Dr B38.....19 F3
Pineridge Dr DY11....27 B5
Pines The B45........18 A1
Pine Tree Cl B97.....69 F3
Pinetree Rd 1 DY12...25 F2
Pineview B31.........18 F2
Pinewall Ave B38.....20 A1
Pine Way WR4.......115 E6
Pine Wlk
  Birmingham B31.....19 B3
  Stourbridge DY9.....6 D3
  2 Stourport-on-Severn
  DY13..............43 E4
Pinewood Cl
  Birmingham B45.....32 D8
  1 Kidderminster DY11..12 C1
Pinewood Dr B32.....9 A1
Pinewoods
  Birmingham, Hurst Green
  B62...............9 A7
  Birmingham, Woodcock Hill
  B31...............18 F8
Pine Woods B32......9 A2
Pinewoods Ave DY9...14 F4
Pinewoods Cl DY9....14 F4
Pinewoods Ct DY9....14 F4
Pinfield Dr B45.......33 B1
Pinkett St WR3.......115 A7
Pink Green La B97....70 C5
Pinkham DY14........22 D4
Pinkham La DY14.....22 D5
Pinkus Cl 3 WR4.....116 C3
Pinnacle Ho B97......89 E5
Pinner Gr B32........9 E4
PIN'S GREEN.......139 E8
Pinta Dr DY13........44 B3
Pintail Gr DY10.......28 B3
PINVIN.............144 E6
Pinvin CE Fst Sch WR10..144 E6
Pinvin Ho B97........70 A3
Pioneer Cl B97.......70 D4
Piper Pl DY8.........5 F8
Pipers Cl B61........67 D7
Pipers Gn B28........21 F5
PIPER'S HILL........87 A7
Pipers Rd B98........90 D7
Pipit Ct DY10........28 A2
Pippen Field WR4....116 C5
Pippin Ave B63.......7 B7
Pippin Cl
  5 Bidford-on-Avon B50..136 D5
  6 Pershore WR10....144 D2
Pippins Rd GL20......184 F6
Pippins The 2 WR10..171 E4
Pirie Ave WR4........116 C3
PIRTON.............142 C3
Pitcairn Cl B30.......20 B6
Pitcairn Dr B62.......8 B5
Pitchard Cl HR7.......96 D7
Pitchcombe Cl B98...71 A2
Pitchcroft La WR1....115 A5
Pitcheroak Cotts B97..70 A3
Pitcheroak Sch B97...70 B4
Pitcheroak Wood Nature
  Reserve★ B97......70 B3
Pitchers Hill WR11....176 D7
Pitclose Rd B31......19 B1
Pitfields Cl B68.......9 A8
Pitfields Rd B68......9 A8
Pit Leasow Cl B30....20 B8
Pitman Rd B32.......9 C5

Pitmaston Prim Sch
WR2 . . . . 127 F8
Pitmaston Rd WR2. . . . . . 114 F1
Pitmeadow Ho **5** B14. . . . 20 E2
Pitt Ave WR4 . . . . 116 B3
Pitt St DY10 . . . . 13 A1
PIXHAM. 141 A6
Pixham Ferry La WR5 . . . . 141 B5
Planetree Cl B60. . . . . 49 B2
Plane Tree Cl DY10 . . . . . . 27 F7
Plantation Cres **3** GL20 . 184 F6
Plantation Dr WR4 . . . . . 116 C5
Platts Cres DY8 . . . . 5 E8
Platts Dr DY8 . . . . 5 E8
Platts Rd DY8 . . . . 5 E8
Playdon Gr B14 . . . . 21 A3
Players Ave WR14. . . . . . 139 A5
PLAYLEY GREEN 192 C4
Pleasant Harbour DY12. . . 26 B4
Pleasant St DY10 . . . . 27 E7
Pleck Ho B14 . . . . 20 C1
Pleck The
  Bidford-on-Avon B50 . . 136 D4
  Inkberrow WR7 . . . . . . 120 E8
Pleck Wlk B38 . . . . 20 A1
Plimsoll Gr B32. . . . . 9 C5
Plimsoll St DY11 . . . . 27 D5
Plough Ave B32. . . . . 9 C2
Plough Croft **12** WR4 . . 116 B5
Plough La
  Oddingley WR9 . . . . . . 104 B2
  Rock DY14 . . . . 24 C1
Ploughmans Cl **11** WR4. 115 F6
Ploughmans Ct **13** WR9 . 84 D5
Ploughmans Pl **21** WR9. 84 D5
Ploughmans Rise **12** WR9 84 D5
Ploughmans Way **1** WR9 84 D5
Ploughmans Wlk
  Stoke Heath B60 . . . . . . 67 D6
  14 Westlands WR9 . . . 84 D5
Plough Rd WR9 . . . . 117 A7
Plover Gr DY10 . . . . 28 B1
Plovers Rise **7** WR5 . . . 141 C6
Plumstead Cl B97 . . . . 70 C6
Plymouth Cl
  Birmingham B31 . . . . . . 34 A7
  Redditch B97 . . . . 70 C1
Plymouth Ct B97 . . . . 70 C1
Plymouth Dr B45 . . . . 50 A8
Plymouth Ho B60 . . . . 69 B7
Plymouth Rd
  Barnt Green B45 . . . . . . 50 A8
  Birmingham B30 . . . . . . 20 B7
  Redditch B97 . . . . 70 D2
Pochard Cl DY10 . . . . 27 F1
Poden La
  Aston Subedge GL55 . . . 178 A8
  Honeybourne WR11 . . . 164 D4
PODMOOR 45 C6
Pointon Way WR9. . . . . . . 84 C6
Polden Cl B63 . . . . 7 C1
POLE ELM 140 F8
Pole Elm Cl **2** WR2 . . . 140 F8
Polesworth Cl B98 . . . . . . 71 D1
Polly Brooks Yd DY9 . . . . . 6 E5
Polo Fields DY9. . . . . 6 B1
Pomeroy Rd B32. . . . . 9 C1
Pool Bank B98 . . . . 70 E2
POOLBROOK 153 C6
Poolbrook Rd WR14. . . . . 153 C6
Poolbrook Way WR14 . . . 153 A6
Pool Cl WR10 . . . . 159 B4
Pooles Ct DY10 . . . . 27 E7
Poole St DY8 . . . . 5 E4
Pool Field Ave B31. . . . . . 18 E7
Pool Furlong DY9. . . . . . . 15 E1
Poolhead La
  Earlswood B94. . . . . 53 C7
  Tanworth-in-A B94. . . . . 53 E5
Pool Rd
  Halesowen B63 . . . . 8 B3
  Studley B80. . . . . 90 E4
Pooltail Wlk B31. . . . . 18 D1
Pool The **3** WR11. . . . . 161 B3
Pope Iron Rd WR1 . . . . . 115 A5
Popes La
  Astwood Bank B96 . . . . . 89 E2
  Birmingham B30, B31, B38 . 19 D3
Poplar Ave
  Birmingham, King's Heath
  B14. . . . . 20 F8
  Worcester WR4 . . . . . . 115 C5
Poplar Cl
  Catshill B61 . . . . 48 F8
  7 Evesham WR11. . . . 161 F2
Poplar Cres DY8 . . . . 5 D3
Poplar Dr B45 . . . . 50 D8
Poplar La WR7 . . . . 17 A4
Poplar Piece WR7 . . . . . . 120 F6
Poplar Rd
  Kidderminster DY11. . . . 27 C4
  Redditch B97 . . . . 70 A3
  Stourbridge DY8 . . . . . . 5 E3
  Wichenford WR6 . . . . . . 99 E5
Poplar Row WR11 . . . . . . 27 C4
Poplars La
  Astwood Bank B96 . . . . . 89 A1
  Feckenham B96 . . . . . . 107 F8
Poplars The
  Badsey WR11. . . . . . . 162 D3
  Bidford-on-Avon B50 . . 136 D5
Poplars Trad Est B80 . . . . 90 D6
Poplar Trees B47. . . . . . . 36 A6
Poplar Way WR11 . . . . . . 148 A9
Poplarwoods B32. . . . . . . 9 B2
Popular Ave WR10 . . . . . 145 A4
PORCHBROOK 41 B2
Porchbrook Rd DY14. . . . . 41 B2

Porlock Cres B31 . . . . 18 D3
Porlock Rd DY8 . . . . 6 A6
Portefields Rd WR4 . . . . . 115 F4
Porter Rd WR11. . . . . 161 F3
Porters Dr B14 . . . . 20 C4
Portersfield Ind Est B64. . . 7 C8
Portersfield Rd B64 . . . . . . 7 C8
Porters Mill La WR9. . . . . 102 E6
Portland Cres DY9 . . . . 6 B1
Portland Dr DY9 . . . . 6 B1
Portland Rd
  1 Droitwich WR9. . . . . 85 B1
  Malvern WR14. . . . . . . 138 F1
Portland St WR1 . . . . 115 B1
Portland Wlk WR1 . . . . . . 115 B1
Portman Rd B13 . . . . 20 F7
Portrush Ave B38. . . . . . . 19 D1
Portsdown Rd B63 . . . . 7 D2
Portsmouth Cl **3** WR5 . 115 F2
Port St WR11 . . . . 161 E4
PORTWAY
  Pendock. 193 A8
  Redditch. 53 A5
Portway Pl DY10 . . . . 13 A5
Post Office La
  Bransford WR6 . . . . . . 126 D6
  Fernhill Heath WR3 . . . 103 A3
  Kempsey WR5 . . . . 141 D7
  8 Tewkesbury GL20 . . 196 E6
Post Office Wlk B96 . . . . . 89 E1
Poston Croft B14 . . . . 20 D3
Potters Cl WR4 . . . . 115 F6
POTTER'S CROSS 4 A5
Pouk La WR14 . . . . 77 F6
POUND BANK
  Clows Top. 41 B8
  Great Malvern 153 D8
Pound Bank Rd WR14 . . . 153 C8
Pound Cl GL20 . . . . 183 F6
Pound Comm WR14. . . . . 153 C8
POUND GREEN 10 B2
Pound La
  Birmingham B32 . . . . . . 17 F3
  Mickleton GL55 . . . . . . 165 D3
  Rock DY14 . . . . 41 C7
Pound Rd B14 . . . . 20 E2
Poverty B96 . . . . 89 E2
Powderham Ave WR4 . . . 116 C6
Powell Ave B32. . . . . 9 A6
Powell's Row WR2. . . . . . 115 A1
Powell St **7** B63. . . . . . . 8 B3
Power Sta Rd DY13 . . . . . . 44 B2
POWICK. 127 E3
Powick Bridge★ WR2 . . . 127 E5
Powick CE Prim Sch
  WR2 . . . . 127 D3
POWICK HAMS. 127 C5
Powlers Cl DY9 . . . . 6 E2
Powyke Court Cl WR2. . . . 127 D3
Pratts La B80. . . . . 91 A8
Preece Cl WR14. . . . . 138 F6
Premier Bsns Ctr **3** DY9 . 6 F5
Premier Ct B30 . . . . 20 C3
Prescot Rd DY9 . . . . 6 C3
Prescott Dr WR4. . . . . . . 116 A8
Prestbury Cl
  Redditch B98 . . . . 72 A3
  6 Worcester WR4 . . . 115 F6
Presthope B29. . . . . 19 B7
Preston Cl B98 . . . . 71 B6
Prestwich Ave WR5 . . . . . 115 F1
Prestwood Dr
  Kinver DY7 . . . . 4 F8
  Stourbridge DY7 . . . . 5 B7
Prestwood Rd
  Birmingham B29 . . . . . . 19 B8
  Stourton DY7 . . . . 4 E6
Price Rd DY9 . . . . 7 A6
Price's La WR8 . . . . 169 C5
Price St WR3 . . . . 115 B6
Pridzor Rd WR9. . . . . 85 A4
PRIESTFIELD. 154 C6
Priestfield Rd B97 . . . . . . 89 E5
Priest La **6** WR10. . . . . 144 D1
Priestley Cl B63. . . . . 7 B6
Priest Mdw Cl B96 . . . . . . 89 D1
Primrose Cl
  Cradley Heath B64. . . . . . 7 B8
  Lickey End B60. . . . . . . 49 C6
  Malvern WR14. . . . . . . 153 C7
Primrose Cres WR5 . . . . . 128 D5
Primrose Croft B28 . . . . . 21 F5
Primrose Dr **10** WR5 . . 128 D5
Primrose Gdns B38 . . . . . 34 F8
Primrose Hill B38. . . . . . . 35 A8
Primrose Hill Prim Sch **5**
  B38 . . . . 34 F8
Primrose La B28. . . . . 21 F5
Primrose Way DY10 . . . . . 27 F4
Primrose Woods B32. . . . . . 9 B2
PRIMSLAND 104 A8
Primsland Dr **3** WR9 . . 85 B1
Primsland Fields **3**
  WR9. . . . . 104 A8
Prince Andrew Cres B45. . 17 E2
Prince Charles Cl B45. . . . 17 E2
Prince Edward Dr B45. . . . 17 E2
Prince Edward's Cl
  WR11. . . . . 161 E7
Prince Henrys High Sch
  WR11 . . . . 161 E6
Prince of Wales La B14. . . 21 C3
Prince Philip Cl B45. . . . . 17 E2
Prince Rd B30 . . . . 20 A3
Prince Rupert Ave WR2 . 127 B2

Prince Rupert Rd
  3 Stourport-on-Severn
  DY13 . . . . 43 E2
  16 Worcester WR5 . . . 115 C2
Princes Ave **2** WR9. . . 103 F8
Princes Dr B14 . . . . 20 C4
Princes Rd DY8 . . . . 5 D3
Princess Anne Dr B45. . . . 17 E2
Princess Cres B63 . . . . 7 E6
Princess Margaret Ave
  WR14. . . . . 139 C5
Princess of Wales Com Hospl
  B61. . . . . 49 A4
Princess Rd WR11 . . . . . . 161 E6
Princess Way DY13. . . . . . 43 E1
Prince St B64. . . . . 7 D8
Princethorpe Rd B29. . . . . 19 A8
Prior Ave B60. . . . . 67 C3
Prior Cl DY10 . . . . 28 C5
Priors Grange WR11 . . . . 135 E4
Priors Oak B97 . . . . 70 B4
PRIORS PARK 196 F4
Prior's Well★ DY13 . . . . . 62 B4
Priors Wlk
  Evesham WR11 . . . . . . 161 E3
  Pershore WR10 . . . . . . 158 D8
Priory Cl DY8 . . . . 6 B3
Priory Ct
  Malvern WR14 . . . . 152 F8
  Studley B80. . . . . 90 E5
Priory Gdns
  Birmingham B28 . . . . . . 21 D4
  1 Droitwich WR9. . . . . 84 F3
Priory Ho B63. . . . . 7 F5
Priory La WR9 . . . . 84 F3
Priory Rd
  Birmingham, Stirchley
  B14. . . . . 20 C7
  Birmingham, Warstock B28. 21 D3
  Dodford B61 . . . . 48 A6
  Halesowen B62 . . . . 8 F4
  Malvern WR14 . . . . 152 F8
  Stourbridge DY8 . . . . . . 6 B3
  Worcester WR2 . . . . . . 127 F8
Priory Sq B80. . . . . 90 E5
Priory The **1** DY13. . . . 44 A5
Pritchard Cl DY12. . . . . . . 26 C3
Pritchett Rd B31. . . . . 34 B7
Private Way B45. . . . . 33 C4
Proctors Barn La B98 . . . . 71 B4
Proctor's Barn Nature
  Reserve★ B98. . . . . 71 B4
Prophets Cl B97 . . . . 70 D3
Prospect Gdns DY8 . . . . . . 6 A4
Prospect Hill
  Kidderminster DY10. . . . 27 E6
  Redditch B97. . . . . 70 E4
  Stourbridge B97 . . . . . . 6 A4
Prospect La DY10 . . . . 27 E6
Prospect Pl **9** WR5 . . . 115 C1
Prospect Rd
  Halesowen B63 . . . . 8 C5
  Stourport-on-Severn DY13 . 44 B4
Prospect Road N B98. . . . 71 A4
Prospect Road S B98. . . . . 71 A4
Prospect Row DY8 . . . . . . 6 A3
Prospero Cl B45 . . . . 18 A2
Proud Cross Ringway
  DY11 . . . . 27 C6
Providence Ct B64. . . . . . . 7 C8
Providence Dr DY9 . . . . 6 E6
Providence Ind Est DY9 . . . 6 E6
Providence Rd B61. . . . . . 48 F3
Providence St
  Stourbridge DY9 . . . . 6 F6
  5 Worcester WR1 . . . . 115 C2
Pry Cl The WR15 . . . . 59 A8
Pry La WR12 . . . . 190 A8
PUCKRUP 183 D5
Puckrup La GL20. . . . . . . 183 C6
Pudford La
  Martley WR6 . . . . 98 F7
  Shelsley Beauchamp WR6. . 79 E1
PUDLESTON 92 E4
Pulley La WR9 . . . . 103 E7
Pullman Cl **4** DY13. . . . 44 A4
Pulman Cl B97 . . . . 70 C4
Pumphouse La
  Bentley Pauncefoot B97 . . . 88 B8
  Blackwell B45, B60 . . . . 49 F7
  Hanbury B60. . . . . 86 E3
  Redditch B97 . . . . 69 D1
Pump St
  Kidderminster DY10. . . . 27 E4
  Malvern WR14 . . . . 138 E4
  Worcester WR1. . . . . . . 115 C2
Purbeck Cl B63 . . . . 7 D1
Purbeck Croft B32. . . . . . . 9 F4
Purefoy Rd B13 . . . . 21 C5
Purleigh Ave WR4 . . . . . . 116 C5
Purlieu The WR14. . . . . . 152 D5
Purshall Cl B97 . . . . 70 C3
PURSHULL GREEN 47 A3
Purshull Green La
  Elmbridge WR9 . . . . . . 47 A2
  Upton Warren B61. . . . . 66 B8
Purslow Gr B31. . . . . 19 A1
Putney La B62. . . . . 17 B1
Puxton Dr DY11 . . . . 12 D1
Puxton La DY11 . . . . 27 C7
Pyke Rd GL20. . . . . 197 B7
Pyndar Ct WR13 . . . . 139 D5

Q

Quadrangle The WR13 . . . 139 D5
Quadrant Ho B32 . . . . 9 F7
Quail Pk Dr DY10 . . . . 28 A2
Quantock Cl
  Birmingham B45 . . . . . . 18 B2
  Halesowen B63 . . . . 7 D2
Quantock Dr DY10 . . . . . . 28 A6
Quantock Rd DY8 . . . . 6 B6
Quantry La DY9 . . . . 31 F8
Quarrington Gr B14 . . . . . 21 A3
QUARRY BANK 7 A8
Quarry Bank DY11 . . . . . . 45 A2
Quarry Hill B63 . . . . 7 E2
Quarry House Cl B45. . . . . 17 F1
Quarry La
  Birmingham B31 . . . . . . 19 A2
  Bromsgrove B61 . . . . . . 67 D8
  Cleeve Prior WR11 . . . . 149 B7
  Halesowen B63 . . . . 8 A2
Quarry Park Rd DY8. . . . . 15 A8
Quarry Rd
  Birmingham B29 . . . . . . 19 A8
  Rock DY14 . . . . 41 D4
Quarry The DY10. . . . . . . 27 F8
Quarry Wlk B45. . . . . 33 A7
Quay La
  Earl's Croome WR8 . . . . 155 F1
  Great Comberton WR10. . 158 E2
  Hanley Castle WR8 . . . . 169 A8
Quay St
  1 Tewkesbury GL20 . . 196 E6
  Worcester WR1 . . . . . . 115 B2
Quebec St WR1 . . . . 127 E6
Queen Elizabeth Dr
  WR10. . . . . 144 D1
Queen Elizabeth Rd
  Birmingham B45 . . . . . . 17 E2
  Kidderminster DY10. . . . 28 B5
  Malvern WR14 . . . . 139 B5
QUEENHILL 182 D6
Queen Margaret Prim Sch
  GL20 . . . . 196 E4
Queens Ave B14 . . . . 20 E8
Queen's Cl WR14 . . . . . . 138 E4
Queen's Cotts B97 . . . . . . 70 B4
Queens Cres DY8 . . . . 6 A7
Queens Ct GL20 . . . . 196 E6
Queens Dr B30 . . . . 20 A4
Queens Dr The B62 . . . . . . 8 C5
Queens Hill DY9 . . . . 30 D7
Queensmead GL20 . . . . . 185 A6
Queens Mead WR8 . . . . . 169 C4
Queen's Park Rd B32. . . . . 9 F6
Queens Rd GL20 . . . . 196 F4
Queen's Rd
  Evesham WR11 . . . . . . 161 D5
  Malvern WR14 . . . . 138 F4
  Stourbridge DY8 . . . . . . 5 F6
  Stourport-on-Severn DY13 . 43 F1
Queen St
  Astwood Bank B96 . . . . . 89 E1
  Brierley Hill, Quarry Bank
  DY5. . . . . 7 A8
  Droitwich WR9. . . . . . . 85 A3
  3 Halesowen B63 . . . . . 8 A4
  Kidderminster DY10. . . . 27 E7
  Redditch B98 . . . . 70 E4
  Stourbridge DY8 . . . . . . 5 F6
  Worcester WR1 . . . . . . 115 C3
Queen Street Pas **1** DY5. . 7 A8
Queensway
  2 Bidford-on-Avon B50 . 136 C5
  Halesowen B63 . . . . 8 B3
  Stourbridge DY9 . . . . . . 6 E2
  Wichenford WR6 . . . . . 100 B6
Queen's Way DY12 . . . . . . 26 C4
Queenswood Dr **4** WR5 . 128 D5
Queens Wood Ho B14. . . . 20 D4
Quest Hills Rd WR14 . . . . 138 F4
Quibery Cl B98 . . . . 71 F3
Quincy Rise DY5 . . . . 6 C7
Quinneys Ct B50 . . . . 136 E4
Quinneys La
  Bidford-on-Avon B50 . . . 136 E4
  Redditch B98 . . . . 90 B6
QUINTON 8 F5
Quinton Bsns Pk B32. . . . . 9 A4
Quinton Church Prim Sch
  B32 . . . . 9 A6
Quinton Cl B98 . . . . 71 D1
Quinton Expressway B32 . . 9 B4
Quinton La B32 . . . . 9 D6
Quinton Road W B32. . . . . 9 D6
Quisters **13** WR4 . . . . . 116 B5

R

Racecourse La DY8 . . . . . . 5 F1
Racecourse Rd WR10 . . . 144 E4
Race Field **3** WR4 . . . . 116 B5
Racks La WR9 . . . . 83 B5
Radbourne Dr B63 . . . . 7 A7
Radcliffe Dr B62. . . . . 8 E6
Raddens Rd B63 . . . . 8 F3
Raddlebarn Farm Dr B29. . 19 F8
Raddlebarn Rd B29. . . . . . 19 F8
RADFORD 120 D3
Radford Ave DY10. . . . . . . 27 E7
Radford Cl DY10 . . . . 27 E7
Radford Ho **2** B97 . . . . 70 A4
Radford Rd
  Alvechurch B48. . . . . . . 51 D7
  Birmingham B29 . . . . . . 19 A6

Radford Rd continued
  Flyford Flavell WR7 . . . . 119 D2
  Rous Lench WR11 . . . . . 120 D1
Radley Rd DY9 . . . . 6 F4
Radnor Cl B45 . . . . 18 B2
Radnor Croft **3** WR5 . . 115 E7
Radnor House B31 . . . . . . 18 D6
Radnor Rd B68 . . . . 9 B7
Radway Cl B98. . . . . 71 B6
Raglan Ct B60 . . . . 49 A1
Raglan St WR3. . . . . 115 B6
Ragley Cres B60 . . . . 68 A8
Ragley Hall★ B49. . . . . . 122 E4
Ragley Ho **7** B97 . . . . . 70 A4
Ragley Rd WR11 . . . . 148 A2
Raglis Cl B97 . . . . 70 A1
Rail Gd **6** WR10 . . . . . 144 C1
Railway Cl B80. . . . . 90 D4
Railway Wlk B60. . . . . 68 A6
RAINBOW HILL 115 D5
Rainbow Hill WR3. . . . . . 115 D4
Rainbow Hill Terr **7** . . . 115 D4
  WR3. . . . . 115 D4
Rainbow Rise WR3. . . . . . 115 D4
Rainford Way **1** B38. . . 34 C8
Rainthorpe Ave **3** WR5 . 128 E6
Raleigh Cl WR2. . . . . 114 D2
Ralphs Mdw B32. . . . . 9 D2
Ramble Cl WR7 . . . . 120 F6
Ramillies Dr WR5 . . . . . . 128 F4
RAMPLINGS THE 182 C1
RAMSDEN 143 E2
Ramsden Cl B29 . . . . 19 B7
Ramsey Cl B45. . . . . 17 F1
Ramsons Cl WR14. . . . . . 139 C3
Randall Ave B48. . . . . 51 A6
Randle Rd DY9. . . . . 6 C4
Randwick Cl **14** WR4 . . 115 F6
Randwick Dr WR4. . . . . . 115 F7
Ranelagh Rd WR14. . . . . 139 C5
Rangeways Rd DY11. . . . . 27 A8
Rangeworthy Cl B97 . . . . . 89 C7
Rannoch Ave **10** WR5 . 128 E6
Rannoch Cl
  Brierley Hill DY5 . . . . . . 6 B8
  Stourport-on-Severn DY13 . 43 F3
Ransom Ave WR5 . . . . . . 128 D7
Ran-Tan The B97 . . . . 89 E5
Ratcliffe Ave B30 . . . . 20 D3
Rathmore Cl DY8 . . . . 5 E2
Rathvilly Sch B31 . . . . 19 B3
Raven Dr WR5 . . . . 128 D5
Ravenhayes La B32 . . . . . 18 A6
Raven Hays Rd B31 . . . . . 18 C2
RAVENHILLS GREEN 111 E1
Ravens Bank Dr B98 . . . . . 71 E7
Ravenscroft B97 . . . . 5 C6
Raven Scroft Dr **1** WR9. 85 B2
Ravenshill Cl **2** WR5 . . 128 E6
Ravenshill Rd B14. . . . . . . 21 D4
Ravenshill Woodland
  Reserve★ WR6 . . . . . . 124 D8
Ravensmere Rd B98. . . . . 71 B1
Raven St DY13 . . . . 43 F3
Raybon Croft B45. . . . . . . 33 A6
Ray Mercer Way DY10. . . . 27 F7
Rea Ave B45. . . . . 32 E8
Reabrook Rd B31 . . . . 33 F8
Rea Cl B31 . . . . 34 A7
Reades Piece WR11. . . . . 164 A4
Rea Fordway B45. . . . . . . 17 F1
Rear Cotts B48. . . . . 50 F6
Rea Rd B31. . . . . 18 F1
Reaside Cres B14. . . . . . . 20 B5
Reaside Dr B45 . . . . 18 B1
Reaside Jun Sch B45. . . . . 17 E1
Rea Valley Dr B31. . . . . . . 19 B2
Rea Way WR2. . . . . 114 D2
Rebecca Pl WR8. . . . . . . 156 F7
Rebekah Gdns WR9 . . . . . 103 F7
Recreation Rd B61. . . . . . 48 F3
Rectory Cl
  Broadheath WR2 . . . . . 114 A7
  Harvington WR11. . . . . 148 A6
  Stourbridge DY8 . . . . . . 6 B3
Rectory Ct B97 . . . . 70 D1
Rectory Gdns
  Hartlebury DY11 . . . . . . 45 A3
  Stourbridge DY8 . . . . 6 B3
  Worcester WR2 . . . . . . 115 A2
Rectory La
  Birlingham WR10. . . . . . 158 A3
  Guarlford WR13. . . . . . 154 A2
  Hartlebury DY11 . . . . . . 45 A3
  Madresfield WR13. . . . . 139 E3
  Malvern WR13. . . . . . . 153 F6
  Rock DY14 . . . . 41 B5
  Shrawley WR6 . . . . 81 D7
  1 Stourport-on-Severn
  DY13. . . . . 43 E2
  Upton Warren B61. . . . . 67 A4
Rectory Rd
  Birmingham B31 . . . . . . 19 B3
  Broad Heath WR15 . . . . 77 A7
  Redditch B97. . . . . 70 D1
  Stourbridge DY8 . . . . . . 6 B3
  Upton upon Severn WR8 . 169 C4
Red Brick Cl B64. . . . . 7 D7
Redbrook Covert **7** B38. 34 E8
Redburn Dr B14 . . . . 20 D2
Redcar Cl B61 . . . . 32 B1
Redcliffe St WR3. . . . . . . 115 A7
REDCROSS 46 C8
Reddings The B47. . . . . . . 36 A5
REDDITCH. 70 C2

Red Ditch La GL19 . . . . . . **192** A2
Redditch Rd
  Alvechurch, Arrowfield Top
  B48. . . . . **51** B8
  Alvechurch, Rowney Green
  B48. . . . . **51** C3
  Birmingham B31, B38 . . . . **34** C8
  Hopwood B48 . . . . **34** B1
  Stoke Heath B60 . . . . **67** D5
  Studley B80 . . . . **90** D5
Redditch Ringway B97,
  B98 . . . . **70** D4
Redditch Sta B97 . . . . **70** D4
Red Earl La WR14 . . . . . . **153** D8
Redfern Ave WR5 . . . . . . **115** F1
Redgate Ave WR15 . . . . . . **55** E4
Redgate Cl B38 . . . . **19** D2
Redhall Rd B32 . . . . **9** E7
RED HILL
  Redditch. **90** F7
  Worcester **128** F8
Red Hill
  Bewdley DY12 . . . . **26** B2
  Redditch B98 . . . . **70** F2
  Stourbridge DY8 . . . . **6** B4
Red Hill CE Prim Sch
  WR5 . . . . **128** E8
Redhill Cl DY8 . . . . **6** E4
Red Hill Cl B80 . . . . **90** E6
Redhill Ct DY8 . . . . **6** E4
Redhill Gdns B38 . . . . **34** C8
Red Hill Gr B38 . . . . **34** F7
Redhill La B45, B61 . . . . . . **32** C5
Red Hill La WR5 . . . . **128** F7
Red Hill Pl B62 . . . . **17** A7
Redhill Rd B38 . . . . **34** D7
Redhill Sch DY8 . . . . **6** E4
Red House Rd DY13 . . . . . . **62** D8
Red La
  Evesham WR11 . . . . **161** B5
  Tewkesbury GL20 . . . . . . **196** E6
Redlake Dr DY9 . . . . **15** B8
Redlake Rd DY9 . . . . **6** B1
Redland Cl
  Lower Marlbrook B60 . . . . **32** C1
  Malvern WR14 . . . . **139** A4
Redland Dr WR13 . . . . **152** A3
Redland Rd WR14 . . . . **139** A4
Redlands ◳ WR10 . . . . . . **144** D1
Red Leasowes Rd B63 . . . . . **8** A3
Red Lion St
  Alvechurch B48 . . . . **51** B6
  Redditch B98 . . . . **70** E4
Redmarley CE Prim Sch
  GL19 . . . . **192** A3
REDMARLEY D'ABITOT . . **192** A3
Redmead Cl B30 . . . . **19** C4
REDNAL **33** C6
Rednal Hill Jun & Inf Schs
  B45 . . . . **33** C7
Rednal Hill La B45 . . . . . . **33** A6
Rednal Mill Dr B45 . . . . . . **33** C7
Rednal Park Ct B38 . . . . . . **19** F2
Rednal Rd B38 . . . . **19** E1
Red Sands Rd DY10 . . . . . . **27** E8
Redstart Ave DY10 . . . . . . **28** B2
Redstone Cl B98 . . . . **71** C6
Redstone La ◳ DY13 . . . . . **62** F8
Redstone Nature Reserve★
  DY13 . . . . **44** A1
Redwing Cl
  Malvern WR14 . . . . **138** D6
  Walton Cardiff GL20 . . . . **197** A3
Redwing Ct DY10 . . . . **28** A1
Redwood Cl
  Birmingham B30 . . . . **19** E4
  Worcester WR4 . . . . **115** E6
Redwood Croft B14 . . . . . . **20** E7
Redwood Ct ◰ GL20 . . . . **184** E1
Redwood Rd
  Birmingham B30 . . . . **19** E4
  Kinver DY7 . . . . **4** C3
Reedham Cl WR3 . . . . **115** A7
Reedmace Cl B38 . . . . **34** F8
Reed Mace Dr B61 . . . . **49** A5
Reeve Ct DY10 . . . . **28** A1
Reeves Rd B14 . . . . **20** C6
Regan Ho B13 . . . . **21** D7
Regency Dr B38 . . . . **19** F2
Regency Gdns B14 . . . . **21** C3
Regency High Sch WR4 . . **115** F6
Regency Rd WR14 . . . . **139** B5
Regent Cl B63 . . . . **8** A4
Regent Ct ◳ B62 . . . . **9** A7
Regent Mews B61 . . . . **67** E8
Regents Park Rd B60 . . . . . **49** C2
Regent St B30 . . . . **20** A7
Regiment Cl WR5 . . . . **128** E4
Regina Cl
  Birmingham B45 . . . . **17** E2
  Worcester WR2 . . . . **127** F6
Renfrew Gdns DY11 . . . . . . **27** C7
Rennie Gr B32 . . . . **9** D5
Renshaw Ind Est B80. . . . . **90** B4
Reservoir Cl B31 . . . . **18** D5
Reservoir La ◳ WR3 . . . . . **115** D4
Reservoir Rd
  Birmingham, Rednal B45. . . **33** C3
  Kidderminster DY11 . . . . . **27** C3
Resolution Way ◳ DY13. . . **44** B2
Retreat St B96 . . . . **89** E1
Retreat The B64 . . . . **7** E7
Reyde Cl B97 . . . . **70** A2
Reynard Cl B97 . . . . **69** F3
Reynolds Cl WR13 . . . . . . **167** C5

Rhayader Rd B31 . . . . **18** E5
Rhuddlan Way DY10 . . . . . . **27** E1
RHYDD **154** F6
Rhydd Cl WR14 . . . . **153** C7
RHYDD GREEN **154** E7
Rhyse La WR15 . . . . **56** C5
Rian Ct B64 . . . . **7** D8
RIBBESFORD **26** B1
Ribbesford Cl B63 . . . . **7** D6
Ribbesford Dr DY13 . . . . . . **43** E4
Ribbesford Rd DY13 . . . . . . **43** C2
Ribble Cl WR5 . . . . **115** E2
Ribblesdale Rd B29, B30 . . **20** A8
Ribston Cl ◳ WR2 . . . . . . **114** E5
Richard Pl ◳ GL20 . . . . . **196** F3
Richards Cl B31 . . . . **33** F6
Richard's Cl WR14 . . . . . . **138** E6
Richardson Cl WR9 . . . . . . **85** E8
Richardson Dr DY8. . . . . **5** E8
Richmond Cl B47 . . . . **36** C7
Richmond Ct
  ◳ Birmingham, Weoley Castle
  B29. . . . . **19** C7
  Halesowen B63 . . . . **7** E3
  Stourbridge DY9 . . . . **6** B1
Richmond Gdns DY8 . . . . . . **5** F7
Richmond Gr DY8 . . . . **5** E8
Richmond Pl B14 . . . . **20** F8
Richmond Rd
  Bewdley DY12 . . . . **25** F4
  Birmingham B45 . . . . **32** E7
  Malvern WR14 . . . . **139** B4
  ◳ Walton Cardiff GL20 . . **197** A3
  Worcester WR5 . . . . **115** D2
Richmonds Pitch ◳
  WR14 . . . . **166** E7
Richmond St B63 . . . . **8** A4
Rickets Cl DY13 . . . . **44** B7
Rickett's La ◲ WR9 . . . . . **84** F3
Ricketts Pl DY12 . . . . **26** B3
Rickyard Cl B29 . . . . **19** A6
Rickyard La B98 . . . . **71** D5
Rickyard Piece B32 . . . . **9** E4
Riddings Cl DY12 . . . . **26** C5
Riddings The B60 . . . . **6** D2
RIDGACRE **9** D6
Ridgacre La B32 . . . . **9** C6
Ridgacre Rd B32 . . . . **9** C6
Ridgacre Road W B32 . . . . . **9** A6
Ridge Cl B13 . . . . **21** C6
Ridgefield Rd B62 . . . . **8** C7
Ridge Gr DY9 . . . . **6** C5
Ridgemount Dr B38 . . . . . . **34** D8
Ridge Prim Sch The DY8 . . **5** C5
Ridge St DY8 . . . . **5** C6
Ridgewater Cl B45 . . . . **33** B6
Ridgeway
  Eastnor WR13 . . . . **166** B4
  Quinton B32. . . . . **9** A4
Ridgeway Ave B62 . . . . **9** A6
Ridgeway Cl B80. . . . . **90** E2
Ridgeway Mid Sch The
  B96. . . . . **108** E8
Ridgeway The
  Birmingham, Quinton B32 . . **9** A4
  Cookhill B96. . . . . **109** A6
  Droitwich WR9. . . . . **85** B3
  Stourport-on-Severn DY13 . **43** F5
  Worcester WR5 . . . . **128** E7
Ridgeway Trad Est B96. . . . **89** E1
Ridgewood Ave DY8. . . . . . . **5** C7
Ridgewood High Sch DY8 . . **5** C5
Ridgmont Croft B32. . . . . . . **9** E5
Ridings La B98. . . . . **71** B6
Ridleys Cross DY13. . . . . . . **62** E6
Ridsdale Cl WR11 . . . . **135** E4
Rifle Range Nature Reserve★
  DY11. . . . . **27** A2
Rifle Range Rd DY11 . . . . . **27** B3
Rigby Hall B60. . . . . **68** C8
Rigby Hall Specl Sch B60 . . **68** C8
Rigby La B60 . . . . **68** C8
Rightons Ct ◳ WR11 . . . . . **161** D5
Riley Rd B14 . . . . **21** D3
Rilstone Rd B32. . . . . **9** F5
Ringway The DY10 . . . . **27** F5
Ringwood Dr B45 . . . . **18** A1
Ripley Gdns WR4 . . . . **116** D6
Ripon Rd
  Birmingham B14 . . . . **21** C4
  Worcester WR5 . . . . **116** A3
RIPPLE **183** A8
Ripple Rd
  Birmingham B30 . . . . **20** B7
  Droitwich WR9. . . . . **84** E2
Rise Ave B45 . . . . **33** A7
Rise The B48 . . . . **34** B4
Rissington Ave B29 . . . . . . **20** A8
River Brook Dr B30 . . . . . . **20** B8
Riversdale Rd B14 . . . . **21** D3
RIVERSIDE **70** F3
Riverside
  Childswickham WR12. . . . **176** F1
  Studley B80 . . . . **90** F5
  ◳ Tenbury Wells WR15. . . **55** E5
Riverside Cl
  Lickey End B60. . . . . **49** C6
  ◳ Upton upon Severn
  WR8 . . . . **169** C6
Riverside Cres B28. . . . . . . **21** D4
Riverside Ct B38 . . . . **19** D3
Riverside Ind Est B98 . . . . . **90** C8
Riverside N DY12 . . . . **26** B4
Riverside Rd ◳ WR9 . . . . . **85** A3
Riverside Sch WR1. . . . . . . **115** A5
Riverside Sh Ctr WR11 . . **161** F4
Riverside Way WR9 . . . . . . **85** B3
Riversleigh Dr DY8. . . . . **5** E8

Rivers Way ◳ WR12. . . . . **177** A1
Riverview Cl WR2 . . . . **114** F6
Riverway Dr DY12 . . . . **26** B4
Rivington Cl DY8. . . . . **5** E4
Roach Cl ◳ WR5. . . . . **128** C5
Road No 1 DY10. . . . . **27** E2
Road No 2 DY10. . . . . **27** E2
Road No 3 DY10. . . . . **27** E2
Robert Owen Ct ◳ WR1. . **115** C2
Roberts La
  South Littleton WR11. . . . **148** F1
  Stourbridge DY9 . . . . **15** B8
Robeson Cl WR9. . . . . **85** B3
Robina Cl ◳ WR11 . . . . . . **175** D8
Robin Cl
  Northway GL20 . . . . **184** D1
  Worcester WR5 . . . . **128** D5
Robin Ct DY10 . . . . **28** A2
Robin Dr WR3 . . . . **102** E3
Robin Hood Cres B28 . . . . . **21** F7
Robin Hood Croft B28. . . . . **21** F6
Robin Hood La B28 . . . . **21** E7
Robin's Cl DY8. . . . . **6** A3
Robinsfield Dr B31. . . . . . . **34** A7
Robins Hill Dr B48. . . . . . . **51** A5
Robins La B97. . . . . **70** C6
Rochester Cl B97 . . . . **89** C8
Rochester Rd B31. . . . . **19** A4
Rochester Wlk DY10 . . . . . **28** C5
ROCHFORD **57** A6
Rochford Cl
  Birmingham B45 . . . . **32** E7
  Halesowen B63 . . . . **7** F2
ROCK **41** C3
Rock Ave B45. . . . . **33** C7
Rock Cotts ◳ DY11 . . . . . . **27** D6
Rockford Cl B98. . . . . **89** F5
Rock Hill
  Bromsgrove B61 . . . . **67** D7
  Inkberrow WR7 . . . . **120** F6
Rockhill La B96. . . . . **107** F8
Rockingham Hall Gdns
  DY9 . . . . **15** D7
Rockingham La WR4 . . . . . **116** D6
Rock La WR6 . . . . **78** C4
Rockley Bank ◳ DY14. . . . . **22** D5
Rockley Gr B45 . . . . **33** B7
Rock St GL19 . . . . **195** D2
Rockwell La B48. . . . . **51** E4
Rocky La B61. . . . . **48** E7
Rocky Wall DY7. . . . . **3** E4
Rodborough Cl WR4 . . . . . **116** A7
Rodborough Dr WR4 . . . . . **116** A7
Roden Ave DY10 . . . . **28** A7
Rodway Cl DY5 . . . . **6** D7
Rogers Hill WR3 . . . . **115** C4
Rolan Dr B90 . . . . **36** E8
Roland Rutter Ct ◳
  WR10. . . . . **144** C1
Roman Ct B38 . . . . **35** B8
Roman Rd (Sandy La) DY8. **5** C3
Roman Way
  Bromsgrove B61 . . . . **49** B4
  Droitwich Spa WR9 . . . . . **84** F4
  Malvern WR14 . . . . **139** C5
  Salwarpe WR9. . . . . **84** C1
Roman Way Bsns Ctr
  WR9 . . . . **84** E5
Roman Way Fst Sch B98 . . **71** E3
Romany Rd B45 . . . . **17** D1
Romany Way DY9 . . . . **5** C3
Romilly Cl DY8. . . . . **5** E6
Romney Cl B28 . . . . **21** F7
ROMSLEY
  Halesowen. **17** A4
  Shatterford. **2** A2
Romsley Cl
  Birmingham B45 . . . . **32** E8
  Halesowen B63 . . . . **8** B2
  Redditch B98 . . . . **71** F3
ROMSLEY HILL **17** A2
Romsley Hill Grange B62. . **16** F1
Romsley La
  Romsley WV15. . . . . **2** A2
  Upper Arley DY12 . . . . . . **11** B8
Romsley Rd
  Birmingham B32 . . . . **18** B8
  Stourbridge DY9 . . . . **6** C5
Romsley View WV15 . . . . . . **1** C6
Rona Gdns WR5 . . . . **128** F6
Ronhill Cres DY14. . . . . . . **22** C5
Ronhill La DY14. . . . . **22** C5
RONKSWOOD **115** F2
Ronkswood Cres WR5. . . . **115** E3
Ronkswood Hill WR4. . . . . **115** E3
Ronkswood Hill Mdws
  Nature Reserve★ WR4 . **116** A4
Rookery Cl B97 . . . . **70** D1
Rookery Cl WR5 . . . . **141** E4
Rookery The B62 . . . . **9** A2
Rooks Mdw DY9 . . . . **15** B6
Rope Wlk
  Bewdley DY12 . . . . **26** B3
  Tewkesbury GL20 . . . . . . **196** F6
Rosafield Ave B62 . . . . **8** F6
Rose Ave
  Alvechurch B48 . . . . **51** A5
  Birmingham B68. . . . . **9** C7
  Droitwich WR9. . . . . **85** A3
  Worcester WR4 . . . . **115** E4
Rose Bank
  ◳ Evesham WR11. . . . . . **161** F4
  Worcester WR5 . . . . **115** D1
Rosebay Ave B38 . . . . **34** F8
Roseberry Gdns DY10 . . . . **13** C3
Rosebriars B90 . . . . **36** E7
Rose Cotts B30 . . . . **20** A6
Rosedale WR6 . . . . **60** E4

Rosedale Cl B97 . . . . **70** A4
Rose Dene ◲ DY13 . . . . . . **43** E4
Rosefield Cres GL20. . . . . **197** A6
Rosegardens The B63. . . . . . **7** F2
Rosehall Cl B98. . . . . **89** E6
Rose Hill
  Barnt Green B45 . . . . **33** B4
  Worcester WR5 . . . . **115** D1
Rose La B61 . . . . **48** A6
Roseleigh Rd B45 . . . . **33** B6
Rosemary Ave ◲ WR2. . . . **114** D1
Rosemary Cl WR11 . . . . . . **161** B2
Rosemary Dr B60 . . . . **67** C1
Rosemary La DY8 . . . . **5** D3
Rosemary Rd
  Halesowen B63 . . . . **7** E2
  Kidderminster DY10. . . . . **28** B7
Rosemoor Dr DY5. . . . . **6** B7
Rosemoor Gdns ◳ WR5. **128** E6
Rosemount B32. . . . . **9** E5
Rosenhurst Dr ◳ DY12. . . . **26** A3
Roses Theatre The★
  GL20 . . . . **196** E7
Rose Terr
  Barnt Green B45 . . . . **50** D8
  Worcester WR5 . . . . **115** D1
Rosetti Cl DY10 . . . . **28** C6
Rosewood Cl WR3 . . . . **102** F2
Rosewood Dr B45. . . . . **50** C7
Roslin Cl B60 . . . . **49** B1
Rossees La WR4 . . . . **99** D7
Rossendale Cl
  Fernhill Heath WR3 . . . . **102** F3
  Halesowen B63 . . . . **7** D6
Rothesay Croft B32 . . . . . . **18** B7
Rothley Wlk B38 . . . . **34** C8
Rothwell Rd WR14 . . . . . . **152** F1
Rough Hill Dr B98. . . . . **89** F6
Rough Mdw ◳ WR4. . . . . . **116** B5
Rough The
  Redditch B97 . . . . **89** D8
  Stourport-on-Severn DY13 . **43** F7
Roundabout The B31. . . . . **18** D1
Round Hill Ave DY9 . . . . **6** C1
Roundhills Rd B62 . . . . **8** F8
Round Hill Wharf DY11. . . . **27** D5
Roundlea Rd B31 . . . . **18** E7
Round Saw Croft B45 . . . . . **32** F8
Rousay Cl B45 . . . . **17** F1
ROUS LENCH **133** E1
Rowan Ave B45 . . . . **33** B5
Rowanberry Cl ◲ DY13. . . . **43** E4
Rowan Cl
  Bromsgrove B61 . . . . **48** E2
  Droitwich WR9. . . . . **103** F8
  ◳ Evesham WR11. . . . . . **161** F2
  Hollywood B47. . . . . **36** B5
Rowan Cres B97 . . . . **70** A4
Rowan Ct
  Birmingham B30 . . . . **20** A2
  Tolladine WR4 . . . . **115** E4
Rowan Dr GL20 . . . . **197** B3
Rowan House EMI Facility &
  Day Hospl WR14 . . . . . **139** A4
Rowan Rd B97. . . . . **70** A4
Rowantrees B45 . . . . **33** B5
Rowan Way B31 . . . . **33** F8
Rowberrie Cl B45. . . . . **33** C7
Rowborough Cl B96. . . . . . **89** E2
Rowbrook Cl B90 . . . . **36** E8
Rowcroft Covert B14. . . . . **20** C2
Rowheath Ho B30. . . . . **19** E5
Rowheath Rd B30. . . . . **19** F4
Rowland Ave B80 . . . . **90** E3
Rowland Hill Ave DY11 . . . **27** B5
Rowland Hill Sh Ctr ◳
  DY10. . . . . **27** E6
Rowland Way (Road 1a)
  DY11. . . . . **27** E1
Rowley Hill St WR2 . . . . . . **114** F2
Rowley Hill View B64 . . . . . . **7** F8
Rowney Croft B28. . . . . **21** E4
ROWNEY GREEN **51** E3
Rowney Green La B48. . . . . **51** F5
Rowntree Gdns WR4 . . . . . **116** C2
Rows The GL55 . . . . **178** C7
Roxall Cl DY10 . . . . **14** C2
Roxboro Ho B98 . . . . **70** D2
Royal Albert Ct ◳ WR5. . **115** C1
Royal Cl DY5. . . . . **6** C8
Royal Gram Sch WR1. . . . **115** B4
Royal Oak Gdns WR14. . . . **139** A5
Royal Oak Rd B62. . . . . **8** F5
Royal Orthopaedic Hospl
  B31. . . . . **19** B5
Royal Worcester Cres
  B60 . . . . **49** C1
Rozel Ave DY10 . . . . **13** B1
Rrde Rd WR14 . . . . **153** A6
RUBERY **33** B7
Rubery Farm Gr B45 . . . . . **32** C7
Rubery Field Cl B45. . . . . . . **18** B1
Rubery La B45 . . . . **18** A1
Rubery Lane S B45. . . . . . . **32** C7
Ruckley Rd B29. . . . . **19** B8
Rudd Cl WR5 . . . . **128** C5
Rudge Rd ◳ WR11 . . . . . . **161** D5
Rufford Prim Sch DY9. . . . . . **6** C5
Rufford Rd DY9. . . . . **6** D5
Rufford St DY9. . . . . **6** D5
Rugby Rd DY8 . . . . **5** D7
Rumbow B63. . . . . **8** A4
Rumbow La B62 . . . . **16** D3
RUMBUSH **36** E3
Rumbush La B90, B94. . . . . **36** F5
Rumer Cl CV37. . . . . **151** C7
Runcorn Cl B98. . . . . **89** F8
Rushall Cl DY8. . . . . **5** E8

RUSHBROOK **53** D3
Rushbrook Gr B14 . . . . **20** C4
Rushbrook La B94 . . . . **53** D3
Rusher's Cl WR10 . . . . **144** C1
Rush Gn B32. . . . . **9** E2
Rush La B98. . . . . **71** B6
Rushleigh Rd B90 . . . . **36** E8
Rushmead Gr B45. . . . . **33** A7
RUSHOCK **46** C3
Rushock Cl B98. . . . . **90** C7
Rushock Trad Est WR9. . . . **46** A2
RUSHWICK **127** B8
Rushwick Prim Sch WR2 **127** C8
Rushy Piece B32. . . . . **9** D3
Ruskin Ave DY10 . . . . **28** C6
Ruskin Ct ◳ B68. . . . . **9** B8
Ruskin Glass Ctr★ DY8 . . . . **5** F7
Russel Croft B60 . . . . **68** A7
Russell Cl
  Bowling Green WR2. . . . . **127** C2
  Malvern WR14 . . . . **139** B3
Russell Dr
  Eckington WR10. . . . . . . **171** E8
  Malvern WR14 . . . . **139** B3
Russell Rd DY10 . . . . **27** F4
Russell Sq ◳ WR12 . . . . . . **190** D8
Russell St WR10 . . . . **158** F1
Russet Cl
  ◳ Bredon GL20 . . . . **184** D5
  ◳ Worcester WR2 . . . . . **114** E5
Russett Way ◳ DY12 . . . . . **25** F4
Russet Way B31 . . . . **18** E6
Ruthall Cl B29 . . . . **19** C7
Ruth Chamberlain Ct ◳
  DY11 . . . . **27** D6
Rutherford Rd B60. . . . . . . **68** B7
Rutland Ct ◲ B29. . . . . **19** C7
Rutland Dr B60 . . . . **68** A8
Rutland Pl
  Stourbridge DY8 . . . . **5** D8
  ◳ St Peter the Great County
  WR5 . . . . **128** E6
Rutley Gr B32. . . . . **9** F4
Rutters Mdw B32 . . . . **9** B4
RYALL **169** E6
Ryall Gr WR8 . . . . **169** F6
Ryall La WR8 . . . . **169** E5
Ryall Mdw WR8 . . . . **169** E5
Rydal Cl
  Stourport-on-Severn DY13 . **43** F6
  ◳ Worcester WR4 . . . . . **115** F5
Rydal Way B28. . . . . **21** F7
Ryden La WR10 . . . . **160** E8
Ryde Park Rd B45. . . . . **33** C7
Ryebank Cl B30. . . . . **19** C5
Rye Cl WR9. . . . . **85** A2
Rye Croft
  Hollywood B47. . . . . **36** A5
  Stourbridge DY9 . . . . **6** E2
Ryefield Cl DY9 . . . . **15** A4
Ryefields Rd B60. . . . . **67** C3
Ryegrass La B97 . . . . **89** C6
Rye Hill La WR7. . . . . **117** C3
Ryeland Cl ◳ WR3 . . . . . . **115** E7
Ryeland La
  Elmley Lovett WR9. . . . . . **45** F2
  Hartlebury WR9 . . . . **64** F8
Ryelands WR10 . . . . **145** A4
Rye Lea The WR9 . . . . **84** F2
Ryemarket Sh Ctr ◳ DY8. . **6** A5
Rye Pl WR4. . . . . **116** D6
RYE STREET **180** A4
Ryland Cl B63 . . . . **7** E2
Rynal Pl WR11 . . . . **161** E5
Rynal St WR11 . . . . **161** D5
Ryton Cl B98 . . . . **71** D1
Ryvere Cl ◲ DY13. . . . . **43** F2

S

Sabrina Ave WR3 . . . . **115** A6
Sabrina Dr DY12 . . . . **26** A4
Sabrina Terr ◳ WR1 . . . . **115** A5
Sabrina Wlk WR3 . . . . **115** A7
Saddlers Cl B63. . . . . **7** B5
Saddlers Wlk WR4 . . . . . . **115** F6
Saffron Ho ◳ B38 . . . . **34** E4
Saffron Rd ◳ GL20. . . . . . **196** E6
Sagebury Dr B60. . . . . **67** C1
Sage Croft B31 . . . . **18** F5
SAILORS BANK **113** F8
St Agatha's Cl ◳ WR10. . . **144** D1
St Agathas Ct ◳ WR10 . . **144** D1
St Agathas Rd
  ◳ Pershore WR10 . . . . . **144** D1
  ◲ Pershore WR10 . . . . . **158** D8
St Agnes Cl B80. . . . . **90** C4
St Alban's Ave WR11. . . . . . **27** A7
St Albans Cl WR5 . . . . **115** F3
St Albans Ho B32. . . . . **4** F4
St Albans RC Prim Sch
  B14. . . . . **20** F4
St Ambrose Cl B62, B65. . . . **8** C8
St Ambrose's RC Prim Sch
  DY10. . . . . **27** F6
St Andrew Rd WR11. . . . . . **161** A3
St Andrews Cl DY8. . . . . **5** F2
St Andrew's Cl ◳ WR9 . . . . **84** F3
St Andrews Cl WR14. . . . . . **153** A6
St Andrew's Dr WR9 . . . . . . **84** F2
St Andrews Fst Sch
  WR11. . . . . **161** B2
St Andrews Gn DY10 . . . . . **27** E4
St Andrews Gr ◳ WR9 . . . . **84** F3
St Andrew's Rd
  Malvern WR14. . . . . **153** A6
  Pershore WR10 . . . . **158** C7

St Andrews Sq
  [14] Droitwich Spa WR9 .... 84 F3
  [13] Newtown WR9 .... 84 F3
St Andrew's St WR9 .... 84 F3
St Andrews Way B61 .... 67 D8
St Annes CE Prim Sch
  DY12 .... 25 F2
St Anne's CI WR3 .... 102 B1
St Anne's Rd
  Cradley Heath B64 ...... 7 C8
  Worcester WR3 .... 102 B1
St Ann's Rd WR14 ...... 138 E1
St Ann's Well★ WR14 ... 152 E8
St Asaphs Ave B80 ...... 90 D4
St Audrie's Rd WR5 .... 128 C8
St Augustine Dr WR9 .... 85 A4
St Augustine's CI WR9 .. 85 A4
St Augustines RC High Sch
  B97 .... 89 D5
St Barnabas CE Fst & Mid
  Sch WR10 .... 143 F6
St Barnabas CE Prim Sch
  WR3 .... 115 D5
St Bartholomews CE Prim
  Sch DY13 .... 43 E1
St Bartholomew's Rd [5]
  DY13 .... 43 E2
St Bede's RC Mid Sch [1]
  B98 .... 71 A3
St Benedicts CI GL20 .. 196 E4
St Bernard Dr WR14 .... 153 A5
St Brigids RC Prim Sch
  B31 .... 18 F3
SAINTBURY 178 B4
St Catherine CE Prim Sch
  DY11 .... 27 C8
St Catherines CI B60 .... 50 A5
St Catherine's Hill WR5 . 115 D1
St Catherines Rd [2]
  WR11 .... 161 D1
St Catherine's Rd B60.. 50 A5
St Catherine's Vale [2]
  WR5 .... 115 L1
St Cecilia CI DY10 ...... 27 E2
St Chads Rd B80 .... 90 C4
St Chad's Rd B45 .... 32 F7
St Christopher CI WR11 . 161 D6
St Clement's CE Prim Sch
  WR2 .... 114 F2
St Clement's CI [3] WR2 . 115 A2
St Clement's Ct [1] WR2 . 115 A2
St Clement's Gdns [2]
  WR2 .... 115 A2
St Columbas Dr B45..... 33 D7
St Columbas RC Prim Sch
  B45 .... 33 D7
St David's CI
  Habberley DY11 .... 26 F6
  [1] Stourport-on-Severn
    DY13 .... 43 E6
St Davids Dr
  Birmingham B32 .... 9 B5
  Evesham WR11 .... 161 D1
St Davids Rd GL20 ..... 197 F7
St Denis Rd B29 .... 19 B7
St Dunstan's CI WR5 ... 128 C8
St Dunstan's Cres
  [13] Worcester WR5 .... 115 C1
  Worcester WR5 .... 128 C8
St Dunstan's La WR15 ... 57 A4
St Dunstans RC Prim Sch
  B14 .... 20 F8
St Egwine CI WR3 ..... 115 C5
St Egwins CE Mid Sch
  WR11 .... 161 D6
St Egwin's CI WR11 ... 147 D3
St Egwin's Rd [6] WR11 . 161 D5
St Francis CE Prim Sch
  B30 .... 19 D6
ST GEORGE'S 70 F4
St Georges CE Fst Sch
  B98 .... 70 F4
St Georges CE Prim Sch
  WR1 .... 115 B5
St George's CE Prim Sch
  DY10 .... 27 F7
St Georges CI [5] WR11.. 161 E1
St George's Cres [4] WR9 . 85 A3
St Georges Ct [10] DY10 . 27 E6
St George's Ct B30 ..... 19 C7
St Georges Gdns [3] B98.. 70 F4
St Georges Lane N WR1 . 115 B5
St George's Lane S WR1 . 115 B5
St George's PI DY10 ..... 27 F7
St Georges RC Prim Sch
  WR1 .... 115 A5
St Georges Rd
  Northway GL20 .... 197 F7
  Redditch B98 .... 70 F4
St George's Rd DY8 ..... 5 D2
St Georges Sq
  [8] Hill End WR9 ...... 85 A3
  Worcester WR1 .... 115 B5
St George's Terr WR1 ... 27 F6
St Georges Wlk WR1 ... 115 B5
St Giles Row DY8 .... 6 A6
St Giles's Rd GL20 ..... 184 E6
St Godwald's Cres B60 .. 68 B8
St Godwald's Rd B60... 68 C7
St Heliers Rd B31 .... 18 F4
St Huberts RC Prim Sch
  B68 .... 9 C8
St James' CE Prim Sch
  DY8 .... 5 D7
St James CI
  Badsey WR11.......... 162 E3
  Harvington WR11....... 148 B6

St James CI continued
  Norton Juxta Kempsey
    WR5 .... 129 C1
St James Ct
  Blakedown DY10 .... 14 B1
  Bromsgrove B60 .... 49 A3
St James Dr [3] WR11 ... 161 D1
St James RC Prim Sch
  B45 .... 33 A7
St James's Dr WR14 ... 138 F2
St James's Rd WR14 ... 138 F2
St John Fishers RC Prim Sch
  B31 .... 34 B7
ST JOHN'S 114 F1
St John's WR2.......... 115 A1
St John's Ave DY11 .... 27 B6
St John's CE Prim Sch
  DY11 .... 27 B6
St Johns CI [3] WR11 ... 161 E1
St John's CI
  [6] Kidderminster DY11 .. 27 C6
  Worcester WR3 .... 102 B1
St Johns Ct B31........ 19 B1
St John's La DY12 ...... 25 A2
St John's Rd
  Halesowen B63 .... 7 E4
  Stourbridge DY8 .... 6 A5
  Stourport-on-Severn DY13 . 44 A5
St John's Sch B61 ..... 48 E1
St John's Sports Ctr
  WR2 .... 115 A1
St John's St [5] DY11 ... 27 C6
St John St B61.......... 48 F2
St Johns Wood B45 .... 33 B5
St Josephs Ave B31 .... 19 B5
St Josephs Cath Prim Sch
  DY8 .... 5 F2
St Joseph's CI WR9 .... 84 D2
St Josephs RC Prim Sch
  Birmingham B30 .... 19 F5
  Droitwich Spa WR9 ... 84 D2
  Worcester WR4 .... 116 B7
St Joseph's RC Prim Sch
  WR14 .... 138 E3
St Judes Ave B80 ...... 90 D4
St Judes CI B14........ 20 F2
St Judes Ct B14........ 20 F7
St Judes RC Prim Sch [4]
  B14 .... 20 F2
St Kenelms Ave B63..... 7 E1
St Kenelms CE Prim Sch
  B62 .... 17 A4
St Kenelms CE Sch B62 . 17 A4
St Kenelms Rd B62..... 16 E5
St Kitts CI WR14 ...... 138 F5
St Laurence CE Inf Sch
  B31 .... 19 B4
St Laurence CE Jun Sch
  B31 .... 19 B4
St Laurence CI B48..... 51 B6
St Laurence Rd B31..... 19 B5
St Laurence Way [3] B50 . 136 D5
St Lawrence CI WR4 ... 127 F7
St Lawrence Mews B31.. 19 A3
St Lawrence Rd [3]
  WR11 .... 161 C4
St Loye's CI B62 .... 8 D8
St Lukes Bsns Pk B64 ... 7 D8
St Lukes CE Fst Sch B97 . 70 D1
St Lukes CI [7] WR11 ... 161 D1
St Lukes Cotts B97...... 70 D1
St Margarets [3] WR14 .. 153 A8
St Margarets Dr B63..... 7 F2
St Margarets Rd [4]
  WR11 .... 161 D1
St Marks CI [6] WR11 ... 161 D1
St Mark's CI WR5 ...... 128 C7
St Mark's Rd DY9 .... 6 D5
St Martins Ave B80..... 90 D4
St Marys Cath Prim Sch
  Evesham WR11 .... 161 E5
  Studley B80 .... 90 E4
St Marys CE Jun Sch B80. 90 E3
St Marys CE Prim Sch
  Kidderminster DY10..... 27 E8
  Longdon GL20 .... 181 F5
St Mary's CI
  Kempsey WR5 .... 141 B7
  [4] Tenbury Wells WR15.. 55 E5
St Mary's Convent Sch
  WR5 .... 128 E8
St Mary's La
  Stourbridge DY8 .... 6 B3
  [9] Tewkesbury GL20 ... 196 E6
St Marys Pk Cvn Pk B47 . 35 E2
St Mary's PI [1] DY14 ... 22 C4
St Marys RC Prim Sch
  WR12 .... 190 D8
St Mary's Rd
  Droitwich WR9......... 84 F2
  Evesham WR11........ 161 D5
  Tewkesbury GL20 ..... 196 D6
St Mary's Ringway DY10 . 27 E6
St Mary's St WR1 ..... 115 B3
St Matthews CI
  [2] Evesham WR11...... 161 E1
  Salford Priors WR11..... 135 D4
St Matthias CE Prim Sch
  WR14 .... 139 A4
St Matthias Prim Sch [6]
  WR14 .... 139 A4
ST MICHAEL'S 74 C8
St Michaels CI [3] WR11 . 175 D8
St Michael's CI
  B32 .... 18 C8
  [2] South Littleton WR11.. 148 F1

St Michael's CI continued
  [6] Stourport-on-Severn
    DY13 .... 44 A4
St Michael's Coll WR15.. 74 C8
St Michael's Rd WR3.... 115 B8
St Milburgh CI WR11.... 148 A1
St Moritz CI WR3....... 114 F8
St Nicholas CE Mid Sch
  WR10 .... 144 E6
St Nicholas Ho WR14.... 138 D3
St Nicholas La WR4.... 116 D6
St Nicholas Rd WR10.... 131 B2
St Nicholas St
  Droitwich WR9......... 84 E3
  Worcester WR1........ 115 B3
St Nicolas Gdns B38 ... 19 F2
St Oswalds CE Prim Sch
  DY10 .... 13 A1
St Oswalds CI DY10 .... 27 F8
St Oswald's Rd WR1.... 115 B4
St Patricks CI
  Birmingham B14 .... 20 E5
  [9] Evesham WR11...... 161 D1
St Patrick's Ct DY11 ... 27 B1
St Paul's Ave WR11..... 27 A6
St Pauls CI WR11 ..... 175 E8
St Pauls RC Prim Sch
  B38 .... 20 A1
St Paul's St WR1....... 115 C2
St Peters CE Fst Sch WR9 . 85 A2
St Peter's Church La WR9 . 85 A2
St Peters CI
  Birmingham B28 .... 21 D6
  Bromsgrove B61 .... 48 E1
  Kidderminster DY10..... 27 E2
  Malvern Wells WR14 .. 166 F7
St Peter's CI
  Evesham WR11 .... 161 E3
  Hinton on the Green WR11 175 A5
  Redditch B97 .... 89 E5
St Peter's Cres WR9.... 85 A3
St Peter's Dr
  Martley WR6 .... 99 A4
St Peter the Great County
  WR5 .... 128 E5
St Peter's Hill WR5..... 128 D5
St Peters La WR11 .... 187 F4
St Peter's La WR8...... 157 C6
St Peters RC Fst Sch [2]
  B61 .... 67 E8
St Peters RC Prim Sch B32 . 9 C1
St Peter's Rd
  Droitwich WR9......... 84 F2
  Malvern WR14......... 138 E3
  Stourbridge DY9 .... 6 C1
  West Malvern WR14 ... 138 C2
St Peters St [5] WR1.... 115 C1
St Peter's Wlk WR9 .... 85 A3
ST PETER THE GREAT.... 128 E6
St Philips Dr WR11..... 175 D8
St Richards CE Sch
  WR11 .... 161 E2
St Richards CI WR9 .... 85 E8
St Richard's Gdns [9] WR9 84 E3
St Richards Rd
  Dodderhill WR9........ 85 E8
  Evesham WR11........ 161 D1
St Saviour's Ct DY9 ... 15 A6
St Stephan's Ho B97.... 70 E4
St Stephen's CE Fst Sch
  B98 .... 70 F5
St Stephens Gdns B98... 70 F5
St Stephens Rd B29 .... 20 B8
St Stephen's St [3] WR9 . 115 B6
St Stephen's Terr [1]
  WR3 .... 115 B6
St Swithin's St [1] WR1.. 115 C2
St Swithuns CI WR5..... 128 D8
St Thomas Aquinas RC Sch
  B38 .... 19 D3
St Thomas More RC Fst Sch
  B98 .... 90 B7
St Wulstans CI [6] WR11 . 161 E1
St Wulstan's Cres [1]
  WR5 .... 115 D1
St Wulstans Dr WR14.... 166 F7
St Wulstan's Nature
  Reserve★ WR14 ...... 167 A7
St Wulstans RC Prim Sch
  DY13 .... 43 D4
Salamanca Dr WR5 ... 128 F4
Salcombe Dr DY5 ...... 6 C7
SALE GREEN 105 A1
SALEWAY 104 F4
Salford CI B98.......... 90 B6
SALFORD PRIORS 135 F3
Salford Priors CE Prim Sch
  WR11 .... 135 E4
Salisbury CI WR5 ..... 115 F2
Salisbury Dr
  [6] Evesham WR11...... 161 C2
  Kidderminster DY11..... 27 A6
Sallieforth PI [5] B50 ... 136 D4
Sallis CI GL20.......... 184 D2
Sally CI WR11 .... 176 D7
Salop Rd B97........... 70 D3
Saltbox La WR15 ...... 55 F2
Saltbrook Rd B63 ...... 7 A7
Saltbrook Trad Est B63 .. 7 A7
Salters CI WR4......... 115 F6
Salters La
  Besford WR8 .... 143 E1
  Defford WR8........... 157 D6
  Fladbury WR10 .... 145 E2
Salter's La B97 .... 70 B5
Salters Sh Ctr WR9 .... 84 F3
Saltway WR9 .... 84 F3

Salt Way
  Cookhill B96........... 108 D5
  Feckenham B96........ 107 A8
  Hadzor WR9........... 85 F2
Saltwood Ave WR4..... 116 C6
SALWARPE 103 B8
Salwarpe Ct★ WR9..... 84 B1
Salwarpe Gr B29....... 9 F2
Salwarpe Rd
  Bromsgrove B60 .... 67 F8
  Droitwich WR9......... 84 E3
Sambourne La
  Astwood Bank B96 .... 89 F1
  Coughton B49 .... 109 E6
Sambourne Park La B96. 90 A1
Sambourne Pk B96 .... 109 A8
Samsara Rd B60 .... 49 C1
Sam Spencer Ct DY10... 29 A2
Samuels Rd B32 .... 9 A5
Sanctuary CI WR2...... 114 E2
Sandalls CI B31........ 18 D1
Sandals Rise B62 .... 8 D3
Sandbourne Dr DY12.... 26 C3
Sanderling Ct DY10 .... 28 A1
Sanders CI B97 .... 70 B4
Sanderson Ct DY11..... 27 C5
Sanders Rd
  Bromsgrove B61 .... 48 E1
  Salford Priors WR11 ... 135 F3
Sanders Rd Ind Est [1]
  B61 .... 48 E1
Sandfield La WR11..... 174 E2
Sandfield The GL20 .... 184 E1
SANDFORD 155 D7
Sandhampton DY13 .... 62 E6
Sandhills Gn B48 ...... 50 E7
Sandhills La B45........ 50 D7
Sandhills Rd B45....... 50 D8
Sandhurst Ave DY9..... 6 D2
Sandhurst CI B98....... 71 C6
Sandhurst Ho B38 ..... 20 B1
Sandicliffe CI DY11 .... 27 C8
Sandles CI WR9........ 103 F7
Sandles Rd WR9....... 103 F7
Sandmartin Way DY10... 28 A2
Sandmere Gr B14...... 21 D3
Sandmere Rd B14...... 21 D3
Sandon CI B98......... 71 A3
Sandon Rd DY9 .... 6 F4
Sandown CI [18] B29 ... 19 C7
Sandown Dr B61....... 32 B1
Sandown Rd [5] WR11 .. 161 C2
Sandown Twr [3] B31... 19 A1
Sandpiper CI
  Kidderminster DY10..... 28 B2
  Stourbridge DY9 .... 6 F5
  [6] Worcester WR5 .... 128 E6
Sandpiper Cres WR14 .. 138 E6
Sandpiper Gdns B38 ... 34 F7
Sandpits CI WR6........ 99 A3
Sandpits The B30 ..... 19 E8
Sandringham CI
  Evesham WR11 .... 161 D6
  Malvern WR14......... 139 C6
Sandringham Rd B62.... 8 B7
Sandringham Way DY5 .. 6 C8
Sands CI [3] WR12..... 177 D1
Sands Croft Ave WR12 .. 177 E1
Sands La WR11 .... 162 E2
Sands Rd WR7......... 107 F1
Sands The
  [4] Broadway WR12..... 177 D1
  Broadway WR12....... 190 D8
Sandstone Ave B45 .... 33 A8
Sandstone Rd [5] DY12.. 26 C3
Sandway Gr B13....... 21 C7
Sandyacre Way DY8..... 6 B5
Sandy Bank DY12 ...... 26 A3
Sandy Croft B13 .... 21 C7
Sandygate CI B97...... 69 F2
Sandy La
  Blakedown DY10 ...... 29 C7
  Kidderminster Foreign DY11 12 A1
  Kinver DY7............. 3 F1
  Madeley Heath B61, B62... 31 E5
  Stourport-on-Severn DY13 . 44 B1
Sandy Lane Ind Est DY13. 44 B1
Sandy Rd DY9 .... 5 D1
Sandys Ave WR11 ..... 176 D7
Sandys CI [2] WR10.... 146 A1
Sandys Rd WR9........ 83 A5
Sandy's Rd WR14 ..... 139 C3
Sandys' Rd WR1....... 115 A5
SANKYNS GREEN........ 81 D6
Sansome Mews [13] WR1 . 115 B4
Sansome PI WR1....... 115 C3
Sansome Rd B90....... 21 F2
Sansome Rise B90 ..... 21 F2
Sansome Wlk [11] WR1.. 115 B4
Santa Maria Way DY13.. 44 B3
Sant Rd B31 .... 34 B7
Santridge Ct B61....... 49 A4
Santridge La B61....... 49 A4
SAPEY BRIDGE.......... 111 A5
SAPEY COMMON 78 C5
Sapphire Cres WR2 .... 114 D8
Sarah Seager CI [5] DY13 . 43 E6
Sarai CI WR1 .... 115 A5
Sarehole Mill Mus★ B13 . 21 D8
Sargent Turner Trad Est
  DY9.................... 6 F6
Saunders St WR3 ..... 115 C2
Saunderton House B31.. 18 D5
Savernake CI B45...... 18 A2
Saville CI B45.......... 33 B7
Sawmill CI WR5........ 115 E1
Saxelby CI B14......... 20 E2
Saxelby Ho [2] B14 .... 20 E2

Saxifrage PI DY10 ..... 27 F4
Saxilby PI [1] DY13 .... 44 B4
Saxon Bsns Pk B60 .... 67 E2
Saxonbury WR11....... 161 E2
Saxon CI
  Clifton on Teme WR6 ... 97 F7
  Studley B80 .... 90 E5
Saxonfields [2] B50..... 136 D4
Saxons Way B14 ...... 21 A2
Saxon Wood CI [2] B31 . 19 A4
Sayers Ave WR14 ..... 138 E4
Scafell CI WR4......... 116 A5
Scafell Rd DY8......... 6 B6
Scaife Rd B60 .... 68 B7
Scarfield Hill B48...... 50 E5
Schofield Bsns Pk B60 .. 68 A7
Scholars Ct WR9 ...... 27 E4
Scholars Wlk WR9 .... 84 E1
School Ave WR11 ..... 135 E4
School Bank WR9...... 83 B4
School CI B31 .... 18 E2
School Dr
  Bromsgrove B60 .... 49 A3
  Stourbridge DY8 .... 5 F8
  Wythall B47 .... 36 A3
Schoolhouse CI B38.... 20 B2
School La
  Alvechurch B48 .... 51 B5
  Badsey WR11.......... 162 E3
  Bretforton WR11....... 163 C4
  Crowle WR7........... 117 E5
  Eckington WR10....... 171 E7
  Hagley DY9 .... 15 D6
  Halesowen B63 .... 7 F2
  Lickey End B60......... 49 B6
  North & Middle Littleton
    WR11 .... 149 A3
  Overbury GL20......... 185 F7
  South Littleton WR11... 148 F2
  Upton Snodsbury WR7... 131 C8
  Upton upon Severn WR8. 169 C5
  Upton Warren B61...... 66 F3
  Wick WR10 .... 159 A7
School Rd
  Aston Somerville WR12.. 175 E1
  Birmingham B45 ...... 32 E6
  Birmingham, Yardley Wood
    B14 .... 21 C4
  Dodderhill WR9........ 85 E8
  Elmley Lovett WR9..... 65 B6
  Evesham WR11 .... 161 B4
  Hanbury B60 .... 87 A5
  Pebworth CV37 .... 150 E2
  Salford Priors WR11 ... 135 E3
  [9] Worcester WR2 .... 114 F1
School St
  Honeybourne WR11.... 164 A4
  Stourbridge DY8 .... 5 F6
Scobell CI [3] WR10.... 144 C1
Scotland La B32 .... 18 C7
Scotland PI [3] WR15 .. 55 E5
Scotlands The [9] WR9 . 84 D5
Scots Cnr B14 .... 20 E8
Scots La DY13 .... 62 F5
Scott CI B50.......... 136 C5
Scott Rd B97 .... 89 C8
Scott's Rd DY8......... 5 F6
Scribers La B28........ 21 E4
Scribers Mdw B28 .... 21 E4
Sculthorpe Rd DY10.... 14 B2
Seabright Way WV15... 1 C5
Seacole Ho B97........ 70 B2
Seafield La
  Beoley B98............ 53 A2
  Portway B48, B98 ..... 52 E4
Seaford La
  Naunton Beauchamp
    WR10 .... 132 A4
  Peopleton WR10....... 131 F3
Seals Gn B38 .... 34 D7
Sebright Ave [3] WR5... 115 E1
Sebright CI WR10 ..... 144 C1
Sebright Gn DY11...... 12 C3
Sebright Rd DY11 ..... 12 C3
Second Crossing Rd
  GL20.................. 197 B4
Securehold Bsns Ctr B98. 71 B2
Sedge Ave B38 .... 19 F3
SEDGEBERROW 175 A2
Sedgeberrow CE Fst Sch
  WR11 .... 175 A1
Sedgeberrow Covert [4]
  B38 .... 34 E8
Sedgeberrow Rd B63.... 8 A2
Sedgebourne Way B31... 18 C1
Sedge CI WR2 .... 114 D2
Sedge Dr B61.......... 49 A6
Sedgefield Wlk B61..... 32 B1
Sedgeford CI DY5...... 6 D8
Sedgley CI B98 .... 70 F4
Seedgreen CI [3] DY13.. 62 E8
Seedgreen La DY13 .... 63 A5
Seedhouse Ct B64 ..... 7 F8
Segbourne Rd B45..... 32 F8
Selba Dr DY11 .... 27 A6
Selborne Gr B13....... 21 C5
Selborne Rd [7] WR1 ... 115 A5
Selborne Road W WR1 . 115 A5
Selby Gr B13 .... 21 C6
Selcombe Way B38..... 34 E8
Selcroft Ave B32....... 9 F5
Selly Hall Croft B30 ... 20 A6
Selly Manor Mus★ B30.. 19 F7
Selly Oak Hosp B29 .... 19 F8
Selly Oak Rd B30 ..... 19 E5

Shearwater Cl *continued*
  Kidderminster DY10......28 B1
Sheenhill Rd
  Honeybourne WR11......164 A7
  South Littleton WR11......163 F8
Selly Oak Sch B29......19 E8
Sellywood Rd B29, B30...19 E8
Selma Gr B14.........21 D5
Selsdon Cl
  Kidderminster DY11......27 B5
  Wythall B47.........36 C5
Selsey Cl WR4........116 A7
Senneleys Park Rd B31....9 E1
Sensall Rd DY9.........6 F3
Serin Cl DY10........28 A1
Serpentine The DY11......27 C4
Servite Ct B14.........21 A2
Seven Acres WR4......116 A4
Seven Acres La B98.....71 C5
Seven Acres Rd
  Birmingham, Quinton B62...9 A5
  Birmingham, Turves Green
   B31.........19 C1
Sevenhills Dr DY13.....62 D8
Severn Cl B61........49 A8
Severn Ct 10 WR9......84 F3
Severndale WR9......84 D1
Severn Dr
  Aschurch GL20......184 C1
  Malvern WR14......153 D8
  Upton upon Severn WR8..169 C6
Severn Gr DY11.........27 B3
Severn Ho 4 B68........9 B8
Severn Hts WR6......82 B3
Severn Manor Gdns 6
  DY13.........43 E1
Severn Quay DY12.....26 B3
Severn Rd
  Halesowen B63......7 B5
  Stourbridge DY8......5 F3
  Stourport-on-Severn DY13..44 A2
Severn Rise DY13......43 E5
Severnside Bsns Pk DY13..44 A2
Severnside Mill DY12.....26 B3
Severn Side N DY12.....26 B4
Severn Side S DY12......26 B3
Severn St WR1........115 B1
SEVERN STOKE.........155 D5
Severn Terr WR1......115 B3
Severn Valley Ctry Pk★
  WV15.........1 A4
Severn Valley Rly★ DY10,
  DY11.........27 D2
Severn Way
  Bewdley DY12......25 F3
  Wythall B47.........35 E2
Seward Rd WR11......162 D3
Seymour Ave WR3......115 A4
Seymour Cl WR14......139 B6
Seymour Dr B98.......71 A5
Seymour Pl GL20......196 E5
Seymour Rd
  Kidderminster DY11......27 B8
  Stourbridge DY9......7 A4
Shadymoor Dr DY5......6 C8
Shaftesbury Ave DY9....6 C2
Shaftesbury Cl B60......49 B2
Shaftesbury Gn 8 WR4..116 C3
Shaftland Cross WR9....118 B7
Shaftsbury Ave B63......7 B7
Shakels Cl B97........89 E4
Shakespeare Ave B98....71 A2
Shakespeare Ct 4 GL20..196 E6
Shakespeare Dr DY10....28 B6
Shakespeare Ho B31....34 A8
Shakespeare La WR11...148 B6
Shakespeare Rd
  1 Worcester WR2......114 D2
  6 Worcester WR2......114 D1
Shalnecote Gr B14.....20 C5
Shambles The WR1......115 C2
Sham La WV15.........1 F3
Shandon Cl B32.........9 F3
Shannon Pl GL20......197 C8
Shannon Rd B38......34 E7
Shannon Way
  Aschurch GL20......197 C8
  Evesham WR11......162 A3
  Tewkesbury GL20......197 C8
Shap Dr WR4........116 B6
Shapinsay Dr B45......17 F1
Sharman Cl WR1......115 A5
Sharman Rd WR1......115 A5
Sharpe Rd WR2......128 A7
Sharps Cl B45.........33 A7
SHARPWAY GATE......86 E7
Sharpway Gate B60.....86 E7
Sharry La CV37......151 E2
SHATTERFORD......11 C7
Shatterford Lakes Wildlife
  Sanctuary & Fishery★
  DY12.........11 D6
Shaw Ave DY10........28 B6
Shawbank Rd B98......71 B3
Shawbrook Gr 4 B14....21 A3
Shawbury Cl B98......71 E3
Shawfield B47.........36 A5
Shaw Hedge Rd DY12....26 C4
Shawhurst Croft B47....36 A7
Shawhurst Gdns B47.....36 B8
Shawhurst La B47.....36 A6
Shaw La
  Dodderhill B60......86 B8
  Stoke Prior B60......67 C2
Shaw Lane Ind Est B60...67 C2
Shaws Cl B97.........69 F2
Shaw St WR1........115 B3
Shaw Wlk WR14......139 C2
Shearwater Cl
  Birmingham B45......32 F6

Sheenhill Rd
  Honeybourne WR11......164 A7
  South Littleton WR11......163 F8
Sheepcote Grange B61...48 F5
Sheepcroft Cl B97......69 F2
Sheepmoor Cl B17......9 F8
Sheepscombe Dr WR4..116 A6
Sheepwalks La DY7......3 A6
Sheepwash La
  Kinver DY7.........3 C3
  Wolverley & Cookley DY11..12 C8
Sheerwater Dr DY5......6 D7
Sheffield Cl 4 WR5....115 F1
Shelah Rd B63.........8 A6
Shelburns Terr WR14...138 F4
Sheldon Ave WR12......177 E1
Sheldon Cl
  1 Pershore WR10......144 C1
  Wychbold WR9......85 E1
Sheldon Dr B31........18 D2
Sheldon Park Rd WR3...102 A2
Shelduck Cl DY10......28 B3
Shelfield Rd B14......20 C3
SHELL.........105 E4
Shell Coner Trad Est B62..8 D8
Shelley Ave DY10......27 E7
Shelley Cl
  Catshill B61.........49 A8
  Redditch B97.........89 C8
  Stourbridge DY8......6 A8
  Worcester WR3......115 C7
Shelley Ho B63.........7 B5
Shelly Twr B31.........19 C3
SHELSLEY BEAUCHAMP..79 C2
Shelsley Dr WR13......152 D3
SHELSLEY WALSH......79 A3
Shelton La B63.........7 E5
Sheltwood Cl B97......70 A2
Sheltwood La B60, B97...69 A3
Shenley Court Acad B31..18 E7
SHENLEY FIELDS......18 E7
Shenley Fields Dr B31....18 E8
Shenley Fields Rd B29....19 B8
Shenley Gdns B29......19 A7
Shenley Gn B29.........18 F6
Shenley Hill B31......18 F6
Shenley La B29.........18 F7
SHENSTONE.........45 F8
Shenstone Ave
  Halesowen B62......8 E5
  Stourbridge DY8......5 D3
Shenstone Cl
  Bromsgrove B60......49 B3
  Malvern WR14......153 D8
Shenstone Ct
  Bromsgrove B60......49 B3
  Solihull B90.........21 D2
Shenstone Flats B62......8 F5
Shenstone Rd B14......21 A1
Shenstone Trad Est B63...8 C4
Shenstone Valley Rd B62..8 F6
Shephard Mead GL20...196 D5
Shepherds Brook Rd DY9...6 D5
Shepherds Cl 5 WR9....84 D5
Shepherds Ct WR9......84 D5
Shepherds Gn 2 WR9....84 E5
Shepherds Hill 4 WR9...84 E5
Shepherds Pl 3 WR9....84 E5
Shepherds Pool 1
  WR11.........161 D5
Shepherds Rise 22 WR9..84 D5
Shepherds Way WR9....84 D5
Shepherds Wlk B60......67 E7
Shepley Mdw B45......50 B8
Shepley Rd
  Barnt Green B45......50 A7
  Birmingham B45......33 B6
Sheraton Dr DY10......28 B6
Sheraton Grange DY8....5 F2
Sheraton Rd B60......49 C1
Sherbourne Cl B98.....71 D2
Sherbourne Rd
  Cradley Heath B64......8 B8
  Stourbridge DY8......6 A8
Sheridan Row 1 WR4...116 C3
SHERIFF'S LENCH......146 F7
Sheringham Rd
  Birmingham B30......20 B3
  Worcester WR5......128 D6
SHERNAL GREEN......104 D7
SHERRARD'S GREEN....139 D1
Sherrard's Green Rd
  WR14.........139 C1
Sherratts The WR9......65 B6
Sherridge Rd WR13....125 E5
Sherriff St WR4......115 A5
Sherston Covert 11 B30..20 C2
Sherwood Cl B28......21 F5
Sherwood Ho 1 B64......7 B8
Sherwood La WR2......127 F7
Sherwood Mews B28....21 E6
Sherwood Rd
  Birmingham B28......21 E7
  Bromsgrove B60......68 A6
  Stourbridge DY8......5 E7
Sherwood Wlk B45......18 B2
Shetland Cl 2 WR3....115 E7
Shifnal Wlk B31.........33 F8
Shilton Gr B29........18 E8
Shinehill La WR11......149 B1
Shipbourne Cl B32......9 F5
Shipley Dr B29.........19 A8
Shipston Cl
  Birchensale B97......70 A5
  Worcester WR4......115 F8

Shipston Rd B31......19 B1
Shipton Cl B97.........70 A5
Ship Wrights Cl 6 WR4.115 F6
Shire Bsns Pk WR4....116 B8
Shirehampton Cl B97....69 F2
Shireland La B97......70 A4
Shire Way WR9.........85 B1
Shirley WR14......139 B1
Shirley Jones Cl WR9....84 C3
Shirley Rd
  Birmingham, King's Norton
   B30.........20 A5
  Droitwich WR9......84 E1
Shirley Sta B90.........21 F1
Shop La WR11......163 C5
Shor Cl 6 WR1......161 E4
Shorters Ave B14......21 B4
Shorthill WR10......158 B3
Shortlands Cl B30......20 A2
Short St
  Halesowen B63......7 F5
  Stourbridge DY8......5 F5
Shortyard The DY11....12 E4
Shottery Cl B98......71 C3
SHOULTON.........101 A2
Shoulton La WR2......101 A2
Showell Cl WR9......103 E7
Showell Gn WR9......103 E7
Showell Gr WR9......103 E7
Showell Rd WR9......103 E7
SHRAWLEY.........81 E6
Shrawley Ave DY11......27 B3
Shrawley Cl
  Birmingham B45......32 F7
  Halesowen B63......8 A2
Shrawley Rd
  Birmingham B31......19 C2
  Fernhill Heath WR3......102 E3
Shrewsbury Rd DY11....27 A6
Shrewton Ave B14......20 D2
Shrubbery Ave WR1....115 B5
Shrubbery Cl DY10......13 B5
Shrubbery Ct DY10......27 F7
Shrubbery Rd
  Bromsgrove B61......48 E1
  Drakes Broughton WR10..143 F6
  Worcester WR1......115 B5
Shrubbery St DY10......27 F7
Shrub Hill WR4......115 E4
Shrub Hill Ind Est WR4.115 D3
Shrub Hill Rd WR4......115 D3
Shrub Hill Retail Pk
  WR5.........115 D5
Shrublands Ave B68......9 B7
SHURNOCK.........108 B6
SHUTHONGER.........183 D3
Shut Mill La B62......16 D2
Shuttlefast La WR14....153 A1
Sibdon Gr B31.........34 A8
Sidbury WR1........115 C1
SIDEMOOR.........48 F4
Sidemoor Fst Sch B61...48 D4
Sidings La
  Charlton WR10......160 D8
  Fladbury WR10......146 D1
Sidings Rd WR8......142 E2
Sidlaw Cl B63.........7 D2
Sigma Cl GL20......197 C7
Silk Printing Ctr The★
  GL20.........186 D5
Sillins Ave B98......71 A3
Sillins La B97.........88 E6
Silver Birch Ct DY10....28 A4
Silver Birch Dr
  Hollywood B47......36 B6
  Kidderminster DY10......28 C5
  Kinver DY7.........3 F5
Silver Birches Bsns Pk 3
  B60.........67 F6
Silverdale B61.........48 F4
Silverdale Ave WR5....115 F1
Silverfield Cl B14......20 E8
Silver Innage B63......7 C7
Silvermead Ct B47......35 F5
Silver St
  Birmingham B14......20 E8
  Colwall WR13......152 B2
  Hollywood B47......35 E5
  Kidderminster DY10......27 E7
  Redditch B97......70 E4
  Worcester WR1......115 C3
Silverstone Ave DY11....12 D1
Silverstone Ct B30......20 B8
SILVER STREET.........35 F5
Silverthorne La B64......7 B8
Silvester Way DY5......6 B8
Silvington Cl B29......19 C7
Simcox Gdns B32......9 D2
Simeon's Wlk DY5......6 F7
Simmons Dr B32......9 D4
Simmons Leasow B32....9 E2
Simms La B47.........36 A5
Simon De Montfort Dr 1
  WR11.........161 E7
Simon Evans Cl DY14....22 D4
Simon Rd B47.........36 A7
Simons Cl WR7......117 E1
Simon's Way 3 WR1....161 E3
Sinderberry Dr GL20...184 C1
Singer Hill WR9......84 D2
SINTON.........83 B2
SINTON GREEN......101 B6
Sinton La WR9......83 B3
Sinton Terr 3 WR2....114 F1
Sion Ave DY10......13 A1
Sion Gdns 1 DY13......44 A3
Sion Hill DY10......12 F1
Sir George's Mall 6 DY10 27 E6

Sir Hilton's Rd B31......34 C7
Sir Richards Dr B17......9 F7
Sir Walter's Mall 8 DY10.27 E6
Sisefield Rd B38......20 A1
Siskin Rd DY9.........6 C3
Siskin Way DY10......28 B1
Site 7 Trading Est WR9..65 B8
Siviter St B63.........8 B4
Six Acres B32.........9 C4
Six Acres Croft 3 WR4..116 B5
Six Ashes WR14......22 E7
Sixteen Acres La B50...149 E8
Six Ways Ind Est WR14..153 B8
Sixways Stadium (Worcester
  RFC) WR3......116 E7
Skenfrith Pl 6 WR4....116 C6
Skiddaw Cl WR4......116 B5
Skilts Ave WR4......116 B5
Skilts Specl Sch B98....72 C4
Skinner Rd WR2......114 F1
Skinner St WR2......114 F1
Skipton Cres 2 WR4...116 C7
Skomer Cl B45.........17 E1
Skylark Way DY10......28 A2
Skyrrold Rd WR14......153 C8
Sladd La DY11......12 A5
Slade Ave WR4......116 B5
Slade La
  Birmingham B28......21 E3
  Shrawley WR6......62 D3
Sladepool Farm Rd B14..21 A2
Slade Rd B62.........7 C6
SLADES GREEN......182 C2
Slad The DY13......44 D6
SLEDGE GREEN......181 A1
Slideslow Ave B60......49 B2
Slideslow Dr B60......49 B3
Slimbridge Cl
  Redditch B97......89 E5
  5 Worcester WR5......128 E5
Slims Gate B63.........8 A4
Slingfield Mill DY10......27 D6
Slingfield Rd B31......19 C1
Sling La
  Hindlip WR3.........103 B2
  Malvern WR14......139 A1
Slingpool Wlk WR2....115 A1
Slough The B97, B80....90 B4
Smallbrook Bsns Ctr
  B50.........136 F6
Smallbrook Rd WR12...177 D2
Small La B94.........53 E6
Smallshire Way DY8......5 D8
SMALLWOOD.........70 E2
Smallwood Almshouses
  B98.........70 E3
Smallwood Arch 5 B98..70 E3
Smallwood St B98......70 E3
Smedley Crooke Pl B48..34 C2
Smirrells Rd B28......21 E5
SMITE HILL.........103 F2
Smite La WR3......103 E2
SMITH END GREEN....125 F5
Smithfields 4 DY8......6 A5
Smiths Ave 1 WR2....114 E1
Smiths Cl B32.........9 B1
Smiths Cl 10 GL20......196 E6
Smith's La 2 GL20......196 E6
Smiths Way
  Pershore WR10......158 C7
  Stoke Works B60......67 D2
Smokey La WR10......160 B4
Snake La B48.........51 A6
Snakes Lake La B61.....48 D6
Snake Terr B48.........51 A6
SNEACHILL.........130 B7
SNEAD COMMON......60 C7
SNEADS GREEN......64 E4
Sneechill WR7......130 B7
Snowberry Ave WR4....116 A4
Snowberry Cl 8 DY13...43 E4
Snowdon Cl DY11......12 C1
Snowdon Gr B63.........7 D1
Snowdonia Rd GL20...197 A4
Snowdon Rd DY8......6 B6
Snowford Cl B90......21 F1
Snowshill Cl
  Redditch B98......71 B6
  2 Worcester WR4......116 B7
Snowshill Rd WR12......190 D6
Snowshill View WR12....176 F1
SNUFF HILL.........31 D1
Snuff Mill Wlk DY12......26 A2
Solcum La DY11......12 D6
Solent Pl WR11......161 F3
Solent Rd WR5......115 E3
SOLIHULL LODGE.........21 E2
Solitaire Ave WR2......114 D3
Somerdale Rd B31......19 C4
Somerford Rd B29......18 F8
Somerleyton Ave DY10..28 A5
Somerleyton Ct 3 DY10..28 A5
Somers Cl WR13......125 F2
Somers Ct WR14......138 F4
Somerset Dr
  Birmingham B31......33 F7
  Kidderminster DY11......12 C1
  Stourbridge DY8......5 D7
Somerset Pl
  Tewkesbury GL20......196 F3
  Worcester WR1......115 B5
Somers Park Ave WR14..138 F4
Somers Park Prim Sch
  WR14.........138 F4
Somers Rd
  Halesowen B62......8 C5
  Malvern WR14......138 F3
Somers' Rd WR1......115 A5

Somers Sq 9 B63.........8 B3
Somerville Rd WR4......115 A8
Sommerfield Rd B32.....9 D3
Sonata Rd B60......49 C1
Sorrel Cl WR3......102 E3
Sorrell Wlk DY5.........6 B6
Sorrel Way WR14......153 C7
Soudan B97.........70 D2
Souters Ho B32......18 D8
Southall Ave WR3......115 A8
Southall Dr DY11......45 A1
Southam Cl B28......21 E8
Southam Rd B28......21 E8
South Ave DY8.........5 F4
Southbank Rd B64......7 F8
South Birmingham Coll (Hall
  Green Campus) B28....21 E8
South Bromsgrove High Sch
  (Tech & Lang Coll) B60..67 F3
Southcote Gr B38......19 D1
Southcott Ave DY5......6 D8
South Cres B60......49 A1
SOUTHCREST.........70 E1
Southcrest Gdns B97....70 D1
Southcrest Rd B98......71 A2
Southcrest Wood Nature
  Reserve★ B97......70 E1
South Croft WR2......127 E6
Southdown Rd 6 WR5..115 E7
South East Quadrant 8
  B98.........70 E4
Southern Dr B30......20 D3
Southern Ho B13......21 A7
Southfield St WR1......115 C3
Southgate B64.........7 D8
Southgate Cl DY11......27 A4
South Gdns DY9.........15 A4
Southlands Ct B97......70 C1
South Lawn WR14......152 E5
SOUTH LITTLETON......148 E1
Southmead Cres B98....70 F3
Southmead Dr B60......49 B6
Southmead Gdns B80....90 E3
Southminster Dr B14....20 E6
South Par WR1......115 B2
South Park Dr WR9......84 D4
South Quay 9 WR1....115 B1
South Rd
  Birmingham, King's Heath
   B14.........20 E8
  Birmingham, Northfield B31 18 F2
  Bromsgrove B60......68 B7
  Stourbridge DY8......5 E4
  West Hagley DY9......15 A4
South St
  3 Kidderminster DY10....27 F6
  Redditch B98......70 E3
  13 Worcester WR1......115 C2
Southview Ridge DY5....6 D7
Southville Bglws for Old
  People B14......21 B4
Southwick Rd B62......8 D8
South Wlk B31.........19 C1
Southwold Ave B30......20 C3
Southwold Cl 6 WR5..128 D6
Southwood Covert B14..20 C2
Sovereign Fields GL55..165 D4
Sovereign Hts B31......18 C1
Sovereign Rd B30......20 A4
Spadesbourne Rd B60...49 C6
Spa Gdns GL20......197 B3
Spa Gr B30.........20 C8
Spa Rd WR9......84 F2
Sparrey Dr B30......20 A8
Sparrow Cl GL20......197 B3
Sparrowhall La WR2....127 B3
Sparrowhawk Cl WR14..139 C4
Speedwell Gdns DY5......6 B6
Speedwell Ho B38......20 A1
Spencer Ave DY12......26 C4
Spencer Dr WR14......153 A7
Spencer St DY11......27 C4
Spencers Wlk WR14.....139 B5
Spencer Wlk B61......49 A8
SPENNELLS.........28 A2
Spennells Valley Nature
  Reserve★ DY10......28 A3
Spennells Valley Rd DY10 28 A3
Spenser Rd 4 WR2......114 D3
SPERNALL ASH.........90 F1
Spernal Ash B80......90 F1
SPERNALL.........91 B1
Spernal La B80......91 B1
SPETCHLEY.........116 F1
Spetchley Cl B97......89 C6
Spetchley Park Gdns★
  WR5.........129 C3
Spetchley Rd WR5......116 B1
Spiceland Rd B31......18 F6
Spies Cl B62.........8 F6
Spies La B62.........8 F5
Spindle Cl DY11......12 D1
Spindle Rd WR14......139 C3
Spinney Cl
  Birmingham B31......19 B3
  Kidderminster DY11......27 A7
Spinney Gr WR11......161 E1
Spinney Mews B97......70 C1
Spinney The
  Worcester WR2......114 E5
  Wythall B47.........36 B4
Spion Kop WR10......144 E5
Spiral Cl B62.........8 E8
Spiral Ct DY8.........6 A4
Spirehouse La B60......49 E5
Spire South Bank Hospl
  (Private) WR5......128 C8
Spires View B61......48 F3

Spoon Dr B38............19 D2
Spreadbury Cl B17.........9 F8
Springbank WR14........138 F1
Spring Bank
 Defford WR8...........157 D3
 Worcester WR3.........102 E1
Spring Cl
 Colwall WR13..........152 B2
 Kinver DY7...............3 F5
 3 Tenbury Wells WR15... 55 F6
 West Hagley DY9........14 F4
Spring Cres B64...........7 F7
Spring Ct WR14..........139 C3
SPRINGFIELD............21 E8
Springfield GL20........197 B7
Springfield Ave
 Bromsgrove B60........68 A8
 Stourbridge DY9.........6 C4
Springfield Cl **2** WR5...128 C6
Springfield Ct B28.......21 F8
Springfield Dr
 1 Evesham WR11......161 E1
 Halesowen B62...........8 D7
Springfield Glade WR14..138 F1
Springfield Ho DY10.....27 F8
Springfield La
 Broadway WR12........177 C1
 Kidderminster DY10....27 F8
Springfield Rd
 Birmingham, King's Heath
 B14.................20 D7
 Halesowen B62...........8 D7
 Worcester WR5........128 D6
Spring Gdns
 Malvern WR14.........139 B5
 Tenbury Wells WR15....55 F5
 Tewkesbury GL20......196 F6
 Worcester WR1........115 C2
Spring Grove Cres DY11...27 B3
Spring Grove La WR15....55 E2
Spring Grove Rd DY11....27 B3
Spring Hill WR5.........115 D2
Springhill Gdns B97......69 F2
Springhill Rise DY12.....26 C4
Spring La
 Malvern WR14.........139 B4
 Romsley B62............16 D4
 Worcester WR5........115 D2
Spring Lane Ind Est
 WR14................139 C4
Spring Lane N WR14.....139 C4
Spring Lane S WR14.....139 C3
Spring Mdw
 Halesowen B63...........7 F2
 1 Worcester WR4.....116 A4
Springs Ave B61..........32 A1
Springside B98...........90 C8
Springside Pl DY12......26 C5
Springslade B32...........9 F5
Spring St
 Halesowen B63...........7 D6
 Stourbridge DY9.........6 E4
Springvale Dr B97........69 F3
Springvale Rd B97.......69 F2
Springwater Ct **8** GL20..184 E1
Spring Wlk B63...........7 D1
Spruces The DY9.........14 F4
SPURTREE...............56 A7
Square Cl B32............9 C3
Square The B48..........51 B6
Squire's Cl WR5.........141 C7
Squires Ct DY5............6 C8
Squires The
 Childswickham WR12....176 F2
 Evesham WR11........161 C4
 Norton & Lenchwick WR11 147 B1
Squire's Wlk WR5.......141 B6
Squirrel Dr WR5........128 F6
Squirrels Hollow B68.....9 D7
Stableford Cl
 Birmingham B32.........9 F3
 Redditch B97...........89 D7
Stable Way B60..........67 E6
Stacey Dr B13...........21 A5
Stacey Grange Gdns B45. 33 A6
Stadium Cl DY10.........27 F4
Stafford Ave WR4......116 D6
Stagborough Way DY13... 43 E4
Stainburn Ave **1** WR2... 114 D1
Stainburn Cl WR2......114 D2
Staite Dr DY10..........13 A5
STAKENBRIDGE.........14 E3
Stakenbridge La DY10....14 D4
Stallard Cl B97..........70 C5
Stallard Rd WR2........114 E5
Stalls Farm Rd WR9.....84 E3
STAMBERMILL...........6 C4
Stambermill Cl DY9......6 D5
Stambermill Ho DY9......6 E5
Stambermill Ind Est DY9...6 D6
Stamford Rd DY5..........6 C6
Stamford St DY8...........5 F7
Stanage Rd **10** WR4.....116 B5
STANBROOK...........140 E8
Stanbrook House Rd **4**
 WR2................140 F8
Stanbrook Rd WR15.....55 F6
Stanbury Rd B14........21 B4
Standlake House B31.....18 E5
Stanfield Rd B32..........9 E6
STANFORD BRIDGE......78 E8
Stanford Ct B31.........89 B6
Stanford Gr B63..........7 C1
STANFORD ON TEME....78 C8
Stanford Rd
 Great Witley WR6.......60 F1
 Northway GL20........197 B8
Stanhoe Cl DY5...........6 D8

Stanier Rd WR4.........116 B7
STANKLYN...............28 D2
Stanklyn La
 Stone DY10............28 D3
 Summerfield DY10......45 A8
Stanks La WR8.........168 F2
STANLEY................1 A3
Stanley Ave B32..........9 E7
Stanley Cl B98..........71 A5
Stanley Rd
 Birmingham B68.........9 C7
 Birmingham, King's Heath
 B14.................20 D7
 Malvern WR14.........139 B1
 Stourbridge DY8.........5 F3
 Worcester WR5........115 D2
Stanley Road Prim Sch
 WR5................115 D2
Stanley St WR5.........128 C7
Stanmore Gr B62..........9 A3
Stanmore Rd WR2......127 F7
STANTON..............189 D1
Stanton Fields WR10....132 F3
Stanton Rd GL20........196 F7
Stanway Cl WR4........115 F7
Stanway Rd WR12......189 C1
Staple Flat B60..........49 C8
Stapleford Croft B14.....20 C2
Staple Hall Rd B31......19 B2
STAPLE HILL............49 C8
Staplehurst Rd B28......21 F8
Staple Lodge Rd B31....19 C2
Stapleton Cl
 Redditch B98...........71 D3
 Studley B80............90 D3
Stapleton Rd B80........90 D4
Staplow Rd WR5........129 A8
Star La WR14...........114 F1
Starling Cl **2** WR5......128 C5
Starling Rd GL20........197 B3
Star St DY9...............6 F5
Station App
 Barnt Green B45........50 D8
 Kidderminster DY10....27 F5
Station Bglws WR13....152 B1
Station Cl
 Newnham Bridge WR15...57 C7
 Stoulton WR7.........143 D8
Station Cotts B60........50 A4
Station Dr
 Blakedown DY10.......14 C2
 Bredon GL20..........184 F6
 Earlswood B94.........36 D1
 West Hagley DY9.......15 A6
Station Gdns **5** WR10..171 E7
Station Hill **3** DY11....45 B2
Station La GL20........196 F7
Station Rd
 Alvechurch B48........51 A5
 Ashton under Hill WR11. 187 C8
 Beckford GL20........186 D4
 3 Bewdley DY12.....26 C3
 Birmingham, King's Norton
 B30.................19 E4
 Birmingham, Northfield B31 19 E4
 Blackwell B60.........50 A5
 Bretforton WR11......163 B5
 Broadway WR12......177 B1
 Central Engineer Park
 CV37................151 E4
 Cleobury Mortimer DY14.. 22 D5
 Cradley Heath, Haden Cross
 B64.................8 A8
 Drakes Broughton &
 Wadborough WR8......142 E4
 Eckington WR10.......171 E7
 Fernhill Heath WR3....103 A4
 Fladbury WR10.......146 A2
 Hartlebury WR11......45 B2
 Harvington WR11......148 B7
 Hinton on the Green WR11 174 F5
 Honeybourne WR11....164 B5
 Offenham WR11.......162 C7
 Pershore WR10.......144 D2
 Ripple GL20..........183 A8
 Rock DY14............24 A5
 Salford Priors WR11....135 F3
 South Littleton WR11...162 F8
 Stourbridge DY9.........6 E6
 Studley B80...........90 D4
 Tewkesbury GL20......196 F6
 West Hagley DY9.......15 A6
 Wythall B47...........36 B3
Station Rd Ind Est WR8. 169 C5
Station St
 Bromsgrove B60........48 F1
 Cradley Heath B64.......7 C8
 4 Droitwich WR9......84 E3
 Tewkesbury GL20......196 F6
Station Way B97.........70 D3
Station Yard Ind Est
 WR13................152 B2
Staveley Rd B14........20 D6
Steamer Point WR14....139 B2
Steatite Way DY13......43 E5
Steel Cl B60............68 A6
Steelpark Rd B62..........8 C7
Steel Rd B31............18 F2
Steene Gr B31..........18 D3
Steeple Cl **3** DY14......22 C4
Steeples The DY8.........6 B3
Steepwood Croft B30....19 D4
Stennels Ave B62.........8 E4
Stennels Cres B62.........8 E4
Stephenson Pl **2** DY12...26 C3
Stephenson Rd WR1....115 A4
Stephenson Terr WR1...115 A4
Stephenson Way WR11..164 A6

Steppes Piece B50......136 C5
Stepping Stones
 Bidford-on-Avon B50...136 C5
 Stourbridge DY8.........6 B5
Sterrymere Gdns DY7.....4 B4
Stevens Ave B32..........9 D2
Stevenson Ave B98......70 F3
Stevens Rd DY9...........6 D7
Steve Roberts Ct DY11...27 A6
Steward Rd GL20......197 E8
Stewart Ct DY10.........27 F5
Stewarts Rd B62..........8 D7
Stewkins DY8.............5 E8
Stewkins Ct **1** DY8......5 E8
Stewponey The DY7.......4 E6
Steynors Cl WR9.........84 E2
Steynors Cl WR9.........84 E2
Stilthouse Gr B45........33 A7
STIRCHLEY.............20 B7
Stirchley Prim Sch B30...20 A6
Stirchley Trad Est B30...20 B6
Stirling Ave WR4.......116 C6
STITCHIN'S HILL.......125 B4
Stock Coppice Cl **1**
 WR4................116 B6
STOCK GREEN.........106 E2
Stockhill Dr B45.........32 F6
Stocking St DY9..........6 F5
Stockmans Cl B38.......34 E8
Stocks La WR13........126 B2
Stocks Rd WR6........124 E4
Stocks Wood B30.......19 F8
STOCKTON ON TEME....59 E3
Stockton Rd
 Abberley WR6..........60 B3
 Stockton on Teme WR6.. 59 F3
Stockwell Ave DY5.......6 D8
STOCK WOOD.........107 C2
Stockwood La WR7....107 C1
STOKE BLISS...........76 E2
Stoke Cross B60.........68 E7
Stoke Gdns WR8.......155 D4
STOKE HEATH..........67 D5
Stoke Cl
 Dodderhill WR9.........85 E7
 Redditch B98...........71 B7
STOKE POUND.........68 A4
Stoke Pound La
 Stoke Pound B60.......68 A4
 Stoke Prior B60........67 F3
STOKE PRIOR..........67 C4
Stoke Prior Fst Sch B60.. 67 C3
Stoke Rd
 Bromsgrove, Aston Fields
 B60.................68 A7
 Bromsgrove, Charford B60. 67 E7
Stokesay Cl DY10........27 E2
Stokesay Gr B31........33 F8
Stokesay La **5** WR4....116 C6
Stokes Rd GL20........183 A1
Stoke Turn Ct B61......67 D6
STOKE WORKS.........67 C1
STONE.................28 E3
STONEBOW............144 A7
Stonebow Rd
 Drakes Broughton &
 Wadborough WR10....144 A7
 Drakes Broughton WR10. 143 F6
Stonebridge Cross Bsns Pk
 WR9................84 C6
Stonebrook Way B29.....9 F2
Stonechat Cl DY10.......28 B2
Stone Cl
 Birmingham B38.......19 F2
 Colwall WR13.........152 A2
Stone Cotts B31.........19 A3
Stonecroft Ave B45......33 A7
Stonecrop Cl B38........34 F8
Stone Ct WR13.........152 B2
Stone Dr WR13........152 A2
Stoneford La WR11.....163 D2
STONEHALL............142 C6
Stonehenge Croft B14... 20 D1
Stone Hill WR10........28 C3
Stonehouse Cl B97.......5 E6
Stone House Cottage Gdn★
 DY10................28 E3
Stonehouse Gr B32......9 D2
Stonehouse La
 Birmingham B32.........9 E2
 Hopwood B48.........34 E2
Stonehouse Rd B60......49 A1
Stone La DY7............4 A4
Stoneleigh Cl
 Redditch B98...........89 F6
 6 Worcester WR5....128 E5
Stoneleigh Ho B32........9 F5
Stonepit La WR7.......120 E7
STONEPITS............120 D7
Stonepits La B97........89 D4
Stonerwood Ave B28... 21 E8
Stonewell Terr WR10...158 D7
Stoneycroft Cl WR3....102 F2
Stoneyford Gr B14......21 B4
STONEY HILL...........49 A2
Stoney Hill Cl B60.......49 A1
Stoney La
 Birmingham B32.........9 B6
 Blackwell B60.........50 C2
 Hartlebury DY13.......64 A6
 Himbleton WR9.......105 E3
 Kidderminster DY10....27 E8
 Stakenbridge DY10.....14 E3
Stoney La Ind Est DY10.. 27 E8
Stoney Ley WR6........112 B3
Stonnall Ct WR8.......155 D5
STONY CROSS.........54 B3

Stony Furlong La WR10. 171 F7
Storer Ct WR14........153 B7
Storrage La B48..........51 E3
STORRIDGE...........138 A5
Storrs Way The B32.....18 B7
Stotfield Ave WR4......116 C4
Stotfold Rd B14.........20 F2
STOULTON............143 B8
STOURBRIDGE...........5 D4
Stourbridge Coll (Hagley Rd
 Ctr) DY8.............6 A4
Stourbridge Coll (Leasowes
 Centre) B62..........8 E4
Stourbridge Coll (Longlands
 Ctr) DY8.............5 E5
Stourbridge Ind Est DY8.. 6 A6
Stourbridge Juntion Sta
 DY8................6 B3
Stourbridge Rd
 Catshill B61...........48 F7
 Churchill & Blakedown
 DY10................13 D2
 Churchill DY10........14 A6
 Clent DY9.............15 E3
 Fairfield B61..........31 D2
 Hackman's Gate DY9....14 F1
 Hagley DY9...........15 C7
 Halesowen B63..........7 F5
 Kidderminster DY10....27 F8
 Madeley Heath DY9.... 31 B7
 Stourbridge DY9........6 A5
Stourbridge Town Sta DY8. 6 A5
Stour Cl B63.............7 E6
Stour Ct B63.............8 B5
Stourdale Rd B64.........7 C8
Stourdell Rd B63..........7 E6
Stour Hill DY5............7 A8
Stour Ho **2** B68.........9 B8
Stour La **4** DY13.......44 A3
Stourminster Specl Sch
 DY10................28 B4
Stourport High Sch & Sixth
 Form Ctr DY13.......44 A5
STOURPORT-ON-
 SEVERN............43 C6
Stourport-on-Severn Fst Sch
 DY13................44 A4
Stourport Rd
 Bewdley DY12.........26 C3
 Great Witley WR6......61 B1
 Hartlebury DY13.......63 D8
 Kidderminster DY11....27 C2
Stourport Sports Ctr
 DY13................43 F2
STOURTON.............4 F7
Stourton Cres DY7.......4 F7
Stourton Rd B32..........9 B5
Stourvale Ind Est DY9....6 F6
Stourvale Rd DY9.........6 F6
Stourvale Trad Est B63....7 D6
Stour Valley Cl DY5......6 D7
Stouton Croft **1** WR9... 84 E4
Stow La WR13.........166 A8
Stowe La WR13.........166 A8
Strand La WR3.........103 B4
Strand The
 Bromsgrove B61........49 A3
 Charlton WR10.......160 D8
STRATFORD...........170 C2
Stratford Gdns B60......49 A2
Stratford Rd
 Bidford-on-Avon B50...137 A5
 Bromsgrove B60........49 A2
 Harvington WR11......148 B6
 Honeybourne WR11....164 B5
 Mickleton GL55.......165 D6
STRENSHAM...........171 C6
Strensham Bsns Pk WR8 171 A2
Strensham Gate WR8...171 A4
Stretton Dr B45.........33 A2
Stretton Ho **7** B97......70 A4
Stretton Rd DY11.......27 B4
Stroma Ave **13** WR5....128 E6
Stronsay Cl B45.........17 F1
Stroud Rd B90..........21 F2
STRUCTON'S HEATH....80 E8
Stuart Rd B62............8 F5
Stuart Rise WR5.......128 E8
Stuarts Ct DY9..........15 A5
Stuarts Gn DY9.........15 B8
Stuarts Way B32........18 B7
Stud La WR6............60 C4
STUDLEY..............90 F4
Studley Com Inf Sch **4**
 B80................90 E4
STUDLEY COMMON....90 C4
Studley Dr DY5...........6 C8
Studley Gate DY8........5 D5
Studley High Sch B80... 90 E3
Studley Rd B98.........71 A2
SUCKLEY.............124 A3
SUCKLEY GREEN.......123 F7
SUCKLEY KNOWL......123 E7
Suckley Prim Sch WR6.. 124 A4
Suckley Rd
 Bransford WR6.......126 B6
 Leigh WR13..........125 F5
Sudeley Ave **8** WR4....116 C6
Sudeley Cl WR14.......138 F6
Sudgrove Cl **2** WR4.....115 F7
Suffield Cl WR6........126 B4
Suffolk Dr
 Brierley Hill DY5........6 C7
 Worcester WR5........115 E7
Suffolk La WR6.........60 F5
Suffolk Way **1** WR9....104 B8
Sugarbrook Ct **1** B60...67 F6
Sugarbrook La B60......68 A5

Sugarbrook Rd B60......68 A7
Sugar Loaf La DY10.....14 B7
Summercroft **7** DY13... 62 E8
SUMMERFIELD..........45 A8
Summerfield Dr **2** B29.. 19 A7
Summerfield Gdns
 WR11................161 B2
Summerfield La DY11....44 F7
Summerfield Rd
 Holy Cross DY9........15 E2
 Malvern WR14........139 B5
 2 Stourport-on-Severn
 DY13................44 B4
Summerfields Ave B62....8 F7
SUMMERHILL............27 B5
Summer Hill **6** B63......8 B3
Summerhill Ave DY11....27 A5
Summer Hollow WR2...127 A8
Summer Pl DY11.........27 C5
Summer Rd DY11........27 C3
Summer St
 Redditch B98..........70 E3
 Stourbridge DY8........5 F5
 Stourbridge, Lye DY9.... 6 E5
 2 Worcester WR3....115 B6
Summervale Cl DY9.....15 A5
Summervale Rd DY9.....15 A5
Summerway La DY11....44 F6
Summit Gdns B63.........7 F3
Summit Rd DY14........40 E4
Summit The DY9.........6 D4
Sunbury Cotts B31......19 A4
Sunbury Rd B63..........7 F4
Suncroft B32............9 C5
Sundbury Rise B31.......19 B5
Sunderland Dr DY8......6 A8
Sunderton Rd B14.......20 E4
Sundew Cl WR3........102 E3
Sunfield Sch DY9........15 F5
Sunningdale
 Bromsgrove B60........49 A1
 Halesowen B62..........8 E4
Sunningdale Cl
 Redditch B98..........70 F4
 Stourbridge DY8........5 F2
Sunningdale Holiday Est
 WR6................111 D6
Sunningdale Rd B61.....67 D8
Sunny Bank Rd B68......9 C7
Sunnymead B60.........49 A1
Sunnyside Cl WR5......141 C6
Sunnyside Gdns **1** DY11. 12 B1
Sunnyside Rd WR14....115 B5
Sunrise WR14..........139 B1
Sunrise Bsns Pk DY8.....5 E7
Sun St GL20...........196 E2
Surfeit Hill Rd B64.......7 D8
Surman St WR1.........115 B4
Sussex Ct **7** B29.......19 C7
Sutherland Rd B64.......7 E8
Sutton Cl B98...........71 D2
Sutton Com Prim Sch
 DY11................27 B4
SUTTON FARM..........27 B4
Sutton Park Gdns DY11.. 27 B3
Sutton Park Gr DY11....27 C3
Sutton Park Rd DY11....27 B3
Sutton Park Rise DY11.. 27 B3
Sutton Rd DY11.........27 C4
Swaledale Cl B60........67 E6
Swaledale Ct **7** WR4....116 B6
Swale Gr B38...........19 F1
Swallow Cl **1** WR5.....128 D5
Swallow Dr DY10........28 A2
Swallowfall Ave DY8.....5 C4
Swallowfields **5** WR4...116 C4
Swallow Pl WR9........104 B7
Swan Cl
 Blakedown DY10.......14 B1
 9 Tenbury Wells WR15.. 55 F6
Swan Ct
 9 Bengeworth WR11...161 E4
 8 Tenbury Wells WR15.. 55 F6
Swan Dr WR9...........85 B3
Swan La
 Evesham WR11.......161 D5
 Fairfield B61..........31 E3
 Tenbury Wells WR15....55 F6
 Upton Warren B61......66 E5
Swan Lane Fst Sch
 WR11................161 D5
Swanley Cl B62..........9 A3
Swan Orch WR6........125 A7
Swanpool Wlk WR1....115 A1
Swansbrook Gdns **4** B38. 20 C2
Swansbrook La B96......88 E1
Swan Sh Ctr **7** DY10.... 27 E6
Swanshurst Girls Sch B13 21 B7
Swanshurst La B13......21 C8
Swans Length B48.......51 A7
Swan St
 Alvechurch B48........51 B5
 Stourbridge DY8........5 E5
Swans Wlk B48.........51 A6
Swarthmore Rd B29.....19 B7
Sweden La GL20.......186 D2
SWEET GREEN..........76 E2
Sweetpool La DY8.......14 F5
Swift Cl B61............67 E8
Swift Park Gr DY10......28 B2
Swilgate Rd GL20......196 E6
Swinburne Rd B97.......89 C7
Swincross Rd DY8........6 B3

Swindell Rd DY9 . . . . 6 C1
SWINESHERD 129 B8
Swinesherd Way WR5 . . 116 C1
Swinford Old Hall DY8 . . . .6 B3
Swinford Rd DY8 . . . . 6 A3
Swinton Cl **3** WR2 . . . . . . 114 E1
Swinton La **4** WR2 . . . . . . 114 E1
Swiss Hts **3** DY13 . . . . 43 E1
Sycamore Ave
　Evesham WR11 . . . . 161 F2
　Redditch B98 . . . . 70 E2
Sycamore Cl
　Kidderminster DY10 . . . . . . 27 F7
　Malvern WR14 . . . . 139 A5
　Stourbridge DY8 . . . . 5 D2
Sycamore Ct B30 . . . . 19 E4
Sycamore Dr B47 . . . . 36 B6
Sycamore Ho B98 . . . . 89 F8
Sycamore Rd
　Birmingham, Bournville
　　B30 . . . . 19 F7
　11 Northway GL20 . . . . . . 184 E1
　Northway GL20 . . . . 197 E8
　Worcester WR4 . . . . 115 E5
Sycamores The DY9 . . . . . 14 F5
Sycamore Terr B14 . . . . . . 20 C7
Sydnall Cl B97 . . . . 69 F2
Sydney Rd
　Bromsgrove B61 . . . . 48 E3
　Cradley Heath B64 . . . . 7 C8
Sydney St WR3 . . . . 115 B6
Sylvan Ave B31 . . . . 18 F3
Sylvan Gn B62 . . . . 8 D5
Sylvia Ave B31 . . . . 34 B8
Synehurst WR14 . . . . 162 D4
Synehurst Ave WR11 . . . 162 D4
Synehurst Cres WR11 . . . 162 D4
SYTCHAMPTON 64 A1
Sytchampton Endowed Fst
　Sch WR13 . . . . 64 B1

T

Tabberness Cl WR6 . . . . . . 112 C3
Tabbs Gdns DY10 . . . . 28 A6
Tabor Gdns WR14 . . . . . . 139 A3
Tagwell Cl WR9 . . . . 104 B8
Tagwell Rd **2** WR9 . . . . . . 85 A1
Tailor's La CV37 . . . . 151 F1
Talavera Rd WR5 . . . . 128 F3
Talbot Cl **1** DY11 . . . . 45 A1
Talbot Pass **2** DY8 . . . . 6 A5
Talbot Rd B60 . . . . 67 E7
Talbotshill La DY10 . . . . . 13 C4
Talbot St
　Halesowen B63 . . . . 7 C6
　Kidderminster DY11 . . . . . 27 C4
　Stourbridge, Lye DY9 . . . . .6 F5
　Stourbridge, Stambermill DY8 6 A5
Talgarth Covert B38 . . . . . 34 E7
Talladale B32 . . . . 18 B7
Tallow Hill WR5 . . . . 115 D3
Tall Trees Cl B61 . . . . 48 F8
Tall Trees Dr DY9 . . . . 6 D2
Tamar Cl WR5 . . . . 115 E3
Tamarisk Cl
　Birmingham B29 . . . . 19 B8
　North Claines WR3 . . . . . . 102 E3
Tamar Pl WR11 . . . . 161 F3
Tamar Rise DY8 . . . . 6 A8
Tame Rd B68 . . . . .9 B8
Tame Rise B68 . . . . .9 B8
Tamerton Rd B32 . . . . 9 D1
Tamworth Ave **12** WR4 . . . 116 C6
Tandy Ct B14 . . . . 20 F3
Tandy Dr B14 . . . . 20 F3
Tandy's La DY10 . . . . 29 E4
Tanglewood Cl
　Birmingham B32 . . . . 9 B4
　Blackwell B60 . . . . 50 A5
Tanglewood Hts WR14 . . 138 E3
Tanhouse La
　Halesowen B63 . . . . 7 C5
　Malvern WR14 . . . . 138 F6
　Redditch B98 . . . . 71 C6
Tan House La WR2 . . . . . . 127 C7
Tan La **2** DY13 . . . . 43 F4
Tanners Cl **7** WR4 . . . . . . 115 F6
TANNER'S GREEN 36 B1
Tanners Green La B47,
　B94 . . . . 36 B2
Tanner's Hill DY12 . . . . . . 25 E3
Tansy Cl WR5 . . . . 128 C4
Tantallon Dr B32 . . . . 9 D1
TANWOOD 30 B2
Tanwood Barns DY10 . . . . 30 B2
Tanwood Cl B97 . . . . 89 A6
Tanwood Cross DY10 . . . . 30 B2
Tanwood La DY10 . . . . 30 A2
Tanworth La B98 . . . . 72 C7
Tanyard Ct B48 . . . . 51 B6
Tanyard La B48 . . . . 51 B6
Tapenhall Rd WR3 . . . . . . 102 E2
TARDEBIGGE 69 B7
Tardebigge CE Fst Sch
　B60 . . . . 69 B7
Tardebigge Ct B97 . . . . . . 69 C6
Tardebigge Ho B60 . . . . . . 49 B3
Tarragon Gdns B31 . . . . . 18 C2
Tarrant Gr B32 . . . . 9 F5
Tarrington Covert **6** B38 . 34 E8
Tattersall **2** WR4 . . . . . . 116 B3
Taunton Cl B31 . . . . 18 C2
Tavern La WR15 . . . . 57 C7

Tavern Orch WR4 . . . . . . 116 B5
Tawny Cl GL20 . . . . 184 D1
Tay Ave WR5 . . . . 128 E6
Tay Gr
　Birmingham B38 . . . . 34 F8
　Halesowen B62 . . . . 8 E8
Taylor Rd B13 . . . . 20 F5
Taylors La WR5 . . . . 128 D4
Taylor's La **3** WR1 . . . . . 115 B3
Taynton Covert **4** B30 . . . 20 C3
Tay Rd B45 . . . . 18 B1
Taysfield Rd B31 . . . . 18 E6
Tayson Way WR14 . . . . . . 139 A5
Teal Cres DY10 . . . . 28 B3
Teal Rd B80 . . . . 90 F4
Tearne St WR2 . . . . 114 E4
Teasdale Way DY9 . . . . 6 D4
Teasel Cl WR5 . . . . 128 D4
Teasel Way WR3 . . . . 102 D2
Teazel Ave B30 . . . . 19 D6
Ted Preston Cl GL20 . . . . 196 F4
TEDSTONE DELAMERE . . . 97 A2
Tedstone Rd B32 . . . . 9 E5
TEDSTONE WAFER 96 D3
Teesdale Cl **4** WR9 . . . . . 84 D1
Tees Gr B38 . . . . 34 F8
Teeswater Cl
　Bromsgrove B60 . . . . 67 E6
　1 Worcester WR3 . . . . . . 115 E4
Telford Dr DY12 . . . . 26 A3
Teme Ave
　Kidderminster DY11 . . . . . 27 B3
　Malvern WR14 . . . . 153 D8
Teme Cres **7** WR9 . . . . . . 84 D1
Teme La WR6 . . . . 112 E1
Teme Rd
　Halesowen B63 . . . . 7 B5
　Stourbridge DY8 . . . . .5 F3
　Worcester WR4 . . . . 115 E3
Temeside Cl **10** WR15 . . . 55 F6
Temeside Way WR2 . . . . . 127 F5
Teme St WR15 . . . . 55 F5
Temperance St **7** WR1 . 115 C2
Temple Cl B98 . . . . 70 F4
Temple Mews **1** WR11 . 161 D4
TEN ACRES 20 B8
Ten Acres WR9 . . . . 84 E5
Ten Acres End B30 . . . . . . 20 B8
Ten Acres Fst Sch B98 . . . 71 F3
Tenacres La B98 . . . . 71 F3
Ten Acres Mews B29 . . . . 20 B8
Ten Ashes La B45 . . . . 33 C4
Tenbury CE Prim Sch
　WR15 . . . . 55 F4
Tenbury Cl B98 . . . . 71 C6
Tenbury Com Hospl WR15 55 F6
Tenbury High Sch WR15 . 55 E3
Tenbury Ho **2** B63 . . . . 8 A3
Tenbury Mead **6** DY14 . . . 22 C4
Tenbury Mus ★ WR15 . . . 55 F5
Tenbury Rd
　Birmingham B14 . . . . 20 E6
　Cleobury Mortimer DY14 . . 22 B3
Tenbury Swimming Pool
　WR15 . . . . 55 F5
TENBURY WELLS 55 F4
Tenbury Wells Bsns Pk
　WR15 . . . . 56 A3
Tenbury Wells Pump Rms ★
　WR15 . . . . 55 F5
Tenby Twr **2** B31 . . . . . . 19 A1
Tenby Way DY13 . . . . 43 E5
Tench Cl WR5 . . . . 128 C5
Tenlands Rd B63 . . . . .7 F3
Tennal Dr B32 . . . . .9 F6
Tennal Gr B32 . . . . .9 F6
Tennal La B32 . . . . .9 F6
Tennal Rd B32 . . . . .9 F6
Tennis Ct B30 . . . . 19 D4
Tennis Wlk **10** WR1 . . . . . 115 B4
Tennyson Cl WR3 . . . . . . 115 C7
Tennyson Dr WR14 . . . . . 139 A2
Tennyson Ho B31 . . . . 34 A8
Tennyson Rd B97 . . . . 89 C8
Tennyson Way DY10 . . . . 28 C6
Tenter Ct B63 . . . . .8 B4
Tenter Dr B63 . . . . 8 C4
Tenterfields B63 . . . . .8 B4
Tenterfields Prim Sch **4**
　B63 . . . . 8 C4
Tern Gr B38 . . . . 19 E1
Terrace Rd WR10 . . . . . . 144 E4
Terrace The B64 . . . . .7 E8
Terrill Ct **4** WR11 . . . . . . 161 D5
Terrills La WR15 . . . . 55 F1
Terry Cl B98 . . . . 70 F5
TERRY'S GREEN 53 F7
Tessall La B31 . . . . 18 D2
Tetbury Dr WR4 . . . . 116 A6
Tetbury Gr B31 . . . . 18 D3
Teviot Gr B38 . . . . 34 F8
TEWKESBURY 196 D6
Tewkesbury Bsns Ctr
　GL20 . . . . 197 C8
Tewkesbury CE Prim Sch
　GL20 . . . . 196 F6
Tewkesbury Hospl GL20 . 196 F6
Tewkesbury Ind Est
　GL20 . . . . 197 C8
Tewkesbury Rd
　Bredon GL20 . . . . 184 B2
　Eckington WR10 . . . . 171 F6
　Tewkesbury Sch GL20 . . . 197 C7
Thackeray Rd B30 . . . . . . 19 D5
Thackholme **7** WR4 . . . . 116 C5
Thame Ct B47 . . . . 35 E2
Thames Cl WR5 . . . . 115 E2
Thames Dr WR9 . . . . 84 D1

Thane Cl B80 . . . . 90 F4
Thatcham Rd **4** GL20 . . . 197 A3
Thatchers Cl **7** WR9 . . . . 84 D5
Thatchers Ct WR9 . . . . . . 84 D5
Thatchers Piece **11** WR9 . 84 D5
Thatchers Pl WR9 . . . . . . 84 D6
Thatchers The B62 . . . . .8 E8
Thatchers Way WR9 . . . . 84 D5
Thatchway Gdns B38 . . . . 34 E7
Thelbridge Rd B31 . . . . . . 33 E6
Theocs Cl GL20 . . . . 196 E4
Thicknall Dr DY9 . . . . 6 C2
Thicknall La DY9 . . . . 15 B3
Thicknall Rise DY9 . . . . . . 15 B4
Third Rd B61 . . . . 31 F4
Thirlmere Cl **4** WR4 . . . . 116 B6
Thirlmere Dr B13 . . . . 21 D8
Thirlmere Rd DY13 . . . . . . 43 F6
Thirlmere Wlk DY5 . . . . . . .6 B7
Thirlstane Rd WR14 . . . . 152 F6
Thirsk Way B61 . . . . 32 B1
Thistle Cl
　Fernhill Heath WR3 . . . . . 102 E3
　11 Worcester WR5 . . . . . 128 D5
Thistledown WR11 . . . . . . 161 C1
Thistle Downs GL20 . . . . 184 D1
Thistle Gn B38 . . . . 34 E7
Thistle La B32 . . . . 18 B7
Thomas Cl WR3 . . . . 102 E2
THOMAS TOWN 90 E3
Thomson Ave B38 . . . . . . 19 D1
Thorn Ave WR4 . . . . 115 E6
THORNBURY 94 E4
Thornbury La B98 . . . . . . 71 C7
Thorncliffe Cl B97 . . . . . . 89 A6
Thorneloe Rd WR1 . . . . . 115 A5
Thorneloe Wlk WR1 . . . . 115 A4
Thorngrove Rd WR14 . . . 153 A8
Thornham Way B14 . . . . . 20 D1
Thornhill Rd
　Brierley Hill DY5 . . . . .6 F8
　Halesowen B63 . . . . 7 E3
　Redditch B98 . . . . 71 E6
Thornhurst Ave B32 . . . . . .9 E7
Thorn Lea WR11 . . . . 162 A4
Thorn Rd B30 . . . . 19 E7
Thorns Com Coll DY5 . . . . .6 E8
Thorns Prim Sch DY5 . . . . .6 E7
Thorns Rd DY5 . . . . .6 E7
Thornthwaite Cl B45 . . . . 18 B2
Three Acres La B90 . . . . . 36 F6
Three Cocks La WR11 . . . 148 B1
Three Corner Cl B90 . . . . 36 E8
Three Counties
　Showground ★
　WR13 . . . . 153 B2
Three Oaks Rd B47 . . . . . . 36 B4
Three Springs Ind Est
　WR5 . . . . 115 D2
Three Springs Rd **7**
　WR10 . . . . 144 C1
Three Springs Trading Est
　WR5 . . . . 115 D2
Threlfall Dr DY12 . . . . 26 D4
Threshfield Dr WR4 . . . . . 116 A4
THROCKMORTON 145 E8
Throckmorton Rd
　Hill & Moor WR10 . . . . . . 145 E4
　Redditch B98 . . . . 90 A8
Thruxton Cl
　Birmingham B14 . . . . 20 F3
　Redditch B98 . . . . 71 E3
Thurleigh Cl DY9 . . . . 6 C2
Thurlestone Rd B31 . . . . . 33 E7
Thurloe Cres B45 . . . . 17 E1
Tibbats Cl B32 . . . . 9 C3
TIBBERTON 117 A7
Tibberton CE Fst Sch
　WR9 . . . . 117 A8
Tibberton Cl B63 . . . . 8 C4
Tibberton Ct B60 . . . . 67 E7
Tibberton Grange **1**
　WR14 . . . . 153 A8
Tibberton Rd WR14 . . . . . 153 A8
Ticknall Cl B97 . . . . 70 A4
Tidbury Cl B97 . . . . 89 C6
TIDBURY GREEN 36 E4
Tidbury Green Prim Sch
　B90 . . . . 36 E4
Tidworth Croft **2** B14 . . . 21 A3
Tigley Ave B32 . . . . 9 D1
Tilehouse B97 . . . . 70 D2
Tilehouse La B90 . . . . 36 E6
Tillington Cl B98 . . . . 71 E3
Till St WR3 . . . . 115 C5
Tilshead Cl B14 . . . . 20 E3
TILSOP 37 C7
Tiltridge Farm Vineyard ★
　WR8 . . . . 168 F6
Timberdine Ave WR5 . . . 128 C7
Timberdine Cl
　Halesowen B63 . . . . 7 D6
　Worcester WR5 . . . . 128 D7
Timber Down WR10 . . . . 158 F7
Timberdyne Cl DY14 . . . . 41 C3
TIMBERHONGER 47 F1
Timberhonger La
　Bromsgrove B61 . . . . 48 B2
　Dodford with Grafton B61 . . 47 F1
Timber La WR10 . . . . 158 F7
Timbertree Cres B64 . . . . . .7 E7
Timbertree Prim Sch B64 . .7 E7
Timbertree Rd B64 . . . . .7 E7
Timmis Rd DY9 . . . . 6 C6
Timms Gn **1** WR12 . . . . . 177 E4
Tinkers' Cross WR6 . . . . . 113 B5
Tinker's Cross WR3 . . . . . 102 D3

Tinkers Farm Gr B31 . . . . 18 E3
Tinkers Farm Rd B31 . . . . 18 E3
Tinmeadow Cres B45 . . . . 33 C7
Tintern Ave WR3 . . . . 115 D5
Tintern Cl
　Bromsgrove B61 . . . . 48 E1
　Kidderminster DY11 . . . . . 26 F6
Tintern Ho B32 . . . . .9 F5
Tipper Trad Est DY9 . . . . . 7 A5
Tipping's Hill B97 . . . . . . 89 C5
Tiree Ave WR5 . . . . 128 E6
Tirle Bank Way GL20 . . . 197 B6
Tirlebrook Prim Sch
　GL20 . . . . 197 C6
Titania Cl B45 . . . . 18 A3
Tithe Ct WR11 . . . . 148 F3
Titheway WR11 . . . . 148 F3
Titterstone Rd B31 . . . . . . 34 A8
TITTON 63 D8
Tiverton Cl **5** WR4 . . . . . 116 B7
Tixall Rd B28 . . . . 21 E5
Toftdale Gn WR4 . . . . 116 B4
TOLLADINE 115 F4
Tolladine Rd WR4 . . . . . . 115 F4
Tolley Rd DY11 . . . . 27 B1
Tollgate Cl B31 . . . . 33 F8
Toll House Cl WR2 . . . . . . 127 B8
Tollhouse Dr WR2 . . . . . . 114 F3
Tollhouse Rd B60 . . . . 67 E6
Toll House Rd B45 . . . . . . 33 C7
Tolsey La **5** GL20 . . . . . . 196 E6
Tomkinson Dr DY11 . . . . . 27 B4
Tomlan Rd B31 . . . . 34 C7
Toms Town La B80 . . . . . . 90 E3
Topfield Wlk B14 . . . . 20 E1
Top Field Wlk B14 . . . . . . 20 D2
Topham Ave WR4 . . . . . . 116 B3
Topland Gr B31 . . . . 18 C2
Top Rd B61 . . . . 32 A4
Topsham Croft B14 . . . . . 20 D5
Top St WR10 . . . . 160 E8
Toronto Cl **5** WR2 . . . . . 127 E6
Toronto Gdns B32 . . . . 9 E6
Torre Ave B31 . . . . 18 E2
Torridon Cl DY13 . . . . 43 E7
Torridon Wlk WR5 . . . . . 128 F6
Torrs Cl B97 . . . . 70 D2
TORTON 45 B5
Torton La DY10 . . . . 45 B5
Toulouse Dr WR5 . . . . . . 128 F4
Towbury Cl B98 . . . . 89 F5
Tower Croft **4** B50 . . . . . 136 E5
Tower Dr B61 . . . . 49 A6
Tower Hill
　Bidford-on-Avon B50 . . . . 136 E4
　6 Droitwich B97 . . . . . . 85 A3
Tower House Dr GL19 . . . 192 E3
Tower Rd WR3 . . . . 115 A6
Towers Cl DY10 . . . . 28 B5
Towneley Wr4 . . . . 116 C3
Townsend Rd B61 . . . . . . 49 B4
Townsend St **5** WR1 . . . 115 A4
Townsend Way WR14 . . . 139 D4
Toys La B63 . . . . 7 C5
Traceys Mdw B45 . . . . 33 A7
Trafalgar Ct **1** B50 . . . . . 136 D4
Trafalgar Way GL20 . . . . 196 F8
Trafalger Rd GL20 . . . . . . 196 F8
Trafford Pk The B98 . . . . . 70 F3
Tram St DY10 . . . . 27 E5
Transport Mus The ★ B47 . 35 C4
Tranter Ave B48 . . . . 51 A5
Treacle Nook **2** WR4 . . . 116 B5
Tredington Cl
　1 Birmingham B29 . . . . . . 19 A7
　Redditch B98 . . . . 90 B7
Tree Acre Gr B63 . . . . 7 C4
Treeside Way B31 . . . . 19 A2
Trefoil Cl
　Birmingham B29 . . . . 19 A7
　Malvern WR14 . . . . 153 D7
　12 Worcester WR5 . . . . . 128 D5
Trefoil Gdns **2** DY8 . . . . . .5 F6
Treford Ct DY9 . . . . .6 B1
Tregarron Rd B63 . . . . 7 C5
Trehearn Rd WR9 . . . . . . 85 B3
Trehernes Dr DY9 . . . . .6 B1
Trejon Rd B64 . . . . .7 E8
Trelawney Cl **8** WR2 . . . 114 F1
Trench La
　Huddington WR9 . . . . 118 B8
　Oddingley WR9 . . . . 104 D5
Trench Wood Nature
　Reserve ★ WR9 . . . . 104 F2
Trent Cl
　Stourbridge DY8 . . . . 6 A4
　9 Witton WR9 . . . . 84 D1
Trent Cres B47 . . . . 35 E2
Trent Rd WR5 . . . . 115 F3
Tre Rd WR14 . . . . 153 B6
Tresco Cl B45 . . . . 17 F1
Trescott Prim Sch B31 . . . 18 D3
Trescott Rd
　Birmingham B31 . . . . 18 D4
　Redditch B98 . . . . 70 F3
Tretawn Gdns GL20 . . . . 197 B6
Trevanie Ave B32 . . . . 9 C6
Treville Cl B98 . . . . 71 E3
Trevithick Cl
　5 Stourport-on-Severn
　　DY13 . . . . 44 A5
　4 Worcester WR4 . . . . . 116 C4
Trianon Rd B60 . . . . 49 C1
Trickses La B97 . . . . 88 D4
Trimnel Gn WR9 . . . . 84 E2
TRIMPLEY 11 C1

Trimpley Dr DY11 . . . . 27 A7
Trimpley La
　Bewdley DY12 . . . . 26 D5
　Kidderminster Foreign DY12 11 C5
Trimpley Rd B32 . . . . .9 B1
Trinity Cl WR11 . . . . 161 E2
Trinity Ct
　Bromsgrove B60 . . . . 68 B7
　1 Kidderminster DY10 . . 27 F6
Trinity Fields DY10 . . . . . . 27 F6
Trinity Grange DY10 . . . . . 27 F7
Trinity High Sch & Sixth
　Form Ctr B98 . . . . 70 F4
Trinity Pas **4** WR1 . . . . . 115 C3
Trinity Rd
　Malvern WR14 . . . . 138 E2
　Stourbridge DY8 . . . . 6 A8
Trinity St
　3 Tewkesbury GL20 . . . 196 E6
　2 Worcester WR1 . . . . . 115 C2
Trinity The **3** WR1 . . . . . 115 C3
Trinity Wlk **18** GL20 . . . . 196 E6
Trippleton Ave B32 . . . . . 18 B8
Tristram Ave B31 . . . . 19 B1
Trittiford Rd B13 . . . . 21 C6
Tromans Cl B64 . . . . .7 E7
Trostrey Rd B30 . . . . 20 D3
TROTSHILL 116 D4
Trotshill Lane E WR4 . . . . 116 C5
Trotshill Lane W WR4 . . . 116 B5
Trotshill Way WR4 . . . . . 116 D4
Troughton Pl GL20 . . . . . 197 B6
Troutbeck Dr DY5 . . . . .6 B8
Trout Beck Dr WR4 . . . . . 115 F5
Trow Way WR5 . . . . 128 B7
Troy Gr B14 . . . . 20 D4
Troy Ind Est B96 . . . . 90 A3
TRUEMAN'S HEATH. 36 C7
Truemans Heath La B47,
　B90 . . . . 36 C7
Truro Dr DY11 . . . . 27 A5
Tryst The B61 . . . . 49 B5
Tudbury Rd B31 . . . . 18 E6
Tudor Bsns Ctr **9** B98 . . . 70 E3
Tudor Cl
　Birmingham, Highter's Heath
　　B14 . . . . 21 A1
　Birmingham, King's Heath
　　B13 . . . . 20 F6
　Malvern WR14 . . . . 153 D6
Tudor Gdns DY8 . . . . .5 E5
Tudor House Heritage Ctr ★
　WR1 . . . . 115 C2
Tudor House Mus ★
　WR8 . . . . 169 B6
Tudor Pl GL20 . . . . 196 F4
Tudor Rd DY12 . . . . 25 F3
Tudor Way WR2 . . . . 114 C3
Tuer The WR11 . . . . 134 A3
Tuer Way WR7 . . . . 120 E7
Tuffery Cl WR3 . . . . 115 B6
Tugford Rd B29 . . . . 19 C7
Tug Wilson Cl GL20 . . . . 184 E2
Tugwood Cl DY13 . . . . 64 B6
Tulip Gdns B29 . . . . 18 F7
Tunnel Dr B98 . . . . 70 E2
TUNNEL HILL 168 F5
Tunnel Hill
　Upton upon Severn WR8 . 169 B4
　Worcester WR4 . . . . 115 F5
Tunnel La B14 . . . . 20 C4
Turbary Ave WR4 . . . . . . 116 C5
Turgo Gdns WR5 . . . . . . 116 A1
TURLEYGREEN 1 C7
Turner Dr DY5 . . . . 6 D7
Turners Cl WR4 . . . . 115 F6
Turney Rd DY8 . . . . .5 F6
Turnpike Cl WR2 . . . . 114 F3
Turnpike La B97 . . . . 70 A4
Turnstone Rd DY10 . . . . . 28 A1
Turrall St WR3 . . . . 115 B6
Turton Gdns B96 . . . . 107 D7
Turton St DY10 . . . . 28 A8
Turves Gn
　Birmingham, Turves Green
　　B31 . . . . 19 A1
　Birmingham, West Heath
　　B31 . . . . 33 F8
TURVES GREEN 19 A1
Turves Green Boys Tech Coll
　B31 . . . . 34 A8
Turves Green Girls Sch &
　Tech Coll B31 . . . . 19 A1
Turves Green Prim Sch
　B31 . . . . 19 A1
Tutbury Row WR4 . . . . . . 116 D6
Tutnall Cl B60 . . . . 49 F1
Tutnall Grange B60 . . . . . 50 A1
Tutnall La
　Blackwell B60 . . . . 50 A1
　Finstall B60 . . . . 49 F1
Tutors Way DY10 . . . . 27 E4
Twarnley Rise **3** WR4 . . 116 B3
Twatling Rd B45 . . . . 33 A2
Tweed Cl WR5 . . . . 115 E2
Tweeds Well B32 . . . . 18 B7
Twickenham Ct DY8 . . . . . 5 C7
Twinberrow Ct WR14 . . . 138 F5
Twiners Rd B98 . . . . 70 F1
Twitchams La WR12 . . . . 176 E2
Twixtbears GL20 . . . . 196 E7
Two Gates B63 . . . . 7 C5
Two Gates La B63 . . . . 7 C5
TWYFORD 147 E1
TWYNING 183 F7
TWYNING GREEN 184 B6
Twyning Prim Sch GL20 . 184 A6

Twyning Rd
Birmingham, Stirchley B30 . 20 B7
Strensham WR8 . 171 A3
Tybridge St WR2 . 115 A2
Tye Gdns DY9 . 6 B1
Tylers Gn B38 . 20 B1
Tyndale WR4 . 116 C4
Tyndall Wlk B32 . 9 A2
Tyne Cl WR5 . 115 E2
Tyne Dr WR11 . 162 A3
Tynes The B60 . 67 E7
Tynings Cl DY11 . 12 B1
Tyning The WR9 . 84 D1
Tynsall Ave B97 . 69 F2
Tyrol Cl DY8 . 5 D6
Tysoe Cl B98 . 71 D2
Tythe Barn Cl B60 . 67 D6
Tythe Barn La B90 . 36 F6
Tythe Rd [1] WR12 . 177 D1
Tything The WR1 . 115 B4

U

UCKINGHALL . 169 F1
Uffculme Rd B30 . 20 D8
UFFMOOR . 7 E1
Uffmoor Est B63 . 7 E2
Uffmoor La B62 . 16 D7
Ullapool Cl B97 . 89 D5
Ullenhall La B95 . 72 E6
ULLINGTON . 150 A2
Ullswater Ave DY13 . 43 F6
Ullswater Cl
Birmingham B32 . 9 F2
Worcester WR4 . 116 A5
Ulverston Gn [1] WR4 . 115 F5
Ulwine Dr B31 . 19 A4
Umberslade Rd B29 . 20 A8
Underhill Cl B98 . 89 F6
Underwood Cl B97 . 89 A7
Unicorn Hill B97 . 70 D4
Union La WR9 . 84 E3
Union Pl
Tewkesbury GL20 . 196 F6
Worcester WR3 . 115 A7
Union St
Kidderminster DY10 . 27 E7
Redditch B98 . 70 F3
Stourbridge, Lye DY9 . 6 E5
Stourbridge, Stambermill DY8 6 A4
[10] Worcester WR1 . 115 C2
Unitt Dr B64 . 7 E8
Univ of Birmingham (Selly Oak Campus) B29 . 19 D8
Univ of Worcester WR2 . 114 F4
Univ of Worcester (City Campus) WR1 . 115 B3
Unwin Cres DY8 . 5 E5
UPHAMPTON . 82 E6
Upland Gr B61 . 49 A4
Upland Rd B61 . 49 B4
Uplands B63 . 7 E2
Upleadon Cl B97 . 89 A6
UPPER ARLEY . 10 D5
Upper Arley CE Prim Sch DY12 . 10 D5
UPPER BENTLEY . 69 A1
UPPER CATSHILL . 32 B2
Upper Chase Rd WR14 . 153 B8
Upper Cl B32 . 9 D3
UPPER COLWALL . 152 D4
Upper Crossgate Rd B98 . 90 C8
Upper Ct WR13 . 152 B2
Upper End WR10 . 171 F8
Upper End Ct WR11 . 163 C4
Upper Ferry La WR2 . 140 E7
Upper Field Cl B98 . 71 C6
Upper Gambolds La B60 . 68 C5
Upper Gd WR4 . 116 B5
Upper Hall Cl B98 . 71 D2
UPPER HAM . 169 D4
UPPER HAMNISH . 92 A3
UPPER HASELOR . 174 E8
Upper Hook Rd WR8 . 168 E6
Upper House WR6 . 124 F6
UPPER HOWSELL . 138 F6
Upper Howsell Rd WR14 . 138 F5
UPPER LODE . 196 C7
UPPER MARLBROOK . 32 D2
Upper Meadow Rd B32 . 9 C5
UPPER MOOR . 145 C4
Upper Norgrove Ho B97 . 69 F1
Upper Oaks Ct GL20 . 185 D2
Upper Park St WR5 . 115 D1
UPPER ROCHFORD . 57 A4
UPPER SAPEY . 77 E3
Upper St WR8 . 157 E3
UPPER STRENSHAM . 171 A4
Upper Teme Bsns Pk WR15 . 55 E6
Upper Tything WR1 . 115 B4
UPPER WELLAND . 166 F6
Upper Welland Rd WR14 166 F7
UPPER WICK . 127 C7
Upper Wick La WR2 . 127 C8
UPPER WOLVERTON . 130 D3
UPPER WYCHE . 152 F4
Upton Cl B98 . 71 F3
Upton Gdns WR8 . 169 D4
Upton Rd
Callow End WR2 . 140 E8
Kidderminster DY10 . 12 F1
Powick WR2 . 127 E2
UPTON SNODSBURY . 118 C1
Upton Snodsbury CE Fst Sch WR7 . 118 C1
Upton Snodsbury Rd WR10 . 144 E7
UPTON UPON SEVERN . 169 D5
Upton upon Severn CE Prim Sch WR8 . 169 C5
UPTON WARREN . 67 A3
Usmere Rd DY10 . 12 F1
Uxbridge Ct DY11 . 27 D5

V

Valbourne Rd B14 . 20 C4
Vale Bsns Pk WR11 . 175 F8
Vale Cl B32 . 9 F3
Vale Ct B64 . 7 D7
Vale Gr B60 . 68 A7
Vale Ind Est DY11 . 27 C1
Vale Link WR11 . 175 F8
Valencia Rd B60 . 49 D1
Valentines Cl [3] WR9 . 104 B8
Vale of Evesham Specl Sch The WR11 . 161 E2
Vale Rd DY13 . 44 A3
Valerian DY10 . 27 E2
Vale St DY8 . 6 A8
Vallenders Rd GL20 . 184 E6
Valley Cl
Kidderminster Foreign DY11 . 26 E8
Redditch B97 . 89 A6
Valley Farm Rd B45 . 33 A6
Valley Rd
Bournheath B61 . 48 E7
Cradley Heath B64 . 7 E7
Halesowen B62 . 8 F8
Stourbridge DY9 . 6 F6
Valley Stad (Redditch FC) B97 . 70 C4
Valley View DY12 . 25 E2
Valley Way WR9 . 84 D2
Valley Wlk WR9 . 84 D2
Vancouver Cl [1] WR2 . 127 E6
Vandra Cl WR14 . 139 B5
Vardon Way B38 . 19 D1
Varlins Way B38 . 34 D6
Vaughan Rd DY14 . 22 B4
Vauxhall Rd DY8 . 6 A5
Vauxhall St WR3 . 115 D5
Vawdrey Cl
[4] Stourport-on-Severn DY13 . 43 E1
[1] Stourport-on-Severn DY13 . 62 E8
Vaynor Dr B97 . 89 D8
Vaynor Fst Sch The B97 . 89 C7
Ventnor Cl B68 . 9 C7
Venus Bank [1] DY12 . 26 A3
Vera Roberts Way DY11 . 27 B3
Verbena Cl B60 . 67 C1
Verbena Rd B31 . 18 F6
Vernon Cl
Halesowen B62 . 8 D8
Martley WR6 . 99 A4
Redditch B98 . 71 A5
Vernon Gr WR9 . 84 D3
Vernon Park Rd [13] WR2 . 114 F1
Vernon Rd
Halesowen B62 . 8 C8
Stourport-on-Severn DY13 . 44 A4
Vernon Trad Est B62 . 8 C8
Verona Rd B60 . 49 C1
Veronica Cl B29 . 19 A6
Verstone Croft B31 . 19 A3
Vesta Tilley Ct [25] WR1 . 115 C2
Vestry Ct DY8 . 5 E6
Vetch Field Ave WR4 . 116 B4
Vicarage Bank WV15 . 1 B5
Vicarage Cl
Birmingham, Stirchley B30 . 20 C7
Brierley Hill DY5 . 6 C8
Bromsgrove B60 . 68 B8
Hallow WR2 . 101 D1
Vicarage Cres
Kidderminster DY10 . 27 F5
Redditch B97 . 70 C3
Vicarage Ct DY7 . 4 A3
Vicarage Dr DY7 . 4 A3
Vicarage Gdns [1] WR10 . 171 E7
Vicarage Hill B94 . 53 F3
Vicarage La
Childswickham WR12 . 176 E2
North Claines WR3 . 102 C3
Vicarage Rd
Birmingham, King's Heath B14 . 20 D7
Brierley Hill DY5 . 6 C7
Stone DY10 . 28 E2
Stourbridge DY8 . 5 D7
Stourbridge, Lye DY9 . 6 F5
Vicarage Rd S DY9 . 6 E5
Vicarage View B97 . 70 D3
Vicar St
Kidderminster DY10 . 27 E6
Worcester WR3 . 115 D4
Vicars Wlk DY9 . 6 E2
Victor Bsns Ctr B98 . 71 B3
Victoria Ave
Droitwich WR9 . 84 F1
Evesham WR11 . 161 D6
Halesowen B62 . 8 F6
Worcester WR5 . 115 D1
Victoria Ct
[6] Birmingham, Hurst Green B62 . 9 A7
Halesowen B62 . 8 F6
[2] Kidderminster DY10 . 27 F6
Victoria Gdns WR11 . 163 B5
Victoria La WR3 . 115 A6
Victoria Mews B45 . 50 D8
Victoria Park Rd WR14 . 139 B4
Victoria Pas DY9 . 15 A5
Victoria Pass [5] DY8 . 6 A5
Victoria Pl
Kidderminster DY11 . 27 B2
[5] Worcester WR5 . 115 D1
Victoria Rd
Bidford-on-Avon B50 . 136 C5
Birmingham, Stirchley B30 . 20 A7
Bromsgrove B61 . 49 A3
Dodford B61 . 48 A7
Halesowen B62 . 8 D8
Malvern WR14 . 138 F1
Victoria Sch B31 . 19 A5
Victoria Sq [5] WR9 . 84 F3
Victoria St
[2] Halesowen B63 . 8 A4
[7] Redditch B98 . 70 E4
Stourbridge DY8 . 6 A5
Worcester WR3 . 115 A6
Victoria Terr [10] WR10 . 144 D1
Victoria Wlk WR14 . 138 E3
Victory Cl [1] DY13 . 44 B2
Viewfields [6] WR5 . 116 B3
Vigornia Ave WR3 . 115 D5
Village Mews [5] B32 . 9 A6
Village St
Aldington WR11 . 162 C5
Harvington WR11 . 148 B7
Village The WR6 . 97 E8
Villa St DY8 . 6 A8
Villeneuve Mews DY13 . 44 A3
Villette Gr B14 . 21 C4
Villiers Rd B60 . 67 E7
Villiers St DY10 . 28 A5
Vimiera Cl WR5 . 128 F4
Vimy Rd B13 . 21 B8
Vincent Rd WR5 . 115 D2
Vine Ct B64 . 7 D8
Vine La
Clent DY9 . 15 F3
Halesowen B63 . 8 B3
Kyre WR15 . 75 C5
Vines La WR9 . 84 F4
Vines Mews WR9 . 84 F4
Vine St
Evesham WR11 . 161 D4
Kidderminster DY10 . 28 A8
Redditch B97 . 70 D4
Worcester WR3 . 115 A7
Vine Way GL20 . 196 E3
Vineyard Rd B31 . 18 F5
Vinnall Gr B32 . 18 B8
Vintners Cl [5] WR4 . 115 F6
Violet La DY9 . 15 E4
Viols Wlk [4] DY14 . 22 C4
Virginia Rd GL20 . 197 E8
Viscount Cobham Ct WR14 . 139 B2
Vista Gn B38 . 20 B1
Vivian Ave WR2 . 127 C8
Vowchurch Cl B97 . 70 A5
Vyrnwy Gr B38 . 34 E8

W

WADBOROUGH . 143 A4
Wadborough Rd
Norton Juxta Kempsey WR5 . 129 C1
Stoulton WR7 . 143 A7
Wad La GL19 . 194 E4
Wadley Dr WR3 . 102 A2
Wadleys Cl [2] B50 . 136 D5
Waggoners Cl [1] B60 . 67 E6
Waggon La
Churchill & Blakedown DY10 . 13 F3
Churchill DY10 . 14 A3
Waggon Pl [6] WR4 . 116 B5
Waggon Wlk [3] B38 . 34 C8
Wagtail Dr GL20 . 184 D1
Wain Gn WR4 . 116 B5
Wainwright Rd WR4 . 116 B8
Wakefield Cl WR5 . 115 F2
Wakeford Rd B31 . 19 C1
Wakeman Cl [17] GL20 . 197 A4
Wakeman St [10] WR3 . 115 B6
WALCOT . 144 B5
Walcot La WR10 . 143 F5
Waldrons Moor B14 . 20 C5
Walford Gn B32 . 18 B7
Walford Wlk [6] B97 . 70 E3
Walker Ave
Brierley Hill DY5 . 6 D7
Stourbridge DY9 . 6 E3
Walker Dr DY10 . 13 A1
WALKER'S HEATH . 20 B1
Walkers Heath Rd B38 . 20 B1
Walkers La WR5 . 129 A7
Walkers Rd B98 . 71 E6
Walkley Rd GL20 . 196 F7
Walkmill Dr WR9 . 85 D8
WALKWOOD . 89 B6
Walkwood Coppice Nature Reserve★ B97 . 89 B7
Walkwood Cres B97 . 89 C6
Walkwood Rd B97 . 89 D6
Walkworth Ave [6] WR4 . 116 C6
Wallace Rise B64 . 7 E7
Wallcroft Cl WR2 . 114 E4
Wallhouse La
Feckenham B97 . 88 B5
Hanbury B60 . 87 F5
Wall's Rd B60 . 67 C3
Wall Well B63 . 7 F3
Wall Well La B63 . 7 F3
Walmead Croft [1] B17 . 9 F7
Walmers Cres WR4 . 116 C7
Walmers Wlk The B31 . 18 D1
Walmesley Way B31 . 18 E3
Walmley Cl B63 . 7 B7
Walnut Ave WR4 . 115 F5
Walnut Cl
Broadway WR12 . 190 C8
Harvington WR11 . 148 B6
Stourbridge DY9 . 6 B1
Walnut Cres WR14 . 152 F5
Walnut Dr DY13 . 44 C3
Walnut La B60 . 68 D8
Walnuts The WR8 . 154 A2
Walnut Way B31 . 33 F8
WALSHES THE . 43 F1
Walter Nash Road E DY11 27 B2
Walter Nash Road W DY11 . 27 A1
Walters Cl B31 . 33 F6
Walters Rd B68 . 9 B6
Waltham Cl B61 . 48 E1
Waltham Ho B38 . 20 B1
Walton Ave B65 . 8 B8
WALTON CARDIFF . 197 B5
Walton Cl
Halesowen B63 . 7 F2
Kidderminster DY11 . 27 B2
Redditch B98 . 71 E3
[2] Stourport-on-Severn DY13 . 43 D1
Tewkesbury GL20 . 197 B7
Walton Ct B63 . 7 F3
Walton Dr DY9 . 6 C5
Walton Gdns GL20 . 197 B6
Walton Gr B30 . 20 B2
Walton La
Elmley Lovett DY10 . 45 D2
Grimley WR2 . 101 C5
WALTON POOL . 16 A2
Walton Pool La DY9 . 15 F2
Walton Rd
Bromsgrove B61 . 49 B4
Elmley Lovett DY10 . 45 D2
Stourbridge DY8 . 6 A6
Walton Rise DY9 . 16 A3
Walwyn Rd WR13 . 152 B2
Wannerton Rd DY10 . 14 B1
Wansbeck Gr B38 . 34 E8
WANTS GREEN . 112 C7
WAPPING . 90 E5
Wapping La B98 . 72 B7
Warbage La
Belbroughton DY9 . 30 F1
Dodford B61 . 48 A7
Warbank Cl B48 . 51 A6
Warbler Pl DY10 . 28 A2
Wardle Way DY11 . 12 B3
Wardoor Pl [1] WR4 . 116 C5
Ward Rd [2] DY13 . 44 B1
Wards Cl WR11 . 162 A3
Wareham Ho B28 . 21 E3
Wareham Rd B45 . 18 B2
WARESLEY . 64 A8
Waresley Ct Rd DY11 . 45 A1
Waresley Pk DY11 . 64 A8
Waresley Rd DY11 . 45 A1
Warley Croft B68 . 9 E8
Warley Hall Rd B68 . 9 D8
WARLEY WOODS . 9 E8
Warmington Rd B47 . 36 A6
Warmstry Ct [4] WR1 . 115 B2
Warmstry Rd B60 . 49 C1
WARNDON . 116 B6
Warndon Bsns Pk WR4 . 116 A8
Warndon Gn WR4 . 116 A5
Warndon La WR4 . 116 D6
Warndon Prim Sch WR4 . 116 B6
Warndon Way WR4 . 116 D7
Warndon Woodlands Nature Reserve★ WR4 . 116 D5
Warple Rd B32 . 9 C5
Warren La B45 . 33 B3
Warren Rd
Birmingham, Stirchley B30 . 20 A6
Northway GL20 . 197 D8
Warrens End [1] B38 . 19 F1
WARSTOCK . 21 C3
Warstock La B14 . 21 A4
Warstock Rd B14 . 21 A3
Warston Ave B32 . 9 D3
Warstone Cl DY12 . 26 D4
Warstone Mdws DY12 . 26 D5
Warwards La B29 . 20 A8
Warwick Ave B60 . 68 A8
Warwick Cl B80 . 90 D3
Warwick Ct
[1] Birmingham, Weoley Castle B29 . 19 C7
Great Malvern WR14 . 152 F8
Warwick Hall Gdns B60 . 68 A8
Warwick Highway B98 . 71 C2
Warwick Ho WR14 . 152 F8
Warwick Pl GL20 . 196 F5
Warwick Rd B68 . 9 D7
Warwick St DY13 . 44 A5
Wasdale Ct WR4 . 116 B6
Wasdale Rd B31 . 18 F4
Waseley Cl [3] WR5 . 128 E5
Waseley Hills Ctry Pk Nature Reserve★ B45 . 32 C8
Waseley Hills High Sch B45 . 32 D7
Waseley Hills Visitor Ctr★ B45 . 17 C1
Waseley Rd B45 . 32 E8
Washbrook Cl [3] WR4 . 116 B7
WASHFORD . 90 E7
Washford Dr B98 . 90 D7
Washford Ind Est B98 . 90 E8
Washford La B98 . 90 D8
Washington Rd WR11 . 176 D8
Washington St
Kidderminster DY11 . 27 C5
[3] Worcester WR1 . 115 C4
Washpole La WR9 . 104 B4
Wassage Way WR9 . 84 D7
Wassage Way N WR9 . 84 C7
Wassage Way S WR9 . 84 C7
Wassell Ct B63 . 7 E2
Wassell Dr DY12 . 26 C4
Wassell Grove Bsns Ctr DY9 . 7 A2
Wassell Grove La
Hagley DY9 . 15 F8
Lutley DY9 . 7 A2
Wassell Grove Rd DY9 . 15 F8
Wassell Rd
Halesowen B63 . 7 E2
Stourbridge DY9 . 6 E2
Wast Hill Gr B38 . 34 F7
Wasthill La B38, B48 . 34 D5
Watchetts Gn [1] WR4 . 116 C4
Watchman Ave DY5 . 6 F7
Watchtower Rd DY13 . 44 D6
Water Croft [5] WR4 . 116 B5
Waterfall Rd DY5 . 6 D7
Waterford Cl WR3 . 115 A7
Watergrip La GL20 . 186 A7
Waterhaynes Cl B45 . 33 A6
Waterlade Cl [2] DY11 . 45 B2
Waterlaide Rd DY11 . 45 A2
Waterloo Cl WR13 . 139 E4
Waterloo Cres B50 . 136 E5
Waterloo Ind Est B50 . 136 E6
Waterloo Pk B50 . 136 E6
Waterloo Rd
Bewdley DY12 . 25 F2
Bidford-on-Avon B50 . 136 E6
Birmingham, King's Heath B14 . 20 E8
Waterloo St DY10 . 27 E6
Waterloo Way GL20 . 185 A6
Waterside
Droitwich WR9 . 85 A3
Evesham WR11 . 161 D3
Tewkesbury GL20 . 196 E6
Upton upon Severn WR8 . 169 C6
Waterside Cl [2] WR9 . 85 A3
Waterside Grange DY10 . 27 E8
Waterside Orch B48 . 34 B2
Waterside View DY5 . 6 B8
Waterway Ct B14 . 21 C3
Waterworks Dr B31 . 18 D4
Waterworks Rd WR1 . 115 A5
Watery La
Alvechurch B48 . 35 C1
Birmingham B62 . 9 A3
Blakedown DY9 . 29 F7
Hopwood B48 . 34 F2
Kinsham GL20 . 185 A4
Portway B47, B48 . 52 D7
Redditch B98 . 71 B2
Welland WR14 . 166 F5
Worcester WR2 . 114 E1
Watford Rd B30 . 19 F5
Watkins Gdns B31 . 19 C4
Watkins' Way WR14 . 153 C7
Watledge Cl [2] GL20 . 196 F6
Watleys Cl [5] B50 . 136 D5
Watsons La WR11 . 161 E3
Watt Cl B60 . 48 F1
Watt Ct [3] DY13 . 44 A4
Watts Rd B80 . 90 E2
Watwood Rd B28, B90 . 21 F3
Waugh Dr B63 . 16 D8
Wavell Rd DY5 . 6 F7
Waveney Rd [5] WR9 . 84 D1
Waverley Cl DY10 . 28 A8
Waverley Cres B62 . 16 F4
Waverley St WR5 . 128 C7
Waxland Rd B63 . 8 B2
Way Croft DY11 . 44 A8
Waystone La DY9 . 30 D4
Weather La DY13 . 62 F4
Weatheroak Cl B97 . 70 A1
WEATHEROAK HILL . 35 B1
Weatheroak Hill B48 . 35 B1
Weatheroaks B62 . 9 A7
Weaver Cl WR9 . 85 A3
Weavers Cl B97 . 89 D4
WEAVERS HILL . 89 C4
Weavers Hill B97 . 89 D4
Weavers Wharf DY10 . 27 D6
Webb Dr WR9 . 85 E1
Webb La B28 . 21 E6
WEBHEATH . 70 A2
Webheath Fst Sch B97 . 70 A2
Wedderburn Rd WR14 . 153 C8
Wedgberrow Cl WR9 . 84 F2
Wedgewood Rd B32 . 9 D5
Wedley Pl WR4 . 116 C3
WEETHLEY . 122 A4
WEETHLEY BANK . 122 B2
WEETHLEY GATE . 122 B1
Weethley Ho [6] B97 . 70 A4
Weights Farm B97 . 70 C7
Weights La B97 . 70 C7

Weights La Bsns Pk B98.. **70** C7
Weirbrook Cl B29........ **19** C7
Weir La WR2........... **128** A7
Welbeck Cl B62...........**8** E6
Welbeck Dr DY11....... **27** B5
Welches Cl B31........ **19** B5
Welcome Dr B61........ **32** A1
Welford Cl B98........ **89** F5

Welford Rd
  Bidford-on-Avon B50....**137** A3
  Long Marston CV37....**151** C6
Well Alley GL20........ **196** F7
WELLAND............ **167** C4
Welland Cl WR9........ **84** D1
Welland Dr DY8.......... **6** A8
Welland Gdns WR13..... **167** C4
Welland Prim Sch WR13 **167** C5

Welland Rd
  Halesowen B63...........**8** A2
  Upton upon Severn WR8..**168** D4
WELLAND STONE...... **168** B2

Well Cl
  Northway GL20........ **184** E1
  Redditch B97........ **89** E5
Wellesbourne Cl B98.... **70** E4
Wellfield GL20........ **197** B7
Wellington Cl 4 WR1... **115** C2

Wellington Ct
  Birmingham B32..........**9** F5
  Kidderminster DY11.... **27** C5
Wellington Ho B32.......**9** F4

Wellington Lodge Cl
  GL20............... **185** A6

Wellington Rd
  Bromsgrove B60....... **68** A8
  Ombersley WR9....... **83** A5
Wellington St 6 B98..... **70** E4
Wellington Twr 4 B31... **19** A1

Well La
  Little Witley WR6........ **81** B4
  Rushock WR9......... **46** B2
Well Mdw B45......... **33** A6
Wellmead Wlk B45..... **32** F8

Wells Cl
  4 Great Malvern WR14.. **166** E7
  Kidderminster DY11.... **27** A6
Wells Gdns WR12...... **190** E8

Wells Rd
  Great Malvern WR14..... **166** E8
  Malvern WR14........ **152** E4
  Worcester WR5........ **116** A2
Welsh House Farm Com Sch
  B32................... **9** F4
Welsh House Farm Rd B32 .**9** F4
Wendron Cl B60........ **49** B2
Wendron Gr B14........ **20** D4
Wenlock Cl B63...........**7** D2
Wenlock Dr B61........ **49** A5

Wenlock Rd
  Stourbridge DY8...........**6** B6
  Tewkesbury GL20...... **196** F5
Wenlock Way 1 DY13... **43** E1
Wensleydale 2 WR9..... **84** D1
Wensleydale Dr WR3... **115** E2
Wentworth Dr B60..... **50** A5
Wentworth Rise B62...... **8** D3
Wentworth Way B32.......**9** F3
WEOLEY CASTLE...... **19** A8
Weoley Castle Rd B29....**9** F1
Weoley Hill B29........ **19** C8
Weoley Park Rd B29 .... **19** D8
Werstan Cl WR14...... **153** C2
Werth La GL19........ **195** D2

Wesley Ave
  Halesowen B63...........**7** B8
  Stourport-on-Severn DY13 . **43** E1
Wesley Wlk B60....... **67** E7
Wesson Gdns B63........ **8** A3
Wessons Rd B50....... **136** E5
WESTACRE........... **84** D3
Westacre Dr DY5..........**6** F8
Westacre Mid Sch WR9... **84** D3
West Ave B98.......... **70** E3
Westbourne WR11..... **164** B5
Westbourne Cl 3 B61.... **48** E1
Westbourne Rd B62.......**8** E7
Westbourne St 1 DY12 .. **26** C3
Westbourne Terr 2 B61. **48** E1
Westbury Ave WR64.... **84** C1
Westbury Ct 10 WR9.... **84** C1
Westbury Ho B97...... **70** B2
Westbury St WR1...... **115** C3
West Bvd B32............**9** F4
Westcliff Pl B31....... **18** F4
Westcombe Gr B32..... **9** A1
Westcote Ave B31..... **18** C2
Westcroft Ct 11 WR9... **84** E3
Westcroft Gr B38...... **19** D3
Westcroft St 5 WR9... **84** E3
Westcroft Way B14.... **21** B1
West Ct B60.......... **67** F6
Westdean Cl B62........ **8** C4
WEST END............ **190** C6
West End WR11...... **149** A8
West End La WR14.... **190** C7
West End Villas B38.... **19** F2
Western Ave B62.......**8** E4
Western Bsns Pk B62.....**8** B7
Western Hill Cl B96..... **89** E1
Western Hill Rd GL20.... **186** D2

Western Rd
  Cradley Heath B64.......**7** E8
  Stourbridge DY8...........**5** F4

Western Rd continued
  West Hagley DY9......... **15** B4
Western Way DY11..... **27** A5

Westfield Ave
  Birmingham B14....... **21** B1
  Northway GL20....... **197** D8
Westfield Cl WR3...... **102** F3
Westfield La WR8...... **156** B7

Westfield Rd
  Brierley Hill DY5..........**6** F8
  Fernhill Heath WR3.... **102** E3
Westfields B61........ **48** F8
Westford Gr B28....... **21** E3
WEST HAGLEY........ **15** A5
Westhaven Dr B31..... **18** E7
Westhaven Pl 8 WR2.. **114** E5
Westhead Rd DY10..... **13** A4
Westhead Road N DY10 . **13** A4
WEST HEATH......... **34** B7
West Heath Hospl B38 ... **34** C8
West Heath Prim Sch B38 **34** C8
West Heath Rd B31.... **19** B1
West Hill Ct B14....... **20** C4
Westhill Rd B38........ **19** F3
Westholme Croft B30 ... **19** E8
Westholme Rd B50.... **136** D5
Westhouse Ct B14..... **20** D4
Westhouse Gr B14..... **20** D4
Westland Gdns DY8......**5** F7
WESTLANDS.......... **84** D5
Westlands Fst Sch WR9.. **84** D5
Westlands Way WR9 ... **84** D3
Westlea Cl WR2....... **114** C1
Westlyn Cl WR14...... **139** B3
WEST MALVERN...... **138** C1
West Malvern Rd WR14.. **152** D6
West Malvern St James CE
  Prim Sch WR14...... **138** C1
WESTMANCOTE....... **185** B8
Westmead Ave B80.... **90** E4
West Mead Dr B14..... **20** E6
Westmere WR8....... **154** A2
West Midland Saf Pk★
  DY12................ **26** E3
West Midlands Hospl B63 . **7** D5
West Mill Croft B38.... **34** E7
Westminster Bank WR14 **138** C1
Westminster Cl B61.... **48** D1
Westminster Ct 3 B60 .. **49** A2
Westminster Dr B14.... **20** E6
Westminster Pl B31.... **34** B7
Westminster Rd
  Birmingham, Stirchley
   B29................ **20** A8
  Kidderminster DY11.... **27** A6
  Malvern WR14........ **152** E4
  Worcester WR5....... **115** F2
Westmount Cl B30..... **19** D6
Westmount Cl 2 WR2... **127** F6
Westonbirt Cl 1 WR5.. **128** E5
Westonhall Rd B60..... **67** D1
Weston Hill WR6...... **112** D4
Weston Ind Est WR11.. **178** C8
Weston Orch WR10 .... **146** A1
Weston Pk★ GL55..... **178** E3

Weston Rd
  Bretforton WR11...... **163** D3
  Honeybourne WR11.... **164** B3
WESTON-SUB-EDGE... **178** D7
West Park Ave B31..... **18** E2
Westray Cl B45....... **17** F1

West St
  Brierley Hill DY5..........**6** F8
  Droitwich WR9........ **84** E3
  Evesham WR11....... **161** C4
  Redditch B98......... **70** E3
  Stourbridge DY8...........**5** F5
West Stone WR9...... **84** E6
Westview CL WR7..... **114** D2
West View Terr 6 WR15.. **55** E5
Westville Ave WR11.... **27** A5
Westward Rd WR14... **138** E6
West Way B31........ **34** B7

Westwood Ave
  Droitwich WR9........ **84** F1
  Stourbridge DY8...........**5** D3
Westwood Cl WR9..... **84** C2
Westwood Dr B45..... **18** B1
Westwood La HR6..... **94** A3
Westwood Pk★ WR9 ... **84** B4
Westwood Rd WR9.... **84** D4
Westwood Way WR9 ... **84** C3
Weyburn Cl WR2...... **127** E6
Wey Cl WR9.......... **84** D2
Wey Pl WR9.......... **84** D2
Wharfedale Cres 7 WR9. **84** C1
Wharfedale Dr WR4... **116** A5
Wharf La B60......... **50** B1
Wharf Rd B30......... **20** A2
Wharfside WR15...... **55** F7
Wharrad Cl B50....... **136** E5
Wharrington CL B98.... **90** A8
Wharrington Hill B98... **90** A8
WHATMORE.......... **37** C3
Wheal Cl GL20....... **197** B8
Wheal Rd GL20....... **197** E8
Wheatcroft Ave DY12.. **26** C4

Wheatcroft Cl
  Birchenale B97....... **70** A5
  Halesowen B63...........**8** A8
  Redditch B97........ **70** A5
Wheatfield Ave WR5 .. **128** C5

Wheatfield Ct GL55 .... **165** D4
Wheatfield View B31.... **18** D6
Wheatley Cl B97.........**9** C8
Wheatley Rd B68...........**9** C8
Wheatley La WR8...... **168** F3
Wheatley Rd B68.........**9** D8
Wheatmill Cl DY10..... **14** B2
Wheatridge Rd B60.... **67** E6
Wheatstone Cl 5 GL20.. **184** E1
Wheeler Cl WR2...... **114** F2
Wheeler Orch WR15.... **55** E3

Wheelers La
  Birmingham B13...... **20** F7
  Redditch B97........ **70** C6
Wheeler's La B13...... **21** A7
Wheelers Lane Prim Sch
  B13................. **20** F7
Wheelers Lane Tech Coll
  B13................. **20** F7
Wheeler St DY8..........**5** F5
Wheeley Rd B48....... **50** D5
Wheelwright Cl
  Bromsgrove B60...... **67** E6
  Worcester WR4...... **115** C6
Whettybridge Rd B45... **32** E6
Whetty La B45........ **32** F7
Whimbrel Gr DY10..... **28** A1
Whinchat Gr DY10..... **28** A1

Whinfield Rd
  Dodford B61......... **48** B6
  Worcester WR3...... **102** B1
Whiston Gr B29....... **19** B8
Whitborn Cl WR14.... **153** C8
Whitborn End WR14... **153** C8
WHITBOURNE........ **111** A6
WHITBOURNE FORD... **98** A1
Whitbourne VC Prim Sch
  WR6................ **110** F6
Whitburn Cl DY11..... **27** B5
Whitchurch Cl B98..... **89** F6
Whitcomb's Orch DY14.. **22** C3
Whitcot Gr B31....... **33** F8
Whitcroft Rd WR10..... **144** D1
Whitebeam Croft 3 B38 . **19** E1
White Castle WR4..... **116** D6
White Cl DY9...........**6** C2
White Cottage Gdn★
  WR9................ **106** C1
WHITE END.......... **180** B1
Whitefriars Dr B63....... **8** A4
Whitegate Dr DY11.... **27** A3
Whitehall Cl WR2..... **127** C8
Whitehall Dr 1 B63......**7** A8
Whitehall La WR10.... **158** A3

Whitehall Rd
  Cradley Heath B64.......**7** C8
  Halesowen B63...........**8** A4
  Stourbridge DY8...........**6** B2
White Harte Cvn Pk DY7...**4** B3
White Heart Cl 18 DY12.. **25** F3
White Hill
  Birmingham B31...... **19** B6
  Kinver DY7............**3** E5
  Worcester WR4...... **116** A4
Whitehill La B29, B31... **19** A5
Whitehill Rd DY11..... **27** A4
Whitehorse Cl 4 WR2 . **127** E6
White House Ct WR6... **124** A6
White House Dr B45.... **33** A2
Whitehouse La B98.... **71** E4
Whitehouse Pl B45.... **32** F6
Whitehouse Rd DY10... **27** E4
WHITE LADIES ASTON. **130** E6
White Ladies Cl 4 WR1. **115** B4
White Ladies Wlk 6
  WR1............... **115** B4
WHITELEAVED OAK... **179** B4
Whitemoor La B96..... **109** B7
Whitepits La B48....... **52** F4
White Rd B32............**9** D6
Whitesmith Croft B14... **20** E8
Whites Rd 2 WR2..... **127** F7
Whitestone Rd B63....... **8** A6
Whitethorn Gr WR14 .. **139** C3
Whitewood Cl WR5.... **129** A8
Whitewood Way WR5 .. **129** A8
Whitford Bridge Rd B60.. **68** A2

Whitford Cl
  Bretforton WR11...... **163** C4
  Bromsgrove B61...... **67** D8
Whitford Gdns B61..... **48** D2
Whitford Rd B61...... **48** D2
Whitland Cl B45....... **33** B6
Whitland Dr B14...... **20** F3
Whit Lenge Gdns★ DY10 .**45** D4
Whitlenge La DY10.... **45** C3
Whitley Court Rd B32.....**9** C6
Whitlock Gr B14...... **21** A3
WHITLOCK'S END..... **36** E6
Whitlocks End Sta B90.. **36** E7

Whitmore Rd
  Stourbridge DY8...........**5** D5
  Worcester WR2...... **114** D1
Whitney Ave DY7........**5** D6
Whittakers Cl 1 WR10 . **144** D1
Whittal Cl WV15..........**1** C5
Whittall Drive E DY11... **27** B1
Whittall Drive W DY11... **27** A1
Whittingham Rd B63.... **8** A5

WHITTINGTON
  Kinver................**4** D2
  Whittington......... **129** B6
Whittington CE Prim Sch
  WR5............... **129** B6
Whittington Cl B14.... **20** E5
Whittington Hall La
  Kinver DY7.............**4** F2
  Stourbridge DY7.........**5** B3

Whittington Rd
  Stourbridge DY8...........**5** E3
  Worcester WR5...... **129** A8
Whittles Ct DY11...... **27** B8
Whitville Cl DY11..... **27** C7
WHYLE.............. **92** D6
Whyle La HR6......... **92** D5
Whynot Cl B60........ **67** C2
Whynot St B63...........**7** B5
WICHENFORD........ **100** B6
Wichenford Dovecote★
  WR6................ **100** B4
WICK............... **159** A7
Wickham Cl WR11..... **176** D8
Wickham Ct WR12..... **176** D3
WICKHAMFORD...... **176** E8
Wickhamford La WR11.. **162** C1
Wickham Rd B80...... **90** F4
Wick House Cl WR10... **158** F7
Wicklow Cl B63...........**7** D1
Wick Rd WR10....... **159** B2
Wide Acres B45....... **17** F1
Widney Ho B97....... **70** C4
Wigeon La GL20...... **197** A5
Wigland Way B38..... **20** A1
Wigley Bank Rd DY7.....**3** D6
Wigorn Ho B67...........**9** F8
Wigorn La DY9........ **15** B8
Wigton Pl 16 WR4..... **115** F6
Wilberforce Pl 9 WR4 . **116** C3
Wildacres............**5** C6
Wilde Cl B14......... **20** D4
WILDEN............. **44** B6

Wilden La
  Kidderminster DY10... **27** E1
  Stourport-on-Severn B61 . **44** C6
Wilden Top Rd DY13 ... **44** D5
Wild Goose La B98..... **90** D8
Wilding Cl GL20...... **197** A7
WILDMOOR.......... **31** F4
Wildmoor La B61...... **32** A3
Wilfred Cl 3 WR3..... **115** C5
Wilkes Way 8 B50.... **136** D5
WILLERSEY........ **177** E4
Willersey Bsns Pk WR12. **177** E5
Willersey Prim Sch
  WR12.............. **177** F4

Willersey Rd
  Badsey WR11........ **162** F1
  Birmingham B13...... **21** D8
Willes Ct 2 B62...........**9** A7
Willets Rd WR9...... **103** F8
Willetts Dr B63...........**7** B4
Willetts Rd B31....... **19** A1
William Bullock Cl DY13 . **43** F3
William Coley Pl 3 DY13. **43** F1
William Cres WR11.... **161** C4
William Rd B31....... **18** F1
Williams Ct WR14.... **139** C1
William Shakespeare Pl 7
  WR9................ **103** F8
William St 7 B70...... **70** E4

William Tennant Way
  WR8................ **169** D4
Willis St DY11........ **27** C5
Willis Wlk GL20...... **184** D1
Willmore Gr 4 B38.... **34** F8
Willow Bank Cl WR10.. **145** A8
Willow Brook Rd B48... **51** A7
Willowbud Ho B98..... **89** F8

Willow Cl
  Ashton under Hill WR11.. **187** B7
  Bromsgrove B61...... **48** E2
  Fernhill Heath WR3... **103** A3
  4 Pershore WR10.... **144** C1
  Ripple WR8......... **169** F6
  West Hagley DY9..... **14** F5
Willow Coppice B32..... **9** C1

Willow Ct
  Bromsgrove B60...... **48** E3
  Westlands WR9...... **84** D4
Willowdene DY13..... **44** C3
Willow Dr WR9...... **103** F8
Willow End DY9.........**6** D3
Willowfield Dr DY11.... **12** C1
Willow Gdns B61...... **48** E3
Willow Gr WR14...... **139** A3
WILLOW GREEN...... **99** C1
Willow Hts B63.......... **8** A8
Willow Park Dr DY8......**6** B2

Willow Rd
  Birmingham, Bournville B29,
   B30................ **19** F8
  Bromsgrove B61...... **48** E3
  Evesham WR11....... **161** F2
  Kinver DY7............**4** C3
  Martley WR6........ **112** C4
  Wichenford WR6..... **99** D1
  Willersey WR12...... **177** D1
Willowsbrook Rd B62......**8** F8
Willowslea Rd WR3.... **102** A1
Willow St 12 WR1..... **115** C1

Willow Way
  Redditch B97........ **70** B4
  Studley B80......... **90** E2
Willsbridge Covert 8
  B14................ **20** C2

Willson Croft B28...... **21** D3
Wilmcote Cl B61...... **67** D8
Wilmcote Ho B97..... **70** B4
Wilmington Rd B32.......**9** B6
Wilmore La B47....... **35** F4
Wilmot Rd WR14..... **138** F5
Wilsford Cl B14....... **20** D1

Wilson Rd
  Birmingham B68.........**9** D8
  Hartlebury DY11...... **45** A1
Wilson St 4 WR3..... **115** D4
Wilton Ave DY11..... **27** B8
Wilton Rd WR14..... **153** B8
Wiltshire Cl 10 B29... **19** C7
Wiltshire Dr B63..........**7** B7
Wiltshire Ho 3 B63......**5** F8
Wimbledon Dr DY8.......**6** B2
Winbrook DY12....... **26** A3
Winchcombe Dr WR4.. **115** F7
Winchcombe Rd WR11.. **175** B2

Winchester Ave
  Kidderminster DY11... **27** A6
  Worcester WR2...... **127** F8
Winchester Cl DY9.... **15** A6
Winchester Dr B79.......**6** A3
Winchester Gdns B31... **19** A3
Winchfield Dr B17......**9** F7
Windermere Dr WR4.. **115** F7
Windermere Ho DY10.. **27** E4
Windermere Way 1 DY13 **43** F5
Winding Mill N DY5.......**6** E7
Winding Mill S DY5.......**6** E7
Windles Row 8 WR4... **116** B5
Windmeres 4 WR11... **161** F3
Windmill Ave B45..... **32** E8

Windmill Cl
  Birmingham B31...... **19** C5
  1 Stourport-on-Severn
   DY13............... **62** F8
  3 Worcester WR1.... **115** B4
Windmill Dr B97...... **89** C6
Windmill Gdns B97.... **89** B6
WINDMILL HILL...... **143** D7

Windmill Hill
  Birmingham B31...... **19** B5
  Halesowen B63...........**7** D5
  Temple Grafton B50... **137** C8

Windmill La
  Inkberrow WR7...... **120** E7
  Kempsey WR5....... **141** C8
  Stoulton WR7....... **143** D8
Windmill Rd B90...... **21** E2

Windrush Cl
  Redditch B97........ **89** D6
  Worcester WR5...... **115** E2
Windrush Cres WR14... **153** D8
Windrush Gr B29...... **20** A8
Windrush House B31... **18** E5
Windrush Rd B47..... **36** B7
Windsor Ave WR2..... **114** C2

Windsor Cl
  Birmingham, Coft Common
   B31................ **34** A6
  Birmingham, Frankley B45 . **18** A2
  Halesowen B63...........**7** F3
  Malvern WR14....... **139** C6
Windsor Cres DY7........**3** F4
Windsor Ct B38....... **19** F1

Windsor Dr
  Astley & Dunley DY13 ... **62** F8
  Kidderminster DY10... **27** E7
Windsor Gdns B60.... **49** A2
Windsor High Sch 4 B63 . **8** A4
Windsor Holloway DY7.....**4** C1

Windsor Rd
  Birmingham, Stirchley B30 . **20** B5
  Droitwich WR9....... **103** F8
  Evesham WR11...... **161** E6
  Halesowen B63...........**7** F4
  Redditch B97........ **70** D5
  Stourbridge DY8...........**5** E3
Windsor St B60....... **49** A2
Windsor View B32..... **18** B7
Winds Point DY9...... **15** A6
Winforton Cl B98..... **71** E3
Wingate Cl B30....... **19** F4
Wingfield Ave WR4... **116** C7
Wing La GL20........ **185** D8
WINNALL............ **63** B4
Winnall La DY13...... **63** B4
Winnington Cl WR6... **97** E8
Winnington Gdns WR8 . **154** A2
Winnipeg Rd B38..... **35** A8
Winsford Cl B63....... **8** A6
Winslow Ave WR9.... **85** B3
Winslow Cl B98...... **71** F3
Winsmore WR2...... **127** E3
Winston Dr B62....... **17** A4
Winstone Cl B98..... **71** A4
Winston Rd DY11..... **13** A6
Winterborne Cl B98.... **70** F3
Winterbourne Croft B14.. **20** C1
Winterburn Rd WR2... **114** E6
WINTERFOLD........ **46** B8
Winterfold Cl DY10.... **28** B6
Winterfold House Sch
  DY10............... **46** A8
Wintour Wlk B60..... **67** E7
Winward Rd B98..... **71** F1
Winwood Ct DY8.........**5** F4
Winwood Heath Rd B62.. **16** E2
Winwoods Gr B32..... **18** A8
Winyate Hill B98...... **71** A2
WINYATES........... **71** E2
Winyates Crafts Ctr B98.. **71** E3
Winyates Ctr B98..... **71** E3
Winyates Way B98..... **71** E4

WIREHILL 90 B5
Wirehill Dr B98 . . . . 70 F1
Wirlpiece Ave WR4 . . . . . 116 C5
Wirral Rd B31 . . . . 18 F6
Wiseacre Croft B90 . . . . . . 21 E2
Wiselack Pl **7** WR4 . . . 116 B4
Wishaw Cl
  Redditch B98 . . . . 90 A8
  Solihull B90 . . . . 21 E2
Wisley Way B32 . . . . .9 F5
Wistaria Cl B31 . . . . 19 A6
Witherford Cl B29 . . . . 19 C8
Witherford Way B29 . . . . . 19 C8
Withers Rd WR2 . . . . 115 A1
Withincroft **5** WR4 . . . 116 B4
Withington Covert B14 . . . 20 D2
Withybed Cl B48 . . . . 51 A6
WITHYBED GREEN 50 F6
Withybed La
  Alvechurch B48 . . . . 51 A6
  Inkberrow WR7 . . . . 120 D8
Withymoor Rd DY8 . . . . 6 A7
WITHYMOOR VILLAGE . . . 6 C8
Withy Trees Rd WR11 . . . 163 C8
Witley Ave B63 . . . . .7 E4
Witley Cl DY11 . . . . 27 B2
Witley Ct★ WR6 . . . . 80 D6
Witley Rd
  1 Birmingham B31 . . . . 19 D2
  Holt WR6 . . . . 81 E3
Witley Way DY13 . . . . 62 D8
WITNELLS END 11 C8
Witney Ct WR4 . . . . 116 A7
WITTON 84 E1
Witton Ave WR9 . . . . 84 D1
Witton Bank B62 . . . . .8 F7
WITTON HILL 80 D1
Witton Mid Sch WR9 . . . . 84 E1
Witton St DY8 . . . . .5 F4
Wivelden Ave DY13 . . . . . . 44 D6
Wixford Rd B50 . . . . 137 A8
Woburn Cl B61 . . . . 48 D1
Woburn Dr
  Brierley Hill DY5 . . . . 6 B8
  Cradley Heath B62 . . . . 8 B7
WOFFERWOOD
  COMMON 123 A4
Wold Wlk B13 . . . . 21 C6
WOLFERLOW 96 B8
WOLLASTON 5 D6
Wollaston Ct DY8 . . . . 5 C6
Wollaston Rd DY7 . . . . 5 C7
WOLLESCOTE 6 E4
Wollescote Bsns Pk **6** DY9 .6 F4
Wollescote Prim Sch DY9 . .6 F4
Wollescote Rd DY9 . . . . 6 D3
Wolsey Cl WR4 . . . . 115 E3
Wolverhampton Rd
  Kidderminster DY10 . . . . 13 A1
  Stourton DY7 . . . . 4 E7
Wolverhampton Road S
  B32 . . . . .9 E7
WOLVERLEY 12 E4
Wolverley Ave DY8 . . . . 5 C6
Wolverley High Sch DY11 . 12 D4
Wolverley Rd
  Birmingham B32 . . . . 18 B8
  Halesowen B63 . . . . .7 F2
  Kidderminster DY10 . . . . . 12 B1
Wolverley Sebright Fst Sch
  DY11 . . . . 12 D3
Wolverly Rd DY10 . . . . 13 A2
Wolverton Cl B98 . . . . 71 E2
Wolverton Rd
  Birmingham, Rednal B45 . . 33 C6
  5 Rainbow Hill WR1 . . 115 C4
Woodbank Dr B61 . . . . 48 F8
Woodberrow La B97 . . . . . 89 D6
WOOD BEVINGTON 135 B8
Woodbine Rd **6** WR1 . . 115 A5
Woodbridge Cl WR5 . . . . . 128 D6
Woodbrooke Gr B31 . . . . . 19 C6
Woodbrooke Rd B30 . . . . . 19.E7
Woodbury Cl
  Great Witley WR6 . . . . 61 B1
  Halesowen B62 . . . . .8 F8
  Hartlebury DY11 . . . . 45 A1
  Redditch B97 . . . . 89 A6
Woodbury La WR5 . . . . . . 129 C3
Woodbury Pk
  Holt WR6 . . . . 82 B3
  Norton Juxta Kempsey
  WR5 . . . . 129 D3
Woodbury Rd
  Birmingham B62 . . . . 9 A8
  Kidderminster DY11 . . . . . 27 B2
  Stourport-on-Severn DY13 . 43 F5
Woodbury Rise WR14 . . . 138 E4
Woodbury Road N DY13 . . 43 F5
Woodchester DY9 . . . . 15 B4
Woodcock Cl
  Birmingham B31 . . . . 18 C1
  Tanworth-in-A B94 . . . . . 53 E3
WOODCOCK HILL 18 F8
Woodcock Hill Prim Sch
  B31 . . . . 18 E7
Woodcock La B31 . . . . 18 E8
Woodcombe Cl DY5 . . . . . . .6 E8
Woodcote Cl B98 . . . . 71 E3
WOODCOTE GREEN 47 C6
Woodcote La
  Belbroughton DY9 . . . . . . 47 C7
  Dodford with Grafton B61 . 47 D5
Wood Croft B47 . . . . 36 B6
Woodcroft Cl
  Blackwell B60 . . . . 49 F5
  Cradley Heath B64 . . . . . . .7 D8
Wood Ct B97 . . . . 70 C1

WOOD END 53 F3
Wood End WR11 . . . . 161 E1
Woodend Cl B97 . . . . 70 B2
Wood End Dr B45 . . . . 50 A8
Wood End La B94 . . . . 53 F5
Wood End Sta B94 . . . . . . 53 F4
Woodfall Ave B30 . . . . 19 F5
Woodfarm Rd WR14 . . . . 152 F2
Wood Farm Rd WR14 . . . 152 F2
Woodfield DY9 . . . . 30 E7
Woodfield Ave
  Cradley Heath B64 . . . . 7 D8
  Stourbridge DY9 . . . . .6 F2
Woodfield Cl B98 . . . . 71 A5
Woodfield Cres DY11 . . . . 27 D5
Woodfield Ct B14 . . . . 20 F8
Woodfield La
  Madeley Heath B62 . . . . . 31 D8
  Ombersley WR9 . . . . 83 A8
Woodfield Mid Sch B98 . . 71 A2
Woodfield Rd
  Birmingham, King's Heath
  B13 . . . . 20 F8
  1 Droitwich WR9 . . . . 85 A3
Woodfields WR9 . . . . 85 A4
Woodfield St **4** DY11 . . 27 C6
WOODGATE
  Birmingham 9 A1
  Bromsgrove 68 B2
Woodgate Bsns Pk B32 . . .9 B2
Woodgate Dr B32 . . . . 9 A1
Woodgate Gdns B32 . . . . . 9 A2
Woodgate Ho B97 . . . . 70 B4
Woodgate La B32 . . . . 9 A2
Woodgate Prim Sch B32 . .9 B1
Woodgate Rd
  Bentley Pauncefoot B60 . . 87 D8
  Stoke Prior B60 . . . . 68 B1
WOODGATES GREEN 38 A1
WOODGATE VALLEY 9 C3
Woodgate Valley Ctry Pk★
  B32 . . . . .9 D3
Woodgate Way DY9 . . . . . 30 E7
Woodglade Croft B38 . . . . 19 E2
WOODGREEN 116 C5
WOOD GREEN 62 E5
Woodgreen Cl B97 . . . . . . 89 B7
Woodgreen Croft B68 . . . . 9 C7
Woodgreen Dr WR4 . . . . 116 B7
Woodgreen Rd B68 . . . . . . 9 C7
Woodhall Cl WR9 . . . . 83 A5
Woodhall La WR9 . . . . 83 A5
Woodham Cl B45 . . . . 17 E1
WOODHAMPTON 54 E7
Woodhampton Cl **6** DY13 62 F8
Woodhouse Cl WR5 . . . . . 128 B8
Woodhouse Orch DY9 . . . 30 E7
Woodhouse Prim Sch B32 .9 E6
Woodhouse Rd B32 . . . . . . 9 E5
Wood La
  Ashton under Hill WR11 . 174 B2
  Birmingham, Woodgate B32 . 9 A1
  Cookhill B96 . . . . 108 F3
  Earlswood B94 . . . . 36 E1
  Edwyn Ralph HR7 . . . . . . 95 B2
  Fairfield B61 . . . . 31 C3
Woodland Ave
  Kidderminster DY11 . . . . . 27 C7
  West Hagley DY8 . . . . 14 F5
Woodland Cl
  Aston Somerville WR12 . . 175 F1
  2 Drakes Broughton
  WR10 . . . . 143 F6
  Stourbridge DY9 . . . . 6 D2
  Worcester WR3 . . . . 115 D6
Woodland Dr B45 . . . . 33 A2
Woodland Gr DY10 . . . . . . 13 C3
Woodland Piece **5**
  WR11 . . . . 161 F1
Woodland Rd
  Birmingham, Northfield
  B31 . . . . 19 B3
  Brierley Hill DY5 . . . . 7 A8
  Dodford B61 . . . . 48 A7
  Halesowen B62 . . . . 8 D8
  Redditch B97 . . . . 70 B3
  Suckley WR6 . . . . 124 A3
  Worcester WR3 . . . . 115 D6
Woodland Rise
  2 Cleobury Mortimer
  DY14 . . . . 22 D5
  Cradley Heath B64 . . . . . . .7 F8
Woodlands WR11 . . . . 161 E1
Woodlands Cl
  3 Great Malvern WR14 . 166 E7
  1 Hartlebury DY11 . . . . 45 B2
Woodlands Park Rd B30 . . 19 C5
Woodlands Rd
  Birmingham B45 . . . . 32 D7
  Cookley DY10 . . . . 13 A4
Woodlands The
  Cradley Heath B64 . . . . . . 8 A7
  Ryall WR8 . . . . 169 E6
  Stourbridge DY8 . . . . 6 A2
Wood Leason Ave WR4 . . 116 B5
Wood Leasow B32 . . . . 9 D2
Woodleaves B47 . . . . 35 F8
Woodleigh WR10 . . . . 143 F6
Wood Leigh Cl B63 . . . . . . 8 A6
Woodleigh St B38 . . . . 19 F1
Woodleys The B14 . . . . . . 21 B4
Woodman Cl B63 . . . . 8 C3
WOODMANCOTE 157 B2
Woodmancote **10** WR4 . 115 F7
Woodman La DY9 . . . . 15 E4
Woodman Rd
  Birmingham B14 . . . . 21 A1
  Halesowen B63 . . . . 8 C3

Woodmans Cl **23** WR9 . . 84 D5
Woodmans Gn **9** WR9 . . 84 D4
Woodmans Pl **6** WR9 . . . 84 D4
Woodmans Rise **18** WR9. . 84 D5
Woodmans Way WR9 . . . . 84 D5
Woodmeadow Rd B30. . . . 20 B3
WOOD NORTON 146 F3
Woodpecker Gr DY10 . . . . 28 B2
Wood Piece Cl **4** WR4 . . 116 B7
Wood Piece La B98 . . . . . . 71 D7
Woodridge Ave B32. . . . . . .9 B4
Woodridge Rd B63. . . . . . . 8 A5
WOODROW
  Redditch. 90 B7
  Stone 29 D3
Woodrow Cl B98. . . . . 31 F1
Woodrow Ctr B98 . . . . 90 B8
Woodrow Dr B98 . . . . 90 B6
Woodrow Fst Sch B98. . . . 90 B7
Woodrow La
  Bluntington DY10 . . . . . . 29 E3
  Lower Marlbrook B61 . . . . 32 B2
Woodrow N B98 . . . . 90 A7
Woodrow S B98 . . . . 90 A7
Woodrow Wlk B98 . . . . . . 90 A7
Woodrush Com High Sch The
  B47 . . . . 36 A6
Woodrush Dr B47 . . . . 36 A5
Woodrush Rd **16** GL20 . . 197 A4
Woodshears Dr WR14 . . . 153 A7
Woodshears Rd WR14 . . . 153 A7
Woodshill Ave B45 . . . . . . 33 A2
Woodside Ave B97 . . . . . . 70 B2
Woodside Dr B45 . . . . 50 B8
Woodside Pk Mobile Homes
  Pk B94. . . . . 53 B7
Woodside Rd **1** WR5 . . 115 E1
Woodside Way B32 . . . . . . 18 A8
Woods La
  Brierley Hill DY5 . . . . 6 D7
  Cradley Heath B64. . . . . . . 7 C8
Wood St
  Bushley GL20 . . . . 182 E1
  Kidderminster DY11 . . . . . 27 D5
  Stourbridge DY8 . . . . 5 D6
  Stourbridge, Lye DY9. . . . . .6 F5
Woodstock Ho B13. . . . . . 21 A7
Woodstock Rd WR2 . . . . . 114 E3
Wood Terr
  Pershore WR10 . . . . 158 C7
  Worcester WR1 . . . . 115 B4
Woodthorpe Dr
  Bewdley DY12 . . . . 26 A4
  Stourbridge DY9 . . . . .6 F2
Woodthorpe Gdns B14 . . . 20 E5
Woodthorpe Jun & Inf Sch
  B14 . . . . 20 E5
Woodthorpe Rd B14 . . . . . 20 E5
Woodvale Dr B28 . . . . 21 E4
Woodvale Rd
  Birmingham B32 . . . . 9 A1
  Birmingham, Yardley Wood
  B28 . . . . 21 E4
Woodville Rd
  Birmingham, King's Heath
  B14 . . . . 20 F8
  5 Tewkesbury GL20 . . 196 F3
Woodward Cl
  Northway GL20 . . . . 197 E8
  Pershore WR10 . . . . 158 C7
Woodward Parks **5**
  WR10. . . . . 146 A1
Woodward Pl DY9 . . . . 6 C4
Woodward Rd
  Kidderminster DY11. . . . . 27 C4
  Pershore WR10 . . . . 158 C7
Woodyatt Ct WR14 . . . . . 153 A7
Woolaston Rd B98 . . . . . . 90 C8
Woolhope Cl B98 . . . . 71 F3
Woolhope Rd WR5 . . . . . 115 C1
Woollas Hall★ WR10 . . . 172 D6
Woolmead Row WR4. . . . 116 C5
WOOLMERE GREEN 87 A3
WOONTON 73 B1
Wooton Cl B97 . . . . 70 A4
Wootton Rd B31 . . . . 34 A6
Worboys Rd WR2 . . . . 127 F8
WORCESTER. 115 B1
Worcester Bsns Coll **26**
  WR1 . . . . 115 C2
Worcester Cath WR1. . . . 115 C1
Worcester City Art Gall &
  Mus★ **16** WR1 . . . . . . 115 B3
Worcester Cl DY9 . . . . 15 A5
Worcester Coll of Tech
  WR1 . . . . 115 B2
Worcester Cross **3** DY10 . 27 E5
Worcester Cty Mus★
  DY11 . . . . 44 F3
Worcester History Ctr★ **6**
  WR1 . . . . 115 C3
Worcester Ho **4** B63. . . . . 8 A3
Worcester La DY9 . . . . 15 B7
Worcester Porcelain Mus★
  WR1 . . . . 115 B1
Worcester Racecourse★
  WR1 . . . . 115 A3
Worcester Rd
  Birmingham, Brandhall B68. . 9 A8
  Bromsgrove B61 . . . . 48 F1
  Dodderhill WR9 . . . . 66 E1
  Evesham WR11 . . . . 161 C7
  Great Witley WR6 . . . . . . 61 A1
  Harvington DY9, DY10. . . . 29 C4
  Kidderminster DY10. . . . . 27 D4
  Malvern WR13, WR14 . . 139 D6
  Mustow Green DY10 . . . . 28 F1
  Newland WR2 . . . . 126 F1

Worcester Rd continued
  Ombersley WR3. . . . . . . 102 A7
  Pershore WR10 . . . . 144 C1
  Pirton WR8 . . . . 142 B4
  Stoke Heath B61 . . . . 67 B4
  Stone DY10 . . . . 45 D7
  Stourport-on-Severn WR13 . 44 B3
  St Peter the Great County
  WR5 . . . . 128 C4
  West Hagley DY9 . . . . . . 15 A5
  Wyre Piddle WR10 . . . . . 145 A4
Worcestershire Royal Hospl
  WR5 . . . . 116 B2
Worcester Shrub Hill Sta
  WR4 . . . . 115 D3
Worcester Sixth Form Coll
  WR5 . . . . 116 A1
Worcester Sq **1** B97 . . . 70 E4
Worcester St
  Kidderminster DY10. . . . . 27 E6
  Stourbridge DY8 . . . . 6 F1
  Stourport-on-Severn DY13 . 44 A4
Worcester Swimming Pool &
  Fitness Ctr WR1 . . . . . . 115 B4
Worcester Trad Est WR3 . 115 E7
Worcester Woods Ctry Pk★
  WR5 . . . . 116 B1
Word Hill B17 . . . . .9 F7
Wordsley Cl B98 . . . . 71 B7
Wordsworth Ave
  Redditch B97 . . . . 89 C8
  Worcester WR3 . . . . 115 C6
Wordsworth Cres DY10. . . 28 B6
Wordsworth Gn WR14. . . 139 A2
Wordsworth Ho
  Birmingham B31 . . . . 34 A8
  Halesowen B63 . . . . 7 B5
Workman Cl GL20 . . . . . . 196 F7
Workman Rd WR11 . . . . . 161 B3
WORLDS END 101 A4
WORLD'S END 9 D5
World's End Ave B32. . . . . . 9 D6
Worlds End Jun & Inf Sch
  B32 . . . . 9 D5
World's End La B32 . . . . . . 9 D5
WORLES COMMON 60 B6
WORMINGTON 188 D6
WORMS ASH 48 C6
Worth Cres DY13. . . . . 43 D5
Worthen Gr B31 . . . . 34 A8
Worthings The B30 . . . . . . 20 B6
Worthington Gdns **10**
  WR4. . . . . 116 B4
Worton Rd DY9 . . . . .6 F2
Wrekin Cl
  Halesowen B63 . . . . 7 C1
  Kidderminster DY11 . . . . . 27 B2
Wrekin Dr
  Bromsgrove B61 . . . . 49 A5
  Stourbridge DY9 . . . . 6 D4
Wrekin Wlk **5** DY13. . . . . 43 D1
Wren Ave WR14. . . . . 139 C2
WRIBBENHALL 26 B4
Wright St B63 . . . . .8 B4
Wroxall Cl DY5 . . . . .6 C8
Wroxall Gr B13 . . . . 21 A6
Wryflatt **3** WR4 . . . . . . 116 C5
Wychall La B38 . . . . 19 E2
Wychall Park Gr B38 . . . . 19 D2
Wychall Prim Sch B31 . . . 19 C2
Wychall Rd B31. . . . . 19 C3
WYCHBOLD. 66 E1
Wychbold Cl B97 . . . . 89 A6
Wychbold Ct DY9 . . . . 15 C8
Wychbold Fst Sch WR9. . . 85 E8
Wychbury Cl B63 . . . . 8 A3
Wychbury Dr DY9 . . . . 15 C7
Wychbury Grange DY9 . . . 6 C1
Wychbury Rd
  Birmingham B32 . . . . 18 B7
  Brierley Hill DY5 . . . . 6 E8
  Stourbridge DY9 . . . . 6 E2
Wyche Ave B14 . . . . 20 D4
Wyche CE Prim Sch
  WR14 . . . . 152 E5
Wyche CE Sch WR14 . . . . 152 E5
Wyche Cotts B60. . . . . 67 C1
Wychelm Cl **2** WR5. . . . 128 E8
Wychelm Farm Rd B14. . . 21 A1
Wyche Rd WR14 . . . . 152 E5
Wycherley Way B64. . . . . . .7 E8
Wych Rd WR9 . . . . 84 E2
Wychwood Dr B97 . . . . . . 89 D6
Wye Ave WR14. . . . . 153 D8
Wye Cl
  Droitwich WR9. . . . . 103 E8
  Worcester WR5 . . . . 115 E2
Wyekham Ct★ WR12 . . . 176 E2
Wykewane WR14 . . . . 153 D7
Wyld's La WR5 . . . . 115 C2
Wynall La WR5 . . . . .6 F3
Wynall La S DY9 . . . . 7 A3
Wyndbrook La GL19. . . . . 192 F7
Wyndham Gdns B30. . . . . 19 D4
Wynds Covert B14 . . . . . . 20 D2
WYNDS POINT 166 C6
Wynds Point B31 . . . . 19 B5
Wynfield Gdns B14. . . . . . 20 F5
Wynn Cl DY12. . . . . 26 D5
Wynniattes Way WR14 . . . 60 F3
Wynstead Covert **6** B14. . 20 C2
Wynyards Cl **1** GL20 . . 196 F6
Wyre Cl B45 . . . . 18 B1
Wyre Forest Glades Leisure
  Ctr DY10 . . . . 27 E6

Wyre Forest National Nature
  Reserve★ DY12 . . . . 25 B5
Wyre Hill
  Bewdley DY12 . . . . 25 F2
  Pinvin WR10. . . . . 144 F4
Wyre La CV37 . . . . 151 D6
WYRE PIDDLE. 145 B4
Wyre Rd
  Pershore WR10 . . . . 144 E3
  Stourbridge DY8 . . . . 5 E7
WYTHALL 36 B3
WYTHALL GREEN 35 E3
Wythall Gn Way B47 . . . . 35 E3
Wythall Rd B63 . . . . 8 A2
Wythall Sta B47. . . . . 36 C4
Wythwood Cl DY9. . . . . 6 D1
Wythwood Gr B47. . . . . . . 36 C6
Wythwood Rd B47 . . . . . . 36 C6

Y

Yardley Cl B98. . . . . 71 E3
Yardley St DY9. . . . . 6 C6
YARDLEY WOOD 21 E5
Yardley Wood Prim Sch
  B14. . . . . 21 D4
Yardley Wood Rd B13,
  B14 . . . . 21 B5
Yardley Wood Sta B28. . . . 21 D5
Yardley Works DY9. . . . . . . 6 C5
Yard The WR11 . . . . 175 B2
YARHAMPTON 61 F3
YARHAMPTON CROSS. . . . 61 F3
Yarnborough Hill DY8. . . . . 6 A2
Yarnbury Cl B14 . . . . 20 E1
Yarn Cl B47 . . . . 36 A5
Yarningale Cl B98. . . . . . . 89 F6
Yarningale Rd B14. . . . . . . 20 D5
Yarnold La
  Bournheath B61. . . . . 48 C8
  Fairfield B61. . . . . 31 C1
Yarranton Cl **2** DY13. . . 62 E8
Yarr Mill Cl B98. . . . . 89 F5
Yarrow Cl WR5 . . . . 128 D4
Yarrow Dr B38. . . . . 34 F8
Yates Hay Rd WR14 . . . . 138 F5
Yeadon Cl B97. . . . . 70 A1
YEARSETT. 123 C8
Yeldside Gdns DY14. . . . . 22 E5
Yellowhammer Ct DY10 . . 28 A1
Yeoman Cl DY10 . . . . 27 E3
Yeomans Cl B96 . . . . 89 E2
Yeomans Wlk B60 . . . . . . 67 E8
Yessell La WR11 . . . . 160 E6
Yewleigh La WR8 . . . . . . 168 F4
Yew Tree Ave DY9 . . . . . . 30 E8
Yewtree Cl WR11 . . . . . . 161 F2
Yew Tree Cl
  4 Bewdley DY12 . . . . . 25 F3
  Redditch B97 . . . . 70 A4
  Worcester WR5 . . . . 128 F8
Yewtree Dr B60. . . . . 49 B2
Yewtree Hill WR9 . . . . . . 103 F8
Yew Tree La
  Bewdley DY12 . . . . 25 F3
  Birmingham, Frankley B32 . 17 E3
  Fairfield B61 . . . . 31 D2
  Fernhill Heath WR3 . . . . 103 A3
  Malvern Wells WR14 . . . 166 F7
Yew Tree Pl B62 . . . . 17 A5
Yew Tree Rd
  Halesowen B63 . . . . .7 F3
  Kidderminster DY10. . . . . 27 F5
Yew Tree Wlk **10** DY13 . . 43 E4
YIELDINGTREE 29 F8
York Ave
  Bromsgrove B61 . . . . 48 E4
  Droitwich WR9. . . . . 84 F1
York Cl
  Birmingham B30 . . . . 20 A6
  Bromsgrove B61 . . . . 48 E4
  Malvern WR14 . . . . 139 C6
  Studley B80 . . . . 90 C4
York Cres DY8 . . . . 5 D7
York Ct DY10 . . . . 27 E7
York La WR10. . . . . 144 F1
York Pl WR1. . . . . 115 A4
York Pl La WR1 . . . . 115 A4
York Rd
  Bewdley DY12 . . . . 25 F4
  Birmingham, King's Heath
  B14 . . . . 20 E8
  Bromsgrove B61 . . . . 48 F4
  Tewkesbury GL20 . . . . . . 196 F4
York St
  Kidderminster DY10. . . . . 27 E7
  Stourport-on-Severn DY13 . 44 A3
Yvonne Rd B97 . . . . 89 D7

Z

Zermatt Cl **2** WR3. . . . . 115 A8
Zetland Rd WR14 . . . . . . 138 F2
Zortech Ave DY11. . . . . . . 44 A8
Zouche Cl DY8 . . . . .5 E8

PHILIP'S MAPS

the Gold Standard for drivers

◆ **Philip's street atlases cover all of England, Wales, Northern Ireland and much of Scotland**

◆ Every named street is shown, including alleys, lanes and walkways

◆ Thousands of additional features marked: stations, public buildings, car parks, places of interest

◆ Route-planning maps to get you close to your destination

◆ Postcodes on the maps and in the index

◆ Widely used by the emergency services, transport companies and local authorities

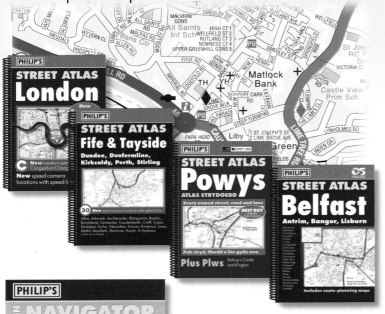

For national mapping, choose
Philip's Navigator Britain
the most detailed road atlas available of England, Wales and Scotland. Hailed by Auto Express as 'the ultimate road atlas', the atlas shows every road and lane in Britain.

'The ultimate in UK mapping'
The Sunday Times

Street atlases currently available

England

Bedfordshire and Luton	Surrey
Berkshire	East Sussex
Birmingham and West Midlands	West Sussex
Bristol and Bath	Tyne and Wear
Buckinghamshire and Milton Keynes	Warwickshire and Coventry
Cambridgeshire and Peterborough	Wiltshire and Swindon
Cheshire	Worcestershire
Cornwall	East Yorkshire Northern Lincolnshire
Cumbria	North Yorkshire
Derbyshire	South Yorkshire
Devon	West Yorkshire
Dorset	
County Durham and Teesside	**Wales**
Essex	Anglesey, Conwy and Gwynedd
North Essex	Cardiff, Swansea and The Valleys
South Essex	Carmarthenshire, Pembrokeshire and Swansea
Gloucestershire and Bristol	
Hampshire	Ceredigion and South Gwynedd
North Hampshire	Denbighshire, Flintshire, Wrexham
South Hampshire	
Herefordshire Monmouthshire	Herefordshire Monmouthshire
Hertfordshire	Powys
Isle of Wight	
Kent	**Scotland**
East Kent	Aberdeenshire
West Kent	Ayrshire
Lancashire	Dumfries and Galloway
Leicestershire and Rutland	Edinburgh and East Central Scotland
Lincolnshire	Fife and Tayside
Liverpool and Merseyside	Glasgow and West Central Scotland
London	Inverness and Moray
Greater Manchester	Lanarkshire
Norfolk	Scottish Borders
Northamptonshire	
Northumberland	**Northern Ireland**
Nottinghamshire	County Antrim and County Londonderry
Oxfordshire	County Armagh and County Down
Shropshire	
Somerset	Belfast
Staffordshire	County Tyrone and County Fermanagh
Suffolk	

How to order

Philip's maps and atlases are available from bookshops, motorway services and petrol stations. You can order direct from the publisher by phoning **0207 531 8473** or online at **www.philips-maps.co.uk**
For bulk orders only, e-mail philips@philips-maps.co.uk